Windows 98 Programming from the Ground Up

About the Author ...

Herbert Schildt is the world's leading programming author. He is an authority on the C and C++ languages, a master Windows programmer, and an expert on Java. His programming books have sold over two million copies worldwide and have been translated into all major foreign languages. He is the author of numerous best-sellers including, *Windows NT 4 Programming from the Ground Up, MFC Programming from the Ground Up, C: The Complete Reference, C++: The Complete Reference, C++ from the Ground Up*, and co-author of *Java: The Complete Reference*. Schildt is president of Universal Computing Laboratories, Inc., a software consulting firm in Mahomet, Illinois. He is a member of both the ANSI C and C++ standardization committees. He holds a master's degree in computer science from the University of Illinois.

Windows 98 Programming from the Ground Up

Herbert Schildt

Osborne **McGraw-Hill**

Berkeley   New York   St. Louis   San Francisco
Auckland   Bogotá   Hamburg   London   Madrid
Mexico City   Milan   Montreal   New Delhi   Panama City
Paris   São Paulo   Singapore   Sydney
Tokyo   Toronto

Osborne **McGraw-Hill**
2600 Tenth Street
Berkeley, California 94710
U.S.A.

For information on translations or book distributors outside the U.S.A., or to arrange bulk purchase discounts for sales promotions, premiums, or fund-raisers, please contact Osborne/**McGraw-Hill** at the above address.

Windows 98 Programming from the Ground Up

  234567890 AGM AGM 901987654321098

ISBN 0-07-882306-4

Microsoft, Windows, the Windows logo, and Windows NT are registered trademarks of Microsoft Corporation.

Publisher
Brandon A. Nordin

Editor-in-Chief
Scott Rogers

Acquisitions Editor
Wendy Rinaldi

Project Editor
Heidi Poulin

Editorial Assistant
Ann Sellers

Technical Editor
Greg Guntle

Copy Editor
Gary Morris

Proofreader
Emily Wolman

Indexer
Sheryl Schildt

Computer Designer
Roberta Steele

Illustrator
Brian Wells

Series Design
Peter Hancik

Contents at a Glance

Contents

Introduction

Windows 98 is the current heir to the Windows legacy. It is the direct descendant of Windows 95 and includes many performance and ease-of-use enhancements. It is safe to say that Windows 98 will be the most widely used operating system on the planet. This fact makes it the single most important operating system for which programs will be written. Programmers that can master this environment will find themselves in great demand well into the new century.

This book teaches you how to write programs for Windows 98. It starts with the basics, covers all of the essentials, and includes many advanced topics. If you have never written a Windows program before, then you will want to read this book in order, starting at Chapter 1. Resist the temptation to skip ahead because each new chapter builds upon material presented earlier. If you have experience programming another version of Windows, such as Windows 95 or Windows NT, then you will be able to advance more quickly. However, you should still skim through the introductory chapters because, in some areas, Windows 98 differs significantly from other versions of Windows.

What Programming Background is Required

To use this book effectively, you must be an experienced C programmer and knowledge of C++ is strongly recommended. C and C++ are *the* languages of Windows 98. If you feel that your C/C++ skills are a little weak, then take some time to fortify them. Programming for Windows 98 relies heavily on such things as structures, unions, and pointers. If you are not comfortable with these items, you will have trouble learning to write Windows 98 programs.

What Software is Needed

To compile the code in this book you will need a C++ compiler capable of producing programs for Windows 98. The compiler used to test the code in this book is Microsoft's latest version of Visual C++.

The examples in this book are written in standard C/C++ and they can be compiled as either C or C++ programs. That is, you may use either the .C or the .CPP extension. Thus, whether you will ultimately write your application in C or C++, the code in this book is compatible.

When compiling the programs in this book, use the default compiler settings suggested for compiling Windows-based code. Also, do not select any class library support, such as MFC or OWL. Specifically, when using Microsoft Visual C++, select Application when creating a new project.

Watch for the In Depth Boxes

Scattered throughout this book you will find special *In Depth* boxes. In Depth boxes delve deeper into specific programming topics. Often they explain options, enhancements, or alternative methods that can be applied to an example described in the book. They also serve as pointers to areas of programming that you will want to explore further on your own.

Source Code Free on the Web

The source code contained in this book is available free online at **http://www.osborne.com**.

For Further Study

Windows 98 Programming from the Ground Up is just one of the many programming books written by Herbert Schildt. Here are some others that you will find of interest.

To learn more about Windows programming, we recommend the following:

Windows NT 4 Programming from the Ground Up
MFC Programming from the Ground Up

If you want to learn more about the C language, then the following titles will be of interest:

C: The Complete Reference
The Annotated ANSI C Standard
Teach Yourself C

To learn more about C++, you will find these books especially helpful:

C++: The Complete Reference
Teach Yourself C++
C++ from the Ground Up
Expert C++
Borland C++: The Complete Reference

If you are interested in Java, then you will want to read

Java: The Complete Reference

co-authored by Herbert Schildt and Patrick Naughton.

When you need solid answers, fast, turn to Herbert Schildt, the recognized authority on programming.

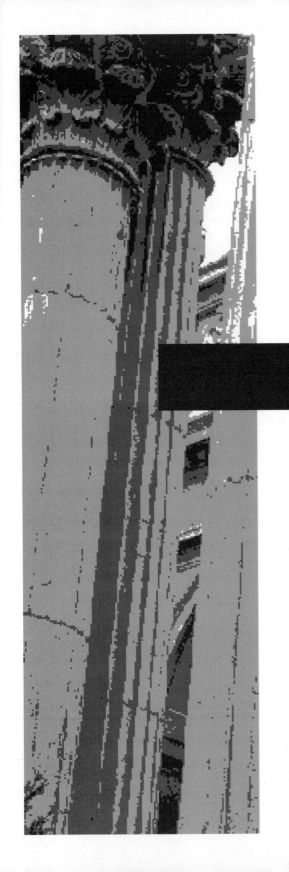

CHAPTER 1

Windows 98
Overview

This book is, first and foremost, a practical "how to" guide to Windows 98 programming. As such, it is not overly concerned with the theoretical aspects of Windows 98 except as they directly relate to writing programs. Instead, this book provides a hands-on approach that will have you writing Windows 98 applications as soon as possible.

The preceding paragraph notwithstanding, before you can become a Windows 98 programmer it is necessary that you understand in a general way how Windows 98 operates, what design concepts it embodies, and how it manages your computer. It is important to understand how Windows 98 differs from its predecessors: Windows 95, Windows 3.1, and DOS. Knowledge of its relationship to Windows NT is also valuable. Therefore, this chapter presents an overview of Windows 98 and discusses ways in which it relates to and differs from these other versions of Windows.

If you have never written a Windows program before, then most of the information in this book will be new to you. Just be patient. If you proceed methodically, you will become an accomplished Windows 98 programmer by the time you finish this book. If you have programmed for some other version of Windows, you will be able to advance more quickly. But be careful. There are some differences between Windows 98 and other versions of Windows that may affect the way that you write programs.

One more point: Windows 98 is a very large, complex programming environment. It cannot be fully described in one book. (Indeed, a full description would require several volumes!) This book covers those elements of Windows 98 programming that are common to all programs, are frequently used, or are important innovations unique to Windows 98. After you have completed this book, you will have sufficient understanding of Windows 98 programming to easily explore any of its other subsystems.

What Is Windows 98?

Windows 98 is the next incarnation of Microsoft's Windows' 32-bit operating system. It is the direct descendent of Windows 95 and contains all of the features found in its predecessors. It also adds several enhancements, refinements, and improvements.

A primary design goal of Windows 98 was compatibility with previous versions of Windows, including Windows 95 and Windows 3.1. It also provides compatibility with DOS. If you have an older program, it can still run just fine under Windows 98. Thus, Windows 98 was designed to be compatible with the large base of existing PC applications. Windows 98 automatically creates the right environment for the type of program you run.

1

For example, when you execute a DOS program, Windows 98 automatically creates a windowed command prompt in which the program runs.

Key Features of Windows 98

From the programmer's perspective, the defining characteristics of Windows 98 are:

1. The 32-bit programming environment
2. Thread-based multitasking
3. The call-based interface
4. Dynamic Link Libraries

Let's look at each.

A 32-bit Operating System

Perhaps the single most important characteristic of Windows 98 is that it is a 32-bit operating system. The original versions of Windows, through Windows 3.1, were 16-bit operating systems. The first 32-bit version of Windows was NT. This was followed by Windows 95. Moving to 32 bits increased the power of Windows and left behind many of the quirks and problems associated with the older 16-bit systems.

While 32-bit environments are now the norm, many older programs were originally written for 16 bits. Although these older programs may still be run under Windows 98, they are not efficient. As you will see as you progress through this book, the 32-bit environment offers many performance improvements.

Windows 98 Uses Thread-based Multitasking

A process is essentially a program that is executing.

As you almost certainly know, Windows 98 is a multitasking operating system. As such, it can run two or more programs concurrently. Of course, the programs share the CPU and do not, technically, run simultaneously. What you may not be aware of is that Windows 98 supports two forms of multitasking: process-based and thread-based. A process is a program that is executing. Because Windows 98 can multitask processes, it can run more than one program at a time. Thus, Windows 98 supports the traditional, process-based multitasking with which you are probably familiar.

A thread is an individual unit of executable code within a process.

Windows 98's second form of multitasking is thread based. A thread is a dispatchable unit of executable code. The name comes from the concept of a "thread of execution." All processes have at least one thread. However, a Windows 98 process may have several.

Since Windows 98 multitasks threads and each process can have more than one thread, it is possible for one process to have two or more pieces of itself executing simultaneously. Therefore, when working with Windows 98, it is possible to multitask both programs and pieces of a single program. As you will see later in this book, this makes it possible to write very efficient programs.

The Windows 98 Call-based Interface

The API defines the programming interface to Windows 98.

Your application programs communicate with Windows 98 through a call-based interface. The Windows 98 call-based interface is an extensive set of system-defined functions that provide access to operating system features. Collectively, these functions are called the *Application Programming Interface*, or API for short. The API contains several hundred functions that your application program calls in order to communicate with Windows 98. These functions perform all necessary operating system-related activities, such as memory allocation, outputting to the screen, creating windows, and the like. For example, if your program wishes to create a window, it calls the API function **CreateWindow( )**. There is a subset to the API called the GDI (Graphics Device Interface), which is the part of Windows that provides device-independent graphics support.

There are two basic flavors of the API in common use: Win16 and Win32. Win16 is the older, 16-bit version of the API. Win32 is the modern, 32-bit version. Win16 is used by Windows 3.1. Windows 98 programs use Win32, as do Windows 95 and Windows NT. Win32 is a superset of Win16. Indeed, for the most part, the functions are called by the same name and are used in the same way.

Even though similar in spirit and purpose, the two APIs differ in two fundamental ways. First, Win32 supports 32-bit, flat addressing while Win16 supports only the 16-bit, segmented memory model. This difference caused several API functions to be widened to accept 32-bit arguments and return 32-bit values. Also, a few API functions were altered to accommodate the 32-bit architecture. Second, API functions were added to support thread-based multitasking, new interface elements, and other enhanced 32-bit features. If you are new to Windows programming in general, these changes will not affect you significantly. However, if you will be porting code from Windows 3.1 to Windows 98, you will need to carefully examine the arguments you pass to each API function.

Dynamic Link Libraries (DLLs)

The Windows 98 API, Win32, is implemented in DLLs.

The Win32 API functions are contained in Dynamic Link Libraries, or DLLs for short, which each program has access to when it is executed. The API functions are stored in a relocatable format within a DLL. During the compilation phase, when your program calls an API function, the linker does not add the code for that function to the executable file for your program. Instead, it adds loading instructions for that function, such as what DLL it resides in and its name. When your program is executed, the necessary API routines are also loaded by the Windows 98 loader. In this way, each application program does not need to contain the actual API code. The API functions are added only when the application is loaded into memory for execution.

Dynamic linking has some very important benefits. First, since virtually all programs will use the API functions, DLLs prevent disk space from being wasted by the significant amount of duplicated object code that would be created if the API functions were actually added to each program's executable file on disk. Second, updates and enhancements to Windows 98 can be accomplished by changing the dynamic link library routines. Existing application programs do not need to be recompiled.

How Windows 98 Differs from Previous Versions

At the time of this writing there are four versions of Windows in common use: Windows 95, Windows 3.1, Windows NT, and, of course, Windows 98. It is important to understand some of the differences between these versions.

Windows 98 vs. Windows 95

From the programmer's perspective, Windows 98 is very similar to Windows 95. In fact, most of the enhancements to Windows 95 that were incorporated into Windows 98 are found "under the hood" and do not affect the way you will write programs. That said, there are a few differences that relate to the computing environment in general, and may indirectly affect how you program. First, Windows 98 supports much tighter Web integration. The Active Desktop is a standard feature, and support for Internet-based services and upgrades is significantly improved over Windows 95. Second is Windows

98's support for multiple monitors. You can put as many as nine monitors in one system. This opens the door to many exciting possibilities. Finally, Windows 98 provides support for additional control elements that can be used by applications.

From the user's perspective, Windows 98 looks like a supercharged version of Windows 95. It provides the user with better access to the Web, better performance and reliability, and the opportunity to access such innovations as WebTV. Users already comfortable with Windows 95 will be at home with Windows 98.

Windows 98 vs. Windows 3.1

Although 32-bit systems have been the norm for several years, 16-bit computers running Windows 3.1 are still commonplace. Although the general approach to programming for Windows 98 is similar to that used to program Windows 3.1, but differences exist. An understanding of these differences will be valuable if you will be working on, or porting, older code, or preparing backward-compatible versions of new programs. Here is an overview of the most important differences.

Windows 98 Does Not Require DOS

Windows 98 does not require DOS. As you probably know, Windows 3.1 was not a completely stand-alone operating system. It ran on top of DOS, which provided support for the file system. Windows 98 is a complete operating system, and DOS is no longer needed. However, Windows 98 still provides support for DOS programs. When you run a DOS program, a windowed command prompt interface is automatically created. Further, this windowed command prompt is fully integrated into the overall Windows 98 graphical interface. For example, you can execute Windows programs directly from the prompt. This was not the case with Windows 3.1.

Windows 98 Supports Long Filenames

Windows 98 supports long filenames. DOS and Windows 3.1 only allowed eight-character filenames followed by a three-character extension. Windows 98 allows filenames to be up to 255 characters long.

32-bit vs. 16-bit Addressing

Windows 98 supports 32-bit, flat addressing and uses virtual memory. Windows 3.1 uses a 16-bit segmented addressing mode. For many application programs, this difference will have little effect. For others, the effect will be substantial.

Because Windows 98 supports full 32-bit addressing, it makes sense that integers are also 32 bits long. This means that types **int** and **unsigned** will be 32 bits, not 16 bits long as is the case for Windows 3.1. If you want to use a 16-bit integer, it must be declared as **short**. (Portable **typedef** names are provided by Windows 98 for these types.) This means that if you will be porting code from the 16-bit environment, you will need to check your use of integers because they will automatically be expanded from 16 to 32 bits and side effects may result.

Another result of 32-bit addressing is that pointers no longer need to be declared as **near** or **far**. Any pointer can access any part of memory.

Multitasking

Preemptive multitasking gives each task a slice of CPU time. Non-preemptive multitasking relies upon each application to relinquish control of the CPU.

Windows 3.1 uses a non-preemptive approach to task switching. This means that a Windows 3.1 task must manually return control to the scheduler in order for another task to run. In other words, a Windows 3.1 program retains control of the CPU until it decides to give it up. Therefore, an ill-behaved program could monopolize the CPU. By contrast, Windows 98 uses preemptive, time-slice-based tasking. In this scheme, tasks are automatically preempted by Windows 98, and the CPU is then assigned to the next task (if one exists). Preemptive multitasking is the superior method because it allows the operating system to fully control tasking and prevents one task from dominating the system.

Windows 3.1 supports process-based multitasking only. That is, the process is Windows 3.1's smallest dispatchable unit. As mentioned earlier, Windows 98 multitasks both threads and processes. While older Windows 3.1 programs will require no changes to run fine under Windows 98, you may want to enhance them to take advantage of thread-based multitasking.

Input Queues

An input queue holds messages sent to your program.

Input queues hold messages, such as a keypress or mouse activity, until they can be sent to your program. In Windows 3.1, there is just one input queue for all tasks running in the system. However, Windows 98 supplies each thread with its own input queue. The advantage to each thread having its own queue is that no one process can reduce system performance by responding to its messages slowly. Although multiple input queues are an important addition, this change has no direct impact on how you program for Windows 98.

Consoles

In Windows 3.1, text-based (i.e., non-windowed) applications were fairly inconvenient to use from Windows. However, Windows 98 supports a special type of window called a console. A console window provides a standard text-based interface, command-prompt environment. However, aside from being text-based, a console acts and can be manipulated like other windows. The text-based console not only allows non-windowed applications to run in a full Windows environment, but also makes it more convenient for you to create short, throwaway utility programs.

Flat Addressing and Virtual Memory

Windows 98 applications have available to them 4 gigabytes of virtual memory in which to run. Further, this address space is flat. Unlike Windows 3.1 and DOS, which use segmented memory, Windows 98 treats memory as linear. And because it virtualizes it, each application has as much memory as it needs. While the change to flat addressing is mostly transparent to the programmer, it does relieve much of the tedium and frustration of dealing with the old, segmented approach.

Changes to Messages and Parameter Types

Because of Windows 98's shift to 32-bit addressing, some messages passed to a Windows 98 program will be organized differently than they are when passed to a Windows 3.1 program. Also, the parameter types used to declare a window function have changed because of the move to 32-bit addressing. The specific changes to the messages and parameters will be discussed later in this book, as they are used.

Windows 98 vs. Windows NT

Windows NT is Microsoft's high-end Windows-based operating system. Windows NT has much in common with Windows 98. Both use the Win32 API; both support 32-bit, flat addressing; both support thread-based multitasking; and both support the console-based interface. However, Windows 98 is not Windows NT. For example, Windows NT uses a special approach to operating system implementation based on the client/server model. Windows 98 does not. Windows NT supports a full security system; Windows 98 does not. While there is no doubt that much of the basic technology developed for use in Windows NT eventually found its way into Windows 98, they are not the same.

Frankly, programming for Windows 98 is very similar to programming for Windows NT (with a few exceptions, security being the most notable). For the most part, a program written for Windows 98 will run under Windows NT and vice versa. However, there are some subtle differences, which you will need to watch for when porting code to Windows NT. Also, in some areas Windows NT is a bit more powerful.

Two Ways to Program for Windows 98

There are two ways you can write programs for Windows 98. The first is to use the API functions defined by Win32. In this approach, your programs directly utilize the API and explicitly handle all of the details associated with a Windows 98 program. This is the method used by this book.

The second way to program for Windows 98 uses a special C++ class library, which encapsulates the API. By far the most popular Windows programming class library is MFC (Microsoft Foundation Classes). MFC is a powerful development tool that offers significant advantages in some situations. But it is best employed after you have gained a firm foundation in Windows programming using the API. The reasons for this are simple.

First, there is a fundamental architecture that all Windows programs share. MFC masks many elements of this architecture. Knowledge of the Windows architecture is crucial to long-term programming success. For example, it makes debugging a Windows application easier. Second, using the API gives you detailed and complete control over how your program executes. Some types of low-level control are not possible using MFC. Third, all Windows 98 programming environments support API-based programming. It is a portable skill. Fourth, the API can be programmed in either C or C++. MFC requires C++. However, many software shops use C, which prevents their use of MFC. Finally, if you can program for Windows 98 using the API, you can more easily learn to use MFC or any other class library. Simply put: You cannot be a top-notch, professional Windows 98 programmer unless you know how to program using the API.

 NOTE: If you are interested in MFC programming, I suggest my book, *MFC Programming from the Ground Up* (Osborne/McGraw-Hill, Berkeley, CA). It contains a detailed description of MFC programming.

Challenging but Rewarding

Now that the stage has been set, we are ready to begin writing programs. If you have never written any type of Windows program before, the next few chapters will contain many unfamiliar concepts and require the use of several new programming techniques. Just be patient. Although it might be a bit overwhelming at first, before long, writing programs for Windows 98 will be second nature. Even though Windows 98 is a challenging environment, it is also a rewarding one. Once you master it, you will possess some of the most highly sought-after skills in the programming profession.

CHAPTER 2

Windows 98 Programming Overview

This chapter introduces Windows 98 programming. It has two main purposes. First, it discusses how a program must interact with Windows 98 and what rules must be followed by every Windows 98 application. Second, it develops an application skeleton that will be used as a basis for the other Windows 98 programs developed in this book. As you will see, all Windows 98 programs share several common traits. It is these shared attributes that will be contained in the application skeleton.

As the preceding chapter mentioned, although they are similar in spirit, there are significant differences between Windows 98 and Windows 3.1. Windows 98 also deviates from Windows 95 and Windows NT in a few ways. These differences will be discussed as they occur, in the Portability tips found throughout this book. Pay special attention to these if you will be porting older applications or writing new ones that must run on other versions of Windows.

To begin, this chapter presents the Windows 98 programming perspective.

Windows 98 Programming Perspective

The goal of Windows 98 (and Windows in general) is to enable a person who has basic familiarity with the system to sit down and run virtually any application without prior training. Toward this end, Windows provides a consistent interface to the user. In theory, if you can run one Windows-based program, you can run them all. Of course, in actuality, most useful programs will still require some sort of training in order to be used effectively, but at least this instruction can be restricted to *what* the program *does*, not *how* the user must *interact* with it. In fact, much of the code in a Windows application is there just to support the user interface.

Before continuing, it must be stated that not every program that runs under Windows 98 will necessarily present the user with a Windows-style interface. It is possible to write Windows programs that do not take advantage of the standard interface elements. To create a Windows-style program, you must purposely do so using the techniques described in this book. Only those programs written to take advantage of Windows will look and feel like Windows programs. While you can override the basic Windows design philosophy, you had better have a good reason to do so, because the users of your programs will, most often, be very disappointed. In general, if you are writing application programs for Windows 98, they should utilize the normal Windows interface and conform to the standard Windows design practices.

Windows 98 is graphics oriented, which means that it provides a graphical user interface (GUI). While graphics hardware and video modes are quite

2

diverse, many of the differences are handled by Windows. This means that, for the most part, your program does not need to worry about what type of graphics hardware or video mode is being used. However, because of its graphical orientation, you (the programmer) have added responsibility when creating Windows applications. As you will see, many chapters in this book are devoted to the correct management of the screen.

Let's look at a few of the more important features of Windows 98.

The Desktop Model

With few exceptions, the point of a window-based user interface is to provide on the screen the equivalent of a desktop. On a desk may be found several different pieces of paper, one on top of another, often with fragments of different pages visible beneath the top page. The equivalent of the desktop in Windows 98 is the screen. The equivalents of pieces of paper are windows on the screen. On a desk you may move pieces of paper about, maybe switching which piece of paper is on top or how much of another is exposed to view. Windows 98 allows the same type of operations on its windows. By selecting a window you can make it current, which means putting it on top of all other windows. You can enlarge or shrink a window, or move it about on the screen. In short, Windows lets you control the surface of the screen the way you control the surface of your desk.

While the desktop model forms the foundation of the Windows 98 user interface, Windows 98 is not limited by it. In fact, several of the Windows 98 interface elements emulate other types of familiar devices, such as slider controls, spin controls, tree lists, and toolbars. As you will see, Windows 98 gives you, the programmer, a large array of features from which to choose those most appropriate to your specific application.

Windows 98 also offers the user the option of viewing the desktop in its traditional format or as a web page. The web page option allows a user to give the desktop the look and feel of the Web while still retaining the advantages of a windowed interface.

The Mouse

Like preceding versions of Windows, Windows 98 allows the use of the mouse for almost all control, selection, and drawing operations. Of course, to say that it *allows* the use of the mouse is an understatement. The fact is that the Windows 98 interface was *designed for the mouse*—it *allows* the use of the keyboard! Although it is certainly possible for an application program to ignore the mouse, it does so in violation of a basic Windows design principle.

Icons, Bitmaps, and Graphics

Icons and
bitmaps are
graphical
images.

Windows 98 encourages the use of icons, bitmaps, and other types of graphics. The theory behind these items is found in the old adage, "A picture is worth a thousand words." An *icon* is a small symbol that represents some operation, resource, or program. A *bitmap* is a rectangular graphics image often used to simply convey information quickly to the user. However, bitmaps can also be used as menu elements. Windows 98 supports a full range of graphics capabilities, including the ability to draw lines, rectangles, and circles. The proper use of these graphical elements is an important part of successful Windows programming.

Menus, Controls, and Dialog Boxes

A menu is a list
from which the
user may select
an option.

Windows provides several standard items that allow user input. They are the menu, various types of controls, and the dialog box. Briefly, a *menu* displays options from which the user makes a selection. Since menus are standard elements in Windows programming, support for them is built in. Your program does not need to handle all of the clerical overhead associated with menus itself.

A control allows
a specific
type of user
interaction.

A *control* is a special type of window that allows a specific type of user interaction. Examples are *push buttons, scroll bars, edit windows,* and *check boxes.* Like menus, the controls defined by Windows are nearly completely automated. Your program can use one without having to handle the details.

A dialog box
is used when
non-menu input
is required.

A *dialog box* is a special window that allows more complex interaction with the application than that found in a menu. For example, your application might use a dialog box to input a filename. Dialog boxes are typically used to house controls. With few exceptions, non-menu input is accomplished via a dialog box.

Internet Integration

Windows 98 provides the user with tight integration with the online environment of the Internet. Items such as the Channel Bar and the Active Desktop offer seamless integration with the Web. Fortunately, much of the Internet integration is provided automatically by Windows 98, and it is not something you will typically need to deal with explicitly in your programs. However, some Internet-related programming issues are discussed later in this book.

The Components of a Window

Before moving on to specific aspects of Windows 98 programming, a few important terms need to be defined. Figure 2-1 shows a standard window with each of its elements pointed out.

2

All windows have a border that defines the limits of the window and is used to resize the window. At the top of the window are several items. On the far left is the system menu icon (also called the title bar icon). Clicking on this box causes the system menu to be displayed. To the right of the system menu box is the window's title. At the far right are the minimize, maximize, and close boxes. The client area is the part of the window in which your program activity takes place. Most windows also have horizontal and vertical scroll bars that are used to move text through the window.

How Windows 98 and Your Program Interact

When you write a program for many operating systems, it is your program that initiates interaction with the operating system. For example, in a DOS program, it is the program that requests such things as input and output. Put differently, programs written in the "traditional way" call the operating system. The operating system does not call your program. However, in a large measure, Windows 98 works in the opposite way. It is Windows 98 that calls your program. The process works like this: a Windows 98 program waits until

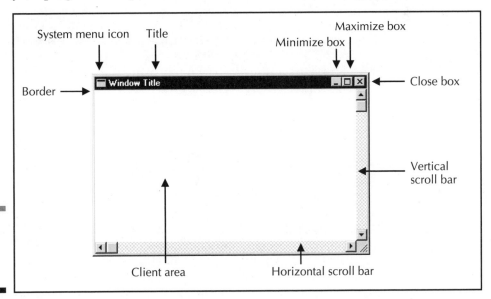

The elements
of a standard
window

Figure 2-1.

it is sent a *message* by Windows. The message is passed to your program through a special function that is called by Windows. Once a message is received, your program is expected to take an appropriate action. While your program may call one or more Windows 98 API functions when responding to a message, it is still Windows 98 that initiates the activity. More than anything else, it is the message-based interaction with Windows 98 that dictates the general form of all Windows 98 programs.

There are many different types of messages that Windows 98 may send your program. For example, each time the mouse is clicked on a window belonging to your program, a mouse-clicked message will be sent. Another type of message is sent each time a window belonging to your program must be redrawn. Still another message is sent each time the user presses a key when your program is the focus of input. Keep one fact firmly in mind: as far as your program is concerned, messages arrive randomly. This is why Windows 98 programs resemble interrupt-driven programs. You can't know what message will be next.

Some Windows 98 Application Basics

Before developing the Windows 98 application skeleton, some basic concepts common to all Windows 98 programs need to be discussed.

WinMain( )

All Windows 98 programs begin execution with a call to **WinMain( )**. (Windows programs do not have a **main( )** function.) **WinMain( )** has some special properties that differentiate it from other functions in your application. First, it must be compiled using the **WINAPI** calling convention. (You will see **APIENTRY** used as well. They both mean the same thing.) By default, functions in your C or C++ programs use the C calling convention. However, it is possible to compile a function so that it uses a different calling convention. For example, a common alternative is to use the Pascal calling convention. For various technical reasons, the calling convention Windows 98 uses to call **WinMain( )** is **WINAPI**. The return type of **WinMain( )** should be **int**.

PORTABILITY: In older Windows 3.1 programs, the calling convention used for **WinMain( )** was **PASCAL**. However, this should be changed to **WINAPI** when porting 3.1 applications to Windows 98.

The Window Procedure

A window procedure is a function called by Windows, not by your program.

All Windows 98 programs must contain a special function that is *not* called by your program, but is called by Windows 98. This function is generally referred to as the *window procedure* or *window function*. The window function is called by Windows 98 when it needs to pass a message to your program. It is through this function that Windows 98 communicates with your program. The window function receives the message in its parameters. All window functions must be declared as returning type **LRESULT CALLBACK**. The type **LRESULT** is a **typdef** that (at the time of this writing) is another name for a long integer. The **CALLBACK** calling convention is used with those functions that will be called by Windows 98. In Windows terminology, any function that is called by Windows is referred to as a callback function.

2

PORTABILITY: Windows 3.1 code specifies the window function as **LONG FAR PASCAL**. You should use **CALLBACK** when porting to Windows 98.

In addition to receiving the messages sent by Windows 98, the window function must initiate any actions indicated by a message. Typically, a window function's body consists of a **switch** statement that links a specific response to each message that the program will respond to. Your program need not respond to every message that Windows 98 will send. For messages that your program doesn't care about, you can let Windows 98 provide default processing. Since there are hundreds of different messages that Windows 98 can generate, it is common for most messages to simply be processed by Windows 98 and not by your program.

All messages are 32-bit integer values. Further, all messages are linked with any additional information that the message requires.

Window Classes

A window class defines the style of a window.

When your Windows 98 program first begins execution, it will need to define and register a *window class*. (Here, the word *class* is not being used in its C++ sense. Rather, it means *style* or *type*.) When you register a window class, you are telling Windows 98 about the form and function of the window. However, registering the window class does not cause a window to come into existence. To actually create a window requires additional steps.

The Message Loop

As explained earlier, Windows 98 communicates with your program by sending it messages. All Windows 98 applications must establish a *message loop* inside the **WinMain( )** function. This loop reads any pending message from the application's message queue and then dispatches that message back to Windows 98, which then calls your program's window function with that message as a parameter. This may seem to be an overly complex way of passing messages, but it is, nevertheless, the way that all Windows programs must function. (Part of the reason for this procedure is to return control to Windows 98 so that the scheduler can allocate CPU time as it sees fit rather than waiting for your application's time slice to end.)

Windows Data Types

As you will soon see, Windows 98 programs do not make extensive use of standard C/C++ data types, such as **int** or **char ***. Instead, all data types used by Windows 98 have been **typdef**ed within the WINDOWS.H file and/or its related files. This file is supplied by Microsoft (and any other company that makes a Windows 98 C++ compiler) and must be included in all Windows 98 programs. Some of the most common types are **HANDLE**, **HWND**, **UINT**, **BYTE**, **WORD**, **DWORD**, **LONG**, **BOOL**, **LPSTR**, and **LPCSTR**. **HANDLE** is a 32-bit integer that is used as a handle. As you will see, there are a number of handle types, but they all are the same size as **HANDLE**. A *handle* is simply a value that identifies some resource. For example, **HWND** is a 32-bit integer that is used as a window handle. Also, all handle types begin with an "H". **BYTE** is an 8-bit unsigned character. **WORD** is a 16-bit unsigned short integer. **DWORD** is an unsigned long integer. **UINT** is an unsigned 32-bit integer. **LONG** is another name for **long**. **BOOL** is an integer. This type is used to indicate values that are either true or false. **LPSTR** is a pointer to a string, and **LPCSTR** is a **const** pointer to a string.

In addition to the basic types described above, Windows 98 defines several structures. The two that are needed by the skeleton program are **MSG** and **WNDCLASSEX**. The **MSG** structure holds a Windows 98 message, and **WNDCLASSEX** is a structure that defines a window class. These structures will be discussed later in this chapter

 PORTABILITY: **UINT** is a 32-bit unsigned integer when compiling Windows 98 programs. It is also a 32-bit integer under Windows 95 and Windows NT. But it is a 16-bit unsigned integer if you compile your code for Windows 3.1.

A Windows 98 Skeleton

Now that the necessary background information has been covered, it is time to develop a minimal Windows 98 application. As stated, all Windows 98 programs have certain things in common. In this section a Windows 98 skeleton is developed that provides these necessary features. In the world of Windows programming, application skeletons are commonly used because there is a substantial "price of admission" when creating a Windows program. Unlike DOS programs that you may have written, in which a minimal program is about five lines long, a minimal Windows program is approximately 50 lines long. Therefore, application skeletons are commonly used when developing Windows applications.

A minimal Windows 98 program contains two functions: **WinMain( )** and the window function. The **WinMain( )** function must perform the following general steps:

1. Define a window class.
2. Register that class with Windows 98.
3. Create a window of that class.
4. Display the window.
5. Begin running the message loop.

The window function must respond to all relevant messages. Since the skeleton program does nothing but display its window, the only message that it must respond to is the one that tells the application that the user has terminated the program.

Before discussing the specifics, examine the following program, which is a minimal Windows 98 skeleton. It creates a standard window that includes a title. The window also contains the system menu and is, therefore, capable of being minimized, maximized, moved, resized, and closed. It also contains the standard minimize, maximize, and close boxes. Remember, the code in this book can be compiled as either a C or C++ program.

```
/* A minimal Windows 98 skeleton. */

#include <windows.h>

LRESULT CALLBACK WindowFunc(HWND, UINT, WPARAM, LPARAM);

char szWinName[] = "MyWin"; /* name of window class */
```

```
int WINAPI WinMain(HINSTANCE hThisInst, HINSTANCE hPrevInst,
                   LPSTR lpszArgs, int nWinMode)
{
  HWND hwnd;
  MSG msg;
  WNDCLASSEX wcl;

  /* Define a window class. */
  wcl.cbSize = sizeof(WNDCLASSEX);

  wcl.hInstance = hThisInst; /* handle to this instance */
  wcl.lpszClassName = szWinName; /* window class name */
  wcl.lpfnWndProc = WindowFunc; /* window function */
  wcl.style = 0; /* default style */

  wcl.hIcon = LoadIcon(NULL, IDI_APPLICATION); /* standard icon */
  wcl.hIconSm = LoadIcon(NULL, IDI_WINLOGO); /* small icon */
  wcl.hCursor = LoadCursor(NULL, IDC_ARROW); /* cursor style */

  wcl.lpszMenuName = NULL; /* no menu */
  wcl.cbClsExtra = 0; /* no extra information needed */
  wcl.cbWndExtra = 0; /* no extra information needed */

  /* Make the window background white. */
  wcl.hbrBackground = (HBRUSH) GetStockObject(WHITE_BRUSH);

  /* Register the window class. */
  if(!RegisterClassEx(&wcl)) return 0;

  /* Now that a window class has been registered, a window
     can be created. */
  hwnd = CreateWindow(
    szWinName, /* name of window class */
    "Windows 98 Skeleton", /* title */
    WS_OVERLAPPEDWINDOW, /* window style - normal */
    CW_USEDEFAULT, /* X coordinate - let Windows decide */
    CW_USEDEFAULT, /* Y coordinate - let Windows decide */
    CW_USEDEFAULT, /* width - let Windows decide */
    CW_USEDEFAULT, /* height - let Windows decide */
    HWND_DESKTOP, /* no parent window */
    NULL, /* no menu */
    hThisInst, /* handle of this instance of the program */
    NULL /* no additional arguments */
  );

  /* Display the window. */
```

2

```
  ShowWindow(hwnd, nWinMode);
  UpdateWindow(hwnd);

  /* Create the message loop. */
  while(GetMessage(&msg, NULL, 0, 0))
  {
    TranslateMessage(&msg); /* translate keyboard messages */
    DispatchMessage(&msg); /* return control to Windows 98 */
  }
  return msg.wParam;
}

/* This function is called by Windows 98 and is passed
   messages from the message queue.
*/
LRESULT CALLBACK WindowFunc(HWND hwnd, UINT message,
                            WPARAM wParam, LPARAM lParam)
{
  switch(message) {
    case WM_DESTROY: /* terminate the program */
      PostQuitMessage(0);
      break;
    default:
      /* Let Windows 98 process any messages not specified in
         the preceding switch statement. */
      return DefWindowProc(hwnd, message, wParam, lParam);
  }
  return 0;
}
```

Let's go through this program step by step.

First, all Windows 98 programs must include the header file WINDOWS.H. As stated, this file (along with its support files) contains the API function prototypes and various types, macros, and definitions used by Windows 98. For example, the data types **HWND** and **WNDCLASSEX** are defined in WINDOWS.H.

The window function used by the program is called **WindowFunc( )**. It is declared as a callback function because this is the function that Windows 98 calls to communicate with the program.

As explained, program execution begins with **WinMain( )**. **WinMain( )** is passed four parameters. **hThisInst** and **hPrevInst** are handles. **hThisInst** refers to the current instance of the program. Remember, Windows 98 is a multitasking system, so it is possible that more than one instance of your program may be running at the same time. **hPrevInst** will always be **NULL**. The **lpszArgs** parameter is a pointer to a string that holds any command-line arguments specified when the application was begun. The **nWinMode** parameter contains a value that determines how the window will be displayed when your program begins execution.

Inside the function, three variables are created. The **hwnd** variable will hold the handle to the program's window. The **msg** structure variable will hold window messages, and the **wcl** structure variable will be used to define the window class.

PORTABILITY: As mentioned above, the **hPrevInst** parameter will always be **NULL** in a Windows 98 program. It will also always be **NULL** in a Windows 95 program or a Windows NT program. But in a Windows 3.1 program, **hPrevInst** will be nonzero if there are other instances of the program currently executing. This reflects a fundamental difference between Windows 3.1 and Windows 98. In Windows 3.1, multiple instances of a program share window classes and various other bits of data. Therefore, it was important for an application to know if another version of itself was running in the system. However, in Windows 98 each process is isolated from the next and there is no automatic sharing of window classes and the like. The only reason that **hPrevInst** exists in Windows 98 is for the sake of compatibility.

Defining the Window Class

The first two actions that **WinMain( )** takes is to define a window class and then register it. A window class is defined by filling in the fields defined by the **WNDCLASSEX** structure. Its fields are shown here.

```
UINT cbSize; /* size of the WNDCLASSEX structure */
UINT style; /* type of window */
WNDPROC lpfnWndProc; /* address to window func */
int cbClsExtra; /* extra class info */
int cbWndExtra; /* extra window info */
HINSTANCE hInstance; /* handle of this instance */
HICON hIcon; /* handle of standard icon */
HICON hIconSm; /* handle of small icon */
HCURSOR hCursor; /* handle of mouse cursor */
HBRUSH hbrBackground; /* background color */
LPCSTR lpszMenuName; /* name of main menu */
LPCSTR lpszClassName; /* name of window class */
```

As you can see by looking at the program, **cbSize** is assigned the size of the **WNDCLASSEX** structure. The **hInstance** member is assigned the current instance handle as specified by **hThisInst**. The name of the window class is pointed to by **lpszClassName**, which points to the string "MyWin" in this case. The address of the window function is assigned to **lpfnWndProc**. No default style is specified. No extra information is needed.

2

PORTABILITY: In Windows 3.1, each window class must only be registered once. Therefore, if another instance of the program is running, then the current instance must not define and register the window class. To avoid this possibility, the value of **hPrevInst** is tested. If it is nonzero, then the window class has already been registered by a previous instance. If not, then the window class is defined and registered. However, this test is not needed by Windows 98 and is not included in any of the examples in this book. For downward compatibility with Windows 3.1, you may wish to include it, and doing so causes no harm.

All Windows applications need to define a default shape for the mouse cursor and for the application's icons. An application can define its own custom version of these resources or it may use one of the built-in styles, as the skeleton does. In either case, handles to these resources must be assigned to the appropriate members of the **WNDCLASSEX** structure. To see how this is done, let's begin with icons.

A Windows 98 application has two icons associated with it, one standard size and one small. (Windows 3.1 and early versions of Windows NT only supported the standard icon.) The small icon is used when the application is minimized, and it is also the icon that is used for the system menu. The standard icon (also called the large icon) is displayed when you move or copy an application to the desktop. Typically, standard icons are 32 x 32 bitmaps and small icons are 16 x 16 bitmaps. Standard icons are loaded by the API function **LoadIcon( )**, whose prototype is shown here:

HICON LoadIcon(HINSTANCE *hInst*, LPCSTR *lpszName*);

This function returns a handle to an icon. Here, *hInst* specifies the handle of the module that contains the icon, and its name is specified in *lpszName*. However, to use one of the built-in icons, you must use **NULL** for the first parameter and the name of a built-in icon for the second. Here are the names of some of the built-in icons.

Icon Macro	Shape
IDI_APPLICATION	Default icon
IDI_ERROR	Error symbol
IDI_INFORMATION	Information
IDI_QUESTION	Question mark
IDI_WARNING	Exclamation point
IDI_WINLOGO	Windows logo

Here are two important points about loading icons. First, if your application does not specify a small icon, then the standard icon is simply shrunk when the small icon is needed. If you don't want to specify a small icon, then assign **hIconSm** the value **NULL**. Second, in general, **LoadIcon( )** can only be used to load the standard-size icon. However, as the skeleton shows, it can also be used to load the small icon if that icon is built in. Later in this book, you will see how to create your own custom icons, including the small icon.

To load the mouse cursor, use the API **LoadCursor( )** function. This function has the following prototype:

HCURSOR LoadCursor(HINSTANCE *hInst*, LPCSTR *lpszName*);

This function returns a handle to a cursor resource. Here, *hInst* specifies the handle of the module that contains the mouse cursor, and its name is specified in *lpszName*. However, to use one of the built-in cursors, you must use **NULL** for the first parameter and specify one of the built-in cursors using its macros for the second parameter. Some of the most common built-in cursors are shown here.

Cursor Macro	Shape
IDC_ARROW	Default arrow pointer
IDC_CROSS	Cross hairs
IDC_IBEAM	Vertical I-beam
IDC_WAIT	Hourglass

The background color of the window created by the skeleton is specified as white, and a handle to this *brush* is obtained using the API function

GetStockObject( ). A brush is a resource that paints the screen using a predetermined size, color, and pattern. The function **GetStockObject( )** is used to obtain a handle to a number of standard display objects, including brushes, pens (which draw lines), and character fonts. It has this prototype:

HGDIOBJ GetStockObject(int *object*);

The function returns a handle to the object specified by *object*. (The type **HGDIOBJ** is a GDI handle.) Here are some of the built-in brushes available to your program:

Macro Name	Background Type
BLACK_BRUSH	Black
DKGRAY_BRUSH	Dark gray
HOLLOW_BRUSH	See-through window
LTGRAY_BRUSH	Light gray
WHITE_BRUSH	White

You can use these macros as parameters to **GetStockObject( )** to obtain a brush.

Once the window class has been fully specified, it is registered with Windows 98 using the API function **RegisterClassEx( )**, whose prototype is shown here:

ATOM RegisterClassEx(CONST WNDCLASSEX *lpWClass*);

The function returns a value that identifies the window class. **ATOM** is a **typedef** that means **WORD**. Each window class is given a unique value. *lpWClass* must be the address of a **WNDCLASSEX** structure.

PORTABILITY: Windows 3.1 and early Windows NT programs defined only one icon, the window class was defined by a **WNDCLASS** structure, and the class was registered using **RegisterClass( )**. The **WNDCLASS** structure is similar to **WNDCLASSEX** except that it does not define the **cbSize** or **hIconSm** members.

Creating a Window

Once a window class has been defined and registered, your application can actually create a window of that class using the API function **CreateWindow( )**, whose prototype is shown here.

```
HWND CreateWindow(
    LPCSTR lpszClassName,      /* name of window class */
    LPCSTR lpszWinName,        /* title of window */
    DWORD dwStyle,             /* type of window */
    int X, int Y,              /* upper-left coordinates */
    int Width, int Height,     /* dimensions of window */
    HWND hParent,              /* handle of parent window */
    HMENU hMenu,               /* handle of main menu */
    HINSTANCE hThisInst,       /* handle of creator */
    LPVOID lpszAdditional      /* pointer to additional info */
);
```

As you can see by looking at the skeleton program, many of the parameters to **CreateWindow( )** may be defaulted or specified as **NULL**. In fact, most often the *X,Y*, *Width*, and *Height* parameters will simply use the macro **CW_USEDEFAULT**, which tells Windows 98 to select an appropriate size and location for the window. If the window has no parent, which is the case in the skeleton, then *hParent* must be specified as **HWND_DESKTOP**. (You may also use **NULL** for this parameter.) If the window does not contain a main menu, then *hMenu* must be **NULL**. Also, if no additional information is required, as is most often the case, then *lpszAdditional* is **NULL**. (The type **LPVOID** is **typedef**ed as **void ***. Historically, **LPVOID** stands for long pointer to **void**.)

The remaining four parameters must be explicitly set by your program. First, *lpszClassName* must point to the name of the window class. (This is the name you gave it when it was registered.) The title of the window is a string pointed to by *lpszWinName*. This can be a null string, but usually a window will be given a title. The style (or type) of window actually created is determined by the value of *dwStyle*. The macro **WS_OVERLAPPED-WINDOW** specifies a standard window that has a system menu, a border, and minimize, maximize, and close boxes. While this style of window is the most common, you can construct one to your own specifications. To accomplish this, you simply OR together the various style macros that you want. Some other common styles are shown here.

Style Macros	Window Feature
WS_OVERLAPPED	Overlapped window with border
WS_MAXIMIZEBOX	Maximize box
WS_MINIMIZEBOX	Minimize box
WS_SYSMENU	System menu
WS_HSCROLL	Horizontal scroll bar
WS_VSCROLL	Vertical scroll bar

The *hThisInst* parameter must contain the current instance handle of the application.

The **CreateWindow( )** function returns the handle of the window it creates or **NULL** if the window cannot be created.

Once the window has been created, it is still not displayed on the screen. To cause the window to be displayed, call the **ShowWindow( )** API function. This function has the following prototype:

    BOOL ShowWindow(HWND *hwnd*, int *nHow*);

The handle of the window to display is specified in *hwnd*. The display mode is specified in *nHow*. The first time the window is displayed, you will want to pass **WinMain( )**'s **nWinMode** as the *nHow* parameter. Remember, the value of **nWinMode** determines how the window will be displayed when the program begins execution. Subsequent calls can display (or remove) the window as necessary. Some common values for *nHow* are shown here.

Display Macros	Effect
SW_HIDE	Removes the window
SW_MINIMIZE	Minimizes the window into an icon
SW_MAXIMIZE	Maximizes the window
SW_RESTORE	Returns a window to normal size

The **ShowWindow( )** function returns the previous display status of the window. If the window was displayed, then nonzero is returned. If the window was not displayed, zero is returned.

Although not technically necessary for the skeleton, a call to **UpdateWindow( )** is included because it is needed by virtually every Windows 98 application that you will create. It essentially tells Windows 98 to send a message to your application that the main window needs to be updated. (This message will be discussed in the next chapter.)

The Message Loop

The final part of the skeletal **WinMain( )** is the *message loop*. The message loop is a part of all Windows applications. Its purpose is to receive and process messages sent by Windows 98. When an application is running, it is continually being sent messages. These messages are stored in the application's message queue until they can be read and processed. Each time your application is ready to read another message, it must call the API function **GetMessage( )**, which has this prototype:

BOOL GetMessage(LPMSG *msg*, HWND *hwnd*, UINT *min*, UINT *max*);

The message will be received by the structure pointed to by *msg*. All Windows messages are of structure type **MSG**, shown here.

```
/* Message structure */
typedef struct tagMSG
{
  HWND hwnd; /* window that message is for */
  UINT message; /* message */
  WPARAM wParam; /* message-dependent info */
  LPARAM lParam; /* more message-dependent info */
  DWORD time; /* time message posted */
  POINT pt; /* X,Y location of mouse */
} MSG;
```

In **MSG**, the handle of the window for which the message is intended is contained in **hwnd**. All Windows 98 messages are 32-bit integers, and the message is contained in **message**. Additional information relating to each message is passed in **wParam** and **lParam**. The type **WPARAM** is a **typedef** for **UINT**, and **LPARAM** is a **typedef** for **LONG**.

PORTABILITY: The **message** field of **MSG** is 16 bits long in Windows 3.1. Also, the **wparam** field, which is 16 bits in Windows 3.1, has been widened to 32 bits in Windows 98. Be aware of these changes when porting code.

The time the message was sent (posted) is specified in milliseconds in the **time** field.

The **pt** member will contain the coordinates of the mouse when the message was sent. The coordinates are held in a **POINT** structure that is defined like this:

```
typedef struct tagPOINT {
  LONG x, y;
} POINT;
```

PORTABILITY: In Windows 3.1, the **x** and **y** in the **POINT** structure are declared as integers. However, in Windows 98, they are widened to **LONG**.

If there are no messages in the application's message queue, then a call to **GetMessage( )** will pass control back to Windows 98. (We will explore messages in greater detail in the next chapter.)

The *hwnd* parameter to **GetMessage( )** specifies for which window messages will be obtained. It is possible (even likely) that an application will contain several windows, and you may only want to receive messages for a specific window. If you want to receive all messages directed at your application, this parameter must be **NULL**. This is the approach used by the programs in this book.

The remaining two parameters to **GetMessage( )** specify a range of messages that will be received. Generally, you want your application to receive all messages. To accomplish this, specify both *min* and *max* as 0, as the skeleton does.

GetMessage( ) returns zero when the user terminates the program, causing the message loop to terminate. Otherwise it returns nonzero. It will return –1 if an error occurs. (Errors can only occur under unusual circumstances; see the following "In Depth" box.) Even though the return type is specified as **BOOL**, it can hold any integer value; **BOOL** is not the same as the **bool** data type in C++.

Inside the message loop two functions are called. The first is the API function **TranslateMessage( )**. This function translates virtual key codes generated by Windows 98 into character messages. (Virtual keys are discussed later in this book.) Although it is not necessary for all applications, most call **TranslateMessage( )** because it is needed to allow full integration of the keyboard into your application program.

Once the message has been read and translated, it is dispatched back to Windows 98 using the **DispatchMessage( )** API function. Windows 98 then holds this message until it can pass it to the program's window function.

Once the message loop terminates, the **WinMain( )** function ends by returning the value of **msg.wParam** to Windows 98. This value contains the return code generated when your program terminates.

The Window Function

The second function in the application skeleton is its window function. In this case the function is called **WindowFunc( )**, but it could have any name you like. The window function is passed the first four members of the **MSG** structure as parameters. For the skeleton, the only parameter that is used is the message itself. However, in the next chapter you will learn more about the parameters to this function.

The skeleton's window function responds explicitly to only one message: **WM_DESTROY**. This message is sent when the user terminates the program. When this message is received, your program must execute a call to the API function **PostQuitMessage( )**. The argument to this function is an exit code that is returned in **msg.wParam** inside **WinMain( ).** Calling **PostQuitMessage( )** causes a **WM_QUIT** message to be sent to your application, which causes **GetMessage( )** to return false and thus stops your program.

Any other messages received by **WindowFunc( )** are passed along to Windows 98, via a call to **DefWindowProc( )**, for default processing. This step is necessary because all messages must be dealt with in one fashion or another.

Definition Files

Definition files are not usually needed by a Windows 98 program.

If you are familiar with Windows 3.1 programming, then you have used *definition files*. For Windows 3.1, all programs need to have a definition file associated with them. A *definition file* is simply a text file that specifies certain information and settings needed by your Windows 3.1 program. However, because of the 32-bit architecture of Windows 98 (and other improvements), definition files are not needed for Windows 98 programs. (They are also not used by Windows 95 or Windows NT.) If you are new to Windows programming in general and you don't know what a definition file is, the following discussion will give you a brief overview.

IN DEPTH

Handling Errors Returned by GetMessage( )

As you may have noticed when reading the description of **GetMessage( )**, even though its return type is specified as **BOOL**, it can actually return three values: true, false, and −1. A −1 indicates that some error has occurred. For the most part, −1 is returned only when the *hwnd* parameter is invalid. Since all of the examples in this book use **NULL** for this parameter, this type of error cannot occur. However, in real-world applications, it is something for which you may need to watch. Of course, errors could also occur because of a system crash, which is beyond the control of your program. (If the computer is crashing, you can't expect your programs to run correctly anyway!) To watch for errors returned by **GetMessage( )**, use a message loop like the one shown here.

```
BOOL result;
/* ... */
while(result = GetMessage(&msg, WinHandle, 0, 0))
{
  if(result == -1) { /* process error */ }
  TranslateMessage(&msg); /* translate keyboard messages */
  DispatchMessage(&msg); /* return control to Windows 98 */
}
```

Here, if **WinHandle** is invalid, **GetMessage( )** will return −1 and the error will be caught by the **if** statement inside the loop. Of course, the **if** statement adds overhead to the message loop that can affect the performance of your program. However, in cases where an error is possible, you must include the necessary error-handling code. If an error does occur, you can use the **GetLastError( )** API function to determine precisely what happened.

As stated, since the programs in this book always pass a valid window handle to **GetMessage( )**, no check is provided for an error return. But be sure to take the possibility of errors into account when creating actual applications.

All definition files use the extension .DEF. For example, the definition file for the skeleton program could be called SKEL.DEF. Here is a definition file that you can use to provide downward compatibility with Windows 3.1.

```
DESCRIPTION 'Skeleton Program'
EXETYPE WINDOWS
CODE PRELOAD MOVEABLE DISCARDABLE
DATA PRELOAD MOVEABLE MULTIPLE
HEAPSIZE 8192
STACKSIZE 8192
EXPORTS WindowFunc
```

This file specifies the name of the program and its description, both of which are optional. It also states that the executable file will be compatible with Windows (rather than DOS, for example). The **CODE** statement tells Windows 98 to load all of the program at startup (PRELOAD), that the code may be moved in memory (MOVEABLE), and that the code may be removed from memory and reloaded if (and when) necessary (DISCARDABLE). The file also states that your program's data must be loaded upon execution and may be moved about in memory. It also specifies that each instance of the program has its own data (MULTIPLE). Next, the size of the heap and stack allocated to the program are specified. Finally, the name of the window function is exported. Exporting allows Windows 3.1 to call the function.

REMEMBER: Definition files are not needed when programming for Windows 98.

Naming Conventions

Before finishing this chapter, a short comment on naming functions and variables is needed. If you are new to Windows 98 programming, several of the variable and parameter names in the skeleton program and its description probably seem rather unusual. The reason for this is that they follow a set of naming conventions invented by Microsoft for Windows programming. For functions, the name consists of a verb followed by a noun. The first character of the verb and noun are capitalized. For the most part, this book will use this convention for function names.

For variable names, Microsoft chose to use a rather complex system of embedding the data type into a variable's name. To accomplish this, a lowercase type prefix is added to the start of the variable's name. The name itself begins with a capital letter. The type prefixes are shown in Table 2-1. Frankly, the use of type prefixes is controversial and is not universally accepted. Many Windows programmers use this method, many do not. This method will be used by the Windows 98 programs in this book when it seems reasonable to do so. However, you are free to use any naming convention you like.

2

Prefix	Data Type
b	Boolean (one byte)
c	Character (one byte)
dw	Long unsigned integer
f	16-bit bitfield (flags)
fn	Function
h	Handle
l	Long integer
lp	Long pointer
n	Short integer
p	Pointer
pt	Long integer holding screen coordinates
w	Short unsigned integer
sz	Pointer to null-terminated string
lpsz	Long pointer to null-terminated string
rgb	Long integer holding RGB color values

Variable Type
Prefix
Characters

Table 2-1.

CHAPTER 3

Processing Messages

35

This chapter introduces Windows 98's messaging system and discusses some of its most commonly used messages. As explained in Chapter 2, Windows 98 communicates with your application by sending it messages. For this reason, the processing of these messages is at the core of all Windows 98 applications. In the previous chapter you learned how to create a skeletal Windows 98 application. In this chapter, that skeleton will be expanded to receive and process various messages.

What Are Messages?

Messages correspond to events.

There are a large number of Windows 98 messages. Each message is represented by a unique 32-bit integer value, and each message corresponds to some event. For example, there are messages to indicate that the user pressed a key or clicked the mouse. There are standard macro names for these messages. Generally, you will use the macro name, not the actual integer value, when referring to a message. Here are some common Windows 98 message macros:

WM_CHAR   WM_PAINT   WM_MOVE   WM_CLOSE

WM_LBUTTONUP WM_LBUTTONDOWN WM_COMMAND WM_SIZE

Two other values accompany each message and contain information related to the specific message. One of these values is of type **WPARAM**; the other is of type **LPARAM**. For Windows 98, both of these types translate into 32-bit integers. These values are commonly called **wParam** and **lParam**, respectively. They typically hold things like cursor or mouse coordinates; the value of a keypress; or a system-related value. As each message is discussed, the meaning of the values contained in **wParam** and **lParam** will be described.

 PORTABILITY: In Windows 3.1, **wParam** is a 16-bit value. In Windows 98, it is a 32-bit value. This change causes a few messages to be different between the two versions of Windows. These differences will be noted as needed.

As mentioned in Chapter 2, the function that actually processes messages is your program's window function. As you should recall, this function is passed four parameters: the handle of the window that the message is for; the message itself; and the last two parameters, **wParam** and **lParam**.

Sometimes two pieces of information are encoded into the two words that comprise the **wParam** and **lParam** parameters. To provide easy access to each half of **wParam** and **lParam**, Windows defines two macros called **LOWORD** and **HIWORD**. They return the low-order and high-order words of a long integer, respectively. They are used like this:

```
x = LOWORD(lParam);
y = HIWORD(lParam);
```

You will soon see these macros in use.

Responding to a Keypress

One of the most common Windows 98 messages is generated when a key is pressed. This message is called **WM_CHAR**. It is important to understand that your application never receives keystrokes, per se, directly from the keyboard. Instead, each time a key is pressed, a **WM_CHAR** message is sent to the active window. To see how this process works, this section extends the skeletal application developed in Chapter 2 so that it processes keystroke messages.

Each time **WM_CHAR** is sent, **wParam** contains the ASCII value of the respective key pressed. **LOWORD(lParam)** contains the number of times the key has been repeated as a result of the key being held down. The bits of **HIWORD(lParam)** are encoded as shown in Table 3-1.

Bit	Meaning
15	Set if the key is being released; cleared if the key is being pressed.
14	Set if the key was pressed before the message was sent; cleared if it was not pressed.
13	Set if the ALT key is also being pressed; cleared if ALT is not pressed.
12	Used by Windows.
11	Used by Windows.
10	Used by Windows.
9	Used by Windows.
8	Set if the key pressed is an extended key provided by an enhanced keyboard; cleared otherwise.
7-0	Manufacturer-dependent key code (i.e., the scan code)

How **lParam** Is Encoded for Keyboard Data

Table 3-1.

For our purposes, the only value that is important at this time is **wParam**, since it holds the key that was pressed. However, notice how detailed the information is that Windows 98 supplies about the state of the system. Of course, you are free to use as much or as little of this information as you like.

To process a **WM_CHAR** message, you must add it to the **switch** statement inside your program's window function. For example, here is a window function that processes a keystroke by displaying it on the screen.

```
char str[255] = "";  /* holds output string */

LRESULT CALLBACK WindowFunc(HWND hwnd, UINT message,
                            WPARAM wParam, LPARAM lParam)
{
  HDC hdc;

  switch(message) {
    case WM_CHAR: /* process keystroke */
      hdc = GetDC(hwnd); /* get device context */
      TextOut(hdc, 1, 1, "    ", 3); /* erase old character */
      sprintf(str, "%c", (char) wParam); /* stringize character */
      TextOut(hdc, 1, 1, str, strlen(str)); /* output char */
      ReleaseDC(hwnd, hdc); /* release device context */
      break;
    case WM_DESTROY: /* terminate the program */
      PostQuitMessage(0);
      break;
    default:
      /* Let Windows 98 process any messages not specified in
         the preceding switch statement. */
      return DefWindowProc(hwnd, message, wParam, lParam);
  }
  return 0;

}
```

The purpose of the code inside the **WM_CHAR** case is very simple: it echoes the key to the screen! You are probably surprised that it takes so many lines of code to accomplish this seemingly trivial feat. The reason for this is that Windows must establish a link between your program and the screen. This is called a *device context* (DC for short), and it is acquired by calling **GetDC( )**. For now, don't worry about precisely what a device context is. It will be discussed in the next section. However, once you obtain a device context, you may write to the screen. At the end of the process, the device context is released using **ReleaseDC( )**. Your program must release the device context when it is done with it. Although the number of device contexts is limited only by the amount of free memory, the number is still finite. If your program doesn't release the DC, eventually the available DCs will be exhausted and a subsequent call to **GetDC( )** will fail. Both **GetDC( )** and **ReleaseDC( )** are API functions. Their prototypes are shown here:

HDC GetDC(HWND *hwnd*);

int ReleaseDC(HWND *hwnd*, HDC *hdc*);

To obtain a device context, call GetDC( ).

GetDC( ) returns a device context associated with the window whose handle is specified by *hwnd*. The type **HDC** specifies a handle to a device context. If a device context cannot be obtained, **NULL** is returned.

To release a device context, call ReleaseDC( ).

ReleaseDC( ) returns true if the device context was released, false otherwise. The *hwnd* parameter is the handle of the window for which the device context is released. The *hdc* parameter is the handle of device context obtained through the call to **GetDC( )**.

PORTABILITY: In Windows 3.1, there are only five device contexts available. In Windows 98, the number is limited only by the amount of free memory. Be aware of this difference if you will be porting programs to 16-bit environments.

The function that actually outputs the character is the API function **TextOut( )**. Its prototype is shown here:

BOOL TextOut(HDC *DC*, int *X*, int *Y*, LPCSTR *lpstr*, int *length*);

The **TextOut( )** function outputs the string pointed to by *lpstr* at the window coordinates specified by *X,Y*. (By default, these coordinates are in terms of pixels.) The length of the string is specified in *length*. The **TextOut( )** function returns nonzero if successful, zero otherwise.

In the window function, each time a **WM_CHAR** message is received, the character that is typed by the user is converted, using **sprintf( )**, into a string that is one character long and then displayed using **TextOut( )** at location 1,1. (The string **str** is global because it will need to keep its value between function calls in later examples.) In a window, the upper-left corner of the client area is location 0,0. Window coordinates are always relative to the

3

window, not the screen. Therefore, as characters are entered, they are displayed in the upper-left corner no matter where the window is physically located on the screen.

The reason for the first call to **TextOut( )** is to erase whatever previous character was just displayed. Because Windows is a graphics-based system, characters are of different sizes and the overwriting of one character by another does not necessarily cause all of the previous character to be erased. For example, if you typed a "w" followed by an "i", part of the "w" would still be displayed if it wasn't manually erased. (Try commenting out the first call to **TextOut( )** and observe what happens.)

It is important to understand that no Windows 98 API function will allow output beyond the borders of a window. Output will automatically be clipped to prevent the boundaries from being crossed.

At first you might think that using **TextOut( )** to output a single character is not an efficient application of the function. The fact is that Windows 98 (and Windows, in general) does not contain a function that simply outputs a character. As you will see, Windows 98 performs much of its user interaction through dialog boxes, menus, toolbars, etc. For this reason it contains only a few functions that output text to the client area.

Here is the entire program that handles **WM_CHAR** messages. Figure 3-1 shows the window produced by this program.

```
/* Process WM_CHAR messages. */

#include <windows.h>
#include <string.h>
#include <stdio.h>

LRESULT CALLBACK WindowFunc(HWND, UINT, WPARAM, LPARAM);

char szWinName[] = "MyWin"; /* name of window class */

char str[255] = ""; /* holds output string */

int WINAPI WinMain(HINSTANCE hThisInst, HINSTANCE hPrevInst,
                   LPSTR lpszArgs, int nWinMode)
{
  HWND hwnd;
  MSG msg;
  WNDCLASSEX wcl;
```

```
/* Define a window class. */
wcl.cbSize = sizeof(WNDCLASSEX);

wcl.hInstance = hThisInst; /* handle to this instance */
wcl.lpszClassName = szWinName; /* window class name */
wcl.lpfnWndProc = WindowFunc; /* window function */
wcl.style = 0; /* default style */

wcl.hIcon = LoadIcon(NULL, IDI_APPLICATION); /* standard icon */
wcl.hIconSm = LoadIcon(NULL, IDI_WINLOGO); /* small icon */
wcl.hCursor = LoadCursor(NULL, IDC_ARROW); /* cursor style */

wcl.lpszMenuName = NULL; /* no menu */
wcl.cbClsExtra = 0; /* no extra */
wcl.cbWndExtra = 0; /* information needed */

/* Make the window white. */
wcl.hbrBackground = (HBRUSH) GetStockObject(WHITE_BRUSH);

/* Register the window class. */
if(!RegisterClassEx(&wcl)) return 0;

/* Now that a window class has been registered, a window
   can be created. */
hwnd = CreateWindow(
  szWinName, /* name of window class */
  "Processing WM_CHAR Messages", /* title */
  WS_OVERLAPPEDWINDOW, /* window style - normal */
  CW_USEDEFAULT, /* X coordinate - let Windows decide */
  CW_USEDEFAULT, /* Y coordinate - let Windows decide */
  CW_USEDEFAULT, /* width - let Windows decide */
  CW_USEDEFAULT, /* height - let Windows decide */
  HWND_DESKTOP, /* no parent window */
  NULL, /* no menu */
  hThisInst, /* handle of this instance of the program */
  NULL /* no additional arguments */
);

/* Display the window. */
ShowWindow(hwnd, nWinMode);
UpdateWindow(hwnd);

/* Create the message loop. */
while(GetMessage(&msg, NULL, 0, 0))
{
```

```
      TranslateMessage(&msg); /* translate keyboard messages */
      DispatchMessage(&msg); /* return control to Windows 98 */
  }
  return msg.wParam;
}

/* This function is called by Windows 98 and is passed
   messages from the message queue.
*/
LRESULT CALLBACK WindowFunc(HWND hwnd, UINT message,
                            WPARAM wParam, LPARAM lParam)
{
  HDC hdc;

  switch(message) {
    case WM_CHAR: /* process keystroke */
      hdc = GetDC(hwnd); /* get device context */
      TextOut(hdc, 1, 1, "   ", 3); /* erase old character */
      sprintf(str, "%c", (char) wParam); /* stringize character */
      TextOut(hdc, 1, 1, str, strlen(str)); /* output char */
      ReleaseDC(hwnd, hdc); /* release device context */
      break;
    case WM_DESTROY: /* terminate the program */
      PostQuitMessage(0);
      break;
    default:
      /* Let Windows 98 process any messages not specified in
         the preceding switch statement. */
      return DefWindowProc(hwnd, message, wParam, lParam);
  }
  return 0;
}
```

Device Contexts

A device context is a structure that describes a window's output environment.

The program in the previous section had to obtain a device context prior to outputting to the window. Also, that device context had to be released when it was no longer needed. It is now time to understand what a device context is. A *device context* is a structure that describes the display environment of a window, including its device driver and various display parameters, such as the current type font. As you will see later in this book, you have substantial control over the display environment of a window.

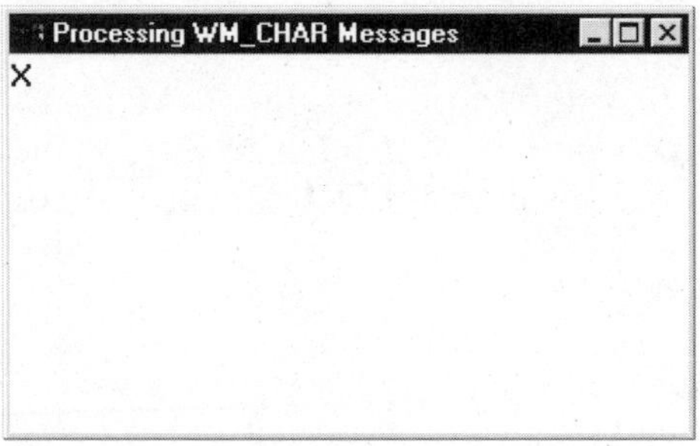

Sample
window
produced
by the
WM_CHAR
program
Figure 3-1.

3

Before your application can output information to the client area of the
window, a device context must be obtained. Until this is done, there is no
linkage between your program and the window relative to output. Thus, it is
necessary to obtain a device context prior to performing any output to a
window. Since **TextOut( )**, and other output functions, require a handle to a
device context, this is a self-enforcing rule.

Processing the WM_PAINT Message

Before continuing, again run the program from the previous section and enter
a few characters. Next, minimize and then restore the window. As you will see,
the last character typed is not displayed after the window is restored. Also, if
the window is overwritten by another window and then redisplayed, the
character is not redisplayed. The reason for this is simple: in general, Windows
does not keep a record of what a window contains. Instead, it is your program's
job to maintain the contents of a window. To help your program accomplish
this, each time the contents of a window must be redisplayed, your program
will be sent a **WM_PAINT** message. (This message will also be sent when your
window is first displayed.) Each time your program receives this message it
must redisplay the contents of the window. In this section, you will add a
WM_PAINT handler to the preceding program.

Before explaining how to respond to a **WM_PAINT** message, it might be
useful to explain why Windows does not automatically rewrite your window.
The answer is short and to the point. In many situations, it is easier for your
program, which has intimate knowledge of the contents of the window, to
rewrite it than it would be for Windows to do so. While the merits of this

approach have been much debated by programmers, you should simply accept it, because it is unlikely to change.

The first step to processing a **WM_PAINT** message is to add its **case** to the **switch** statement inside the window function. For example, the following will handle **WM_PAINT** for the preceding program.

```
case WM_PAINT: /* process a repaint request */
  hdc = BeginPaint(hwnd, &paintstruct); /* get DC */
  TextOut(hdc, 1, 1, str, strlen(str)); /* output string */
  EndPaint(hwnd, &paintstruct); /* release DC */
  break;
```

Let's look at this closely. First, notice that a device context is obtained using a call to **BeginPaint( )** instead of **GetDC( )**. For various reasons, when you process a **WM_PAINT** message, you must obtain a device context using **BeginPaint( )**, which has this prototype:

HDC BeginPaint(HWND *hwnd*, LPPAINTSTRUCT *lpPS*);

BeginPaint( ) returns a handle to the current device context or **NULL** if an error occurs. Here, *hwnd* is the handle of the window for which the device context is being obtained. The second parameter is a pointer to a structure of type **PAINTSTRUCT**. On return, the structure pointed to by *lpPS* will contain information that your program can use to repaint the window. **PAINTSTRUCT** is defined like this:

```
typedef struct tagPAINTSTRUCT {
  HDC hdc; /* handle to device context */
  BOOL fErase; /* true if background must be erased */
  RECT rcPaint; /* coordinates of region to redraw */
  BOOL fRestore;  /* reserved */
  BOOL fIncUpdate; /* reserved */
  BYTE rgbReserved[32]; /* reserved */
} PAINTSTRUCT;
```

Here, **hdc** will contain the device context of the window that needs to be repainted. This DC is also returned by the call to **BeginPaint( )**. **fErase** will be nonzero if the background of the window needs to be erased. However, as long as you specified a background brush when you created the window, you can ignore the **fErase** member. Windows 98 will erase the window for you.

The type **RECT** is a structure that specifies the upper-left and lower-right coordinates of a rectangular region. This structure is shown here:

```
typedef tagRECT {
  LONG left, top; /* upper left */
  LONG right, bottom; /* lower right */
} RECT;
```

In **PAINTSTRUCT**, the **rcPaint** element contains the coordinates of the region of the window that needs to be repainted. For now, you will not need to use the contents of this structure because you can assume that the entire window must be redisplayed.

Once the device context has been obtained, output can be written to the window. After the window has been repainted, you must release the device context using a call to **EndPaint( )**, which has this prototype.

BOOL EndPaint(HWND *hwnd*, CONST PAINTSTRUCT **lpPS*);

When handling
WM_PAINT, use
BeginPaint( ) to
obtain a device
context. Use
EndPaint( ) to
release it.

EndPaint( ) returns nonzero. (It cannot fail.) Here, *hwnd* is the handle of the window that was repainted. The second parameter is a pointer to the **PAINTSTRUCT** structure used in the call to **BeginPaint( )**.

It is critical to understand that a device context obtained using **BeginPaint( )** must be released only through a call to **EndPaint( )**. Further, **BeginPaint( )** must only be used when a **WM_PAINT** message is being processed.

Here is the full program that now processes **WM_PAINT** messages.

```
/* Process WM_PAINT messages. */

#include <windows.h>
#include <string.h>
#include <stdio.h>

LRESULT CALLBACK WindowFunc(HWND, UINT, WPARAM, LPARAM);

char szWinName[] = "MyWin"; /* name of window class */

char str[255] = "Sample Output"; /* holds output string */

int WINAPI WinMain(HINSTANCE hThisInst, HINSTANCE hPrevInst,
                    LPSTR lpszArgs, int nWinMode)
{
```

```
  HWND hwnd;
  MSG msg;
  WNDCLASSEX wcl;

/* Define a window class. */
  wcl.cbSize = sizeof(WNDCLASSEX);

  wcl.hInstance = hThisInst; /* handle to this instance */
  wcl.lpszClassName = szWinName; /* window class name */
  wcl.lpfnWndProc = WindowFunc; /* window function */
  wcl.style = 0; /* default style */

  wcl.hIcon = LoadIcon(NULL, IDI_APPLICATION); /* standard icon */
  wcl.hIconSm = LoadIcon(NULL, IDI_WINLOGO); /* small icon */
  wcl.hCursor = LoadCursor(NULL, IDC_ARROW); /* cursor style */

  wcl.lpszMenuName = NULL; /* no menu */
  wcl.cbClsExtra = 0; /* no extra */
  wcl.cbWndExtra = 0; /* information needed */

  /* Make the window white. */
  wcl.hbrBackground = (HBRUSH) GetStockObject(WHITE_BRUSH);

  /* Register the window class. */
  if(!RegisterClassEx(&wcl)) return 0;

  /* Now that a window class has been registered, a window
     can be created. */
  hwnd = CreateWindow(
    szWinName, /* name of window class */
    "Processing WM_PAINT Messages", /* title */
    WS_OVERLAPPEDWINDOW, /* window style - normal */
    CW_USEDEFAULT, /* X coordinate - let Windows decide */
    CW_USEDEFAULT, /* Y coordinate - let Windows decide */
    CW_USEDEFAULT, /* width - let Windows decide */
    CW_USEDEFAULT, /* height - let Windows decide */
    HWND_DESKTOP, /* no parent window */
    NULL, /* no menu */
    hThisInst, /* handle of this instance of the program */
    NULL /* no additional arguments */
  );

  /* Display the window. */
  ShowWindow(hwnd, nWinMode);
  UpdateWindow(hwnd);
```

```
  /* Create the message loop. */
  while(GetMessage(&msg, NULL, 0, 0))
  {
    TranslateMessage(&msg); /* translate keyboard messages */
    DispatchMessage(&msg); /* return control to Windows 98 */
  }
  return msg.wParam;
}

/* This function is called by Windows 98 and is passed
   messages from the message queue.
*/
LRESULT CALLBACK WindowFunc(HWND hwnd, UINT message,
                            WPARAM wParam, LPARAM lParam)
{
  HDC hdc;
  PAINTSTRUCT paintstruct;

  switch(message) {
    case WM_CHAR: /* process keystroke */
      hdc = GetDC(hwnd); /* get device context */
      TextOut(hdc, 1, 1, "    ", 3); /* erase old character */
      sprintf(str, "%c", (char) wParam); /* stringize character */
      TextOut(hdc, 1, 1, str, strlen(str)); /* output char */
      ReleaseDC(hwnd, hdc); /* release device context */
      break;
    case WM_PAINT: /* process a repaint request */
      hdc = BeginPaint(hwnd, &paintstruct); /* get DC */
      TextOut(hdc, 1, 1, str, strlen(str)); /* output string */
      EndPaint(hwnd, &paintstruct); /* release DC */
      break;
    case WM_DESTROY: /* terminate the program */
      PostQuitMessage(0);
      break;
    default:
      /* Let Windows 98 process any messages not specified in
         the preceding switch statement. */
      return DefWindowProc(hwnd, message, wParam, lParam);
  }
  return 0;
}
```

Before continuing, enter, compile, and run this program. Try typing a few characters and then minimizing and restoring the window. As you will see, each time the window is redisplayed, the last character you typed is automatically redrawn. Notice that the global array **str** is initialized to **Sample Output** and that this is displayed when the program begins execution. The reason for this is that when a window is created, a **WM_PAINT** message is automatically generated.

While the handling of the **WM_PAINT** message in the preceding example is quite simple, it must be emphasized that most real-world applications will be more complex because most windows contain considerably more output.

Since it is your program's responsibility to restore the window if it is resized or overwritten, you must always provide some mechanism to accomplish this. In real-world programs, this is usually done in one of three ways. First, your program can simply regenerate the output by computational means. This is most feasible when no user input is used. Second, in some instances, you can keep a record of events and replay the events when the window needs to be redrawn. Finally, your program can maintain a virtual window that you simply copy to the window each time it must be redrawn. This is the most general method. (The implementation of this approach is described later in this book.) Which approach is best depends completely upon the application. Most of the examples in this book won't bother to redraw the window because doing so typically involves substantial additional code, which often just muddies the point of an example. However, your programs will need to restore their windows in order to be conforming Windows 98 applications.

Responding to Mouse Messages

Since Windows is, to a great extent, a mouse-based operating system, all Windows programs should respond to mouse input. Windows 98 is no exception. Because the mouse is so important, there are several different types of mouse messages. The ones discussed in this chapter are

WM_LBUTTONDOWN   WM_LBUTTONUP   WM_LBUTTONDBLCLK

WM_RBUTTONDOWN   WM_RBUTTONUP   WM_RBUTTONDBLCLK

While most computers use a two-button mouse, Windows 98 is capable of handling a mouse with up to three buttons. These buttons are called the left, middle, and right. For the rest of this chapter we will be concerned only with the left and right buttons.

Let's start with the two most common mouse messages, **WM_LBUTTONDOWN** and **WM_RBUTTONDOWN**. They are generated when the left and right buttons are pressed, respectively.

When either the **WM_LBUTTONDOWN** or **WM_RBUTTONDOWN** message is received, the mouse's current *X,Y* location is specified in **LOWORD(lParam)** and **HIWORD(lParam)**, respectively. The value of **wParam** contains various pieces of status information, which are described in the next section.

3

The following program responds to mouse messages. Each time you press a mouse button when the program's window contains the mouse, a message will be displayed at the current location of the mouse pointer.

```
/* Process Mouse Messages. */

#include <windows.h>
#include <string.h>
#include <stdio.h>

LRESULT CALLBACK WindowFunc(HWND, UINT, WPARAM, LPARAM);

char szWinName[] = "MyWin"; /* name of window class */

char str[255] = ""; /* holds output string */

int WINAPI WinMain(HINSTANCE hThisInst, HINSTANCE hPrevInst,
                   LPSTR lpszArgs, int nWinMode)
{
  HWND hwnd;
  MSG msg;
  WNDCLASSEX wcl;

  /* Define a window class. */
  wcl.cbSize = sizeof(WNDCLASSEX);

  wcl.hInstance = hThisInst; /* handle to this instance */
  wcl.lpszClassName = szWinName; /* window class name */
  wcl.lpfnWndProc = WindowFunc; /* window function */
  wcl.style = 0; /* default style */
```

```
wcl.hIcon = LoadIcon(NULL, IDI_APPLICATION); /* standard icon */
wcl.hIconSm = LoadIcon(NULL, IDI_WINLOGO); /* small icon */
wcl.hCursor = LoadCursor(NULL, IDC_ARROW); /* cursor style */

wcl.lpszMenuName = NULL; /* no main menu */
wcl.cbClsExtra = 0; /* no extra */
wcl.cbWndExtra = 0; /* information needed */

/* Make the window white. */
wcl.hbrBackground = (HBRUSH) GetStockObject(WHITE_BRUSH);

/* Register the window class. */
if(!RegisterClassEx(&wcl)) return 0;

/* Now that a window class has been registered, a window
   can be created. */
hwnd = CreateWindow(
  szWinName, /* name of window class */
  "Processing Mouse Messages", /* title */
  WS_OVERLAPPEDWINDOW, /* window style - normal */
  CW_USEDEFAULT, /* X coordinate - let Windows decide */
  CW_USEDEFAULT, /* Y coordinate - let Windows decide */
  CW_USEDEFAULT, /* width - let Windows decide */
  CW_USEDEFAULT, /* height - let Windows decide */
  HWND_DESKTOP, /* no parent window */
  NULL, /* no menu */
  hThisInst, /* handle of this instance of the program */
  NULL /* no additional arguments */
);

/* Display the window. */
ShowWindow(hwnd, nWinMode);
UpdateWindow(hwnd);

/* Create the message loop. */
while(GetMessage(&msg, NULL, 0, 0))
{
  TranslateMessage(&msg); /* translate keyboard messages */
  DispatchMessage(&msg); /* return control to Windows 98 */
}
return msg.wParam;
}
```

```
/* This function is called by Windows 98 and is passed
   messages from the message queue.
*/
LRESULT CALLBACK WindowFunc(HWND hwnd, UINT message,
                            WPARAM wParam, LPARAM lParam)
{
  HDC hdc;

  switch(message) {
    case WM_RBUTTONDOWN: /* process right button */
      hdc = GetDC(hwnd); /* get DC */
      sprintf(str, "Right button is down at %d, %d",
              LOWORD(lParam), HIWORD(lParam));
      TextOut(hdc, LOWORD(lParam), HIWORD(lParam),
              str, strlen(str));
      ReleaseDC(hwnd, hdc); /* Release DC */
      break;
    case WM_LBUTTONDOWN: /* process left button */
      hdc = GetDC(hwnd); /* get DC */
      sprintf(str, "Left button is down at %d, %d",
              LOWORD(lParam), HIWORD(lParam));
      TextOut(hdc, LOWORD(lParam), HIWORD(lParam),
              str, strlen(str));
      ReleaseDC(hwnd, hdc); /* Release DC */
      break;
    case WM_DESTROY: /* terminate the program */
      PostQuitMessage(0);
      break;
    default:
      /* Let Windows 98 process any messages not specified in
         the preceding switch statement. */
      return DefWindowProc(hwnd, message, wParam, lParam);
  }
  return 0;
}
```

Figure 3-2 shows sample output from this program.

A Closer Look at Mouse Messages

For all of the mouse messages described in this chapter, the meaning of **lParam** and **wParam** is the same. As described earlier, the value of **lParam** contains the coordinates of the mouse when the message was generated. The value of **wParam** supplies information about the state of the mouse and keyboard. It may contain any combination of the following values:

MK_CONTROL

MK_SHIFT

MK_MBUTTON

MK_RBUTTON

MK_LBUTTON

If the CTRL key is pressed when a mouse button is pressed, then **wParam** will contain **MK_CONTROL**. If the SHIFT key is pressed when a mouse button is pressed, then **WParam** will contain **MK_SHIFT.** If the right button is down when the left button is pressed, then **wParam** will contain **MK_RBUTTON.** If the left button is down when the right button is pressed, then **wParam** will contain **MK_LBUTTON.** If the middle button (if it exists) is down when one of the other buttons is pressed, then **wParam** will contain **MK_MBUTTON.** Before moving on, you might want to try experimenting with these messages.

Using Button-up Messages

When a mouse button is clicked, your program actually receives two messages. The first is a button-down message, such as

WM_LBUTTONDOWN, when the button is pressed. The second is a button-up message, when the button is released. The button-up messages for the left and right buttons are called **WM_LBUTTONUP** and **WM_RBUTTONUP**. For some applications, such as selecting an item, it is better to process button-up rather than button-down messages. This gives the user a chance to change his or her mind after the mouse button has been pressed.

Responding to a Double-Click

While it is easy to respond to a single-click, handling double-clicks requires a bit more work. First, you must enable your program to receive double-click messages. By default, double-click messages are not sent to your program. Second, you will need to add message response code for the double-click message you want to respond to.

To allow your program to receive double-click messages, you will need to specify **CS_DBLCLKS** in the **style** member of the **WNDCLASSEX** structure prior to registering the window class. That is, you must use a line of code like that shown here.

```
wcl.style = CS_DBLCLKS; /* allow double-clicks */
```

After you have enabled double-clicks, your program can receive these double-click messages: **WM_LBUTTONDBLCLK** and **WM_RBUTTONDBLCLK**. The contents of the **lParam** and **wParam** parameters are the same as they are for the other mouse messages.

As you know, a double-click is two presses of a mouse button in quick succession. You can obtain and/or set the time interval in which two presses of a mouse button must occur in order for a double-click message to be generated. To obtain the double-click interval, use the API function **GetDoubleClickTime( )**, whose prototype is shown here:

```
UINT GetDoubleClickTime(void);
```

This function returns the interval of time (specified in milliseconds) in which a double-click must occur. To set the double-click interval, use **SetDoubleClickTime( )**. Its prototype is shown here:

```
BOOL SetDoubleClickTime(UINT interval);
```

Here, *interval* specifies the number of milliseconds in which two presses of a mouse button must occur in order for a double-click to be generated. If you specify zero, then the default double-click time is used. (The default interval is approximately half a second.) The function returns nonzero if successful and zero on failure.

The following program responds to double-click messages. This program also demonstrates the use of **GetDoubleClickTime( )** and **SetDoubleClickTime( )**. Each time you press the "S" key, the double-click interval is increased. Each time you press the "F" key, the interval is decreased. Each time you double-click either the right or left mouse button, the current double-click interval is displayed at the location of the mouse pointer. Since the double-click interval is a system-wide setting, changes to it will affect all other programs in the system. For this reason, when the program begins, it saves the current double-click interval. When the program ends, the original interval is restored. In general, if your program changes a system-wide setting, it should be restored before the program ends. Sample output is shown in Figure 3-3.

```
/* Respond to double clicks and set
   the double-click interval. */

#include <windows.h>
#include <string.h>
#include <stdio.h>
#include <ctype.h>

LRESULT CALLBACK WindowFunc(HWND, UINT, WPARAM, LPARAM);

char szWinName[] = "MyWin"; /* name of window class */

char str[255] = ""; /* holds output string */

UINT OrgDblClkTime; /* holds original double-click interval. */

int WINAPI WinMain(HINSTANCE hThisInst, HINSTANCE hPrevInst,
                   LPSTR lpszArgs, int nWinMode)
{
  HWND hwnd;
  MSG msg;
  WNDCLASSEX wcl;

  /* Define a window class. */
  wcl.cbSize = sizeof(WNDCLASSEX);
```

```
wcl.hInstance = hThisInst; /* handle to this instance */
wcl.lpszClassName = szWinName; /* window class name */
wcl.lpfnWndProc = WindowFunc; /* window function */

wcl.style = CS_DBLCLKS; /* enable double clicks */

wcl.hIcon = LoadIcon(NULL, IDI_APPLICATION); /* standard icon */
wcl.hIconSm = LoadIcon(NULL, IDI_WINLOGO); /* small icon */
wcl.hCursor = LoadCursor(NULL, IDC_ARROW); /* cursor style */

wcl.lpszMenuName = NULL; /* no main menu */
wcl.cbClsExtra = 0; /* no extra */
wcl.cbWndExtra = 0; /* information needed */

/* Make the window white. */
wcl.hbrBackground = (HBRUSH) GetStockObject(WHITE_BRUSH);

/* Register the window class. */
if(!RegisterClassEx(&wcl)) return 0;

/* Now that a window class has been registered, a window
   can be created. */
hwnd = CreateWindow(
  szWinName, /* name of window class */
  "Processing Double-Clicks", /* title */
  WS_OVERLAPPEDWINDOW, /* window style - normal */
  CW_USEDEFAULT, /* X coordinate - let Windows decide */
  CW_USEDEFAULT, /* Y coordinate - let Windows decide */
  CW_USEDEFAULT, /* width - let Windows decide */
  CW_USEDEFAULT, /* height - let Windows decide */
  HWND_DESKTOP, /* no parent window */
  NULL, /* no menu */
  hThisInst, /* handle of this instance of the program */
  NULL /* no additional arguments */
);

/* save original double-click time interval */
OrgDblClkTime = GetDoubleClickTime();

/* Display the window. */
ShowWindow(hwnd, nWinMode);
UpdateWindow(hwnd);

/* Create the message loop. */
while(GetMessage(&msg, NULL, 0, 0))
```

3

```
  {
    TranslateMessage(&msg); /* translate keyboard messages */
    DispatchMessage(&msg); /* return control to Windows 98 */
  }
  return msg.wParam;
}


/* This function is called by Windows 98 and is passed
   messages from the message queue.
*/
LRESULT CALLBACK WindowFunc(HWND hwnd, UINT message,
                            WPARAM wParam, LPARAM lParam)
{
  HDC hdc;
  UINT interval;

  switch(message) {
    case WM_CHAR:
      if(toupper((char)wParam) == 'S') { /* increase interval */
        interval = GetDoubleClickTime();
        interval += 100;
        SetDoubleClickTime(interval);
      } else if(toupper((char)wParam) == 'F') { /* decrease interval */
        interval = GetDoubleClickTime();
        interval -= 100;
        if(interval < 0) interval = 0;
        SetDoubleClickTime(interval);
      } else /* no change */
          interval = GetDoubleClickTime();

      sprintf(str, "Interval is %u milliseconds. ",
              interval);
      hdc = GetDC(hwnd); /* get DC */
      TextOut(hdc, 1, 1, str, strlen(str));
      ReleaseDC(hwnd, hdc); /* Release DC */
      break;
    case WM_RBUTTONDOWN: /* process right button */
      hdc = GetDC(hwnd); /* get DC */
      sprintf(str, "Right button is down at %d, %d",
              LOWORD(lParam), HIWORD(lParam));
      TextOut(hdc, LOWORD(lParam), HIWORD(lParam),
              str, strlen(str));
      ReleaseDC(hwnd, hdc); /* Release DC */
      break;
```

```
case WM_LBUTTONDOWN: /* process left button */
  hdc = GetDC(hwnd); /* get DC */
  sprintf(str, "Left button is down at %d, %d",
          LOWORD(lParam), HIWORD(lParam));
  TextOut(hdc, LOWORD(lParam), HIWORD(lParam),
          str, strlen(str));
  ReleaseDC(hwnd, hdc); /* Release DC */
  break;
case WM_LBUTTONDBLCLK: /* process left button double-click */
  interval = GetDoubleClickTime();
  sprintf(str, "Left Button Double-click is %u milliseconds. ",
          interval);
  hdc = GetDC(hwnd); /* get DC */
  TextOut(hdc, LOWORD(lParam), HIWORD(lParam),
          str, strlen(str));
  ReleaseDC(hwnd, hdc); /* Release DC */
  break;
case WM_RBUTTONDBLCLK: /* process right button double-click */
  interval = GetDoubleClickTime();
  sprintf(str, "Right Button Double-click is %u milliseconds. ",
          interval);
  hdc = GetDC(hwnd); /* get DC */
  TextOut(hdc, LOWORD(lParam), HIWORD(lParam),
          str, strlen(str));
  ReleaseDC(hwnd, hdc); /* Release DC */
  break;
case WM_DESTROY: /* terminate the program */
  SetDoubleClickTime(OrgDblClkTime); /* restore interval */
  PostQuitMessage(0);
  break;
default:
  /* Let Windows 98 process any messages not specified in
     the preceding switch statement. */
  return DefWindowProc(hwnd, message, wParam, lParam);
}
  return 0;
}
```

More Keyboard Messages

While **WM_CHAR** is probably the most commonly handled keyboard message, it is not the only one. In fact, **WM_CHAR** is actually a synthetic message that is constructed by the **TranslateMessage( )** function inside your program's message loop. At the lowest level, Windows 98 generates two

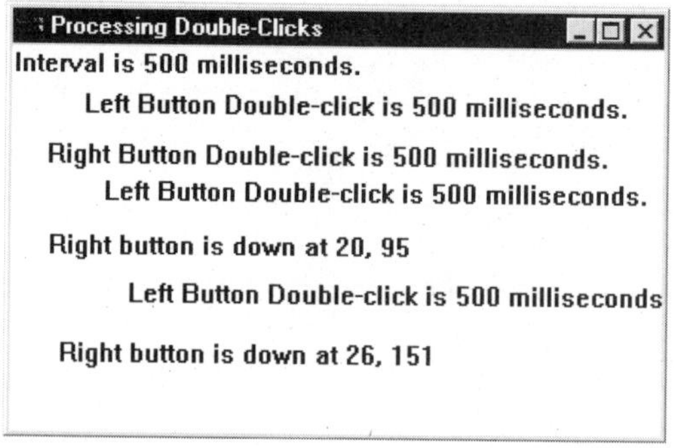

Sample output
from the
Double-Click
program
Figure 3-3.

messages each time you press a key. Whenever a key is pressed, a
WM_KEYDOWN message is sent. When the key is released, a **WM_KEYUP**
message is posted. If possible, a **WM_KEYDOWN** message is translated into
a **WM_CHAR** message by **TranslateMessage( )**. Thus, unless you include
TranslateMessage( ) in your message loop, your program will not receive
WM_CHAR messages. To prove this to yourself, try commenting out the call
to **TranslateMessage( )** in the preceding program. After doing so, it will no
longer respond to your keypresses.

The reason that you will seldom use **WM_KEYDOWN** or **WM_KEYUP** for
character input is that the information they contain is in a raw format. For
example, the value in **wParam** contains the *virtual key code*, not the key's
ASCII value. Part of what **TranslateMessage( )** does is transform the virtual
key codes into ASCII characters, taking into account the state of the SHIFT key,
etc. Also, **TranslateMessage( )** automatically handles auto-repeat.

Virtual keys are
device-
independent
key mappings.

A virtual key is a device-independent key code. As you may know, there are
keys on nearly all computer keyboards that do not correspond to the ASCII
character set—for example, the arrow keys and the function keys. Each key
that can be generated has been assigned a value, which is its virtual key
code. All of the virtual key codes are defined as macros in the header file
WINUSER.H (which is automatically part of your program when you include
WINDOWS.H). The codes begin with **VK_**. Here are some examples.

Virtual Key Code	Corresponding Key
VK_DOWN	DOWN ARROW
VK_LEFT	LEFT ARROW
VK_RIGHT	RIGHT ARROW

Virtual Key Code	Corresponding Key
VK_UP	UP ARROW
VK_SHIFT	SHIFT
VK_CONTROL	CTRL
VK_ESCAPE	ESCAPE
VK_F1 through VK_F24	FUNCTION KEYS
VK_HOME	HOME
VK_END	END
VK_INSERT	INSERT
VK_DELETE	DELETE
VK_PRIOR	PAGE UP
VK_NEXT	PAGE DOWN
VK_A through VK_Z	The letters of the alphabet
VK_0 through VK_9	The digits 0 through 9

3

For keys that have ASCII equivalents, **TranslateMessage( )** converts the virtual key code into its ASCII code and sends it in a **WM_CHAR** message. Of course, the non-ASCII keys are not converted. This means that if your program wants to handle non-ASCII keypresses, it must use **WM_KEYDOWN** or **WM_KEYUP** (or both).

Here is a program that handles **WM_KEYDOWN**, **WM_KEYUP**, and **WM_CHAR** messages. The handler for **WM_KEYDOWN** reports if the key is an arrow, shift, or control key. The handler for **WM_CHAR** displays a normal character. The **WM_KEYUP** handler simply reports when the key is released. Sample output is shown in Figure 3-4.

```
/* Processing WM_KEYDOWN, WM_KEYUP, and WM_CHAR messages. */

#include <windows.h>
#include <string.h>
#include <stdio.h>

LRESULT CALLBACK WindowFunc(HWND, UINT, WPARAM, LPARAM);

char szWinName[] = "MyWin"; /* name of window class */
```

```
char str[255] = ""; /* holds output string */

int WINAPI WinMain(HINSTANCE hThisInst, HINSTANCE hPrevInst,
                   LPSTR lpszArgs, int nWinMode)
{
  HWND hwnd;
  MSG msg;
  WNDCLASSEX wcl;

  /* Define a window class. */
  wcl.cbSize = sizeof(WNDCLASSEX);

  wcl.hInstance = hThisInst; /* handle to this instance */
  wcl.lpszClassName = szWinName; /* window class name */
  wcl.lpfnWndProc = WindowFunc; /* window function */
  wcl.style = 0; /* default style */

  wcl.hIcon = LoadIcon(NULL, IDI_APPLICATION); /* standard icon */
  wcl.hIconSm = LoadIcon(NULL, IDI_WINLOGO); /* small icon */
  wcl.hCursor = LoadCursor(NULL, IDC_ARROW); /* cursor style */

  wcl.lpszMenuName = NULL; /* no main menu */
  wcl.cbClsExtra = 0; /* no extra */
  wcl.cbWndExtra = 0; /* information needed */

  /* Make the window white. */
  wcl.hbrBackground = (HBRUSH) GetStockObject(WHITE_BRUSH);

  /* Register the window class. */
  if(!RegisterClassEx(&wcl)) return 0;

  /* Now that a window class has been registered, a window
     can be created. */
  hwnd = CreateWindow(
    szWinName, /* name of window class */
    "Processing WM_CHAR, WM_KEYDOWN, and WM_KEYUP Messages",
    WS_OVERLAPPEDWINDOW, /* window style - normal */
    CW_USEDEFAULT, /* X coordinate - let Windows decide */
    CW_USEDEFAULT, /* Y coordinate - let Windows decide */
    CW_USEDEFAULT, /* width - let Windows decide */
    CW_USEDEFAULT, /* height - let Windows decide */
    HWND_DESKTOP, /* no parent window */
    NULL, /* no menu */
    hThisInst, /* handle of this instance of the program */
    NULL /* no additional arguments */
```

```
    );

    /* Display the window. */
    ShowWindow(hwnd, nWinMode);
    UpdateWindow(hwnd);

    /* Create the message loop. */
    while(GetMessage(&msg, NULL, 0, 0))
    {
      TranslateMessage(&msg); /* translate keyboard messages */
      DispatchMessage(&msg); /* return control to Windows 98 */
    }
    return msg.wParam;
}

/* This function is called by Windows 98 and is passed
   messages from the message queue.
*/
LRESULT CALLBACK WindowFunc(HWND hwnd, UINT message,
                            WPARAM wParam, LPARAM lParam)
{
  HDC hdc;

  switch(message) {
    case WM_CHAR: /* process character */
      hdc = GetDC(hwnd); /* get device context */
      sprintf(str, "WM_CHAR received: %c   ",
            (char) wParam);
      TextOut(hdc, 1, 1, str, strlen(str)); /* show string */
      ReleaseDC(hwnd, hdc); /* release device context */
      break;
    case WM_KEYDOWN: /* process raw keystroke */
      strcpy(str, "WM_KEYDOWN received. Key is ");
      switch((char)wParam) {
        case VK_UP:
          strcat(str, "Up Arrow");
          break;
        case VK_DOWN:
          strcat(str, "Down Arrow");
          break;
        case VK_LEFT:
          strcat(str, "Left Arrow");
          break;
        case VK_RIGHT:
          strcat(str, "Right Arrow");
```

3

```
            break;
          case VK_SHIFT:
            strcat(str, "Shift");
            break;
          case VK_CONTROL:
            strcat(str, "Control");
            break;
          default:
            strcat(str, "Other");
        }
        strcat(str, "               "); /* erase previous output */
        hdc = GetDC(hwnd); /* get device context */
        TextOut(hdc, 1, 20, str, strlen(str)); /* show string */

        /* erase WM_KEYUP output */
        strcpy(str, "                              ");
        TextOut(hdc, 1, 40, str, strlen(str));

        /* erase WM_CHAR output */
        strcpy(str, "                              ");
        TextOut(hdc, 1, 1, str, strlen(str));

        ReleaseDC(hwnd, hdc); /* release device context */
        break;
      case WM_KEYUP: /* process a key release */
        hdc = GetDC(hwnd); /* get device context */
        sprintf(str, "WM_KEYUP received.");
        TextOut(hdc, 1, 40, str, strlen(str)); /* show string */
        ReleaseDC(hwnd, hdc); /* release device context */
        break;
      case WM_DESTROY: /* terminate the program */
        PostQuitMessage(0);
        break;
      default:
        /* Let Windows 98 process any messages not specified in
           the preceding switch statement. */
        return DefWindowProc(hwnd, message, wParam, lParam);
    }
    return 0;
}
```

When you try this program, notice one important point. When you press a standard ASCII key, such as "X", the program will receive two messages: one will be **WM_CHAR** and the other will be **WM_KEYDOWN**. The reason for

```
: Processing WM_CHAR, WM_KEYDOWN, and WM_KEYUP Messages  _ □ ✕
WM_CHAR received: X
WM_KEYDOWN received. Key is Other
WM_KEYUP received.
```

3

this is easy to understand. Each time you press a key, a **WM_KEYDOWN** message is generated. (That is, all keystrokes generate a key-down message.) If the key is an ASCII key, it is transformed into a **WM_CHAR** message by **TranslateMessage( )**. For all keys, when you release the key, a **WM_KEYUP** message is generated.

Other Keyboard Messages

In addition to **WM_KEYDOWN** and **WM_KEYUP**, other keyboard messages are shown here.

WM_SYSKEYDOWN	Raw keyboard message when a system key is pressed. **wParam** contains virtual key code.
WM_SYSKEYUP	Raw keyboard message when a system key is released. **wParam** contains virtual key code.
WM_DEADCHAR	Message generated by **TranslateMessage( )** when a key has no translation into the current environment. **wParam** contains ASCII code.
WM_SYSCHAR	Message generated by **TranslateMessage( )** when a system key is pressed. **wParam** contains ASCII code.
WM_SYSDEADCHAR	Message generated by **TranslateMessage( )** when a system key has no translation into the current environment. **wParam** contains ASCII code.

A system key is generated by holding down the ALT key, for example, ALT-F. For all keyboard messages, the value of **lParam** is similar to that shown in Table 3-1.

For most applications, you will include **TranslateMessage( )** in your message loop and process messages for **WM_CHAR**. The other messages are available for those few programs that have specialized keyboard needs. Although the low-level control of keyboard input may have been essential in other programming environments in which you have worked, it is seldom necessary in Windows. The main reason for this is that Windows contains several controls, such as edit boxes and list controls, that automate the handling of keyboard input.

Generating a WM_PAINT Message

In addition to receiving messages, your program can also generate them. The most frequently generated message is **WM_PAINT**. At first, you might wonder why your program would need to generate a **WM_PAINT** message, since it seems that it can repaint its window whenever it wants. However, this is a false assumption. Remember, updating a window is costly in terms of time. Because Windows is a multitasking system that might be running other programs that are also demanding CPU time, your program should simply tell Windows that it wants to output information, but let Windows decide when it is best to actually perform that output. This allows Windows to better manage the system and efficiently allocate CPU time to all the tasks in the system. Using this approach, your program simply holds all output until a **WM_PAINT** message is received.

*To cause the window to be repainted, call **InvalidateRect( )**.*

In the previous examples, the **WM_PAINT** message was received only when the window was resized or uncovered. However, if all output is held until a **WM_PAINT** message is received, then to achieve interactive I/O, there must be some way to tell Windows that it needs to send a **WM_PAINT** to your window whenever output is pending. As expected, Windows 98 includes such a feature. Thus, when your program has information to output, it simply requests that a **WM_PAINT** message be sent when Windows is ready to do so.

To cause Windows to send a **WM_PAINT** message, your program will call the **InvalidateRect( )** API function. Its prototype is shown here:

BOOL InvalidateRect(HWND *hwnd*, CONST RECT **lpRect*, BOOL *bErase*);

Here, *hwnd* is the handle of the window to which you want to send the **WM_PAINT** message. The **RECT** structure pointed to by *lpRect* specifies the coordinates within the window that must be redrawn. If this value is **NULL**, then the entire window will be specified. If *bErase* is true, then the background will be erased. If it is 0, then the background is left unchanged.

The function returns nonzero if successful; it returns zero otherwise. (In general, this function will always succeed.)

When **InvalidateRect( )** is called, it tells Windows that the window is invalid and must be redrawn. This, in turn, causes Windows to send a **WM_PAINT** message to the program's window function.

Here is an example that responds to **WM_CHAR**, **WM_LBUTTONDOWN**, **WM_RBUTTONDOWN**, and **WM_PAINT** messages. All output is routed through the **WM_PAINT** handler. The other message response code simply prepares the information to be displayed and then calls **InvalidateRect( )**.

3

```c
/* An example that routes all output through
   the WM_PAINT message. */

#include <windows.h>
#include <string.h>
#include <stdio.h>

LRESULT CALLBACK WindowFunc(HWND, UINT, WPARAM, LPARAM);

char szWinName[] = "MyWin"; /* name of window class */

char str[255] = "Sample Output"; /* holds output string */

int X = 1, Y = 1; /* screen location */

int WINAPI WinMain(HINSTANCE hThisInst, HINSTANCE hPrevInst,
                   LPSTR lpszArgs, int nWinMode)
{
  HWND hwnd;
  MSG msg;
  WNDCLASSEX wcl;

  /* Define a window class. */
  wcl.cbSize = sizeof(WNDCLASSEX);

  wcl.hInstance = hThisInst; /* handle to this instance */
  wcl.lpszClassName = szWinName; /* window class name */
  wcl.lpfnWndProc = WindowFunc; /* window function */
  wcl.style = 0; /* default style */

  wcl.hIcon = LoadIcon(NULL, IDI_APPLICATION); /* standard icon */
  wcl.hIconSm = LoadIcon(NULL, IDI_WINLOGO); /* small icon */
  wcl.hCursor = LoadCursor(NULL, IDC_ARROW); /* cursor style */
```

```
wcl.lpszMenuName = NULL; /* no main menu */
wcl.cbClsExtra = 0; /* no extra */
wcl.cbWndExtra = 0; /* information needed */

/* Make the window white. */
wcl.hbrBackground = (HBRUSH) GetStockObject(WHITE_BRUSH);

/* Register the window class. */
if(!RegisterClassEx(&wcl)) return 0;

/* Now that a window class has been registered, a window
   can be created. */
hwnd = CreateWindow(
  szWinName, /* name of window class */
  "Routing Output Through WM_PAINT", /* title */
  WS_OVERLAPPEDWINDOW, /* window style - normal */
  CW_USEDEFAULT, /* X coordinate - let Windows decide */
  CW_USEDEFAULT, /* Y coordinate - let Windows decide */
  CW_USEDEFAULT, /* width - let Windows decide */
  CW_USEDEFAULT, /* height - let Windows decide */
  HWND_DESKTOP, /* no parent window */
  NULL, /* no menu */
  hThisInst, /* handle of this instance of the program */
  NULL /* no additional arguments */
);

/* Display the window. */
ShowWindow(hwnd, nWinMode);
UpdateWindow(hwnd);

/* Create the message loop. */
while(GetMessage(&msg, NULL, 0, 0))
{
  TranslateMessage(&msg); /* Translate keyboard messages */
  DispatchMessage(&msg); /* return control to Windows 98 */
}
return msg.wParam;
}

/* This function is called by Windows 98 and is passed
   messages from the message queue.
*/
LRESULT CALLBACK WindowFunc(HWND hwnd, UINT message, WPARAM wParam,
              LPARAM lParam)
```

```
{
  HDC hdc;
  PAINTSTRUCT paintstruct;

  switch(message) {
    case WM_CHAR: /* process keystroke */
      X = Y = 1; /* display chars in upper left corner */
      sprintf(str, "%c", (char) wParam); /* stringize character */
      InvalidateRect(hwnd, NULL, 1); /* paint the screen */
      break;
    case WM_PAINT: /* process a repaint request */
      hdc = BeginPaint(hwnd, &paintstruct); /* get DC */
      TextOut(hdc, X, Y, str, strlen(str)); /* output string */
      EndPaint(hwnd, &paintstruct); /* release DC */
      break;
    case WM_RBUTTONDOWN: /* process right button */
      strcpy(str, "Right button is down.");
      X = LOWORD(lParam); /* set X,Y to current */
      Y = HIWORD(lParam); /* mouse location */
      InvalidateRect(hwnd, NULL, 1); /* paint the screen */
      break;
    case WM_LBUTTONDOWN: /* process left button */
      strcpy(str, "Left button is down.");
      X = LOWORD(lParam); /* set X,Y to current */
      Y = HIWORD(lParam); /* mouse location */
      InvalidateRect(hwnd, NULL, 1); /* paint the screen */
      break;
    case WM_DESTROY: /* terminate the program */
      PostQuitMessage(0);
      break;
    default:
      /* Let Windows 98 process any messages not specified in
         the preceding switch statement. */
      return DefWindowProc(hwnd, message, wParam, lParam);
  }
  return 0;
}
```

Notice that the program adds two new global variables called **X** and **Y** that hold the location at which the text will be displayed when a **WM_PAINT** message is received.

As you can see, by channeling all output through **WM_PAINT**, the program is actually smaller and, in some ways, easier to understand than if output had been performed inside the other message handlers. Also, as stated at the start of this section, the program allows Windows 98 to decide when it is most appropriate to update the window.

Many Windows applications route all (or most) output through **WM_PAINT**, for the reasons already stated. However, there is nothing technically wrong with outputting text or graphics as needed. Which method you use will depend on the exact nature of each situation.

Generating Timer Messages

A timer sends a message to your program at predetermined intervals.

The last message that will be discussed here is **WM_TIMER**. Using Windows, it is possible to establish a timer that will interrupt your program at periodic intervals. Each time the timer goes off, it sends a **WM_TIMER** message to your window function. Using a timer is a good way to "wake up your program" every so often. This is particularly useful when your program is running as a background task.

To start a timer, use the **SetTimer( )** API function, whose prototype is shown here:

UINT SetTimer(HWND *hwnd*, UINT *ID*, UINT *length*, TIMERPROC *lpTFunc*);

Here, *hwnd* is the handle of the window that uses the timer. The value of *ID* specifies a value that will be associated with this timer. (More than one timer can be active.) The value of *length* specifies the length of the period, in milliseconds. That is, *length* specifies how long a time there is between interrupts. The function pointed to by *lpTFunc* is the function that will be called when the timer goes off. This must be a callback function that returns **VOID CALLBACK** and takes the same type of parameters as the window function. However, if the value of *lpTFunc* is **NULL**, as it commonly is, then your program's window function will be used for this purpose. In this case, each time the timer goes off, a **WM_TIMER** message is put into the message queue for your program and your program's window function processes it like any other message. This is the approach used by the example that follows. The function returns *ID* if successful. If the timer cannot be allocated, zero is returned.

Once a timer has been started, it continues to interrupt your program until either you terminate the application or your program executes a call to the **KillTimer( )** API function, whose prototype is shown here:

BOOL KillTimer(HWND *hwnd*, UINT *ID*);

Here, *hwnd* is the window that contains the timer, and *ID* is the value that identifies that particular timer. **KillTimer( )** returns nonzero if the timer is stopped and zero on error.

Each time a **WM_TIMER** message is generated, the value of **wParam** contains the ID of the timer and **lParam** contains the address of the timer callback function (if it is specified). For the example that follows, **lParam** will be **NULL**.

To demonstrate the use of a timer, the following program uses a timer to create a clock. It uses the standard C/C++ time and date functions to obtain and display the current system time and date. Each time the timer goes off, which is approximately once each second, the time is updated. Thus, the time displayed is accurate to within one second. Notice that output is performed only through the **WM_PAINT** handler. **WM_TIMER** simply calls **InvalidateRect( )**.

3

```
/* A clock program. */

#include <windows.h>
#include <string.h>
#include <stdio.h>
#include <time.h>

LRESULT CALLBACK WindowFunc(HWND, UINT, WPARAM, LPARAM);

char szWinName[] = "WinClock"; /* name of window class */

char str[255] = ""; /* holds output string */

int WINAPI WinMain(HINSTANCE hThisInst, HINSTANCE hPrevInst,
                   LPSTR lpszArgs, int nWinMode)
{
  HWND hwnd;
  MSG msg;
  WNDCLASSEX wcl;

  /* Define a window class. */
  wcl.cbSize = sizeof(WNDCLASSEX);

  wcl.hInstance = hThisInst; /* handle to this instance */
  wcl.lpszClassName = szWinName; /* window class name */
  wcl.lpfnWndProc = WindowFunc; /* window function */
  wcl.style = 0; /* default style */
```

```
wcl.hIcon = LoadIcon(NULL, IDI_APPLICATION); /* standard icon */
wcl.hIconSm = LoadIcon(NULL, IDI_WINLOGO); /* small icon */
wcl.hCursor = LoadCursor(NULL, IDC_ARROW); /* cursor style */

wcl.lpszMenuName = NULL; /* no menu */
wcl.cbClsExtra = 0; /* no extra */
wcl.cbWndExtra = 0; /* information needed */

/* Make the window white. */
wcl.hbrBackground = (HBRUSH) GetStockObject(WHITE_BRUSH);

/* Register the window class. */
if(!RegisterClassEx(&wcl)) return 0;

/* Now that a window class has been registered, a window
   can be created. */
hwnd = CreateWindow(
  szWinName, /* name of window class */
  "Clock", /* title */
  WS_OVERLAPPEDWINDOW, /* window style - normal */
  CW_USEDEFAULT, /* X coordinate - let Windows decide */
  CW_USEDEFAULT, /* Y coordinate - let Windows decide */
  CW_USEDEFAULT, /* width - let Windows decide */
  CW_USEDEFAULT, /* height - let Windows decide */
  HWND_DESKTOP, /* no parent window */
  NULL, /* no menu */
  hThisInst, /* handle of this instance of the program */
  NULL /* no additional arguments */
);

/* Display the window. */
ShowWindow(hwnd, nWinMode);

/* start a timer -- interrupt once per second */
SetTimer(hwnd, 1, 1000, NULL);

UpdateWindow(hwnd);

/* Create the message loop. */
while(GetMessage(&msg, NULL, 0, 0))
{
  TranslateMessage(&msg); /* translate keyboard messages */
  DispatchMessage(&msg); /* return control to Windows 98 */
}
```

```
      KillTimer(hwnd, 1); /* stop the timer */

      return msg.wParam;
}

/* This function is called by Windows 98 and is passed
   messages from the message queue.
*/
LRESULT CALLBACK WindowFunc(HWND hwnd, UINT message,
                            WPARAM wParam, LPARAM lParam)
{
  HDC hdc;
  PAINTSTRUCT paintstruct;
  struct tm *newtime;
  time_t t;

  switch(message) {
    case WM_PAINT: /* process a repaint request */
      hdc = BeginPaint(hwnd, &paintstruct); /* get DC */
      TextOut(hdc, 1, 1, str, strlen(str)); /* output string */
      EndPaint(hwnd, &paintstruct); /* release DC */
      break;
    case WM_TIMER: /* timer went off */
      /* get the new time */
      t = time(NULL);
      newtime = localtime(&t);

      /* display the new time */
      strcpy(str, asctime(newtime));
      str[strlen(str)-1] = '\0'; /* remove /r/n */
      InvalidateRect(hwnd, NULL, 0); /* update screen */
      break;
    case WM_DESTROY: /* terminate the program */
      PostQuitMessage(0);
      break;
    default:
      /* Let Windows 98 process any messages not specified in
         the preceding switch statement. */
      return DefWindowProc(hwnd, message, wParam, lParam);
  }
  return 0;
}
```

Sample output from this program is shown in Figure 3-5.

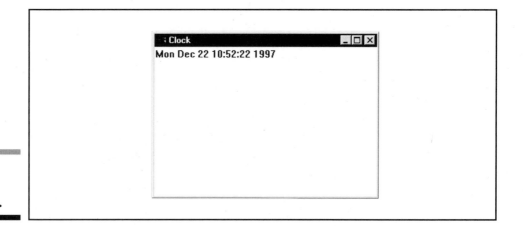

The clock
window
Figure 3-5.

Now that you have learned how a Windows 98 program processes messages,
you can move on to creating message boxes and menus, which are the
subject of the next chapter.

IN DEPTH

Positioning a Window

In most of the programs in this book, Windows 98 is allowed to choose a
position and size for the main window when a program begins execution.
While this is the way many applications work, it is possible to explicitly
specify these attributes. To do so, simply pass the coordinates of the
window's upper-left corner and its width and height to **CreateWindow( )**.
For example, if you substitute the following call to **CreateWindow( )**
into the clock program, the window will be displayed in the upper-left
corner of the screen and will be 200 units wide and 50 units tall.

```
hwnd = CreateWindow(
  szWinName, /* name of window class */
  "Clock", /* title */
  WS_OVERLAPPEDWINDOW, /* window style - normal */
  0, /* X coordinate */
  0, /* Y coordinate */
  200, /* width */
  50, /* height */
  HWND_DESKTOP, /* no parent window */
```

```
      NULL, /* no menu */
      hThisInst, /* handle of this instance of the program */
      NULL /* no additional arguments */
);
```

The clock window will now look like the one shown here:

When determining the location and dimensions of a window, keep in mind that these are specified in *device units,* which are the physical units used by the device (in this case, pixels). This means that the coordinates and dimensions are relative to the screen. The coordinates of the upper-left corner are 0,0. As you will see later in this book, output to a window is generally specified in terms of *logical units,* which are mapped to a window according to the current mapping mode. However, since the position of a window is relative to the entire screen, it makes sense that **CreateWindow( )** would require physical units rather than logical ones.

3

CHAPTER 4

Message Boxes
and Menus

75

Now that you know how to construct a basic Windows 98 skeleton and receive and process messages, it is time to begin exploration of Windows' user interface components. If you are learning to program Windows for the first time, it is important to understand that your application will most often communicate with the user through one or more predefined interface components. There are several different types of interface elements supported by Windows 98. This chapter discusses two: message boxes and menus. These are the most fundamental. Virtually any program you write will use both of them. As you will see, the basic style of the message box and the menu is predefined. You need only supply the specific information that relates to your application.

This chapter also introduces the resource. A resource is, essentially, an object defined outside your program but used by your program. Icons, cursors, menus, and bitmaps are common resources. Resources are a crucial part of nearly all Windows applications.

Message Boxes

A message box is a predefined window that displays simple output.

By far, the simplest interface window is the message box. A *message box* simply displays a message to the user and waits for an acknowledgement. It is possible to construct message boxes that allow the user to select among a few basic alternatives, but in general, the purpose of a message box is to inform the user that some event has taken place.

NOTE: In the term *message box*, the word *message* refers to human-readable text that is displayed on the screen. It does not refer to Windows 98 messages that are sent to your program's window function. Although the terms sound similar, *message boxes* and *messages* are two entirely separate concepts.

To create a message box, use the **MessageBox( )** API function. Its prototype is shown here:

    int MessageBox(HWND *hwnd*, LPCSTR *lpszText*, LPCSTR *lpszCaption*, UINT *MBType*);

Here, *hwnd* is the handle to the parent window. The *lpszText* parameter is a pointer to a string that will appear inside the message box. The string pointed to by *lpszCaption* is used as the title for the box. The value of *MBType* determines the exact nature of the message box, including what type of buttons and icons will be present. Some of its most common values are shown in Table 4-1. These macros are defined by including WINDOWS.H, and you can OR together two or more of these macros so long as they are not mutually exclusive.

MessageBox( ) returns the user's response to the box. The possible return values are shown here:

4

Button Pressed	Return Value
Abort	IDABORT
Retry	IDRETRY
Ignore	IDIGNORE
Cancel	IDCANCEL
No	IDNO
Yes	IDYES
OK	IDOK

Value	Effect
MB_ABORTRETRYIGNORE	Displays Abort, Retry, and Ignore push buttons
MB_ICONEXCLAMATION	Displays an exclamation point icon
MB_ICONERROR	Displays a stop sign icon
MB_ICONINFORMATION	Displays an information icon
MB_ICONQUESTION	Displays a question mark icon
MB_ICONSTOP	Displays a stop sign
MB_OK	Displays OK button
MB_OKCANCEL	Displays OK and Cancel push buttons
MB_RETRYCANCEL	Displays Retry and Cancel push buttons
MB_YESNO	Displays Yes and No push buttons
MB_YESNOCANCEL	Displays Yes, No, and Cancel push buttons

Some Common Values for *MBType*

Table 4-1.

Remember, depending upon the value of *MBType*, only certain buttons will be present. Quite often message boxes are simply used to display an item of information, and the only response offered to the user is the OK button. In these cases, the return value of a message box is usually ignored by the program.

To display a message box, simply call the **MessageBox( )** function. Windows 98 will display it at its first opportunity. You don't have to obtain a device context because **MessageBox( )** automatically creates a window and displays your message in it. For example, this call to **MessageBox( )**:

```
i = MessageBox(hwnd, "This is Caption", "This is Title", MB_OKCANCEL);
```

produces the following message box.

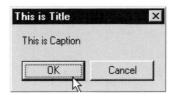

Depending upon which button the user presses, **i** will receive either **IDOK** or **IDCANCEL**.

Message boxes are typically used to notify the user that some event has occurred. However, because they are so easy to use, they make excellent debugging tools when you need a simple way to output something to the screen. As you will see, examples in this book will use a message box whenever a simple means of displaying information is needed.

Here is an example that displays a message box when you press a mouse button.

```
/* Demonstrate a Message Box. */

#include <windows.h>

LRESULT CALLBACK WindowFunc(HWND, UINT, WPARAM, LPARAM);

char szWinName[] = "MyWin"; /* name of window class */

int WINAPI WinMain(HINSTANCE hThisInst, HINSTANCE hPrevInst,
                   LPSTR lpszArgs, int nWinMode)
```

4

```
{
  HWND hwnd;
  MSG msg;
  WNDCLASSEX wcl;

  /* Define a window class. */
  wcl.cbSize = sizeof(WNDCLASSEX);

  wcl.hInstance = hThisInst; /* handle to this instance */
  wcl.lpszClassName = szWinName; /* window class name */
  wcl.lpfnWndProc = WindowFunc; /* window function */
  wcl.style = 0; /* default style */

  wcl.hIcon = LoadIcon(NULL, IDI_APPLICATION); /* standard icon */
  wcl.hIconSm = LoadIcon(NULL, IDI_WINLOGO); /* small icon */
  wcl.hCursor = LoadCursor(NULL, IDC_ARROW); /* cursor style */

  wcl.lpszMenuName = NULL; /* no menu */
  wcl.cbClsExtra = 0; /* no extra */
  wcl.cbWndExtra = 0; /* information needed */

  /* Make the window white. */
  wcl.hbrBackground = (HBRUSH) GetStockObject(WHITE_BRUSH);

  /* Register the window class. */
  if(!RegisterClassEx(&wcl)) return 0;

  /* Now that a window class has been registered, a window
     can be created. */
  hwnd = CreateWindow(
    szWinName, /* name of window class */
    "Using Message Boxes", /* title */
    WS_OVERLAPPEDWINDOW, /* window style - normal */
    CW_USEDEFAULT, /* X coordinate - let Windows decide */
    CW_USEDEFAULT, /* Y coordinate - let Windows decide */
    CW_USEDEFAULT, /* width - let Windows decide */
    CW_USEDEFAULT, /* height - let Windows decide */
    HWND_DESKTOP, /* no parent window */
    NULL, /* no menu */
    hThisInst, /* handle of this instance of the program */
    NULL /* no additional arguments */
  );

  /* Display the window. */
  ShowWindow(hwnd, nWinMode);
```

```
  UpdateWindow(hwnd);

  /* Create the message loop. */
  while(GetMessage(&msg, NULL, 0, 0))
  {
    TranslateMessage(&msg); /* translate keyboard messages */
    DispatchMessage(&msg); /* return control to Windows 98 */
  }
  return msg.wParam;
}

/* This function is called by Windows 98 and is passed
   messages from the message queue.
*/
LRESULT CALLBACK WindowFunc(HWND hwnd, UINT message,
                            WPARAM wParam, LPARAM lParam)
{
  int response;

  switch(message) {
    case WM_RBUTTONDOWN: /* process right button */
      response = MessageBox(hwnd, "Press One:", "Right Button",
                            MB_ABORTRETRYIGNORE);
      switch(response) {
        case IDABORT:
          MessageBox(hwnd, "Press Button", "Abort", MB_OK);
          break;
        case IDRETRY:
          MessageBox(hwnd, "Press Button", "Retry", MB_OK);
          break;
        case IDIGNORE:
          MessageBox(hwnd, "Press Button", "Ignore", MB_OK);
          break;
      }
      break;
    case WM_LBUTTONDOWN: /* process left button */
      response = MessageBox(hwnd, "Continue?", "Left Button",
                  MB_ICONSTOP | MB_YESNO);
      switch(response) {
        case IDYES:
          MessageBox(hwnd, "Press Button", "Yes", MB_OK);
          break;
        case IDNO:
          MessageBox(hwnd, "Press Button", "No", MB_OK);
          break;
```

```
    }
    break;
  case WM_DESTROY: /* terminate the program */
    PostQuitMessage(0);
    break;
  default:
    /* Let Windows 98 process any messages not specified in
       the preceding switch statement. */
    return DefWindowProc(hwnd, message, wParam, lParam);
  }
  return 0;
}
```

4

Each time a button is pressed, a message box is displayed. For example, pressing the right button displays the message box shown in Figure 4-1. Depending upon your response, a second message box will be displayed that indicates which button you pressed. Pressing the left mouse button causes a message box to be displayed that contains a stop sign. This box allows a Yes or a No response.

Before continuing, experiment with message boxes, trying different types.

Introducing Menus

In Windows, the most common element of control is the menu. Windows 98 supports three general types:

1. The menu bar (or main menu)
2. Pop-up submenus
3. Floating, stand-alone pop-up menus

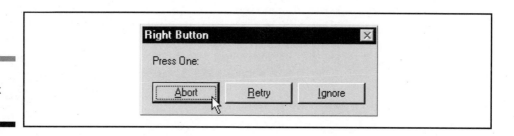

A sample
message box
Figure 4-1.

The menu bar is an application's topmost menu.

In a Windows application, the menu bar is displayed across the top of the window. This is frequently called the main menu. The menu bar is your application's top-level menu. Submenus descend from the menu bar and are displayed as pop-up menus. (You should be accustomed to this approach because it is used by virtually all Windows programs.) Floating pop-up menus are freestanding pop-up menus that are typically activated by pressing the right mouse button. In this chapter, we will explore the first two types: the menu bar and pop-up submenus. Floating menus are described in a later chapter.

A pop-up submenu drops down from the main menu.

Because menus are so common and important in Windows applications, Windows provides substantial built-in support for them. Adding a menu to a window involves these relatively few steps:

A floating pop-up menu is a freestanding menu.

1. Define the form of the menu in a resource file.
2. Load the menu when your program creates its main window.
3. Process menu selections.

The next few sections show how to implement these steps.

Before beginning, it is necessary to explain what resources and resource files are.

Using Resources

A resource is an object used by your program, but defined outside of it. A menu is one type of resource.

Windows defines several common types of objects as *resources*. As mentioned at the beginning of this chapter, resources are essentially objects that are used by your program, but are defined outside your program. They include things such as menus, icons, dialog boxes, and bitmapped graphics. Since a menu is a resource, you need to understand resources before you can add a menu to your program.

Resources are contained within a resource file, which uses the .RC extension.

A resource is created separately from your program, but is added to the .EXE file when your program is linked. Resources are contained in *resource files*, which have the extension .RC. For small projects, the name of the resource file is often the same as that of your program's .EXE file. For example, if your program is called PROG.EXE, then its resource file will typically be called PROG.RC. Of course, you can call a resource file by any name you please as long as it has the .RC extension.

Depending upon the resource, some are text-based and are created using a standard text editor. Text resources are typically defined within the resource file. Others, such as icons, are most easily generated using a resource editor, but they still must be referred to in the .RC file that is associated with your application. The example resource files in this chapter are simply text files because menus are text-based resources.

Resource files do not contain C or C++ statements. Instead, resource files consist of special resource statements. In the course of this chapter, the resource commands needed to support menus are discussed. Others are described as needed throughout this book.

4

Compiling .RC files

Resource files are not used directly by your program. Instead, they must be converted into a linkable format. Once you have created a .RC file, you compile it into a .RES file using the resource compiler. (Often, the resource compiler is called RC.EXE, but this varies.) Exactly how you compile a resource file will depend upon what compiler you are using. Also, some integrated development environments, such as Visual C++ and Borland C++, automatically handle this phase for you. In any event, the output of the resource compiler will be a .RES file, and it is this file that you will link with your program to build the final Windows 98 application.

Creating a Simple Menu

Before a menu can be included, you must define its content in a resource file. All menu definitions have this general form:

MenuName MENU [*options*]
{
   menu items
}

Here, *MenuName* is the name of the menu. (It may also be an integer value identifying the menu, but all examples in this book will use the name when referring to the menu.) The keyword **MENU** tells the resource compiler that a menu is being created. There are only a few options that apply to Windows 98 programs. They are shown here.

The MENU Options:

Option	Meaning
DISCARDABLE	Menu may be removed from memory when no longer needed.
CHARACTERISTICS *info*	Application-specific information, which is specified as a LONG value in *info*.
LANGUAGE *lang, sub-lang*	The language used by the resource is specified by *lang* and *sub-lang*. This is used by internationalized menus.
VERSION *ver*	Application-defined version number is specified in *ver*.

Most simple applications do not require the use of any options and simply use the default settings.

PORTABILITY: Windows 3.1 defines several additional options that may be applied to a MENU statement, such as PRELOAD. But they have no effect for Windows 98, Windows 95, or Windows NT programs. When porting code, you can eliminate these obsolete options.

There are two types of items that can be used to define the menu: **MENUITEM**s and **POPUP**s. A **MENUITEM** specifies a final selection. A **POPUP** specifies a pop-up submenu, which may, in itself, contain other **MENUITEM**s or **POPUP**s. The general form of these two statements is shown here:

MENUITEM *"ItemName"*, *MenuID* [,*Options*]

POPUP *"PopupName"* [,*Options*]

Here, *ItemName* is the name of the menu selection, such as "Help" or "Open". *MenuID* is a unique integer associated with a menu item that will be sent to your application when a selection is made. Typically, these values are defined as macros inside a header file that is included in both your application code

4

and in the .RC resource file. *PopupName* is the name of the pop-up menu. For both cases, the values for *Options* (defined by including WINDOWS.H) are shown in Table 4-2.

Here is an example of a simple menu that you should enter at this time. Call the file MENU.RC.

```
// Sample menu resource file.
#include "menu.h"

MyMenu MENU
{
  POPUP "&One"
  {
    MENUITEM "&Alpha", IDM_ALPHA
    MENUITEM "&Beta", IDM_BETA
    MENUITEM "E&xit", IDM_EXIT
  }
  POPUP "&Two"
  {
    MENUITEM "&Gamma", IDM_GAMMA
    POPUP "&Delta"
    {
      MENUITEM "&Epsilon", IDM_EPSILON
      MENUITEM "&Zeta", IDM_ZETA
    }
    MENUITEM "&Eta", IDM_ETA
    MENUITEM "&Theta", IDM_THETA
  }
  MENUITEM "&Help", IDM_HELP
}
```

This menu, called **MyMenu**, contains three top-level, menu bar options: One, Two, and Help. The One and Two options contain pop-up submenus. The Delta option activates a pop-up submenu of its own. Notice that options that activate submenus do not have menu ID values associated with them. Only actual menu items have ID numbers. In this menu, all menu ID values are specified as macros beginning with **IDM**. (These macros are defined in the header file MENU.H.) What names you give these values is arbitrary.

An **&** in an item's name causes the key that it precedes to become the shortcut key associated with that option. That is, once that menu is active, pressing that key causes that menu item to be selected. It doesn't have to be the first key in the name, but it should be unless a conflict with another

Option	Meaning
CHECKED	A check mark is displayed next to the name. Not applicable to top-level menus.
GRAYED	The name is shown in gray and may not be selected.
HELP	May be associated with a help selection. Applies to MENUITEMs only.
INACTIVE	The option may not be selected.
MENUBARBREAK	For menu bar, causes the item to be put on a new line. For pop-up menus, causes the item to be put in a different column. In this case, the item is separated using a bar.
MENUBREAK	Same as MENUBARBREAK except that no separator bar is used.
SEPARATOR	Creates an empty menu item that acts as a separator. Applies to MENUITEMs only.

The
MENUITEM
and POPUP
Options
Table 4-2.

name exists. Also, by convention, the Exit option usually uses "X" as the shortcut key.

NOTE: You can embed C and C++ style comments into the resource file as the first line of the resource file shows.

The MENU.H header file, which is included in MENU.RC, contains the macro definitions of the menu ID values. It is shown here. Enter it at this time.

```
#define IDM_ALPHA     100
#define IDM_BETA      101
#define IDM_EXIT      102
#define IDM_GAMMA     103
#define IDM_DELTA     104
#define IDM_EPSILON   105
#define IDM_ZETA      106
#define IDM_ETA       107
#define IDM_THETA     108
#define IDM_HELP      109
```

This file defines the menu ID values that will be returned when the various menu items are selected. This file will also be included in the program that uses the menu. Remember, the actual names and values you give the menu items are arbitrary, but each value must be unique. Also, the valid range for ID values is 0 through 65,565.

Including a Menu in Your Program

Once you have created a menu, you include it in a program by specifying its name when you create the window's class. Specifically, you assign the **lpszMenuName** field a pointer to a string that contains the name of the menu. For example, to load the menu **MyMenu**, you would use this line when defining the window's class.

```
wcl.lpszMenuName = "MyMenu"; // main menu
```

Now, **MyMenu** is the default main menu for all windows of its class. This means that all windows of this type will have the menu defined by **MyMenu**. (As you will see, you can override this class menu, if you like.)

Responding to Menu Selections

Each time the user makes a menu selection, your program's window function is sent a **WM_COMMAND** message. When that message is received, the value of **LOWORD(wParam)** corresponds to the menu item's ID constant. (That is, **LOWORD(wParam)** contains the value you associated with the item when you defined the menu in its .RC file.) Since **WM_COMMAND** is sent whenever a menu item is selected and the value associated with that item is contained in **LOWORD(wParam)**, you will need to use a nested **switch** statement to determine which item
was selected. For example, this fragment responds to a selection made from **MyMenu**.

```
switch(message) {
  case WM_COMMAND:
    switch(LOWORD(wParam)) {
      case IDM_ALPHA:
        MessageBox(hwnd, "Alpha", "Alpha", MB_OK);
        break;
      case IDM_BETA:
        MessageBox(hwnd, "Beta", "Beta", MB_OK);
        break;
```

4

```
    case IDM_EXIT:
      response = MessageBox(hwnd, "Quit the Program?",
                            "Exit", MB_YESNO);
      if(response == IDYES) PostQuitMessage(0);
      break;
    case IDM_GAMMA:
      MessageBox(hwnd, "Gamma", "Gamma", MB_OK);
      break;
    case IDM_EPSILON:
      MessageBox(hwnd, "Epsilon", "Epsilon", MB_OK);
      break;
    case IDM_ZETA:
      MessageBox(hwnd, "Zeta", "Zeta", MB_OK);
      break;
    case IDM_ETA:
      MessageBox(hwnd, "Eta", "Eta", MB_OK);
      break;
    case IDM_THETA:
      MessageBox(hwnd, "Theta", "Theta", MB_OK);
      break;
    case IDM_HELP:
      MessageBox(hwnd, "No Help", "Help", MB_OK);
      break;
  }
  break;
```

For the sake of illustration, the response to each selection simply displays an acknowledgment of that selection on the screen. However, in real applications, the response to menu selections will generally be more complex.

A Sample Menu Program

Here is a program that uses the menu just described. Enter it at this time. Sample output from the program is shown in Figure 4-2.

```
/* Demonstrate menus. */

#include <windows.h>
#include "menu.h"

LRESULT CALLBACK WindowFunc(HWND, UINT, WPARAM, LPARAM);

char szWinName[] = "MyWin"; /* name of window class */
```

```
int WINAPI WinMain(HINSTANCE hThisInst, HINSTANCE hPrevInst,
                   LPSTR lpszArgs, int nWinMode)
{
  HWND hwnd;
  MSG msg;
  WNDCLASSEX wcl;

  /* Define a window class. */
  wcl.cbSize = sizeof(WNDCLASSEX);

  wcl.hInstance = hThisInst; /* handle to this instance */
  wcl.lpszClassName = szWinName; /* window class name */
  wcl.lpfnWndProc = WindowFunc; /* window function */
  wcl.style = 0; /* default style */

  wcl.hIcon = LoadIcon(NULL, IDI_APPLICATION); /* standard icon */
  wcl.hIconSm = LoadIcon(NULL, IDI_WINLOGO); /* small icon */
  wcl.hCursor = LoadCursor(NULL, IDC_ARROW); /* cursor style */

  /* Specify name of menu resource. */
  wcl.lpszMenuName = "MyMenu"; /* main menu */

  wcl.cbClsExtra = 0; /* no extra */
  wcl.cbWndExtra = 0; /* information needed */

  /* Make the window white. */
  wcl.hbrBackground = (HBRUSH) GetStockObject(WHITE_BRUSH);

  /* Register the window class. */
  if(!RegisterClassEx(&wcl)) return 0;

  /* Now that a window class has been registered, a window
     can be created. */
  hwnd = CreateWindow(
    szWinName, /* name of window class */
    "Using Menus", /* title */
    WS_OVERLAPPEDWINDOW, /* window style - normal */
    CW_USEDEFAULT, /* X coordinate - let Windows decide */
    CW_USEDEFAULT, /* Y coordinate - let Windows decide */
    CW_USEDEFAULT, /* width - let Windows decide */
    CW_USEDEFAULT, /* height - let Windows decide */
    HWND_DESKTOP, /* no parent window */
    NULL,
    hThisInst, /* handle of this instance of the program */
```

```
      NULL /* no additional arguments */
  );

  /* Display the window. */
  ShowWindow(hwnd, nWinMode);
  UpdateWindow(hwnd);

  /* Create the message loop. */
  while(GetMessage(&msg, NULL, 0, 0))
  {
    TranslateMessage(&msg); /* translate keyboard messages */
    DispatchMessage(&msg); /* return control to Windows */
  }
  return msg.wParam;
}

/* This function is called by Windows 98 and is passed
   messages from the message queue.
*/
LRESULT CALLBACK WindowFunc(HWND hwnd, UINT message,
                            WPARAM wParam, LPARAM lParam)
{
  int response;

  switch(message) {
    case WM_COMMAND:
      switch(LOWORD(wParam)) {
        case IDM_ALPHA:
          MessageBox(hwnd, "Alpha", "Alpha", MB_OK);
          break;
        case IDM_BETA:
          MessageBox(hwnd, "Beta", "Beta", MB_OK);
          break;
        case IDM_EXIT:
          response = MessageBox(hwnd, "Quit the Program?",
                                "Exit", MB_YESNO);
          if(response == IDYES) PostQuitMessage(0);
          break;
        case IDM_GAMMA:
          MessageBox(hwnd, "Gamma", "Gamma", MB_OK);
          break;
        case IDM_EPSILON:
          MessageBox(hwnd, "Epsilon", "Epsilon", MB_OK);
```

4

```
          break;
        case IDM_ZETA:
          MessageBox(hwnd, "Zeta", "Zeta", MB_OK);
          break;
        case IDM_ETA:
          MessageBox(hwnd, "Eta", "Eta", MB_OK);
          break;
        case IDM_THETA:
          MessageBox(hwnd, "Theta", "Theta", MB_OK);
          break;
        case IDM_HELP:
          MessageBox(hwnd, "No Help", "Help", MB_OK);
          break;
      }
      break;
    case WM_DESTROY: /* terminate the program */
      PostQuitMessage(0);
      break;
    default:
      /* Let Windows 98 process any messages not specified in
         the preceding switch statement. */
      return DefWindowProc(hwnd, message, wParam, lParam);
  }
  return 0;
}
```

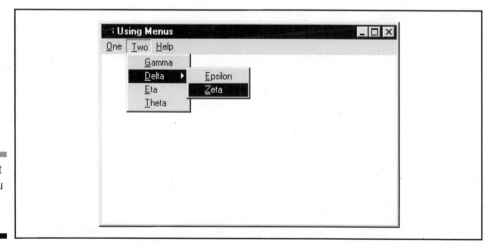

Sample output
from the menu
example

Figure 4-2.

Adding Menu Accelerator Keys

An accelerator
key allows you
to select a
menu item using
the keyboard,
bypassing
the menus
themselves.

There is an important feature that is often used in conjunction with a menu: the accelerator key. *Accelerator keys* are special keystrokes that you define that, when pressed, automatically select a menu option even though the menu in which that option resides is not displayed. Put differently, you can select an item directly by pressing an accelerator key, bypassing the menu entirely. The term *accelerator keys* is an accurate description because pressing one is generally a faster way to select a menu item than first activating its menu and then selecting the item.

To define accelerator keys relative to a menu, you must add an accelerator key table to your resource file. All accelerator table definitions have this general form:

```
TableName ACCELERATORS
{
  Key1, MenuID1 [,type] [option]
  Key2, MenuID2 [,type] [option]
  Key3, MenuID3 [,type] [option]
  .
  .
  .
  Keyn, MenuIDn [,type] [option]
}
```

Here, *TableName* is the name of the accelerator table. *Key* is the keystroke that selects the item, and *MenuID* is the ID value associated with the desired item. The *type* specifies whether the key is a standard key (the default) or a virtual key. The options may be one of the following macros: **NOINVERT**, **ALT**, **SHIFT**, and **CONTROL**. **NOINVERT** prevents the selected menu item from being highlighted when its accelerator key is pressed. **ALT** specifies an ALT key. **SHIFT** specifies a SHIFT key. **CONTROL** specifies a CTRL key.

The value of *Key* will be either a quoted character, an ASCII integer value corresponding to a key, or a virtual key code. If a quoted character is used, then it is assumed to be an ASCII character. If it is an integer value, then you must tell the resource compiler explicitly that this is an ASCII character by specifying *type* as **ASCII**. If it is a virtual key, then *type* must be **VIRTKEY**.

If the key is an uppercase quoted character, then its corresponding menu item will be selected if it is pressed while holding down the SHIFT key. If it is a lowercase character, then its menu item will be selected if the key is pressed by ítself. If the key is specified as a lowercase character and **ALT** is specified as an option, then pressing ALT and the character will select the item. (If the key is uppercase and ALT is specified, then you must press SHIFT and ALT to select the item.) Finally, if you want the user to press CTRL and the character to select an item, precede the key with a ^.

As explained in Chapter 3, a virtual key is a system-independent code for a variety of keys. To use a virtual key as an accelerator, simply specify its macro for the *key* and specify **VIRTKEY** for its *type*. You may also specify **ALT**, **SHIFT**, or **CONTROL** to achieve the desired key combination.

Here are some examples:

4

```
"A", IDM_x            ; select by pressing Shift-A
"a", IDM_x            ; select by pressing a
"^a", IDM_x           ; select by pressing Ctrl-a
"a", IDM_x, ALT       ; select by pressing Alt-a
VK_F2, IDM_x          ; select by pressing F2
VK_F2, IDM_x, SHIFT   ; select by pressing Shift-F2
```

Here is the MENU.RC resource file that also contains accelerator key definitions for the menu specified in the previous section.

```
// Sample menu resource file
#include <windows.h>
#include "menu.h"

MyMenu MENU
{
  POPUP "&One"
  {
    MENUITEM "&Alpha\tF2", IDM_ALPHA
    MENUITEM "&Beta\tF3", IDM_BETA
    MENUITEM "E&xit\tCtrl+X", IDM_BETA
  }
  POPUP "&Two"
  {
    MENUITEM "&Gamma\tShift+G", IDM_GAMMA
    POPUP "&Delta"
    {
      MENUITEM "&Epsilon\tCtrl+E", IDM_EPSILON
      MENUITEM "&Zeta\tCtrl+Z", IDM_ZETA
    }
    MENUITEM "&Eta\tCtrl+F4", IDM_ETA
```

```
    MENUITEM "&Theta\tF5", IDM_THETA
  }
  MENUITEM "&Help", IDM_HELP
}

// Define menu accelerators
MyMenu ACCELERATORS
{
  VK_F2, IDM_ALPHA, VIRTKEY
  VK_F3, IDM_BETA, VIRTKEY
  "^X", IDM_EXIT
  "G", IDM_GAMMA
  "^E", IDM_EPSILON
  "^Z", IDM_ZETA
  VK_F4, IDM_ETA, VIRTKEY, CONTROL
  VK_F5, IDM_THETA, VIRTKEY
  VK_F1, IDM_HELP, VIRTKEY
}
```

Notice that the menu definition has been enhanced to display which accelerator key selects which option. Each item is separated from its accelerator key using a tab. The header file WINDOWS.H is included because it defines the virtual key macros.

Loading the Accelerator Table

Even though the accelerators are contained in the same resource file as the menu, they must be loaded separately using another API function called **LoadAccelerators( )**, whose prototype is shown here:

HACCEL LoadAccelerators(HINSTANCE *ThisInst*, LPCSTR *Name*);

where *ThisInst* is the handle of the application and *Name* is the name of the accelerator table. The function returns a handle to the accelerator table or **NULL** if the table cannot be loaded.

You must call **LoadAccelerators( )** soon after the window is created. For example, this shows how to load the **MyMenu** acclerator table:

```
HACCEL hAccel;

hAccel = LoadAccelerators(hThisInst, "MyMenu");
```

The value of **hAccel** will be used later to help process accelerator keys.

Although the **LoadAccelerators( )** function loads the accelerator table, your program still cannot process the accelerators until you add another API function to the message loop. This function is called **TranslateAccelerator( )**, and its prototype is shown here:

int TranslateAccelerator(HWND *hwnd*, HACCEL *hAccel*, LPMSG *lpMess*);

Here, *hwnd* is the handle of the window for which accelerator keys will be translated. *hAccel* is the handle to the accelerator table that will be used. This is the handle returned by **LoadAccelerator( )**. Finally, *lpMess* is a pointer to the message. The **TranslateAccelerator( )** function returns true if an accelerator key was pressed and false otherwise.

TranslateAccelerator( ) translates an accelerator keystroke into its corresponding **WM_COMMAND** message and sends that message to the window. In this message, the value of **LOWORD(wParam)** will contain the ID associated with the accelerator key. Thus, to your program, the **WM_COMMAND** message will appear to have been generated by a menu selection.

Since **TranslateAccelerator( )** sends a **WM_COMMAND** message whenever an accelerator key is pressed, your program must not execute **TranslateMessage( )** or **DispatchMessage( )** when such a translation takes place. When using **TranslateAccelerator( )**, your message loop should look like this:

```
while(GetMessage(&msg, NULL, 0, 0))
{
  if(!TranslateAccelerator(hwnd, hAccel, &msg)) {
    TranslateMessage(&msg); /* translate keyboard messages */
    DispatchMessage(&msg); /* return control to Windows */
  }
}
```

To try using accelerators, substitute the following version of **WinMain( )** in the preceding application and add the accelerator table to your resource file.

```
/* Process accelerator keys. */
int WINAPI WinMain(HINSTANCE hThisInst, HINSTANCE hPrevInst,
                   LPSTR lpszArgs, int nWinMode)
{
  HWND hwnd;
  MSG msg;
```

```
WNDCLASSEX wcl;
HACCEL hAccel;

/* Define a window class. */
wcl.cbSize = sizeof(WNDCLASSEX);

wcl.hInstance = hThisInst; /* handle to this instance */
wcl.lpszClassName = szWinName; /* window class name */
wcl.lpfnWndProc = WindowFunc; /* window function */
wcl.style = 0; /* default style */

wcl.hIcon = LoadIcon(NULL, IDI_APPLICATION); /* standard icon */
wcl.hIconSm = LoadIcon(NULL, IDI_WINLOGO); /* small icon */
wcl.hCursor = LoadCursor(NULL, IDC_ARROW); /* cursor style */

/* Specify name of menu resource. */
wcl.lpszMenuName = "MyMenu"; /* main menu */

wcl.cbClsExtra = 0; /* no extra */
wcl.cbWndExtra = 0; /* information needed */

/* Make the window white. */
wcl.hbrBackground = (HBRUSH) GetStockObject(WHITE_BRUSH);

/* Register the window class. */
if(!RegisterClassEx(&wcl)) return 0;

/* Now that a window class has been registered, a window
   can be created. */
hwnd = CreateWindow(
  szWinName, /* name of window class */
  "Using Menus with Accelerators", /* title */
  WS_OVERLAPPEDWINDOW, /* window style - normal */
  CW_USEDEFAULT, /* X coordinate - let Windows decide */
  CW_USEDEFAULT, /* Y coordinate - let Windows decide */
  CW_USEDEFAULT, /* width - let Windows decide */
  CW_USEDEFAULT, /* height - let Windows decide */
  HWND_DESKTOP, /* no parent window */
  NULL,
  hThisInst, /* handle of this instance of the program */
  NULL /* no additional arguments */
);

/* Load the keyboard accelerators. */
hAccel = LoadAccelerators(hThisInst, "MyMenu");
```

```
/* Display the window. */
ShowWindow(hwnd, nWinMode);
UpdateWindow(hwnd);

/* Create the message loop. */
while(GetMessage(&msg, NULL, 0, 0))
{
  if(!TranslateAccelerator(hwnd, hAccel, &msg)) {
    TranslateMessage(&msg); /* translate keyboard messages */
    DispatchMessage(&msg); /* return control to Windows */
  }
}
return msg.wParam;
}
```

4

One last point about accelerators: Although they are most commonly used to provide a fast means of selecting a menu item, they are not limited to this role. For example, you can define an accelerator key for which there is no corresponding menu item. You might use such a key to activate a keyboard macro or to initiate some frequently used option. To define a nonmenu accelerator key, simply add it to the accelerator table, assigning it a unique ID value.

Overriding the Class Menu

In the preceding programs the main menu has been specified in the **lpszMenuName** member of the **WNDCLASSEX** structure. As mentioned, this specifies a class menu that will be used by all windows that are created of its class. This is the way that most main menus are specified for simple applications. However, there is another way to specify a main menu that uses the **CreateWindow( )** function. As you may recall from Chapter 2, **CreateWindow( )** is defined like this:

```
HWND CreateWindow(
  LPCSTR lpszClassName, /* name of window class */
  LPCSTR lpszWinName, /* title of window */
  DWORD dwStyle, /* type of window */
  int X, int Y, /* upper-left coordinates */
  int Width, int Height, /* dimensions of window */
  HWND hParent, /* handle of parent window */
  HMENU hMenu, /* handle of main menu */
  HINSTANCE hThisInst, /* handle of creator */
  LPVOID lpszAdditional /* pointer to additional info */
);
```

IN DEPTH

A Closer Look at WM_COMMAND

As explained, each time you make a menu selection or press an accelerator key, a **WM_COMMAND** message is sent and the value in **LOWORD(wParam)** contains the ID of the menu item selected or the accelerator key pressed. However, using only the value in **LOWORD(wParam)**, it is not possible to determine which event occurred. In most situations, it doesn't matter whether the user actually made a menu selection or just pressed an accelerator key. But in those situations in which it does, you can find out because Windows provides this information in the high-order word of **wParam**. If the value in **HIWORD(wParam)** is zero, then the user has made a menu selection. If this value is 1, then the user pressed an accelerator key. For example, try substituting the following fragment into the menu program. It reports whether the Alpha option was selected using the menu or by pressing an accelerator key.

```
case IDM_ALPHA:
  if(HIWORD(wParam))
    MessageBox(hwnd, "Alpha via Accelerator", "Alpha", MB_OK);
  else
    MessageBox(hwnd, "Alpha via Menu Selection", "Alpha",
MB_OK);
  break;
```

The value of **lParam** for **WM_COMMAND** messages generated by menu selections or accelerator keys is unused and always contains **NULL**.

As you will see in the next chapter, **WM_COMMAND** is also generated when the user interacts with various types of controls. In this case, the meaning of **lParam** and **wParam** is somewhat different. For example, the value of **lParam** will contain the handle of the control.

Notice the *hMenu* parameter. It can be used to specify a main menu for the window being created. In the preceding programs, this parameter has been specified as **NULL**. When *hMenu* is **NULL**, the class menu is used. However, if it contains the handle to a menu, then that menu will be used as the main menu for the window being created. In this case, the menu specified by *hMenu* overrides the class menu. Although simple applications, such as those shown in this book, do not need to override the class menu, there can be times when this is beneficial. For example, you might want to define a generic window class that your application will tailor to specific needs.

To specify a main menu using **CreateWindow( )**, you need a handle to the menu. The easiest way to obtain one is by calling the **LoadMenu( )** API function, shown here.

> HMENU LoadMenu(HINSTANCE *hInst*, LPCSTR *lpszName*);

Here, *hInst* is the instance handle of your application. A pointer to the name of the menu is passed in *lpszName*. **LoadMenu( )** returns a handle to the menu if successful or **NULL** on failure. Once you have obtained a handle to a menu, it can be used as the *hMenu* parameter to **CreateWindow( )**.

When you load a menu using **LoadMenu( )**, you are creating an object that allocates memory. This memory must be released before your program ends. If the menu is linked to a window, then this is done automatically. However, if it is not, you must free the memory explicitly. This is accomplished using the **DestroyMenu( )** API function. Its prototype is shown here:

> BOOL DestroyMenu(HMENU *hMenu*);

Here, *hMenu* is the handle of the menu being destroyed. The function returns nonzero if successful and zero on failure. As stated, you will not need to use **DestroyMenu( )** if the menu you load is linked to a window.

An Example That Overrides the Class Menu

To illustrate how the class menu can be overridden, let's modify the preceding menu program. To do so, add a second menu, called **PlaceHolder**, to the MENU.RC file, as shown here.

```
// Define two menus.
#include <windows.h>
#include "menu.h"

// Placeholder menu.
PlaceHolder MENU
{
  POPUP "&Options"
  {
    MENUITEM "E&xit\tCtrl+X", IDM_EXIT
  }
  MENUITEM "&Help", IDM_HELP
```

```
}

MyMenu MENU
{
  POPUP "&One"
  {
    MENUITEM "&Alpha\tF2", IDM_ALPHA
    MENUITEM "&Beta\tF3", IDM_BETA
    MENUITEM "E&xit\tCtrl+X", IDM_BETA
  }
  POPUP "&Two"
  {
    MENUITEM "&Gamma\tShift+G", IDM_GAMMA
    POPUP "&Delta"
    {
      MENUITEM "&Epsilon\tCtrl+E", IDM_EPSILON
      MENUITEM "&Zeta\tCtrl+Z", IDM_ZETA
    }
    MENUITEM "&Eta\tCtrl+F4", IDM_ETA
    MENUITEM "&Theta\tF5", IDM_THETA
  }
  MENUITEM "&Help", IDM_HELP
}

// Define menu accelerators
MyMenu ACCELERATORS
{
  VK_F2, IDM_ALPHA, VIRTKEY
  VK_F3, IDM_BETA, VIRTKEY
  "^X", IDM_EXIT
  "G", IDM_GAMMA
  "^E", IDM_EPSILON
  "^Z", IDM_ZETA
  VK_F4, IDM_ETA, VIRTKEY, CONTROL
  VK_F5, IDM_THETA, VIRTKEY
  VK_F1, IDM_HELP, VIRTKEY
}
```

The **PlaceHolder** menu will be used as the class menu. That is, it will be assigned to the **lpszMenuName** member of **WNDCLASSEX**. **MyMenu** will be loaded separately and its handle will be used in the *hMenu* parameter of **CreateWindow( )**. Thus, **MyMenu** will override **PlaceHolder**.

The contents of MENU.H are the same as the previous program.

Here is the complete program that overrides the class menu. This program incorporates all of the features discussed in this chapter. Since we have made so many changes to the menu program throughout the course of this chapter, the entire program is shown here for your convenience.

```
/* Overriding the class menu. */

#include <windows.h>
#include "menu.h"

LRESULT CALLBACK WindowFunc(HWND, UINT, WPARAM, LPARAM);

char szWinName[] = "MyWin"; /* name of window class */

int WINAPI WinMain(HINSTANCE hThisInst, HINSTANCE hPrevInst,
                   LPSTR lpszArgs, int nWinMode)
{
  HWND hwnd;
  MSG msg;
  WNDCLASSEX wcl;
  HACCEL hAccel;
  HMENU hmenu;

  /* Define a window class. */
  wcl.cbSize = sizeof(WNDCLASSEX);

  wcl.hInstance = hThisInst; /* handle to this instance */
  wcl.lpszClassName = szWinName; /* window class name */
  wcl.lpfnWndProc = WindowFunc; /* window function */
  wcl.style = 0; /* default style */

  wcl.hIcon = LoadIcon(NULL, IDI_APPLICATION); /* standard icon */
  wcl.hIconSm = LoadIcon(NULL, IDI_WINLOGO); /* small icon */
  wcl.hCursor = LoadCursor(NULL, IDC_ARROW); /* cursor style */

  /* Specify name of menu resource.  This will be overridden. */
  wcl.lpszMenuName = "PlaceHolder";  /* class menu */

  wcl.cbClsExtra = 0; /* no extra */
  wcl.cbWndExtra = 0; /* information needed */

  /* Make the window white. */
  wcl.hbrBackground = (HBRUSH) GetStockObject(WHITE_BRUSH);

  /* Register the window class. */
```

```
   if(!RegisterClassEx(&wcl)) return 0;

   /* Load the menu. */
   hmenu = LoadMenu(hThisInst, "MyMenu");

   /* Now that a window class has been registered, a window
      can be created. */
   hwnd = CreateWindow(
     szWinName, /* name of window class */
     "Override Class Menu", /* title */
     WS_OVERLAPPEDWINDOW, /* window style - normal */
     CW_USEDEFAULT, /* X coordinate - let Windows decide */
     CW_USEDEFAULT, /* Y coordinate - let Windows decide */
     CW_USEDEFAULT, /* width - let Windows decide */
     CW_USEDEFAULT, /* height - let Windows decide */
     HWND_DESKTOP, /* no parent window */
     hmenu, /* specify alternative main menu */
     hThisInst, /* handle of this instance of the program */
     NULL /* no additional arguments */
   );

   /* Load the keyboard accelerators. */
   hAccel = LoadAccelerators(hThisInst, "MyMenu");

   /* Display the window. */
   ShowWindow(hwnd, nWinMode);
   UpdateWindow(hwnd);

   /* Create the message loop. */
   while(GetMessage(&msg, NULL, 0, 0))
   {
     if(!TranslateAccelerator(hwnd, hAccel, &msg)) {
       TranslateMessage(&msg); /* translate keyboard messages */
       DispatchMessage(&msg); /* return control to Windows */
     }
   }
   return msg.wParam;
}

/* This function is called by Windows 98 and is passed
   messages from the message queue.
*/
LRESULT CALLBACK WindowFunc(HWND hwnd, UINT message,
                            WPARAM wParam, LPARAM lParam)
{
```

```
    int response;

    switch(message) {
      case WM_COMMAND:
        switch(LOWORD(wParam)) {
          case IDM_ALPHA:
            MessageBox(hwnd, "Alpha", "Alpha", MB_OK);
            break;
          case IDM_BETA:
            MessageBox(hwnd, "Beta", "Beta", MB_OK);
            break;
          case IDM_EXIT:
            response = MessageBox(hwnd, "Quit the Program?",
                                  "Exit", MB_YESNO);
            if(response == IDYES) PostQuitMessage(0);
            break;
          case IDM_GAMMA:
            MessageBox(hwnd, "Gamma", "Gamma", MB_OK);
            break;
          case IDM_EPSILON:
            MessageBox(hwnd, "Epsilon", "Epsilon", MB_OK);
            break;
          case IDM_ZETA:
            MessageBox(hwnd, "Zeta", "Zeta", MB_OK);
            break;
          case IDM_ETA:
            MessageBox(hwnd, "Eta", "Eta", MB_OK);
            break;
          case IDM_THETA:
            MessageBox(hwnd, "Theta", "Theta", MB_OK);
            break;
          case IDM_HELP:
            MessageBox(hwnd, "No Help", "Help", MB_OK);
            break;
        }
        break;
      case WM_DESTROY: /* terminate the program */
        PostQuitMessage(0);
        break;
      default:
        /* Let Windows 98 process any messages not specified in
           the preceding switch statement. */
        return DefWindowProc(hwnd, message, wParam, lParam);
    }
    return 0;
}
```

4

Pay special attention to the code inside **WinMain( )**. It creates a window class that specifies **PlaceHolder** as its class menu. However, before a window is actually created, **MyMenu** is loaded and its handle is used in the call to **CreateWindow( )**. This causes the class menu to be overridden and **MyMenu** to be displayed. You might want to experiment with this program a little. For example, since the class menu is being overridden, there is no reason to specify one at all. To prove this, assign **lpszMenuName** the value **NULL**. The operation of the program is unaffected.

In this example, both **MyMenu** and **PlaceHolder** contain menus that can be processed by the same window function. That is, they both use the same set of menu IDs. (Of course, **PlaceHolder** only contains two selections.) This allows either menu to work in the preceding program. Although you are not restricted in the form or structure of an overriding menu, you must always make sure that whatever menu you use, your window function contains the proper code to respond to it.

REMEMBER: It is usually easier to specify the main menu using **WNDCLASSEX** rather than **CreateWindow( )**. This is the approach used by the rest of the programs in this book.

One last point: since **MyMenu** is linked to the window created by **CreateWindow( )**, it is destroyed automatically when the program terminates. There is no need to call **DestroyMenu( )**.

Before moving on the next chapter, you should experiment on your own using message boxes, menus, and accelerators. Try the various options and see what they do. Menus and message boxes will be used by most of the other programs in this book, so a thorough understanding is important.

Some Menu Style Rules

While the precise structure and functionality of the menus associated with your applications is under your control, there are some guidelines that you should follow. By following these suggestions, your applications will give the user the same look and feel as most other Windows programs. Here are a few of the most important rules.

First, menu bar options should activate pop-up menus. They should not directly activate program functionality. That is, a menu bar option should only act as a gateway to another menu. The selection of menu items is best left to pop-up menus. This is the way most Windows applications function.

Second, if your application performs any type of file operations, such as opening, saving, or closing, then it should include a File menu bar item. This should be the first entry in the menu bar (that is, it should be on the far left). It should also include the Exit option. If your application does not have a File menu bar entry, then the leftmost pop-up menu should include the Exit option.

Third, if your application supports editing, such as Cut and Paste, then the menu bar should include the Edit option.

Fourth, if your application supports different viewing options, the menu bar should support the View item.

Finally, all applications should provide the Help option on the far right side of the menu bar.

While there certainly are going to be exceptions to these rules, they apply to the vast majority of Windows applications. Also, if you will be designing the menus for a sophisticated application, you will want to consult Microsoft's standard style guide for further suggestions.

4

CHAPTER 5

Introducing Dialog Boxes

This chapter introduces the dialog box. After menus, there is no more important interface element than the dialog box. A *dialog box* is a type of window that provides a more flexible means by which the user can interact with your application. In general, dialog boxes allow the user to select or enter information in a way that would be difficult or impossible using a menu.

Dialog boxes (and the controls that occur within them) are a large topic. In this chapter you will learn the basics of dialog box management, including how to create a dialog box and process dialog box messages. In subsequent chapters, we will use a dialog box to explore several elements of the Windows 98 interface.

Dialog Boxes Interact with the User Through Controls

A control is a special window that provides for input or output.

A dialog box interacts with the user through one or more *controls*. A control is a specific type of input or output window that is owned by its parent window, which, for the examples presented in this chapter, is the dialog box. Windows 98 supports several standard controls, including push buttons, check boxes, radio buttons, list boxes, edit boxes, combo boxes, scroll bars, and static controls. (Windows 98 also supports several enhanced controls called *common controls*, which are discussed later in this book.) Each standard control is briefly described here.

A *push button* is a control that the user "pushes on" to activate some response. You have seen push buttons in message boxes. For example, the OK button that we have been using in most message boxes is a push button.

A *check box* contains one or more items that are either checked or not checked. If the item is checked, it means that it is selected. If there is more than one check box in a dialog box, more than one item may be selected.

A *radio button* is essentially a special type of check box. However, when there is more than one radio button, one and only one item may be selected. Thus, radio buttons are mutually exclusive check boxes.

A *list box* displays a list of items from which the user selects one (or more). List boxes are commonly used to display things such as filenames.

An *edit box* allows the user to enter a string. Edit boxes provide all necessary text editing features required by the user. Therefore, to input a string, your program simply displays an edit box and waits until the user has finished typing in the string.

A *combo box* is a combination of a list box and an edit box.

As you know, a *scroll bar* is used to scroll text in a window.

A *static control* is used to output text (or graphics) that provides information to the user, but accepts no input.

In the course of explaining how to use dialog boxes with Windows, the examples in this chapter illustrate three of these controls: push buttons, the list box, and the edit box. Later in this book, the other controls will be examined.

It is important to understand that controls both generate messages (when accessed by the user) and receive messages (from your application). A message generated by a control indicates what type of interaction the user has had with the control. A message sent to the control is essentially an instruction to which the control must respond. You will see examples of this type of message passing later in this chapter.

5

Modal vs. Modeless Dialog Boxes

There are two types of dialog boxes: *modal* and *modeless*. The most common dialog boxes are modal. A modal dialog box demands a response from the user before the program will continue. When a modal dialog box is active, the user cannot refocus input to another part of the application without first closing the dialog box. More precisely, the *owner window* of a modal dialog box is deactivated until the dialog box is closed. (The owner window is usually the one that activates the dialog box.)

A modal dialog box must be closed before its owner window can be reactivated.

A modeless dialog box does not prevent other parts of the program from being used. That is, it does not need to be closed before input can be refocused to another part of the program. The owner window of a modeless dialog box remains active. In essence, modeless dialog boxes are more independent than modal ones.

A modeless dialog box allows its owner window to remain active.

We will examine modal dialog boxes first, since they are the most common. A modeless dialog box example concludes this chapter.

Receiving Dialog Box Messages

A dialog box is a window (albeit a special kind of window). Events that occur within it are sent to your program using the same message-passing mechanism the main window uses. However, dialog box messages are not sent to your program's main window function. Instead, each dialog box that you define will need its own window function, which is generally called a *dialog function* or *dialog procedure*. This function must have the following prototype. (Of course, the name of the function may be anything you like.)

BOOL CALLBACK DFunc(HWND *hdwnd*, UINT *message*,
WPARAM *wParam*, LPARAM *lParam*);

Dialog box messages are handled by a dialog procedure.

As you can see, a dialog function receives the same parameters as your program's main window function. However, it differs from the main window function in that it returns a true or false result. Like your program's main window function, the dialog box window function will receive many messages. If it processes a message, then it must return true. If it does not respond to a message, it must return false.

In general, each control within a dialog box will be given its own resource ID. Each time that control is accessed by the user, a **WM_COMMAND** message will be sent to the dialog function, indicating the ID of the control and the type of action the user has taken. That function will then decode the message and take appropriate actions. This process parallels the way messages are decoded by your program's main window function.

PORTABILITY: In Windows 3.1, the dialog function must be exported in the .DEF file associated with your program. However, this is not required by Windows 98. (In fact, as mentioned earlier, DEF files are not used by Windows 98.) Also, as mentioned in Chapter 3, Windows 3.1 organizes the **lParam** and **wParam** components of **WM_COMMAND** differently than does Windows 98.

Activating a Dialog Box

To activate a modal dialog box, use DialogBox( ).

To activate a modal dialog box (to cause it to be displayed), you must call the **DialogBox( )** API function, whose prototype is shown here:

int DialogBox(HINSTANCE *hThisInst*, LPCSTR *lpszName*,
HWND *hwnd*, DLGPROC *lpDFunc*)

hThisInst is a handle to the current application that is passed to your program in the instance parameter to **WinMain( )**. The name of the dialog box as defined in the resource file is pointed to by *lpszName*. The handle to the parent window that activates the dialog box is passed in *hwnd*. The *lpDFunc* parameter contains a pointer to the dialog function described in the preceding section. If **DialogBox( )** fails, then it returns –1. Otherwise, the return value is that specified by **EndDialog( )**, discussed next.

PORTABILITY: In Windows 3.1, *the lpDFunc* parameter to the **DialogBox( )** is a pointer to a procedure-instance, which is a short piece of code that links the dialog function with the data segment that the program is currently using. A procedure-instance is obtained using the **MakeProc-Instance( )** API function. However, this does not apply to Windows 98 (or any 32-bit version of Windows). Instead, the *lpDFunc* parameter is a pointer to the dialog function itself, and **MakeProcInstance( )** is not needed. You should remove calls to **MakeProcInstance( )** if you are converting older 3.1 code.

5

Deactivating a Dialog Box

To close a modal dialog box, use EndDialog( ).

To deactivate (that is, destroy and remove from the screen) a modal dialog box, use **EndDialog( )**. It has this prototype:

    BOOL EndDialog(HWND *hdwnd*, int *Status*);

Here, *hdwnd* is the handle to the dialog box, and *Status* is a status code returned by the **DialogBox( )** function. (The value of *Status* may be ignored, if it is not relevant to your program.) This function returns nonzero if successful and zero otherwise. (In normal situations, the function is successful.)

Creating a Simple Dialog Box

For a first dialog box, a simple example will be created. This dialog box will contain three push buttons called Red, Green, and Cancel. When either the Red or Green button is pressed, it will activate a message box indicating the choice selected. The box will be removed from the screen when the Cancel button is pressed.

The program will have a menu bar containing two options: Dialog and Help. The submenu under Dialog will contain three options: Dialog 1, Dialog 2, and Exit. Only Dialog 1 will have a dialog box associated with it. The Dialog 2 entry is a placeholder, so you can try defining your own dialog box as you work through the examples.

While this, and other examples in this chapter, don't do much with the information provided by the dialog box, they do illustrate the central features that you will use in your own applications.

The Dialog Box Resource File

A dialog box is another resource that is contained in your program's resource file. Before developing a program that uses a dialog box, you will need a resource file that specifies one. Although it is possible to specify the contents of a dialog box using a text editor, entering its specifications as you do when creating a menu, this is seldom done. Instead, most programmers use a dialog editor. The main reason for this is that dialog box definitions involve the positioning of the various controls inside the dialog box, which is best done interactively. However, since the complete .RC files for the examples in this chapter are supplied in their text form, you should simply enter them as text. Just remember that when creating your own dialog boxes, you will want to use a dialog editor.

NOTE: Since, in practice, most dialog boxes are created using a dialog editor, only a brief explanation of the dialog box definition in the resource file is given for the examples in this chapter.

Dialog boxes are defined within your program's resource file using the **DIALOG** statement. Its general form is shown here:

Dialog-name DIALOG [DISCARDABLE] *X, Y, Width, Height*
Features
{
   Dialog-items
}

The *Dialog-name* is the name of the dialog box. The box's upper-left corner will be at *X,Y, and the box will have the dimensions specified by Width × Height.* If the box may be removed from memory when not in use, then specify it as **DISCARDABLE**. One or more features of the dialog box may be specified. As you will see, two of these are the caption and the style of the box. The *Dialog-items* are the controls that comprise the dialog box.

The following resource file defines the dialog box that will be used by the first example program. It includes a menu that is used to activate the dialog box, the menu accelerator keys, and then the dialog box itself. You should enter it into your computer at this time, calling it MYDIALOG.RC.

```
// Sample dialog box and menu resource file.
#include <windows.h>
#include "mydialog.h"

MyMenu MENU
{
  POPUP "&Dialog"
  {
    MENUITEM "Dialog &1\tF2", IDM_DIALOG1
    MENUITEM "Dialog &2\tF3", IDM_DIALOG2
    MENUITEM "E&xit\tCtrl+X", IDM_EXIT
  }
  MENUITEM "&Help", IDM_HELP
}

MyMenu ACCELERATORS
{
  VK_F2, IDM_DIALOG1, VIRTKEY
  VK_F3, IDM_DIALOG2, VIRTKEY
  "^X", IDM_EXIT
  VK_F1, IDM_HELP, VIRTKEY
}

MyDB DIALOG 18, 18, 142, 92
CAPTION "Test Dialog Box"
STYLE DS_MODALFRAME | WS_POPUP | WS_CAPTION | WS_SYSMENU
{
  DEFPUSHBUTTON "Red", IDD_RED, 32, 40, 30, 14,
            WS_CHILD | WS_VISIBLE | WS_TABSTOP
  PUSHBUTTON "Green", IDD_GREEN, 74, 40, 30, 14,
            WS_CHILD | WS_VISIBLE | WS_TABSTOP
  PUSHBUTTON "Cancel", IDCANCEL, 52, 65, 37, 14,
            WS_CHILD | WS_VISIBLE | WS_TABSTOP
}
```

This defines a dialog box called **MyDB** that has its upper-left corner at location 18, 18. Its width is 142 and its height is 92. The string after **CAPTION** becomes the title of the dialog box. The **STYLE** statement determines what type of dialog box is created. Some common style values, including those used in this chapter, are shown if Table 5-1. You can OR

Value	Meaning
DS_MODALFRAME	Dialog box has a modal frame (i.e., a border).
WS_BORDER	Include a border.
WS_CAPTION	Include title bar.
WS_CHILD	Create as child window.
WS_POPUP	Create as pop-up window.
WS_MAXIMIZEBOX	Include maximize box.
WS_MINIMIZEBOX	Include minimize box.
WS_SYSMENU	Include system menu (or close box when used with a child window).
WS_TABSTOP	Control may be tabbed to.
WS_VISIBLE	Box is visible when activated.

Some
Common
Dialog Box
Style Options
Table 5-1.

together the values that are appropriate for the style of dialog box that you desire. These style values may also be used by other controls.

Within the **MyDB** definition are defined three push buttons. The first is the default push button. This button is automatically highlighted when the dialog box is first displayed. The general form of a push button declaration is shown here:

PUSHBUTTON "*string*", *PBID, X, Y, Width, Height* [, *Style*]

Here, *string* is the text that will be shown inside the push button. *PBID* is the value associated with the push button. It is this value that is returned to your program when the button is pushed. The button's upper-left corner will be at *X,Y,* and the button will have the dimensions specified by *Width* × *Height*. The *Style* determines the exact nature of the push button. To define a default push button, use the **DEFPUSHBUTTON** statement. It has the same parameters as the regular push buttons.

The header file MYDIALOG.H, which is also used by the example program, is shown here:

```
#define IDM_DIALOG1   100
#define IDM_DIALOG2   101
```

```
#define IDM_EXIT     102
#define IDM_HELP     103

#define IDD_RED      104
#define IDD_GREEN    105
```

Enter this file now.

The Dialog Box Window Function

As stated earlier, events that occur within a dialog box are passed to the window function associated with that dialog box and not to your program's main window function. The following dialog box window function responds to the events that occur within the **MyDB** dialog box.

5

```
/* A simple dialog function. */
BOOL CALLBACK DialogFunc(HWND hdwnd, UINT message,
                         WPARAM wParam, LPARAM lParam)
{
  switch(message) {
    case WM_COMMAND:
      switch(LOWORD(wParam)) {
        case IDCANCEL:
          EndDialog(hdwnd, 0);
          return 1;
        case IDD_RED:
          MessageBox(hdwnd, "You Picked Red", "RED", MB_OK);
          return 1;
        case IDD_GREEN:
          MessageBox(hdwnd, "You Picked Green", "GREEN", MB_OK);
          return 1;
      }
  }
  return 0;
}
```

Each time a control within the dialog box is accessed, a **WM_COMMAND** message is sent to **DialogFunc( )**, and **LOWORD(wParam)** contains the ID of the control affected.

DialogFunc( ) processes the three messages that can be generated by the box. If the user presses **Cancel**, then **IDCANCEL** is sent, causing the dialog box to be closed using a call to the API function **EndDialog( )**. (**IDCANCEL** is a standard ID defined by including WINDOWS.H.) Pressing either of the other two buttons causes a message box to be displayed that confirms the selection.

A First Dialog Box Sample Program

Here is the entire dialog box example. By selecting **Dialog 1** from the **Dialog** pop-up menu, the user causes the dialog box to be displayed. Once the dialog box is displayed, selecting a push button causes the appropriate response. Sample output is shown in Figure 5-1.

```
/* Demonstrate a Modal Dialog box. */

#include <windows.h>
#include <string.h>
#include <stdio.h>
#include "mydialog.h"

LRESULT CALLBACK WindowFunc(HWND, UINT, WPARAM, LPARAM);
BOOL CALLBACK DialogFunc(HWND, UINT, WPARAM, LPARAM);

char szWinName[] = "MyWin"; /* name of window class */

HINSTANCE hInst;

int WINAPI WinMain(HINSTANCE hThisInst, HINSTANCE hPrevInst,
                   LPSTR lpszArgs, int nWinMode)
{
  HWND hwnd;
  MSG msg;
  WNDCLASSEX wcl;
  HACCEL hAccel;

  /* Define a window class. */
  wcl.cbSize = sizeof(WNDCLASSEX);

  wcl.hInstance = hThisInst; /* handle to this instance */
  wcl.lpszClassName = szWinName; /* window class name */
  wcl.lpfnWndProc = WindowFunc; /* window function */
  wcl.style = 0; /* default style */

  wcl.hIcon = LoadIcon(NULL, IDI_APPLICATION); /* standard icon */
  wcl.hIconSm = LoadIcon(NULL, IDI_WINLOGO); /* small icon */
  wcl.hCursor = LoadCursor(NULL, IDC_ARROW); /* cursor style */
```

```
    wcl.lpszMenuName = "MyMenu"; /* main menu */
    wcl.cbClsExtra = 0; /* no extra */
    wcl.cbWndExtra = 0; /* information needed */

    /* Make the window white. */
    wcl.hbrBackground = (HBRUSH) GetStockObject(WHITE_BRUSH);

    /* Register the window class. */
    if(!RegisterClassEx(&wcl)) return 0;

    /* Now that a window class has been registered, a window
       can be created. */
    hwnd = CreateWindow(
      szWinName, /* name of window class */
      "Dialog Boxes", /* title */
      WS_OVERLAPPEDWINDOW, /* window style - normal */
      CW_USEDEFAULT, /* X coordinate - let Windows decide */
      CW_USEDEFAULT, /* Y coordinate - let Windows decide */
      CW_USEDEFAULT, /* width - let Windows decide */
      CW_USEDEFAULT, /* height - let Windows decide */
      HWND_DESKTOP, /* no parent window */
      NULL, /* no override of class menu */
      hThisInst, /* handle of this instance of the program */
      NULL /* no additional arguments */
    );

    hInst = hThisInst; /* save the current instance handle */

    /* Load accelerators. */
    hAccel = LoadAccelerators(hThisInst, "MyMenu");

    /* Display the window. */
    ShowWindow(hwnd, nWinMode);
    UpdateWindow(hwnd);

    /* Create the message loop. */
    while(GetMessage(&msg, NULL, 0, 0))
    {
      if(!TranslateAccelerator(hwnd, hAccel, &msg)) {
        TranslateMessage(&msg); /* Translate keyboard messages */
        DispatchMessage(&msg); /* return control to Windows 98 */
      }
    }
    return msg.wParam;
}
```

```
/* This function is called by Windows 98 and is passed
   messages from the message queue.
*/
LRESULT CALLBACK WindowFunc(HWND hwnd, UINT message,
                            WPARAM wParam, LPARAM lParam)
{
  int response;

  switch(message) {
    case WM_COMMAND:
      switch(LOWORD(wParam)) {
        case IDM_DIALOG1:
          DialogBox(hInst, "MyDB", hwnd, (DLGPROC) DialogFunc);
          break;
        case IDM_DIALOG2:
          MessageBox(hwnd, "Dialog Not Implemented", "Dialog 2",
                     MB_OK);
          break;
        case IDM_EXIT:
          response = MessageBox(hwnd, "Quit the Program?",
                                "Exit", MB_YESNO);
          if(response == IDYES) PostQuitMessage(0);
          break;
        case IDM_HELP:
          MessageBox(hwnd, "Not Implemented", "Help", MB_OK);
          break;
      }
      break;
    case WM_DESTROY: /* terminate the program */
      PostQuitMessage(0);
      break;
    default:
      /* Let Windows 98 process any messages not specified in
         the preceding switch statement. */
      return DefWindowProc(hwnd, message, wParam, lParam);
  }
  return 0;
}

/* A simple dialog function. */
BOOL CALLBACK DialogFunc(HWND hdwnd, UINT message,
                         WPARAM wParam, LPARAM lParam)
{
  switch(message) {
    case WM_COMMAND:
```

```
        switch(LOWORD(wParam)) {
          case IDCANCEL:
            EndDialog(hdwnd, 0);
            return 1;
          case IDD_RED:
            MessageBox(hdwnd, "You Picked Red", "RED", MB_OK);
            return 1;
          case IDD_GREEN:
            MessageBox(hdwnd, "You Picked Green", "GREEN", MB_OK);
            return 1;
        }
      }
    return 0;
  }
```

5

Notice the global variable **hInst**. This variable is assigned a copy of the current instance handle passed to **WinMain( )**. The reason for this variable is that the dialog box needs access to the current instance handle. However, the dialog box is not created in **WinMain( )** but in **WindowFunc( )**. Therefore, a copy of the instance parameter must be made so that it can be accessible outside of **WinMain( )**.

Adding a List Box

To continue exploring dialog boxes, let's add another control to the dialog box defined in the previous program. One of the most common controls after the push button is the list box. The **LISTBOX** statement has this general form:

LISTBOX *LBID, X, Y, Width, Height* [,*Style*]

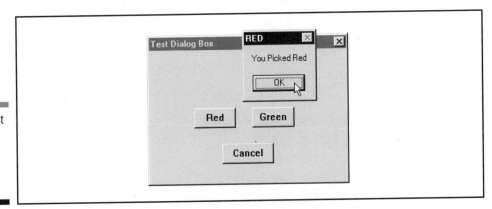

Sample output from the first dialog box program

Figure 5-1.

Here, *LBID* is the value that identifies the list box. The box's upper-left corner will be at *X,Y*, and the box will have the dimensions specified by *Width* × *Height*. The *Style* determines the exact nature of the list box. (The *Style* values used here are described in Table 5-1.)

To add a list box, you must change the dialog box definition in MYDIALOG.RC. First, add this list box description to the dialog box definition.

```
LISTBOX ID_LB1, 2, 10, 47, 28, LBS_NOTIFY | WS_CHILD |
           WS_VISIBLE | WS_BORDER | WS_VSCROLL | WS_TABSTOP
```

Second, add this push button to the dialog box definition.

```
PUSHBUTTON "Select Fruit", IDD_SELFRUIT, 5, 45, 42, 14,
           WS_CHILD | WS_VISIBLE | WS_TABSTOP
```

Finally, the positions of the Red and Green push buttons must be changed slightly, with the Red button located at 57,45 and the Green button located at 95,45. After these changes, your dialog box definition should now look like this:

```
MyDB DIALOG 18, 18, 142, 92
CAPTION "Test Dialog Box"
STYLE DS_MODALFRAME | WS_POPUP | WS_CAPTION | WS_SYSMENU
{
  DEFPUSHBUTTON "Red", IDD_RED, 57, 45, 30, 14,
           WS_CHILD | WS_VISIBLE | WS_TABSTOP
  PUSHBUTTON "Green", IDD_GREEN, 95, 45, 30, 14,
           WS_CHILD | WS_VISIBLE | WS_TABSTOP
  PUSHBUTTON "Cancel", IDCANCEL, 52, 65, 37, 14,
           WS_CHILD | WS_VISIBLE | WS_TABSTOP
  PUSHBUTTON "Select Fruit", IDD_SELFRUIT, 5, 45, 42, 14,
           WS_CHILD | WS_VISIBLE | WS_TABSTOP
  LISTBOX ID_LB1, 2, 10, 47, 28, LBS_NOTIFY | WS_CHILD |
         WS_VISIBLE | WS_BORDER | WS_VSCROLL | WS_TABSTOP
}
```

You will also need to add these macros to MYDIALOG.H:

```
#define IDD_SELFRUIT 106
#define ID_LB1       107
```

ID_LB1 identifies the list box specified in the dialog box definition in the resource file. **IDD_SELFRUIT** is the ID value of the Select Fruit push button.

List Box Basics

A notification
message
describes a
control event.

When using a list box, you must perform two basic operations. First, you must initialize the list box when the dialog box is first displayed. This consists of sending the list box the list that it will display. (By default, the list box will be empty.) Second, once the list box has been initialized, your program will need to respond to the user selecting an item from the list.

List boxes generate various types of *notification messages*. A notification message describes what type of control event occurred. The only one we will use here is **LBN_DBLCLK**. This message is sent when the user has double-clicked on an entry in the list. This message is contained in **HIWORD(wParam)** each time a **WM_COMMAND** is generated for the list box. (The list box must have the **LBS_NOTIFY** style flag included in its definition in order to generate **LBN_DBLCLK** messages.) Once a selection has been made, you will need to query the list box to find out which item has been selected.

To receive
double-click
messages,
a list box must
include the
LBS_NOTIFY
style.

5

Unlike a push button, a list box is a control that receives messages as well as generating them. You can send a list box several different messages. However, our example only sends these two:

Macro	Purpose
LB_ADDSTRING	Adds a string (selection) to the list box.
LB_GETCURSEL	Requests the index of the selected item.

LB_ADDSTRING is a message that tells the list box to add a specified string to the list. That is, the specified string becomes another selection within the box. You will see how to use this message shortly. **LB_GETCURSEL** causes the list box to return the index of the item within the list box that the user selects. All list box indexes begin with 0.

To send a message to the list box (or any other control), use the **SendDlgItemMessage( )** API function. Its prototype is shown here:

LONG SendDlgItemMessage(HWND *hdwnd*, int *ID*, UINT *IDMsg*,
WPARAM *wParam*, LPARAM *lParam*);

SendDlgItemMessage( ) sends the message specified by *IDMsg* to the control whose ID is specified by *ID*. The handle of the dialog box is specified in *hdwnd*. Any additional information required by the message is specified in *wParam* and *lParam*. The additional information, if any, varies from message to message. If there is no additional information to pass to a control, the *wParam* and *lParam* arguments should be 0. The value returned by **SendDlgItemMessage( )** contains the information requested by *IDMsg*.

Initializing the List Box

Since a list box is by default empty, you will need to initialize it each time the dialog box that contains it is displayed. This proves to be quite simple because each time a dialog box is activated, its window function is sent a **WM_INITDIALOG** message. Therefore, you will need to add this case to the outer **switch** statement in **DialogFunc( )**.

```
case WM_INITDIALOG: // initialize list box
  SendDlgItemMessage(hdwnd, ID_LB1,
                     LB_ADDSTRING, 0, (LPARAM)"Apple");
  SendDlgItemMessage(hdwnd, ID_LB1,
                     LB_ADDSTRING, 0, (LPARAM)"Orange");
  SendDlgItemMessage(hdwnd, ID_LB1,
                     LB_ADDSTRING, 0, (LPARAM)"Pear");
  SendDlgItemMessage(hdwnd, ID_LB1,
                     LB_ADDSTRING, 0, (LPARAM)"Grape");
  return 1;
```

This code loads the list box with the strings "Apple, "Orange", "Pear", and "Grape". Each string is added to the list box by calling **SendDlgItem-Message( )** with the **LB_ADDSTRING** message. The string to add is pointed to by the *lParam* parameter. (The type cast to **LPARAM** is necessary in this case in order to convert a pointer into an unsigned integer.) In this case, each string is added to the list box in the order it is sent. (However, depending upon how you construct the list box, it is possible to have the items displayed in alphabetical order.) If the number of items you send to a list box exceeds what it can display in its window, vertical scroll bars will be added automatically.

Processing a Selection

After the list box has been initialized, it is ready for use. There are essentially two ways a user makes a selection from a list box. First, the user may double-click on an item in the list box. This causes a **WM_COMMAND** message to be passed to the dialog box's window function. In this case, **LOWORD(wParam)** contains the ID associated with the list box, and

HIWORD(wParam) contains the **LBN_DBLCLK** message. Double-clicking causes your program to be immediately aware of the user's selection. The other way to use a list box is to simply highlight a selection (either by single-clicking or by using the arrow keys to move the highlight). This does not cause a message to be sent to your program, but the list box remembers the selection and waits until your program requests it. Both methods are demonstrated in the example program.

Once an item has been selected, you determine which item was chosen by sending the **LB_GETCURSEL** message to the list box. The list box then returns the index of the selected item. If this message is sent before an item has been selected, the list box returns **LB_ERR**.

To demonstrate how to process a list box selection, add these cases to the inner switch inside **DialogFunc( )**. Each time a selection is made because of a double-click, a message box will display the index of the item selected. If the user presses the "Select Fruit" push button, the currently selected item is also reported.

5

```
case ID_LB1: /* process a list box LBN_DBLCLK */
  /* see  if user made a selection */
  if(HIWORD(wParam)==LBN_DBLCLK) {
    i = SendDlgItemMessage(hdwnd, ID_LB1,
           LB_GETCURSEL, 0, 0);  // get index
    sprintf(str, "Index in list is: %d", i);
    MessageBox(hdwnd, str, "Selection Made", MB_OK);
  }
  return 1;
case IDD_SELFRUIT: /* Select Fruit has been pressed */
  i = SendDlgItemMessage(hdwnd, ID_LB1,
         LB_GETCURSEL, 0, 0);  // get index
  if(i != LB_ERR) sprintf(str, "Index in list is: %d", i);
  else sprintf(str, "No Fruit Selected");
  MessageBox(hdwnd, str, "Selection Made", MB_OK);
  return 1;
```

The Entire List Box Example

For your convenience, the entire expanded dialog box program is shown here. (Be sure to update MYDIALOG.H and MYDIALOG.RC before compiling this program.)

```
/* Demonstrate List Boxes */
```

```c
#include <windows.h>
#include <string.h>
#include <stdio.h>
#include "mydialog.h"

LRESULT CALLBACK WindowFunc(HWND, UINT, WPARAM, LPARAM);
BOOL CALLBACK DialogFunc(HWND, UINT, WPARAM, LPARAM);

char szWinName[] = "MyWin"; /* name of window class */

HINSTANCE hInst;

int WINAPI WinMain(HINSTANCE hThisInst, HINSTANCE hPrevInst,
                   LPSTR lpszArgs, int nWinMode)
{
  HWND hwnd;
  MSG msg;
  WNDCLASSEX wcl;
  HACCEL hAccel;

  /* Define a window class. */
  wcl.cbSize = sizeof(WNDCLASSEX);

  wcl.hInstance = hThisInst; /* handle to this instance */
  wcl.lpszClassName = szWinName; /* window class name */
  wcl.lpfnWndProc = WindowFunc; /* window function */
  wcl.style = 0; /* default style */

  wcl.hIcon = LoadIcon(NULL, IDI_APPLICATION); /* standard icon */
  wcl.hIconSm = LoadIcon(NULL, IDI_WINLOGO); /* small icon */
  wcl.hCursor = LoadCursor(NULL, IDC_ARROW); /* cursor style */

  wcl.lpszMenuName = "MyMenu"; /* main menu */
  wcl.cbClsExtra = 0; /* no extra */
  wcl.cbWndExtra = 0; /* information needed */

  /* Make the window white. */
  wcl.hbrBackground = (HBRUSH) GetStockObject(WHITE_BRUSH);

  /* Register the window class. */
  if(!RegisterClassEx(&wcl)) return 0;
```

```
    /* Now that a window class has been registered, a window
       can be created. */
    hwnd = CreateWindow(
      szWinName, /* name of window class */
      "Using a List Box", /* title */
      WS_OVERLAPPEDWINDOW, /* window style - normal */
      CW_USEDEFAULT, /* X coordinate - let Windows decide */
      CW_USEDEFAULT, /* Y coordinate - let Windows decide */
      CW_USEDEFAULT, /* width - let Windows decide */
      CW_USEDEFAULT, /* height - let Windows decide */
      HWND_DESKTOP, /* no parent window */
      NULL, /* no override of class menu */
      hThisInst, /* handle of this instance of the program */
      NULL /* no additional arguments */
    );

    hInst = hThisInst; /* save the current instance handle */

    /* Load accelerators. */
    hAccel = LoadAccelerators(hThisInst, "MyMenu");

    /* Display the window. */
    ShowWindow(hwnd, nWinMode);
    UpdateWindow(hwnd);

    /* Create the message loop. */
    while(GetMessage(&msg, NULL, 0, 0))
    {
      if(!TranslateAccelerator(hwnd, hAccel, &msg)) {
        TranslateMessage(&msg); /* translate keyboard messages */
        DispatchMessage(&msg); /* return control to Windows 98 */
      }
    }
    return msg.wParam;
}

/* This function is called by Windows 98 and is passed
   messages from the message queue.
*/
LRESULT CALLBACK WindowFunc(HWND hwnd, UINT message,
                            WPARAM wParam, LPARAM lParam)

{
```

5

```
int response;

switch(message) {
  case WM_COMMAND:
    switch(LOWORD(wParam)) {
      case IDM_DIALOG1:
        DialogBox(hInst, "MyDB", hwnd, (DLGPROC) DialogFunc);
        break;
      case IDM_DIALOG2:
        MessageBox(hwnd, "Dialog Not Implemented",
                   "Dialog 2", MB_OK);
        break;
      case IDM_EXIT:
        response = MessageBox(hwnd, "Quit the Program?",
                              "Exit", MB_YESNO);
        if(response == IDYES) PostQuitMessage(0);
        break;
      case IDM_HELP:
        MessageBox(hwnd, "Not Implemented", "Help", MB_OK);
        break;
    }
    break;
  case WM_DESTROY: /* terminate the program */
    PostQuitMessage(0);
    break;
  default:
    /* Let Windows 98 process any messages not specified in
       the preceding switch statement. */
    return DefWindowProc(hwnd, message, wParam, lParam);
}
return 0;
}

/* A simple dialog function. */
BOOL CALLBACK DialogFunc(HWND hdwnd, UINT message,
                         WPARAM wParam, LPARAM lParam)
{
  long i;
  char str[80];

  switch(message) {
    case WM_COMMAND:
      switch(LOWORD(wParam)) {
        case IDCANCEL:
          EndDialog(hdwnd, 0);
```

```
          return 1;
        case IDD_RED:
          MessageBox(hdwnd, "You Picked Red", "RED", MB_OK);
          return 1;
        case IDD_GREEN:
          MessageBox(hdwnd, "You Picked Green", "GREEN", MB_OK);
          return 1;
        case ID_LB1: /* process a list box LBN_DBLCLK */
          /* see if user made a selection */
          if(HIWORD(wParam)==LBN_DBLCLK) {
            i = SendDlgItemMessage(hdwnd, ID_LB1,
                    LB_GETCURSEL, 0, 0);  // get index
            sprintf(str, "Index in list is: %d", i);
            MessageBox(hdwnd, str, "Selection Made", MB_OK);
          }
          return 1;
        case IDD_SELFRUIT: /* Select Fruit has been pressed */
          i = SendDlgItemMessage(hdwnd, ID_LB1,
                  LB_GETCURSEL, 0, 0);  // get index
          if(i != LB_ERR) sprintf(str, "Index in list is: %d", i);
          else sprintf(str, "No Fruit Selected");
          MessageBox(hdwnd, str, "Selection Made", MB_OK);
          return 1;
      }
      break;
    case WM_INITDIALOG: // initialize list box
      SendDlgItemMessage(hdwnd, ID_LB1,
                    LB_ADDSTRING, 0, (LPARAM)"Apple");
      SendDlgItemMessage(hdwnd, ID_LB1,
                    LB_ADDSTRING, 0, (LPARAM)"Orange");
      SendDlgItemMessage(hdwnd, ID_LB1,
                    LB_ADDSTRING, 0, (LPARAM)"Pear");
      SendDlgItemMessage(hdwnd, ID_LB1,
                    LB_ADDSTRING, 0, (LPARAM)"Grape");
      return 1;
  }
  return 0;
}
```

Sample output from this program is shown in Figure 5-2.

Adding an Edit Box

The last control that we will add to the sample dialog box in this chapter is
the edit box. Edit boxes are particularly useful because they allow users to

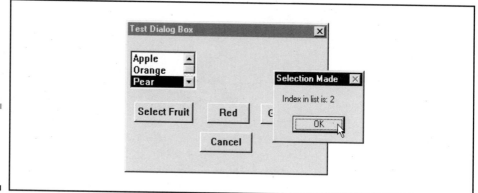

Sample output
that includes a
list box
Figure 5-2.

enter a string of their own choosing. Before you can use an edit box, you
must define one in your resource file. For this example, change
MYDIALOG.RC so that it looks like this:

```
MyDB DIALOG 18, 18, 142, 92
CAPTION "Test Dialog Box"
STYLE DS_MODALFRAME | WS_POPUP | WS_CAPTION | WS_SYSMENU
{
  DEFPUSHBUTTON "Red", IDD_RED, 57, 45, 30, 14,
               WS_CHILD | WS_VISIBLE | WS_TABSTOP
  PUSHBUTTON "Green", IDD_GREEN, 95, 45, 30, 14,
               WS_CHILD | WS_VISIBLE | WS_TABSTOP
  PUSHBUTTON "Cancel", IDCANCEL, 52, 65, 37, 14,
               WS_CHILD | WS_VISIBLE | WS_TABSTOP
  PUSHBUTTON "Select Fruit", IDD_SELFRUIT, 5, 45, 42, 14,
               WS_CHILD | WS_VISIBLE | WS_TABSTOP
  PUSHBUTTON "Edit OK", IDOK, 68, 22, 30, 14,
               WS_CHILD | WS_VISIBLE | WS_TABSTOP
  LISTBOX ID_LB1, 2, 10, 47, 28, LBS_NOTIFY | WS_CHILD |
          WS_VISIBLE | WS_BORDER | WS_VSCROLL | WS_TABSTOP
  EDITTEXT ID_EB1, 68, 8, 72, 12, ES_LEFT | ES_AUTOHSCROLL |
             WS_CHILD | WS_VISIBLE | WS_BORDER | WS_TABSTOP
}
```

This version adds a push button called **Edit OK** that will be used to tell the
program that you are done editing text in the edit box. It also adds the edit
box itself. The ID for the edit box is **ID_EB1**. This definition causes a
standard edit box to be created.

The **EDITTEXT** statement has this general form:

EDITTEXT *EDID, X, Y, Width, Height* [*,Style*]

Here, *EDID* is the value that identifies the edit box. The box's upper-left corner will be at *X,Y,* and its dimensions are specified by *Width × Height. Style* determines the exact nature of the list box. (The *Style* values used here are described Table 5-1)

Next, add this macro definition to MYDIALOG.H:

```
#define ID_EB1     108
```

Edit boxes recognize many messages and generate several of their own. However, for the purposes of this example, there is no need for the program to respond to any messages. As you will see, edit boxes perform the editing function on their own. There is no need for program interaction when text is edited. Your program simply decides when it wants to obtain the current contents of the edit box.

5

To obtain the current contents of the edit box, use the API function **GetDlgItemText( )**. It has this prototype:

UINT GetDlgItemText(HWND *hdwnd*, int *ID*, LPSTR *lpstr*, int *Max*);

This function causes the edit box to copy the current contents of the box to the string pointed to by *lpstr*. The handle of the dialog box is specified by *hdwnd*. The ID of the edit box is specified by *ID*. The maximum number of characters to copy is specified by *Max*. The function returns the length of the string.

To add an edit box to the sample program, add this **case** statement to the inner **switch** of the **DialogFunc( )** function. Each time the **Edit OK** button is pressed, a message window will be displayed that contains the contents of the edit box.

```
case IDOK: /* edit box OK button selected */
  /* display contents of the edit box */
  GetDlgItemText(hdwnd, ID_EB1, str, 80);
  MessageBox(hdwnd, str, "Edit Box Contains", MB_OK);
  return 1;
```

The macro **IDOK** is a built-in value defined by including WINDOWS.H.

Figure 5-3 shows sample output created by the edit box.

Using a Modeless Dialog Box

A modeless dialog box is created using CreateDialog( ).

To conclude this chapter, the modal dialog box used by the preceding program will be converted into a modeless dialog box. As you will see, using a modeless dialog box requires a little more work than using a modal one. The main reason for this is that a modeless dialog box is a more independent window than a modal dialog box. Specifically, the rest of your program is still active when a modeless dialog box is displayed. Also, both it and your application's window function continue to receive messages. Thus, some additional overhead is required in your application's message loop to accommodate the modeless dialog box.

To create a modeless dialog box, you do not use **DialogBox( )**. Instead, you must use the **CreateDialog( )** API function. Its prototype is shown here:

HWND CreateDialog(HINSTANCE *hThisInst*, LPCSTR *lpszName*,
HWND *hwnd*, DLGPROC *lpDFunc*);

Here, *hThisInst* is a handle to the current application that is passed to your program in the instance parameter to **WinMain( )**. The name of the dialog box as defined in the resource file is pointed to by *lpszName*. The handle to the owner of the dialog box is passed in *hwnd*. (This is typically the handle to the window that calls **CreateDialog( )**.) The *lpDFunc* parameter contains a pointer to the dialog function. The dialog function is of the same type as that used for a modal dialog box. **CreateDialog( )** returns a handle to the dialog box. If the dialog box cannot be created, **NULL** is returned.

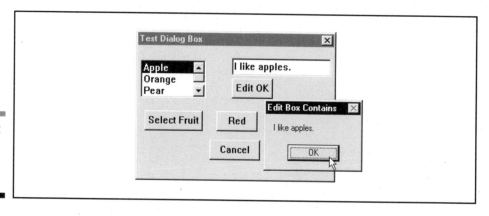

Sample output using the edit box

Figure 5-3.

IN DEPTH

Exploring Edit and List Box Messages

Both list boxes and edit boxes respond to a wide range of messages. While none of the examples in this chapter require the use of any messages not already described, you will want to explore these two controls more thoroughly on your own. To understand why, here is a list of just a few of the messages to which these controls can respond.

EM_GETLIMITTEXT	Gets the current text limit in an edit box.
EM_GETLINE	Obtains a line of text from the edit box.
EM_GETLINECOUNT	Obtains the number of lines of text currently in a multiline edit control.
EM_GETMODIFY	Determines if the text in an edit box has been modified.
EM_LIMITTEXT	Limits the number of characters that the user can enter into an edit box.
EM_LINELENGTH	Obtains the number of characters currently in the edit box.
EM_SETLIMITTEXT	Limits the number of characters that an edit box can hold.
EM_UNDO	Undoes the last edit operation.
LB_DELETESTRING	Removes a string from the list box.
LB_DIR	Adds filenames to the list box.
LB_FINDSTRING	Finds a matching entry.
LB_FINDSTRINGEXACT	Finds a string in the list box that exactly matches the one specified.
LB_GETCOUNT	Obtains the number of items in a list box.
LB_GETTEXT	Obtains the text associated with an item.

5

LB_GETTEXTLEN	Obtains the length of the specified string in a list box.
LB_INSERTSTRING	Inserts a string into a list box.
LB_SELECTSTRING	Finds a matching entry and selects it.
LB_SETCURSEL	Selects an item.

Unlike a modal dialog box, a modeless dialog box is not automatically visible, so you may need to call **ShowWindow( )** to cause it to be displayed after it has been created. However, if you add **WS_VISIBLE** to the dialog box's definition in its resource file, then it will be automatically displayed.

A modeless dialog box must be closed using **Destroy-Window( )**.

To close a modeless dialog box, your program must call **DestroyWindow( )** rather than **EndDialog( )**. The prototype for **DestroyWindow( )** is shown here:

BOOL DestroyWindow(HWND *hwnd*);

Here, *hwnd* is the handle to the window (in this case, dialog box) being closed.

Since your application's window function will continue receiving messages while a modeless dialog box is active, you must make a change to your program's message loop. Specifically, you must add a call to **IsDialog-Message( )**. This function routes dialog box messages to your modeless dialog box. It has this prototype:

BOOL IsDialogMessage(HWND *hdwnd*, LPMSG *msg*);

Here, *hdwnd* is the handle of the modeless dialog box, and **msg** is the message obtained from **GetMessage( )** within your program's message loop. The function returns nonzero if the message is for the dialog box. It returns false otherwise. If the message is for the dialog box, then it is automatically passed to the dialog box function. Therefore, to process modeless dialog box messages, your program's message loop must look something like this:

```
while(GetMessage(&msg, NULL, 0, 0))
{
  if(!IsDialogMessage(hDlg, &msg)) {
    /* not for dialog box */
    if(!TranslateAccelerator(hwnd, hAccel, &msg)) {
      TranslateMessage(&msg); /* translate keyboard messages */
      DispatchMessage(&msg); /* return control to Windows 98 */
    }
  }
}
```

As you can see, the message is processed by the rest of the message loop only if it is not a dialog box message.

Creating a Modeless Dialog Box

5

To convert the modal dialog box shown in the preceding example into a modeless one, surprisingly few changes are needed. The first change that you need to make is to the dialog box definition in the MYDIALOG.RC resource file. Since a modeless dialog box is not automatically visible, add **WS_VISIBLE** to the dialog box definition. Also, instead of using the **DS_MODALFRAME** style, you should use **WS_BORDER**. Because we have made many changes to MYDIALOG.RC since the start of this chapter, the entire file is shown here for your convenience.

```
// Sample dialog box and menu resource file.
#include <windows.h>
#include "mydialog.h"

MyMenu MENU
{
  POPUP "&Dialog"
  {
    MENUITEM "Dialog &1\tF2", IDM_DIALOG1
    MENUITEM "Dialog &2\tF3", IDM_DIALOG2
    MENUITEM "E&xit\tCtrl+X", IDM_EXIT
  }
  MENUITEM "&Help", IDM_HELP
}

MyMenu ACCELERATORS
{
  VK_F2, IDM_DIALOG1, VIRTKEY
  VK_F3, IDM_DIALOG2, VIRTKEY
  "^X", IDM_EXIT
  VK_F1, IDM_HELP, VIRTKEY
```

```
}

MyDB DIALOG 18, 18, 142, 92
CAPTION "Test Dialog Box"
STYLE WS_BORDER | WS_POPUP | WS_CAPTION
      | WS_SYSMENU | WS_VISIBLE
{
  DEFPUSHBUTTON "Red", IDD_RED, 57, 45, 30, 14,
            WS_CHILD | WS_VISIBLE | WS_TABSTOP
  PUSHBUTTON "Green", IDD_GREEN, 95, 45, 30, 14,
            WS_CHILD | WS_VISIBLE | WS_TABSTOP
  PUSHBUTTON "Cancel", IDCANCEL, 52, 65, 37, 14,
            WS_CHILD | WS_VISIBLE | WS_TABSTOP
  PUSHBUTTON "Select Fruit", IDD_SELFRUIT, 5, 45, 42, 14,
            WS_CHILD | WS_VISIBLE | WS_TABSTOP
  PUSHBUTTON "Edit OK", IDOK, 68, 22, 30, 14,
            WS_CHILD | WS_VISIBLE | WS_TABSTOP
  LISTBOX ID_LB1, 2, 10, 47, 28, LBS_NOTIFY | WS_CHILD |
          WS_VISIBLE | WS_BORDER | WS_VSCROLL | WS_TABSTOP
  EDITTEXT ID_EB1, 68, 8, 72, 12, ES_LEFT | ES_AUTOHSCROLL |
            WS_CHILD | WS_VISIBLE | WS_BORDER | WS_TABSTOP
}
```

Next, you must make the following changes to the program:

1. Add **IsDialogMessage( )** to the message loop.
2. Create the dialog box using **CreateDialog( )** rather than **DialogBox( )**.
3. Close the dialog box using **DestroyWindow( )** instead of **EndDialog( )**.

The entire listing (which incorporates these changes) for the modeless dialog box example is shown here. Sample output from this program is shown in Figure 5-4. You should try this program on your own to fully understand the difference between modal and modeless dialog boxes.

```
/* Demonstrate modeless dialog box. */

#include <windows.h>
#include <string.h>
#include <stdio.h>
#include "mydialog.h"

LRESULT CALLBACK WindowFunc(HWND, UINT, WPARAM, LPARAM);
BOOL CALLBACK DialogFunc(HWND, UINT, WPARAM, LPARAM);
```

```
char szWinName[] = "MyWin"; /* name of window class */

HINSTANCE hInst;

HWND hDlg; /* dialog box handle */

int WINAPI WinMain(HINSTANCE hThisInst, HINSTANCE hPrevInst,
                   LPSTR lpszArgs, int nWinMode)
{
  HWND hwnd;
  MSG msg;
  WNDCLASSEX wcl;
  HACCEL hAccel;

  /* Define a window class. */
  wcl.cbSize = sizeof(WNDCLASSEX);

  wcl.hInstance = hThisInst; /* handle to this instance */
  wcl.lpszClassName = szWinName; /* window class name */
  wcl.lpfnWndProc = WindowFunc; /* window function */
  wcl.style = 0; /* default style */

  wcl.hIcon = LoadIcon(NULL, IDI_APPLICATION); /* standard icon */
  wcl.hIconSm = LoadIcon(NULL, IDI_WINLOGO); /* small icon */
  wcl.hCursor = LoadCursor(NULL, IDC_ARROW); /* cursor style */

  wcl.lpszMenuName = "MyMenu"; /* main menu */
  wcl.cbClsExtra = 0; /* no extra */
  wcl.cbWndExtra = 0; /* information needed */

  /* Make the window white. */
  wcl.hbrBackground = (HBRUSH) GetStockObject(WHITE_BRUSH);

  /* Register the window class. */
  if(!RegisterClassEx(&wcl)) return 0;

  /* Now that a window class has been registered, a window
     can be created. */
  hwnd = CreateWindow(
    szWinName, /* name of window class */
    "A Modeless Dialog Box", /* title */
    WS_OVERLAPPEDWINDOW, /* window style - normal */
    CW_USEDEFAULT, /* X coordinate - let Windows decide */
    CW_USEDEFAULT, /* Y coordinate - let Windows decide */
```

5

```
      CW_USEDEFAULT, /* width - let Windows decide */
      CW_USEDEFAULT, /* height - let Windows decide */
      HWND_DESKTOP, /* no parent window */
      NULL, /* no override of class menu */
      hThisInst, /* handle of this instance of the program */
      NULL /* no additional arguments */
  );

  hInst = hThisInst; /* save the current instance handle */

  /* Load accelerators. */
  hAccel = LoadAccelerators(hThisInst, "MyMenu");

  /* Display the window. */
  ShowWindow(hwnd, nWinMode);
  UpdateWindow(hwnd);

  /* Create the message loop. */
  while(GetMessage(&msg, NULL, 0, 0))
  {
    if(!IsDialogMessage(hDlg, &msg)) {
      /* not for dialog box */
      if(!TranslateAccelerator(hwnd, hAccel, &msg)) {
        TranslateMessage(&msg); /* translate keyboard messages */
        DispatchMessage(&msg); /* return control to Windows 98 */
      }
    }
  }
  return msg.wParam;
}


/* This function is called by Windows 98 and is passed
   messages from the message queue.
*/
LRESULT CALLBACK WindowFunc(HWND hwnd, UINT message,
                            WPARAM wParam, LPARAM lParam)
{
  int response;

  switch(message) {
    case WM_COMMAND:
      switch(LOWORD(wParam)) {
```

```
      case IDM_DIALOG1: /* this creates modeless dialog box */
        hDlg = CreateDialog(hInst, "MyDB", hwnd, (DLGPROC)
        DialogFunc);
        break;
      case IDM_DIALOG2:
        MessageBox(hwnd, "Dialog Not Implemented", "Dialog 2",
                   MB_OK);
        break;
      case IDM_EXIT:
        response = MessageBox(hwnd, "Quit the Program?",
                              "Exit", MB_YESNO);
        if(response == IDYES) PostQuitMessage(0);
        break;
      case IDM_HELP:
        MessageBox(hwnd, "Not Implemented", "Help", MB_OK);
        break;
    }
    break;
  case WM_DESTROY: /* terminate the program */
    PostQuitMessage(0);
    break;
  default:
    /* Let Windows 98 process any messages not specified in
       the preceding switch statement. */
    return DefWindowProc(hwnd, message, wParam, lParam);
  }
  return 0;
}

/* A simple dialog function. */
BOOL CALLBACK DialogFunc(HWND hdwnd, UINT message,
                         WPARAM wParam, LPARAM lParam)
{
  long i;
  char str[80];

  switch(message) {
    case WM_COMMAND:
      switch(LOWORD(wParam)) {
        case IDOK: /* edit box OK button selected */
          /* display contents of the edit box */
          GetDlgItemText(hdwnd, ID_EB1, str, 80);
```

5

```
        MessageBox(hdwnd, str, "Edit Box Contains", MB_OK);
        return 1;
      case IDCANCEL:
        DestroyWindow(hdwnd);
        return 1;
      case IDD_RED:
        MessageBox(hdwnd, "You Picked Red", "RED", MB_OK);
        return 1;
      case IDD_GREEN:
        MessageBox(hdwnd, "You Picked Green", "GREEN", MB_OK);
        return 1;
      case ID_LB1: /* process a list box LBN_DBLCLK */
        // see if user made a selection
        if(HIWORD(wParam)==LBN_DBLCLK) {
          i = SendDlgItemMessage(hdwnd, ID_LB1,
                LB_GETCURSEL, 0, 0);  // get index
          sprintf(str, "Index in list is: %d", i);
          MessageBox(hdwnd, str, "Selection Made", MB_OK);
        }
        return 1;
      case IDD_SELFRUIT: /* Select Fruit has been pressed */
        i = SendDlgItemMessage(hdwnd, ID_LB1,
                LB_GETCURSEL, 0, 0);  // get index
        if(i != LB_ERR) sprintf(str, "Index in list is: %d", i);
        else sprintf(str, "No Fruit Selected");
        MessageBox(hdwnd, str, "Selection Made", MB_OK);
        return 1;
    }
    break;
  case WM_INITDIALOG: // initialize list box
    SendDlgItemMessage(hdwnd, ID_LB1,
                       LB_ADDSTRING, 0, (LPARAM)"Apple");
    SendDlgItemMessage(hdwnd, ID_LB1,
                       LB_ADDSTRING, 0, (LPARAM)"Orange");
    SendDlgItemMessage(hdwnd, ID_LB1,
                       LB_ADDSTRING, 0, (LPARAM)"Pear");
    SendDlgItemMessage(hdwnd, ID_LB1,
                       LB_ADDSTRING, 0, (LPARAM)"Grape");
    return 1;
  }
  return 0;
}
```

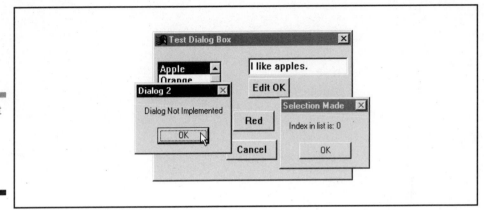

Sample output
using the
modeless
dialog box
Figure 5-4.

This chapter only scratches the surface of what you can do using dialog boxes
and controls. Additional controls are covered throughout this book. Also, you
will want to experiment on your own, exploring how the various controls
function and interact with your program.

CHAPTER 6

A Closer Look at Controls

Controls were introduced in the preceding chapter, when dialog boxes were first discussed. This chapter continues the discussion by examining several more controls, including check boxes, radio buttons, group boxes, static text controls, and scroll bars. As you will see, many of the techniques that you learned when using the controls in Chapter 5 will apply to the controls discussed here.

Using Check Boxes

A *check box* is a control that is used to turn an option on or off. It consists of a small rectangle that may or may not contain a check mark. A check box has associated with it a label that describes what option the box represents. If the box contains a check mark, the box is said to be "checked" and the option is selected. If the box is empty, then the box is unchecked and the option will be deselected. A check box is a control that is typically part of a dialog box and is generally defined within the dialog box's definition in your program's resource file. To add a check box to a dialog box definition, use the **CHECKBOX** command, which has this general form:

A check box is used to turn on or off an option.

CHECKBOX "*string*", *CBID*, *X*, *Y*, *Width*, *Height*, [, *Style*]

Here, *string* is the text that will be shown alongside the check box. *CBID* is the value associated with the checkbox. The box's upper-left corner will be at *X,Y*, and the box plus its associated text will have the dimensions specified by *Width* × *Height*. *Style* determines the exact nature of the check box. If no explicit style is specified, the check box defaults to displaying the *string* on the right and allowing the box to be tabbed to. As you know from using Windows 98, check boxes are toggles. Each time you select a check box, its state changes from checked to unchecked, and vice versa. However, this is not necessarily automatically accomplished. When you use the **CHECKBOX** resource command, you are creating a *manual check box*, which your program must manage by checking and unchecking the box each time it is selected. (You will see how, shortly.) However, you can have Windows 98 perform this housekeeping function for you if you create an *automatic check box*. This is done using the **AUTOCHECKBOX** resource command. It has exactly the same form as the **CHECKBOX** command. When you use an automatic check box, Windows 98 automatically toggles its state (between checked and not checked) each time it is selected.

PORTABILITY: The resource compiler for Windows 3.1 does not support the **AUTOCHECKBOX** resource command. When converting from Windows 3.1, you will want to watch for check boxes that can be converted to automatic check boxes.

6

Before continuing, you need to create the following resource file, which defines a dialog box that contains both a manual and an automatic check box. The file also defines a top-level menu. Enter this file into your computer now.

```
#include <windows.h>
#include "mydialog.h"

MyMenu MENU
{
  POPUP   "&Demo"
  {
    MENUITEM "&Dialog\tF2", IDM_DIALOG
    MENUITEM "&Status\tF3", IDM_STATUS
    MENUITEM "E&xit\tCtrl+X", IDM_EXIT
  }
  MENUITEM "&Help", IDM_HELP
}

MyMenu ACCELERATORS
{
  VK_F2, IDM_DIALOG, VIRTKEY
  VK_F3, IDM_STATUS, VIRTKEY
  "^X", IDM_EXIT
  VK_F1, IDM_HELP, VIRTKEY
}

MyDB DIALOG 18, 18, 110, 92
CAPTION "Test Dialog Box"
STYLE DS_MODALFRAME | WS_POPUP | WS_CAPTION | WS_SYSMENU
{
  PUSHBUTTON "OK", IDOK, 67, 40, 30, 13, WS_TABSTOP
```

```
PUSHBUTTON "Cancel", IDCANCEL, 64, 65, 37, 14, WS_TABSTOP
CHECKBOX "Checkbox 1" , ID_CB1, 3, 10, 48, 12
AUTOCHECKBOX "Checkbox 2" , ID_CB2, 3, 22, 48, 12
}
```

You will also need to create the header file MYDIALOG.H, which is shown here. This file also defines values that will be needed by other examples later in this chapter.

```
#define IDM_DIALOG    100
#define IDM_STATUS    101
#define IDM_EXIT      102
#define IDM_HELP      103

#define ID_CB1        104
#define ID_CB2        105

#define ID_CT1        106

#define ID_RB1        107
#define ID_RB2        108

#define ID_GB1        200
#define ID_GB2        201
```

Check Box Messages

Each time the user clicks on a check box or selects the check box and then presses the space bar, a **WM_COMMAND** message is sent to the dialog function and the low-order word of **wParam** contains the identifier associated with that check box. If you are using a manual check box, you will want to respond to this command by changing the state of the box.

To check a box, send the check box a **BM_SETCHECK** message using the **SendDlgItemMessage( )** API function. This function was discussed in Chapter 5. Its prototype is shown here again for your convenience.

LONG SendDlgItemMessage(HWND *hdwnd*, int *ID*, UINT *IDMsg*,
                                    WPARAM *wParam*, LPARAM *lParam*);

When the **BM_SETCHECK** message is sent, the value of *wParam* determines whether the box will be checked or cleared. If *wParam* is **BST_CHECKED**, then the box will be checked. If it is **BST_UNCHECKED**, the box will be cleared. By default, when a dialog box is first displayed, all check boxes will be unchecked. When sending **BM_SETCHECK**, *lParam* is unused.

You can determine the status of a check box by sending it the message **BM_GETCHECK**. In this case, both *wParam* and *lParam* are 0. The check box returns **BST_CHECKED** if the box is checked and **BST_UNCHECKED** if it is cleared.

REMEMBER: If you use an automatic check box, then the state of the box will be changed automatically each time it is selected.

Here is a program that demonstrates both an automatic and a manual check box. For the sake of illustrating the difference between the two, when the manual check box is selected, it is always checked. It is not possible to uncheck the box. You will see how to manage a manual check box in the next example.

6

```
/* Demonstrate check boxes. */

#include <windows.h>
#include <string.h>
#include <stdio.h>
#include "mydialog.h"

LRESULT CALLBACK WindowFunc(HWND, UINT, WPARAM, LPARAM);
LRESULT CALLBACK DialogFunc(HWND, UINT, WPARAM, LPARAM);

char szWinName[] = "MyWin"; /* name of window class */

HINSTANCE hInst;

/* holds status of check boxes */
int cbstatus1=BST_UNCHECKED, cbstatus2=BST_UNCHECKED;

int WINAPI WinMain(HINSTANCE hThisInst, HINSTANCE hPrevInst,
                   LPSTR lpszArgs, int nWinMode)
{
  HWND hwnd;
  MSG msg;
  WNDCLASSEX wcl;
```

```
HACCEL hAccel;

/* Define a window class. */
wcl.cbSize = sizeof(WNDCLASSEX);

wcl.hInstance = hThisInst; /* handle to this instance */
wcl.lpszClassName = szWinName; /* window class name */
wcl.lpfnWndProc = WindowFunc; /* window function */
wcl.style = 0; /* default style */

wcl.hIcon = LoadIcon(NULL, IDI_APPLICATION); /* standard icon */
wcl.hIconSm = LoadIcon(NULL, IDI_WINLOGO); /* small icon */
wcl.hCursor = LoadCursor(NULL, IDC_ARROW); /* cursor style */

wcl.lpszMenuName = "MyMenu"; /* main menu */
wcl.cbClsExtra = 0; /* no extra */
wcl.cbWndExtra = 0; /* information needed */

/* Make the window white. */
wcl.hbrBackground = (HBRUSH) GetStockObject(WHITE_BRUSH);

/* Register the window class. */
if(!RegisterClassEx(&wcl)) return 0;

/* Now that a window class has been registered, a window
   can be created. */
hwnd = CreateWindow(
  szWinName, /* name of window class */
  "Using Check Boxes", /* title */
  WS_OVERLAPPEDWINDOW, /* window style - normal */
  CW_USEDEFAULT, /* X coordinate - let Windows decide */
  CW_USEDEFAULT, /* Y coordinate - let Windows decide */
  CW_USEDEFAULT, /* width - let Windows decide */
  CW_USEDEFAULT, /* height - let Windows decide */
  HWND_DESKTOP, /* no parent window */
  NULL, /* no override of class menu */
  hThisInst, /* handle of this instance of the program */
  NULL /* no additional arguments */
);

hInst = hThisInst; /* save the current instance handle */

/* Load accelerators. */
hAccel = LoadAccelerators(hThisInst, "MyMenu");
```

```
      /* Display the window. */
      ShowWindow(hwnd, nWinMode);
      UpdateWindow(hwnd);

      /* Create the message loop. */
      while(GetMessage(&msg, NULL, 0, 0))
      {
        if(!TranslateAccelerator(hwnd, hAccel, &msg)) {
          TranslateMessage(&msg); /* translate keyboard messages */
          DispatchMessage(&msg); /* return control to Windows 98 */
        }
      }
      return msg.wParam;
}

/* This function is called by Windows 98 and is passed
   messages from the message queue.
*/
LRESULT CALLBACK WindowFunc(HWND hwnd, UINT message,
                            WPARAM wParam, LPARAM lParam)
{
  char str[255];
  int response;

  switch(message) {
    case WM_COMMAND:
      switch(LOWORD(wParam)) {
        case IDM_DIALOG:
          DialogBox(hInst, "MyDB", hwnd, (DLGPROC) DialogFunc);
          break;
        case IDM_EXIT:
          response = MessageBox(hwnd, "Quit the Program?",
                                "Exit", MB_YESNO);
          if(response == IDYES) PostQuitMessage(0);
          break;
        case IDM_STATUS: /* show check box status */
          if(cbstatus1 == BST_CHECKED)
            strcpy(str, "Checkbox 1 is checked\n");
          else strcpy(str, "Checkbox 1 is not checked\n");
          if(cbstatus2 == BST_CHECKED)
            strcat(str, "Checkbox 2 is checked");
          else strcat(str, "Checkbox 2 is not checked");
          MessageBox(hwnd, str, "Status", MB_OK);
          break;
        case IDM_HELP:
```

6

```
          MessageBox(hwnd, "Not Implemented", "Help", MB_OK);
          break;
      }
      break;
    case WM_DESTROY: /* terminate the program */
      PostQuitMessage(0);
      break;
    default:
      /* Let Windows 98 process any messages not specified in
         the preceding switch statement. */
      return DefWindowProc(hwnd, message, wParam, lParam);
  }
  return 0;
}

/* A simple dialog function. */
LRESULT CALLBACK DialogFunc(HWND hdwnd, UINT message,
                            WPARAM wParam, LPARAM lParam)
{
  switch(message) {
    case WM_COMMAND:
      switch(LOWORD(wParam)) {
        case IDCANCEL:
          EndDialog(hdwnd, 0);
          return 1;
        case IDOK:
          /* update global checkbox status variables */
          cbstatus1 = SendDlgItemMessage(hdwnd, ID_CB1,
                                         BM_GETCHECK, 0, 0);
          cbstatus2 = SendDlgItemMessage(hdwnd, ID_CB2,
                                         BM_GETCHECK, 0, 0);
          EndDialog(hdwnd, 0);
          return 1;
        case ID_CB1:
          /* user selected 1st check box, so check it */
          SendDlgItemMessage(hdwnd, ID_CB1,
                             BM_SETCHECK, BST_CHECKED, 0);
          return 1;
      }
  }
  return 0;
}
```

This program contains two global variables, called **cbstatus1** and
cbstatus2, that hold the state of the two check boxes. These variables are set

when the OK button is selected inside the dialog box. To set the state of the check boxes, select the **Dialog** menu option. To see the status of the check boxes, select the **Status** menu option.

When you run this program and select the **Dialog** menu option, you will see the dialog box shown in Figure 6-1.

Managing Check Boxes

The check box program, as it stands, has two serious flaws. First, the state of each check box is reset each time the dialog box is displayed. That is, the previous setting of each box is lost. Secondly, while the manual check box can be set, it cannot be cleared. That is, the manual check box is not fully implemented as a toggle, the way check boxes are expected to function. In this section, you will see how to manage check boxes more effectively.

Toggling a Check Box

First, while it is far easier to simply use automatic check boxes, it is possible to implement a toggled check box by managing a manual check box. To do this means that your program will have to perform all the necessary overhead itself, instead of letting Windows 98 handle it. To accomplish this, the program first finds out the current state of the check box and then sets it to the opposite state. The following change to the dialog function accomplishes this.

6

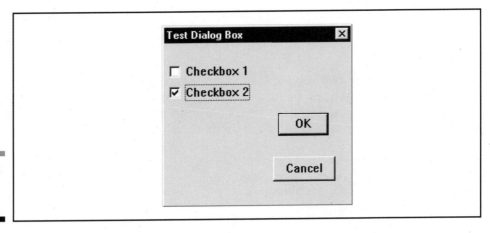

The Checkbox
dialog box
Figure 6-1.

```
case ID_CB1: /* This is a manually managed check box. */
  /* user selected 1st check box, so change its state */
  if(SendDlgItemMessage(hdwnd, ID_CB1,
         BM_GETCHECK, 0, 0) == BST_UNCHECKED)
    SendDlgItemMessage(hdwnd, ID_CB1,
                       BM_SETCHECK, BST_CHECKED, 0);
  else /* turn it off */
    SendDlgItemMessage(hdwnd, ID_CB1,
                       BM_SETCHECK, BST_UNCHECKED, 0);
  return 1;
```

Initializing a Check Box

As mentioned, both the manual and the automatic check boxes are cleared (that is, unchecked) each time the dialog box that contains them is activated. While this might be desirable in some situations, it is not what is normally expected. Generally, check boxes are set to their previous state each time the dialog box is displayed. If you want the check boxes to reflect their previous state, you must initialize them each time the dialog box is activated. The easiest way to do this is to send them the appropriate **BM_SETCHECK** messages when the dialog box is created. Remember, each time a dialog box is activated, it is sent a **WM_INITDIALOG** message. When this message is received, you can set the state of the check boxes (and anything else) inside the dialog box.

The code to initialize the check boxes is shown here.

```
case WM_INITDIALOG:
  /* The dialog box has just been displayed.  Set
     the check boxes appropriately. */
  SendDlgItemMessage(hdwnd, ID_CB1, BM_SETCHECK, cbstatus1, 0);
  SendDlgItemMessage(hdwnd, ID_CB2, BM_SETCHECK, cbstatus2, 0);
  return 1;
```

The entire program listing that incorporates the check box initialization and manages the manual check box is shown here. You should compare its operation to the preceding example. As you might expect, it now behaves in a way that is common to most all other Windows applications.

```
/* Demonstrate checkboxes with enhancements. */

#include <windows.h>
#include <string.h>
```

```c
#include <stdio.h>
#include "mydialog.h"

LRESULT CALLBACK WindowFunc(HWND, UINT, WPARAM, LPARAM);
LRESULT CALLBACK DialogFunc(HWND, UINT, WPARAM, LPARAM);

char szWinName[] = "MyWin"; /* name of window class */

HINSTANCE hInst;

/* holds status of check boxes */
int cbstatus1=BST_UNCHECKED, cbstatus2=BST_UNCHECKED;

int WINAPI WinMain(HINSTANCE hThisInst, HINSTANCE hPrevInst,
                   LPSTR lpszArgs, int nWinMode)
{
  HWND hwnd;
  MSG msg;
  WNDCLASSEX wcl;
  HACCEL hAccel;

  /* Define a window class. */
  wcl.cbSize = sizeof(WNDCLASSEX);

  wcl.hInstance = hThisInst; /* handle to this instance */
  wcl.lpszClassName = szWinName; /* window class name */
  wcl.lpfnWndProc = WindowFunc; /* window function */
  wcl.style = 0; /* default style */

  wcl.hIcon = LoadIcon(NULL, IDI_APPLICATION); /* standard icon */
  wcl.hIconSm = LoadIcon(NULL, IDI_WINLOGO); /* small icon */
  wcl.hCursor = LoadCursor(NULL, IDC_ARROW); /* cursor style */

  wcl.lpszMenuName = "MyMenu"; /* main menu */
  wcl.cbClsExtra = 0; /* no extra */
  wcl.cbWndExtra = 0; /* information needed */

  /* Make the window white. */
  wcl.hbrBackground = (HBRUSH) GetStockObject(WHITE_BRUSH);

  /* Register the window class. */
  if(!RegisterClassEx(&wcl)) return 0;

  /* Now that a window class has been registered, a window
     can be created. */
```

```
hwnd = CreateWindow(
  szWinName, /* name of window class */
  "Using Check Boxes", /* title */
  WS_OVERLAPPEDWINDOW, /* window style - normal */
  CW_USEDEFAULT, /* X coordinate - let Windows decide */
  CW_USEDEFAULT, /* Y coordinate - let Windows decide */
  CW_USEDEFAULT, /* width - let Windows decide */
  CW_USEDEFAULT, /* height - let Windows decide */
  HWND_DESKTOP, /* no parent window */
  NULL, /* no override of class menu */
  hThisInst, /* handle of this instance of the program */
  NULL /* no additional arguments */
);

hInst = hThisInst; /* save the current instance handle */

/* Load accelerators. */
hAccel = LoadAccelerators(hThisInst, "MyMenu");

/* Display the window. */
ShowWindow(hwnd, nWinMode);
UpdateWindow(hwnd);

/* Create the message loop. */
while(GetMessage(&msg, NULL, 0, 0))
{
  if(!TranslateAccelerator(hwnd, hAccel, &msg)) {
    TranslateMessage(&msg); /* translate keyboard messages */
    DispatchMessage(&msg); /* return control to Windows 98 */
  }
}
return msg.wParam;
}

/* This function is called by Windows 98 and is passed
   messages from the message queue.
*/
LRESULT CALLBACK WindowFunc(HWND hwnd, UINT message,
                            WPARAM wParam, LPARAM lParam)
{
  char str[255];
  int response;

  switch(message) {
    case WM_COMMAND:
```

```
          switch(LOWORD(wParam)) {
            case IDM_DIALOG:
              DialogBox(hInst, "MyDB", hwnd, (DLGPROC) DialogFunc);
              break;
            case IDM_EXIT:
              response = MessageBox(hwnd, "Quit the Program?",
                                    "Exit", MB_YESNO);
              if(response == IDYES) PostQuitMessage(0);
              break;
            case IDM_STATUS:
              if(cbstatus1 == BST_CHECKED)
                strcpy(str, "Checkbox 1 is checked\n");
              else strcpy(str, "Checkbox 1 is not checked\n");
              if(cbstatus2 == BST_CHECKED)
                strcat(str, "Checkbox 2 is checked");
              else strcat(str, "Checkbox 2 is not checked");
              MessageBox(hwnd, str, "", MB_OK);
              break;
            case IDM_HELP:
              MessageBox(hwnd, "Not Implemented", "Help", MB_OK);
              break;
          }
          break;
      case WM_DESTROY: /* terminate the program */
        PostQuitMessage(0);
        break;
      default:
        /* Let Windows 98 process any messages not specified in
           the preceding switch statement. */
        return DefWindowProc(hwnd, message, wParam, lParam);
    }
    return 0;
}

/* A simple dialog function. */
LRESULT CALLBACK DialogFunc(HWND hdwnd, UINT message,
                            WPARAM wParam, LPARAM lParam)
{
  switch(message) {
    case WM_INITDIALOG:
      /* The dialog box has just been displayed.  Set
         the check boxes appropriately. */
      SendDlgItemMessage(hdwnd, ID_CB1, BM_SETCHECK, cbstatus1, 0);
      SendDlgItemMessage(hdwnd, ID_CB2, BM_SETCHECK, cbstatus2, 0);
      return 1;
```

```
case WM_COMMAND:
  switch(LOWORD(wParam)) {
    case IDCANCEL:
      EndDialog(hdwnd, 0);
      return 1;
    case IDOK:
      /* update global checkbox status variables */
      cbstatus1 = SendDlgItemMessage(hdwnd, ID_CB1,
                                     BM_GETCHECK, 0, 0);
      cbstatus2 = SendDlgItemMessage(hdwnd, ID_CB2,
                                     BM_GETCHECK, 0, 0);
      EndDialog(hdwnd, 0);
      return 1;
    case ID_CB1: /* This is a manually managed check box. */
      /* user selected 1st check box, so change its state */
      if(SendDlgItemMessage(hdwnd, ID_CB1,
            BM_GETCHECK, 0, 0) == BST_UNCHECKED)
        SendDlgItemMessage(hdwnd, ID_CB1,
                           BM_SETCHECK, BST_CHECKED, 0);
      else /* turn it off */
        SendDlgItemMessage(hdwnd, ID_CB1,
                           BM_SETCHECK, BST_UNCHECKED, 0);
      return 1;
  }
}
return 0;
}
```

IN DEPTH

The 3-State Check Box

Windows 98 provides an interesting variation of the check box called the *3-state box*. This check box has three possible states: checked, cleared, or grayed. (When the control is grayed, it is disabled.) Like its relative, the 3-state check box can be implemented as either an automatic or manually managed control using the **AUTO3STATE** and **STATE3** resource commands, respectively. The general forms are shown here:

STATE3 "*string*", *ID*, *X*, *Y*, *Width*, *Height* [, *Style*]

AUTO3STATE "*string*", *ID*, *X*, *Y*, *Width*, *Height* [, *Style*]

Here, *string* is the text that will be shown alongside the check box. *ID* is the value associated with the check box. The box's upper-left corner will be at *X,Y*, and the box plus its associated text will have the dimensions specified by *Width × Height*. *Style* determines the exact nature of the check box. If no explicit style is specified, the check box defaults to displaying the *string* on the right and allowing the box to be tabbed to. When a 3-state check box is first created, it is unchecked.

In response to a **BM_GETCHECK** message, 3-state check boxes return **BST_UNCHECKED** if unchecked, **BST_CHECKED** if checked, and **BST_INDETERMINATE** if grayed. Correspondingly, when setting a 3-state check box using **BM_SETCHECK**, use **BST_UNCHECKED** to clear it, **BST_CHECKED** to check it, and **BST_INDETERMINATE** to gray it.

6

Adding Static Controls

Static controls do not generate or receive messages.

A static control is one that neither receives nor generates any messages. In short, the term "static control" is simply a formal way of describing something that is displayed in a dialog box, such as a text message or a simple box used to group other controls. The two static controls that we will look at here are the centered text box and the group box. Both of these controls are included in the dialog definition in your program's resource file using the commands **CTEXT** and **GROUPBOX**, respectively.

The **CTEXT** control outputs a string that is centered within a predefined area. The general form for **CTEXT** is shown here:

CTEXT "*string*" *CTID, X, Y, Width, Height* [, *Style*]

Here, *string* is the text that will be displayed. *CTID* is the value associated with the text. The text will be shown in a box whose upper-left corner will be at *X, Y*, and dimensions are specified by *Width × Height*. *Style* determines the exact nature of the text box. If no explicit style is specified, the check box defaults to displaying the text centered within the box. Understand that the box itself is not displayed. The box simply defines the space that the text is allowed to occupy.

The **GROUPBOX** control draws a box. This box is generally used to visually group other controls. The box may contain a title. The general form for **GROUPBOX** is shown here:

GROUPBOX "*title*", *GBID, X, Y, Width, Height* [, *Style*]

Here, *title* is the title to the box. *GBID* is the value associated with the box. The upper-left corner will be at *X,Y,* and its dimensions are specified by *Width* × *Height. Style* determines the exact nature of the group box. Generally, the default setting is sufficient.

To see the effects of using these two static controls, add the following definitions to the resource file you created for the preceding examples.

```
GROUPBOX "Checkboxes", ID_GB1, 1, 1, 51, 34
CTEXT "This is text", ID_CT1, 1, 44, 50, 24
```

After you have added these lines, recompile the preceding example, execute the program, and select the Dialog menu option. The dialog box will now look like that shown in Figure 6-2. Remember that although the static controls make the dialog box look different, its function has not changed.

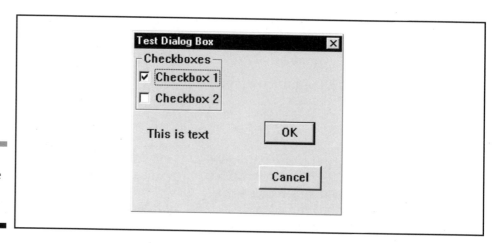

Adding static controls to the dialog box

Figure 6-2.

Adding Radio Buttons

The next control that we will examine is the *radio button*. Radio buttons are used to present mutually exclusive options. A radio button consists of a label and a small circle. If the circle is empty, the option is not selected. If the circle is filled, the option is selected. Windows 98 supports two types of radio buttons: manual and automatic. The manual radio button (like the manual check box) requires that you perform all management functions. The automatic radio button performs the management functions for you. Because managing radio buttons is more complex than managing check boxes, and because automatic radio buttons are the type generally used by applications, they are the only ones examined here.

Like other controls, automatic radio buttons are usually defined in your program's resource file, within a dialog definition. To create an automatic radio button, use **AUTORADIOBUTTON**, which has this general form:

AUTORADIOBUTTON "*string*", *RBID*, *X*, *Y*, *Width*, *Height* [, *Style*]

6

Here, *string* is the text that will be shown alongside the button. *RBID* is the value associated with the radio button. The button's upper-left corner will be at *X,Y*, and the button plus its associated text will have the dimensions specified by *Width* × *Height*. *Style* determines the exact nature of the radio button. If no explicit style is specified, the button defaults to displaying the *string* on the right and allowing the button to be tabbed to.

PORTABILITY: The resource compiler for Windows 3.1 does not support the **AUTORADIOBUTTON** resource command. Watch for opportunities to use **AUTORADIOBUTTON** when converting from Windows 3.1.

As stated, radio buttons are generally used to create groups of mutually exclusive options. When you use automatic radio buttons to create such a group, Windows 98 automatically manages the buttons in a mutually exclusive manner. That is, each time you select one button, the previously selected button is turned off. Also, it is not possible to select more than one button at any one time.

A radio button (even an automatic one) may be set to a known state by your program by sending it the **BM_SETCHECK** message using the **SendDlgItemMessage( )** API function. The value of *wParam* determines whether the button will be checked or cleared. If *wParam* is **BST_CHECKED**, then the button will be checked. If it is **BST_UNCHECKED**, the box will be cleared. By default, all buttons are cleared.

NOTE: It is possible to manually set more than one radio button or to clear all buttons using **SendDlgItemMessage( )**. However, normal Windows style dictates that radio buttons be used in a mutually exclusive fashion, with one (and only one) option selected. It is strongly suggested that you do not violate this rule.

You can obtain the status of a radio button by sending it the **BM_GETCHECK** message. The button returns **BST_CHECKED** if the button is selected and **BST_UNCHECKED** if it is not.

To add radio buttons to the example program, first add these lines to your resource file. Notice that another group box is added to surround the radio buttons. This is not necessary, of course, but such groupings are common in dialog boxes.

```
AUTORADIOBUTTON "Radio 1", ID_RB1, 60, 10, 48, 12
AUTORADIOBUTTON "Radio 2", ID_RB2, 60, 22, 48, 12
GROUPBOX "Radio Group", ID_GB2, 58, 1, 51, 34
```

Here is the preceding sample program, expanded to accommodate the two radio buttons. Notice that since the radio buttons are automatic, there are only a few additions to the program. First, the state of the radio buttons is stored in two global variables, **rbstatus1** and **rbstatus2**. The values of these variables are used to set the initial button states and to display the status of the buttons when the **Status** main menu option is selected.

```
/* Demonstrate radio buttons. */

#include <windows.h>
#include <string.h>
#include <stdio.h>
#include "mydialog.h"
```

```
LRESULT CALLBACK WindowFunc(HWND, UINT, WPARAM, LPARAM);
LRESULT CALLBACK DialogFunc(HWND, UINT, WPARAM, LPARAM);

char szWinName[] = "MyWin"; /* name of window class */

HINSTANCE hInst;

/* holds status of check boxes and radio buttons */
int cbstatus1=BST_UNCHECKED, cbstatus2=BST_UNCHECKED;
int rbstatus1=BST_CHECKED, rbstatus2=BST_UNCHECKED;

int WINAPI WinMain(HINSTANCE hThisInst, HINSTANCE hPrevInst,
                   LPSTR lpszArgs, int nWinMode)
{
  HWND hwnd;
  MSG msg;
  WNDCLASSEX wcl;
  HACCEL hAccel;

  /* Define a window class. */
  wcl.cbSize = sizeof(WNDCLASSEX);

  wcl.hInstance = hThisInst; /* handle to this instance */
  wcl.lpszClassName = szWinName; /* window class name */
  wcl.lpfnWndProc = WindowFunc; /* window function */
  wcl.style = 0; /* default style */

  wcl.hIcon = LoadIcon(NULL, IDI_APPLICATION); /* standard icon */
  wcl.hIconSm = LoadIcon(NULL, IDI_WINLOGO); /* small icon */
  wcl.hCursor = LoadCursor(NULL, IDC_ARROW); /* cursor style */

  wcl.lpszMenuName = "MyMenu"; /* main menu */
  wcl.cbClsExtra = 0; /* no extra */
  wcl.cbWndExtra = 0; /* information needed */

  /* Make the window white. */
  wcl.hbrBackground = (HBRUSH) GetStockObject(WHITE_BRUSH);

  /* Register the window class. */
  if(!RegisterClassEx(&wcl)) return 0;

  /* Now that a window class has been registered, a window
     can be created. */
  hwnd = CreateWindow(
    szWinName, /* name of window class */
```

6

```
    "Try Radio Buttons", /* title */
    WS_OVERLAPPEDWINDOW, /* window style - normal */
    CW_USEDEFAULT, /* X coordinate - let Windows decide */
    CW_USEDEFAULT, /* Y coordinate - let Windows decide */
    CW_USEDEFAULT, /* width - let Windows decide */
    CW_USEDEFAULT, /* height - let Windows decide */
    HWND_DESKTOP, /* no parent window */
    NULL, /* no override of class menu */
    hThisInst, /* handle of this instance of the program */
    NULL /* no additional arguments */
  );

  hInst = hThisInst; /* save the current instance handle */

  /* Load accelerators. */
  hAccel = LoadAccelerators(hThisInst, "MyMenu");

  /* Display the window. */
  ShowWindow(hwnd, nWinMode);
  UpdateWindow(hwnd);

  /* Create the message loop. */
  while(GetMessage(&msg, NULL, 0, 0))
  {
    if(!TranslateAccelerator(hwnd, hAccel, &msg)) {
      TranslateMessage(&msg); /* translate keyboard messages */
      DispatchMessage(&msg); /* return control to Windows 98 */
    }
  }
  return msg.wParam;
}

/* This function is called by Windows 98 and is passed
   messages from the message queue.
*/
LRESULT CALLBACK WindowFunc(HWND hwnd, UINT message,
                            WPARAM wParam, LPARAM lParam)
{
  char str[255];
  int response;

  switch(message) {
    case WM_COMMAND:
      switch(LOWORD(wParam)) {
        case IDM_DIALOG:
```

```
          DialogBox(hInst, "MyDB", hwnd, (DLGPROC) DialogFunc);
          break;
        case IDM_EXIT:
          response = MessageBox(hwnd, "Quit the Program?",
                                "Exit", MB_YESNO);
          if(response == IDYES) PostQuitMessage(0);
          break;
        case IDM_STATUS:
          if(cbstatus1 == BST_CHECKED)
            strcpy(str, "Checkbox 1 is checked\n");
          else strcpy(str, "Checkbox 1 is not checked\n");
          if(cbstatus2 == BST_CHECKED)
            strcat(str, "Checkbox 2 is checked\n");
          else strcat(str, "Checkbox 2 is not checked\n");
          if(rbstatus1 == BST_CHECKED)
            strcat(str, "Radio 1 is checked\n");
          else strcat(str, "Radio 1 is not checked\n");
          if(rbstatus2 == BST_CHECKED)
            strcat(str, "Radio 2 is checked");
          else strcat(str, "Radio 2 is not checked");
          MessageBox(hwnd, str, "", MB_OK);
          break;
        case IDM_HELP:
          MessageBox(hwnd, "Not Implemented", "Help", MB_OK);
          break;
      }
      break;
    case WM_DESTROY: /* terminate the program */
      PostQuitMessage(0);
      break;
    default:
      /* Let Windows 98 process any messages not specified in
      the preceding switch statement. */
      return DefWindowProc(hwnd, message, wParam, lParam);
  }
  return 0;
}

/* A simple dialog function. */
LRESULT CALLBACK DialogFunc(HWND hdwnd, UINT message,
                            WPARAM wParam, LPARAM lParam)
{
  switch(message) {
    case WM_INITDIALOG:
      /* The dialog box has just been displayed.  Set
```

```
          the check boxes and radio buttons appropriately. */
      SendDlgItemMessage(hdwnd, ID_CB1, BM_SETCHECK, cbstatus1, 0);
      SendDlgItemMessage(hdwnd, ID_CB2, BM_SETCHECK, cbstatus2, 0);
      SendDlgItemMessage(hdwnd, ID_RB1, BM_SETCHECK, rbstatus1, 0);
      SendDlgItemMessage(hdwnd, ID_RB2, BM_SETCHECK, rbstatus2, 0);
      return 1;
    case WM_COMMAND:
      switch(LOWORD(wParam)) {
        case IDCANCEL:
          EndDialog(hdwnd, 0);
          return 1;
        case IDOK:
          /* update global checkbox status variables */
          cbstatus1 = SendDlgItemMessage(hdwnd, ID_CB1,
                                    BM_GETCHECK, 0, 0);
          cbstatus2 = SendDlgItemMessage(hdwnd, ID_CB2,
                                    BM_GETCHECK, 0, 0);

          /* now, update global checkbox status variables */
          rbstatus1 = SendDlgItemMessage(hdwnd, ID_RB1,
                                    BM_GETCHECK, 0, 0);
          rbstatus2 = SendDlgItemMessage(hdwnd, ID_RB2,
                                    BM_GETCHECK, 0, 0);

          EndDialog(hdwnd, 0);
          return 1;
        case ID_CB1: /* This is a manually managed check box. */
          /* user selected 1st check box, so change its state */
          if(SendDlgItemMessage(hdwnd, ID_CB1,
                BM_GETCHECK, 0, 0) == BST_UNCHECKED)
            SendDlgItemMessage(hdwnd, ID_CB1,
                            BM_SETCHECK, BST_CHECKED, 0);
          else /* turn it off */
            SendDlgItemMessage(hdwnd, ID_CB1,
                            BM_SETCHECK, BST_UNCHECKED, 0);
          return 1;
      }
  }
  return 0;
}
```

When you run this program, the dialog box will now look like that shown in Figure 6-3.

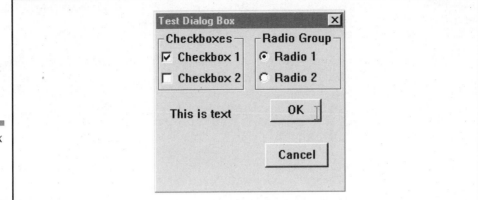

The dialog box
with radio
buttons
Figure 6-3.

Scroll Bars

6

The *scroll bar* is one of Windows 98's most important controls. Scroll bars
exist in two forms. The first is an integral part of a normal window or dialog
box and is called a *standard scroll bar*. The second exists separately as a control
and is called a *scroll bar control*. Both types of scroll bars are managed in much
the same way.

Standard
scroll bars are
attached to
a window.

A scroll bar
control is a
freestanding
scroll bar.

Activating the Standard Scroll Bars

For a window to include standard scroll bars, you must explicitly request it.
For windows created using **CreateWindow( )**, such as your application's
main window, you do this by including the styles **WS_VSCROLL** and/or
WS_HSCROLL in the style parameter. In the case of a dialog box, you
include the **WS_VSCROLL** and/or **WS_HSCROLL** styles in the dialog box's
definition inside its resource file. As expected, the **WS_VSCROLL** causes a
standard vertical scroll bar to be included, and **WS_HSCROLL** activates a
horizontal scroll bar. After you have added these styles, the window will
automatically display the standard vertical and horizontal scroll bars.

To add
standard
scroll bars
to a window,
specify the
WS_VSCROLL
and/or
WS_HSCROLL
styles.

Receiving Scroll Bar Messages

Unlike other controls, a scroll bar control does not generate a
WM_COMMAND message. Instead, scroll bars send either a **WM_VSCROLL**
or a **WM_HSCROLL** message when either a vertical or horizontal scroll bar
is accessed, respectively. The value of the low-order word of **wParam**

contains a code that describes the activity. For the standard window scroll bars, **lParam** is 0. However, if a scroll bar control generates the message, then **lParam** contains its handle.

As mentioned, the value in **LOWORD(wParam)** specifies what type of scroll bar action has taken place. Here are some common scroll bar values.

SB_LINEUP

SB_LINEDOWN

SB_PAGEUP

SB_PAGEDOWN

SB_LINELEFT

SB_LINERIGHT

SB_PAGELEFT

SB_PAGERIGHT

SB_THUMBPOSITION

SB_THUMBTRACK

For vertical scroll bars, each time the user moves the scroll bar up one position, **SB_LINEUP** is sent. Each time the scroll bar is moved down one position, **SB_LINEDOWN** is sent. **SB_PAGEUP** and **SB_PAGEDOWN** are sent when the scroll bar is moved up or down one page.

For horizontal scroll bars, each time the user moves the scroll bar left one position, **SB_LINELEFT** is sent. Each time the scroll bar is moved right one position, **SB_LINERIGHT** is sent. **SB_PAGELEFT** and **SB_PAGERIGHT** are sent when the scroll bar is moved left or right one page.

For both types of scroll bars, the **SB_THUMBPOSITION** value is sent after the slider box (thumb) of the scroll bar has been dragged to a new position. The **SB_THUMBTRACK** message is also sent when the thumb is dragged to a new position. However, it is sent each time the thumb passes over a new position. This allows you to "track" the movement of the thumb before it is released. When **SB_THUMBPOSITION** or **SB_THUMBTRACK** is received, the high-order word of **wParam** contains the current slider box position.

PORTABILITY: In Windows 3.1, the organization of **lParam** and **wParam** differ from their equivalents in 32-bit versions of Windows, including Windows 95, Windows 98, and Windows NT. Specifically, the handle of the scroll bar is in the high-order word of **lParam**. The position of the slider box is in the low-order word of **lParam**. The nature of the scroll bar action is in **wParam**. Because of these differences, you must rewrite all scroll bar message-handling code when porting from Windows 3.1.

SetScrollInfo( ) and GetScrollInfo( )

Scroll bars are, for the most part, manually managed controls. This means that in addition to responding to scroll bar messages, your program will also need to update various attributes associated with a scroll bar. For example, your program must update the position of the slider box manually. Windows 98 contains two functions that help you manage scroll bars. The first is **SetScrollInfo( )**, which is used to set various attributes associated with a scroll bar. Its prototype is shown here:

6

int SetScrollInfo(HWND *hwnd*, int *which*, LPSCROLLINFO *lpSI*, BOOL *repaint*);

Here, *hwnd* is the handle that identifies the scroll bar. For window scroll bars, this is the handle of the window that owns the scroll bar. For scroll bar controls, this is the handle of the scroll bar itself. The value of *which* determines which scroll bar is affected. If you are setting the attributes of the vertical window scroll bar, then this parameter must be **SB_VERT**. If you are setting the attributes of the horizontal window scroll bar, this value must be **SB_HORZ**. However, to set a scroll bar control, this value must be **SB_CTL** and *hwnd* must be the handle of the control. The attributes are set according to the information pointed to by *lpSI* (discussed shortly). If *repaint* is true, then the scroll bar is redrawn; if false, the bar is not redisplayed. The function returns the position of the slider box.

To obtain the attributes associated with a scroll bar, use **GetScrollInfo( )**, shown here:

BOOL GetScrollInfo(HWND *hwnd*, int *which*, LPSCROLLINFO *lpSI*);

The *hwnd* and *which* parameters are the same as those just described for **SetScrollInfo( )**. The information obtained by **GetScrollInfo( )** is put into the structure pointed to by *lpSI*. The function returns nonzero if successful and zero on failure.

The *lpSI* parameter of both functions points to a structure of type
SCROLLINFO, which is defined like this.

```
typedef struct tagSCROLLINFO
{
  UINT cbSize; /* size of SCROLLINFO */
  UINT fMask; /* Operation performed */
  int nMin; /* minimum range */
  int nMax; /* maximum range */
  UINT nPage; /* Page value */
  int nPos; /* slider box position */
  int nTrackPos; /* current tracking position */
} SCROLLINFO;
```

Here, **cbSize** must contain the size of the **SCROLLINFO** structure. The value
or values contained in **fMask** determine which of the remaining members
are meaningful. Specifically, when used in a call to **SetScrollInfo( )**, the
value in **fMask** specifies which scroll bar values will be updated. When used
with **GetScrollInfo( )**, the value in **fMask** determines which settings will
be obtained. **fMask** must be one or more of these values. (To combine
values, simply OR them together.)

SIF_ALL	Same as SIF_PAGE I SIF_POS I SIF_RANGE I SIF_TRACKPOS.
SIF_DISABLENOSCROLL	Scroll bar is disabled rather than removed if its range is set to zero.
SIF_PAGE	**nPage** contains valid information.
SIF_POS	**nPos** contains valid information.
SIF_RANGE	**nMin** and **nMax** contain valid information.
SIF_TRACKPOS	**nTrackPos** contains valid information.

nPage contains the current page setting for proportional scroll bars. **nPos**
contains the position of the slider box. **nMin** and **nMax** contain the
minimum and maximum range of the scroll bar. **nTrackPos** contains the
current tracking position. The tracking position is the current position of the
slider box while it is being dragged by the user. This value cannot be set.

Working with Scroll Bars

As stated, scroll bars are manually managed controls. This means that your program will need to update the position of the slider box within the scroll bar each time it is moved. To do this you will need to assign **nPos** the value of the new position, assign **fMask** the value **SIF_POS**, and then call **SetScrollInfo( )**. For example, to update the slider box for the vertical scroll bar, your program will need to execute a sequence like the following.

```
SCROLLINFO si;
/* ... */
si.cbSize = sizeof(SCROLLINFO);
si.fMask = SIF_POS;
si.nPos = newposition;
SetScrollInfo(hwnd, SB_VERT, &si, 1);
```

The range of the scroll bar determines how many positions there are between one end and the other. By default, window scroll bars have a range of 0 to 100. However, you can set their range to meet the needs of your program. Control scroll bars have a default range of 0 to 0, which means that the range must be set before the scroll bar control can be used. (A scroll bar that has a zero range is inactive.) Setting the range can make it easier for your application to maintain the position of the slider box.

6

A Sample Scroll Bar Program

The following program demonstrates both vertical and horizontal standard scroll bars. The scroll bar program requires the following resource file.

```
/* Demonstrate Scroll Bars */
#include <windows.h>
#include "scroll.h"

MyMenu MENU
{
  POPUP "&Dialog"
  {
    MENUITEM "&Scroll Bars\tF2", IDM_DIALOG
    MENUITEM "&Exit\tCtrl+X", IDM_EXIT
  }
```

```
    MENUITEM "&Help", IDM_HELP
}

MyMenu ACCELERATORS
{
  VK_F2, IDM_DIALOG, VIRTKEY
  "^X", IDM_EXIT
  VK_F1, IDM_HELP, VIRTKEY
}

MyDB DIALOG 18, 18, 142, 92
CAPTION "Using Standard Scroll Bars"
STYLE DS_MODALFRAME | WS_POPUP | WS_CAPTION | WS_SYSMENU
     | WS_VSCROLL | WS_HSCROLL
{
  GROUPBOX "Slider Positions", ID_GB1, 2, 2, 100, 60
}
```

As you can see, the dialog box contains only a group box. The scroll bars are added automatically because of the **WS_VSCROLL** and **WS_HSCROLL** style specifications.

You will also need to create this header file, called SCROLL.H.

```
#define IDM_DIALOG    100
#define IDM_EXIT      101
#define IDM_HELP      102

#define ID_GB1        200
```

The entire scroll bar demonstration program is shown here. The vertical scroll bar responds to the **SB_LINEUP**, **SB_LINEDOWN**, **SB_PAGEUP**, **SB_PAGEDOWN**, **SB_THUMBPOSITION**, and **SB_THUMBTRACK** messages by moving the slider box appropriately. It also displays the current position of the thumb. The position will change as you move the slider. The horizontal scroll bar only responds to **SB_LINELEFT** and **SB_LINERIGHT**. Its thumb position is also displayed. (On your own, you might try adding the necessary code to make the horizontal scroll bar respond to other messages.) Notice that the range of both the horizontal and vertical scroll bars is set when the dialog box receives a **WM_INITDIALOG** message. You might want to try changing the range of the scroll bars and observing the results. Sample output from the program is shown in Figure 6-4.

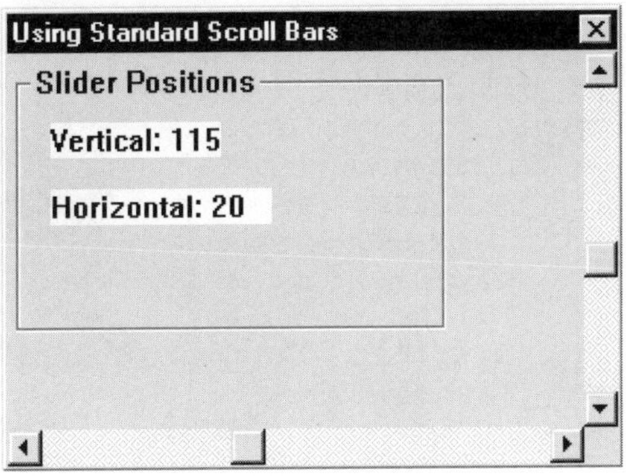

Sample
output from
the standard
scroll bar
demonstration
program
Figure 6-4.

One other point: notice that the thumb position of each scroll bar is displayed by outputting text into the client area of the dialog box using **TextOut( )**. Although a dialog box performs a special purpose, it is still a window with the same basic characteristics as the main window. Also notice that the background of the text is white, but the background of the dialog box is light gray. In the next chapter you will learn how to control the color of both the text and the background when outputting text.

```c
/* Demonstrate Standard Scroll Bars */

#include <windows.h>
#include <string.h>
#include <stdio.h>
#include "scroll.h"

#define VERTRANGEMAX 200
#define HORZRANGEMAX  50

LRESULT CALLBACK WindowFunc(HWND, UINT, WPARAM, LPARAM);
BOOL CALLBACK DialogFunc(HWND, UINT, WPARAM, LPARAM);

char szWinName[] = "MyWin"; /* name of window class */

HINSTANCE hInst;

int WINAPI WinMain(HINSTANCE hThisInst, HINSTANCE hPrevInst,
```

6

```
                    LPSTR lpszArgs, int nWinMode)
{
  HWND hwnd;
  MSG msg;
  WNDCLASSEX wcl;
  HACCEL hAccel;

  /* Define a window class. */
  wcl.cbSize = sizeof(WNDCLASSEX);

  wcl.hInstance = hThisInst; /* handle to this instance */
  wcl.lpszClassName = szWinName; /* window class name */
  wcl.lpfnWndProc = WindowFunc; /* window function */
  wcl.style = 0; /* default style */

  wcl.hIcon = LoadIcon(NULL, IDI_APPLICATION); /* standard icon */
  wcl.hIconSm = LoadIcon(NULL, IDI_WINLOGO); /* small icon */
  wcl.hCursor = LoadCursor(NULL, IDC_ARROW); /* cursor style */

  /* specify name of menu resource */
  wcl.lpszMenuName = "MyMenu"; /* main menu */

  wcl.cbClsExtra = 0; /* no extra */
  wcl.cbWndExtra = 0; /* information needed */

  /* Make the window white. */
  wcl.hbrBackground = (HBRUSH) GetStockObject(WHITE_BRUSH);

  /* Register the window class. */
  if(!RegisterClassEx(&wcl)) return 0;

  /* Now that a window class has been registered, a window
     can be created. */
  hwnd = CreateWindow(
    szWinName, /* name of window class */
    "Managing Standard Scroll Bars", /* title */
    WS_OVERLAPPEDWINDOW, /* window style - normal */
    CW_USEDEFAULT, /* X coordinate - let Windows decide */
    CW_USEDEFAULT, /* Y coordinate - let Windows decide */
    CW_USEDEFAULT, /* width - let Windows decide */
    CW_USEDEFAULT, /* height - let Windows decide */
    HWND_DESKTOP, /* no parent window */
    NULL, /* no override of class menu */
    hThisInst, /* handle of this instance of the program */
    NULL /* no additional arguments */
```

```
       );

       hInst = hThisInst; /* save the current instance handle */

       /* Load accelerators. */
       hAccel = LoadAccelerators(hThisInst, "MyMenu");

       /* Display the window. */
       ShowWindow(hwnd, nWinMode);
       UpdateWindow(hwnd);

       /* Create the message loop. */
       while(GetMessage(&msg, NULL, 0, 0))
       {
         if(!TranslateAccelerator(hwnd, hAccel, &msg)) {
           TranslateMessage(&msg); /* translate keyboard messages */
           DispatchMessage(&msg); /* return control to Windows 98 */
         }
       }
       return msg.wParam;
}

/* This function is called by Windows 98 and is passed
   messages from the message queue.
*/
LRESULT CALLBACK WindowFunc(HWND hwnd, UINT message,
                            WPARAM wParam, LPARAM lParam)
{
  int response;

  switch(message) {
    case WM_COMMAND:
      switch(LOWORD(wParam)) {
        case IDM_DIALOG:
          DialogBox(hInst, "MyDB", hwnd, (DLGPROC) DialogFunc);
          break;
        case IDM_EXIT:
          response = MessageBox(hwnd, "Quit the Program?",
                                "Exit", MB_YESNO);
          if(response == IDYES) PostQuitMessage(0);
          break;
        case IDM_HELP:
          MessageBox(hwnd, "Not Implemented", "Help", MB_OK);
          break;
      }
```

6

```
      break;
    case WM_DESTROY: /* terminate the program */
      PostQuitMessage(0);
      break;
    default:
      /* Let Windows 98 process any messages not specified in
         the preceding switch statement. */
      return DefWindowProc(hwnd, message, wParam, lParam);
  }
  return 0;
}


/* Dialog function */
BOOL CALLBACK DialogFunc(HWND hdwnd, UINT message,
                          WPARAM wParam, LPARAM lParam)
{
  char str[255];
  static int vpos = 0; /* vertical slider box position */
  static int hpos = 0; /* horizontal slider box position */
  static SCROLLINFO si; /* scroll bar info structure */

  HDC hdc;
  PAINTSTRUCT paintstruct;

  switch(message) {
    case WM_COMMAND:
      switch(LOWORD(wParam)) {
        case IDCANCEL:
          EndDialog(hdwnd, 0);
          return 1;
      }
      break;
    case WM_INITDIALOG:
      si.cbSize = sizeof(SCROLLINFO);
      si.fMask = SIF_RANGE;
      si.nMin = 0; si.nMax = VERTRANGEMAX;
      SetScrollInfo(hdwnd, SB_VERT, &si, 1);
      si.nMax = HORZRANGEMAX;
      SetScrollInfo(hdwnd, SB_HORZ, &si, 1);
      vpos = hpos = 0;
      return 1;
    case WM_PAINT:
      hdc = BeginPaint(hdwnd, &paintstruct);
      sprintf(str, "Vertical: %d", vpos);
      TextOut(hdc, 20, 30, str, strlen(str));
```

```
          sprintf(str, "Horizontal: %d", hpos);
          TextOut(hdc, 20, 60, str, strlen(str));
          EndPaint(hdwnd, &paintstruct);
          return 1;
       case WM_VSCROLL:
         switch(LOWORD(wParam)) {
           case SB_LINEDOWN:
             vpos++;
             if(vpos>VERTRANGEMAX) vpos = VERTRANGEMAX;
             break;
           case SB_LINEUP:
             vpos--;
             if(vpos<0) vpos = 0;
             break;
           case SB_THUMBPOSITION:
             vpos = HIWORD(wParam); /* get current position */
             break;
           case SB_THUMBTRACK:
             vpos = HIWORD(wParam); /* get current position */
             break;
           case SB_PAGEDOWN:
             vpos += 5;
             if(vpos>VERTRANGEMAX) vpos = VERTRANGEMAX;
             break;
           case SB_PAGEUP:
             vpos -= 5;
             if(vpos<0) vpos = 0;
         }
         /* update vertical bar position */
         si.fMask = SIF_POS;
         si.nPos = vpos;
         SetScrollInfo(hdwnd, SB_VERT, &si, 1);
         hdc = GetDC(hdwnd);
         sprintf(str, "Vertical: %d    ", vpos);
         TextOut(hdc, 20, 30, str, strlen(str));
         ReleaseDC(hdwnd, hdc);
         return 1;
       case WM_HSCROLL:
         switch(LOWORD(wParam)) {
           /* Try adding the other event handling code
              for the horizontal scroll bar, here. */
           case SB_LINERIGHT:
             hpos++;
             if(hpos>HORZRANGEMAX) hpos = HORZRANGEMAX;
             break;
```

6

```
      case SB_LINELEFT:
        hpos--;
        if(hpos<0) hpos = 0;
    }
    /* update horizontal bar position */
    si.fMask = SIF_POS;
    si.nPos = hpos;
    SetScrollInfo(hdwnd, SB_HORZ, &si, 1);
    hdc = GetDC(hdwnd);
    sprintf(str, "Horizontal: %d   ", hpos);
    TextOut(hdc, 20, 60, str, strlen(str));
    ReleaseDC(hdwnd, hdc);
    return 1;
  }
  return 0;
}
```

IN DEPTH

The Old Scroll Bar API Functions

For Windows 3.1 programs, the functions **SetScrollInfo( )** and
GetScrollInfo( ) are not available. Instead, Windows 3.1 programs must
use these API functions to manage scroll bars.

GetScrollRange( )	Obtains the scroll bar range.
SetScrollRange( )	Sets the scroll bar range.
GetScrollPos( )	Obtains the position of the slider box.
SetScrollPos( )	Sets the position of the slider box.

Although these functions are still supported under Win32, their use is not
recommended and you should upgrade them to calls to **SetScrollInfo( )**
when porting older programs. Since these functions are still widely used,
they are described here.

The **SetScrollRange( )** API function has this prototype:

BOOL SetScrollRange(HWND *hwnd*, int *which*, int *min*, int *max*,
BOOL *repaint*);

Here, *hwnd* is the handle that identifies the scroll bar. For window scroll bars, this is the handle of the window. For scroll bar controls, this is the handle of the scroll bar. The value of *which* determines which scroll bar is having its range set. If you are setting the range of the vertical window scroll bar, this parameter must be **SB_VERT**. If you are setting the range of the horizontal window scroll bar, this value must be **SB_HORZ**. However, to set a scroll bar control, this value must be **SB_CTL**. The values of *min* and *max* determine the range. These values must lie between 0 and 32,767. If *repaint* is true, then the scroll bar is redrawn after the range is set. If it is false, the bar is not redisplayed. The function returns nonzero if successful and zero on failure.

GetScrollRange( ) has the following prototype:

BOOL GetScrollRange(HWND *hwnd*, int *which*, int **min*, int **max*);

Here, *hwnd* is the handle that identifies the scroll bar. For window scroll bars, this is the handle of the window. For scroll bar controls, this is the handle of the scroll bar. The value of *which* determines which scroll bar's range is being obtained. It must be **SB_VERT**, **SB_HORZ**, or **SB_CTL**. The values of *min* and *max* are pointers to integers that receive the range. The function returns nonzero if successful and zero on failure.

SetScrollPos( ) has this prototype:

int SetScrollPos(HWND *hwnd*, int *which*, int *pos*, BOOL *repaint*);

Here, *hwnd* is the handle that identifies the scroll bar. For window scroll bars, this is the handle of the window. For scroll bar controls, this is the handle of the scroll bar. The value of *which* determines which scroll bar is having its slider box set. It must be **SB_VERT**, **SB_HORZ**, or **SB_CTL**. The value of *pos* determines where the slider box will be positioned. It must contain a value that is within the range of the scroll bar. If *repaint* is true, the scroll bar is redrawn after the box is set; if false, the bar is not redisplayed. It returns the previous slider box position or zero on error.

GetScrollPos( ) has this prototoype:

int GetScrollPos(HWND *hwnd*, int *which*);

Here, *hwnd* is the handle that identifies the scroll bar. For window scroll bars, this is the handle of the window. For scroll bar controls, this is the handle of the scroll bar. The value of *which* determines which scroll bar's position is being obtained. It must be **SB_VERT**, **SB_HORZ**, or **SB_CTL**. The function returns the current position of the slider box. It returns zero if an error occurs.

Remember, these functions are now obsolete and not recommended for new 32-bit code.

Using a Scroll Bar Control

A scroll bar control is a stand-alone scroll bar; it is not attached to a window. Scroll bar controls are handled much like standard scroll bars, with two important differences. First, the range of a scroll bar control must be set because it has a default range of zero. Thus, it is initially inactive. This differs from standard scroll bars, whose default range is 0 through 100.

When a control scroll bar generates a message, its handle is passed in **lParam**.

The second difference has to do with the meaning of **lParam** when a scroll bar message is received. Recall that all scroll bars—standard or control—generate a **WM_HSCROLL** or a **WM_VSCROLL** message, depending upon whether the scroll bar is horizontal or vertical. When these messages are generated by a standard scroll bar, **lParam** is always zero. However, when they are generated by a scroll bar control, the handle of the control is passed in **lParam**. In windows that contain both standard and control scroll bars, you will need to make use of this fact to determine which scroll bar generated the message.

Creating a Scroll Bar Control

To create a scroll bar control in a dialog box, use the **SCROLLBAR** statement, which has this general form:

SCROLLBAR *SBID, X, Y, Width, Height* [, *Style*]

Here, *SBID* is the value associated with the scroll bar. The scroll bar's upper-left corner will be at *X,Y*, and the scroll bar will have the dimensions specified by *Width* × *Height*. *Style* determines the exact nature of the scroll bar. Its default style is **SBS_HORZ**, which creates a horizontal scroll bar. For a vertical scroll bar, specify the **SBS_VERT** style. If you want the scroll bar to be able to receive keyboard focus, include the **WS_TABSTOP** style.

Obtaining the Handle of Scroll Bar Control

To determine if a scroll bar message was generated by a scroll bar control, you will need to compare the value in **lParam** to the handle of the scroll bar control. To do this means that you will need to obtain a handle to the scroll bar control. You can do this using the **GetDlgItem( )** API. It returns a handle to a control given its ID. Its prototype is:

HWND GetDlgItem(HWND *hDwnd*, int *ID*);

Here, *hDwnd* is the handle of the dialog box that owns the control. The control ID is passed in *ID*. This is the value that you associate with the control in its resource file. The function returns the handle of the specified control or **NULL** on failure.

6

Demonstrating a Scroll Bar Control

To demonstrate a control scroll bar, one will be added to the preceding program. First, change the dialog box definition as shown here. This version adds a vertical scroll bar control.

```
MyDB DIALOG 18, 18, 142, 92
CAPTION "Adding a Control Scroll Bar"
STYLE DS_MODALFRAME | WS_POPUP | WS_CAPTION | WS_SYSMENU
     | WS_VSCROLL | WS_HSCROLL
{
  GROUPBOX "Slider Positions", ID_GB1, 2, 2, 100, 60
  SCROLLBAR ID_SB1, 110, 10, 10, 70, SBS_VERT | WS_TABSTOP
}
```

Then, add this line to SCROLL.H:

```
#define ID_SB1    300
```

Next, you will need to add the code that handles the control scroll bar. This code will need to distinguish between the standard scroll bar and the scroll bar control, since both generate **WM_VSCROLL** messages. To do this, just remember that a scroll bar control passes its handle in **lParam**. For standard

scroll bars, **lParam** is zero. For example, here is the **SB_LINEDOWN** case
that distinguishes between the standard scroll bar and the control scroll bar.

```
case SB_LINEDOWN:
  if((HWND)lParam==GetDlgItem(hdwnd, ID_SB1)) {
    /* is control scroll bar */
    cntlpos++;
    if(cntlpos>VERTRANGEMAX) cntlpos = VERTRANGEMAX;
  }
  else {
    /* is window scroll bar */
    vpos++;
    if(vpos>VERTRANGEMAX) vpos = VERTRANGEMAX;
  }
  break;
```

Here, the handle in **lParam** is compared with the handle of the scroll bar
control, as obtained using **GetDlgItem( )**. If the handles are the same, the
message was generated by the scroll bar control. If not, the message came
from the standard scroll bar.

Here is the entire program that includes the vertical scroll bar control. It is
the same as the preceding program except for the following additions. First,
DialogFunc( ) defines the static variable **cntlpos**, which holds the position
of the control scroll bar. Second, the control scroll bar is initialized inside
WM_INITDIALOG. Third, the handlers that process **WM_VSCROLL**
messages determine whether the message came from the standard scroll bar
or the control scroll bar. Finally, code has been added to display the current
position of the control scroll bar.

Sample output is shown in Figure 6-5. On your own, try adding a horizontal
control scroll bar.

```
/* Demonstrate a Control Scroll Bar */

#include <windows.h>
#include <string.h>
#include <stdio.h>
#include "scroll.h"

#define VERTRANGEMAX 200
#define HORZRANGEMAX  50
```

```
LRESULT CALLBACK WindowFunc(HWND, UINT, WPARAM, LPARAM);
BOOL CALLBACK DialogFunc(HWND, UINT, WPARAM, LPARAM);

char szWinName[] = "MyWin"; /* name of window class */

HINSTANCE hInst;

int WINAPI WinMain(HINSTANCE hThisInst, HINSTANCE hPrevInst,
                   LPSTR lpszArgs, int nWinMode)
{
  HWND hwnd;
  MSG msg;
  WNDCLASSEX wcl;
  HACCEL hAccel;

  /* Define a window class. */
  wcl.cbSize = sizeof(WNDCLASSEX);

  wcl.hInstance = hThisInst; /* handle to this instance */
  wcl.lpszClassName = szWinName; /* window class name */
  wcl.lpfnWndProc = WindowFunc; /* window function */
  wcl.style = 0; /* default style */

  wcl.hIcon = LoadIcon(NULL, IDI_APPLICATION); /* standard icon */
  wcl.hIconSm = LoadIcon(NULL, IDI_WINLOGO); /* small icon */
  wcl.hCursor = LoadCursor(NULL, IDC_ARROW); /* cursor style */

  /* specify name of menu resource */
  wcl.lpszMenuName = "MyMenu"; /* main menu */

  wcl.cbClsExtra = 0; /* no extra */
  wcl.cbWndExtra = 0; /* information needed */

  /* Make the window white. */
  wcl.hbrBackground = (HBRUSH) GetStockObject(WHITE_BRUSH);

  /* Register the window class. */
  if(!RegisterClassEx(&wcl)) return 0;

  /* Now that a window class has been registered, a window
     can be created. */
  hwnd = CreateWindow(
    szWinName, /* name of window class */
    "Managing Scroll Bars", /* title */
    WS_OVERLAPPEDWINDOW, /* window style - normal */
```

6

```
      CW_USEDEFAULT, /* X coordinate - let Windows decide */
      CW_USEDEFAULT, /* Y coordinate - let Windows decide */
      CW_USEDEFAULT, /* width - let Windows decide */
      CW_USEDEFAULT, /* height - let Windows decide */
      HWND_DESKTOP, /* no parent window */
      NULL, /* no override of class menu */
      hThisInst, /* handle of this instance of the program */
      NULL /* no additional arguments */
    );

    hInst = hThisInst; /* save the current instance handle */

    /* Load accelerators. */
    hAccel = LoadAccelerators(hThisInst, "MyMenu");

    /* Display the window. */
    ShowWindow(hwnd, nWinMode);
    UpdateWindow(hwnd);

    /* Create the message loop. */
    while(GetMessage(&msg, NULL, 0, 0))
    {
      if(!TranslateAccelerator(hwnd, hAccel, &msg)) {
        TranslateMessage(&msg); /* translate keyboard messages */
        DispatchMessage(&msg); /* return control to Windows 98 */
      }
    }
    return msg.wParam;
}

/* This function is called by Windows 98 and is passed
   messages from the message queue.
*/
LRESULT CALLBACK WindowFunc(HWND hwnd, UINT message,
                            WPARAM wParam, LPARAM lParam)
{
  int response;

  switch(message) {
    case WM_COMMAND:
      switch(LOWORD(wParam)) {
        case IDM_DIALOG:
          DialogBox(hInst, "MyDB", hwnd, (DLGPROC) DialogFunc);
          break;
        case IDM_EXIT:
```

```
        response = MessageBox(hwnd, "Quit the Program?",
                              "Exit", MB_YESNO);
        if(response == IDYES) PostQuitMessage(0);
        break;
      case IDM_HELP:
        MessageBox(hwnd, "Not Implemented", "Help", MB_OK);
        break;
    }
    break;
  case WM_DESTROY: /* terminate the program */
    PostQuitMessage(0);
    break;
  default:
    /* Let Windows 98 process any messages not specified in
       the preceding switch statement. */
    return DefWindowProc(hwnd, message, wParam, lParam);
  }
  return 0;
}

/* Dialog function */
BOOL CALLBACK DialogFunc(HWND hdwnd, UINT message,
                         WPARAM wParam, LPARAM lParam)
{
  char str[255];
  static int vpos = 0; /* vertical slider box position */
  static int hpos = 0; /* horizontal slider box position */
  static int cntlpos = 0; /* control slider box position */
  static SCROLLINFO si; /* scroll bar info structure */

  HDC hdc;
  PAINTSTRUCT paintstruct;

  switch(message) {
    case WM_COMMAND:
      switch(LOWORD(wParam)) {
        case IDCANCEL:
          EndDialog(hdwnd, 0);
          return 1;
      }
      break;
    case WM_INITDIALOG:
      si.cbSize = sizeof(SCROLLINFO);
      si.fMask = SIF_RANGE;
      si.nMin = 0; si.nMax = VERTRANGEMAX;
```

```
      /* set range of standard vertical scroll bar */
      SetScrollInfo(hdwnd, SB_VERT, &si, 1);

      /* set range of scroll bar control */
      SetScrollInfo(GetDlgItem(hdwnd, ID_SB1), SB_CTL, &si, 1);

      si.nMax = HORZRANGEMAX;
      /* set range of standard horizontal scroll bar */
      SetScrollInfo(hdwnd, SB_HORZ, &si, 1);

      vpos = hpos = cntlpos = 0;
      return 1;
    case WM_PAINT:
      hdc = BeginPaint(hdwnd, &paintstruct);
      sprintf(str, "Vertical: %d", vpos);
      TextOut(hdc, 20, 30, str, strlen(str));
      sprintf(str, "Horizontal: %d", hpos);
      TextOut(hdc, 20, 60, str, strlen(str));
      sprintf(str, "Scroll Bar Control: %d    ", cntlpos);
      TextOut(hdc, 20, 90, str, strlen(str));
      EndPaint(hdwnd, &paintstruct);
      return 1;
    case WM_VSCROLL:
      /* Now we must determine whether the control
         scroll bar or the standard scroll bar generated
         the message. */
      switch(LOWORD(wParam)) {
        case SB_LINEDOWN:
          if((HWND)lParam==GetDlgItem(hdwnd, ID_SB1)) {
            /* is control scroll bar */
            cntlpos++;
            if(cntlpos>VERTRANGEMAX) cntlpos = VERTRANGEMAX;
          }
          else {
            /* is window scroll bar */
            vpos++;
            if(vpos>VERTRANGEMAX) vpos = VERTRANGEMAX;
          }
          break;
        case SB_LINEUP:
          if((HWND)lParam==GetDlgItem(hdwnd, ID_SB1)) {
            /* is control scroll bar */
            cntlpos--;
            if(cntlpos<0) cntlpos = 0;
```

```
      }
      else {
        /* is window scroll bar */
        vpos--;
        if(vpos<0) vpos = 0;
      }
      break;
  case SB_THUMBPOSITION:
      if((HWND)lParam==GetDlgItem(hdwnd, ID_SB1)) {
        /* is control scroll bar */
        cntlpos = HIWORD(wParam); /* get current position */
      }
      else {
        /* is window scroll bar */
        vpos = HIWORD(wParam); /* get current position */
      }
      break;
  case SB_THUMBTRACK:
      if((HWND)lParam==GetDlgItem(hdwnd, ID_SB1)) {
        /* is control scroll bar */
        cntlpos = HIWORD(wParam); /* get current position */
      }
      else {
        /* is window scroll bar */
        vpos = HIWORD(wParam); /* get current position */
      }
      break;
  case SB_PAGEDOWN:
      if((HWND)lParam==GetDlgItem(hdwnd, ID_SB1)) {
        /* is control scroll bar */
        cntlpos += 5;
        if(cntlpos>VERTRANGEMAX) cntlpos = VERTRANGEMAX;
      }
      else {
        /* is window scroll bar */
        vpos += 5;
        if(vpos>VERTRANGEMAX) vpos = VERTRANGEMAX;
      }
      break;
  case SB_PAGEUP:
      if((HWND)lParam==GetDlgItem(hdwnd, ID_SB1)) {
        /* is control scroll bar */
        cntlpos -= 5;
        if(cntlpos<0) cntlpos = 0;
      }
```

6

```
      else {
        /* is window scroll bar */
        vpos -= 5;
        if(vpos<0) vpos = 0;
      }
      break;
  }

  if((HWND)lParam==GetDlgItem(hdwnd, ID_SB1)) {
    /* update control scroll bar position */
    si.fMask = SIF_POS;
    si.nPos = cntlpos;
    SetScrollInfo((HWND)lParam, SB_CTL, &si, 1);
    hdc = GetDC(hdwnd);
    sprintf(str, "Scroll Bar Control: %d   ", cntlpos);
    TextOut(hdc, 20, 90, str, strlen(str));
    ReleaseDC(hdwnd, hdc);
  }
  else {
    /* update standard scroll bar position */
    si.fMask = SIF_POS;
    si.nPos = vpos;
    SetScrollInfo(hdwnd, SB_VERT, &si, 1);
    hdc = GetDC(hdwnd);
    sprintf(str, "Vertical: %d   ", vpos);
    TextOut(hdc, 20, 30, str, strlen(str));
    ReleaseDC(hdwnd, hdc);
  }
  return 1;
case WM_HSCROLL:
  switch(LOWORD(wParam)) {
    /* Try adding the other event handling code
       for the horizontal scroll bar, here. */
    case SB_LINERIGHT:
      hpos++;
      if(hpos>HORZRANGEMAX) hpos = HORZRANGEMAX;
      break;
    case SB_LINELEFT:
      hpos--;
      if(hpos<0) hpos = 0;
  }
  /* update horizontal scroll bar position */
  si.fMask = SIF_POS;
  si.nPos = hpos;
  SetScrollInfo(hdwnd, SB_HORZ, &si, 1);
```

```
        hdc = GetDC(hdwnd);
        sprintf(str, "Horizontal: %d    ", hpos);
        TextOut(hdc, 20, 60, str, strlen(str));
        ReleaseDC(hdwnd, hdc);
        return 1;
    }
    return 0;
}
```

Frankly, many beginning Windows programmers have the impression that using scroll bars is difficult. Actually, scroll bars are one of Windows' easiest controls. It's just that they require the handling of several contingencies.

In the next chapter, you will learn how to create and use bitmaps, icons, and cursors.

6

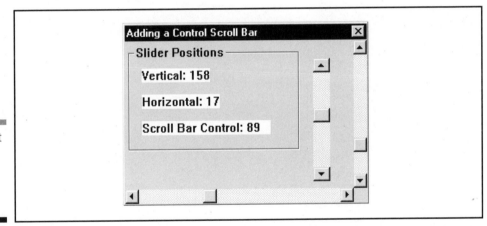

Sample output from the control scroll bar program

Figure 6-5.

CHAPTER 7

Creating Custom Icons, Cursors, and Bitmaps

This chapter explains how to control the appearance of two important items linked with all Windows applications: the icons and the mouse cursor. It also shows how to display a bitmap. The attribute that icons, cursors, and bitmaps have in common is that they are resources that consist of graphical images.

Icons, cursors, and bitmaps are created using an *image editor*. An image editor is generally supplied with a compiler that is capable of creating Windows 98 programs. It displays an enlarged view of your icon, cursor, or bitmap. This allows you to easily construct or alter the image. Once you have defined an icon, cursor, or bitmap, the image must be incorporated into the resource file associated with your program. Finally, before the image is used, it must be loaded by your program. This chapter discusses the necessary details required to accomplish this.

Defining Icons and Cursors

To use a custom icon and mouse cursor, you must first define their images using an image editor. Remember, you will need to make both a small and a standard-size icon. Actually, icons come in three sizes: small, standard, and large. The small icon is 16×16, the standard icon is 32×32, and the large icon is 48×48. However, the large icon is seldom used. In fact, most programmers mean the 32×32 icon when they use the term "large icon." All three sizes of icons are defined within a single icon file. Of course, you don't need to define the large icon. If one is ever needed, Windows will automatically enlarge the standard icon. All cursors are the same size, 32×32.

PORTABILITY: Windows 3.1 defines only the standard icon. You will want to add the small icon when porting to Windows 98.

For the examples that follow, you should call the file that holds your icons ICON.ICO. Be sure to create both the 32×32 and the 16×16 icons. Call the file that holds your cursor CURSOR.CUR. Figure 7-1 shows the icons and cursor used by the examples in this chapter.

Once you have defined the icon and cursor images, you will need to add an **ICON** and a **CURSOR** statement to your program's resource file. These statements have these general forms:

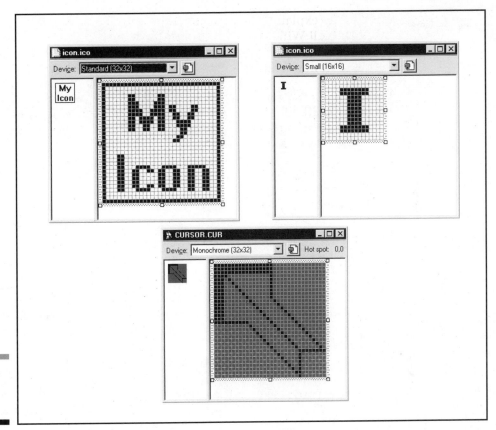

Custom icons
and cursor
Figure 7-1.

IconName ICON *filename*

CursorName CURSOR *filename*

Here, the *IconName* is the name that identifies the icon, and *CursorName* is
the name that identifies the cursor. These names are used by your program to
refer to the icon and cursor. The *filename* specifies the file that holds the
custom icon or cursor.

For the example program, you will need a resource file that contains the
following statements:

```
MyCursor CURSOR CURSOR.CUR
MyIcon ICON ICON.ICO
```

Loading Your Icons and Cursor

To use your custom icons and cursor, you must load them and assign their handles to the appropriate fields in the **WNDCLASSEX** structure before the window class is registered. To accomplish this, you can use the API functions **LoadIcon( )** and **LoadCursor( )**, which you learned about in Chapter 2. For example, the following loads the icon identified as **MyIcon** and the cursor called **MyCursor** and stores their handles in the appropriate fields of **WNDCLASSEX**.

```
wcl.hIcon = LoadIcon(hThisInst, "MyIcon"); /* standard icon */
wcl.hIconSm = NULL; /* use small icon in MyIcon */
wcl.hCursor = LoadCursor(hThisInst, "MyCursor"); /* load cursor */
```

Here, **hThisInst** is the handle of the current instance of the program. In the previous programs in this book, these functions have been used to load default icons and cursors. Here they will be used to load your custom icons and cursor.

You are probably wondering why **hIconSm** is assigned **NULL**. As you should recall, in previous programs the handle of the small icon is assigned to the **hIconSm** field of the **WNDCLASSEX** structure. However, if this value is **NULL**, then the program automatically uses the 16 × 16 icon defined in the file that holds the standard icon. Of course, you are free to specify a different icon resource for this icon if you like.

A Sample Program That Demonstrates Custom Icons and Cursor

The following program uses custom icons and cursor. The small icon is displayed in the main window's system menu box and in the program's entry in the task bar. The standard icon is displayed when you move your program to the desktop. The cursor will be used when the mouse pointer is over the window. That is, the shape of the mouse cursor will automatically change to the one defined by your program when the mouse moves over the program's window. It will automatically revert to its default shape when it moves off the program's window.

Remember, before you try to compile this program, you must define the custom icons and cursor using an image editor and then add these resources to the resource file associated with the program.

```
/* Demonstrate custom icons and mouse cursor. */

#include <windows.h>
#include <string.h>
#include <stdio.h>

LRESULT CALLBACK WindowFunc(HWND, UINT, WPARAM, LPARAM);

char szWinName[] = "MyWin"; /* name of window class */

int WINAPI WinMain(HINSTANCE hThisInst, HINSTANCE hPrevInst,
                   LPSTR lpszArgs, int nWinMode)
{
  HWND hwnd;
  MSG msg;
  WNDCLASSEX wcl;

  /* Define a window class. */
  wcl.cbSize = sizeof(WNDCLASSEX);

  wcl.hInstance = hThisInst; /* handle to this instance */
  wcl.lpszClassName = szWinName; /* window class name */
  wcl.lpfnWndProc = WindowFunc; /* window function */
  wcl.style = 0; /* default style */

  wcl.hIcon = LoadIcon(hThisInst, "MyIcon"); /* standard icon */
  wcl.hIconSm = NULL; /* use small icon in MyIcon */
  wcl.hCursor = LoadCursor(hThisInst, "MyCursor"); /* load cursor */

  wcl.lpszMenuName = NULL; /* no menu */
  wcl.cbClsExtra = 0; /* no extra */
  wcl.cbWndExtra = 0; /* information needed */

  /* Make the window white. */
  wcl.hbrBackground = (HBRUSH) GetStockObject(WHITE_BRUSH);

  /* Register the window class. */
  if(!RegisterClassEx(&wcl)) return 0;

  /* Now that a window class has been registered, a window
     can be created. */
  hwnd = CreateWindow(
    szWinName, /* name of window class */
    "Custom Icons and Cursor", /* title */
```

```
    WS_OVERLAPPEDWINDOW, /* window style - normal */
    CW_USEDEFAULT, /* X coordinate - let Windows decide */
    CW_USEDEFAULT, /* Y coordinate - let Windows decide */
    CW_USEDEFAULT, /* width - let Windows decide */
    CW_USEDEFAULT, /* height - let Windows decide */
    HWND_DESKTOP, /* no parent window */
    NULL, /* no override of class menu */
    hThisInst, /* handle of this instance of the program */
    NULL /* no additional arguments */
  );

  /* Display the window. */
  ShowWindow(hwnd, nWinMode);
  UpdateWindow(hwnd);

  /* Create the message loop. */
  while(GetMessage(&msg, NULL, 0, 0))
  {
    TranslateMessage(&msg); /* translate keyboard messages */
    DispatchMessage(&msg); /* return control to Windows 98 */
  }
  return msg.wParam;
}


/* This function is called by Windows 98 and is passed
   messages from the message queue.
*/
LRESULT CALLBACK WindowFunc(HWND hwnd, UINT message,
                            WPARAM wParam, LPARAM lParam)
{
  switch(message) {
    case WM_DESTROY: /* terminate the program */
      PostQuitMessage(0);
      break;
    default:
      /* Let Windows 98 process any messages not specified in
         the preceding switch statement. */
      return DefWindowProc(hwnd, message, wParam, lParam);
  }
  return 0;
}
```

The small custom icon is shown in Figure 7-2. (Of course, your custom icon may look different.) The custom mouse cursor will appear when you move the mouse over the window. Try this before continuing.

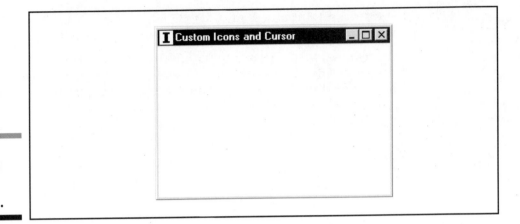

The small customized icon

Figure 7-2.

Using a Bitmap

A *bitmap* is a display object that contains a graphical image. The term comes from the fact that a bitmap contains a set of bits that defines the image. Since Windows is a graphics-based operating system, it makes sense that you can include graphics images in your applications. It is important to understand that you can draw graphics objects, such as lines, circles, and boxes, inside the client area of a window using the rich set of graphics functions contained in the Windows API. (These functions are discussed later in this book.) However, a bitmap, and the mechanism used to display one, are separate from those types of graphics. A bitmap is a self-contained graphical resource that your program utilizes as a single entity. A bitmap contains a bit-by-bit representation of the image that will ultimately be displayed on the screen. Put differently, a bitmap contains a complete image that your program displays in its totality.

A device-dependent bitmap (DDB) is tied to a specific device.

There are two general types of bitmaps supported by Windows 98: device-independent and device-dependent. Device-dependent bitmaps (DDB) are designed for use with a specific device. Device independent-bitmaps (DIB) are not tied to a specific device. Device-dependent bitmaps were initially the only type available in Windows. However, all versions of Windows since 3.0 have included device-independent bitmaps, too.

A device-independent bitmap (DIB) works with different types of devices.

DIBs are most valuable when you are creating a bitmap that will be used in environments other than the one in which it was created. For example, if you want to distribute a bitmap, a device-independent bitmap is the best way to do this. However, DDBs are still commonly used when a program needs to create a bitmap for its own, internal use. In fact, this is the main reason that

7

DDBs remain widely used. Also, Win32 provides various functions that allow you to convert between DDBs and DIBs, should you need to.

The organization of a DDB differs from that of a DIB. However, for the purposes of this chapter, the differences are not important. In fact, the binary format of a bitmap is seldom significant from the application's perspective because Windows provides high-level API functions that manage bitmaps—you will seldom need to "get your hands dirty" with their internals.

For the purposes of this chapter, we will be using device-dependent bitmaps because we will be focussing on bitmaps used by the program that creates them.

In general, to use a bitmap resource you must follow these three steps.

1. The bitmap resource must be specified within your program's resource file.
2. The bitmap resource must be loaded by your program.
3. The bitmap image must be displayed through a device context.

The next few sections describe the procedures necessary to accomplish these steps.

Creating a Bitmap Resource

Bitmap resources are not like the resources described in the preceding chapters, such as menus, dialog boxes, and controls. These resources are defined using textual statements in a resource file. Bitmaps are graphical images that must reside in special bitmap files. However, the bitmap file must still be referred to in your program's resource file.

Like icons and cursors, a bitmap resource is typically created using an image editor. Except for specialized bitmaps, such as icons and cursors, the size of a bitmap is arbitrary and under your control. Within reason, you can create bitmaps as large or as small as you like. To try the example that follows, your bitmap must be 64 × 64 pixels. Call your bitmap file BP.BMP. After you have defined your bitmap, create a resource file called BP.RC that contains this line:

```
MyBP1 BITMAP BP.BMP
```

As you can guess, the **BITMAP** statement defines a bitmap resource called **MyBP1** that is contained in the file BP.BMP. The general form of the **BITMAP** statement is

> *BitmapName* BITMAP *filename*

Here, *BitmapName* is the name that identifies the bitmap. This name is used by your program to refer to the bitmap. The *filename* is the name of the file that contains the bitmap.

Displaying a Bitmap

Once you have created a bitmap resource and included it in your application's resource file, you may display it as many times as you want. However, displaying a bitmap requires a little more work than does a custom cursor or icon. The following discussion explains the proper procedure.

Your main window receives a WM_CREATE message when it is first created.

Before you can use your bitmap, you must load it and store its handle. This can be done inside **WinMain( )** or when your application's main window receives a **WM_CREATE** message. A **WM_CREATE** message is sent to a window when it is first created, but before it is visible. **WM_CREATE** is a good place to perform any initializations that relate to (and are subordinate to) a window. Since the bitmap resource will be displayed within the client area of the main window, it makes sense to load the bitmap when the window receives the **WM_CREATE** message. This is the approach that will be used in this chapter.

To load the bitmap, use the **LoadBitmap( )** API function, whose prototype is shown here.

> HBITMAP LoadBitmap(HINSTANCE *hThisInst*, LPCSTR *lpszName*);

The current instance is specified in *hThisInst* and a pointer to the name of the bitmap as specified in the resource file is passed in *lpszName*. The function returns the handle to the bitmap, or **NULL** if an error occurs. For example:

```
HBITMAP hBit1; /* handle of bitmap */
/* ... */
hBit1 = LoadBitmap(hThisInst, "MyBP1"); /* load bitmap */
```

This fragment loads a bitmap called **MyBP1** and stores a handle to it in **hBit1**.

7

When it comes time to display the bitmap, your program must follow these steps.

1. Obtain the device context so that your program can output to the window.
2. Obtain an equivalent memory device context that will hold the bitmap until it is displayed. (A bitmap is held in memory until it is copied to your window.)
3. Select the bitmap into the memory device context.
4. Finally, copy the bitmap from the memory device context to the window device context. This causes the bitmap to actually be displayed.

To see how the preceding steps can be implemented, consider the following fragment. It causes a bitmap to be displayed each time the left mouse button is pressed. (It assumes that the bitmap has already been loaded.)

```
HDC DC, memDC;

/* ... */

case WM_LBUTTONDOWN:
  DC = GetDC(hwnd); /* get device context */
  memDC = CreateCompatibleDC(DC); /* create compatible DC */
  SelectObject(memDC, hBit1);
  BitBlt(DC, LOWORD(lParam), HIWORD(lParam), 64, 64,
        memDC, 0, 0, SRCCOPY); /* display image */
  ReleaseDC(hwnd, DC); /* free the device context */
  DeleteDC(memDC); /* free the memory context */
  break;
```

Let's examine this code step by step.

First, two device context handles are declared. **DC** will hold the current window device context as obtained by **GetDC( )**. The other, called **memDC**, will hold the device context of the memory that stores the bitmap until it is drawn in the window.

Inside the **case** statement, the window device context is obtained. This is necessary because the bitmap will be displayed in the client area of the window and no output can occur until your program is granted a device context. Next, a memory context is created that will hold the bitmap. This memory device context must be compatible with the window device context. The compatible memory device context is created using the **CreateCompatibleDC( )** API function. Its prototype is shown here.

HDC CreateCompatibleDC(HDC *hdc*);

A bitmap must be selected into a memory device context before it can be displayed.

This function returns a handle to a region of memory that is compatible with the device context of the window, specified by *hdc*. This memory will be used to construct an image before it is actually displayed. The function returns **NULL** if an error occurs.

Before a bitmap can be displayed, it must be selected into the memory device context using the **SelectObject( )** API function. Since there can be several bitmaps associated with an application, you must select the one you want to display before it can actually be output to the window. The **SelectObject( )** prototype is shown here:

HGDIOBJ SelectObject(HDC *hMdc*, HGDIOBJ *hObject*)

Here, *hMdc* is the memory device context that holds the object, and *hObject* is the handle of that object. The function returns the handle of the previously selected object, allowing it to be reselected later, if desired.

To actually display the object once it has been selected, use the **BitBlt( )** API function. This function copies a bitmap from one device context to another. Its prototype is shown here:

BitBlt stands for Bit-Block Transfer.

7

BOOL BitBlt(HDC *hDest*, int *X*, int *Y*, int *Width*, int *Height*,
　　　　　HDC *hSource*, int *Sourcex*, int *Sourcey*, DWORD *dwHow*);

Here, *hDest* is the handle of the target device context, and *X* and *Y* are the upper-left coordinates at which point the bitmap will be drawn. The width and height of the bitmap are specified in *Width* and *Height*. The *hSource* parameter contains the handle of the source device context, which in this case will be the memory context obtained using **CreateCompatibleDC( )**. *Sourcex* and *Sourcey* specify the upper-left coordinates in the bitmap. These values are usually 0. The value of *dwHow* determines how the bit-by-bit contents of the bitmap will actually be drawn on the screen. Some of the most common values are shown here:

Macro	Effect
DSTINVERT	Inverts the bits in the destination bitmap.
SRCAND	ANDs bitmap with current destination.

Macro	Effect
SRCCOPY	Copies bitmap as is, overwriting any preexisting output.
SRCPAINT	ORs bitmap with current destination.
SRCINVERT	XORs bitmap with current destination.

BitBlt( ) returns nonzero if successful and zero otherwise.

In the example, the call to **BitBlt( )** displays the entire bitmap at the destination location at which the left mouse button was pressed, copying the bitmap to the window.

After the bitmap is displayed, both device contexts are released. Only a device context obtained through a call to **GetDC( )** can be released using a call to **ReleaseDC( )**. To release the memory device context obtained using **CreateCompatibleDC( )**, you must use **DeleteDC( )**, which takes as its parameter the handle of the device context to release.

Deleting a Bitmap

A bitmap is a resource that must be removed before your application ends. To do this, your program must call **DeleteObject( )** when the bitmap is no longer needed or when a **WM_DESTROY** message is received. **DeleteObject( )** has this prototype:

```
BOOL DeleteObject(HGDIOBJ hObj);
```

Here, *hObj* is the handle to the object being deleted. The function returns nonzero if successful and zero on failure.

The Complete Bitmap Example Program

Here is a complete program that displays a bitmap each time you press the left mouse button. The bitmap is shown at the location pointed to by the mouse. Sample output is shown in Figure 7-3. Of course, your bitmap will look different than the one shown in the figure.

```
/*   Demonstrate a bitmap. */

#include <windows.h>
#include <string.h>
```

```
#include <stdio.h>

LRESULT CALLBACK WindowFunc(HWND, UINT, WPARAM, LPARAM);

char szWinName[] = "MyWin"; /* name of window class */

HBITMAP hBit1; /* handle of bitmap */
HINSTANCE hInst; /* handle to this instance */

int WINAPI WinMain(HINSTANCE hThisInst, HINSTANCE hPrevInst,
                   LPSTR lpszArgs, int nWinMode)
{
  HWND hwnd;
  MSG msg;
  WNDCLASSEX wcl;

  /* Define a window class. */
  wcl.cbSize = sizeof(WNDCLASSEX);

  wcl.hInstance = hThisInst; /* handle to this instance */
  wcl.lpszClassName = szWinName; /* window class name */
  wcl.lpfnWndProc = WindowFunc; /* window function */
  wcl.style = 0; /* default style */

  wcl.hIcon = LoadIcon(NULL, IDI_APPLICATION); /* standard icon */
  wcl.hIconSm = LoadIcon(NULL, IDI_WINLOGO); /* small icon */
  wcl.hCursor = LoadCursor(NULL, IDC_ARROW); /* cursor style */

  wcl.lpszMenuName = NULL; /* no menu */
  wcl.cbClsExtra = 0; /* no extra */
  wcl.cbWndExtra = 0; /* information needed */

  /* Make the window white. */
  wcl.hbrBackground = (HBRUSH) GetStockObject(WHITE_BRUSH);

  /* Register the window class. */
  if(!RegisterClassEx(&wcl)) return 0;

  hInst = hThisInst; /* save instance handle */

  /* Now that a window class has been registered, a window
     can be created. */
```

```
  hwnd = CreateWindow(
    szWinName, /* name of window class */
    "Custom Bitmap", /* title */
    WS_OVERLAPPEDWINDOW, /* window style - normal */
    CW_USEDEFAULT, /* X coordinate - let Windows decide */
    CW_USEDEFAULT, /* Y coordinate - let Windows decide */
    CW_USEDEFAULT, /* width - let Windows decide */
    CW_USEDEFAULT, /* height - let Windows decide */
    HWND_DESKTOP, /* no parent window */
    NULL, /* no override of class menu */
    hThisInst, /* handle of this instance of the program */
    NULL /* no additional arguments */
  );

  /* Display the window. */
  ShowWindow(hwnd, nWinMode);
  UpdateWindow(hwnd);

  /* Create the message loop. */
  while(GetMessage(&msg, NULL, 0, 0))
  {
    TranslateMessage(&msg); /* translate keyboard messages */
    DispatchMessage(&msg); /* return control to Windows 98 */
  }
  return msg.wParam;
}


/* This function is called by Windows 98 and is passed
   messages from the message queue.
*/
LRESULT CALLBACK WindowFunc(HWND hwnd, UINT message,
                            WPARAM wParam, LPARAM lParam)
{
  HDC DC, memDC;

  switch(message) {
    case WM_CREATE: /* load the bitmap */
      hBit1 = LoadBitmap(hInst, "MyBP1"); /* load bitmap */
      break;
    case WM_LBUTTONDOWN:
      DC = GetDC(hwnd); /* get device context */
      memDC = CreateCompatibleDC(DC); /* create compatible DC */
```

```
            SelectObject(memDC, hBit1);
            BitBlt(DC, LOWORD(lParam), HIWORD(lParam), 64, 64,
                   memDC, 0, 0, SRCCOPY); /* display image */
            ReleaseDC(hwnd, DC); /* free the device context */
            DeleteDC(memDC); /* free the memory context */
            break;
         case WM_DESTROY: /* terminate the program */
            DeleteObject(hBit1); /* remove the bitmap */
            PostQuitMessage(0);
            break;
         default:
            /* Let Windows 98 process any messages not specified in
               the preceding switch statement. */
            return DefWindowProc(hwnd, message, wParam, lParam);
      }
      return 0;
}
```

7

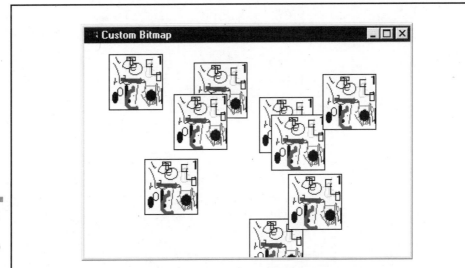

Sample output
using the
custom bitmap

Figure 7-3.

XORing an Image to a Window

As explained, **BltBlt( )** can copy the bitmap contained in one device context into another device context a number of different ways. For example, if you specify **SRCPAINT**, the image is ORed with the destination. Using **SCRAND** causes the bitmap to be ANDed with the destination. Perhaps the most interesting way to copy the contents of one DC to another uses **SCRINVERT**. This method XORs the source with the destination. There are two reasons this is particularly valuable.

First, XORing an image onto a window guarantees that the image will be visible. It doesn't matter what color or colors the source image or the destination use, an XORed image is always visible. Second, XORing the image to the same destination a second time removes the image and restores the destination to its original condition. As you might guess, XORing is an efficient way to temporarily display and then remove an image from a window without disturbing its original contents.

To see the effects of XORing an image to a window, insert the following cases into **WindowFunc( )** in the first bitmap program.

```
case WM_RBUTTONDOWN:
  DC = GetDC(hwnd);
  memDC = CreateCompatibleDC(DC);
  SelectObject(memDC, hBit1);

  /* XOR image onto the window */
  BitBlt(DC, LOWORD(lParam), HIWORD(lParam), 64, 64,
        memDC, 0, 0, SRCINVERT);

  ReleaseDC(hwnd, DC);
  DeleteDC(memDC);
  break;
case WM_RBUTTONUP:
  DC = GetDC(hwnd);
  memDC = CreateCompatibleDC(DC);
  SelectObject(memDC, hBit1);

  /* XOR image onto the window a second time */
  BitBlt(DC, LOWORD(lParam), HIWORD(lParam), 64, 64,
```

```
        memDC, 0, 0, SRCINVERT);
ReleaseDC(hwnd, DC);
DeleteDC(memDC);
break;
```

The code works like this. Each time the right mouse button is pressed, the bitmap is XORed to the window starting at the location of the mouse pointer. This causes an inverted image of the bitmap to be displayed. When the button is released, the image is XORed a second time, causing the bitmap to be removed and the previous contents to be restored.

Using Multiple Bitmaps

Before moving on, one last point must be emphasized: it is possible (indeed, easy) to use more than one bitmap within your program. Your application can include as many bitmaps as necessary. Whenever you need to display one, simply load the desired bitmap and display it using the method described in the previous section.

To illustrate how easy it is to use multiple bitmaps, let's add another one to the preceding program. First, add this line to your resource file:

```
MyBP2 BITMAP BP2.BMP
```

Then, using an image editor, create a second 64 × 64 bitmap. When you are done, save the second bitmap in a file called BP2.BMP.

Next, add a second bitmap handle to your program called **hBit2**. Also, add this line to the **WM_CREATE** message handler to load the second bitmap:

```
hBit2 = LoadBitmap(hThisInst, "MyBP2"); /* load 2nd bitmap */
```

Next, add this **case** to the preceding program. It will cause the second bitmap to be displayed each time the right mouse button is pressed.

7

```
case WM_RBUTTONDOWN: /* display second bitmap */
  DC = GetDC(hwnd); /* get device context */
  memDC = CreateCompatibleDC(DC); /* create compatible DC */
  SelectObject(memDC, hBit2);
  BitBlt(DC, LOWORD(lParam), HIWORD(lParam), 64, 64,
         memDC, 0, 0, SRCCOPY); /* display image */
  ReleaseDC(hwnd, DC); /* free the device context */
  DeleteDC(memDC); /* free the memory context */
  break;
```

Finally, add this line to the **WM_DESTROY case**:

```
DeleteObject(hBit2);
```

After making these changes, your program should look like the one shown here. To display the first bitmap, press the left mouse button. To display the second bitmap, press the right mouse button.

```
/*  Demonstrate two bitmaps. */

#include <windows.h>
#include <string.h>
#include <stdio.h>

LRESULT CALLBACK WindowFunc(HWND, UINT, WPARAM, LPARAM);

char szWinName[] = "MyWin"; /* name of window class */

HBITMAP hBit1, hBit2; /* handle of bitmaps */
HINSTANCE hInst; /* handle to this instance */

int WINAPI WinMain(HINSTANCE hThisInst, HINSTANCE hPrevInst,
                   LPSTR lpszArgs, int nWinMode)
{
  HWND hwnd;
  MSG msg;
  WNDCLASSEX wcl;

  /* Define a window class. */
  wcl.cbSize = sizeof(WNDCLASSEX);

  wcl.hInstance = hThisInst; /* handle to this instance */
  wcl.lpszClassName = szWinName; /* window class name */
  wcl.lpfnWndProc = WindowFunc; /* window function */
```

```
wcl.style = 0; /* default style */

wcl.hIcon = LoadIcon(NULL, IDI_APPLICATION); /* standard icon */
wcl.hIconSm = LoadIcon(NULL, IDI_WINLOGO); /* small icon */
wcl.hCursor = LoadCursor(NULL, IDC_ARROW); /* cursor style */

wcl.lpszMenuName = NULL; /* no menu */
wcl.cbClsExtra = 0; /* no extra */
wcl.cbWndExtra = 0; /* information needed */

/* Make the window white. */
wcl.hbrBackground = (HBRUSH) GetStockObject(WHITE_BRUSH);

hInst = hThisInst; /* save instance handle */

/* Register the window class. */
if(!RegisterClassEx(&wcl)) return 0;

/* Now that a window class has been registered, a window
   can be created. */
hwnd = CreateWindow(
  szWinName, /* name of window class */
  "Two Custom Bitmaps", /* title */
  WS_OVERLAPPEDWINDOW, /* window style - normal */
  CW_USEDEFAULT, /* X coordinate - let Windows decide */
  CW_USEDEFAULT, /* Y coordinate - let Windows decide */
  CW_USEDEFAULT, /* width - let Windows decide */
  CW_USEDEFAULT, /* height - let Windows decide */
  HWND_DESKTOP, /* no parent window */
  NULL, /* no override of class menu */
  hThisInst, /* handle of this instance of the program */
  NULL /* no additional arguments */
);

/* Display the window. */
ShowWindow(hwnd, nWinMode);
UpdateWindow(hwnd);

/* Create the message loop. */
while(GetMessage(&msg, NULL, 0, 0))
{
  TranslateMessage(&msg); /* translate keyboard messages */
  DispatchMessage(&msg); /* return control to Windows 98 */
}
return msg.wParam;
```

7

```
}

/* This function is called by Windows 98 and is passed
   messages from the message queue.
*/
LRESULT CALLBACK WindowFunc(HWND hwnd, UINT message,
                            WPARAM wParam, LPARAM lParam)
{
  HDC DC, memDC;

  switch(message) {
    case WM_CREATE: /* load the bitmaps */
      hBit1 = LoadBitmap(hInst, "MyBP1"); /* load 1st bitmap */
      hBit2 = LoadBitmap(hInst, "MyBP2"); /* load 2nd bitmap */
      break;
    case WM_LBUTTONDOWN: /* display first bitmap */
      DC = GetDC(hwnd); /* get device context */
      memDC = CreateCompatibleDC(DC); /* create compatible DC */
      SelectObject(memDC, hBit1);
      BitBlt(DC, LOWORD(lParam), HIWORD(lParam), 64, 64,
             memDC, 0, 0, SRCCOPY); /* display image */
      ReleaseDC(hwnd, DC); /* free the device context */
      DeleteDC(memDC); /* free the memory context */
      break;
    case WM_RBUTTONDOWN: /* display second bitmap */
      DC = GetDC(hwnd); /* get device context */
      memDC = CreateCompatibleDC(DC); /* create compatible DC */
      SelectObject(memDC, hBit2);
      BitBlt(DC, LOWORD(lParam), HIWORD(lParam), 64, 64,
             memDC, 0, 0, SRCCOPY); /* display image */
      ReleaseDC(hwnd, DC); /* free the device context */
      DeleteDC(memDC); /* free the memory context */
      break;
    case WM_DESTROY: /* terminate the program */
      DeleteObject(hBit1); /* remove the bitmaps */
      DeleteObject(hBit2);
      PostQuitMessage(0);
      break;
    default:
      /* Let Windows 98 process any messages not specified in
         the preceding switch statement. */
      return DefWindowProc(hwnd, message, wParam, lParam);
  }
  return 0;
}
```

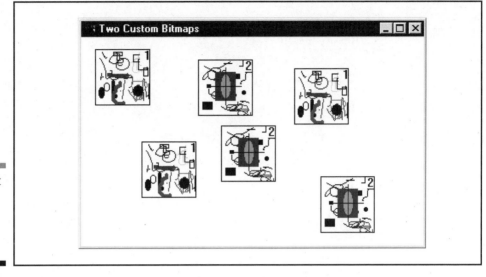

Sample output from the dual-bitmap program is shown in Figure 7-4.

7

Using LoadImage( )

Throughout this book we have been using **LoadIcon( )** and **LoadCursor( )** to load the icons and cursors used by the application examples. As you have just seen, you can use **LoadBitmap( )** to load a bitmapped image. These are the standard functions used to accomplish these tasks since Windows was first invented. They are still perfectly acceptable functions to use. However, Windows 98 includes a new function called **LoadImage( )** that provides a useful alternative. **LoadImage( )** is a more flexible function that can be used to load icons, cursors, and bitmaps of any size and provides more detailed control over how these items are loaded. For example, you can use it to load a small custom icon that is not part of the file specified by the large icon. While we won't need the fine-grained control that **LoadImage( )** offers for the examples in this book, it is a function that you may find useful for your programs. For this reason, it is examined here.

PORTABILITY: **LoadImage( )** is not available for Windows 3.1 or versions of Windows NT prior to 4.0.

LoadImage( ) has the following prototype:

HANDLE LoadImage(HINSTANCE *hThisInst*, LPCSTR *lpszName*,
 UINT *what*, int *width*, int *height*, UINT *how*);

The current instance handle is specified in *hThisInst*. A pointer to the name of the resource being loaded is passed in *lpszName*. The value of *what* determines what type of image is being loaded. It must be one of the following:

IMAGE_ICON   IMAGE_CURSOR   IMAGE_BITMAP

The width and the height of the image are passed in *width* and *height*. The *how* parameter determines how the image is loaded. It can be zero if no options are required. Two commonly used values are

LR_DEFAULTSIZE   LR_LOADFROMFILE

If **LR_DEFAULTSIZE** is specified, and if *width* and *height* are zero, the standard size of an icon or cursor is used for the width and height. If **LR_DEFAULTSIZE** is not specified and *width* and *height* are zero, then the actual size of the image determines its width and height. If **LR_LOADFROMFILE** is specified, then *lpszName* specifies the name of a file that contains the image rather than the name of the resource, itself.

LoadImage( ) returns a handle to the image if successful, or **NULL** if an error occurs.

To try **LoadImage( )**, substitute the following lines into the preceding bitmap example inside the **WM_CREATE** handler:

```
hBit1 = (HBITMAP)LoadImage(hInst, "MyBP1", IMAGE_BITMAP, 64, 64, 0);
hBit2 = (HBITMAP)LoadImage(hInst, "MyBP2", IMAGE_BITMAP, 64, 64, 0);
```

As you will see, the program works the same as before. As an experiment, try changing the dimensions. For example, try using 32×16 and observe the results. As you will see, only part of the bitmaps are loaded.

As stated, while **LoadImage( )** gives you greater control over the way images are loaded by your program, the examples in this book will not make further use of it since they do not require this extended control.

7

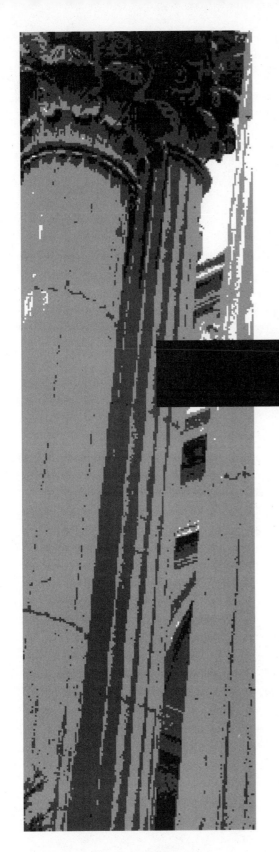

CHAPTER 8

Working with Text and Solving the Repaint Problem

For the past several chapters, most output has been handled using message and dialog boxes—the client area of the window has been ignored. However, this chapter returns to the client area and explores various aspects of how Windows 98 manages text. Also, some important techniques are developed that make it easier for you to repaint the window when it has been overwritten. The chapter concludes with a discussion of the way additional text fonts can be used by your application.

As with most other aspects of the Windows 98 environment, you, the programmer, have virtually unlimited control over the way text is displayed and managed within the client area of a window. Given this fact, it is far beyond the scope of this chapter to cover all aspects of text output using Windows. However, you will be able to easily explore other aspects of text manipulation after understanding the basics introduced here.

This chapter begins with a discussion of the window coordinate system and how text is mapped to it. Then several API functions are described that help you control and manage text output to the client area of a window.

Window Coordinates

Window coordinates are specified in logical units, which by default are equal to pixels.

As you know, **TextOut( )** is Windows' main text output function. It displays a string at the specified coordinates, which are always relative to the window. Therefore, where a window is positioned on the screen has no effect upon the coordinates passed to **TextOut( )**. By default, the upper-left corner of the client area of the window is location 0,0. The *X* value increases to the right, and the *Y* value increases downward.

So far, we have been using window coordinates for **TextOut( )** and for positioning various elements within a dialog box without any specific mention of what those coordinates actually refer to. Now is the time to clarify a few details. First, the coordinates that are specified in **TextOut( )** are *logical coordinates*. That is, the units used by **TextOut( )** (and other window display functions, including the graphics functions described in the next chapter) are *logical units*. Windows maps these logical units onto pixels when output is actually displayed. The reason that we haven't had to worry about this distinction is that, by default, logical units are the same as pixels. In other words, by default, logical units are pixels. It is important to understand, however, that different mapping modes can be selected in which this convenient default will not be the case.

Setting the Text and Background Color

By default, when you output text to the window using **TextOut( )**, it is shown as black text against the current background. You can determine both the color of the text and the background color using the API functions **SetTextColor( )** and **SetBkColor( )**, whose prototypes are shown here.

COLORREF SetTextColor(HDC *hdc*, COLORREF *color*);

COLORREF SetBkColor(HDC *hdc*, COLORREF *color*);

The **SetTextColor( )** function sets the current text color of the device associated with *hdc* to that specified by *color* (or closest color that the device is capable of displaying). The **SetBkcolor( )** function sets the current text background color to that specified by *color* (or nearest possible). For both functions, the previous color setting is returned. If an error occurs, then the value **CLR_INVALID** is returned.

COLORREF
defines a color.

Colors are specified as values of type **COLORREF**, which is a 32-bit integer. Windows allows colors to be specified in three different ways. First, and by far most common, is as an RGB (red, green, blue) value. In an RGB value, the relative intensities of the three colors are combined to produce the actual color. The second way a color can be specified is as an index into a logical palette. The third is as an RGB value relative to a palette. In this chapter, only the first way will be discussed.

8

A 32-bit integer value that holds an RGB color is passed to either **SetTextColor( )** or **SetBkColor( )** using the following encoding:

Byte	Color
byte 0 (low-order byte)	red
byte 1	green
byte 2	blue
byte 3 (high-order byte)	must be zero

Each color in an RGB value is in the range 0 through 255, with 0 being the lowest intensity and 255 being the brightest intensity. For example, the following long integer produces the color bright magenta:

00   255   00   255

Although you are free to manually construct a **COLORREF** value, Windows defines the macro **RGB( )** that does this for you. It has this general form:

COLORREF RGB(int *red*, int *green*, int *blue*);

Here, *red, green,* and *blue* must be values in the range 0 through 255. Therefore, to create magenta, use **RGB(255, 0, 255)**. To create white, use **RGB(255, 255, 255)**. To create the color black, use **RGB(0, 0, 0)**. To create other colors, you combine the three basic colors in varying intensities. For example, this creates a light aqua: **RGB(0, 100, 100)**. You can experiment to determine which colors are best for your application.

Setting the Background Display Mode

You can control the way that the background is affected when text is displayed on the screen by using the **SetBkMode( )** API function, whose prototype is shown here:

int SetBkMode(HDC *hdc*, int *mode*);

This function determines what happens to the current background color when text (and some other types of output) is displayed. The handle of the device context affected is specified by *hdc*. The background mode is specified in *mode* and must be one of these two macros: **OPAQUE** or **TRANSPARENT**. The function returns the previous setting or 0 if an error occurs.

If *mode* is **OPAQUE**, then each time text is output, the window's background is changed to that of the current text background color. If *mode* is **TRANSPARENT**, then the background is not altered. In this case, any effects of a call to **SetBkColor( )** are effectively ignored. By default, the background mode is **OPAQUE**.

Obtaining the Text Metrics

As you know from Chapter 3, characters are not all the same dimension. That is, in Windows, most text fonts are proportional. Therefore, the character "i" is not as wide as the character "w". Also, the height of each character and of descenders varies among fonts. In addition, the amount of space between horizontal lines is also changeable. That these (and other) attributes are variable would not be of too much consequence except for the fact that Windows demands that you, the programmer, manually manage virtually all text output.

Windows provides only the minimal support for text output to the client area of a window. The main output function is **TextOut( )**. This function will only display a string of text beginning at a specified location. It will not format output or even automatically perform a carriage return/linefeed sequence, for example. Instead, managing output to the client window is completely your job.

The fact that the size of each font may be different (and that fonts may be changed while your program is executing) implies that there must some way to determine the dimensions and various other attributes of the currently selected font. For example, the ability to write one line of text after another implies that you have some way of knowing how tall the font is and how many pixels are between lines. The API function that obtains information about the current font is called **GetTextMetrics( )**, and it has this prototype:

BOOL GetTextMetrics(HDC *hdc*, LPTEXTMETRIC *lpTAttrib*);

Here, *hdc* is the handle of the output device, which is generally obtained using **GetDC( )** or **BeginPaint( )**, and *lpTAttrib* is a pointer to a structure of type **TEXTMETRIC** which will, upon return, contain the text metrics for the currently selected font. The **TEXTMETRIC** structure is defined as shown here:

```
typedef struct tagTEXTMETRIC
{
  LONG tmHeight; /* total height of font */
  LONG tmAscent; /* height above base line */
```

8

```
  LONG tmDescent; /* length of descenders */
  LONG tmInternalLeading; /* space above characters */
  LONG tmExternalLeading; /* blank space between rows */
  LONG tmAveCharWidth; /* average width */
  LONG tmMaxCharWidth; /* maximum width */
  LONG tmWeight; /* weight */
  LONG tmOverhang; /* extra width added to special fonts */
  LONG tmDigitizedAspectX; /* horizontal aspect */
  LONG tmDigitizedAspectY; /* vertical aspect */
  BYTE tmFirstChar; /* first character in font */
  BYTE tmLastChar; /* last character in font */
  BYTE tmDefaultChar; /* default character */
  BYTE tmBreakChar; /* character used to break words */
  BYTE tmItalic; /* non-zero if italic */
  BYTE tmUnderlined; /* non-zero if underlined */
  BYTE tmStruckOut; /* non-zero if struckout */
  BYTE tmPitchAndFamily; /* pitch and family of font */
  BYTE tmCharSet; /* character set identifier */
} TEXTMERIC;
```

The vertical distance between lines of text is **tmHeight** plus **tmExternal-Leading**.

While most of the values obtained by this function will not be used in this chapter, two are very important because they are required to compute the vertical distance between lines of text. This value is needed if you want to output more than one line of text to a window. Unlike a console-based application in which there is only one font and its size is fixed, there may be several Windows fonts and they may vary in size. Specifically, each font defines the height of its characters and the amount of space required between lines. This means that it is not possible to know in advance the vertical (*Y*) coordinate of the next line of text. To determine where the next line of text will begin, you must call **GetTextMetrics( )** to acquire two values: the character height and the amount of space between lines. These values are given in the **tmHeight** and **tmExternalLeading** fields, respectively. By adding together these two values, you obtain the number of vertical units between lines.

REMEMBER: The value **tmExternalLeading** contains, in essence, the number of vertical units that should be left blank between lines of text. This value is separate from the height of the font. Thus, both values are needed to compute where the next line of text will begin. You will see this applied shortly.

IN DEPTH

NEWTEXTMETRIC and NEWTEXTMETRICEX

There is an enhanced version of **TEXTMETRIC** called
NEWTEXTMETRIC. NEWTEXTMETRIC is exactly the same as
TEXTMETRIC except that it adds four additional fields at the end.
These fields provide support for TrueType fonts. (TrueType fonts provide
superior scalability features.) The new fields in **NEWTEXTMETRIC** are
shown here.

```
DWORD ntmFlags; /* indicates style of font */
UINT ntmSizeEM; /* size of an em */
UINT ntmCellHeight; /* font height */
UINT ntmAvgWidth; /* average character width */
```

Recently, an extension to **NEWTEXTMETRIC**, called
NEWTEXTMETRICEX, has been added to Win32. It is defined like this.

```
typedef struct tagNEWTEXTMETRICEX
{
  NEWTEXTMETRICA ntmTm;
  FONTSIGNATURE ntmFontSig; /* font signature */
} NEWTEXTMETRICEX;
```

As you can see, it includes all of **NEWTEXTMETRIC** and adds the
structure **FONTSIGNATURE**, which contains information relating to
Unicode and code pages.

For the purposes of this chapter, none of these fields added by
NEWTEXTMETRIC or **NEWTEXTMETRICEX** are needed. However,
they may be of value to applications that you create. You should consult
an API reference for details.

Computing the Length of a String

Windows does not automatically maintain a text cursor or keep track of your
current output location. This means that if you wish to display one string

after another on the same line, you will need to remember where the previous output left off. This implies that you must have some way of knowing the length of a string in logical units. Because characters in most fonts are not the same size, it is not possible to know the length of a string, in logical units, by simply knowing how many characters it contains. That is, the result returned by **strlen( )** is not meaningful to managing output to a window because characters are of differing widths. To solve this problem, Windows 98 includes the API function **GetTextExtentPoint32( )**, whose prototype is shown here.

BOOL GetTextExtentPoint32(HDC *hdc*, LPCSTR *lpszString*,
int *len*, LPSIZE *lpSize*);

Here, *hdc* is the handle of the output device. The string whose length you want is pointed to by *lpszString*. The number of characters in the string is specified in *len*. The width and height of the string, in logical units, is returned in the **SIZE** structure pointed to by *lpSize*. The **SIZE** structure is defined as shown here:

```
typedef struct tagSIZE {
  LONG cx; /* width */
  LONG cy; /* height */
} SIZE;
```

Upon return from a call to **GetTextExtentPoint32( )**, the **cx** field will contain the length of the string. Therefore, this value can be used to determine the starting point for the next string to be displayed if you want to continue on from where the previous output left off.

PORTABILITY: **GetTextExtentPoint32( )** replaces the older **GetTextExtentPoint( )** function. Be aware of this when converting programs from Windows 3.1.

Obtaining the System Metrics

Although Windows maintains and automatically translates logical coordinates into pixels, sometimes you will want to know the resolution of the monitor being used to run your application. To obtain this and other information, use the **GetSystemMetrics( )** API function, whose prototype is shown here:

    int GetSystemMetrics(int *what*);

Here, *what* specifies the value that you want to obtain. **GetSystemMetrics( )** can obtain many different values. The values for screen coordinates are returned in pixel units. Here are the macros for some common values.

Value	Metric Obtained
SM_CXFULLSCREEN	Width of maximized client area.
SM_CYFULLSCREEN	Height of maximized client area.
SM_CXICON	Width of standard icon.
SM_CYICON	Height of standard icon.
SM_CXSMICON	Width of small icon.
SM_CYSMICON	Height of small icon.
SM_CXSCREEN	Width of entire screen.
SM_CYSCREEN	Height of entire screen.

8

A Short Text Demonstration

Now that you have learned about some of Windows 98's text functions, a short demonstration of these features will be useful. Here is a program that does just that.

```
/* Demonstrate Text Output */

#include <windows.h>
#include <string.h>
#include <stdio.h>
#include "text.h"

LRESULT CALLBACK WindowFunc(HWND, UINT, WPARAM, LPARAM);

char szWinName[] = "MyWin"; /* name of window class */

char str[255]; /* holds output strings */
```

```
int X=0, Y=0; /* current output location */
int maxX, maxY; /* screen dimensions */

int WINAPI WinMain(HINSTANCE hThisInst, HINSTANCE hPrevInst,
                   LPSTR lpszArgs, int nWinMode)
{
  HWND hwnd;
  MSG msg;
  WNDCLASSEX wcl;
  HACCEL hAccel;

  /* Define a window class. */
  wcl.cbSize = sizeof(WNDCLASSEX);

  wcl.hInstance = hThisInst; /* handle to this instance */
  wcl.lpszClassName = szWinName; /* window class name */
  wcl.lpfnWndProc = WindowFunc; /* window function */
  wcl.style = 0; /* default style */

  wcl.hIcon = LoadIcon(NULL, IDI_APPLICATION); /* standard icon */
  wcl.hIconSm = LoadIcon(NULL, IDI_APPLICATION); /* small icon */
  wcl.hCursor = LoadCursor(NULL, IDC_ARROW); /* cursor style */

  wcl.lpszMenuName = "MyMenu"; /* main menu */
  wcl.cbClsExtra = 0; /* no extra */
  wcl.cbWndExtra = 0; /* information needed */

  /* Make the window white. */
  wcl.hbrBackground = (HBRUSH) GetStockObject(WHITE_BRUSH);

  /* Register the window class. */
  if(!RegisterClassEx(&wcl)) return 0;

  /* Now that a window class has been registered, a window
     can be created. */
  hwnd = CreateWindow(
    szWinName, /* name of window class */
    "Fun with Text", /* title */
    WS_OVERLAPPEDWINDOW, /* window style - normal */
    CW_USEDEFAULT, /* X coordinate - let Windows decide */
    CW_USEDEFAULT, /* Y coordinate - let Windows decide */
    CW_USEDEFAULT, /* width - let Windows decide */
    CW_USEDEFAULT, /* height - let Windows decide */
    HWND_DESKTOP, /* no handle of parent window */
    NULL, /* no override of class menu */
```

```
      hThisInst, /* handle of this instance of the program */
      NULL /* no additional arguments */
    );

    /* Load accelerators. */
    hAccel = LoadAccelerators(hThisInst, "MyMenu");

    /* Display the window. */
    ShowWindow(hwnd, nWinMode);
    UpdateWindow(hwnd);

    /* Create the message loop. */
    while(GetMessage(&msg, NULL, 0, 0))
    {
      if(!TranslateAccelerator(hwnd, hAccel, &msg)) {
        TranslateMessage(&msg); /* translate keyboard messages */
        DispatchMessage(&msg); /* return control to Windows 98 */
      }
    }
    return msg.wParam;
}

/* This function is called by Windows 98 and is passed
   messages from the message queue.
*/
LRESULT CALLBACK WindowFunc(HWND hwnd, UINT message,
                            WPARAM wParam, LPARAM lParam)
{
  HDC hdc;
  TEXTMETRIC tm;
  SIZE size;
  int response;

  switch(message) {
    case WM_CREATE:
      /* get screen coordinates */
      maxX = GetSystemMetrics(SM_CXSCREEN);
      maxY = GetSystemMetrics(SM_CYSCREEN);
      break;
    case WM_COMMAND:
      switch(LOWORD(wParam)) {
        case IDM_SHOW:
          hdc = GetDC(hwnd); /* get device context */

          /* set text color to black */
```

8

```
   SetTextColor(hdc, RGB(0, 0, 0));
   /* set background color to turquoise */
   SetBkColor(hdc, RGB(0, 255, 255));

   /* get text metrics */
   GetTextMetrics(hdc, &tm);

   sprintf(str, "The font is %ld pixels high.",
           tm.tmHeight);
   TextOut(hdc, X, Y, str, strlen(str)); /* output string */
   Y = Y + tm.tmHeight + tm.tmExternalLeading; /* next line */

   strcpy(str, "This is on the next line. ");
   TextOut(hdc, X, Y, str, strlen(str)); /* output string */

   /* compute length of a string */
   GetTextExtentPoint32(hdc, str, strlen(str), &size);
   sprintf(str, "Previous string is %ld units long",
           size.cx);
   X = size.cx; /* advance to end of previous string */
   TextOut(hdc, X, Y, str, strlen(str));
   Y = Y + tm.tmHeight + tm.tmExternalLeading; /* next line */

   X = 0; /* reset X */

   sprintf(str, "Screen dimensions: %d %d", maxX, maxY);
   TextOut(hdc, X, Y, str, strlen(str));
   Y = Y + tm.tmHeight + tm.tmExternalLeading; /* next line */

   ReleaseDC(hwnd, hdc); /* Release DC */
   break;
case IDM_RESET:
  X = Y = 0;
  break;
case IDM_EXIT:
  response = MessageBox(hwnd, "Quit the Program?",
                        "Exit", MB_YESNO);
  if(response == IDYES) PostQuitMessage(0);
  break;
case IDM_HELP:
  MessageBox(hwnd, "F2: Display\nF3: Reset", "Help",
             MB_OK);
  break;
```

```
      }
      break;
    case WM_DESTROY: /* terminate the program */
      PostQuitMessage(0);
      break;
    default:
      /* Let Windows 98 process any messages not specified in
      the preceding switch statement. */
      return DefWindowProc(hwnd, message, wParam, lParam);
  }
  return 0;
}
```

This program requires the following resource file:

```
#include <windows.h>
#include "text.h"

MyMenu MENU
{
  POPUP "&Demo Text" {
    MENUITEM "&Show\tF2", IDM_SHOW
    MENUITEM "&Reset\tF3", IDM_RESET
    MENUITEM "E&xit\tCtrl+X", IDM_EXIT
  }
  MENUITEM "&Help", IDM_HELP
}


MyMenu ACCELERATORS
{
  VK_F2, IDM_SHOW, VIRTKEY
  VK_F3, IDM_RESET, VIRTKEY
  VK_F1, IDM_HELP, VIRTKEY
  "^X", IDM_EXIT
}
```

It also requires the header file TEXT.H, which is shown here:

```
#define IDM_SHOW      100
#define IDM_RESET     101
#define IDM_HELP      102
#define IDM_EXIT      104
```

Enter these files and compile and run the program. Each time you select Show from the main menu, you will cause a few lines of text to be displayed. The text will be black and the background is turquoise. Sample output is shown in Figure 8-1.

When the window is first created and **WM_CREATE** is received, the global integers **maxX** and **maxY** are initialized to the coordinates of the screen using the **GetSystemMetrics( )** function. While these values serve no purpose in this program, they will be used in later examples.

Notice that the program declares two global variables called **X** and **Y** and initializes both to 0. These variables will contain the current window location at which text will be displayed. They will be continually updated by the program after each output sequence.

The interesting part of this program is mostly contained within the **WM_COMMAND** message. Let's examine it closely, beginning with the **IDM_SHOW** case. Each time an **IDM_SHOW** message is received, a device context is obtained. Then the text color is set to black and the background color is set to turquoise. Since the device context is obtained each time an **IDM_SHOW** message is received, the colors must be set each time. That is, they cannot be set once, at the start of the program, for example.

After the colors have been set, the text metrics are obtained. Next, the first line of text is output. Notice that it is constructed using **sprintf( )** and then actually output using **TextOut( )**. As you know from earlier in this book,

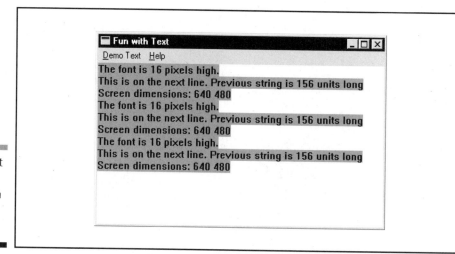

Sample output from the text demonstration program

Figure 8-1.

neither **TextOut( )** nor any other API function performs text formatting, so it is up to you, the programmer, to construct your output first and then display it using **TextOut( )**. After the string is displayed, the **Y** coordinate is advanced to the next line by applying the formula developed earlier.

The program continues by next outputting the line "This is on the next line." Then, before that string is overwritten by the next call to **sprintf( )**, its length is computed using a call to **GetTextExtentPoint32( )**. This value is then used to advance the **X** coordinate to the end of the line before the next line is printed. Notice that here, the **Y** coordinate is unchanged. This causes the next string to be displayed immediately after the previous one. Before continuing, the program advances **Y** to the next line and resets **X** to 0, which is the leftmost coordinate. This causes subsequent output to once again be started at the beginning of the next line.

Finally, the screen dimensions are displayed, and the **Y** coordinate is advanced to the next line.

Each time you select Show, the text is displayed lower in the window and does not overwrite the preceding text. Instead, each set of lines is displayed beneath the previous one.

To start over, select Reset. This causes the coordinates to be reset to 0,0. However, it does not erase what is already in the window.

Solving the Repaint Problem

8

While the preceding program demonstrates some text and system functions, it reintroduces a fundamental problem that was first discussed in Chapter 3. The problem is this: when you run the program, display some text, and then overlay the window with another, the text is lost. When the window is then redisplayed, the part of the text that was covered will be missing. Of course, the reason for this is that each program must repaint its window when it receives a **WM_PAINT** message, and the preceding program does not do this. However, this raises the larger question: What mechanism should you use to restore the contents of a window that has been overwritten? As mentioned earlier, there are three basic methods. To review: First, you can regenerate the output if that output is created by some computational method. Second, you can store a record of display events and "replay" those events. Third, you can maintain a virtual window and simply copy the contents of the virtual window each time a **WM_PAINT** message is received. The most general of these is, of course, the third, and this is the method that will be developed here. As you will see, Windows provides substantial support for this method.

Virtual Window Theory

A virtual window is a memory device context combined with a bitmap that is compatible with the physical device context used by your program.

Here is how output will be accomplished using a virtual window. First, a memory device context is created that is compatible with the physical device context used by your application. Thus, a virtual window is simply a compatible memory DC that has the same characteristics as your program's actual window. Once you have created a virtual window, all output intended for the client area of the main window must also be written to the virtual window. This causes the virtual window to contain a complete and current copy of whatever you output to the physical window. Each time a **WM_PAINT** message is received, the contents of the virtual window are copied into the actual window, restoring its contents. Therefore, a window that has been covered and then uncovered will automatically be redrawn when it receives the **WM_PAINT** message. As you will see, this scheme is surprisingly easy to implement and convenient to use.

Some Additional API Functions

To implement a virtual window requires the use of several API functions. Four have been discussed already. These are **CreateCompatibleDC( )**, **SelectObject( )**, **GetStockObject( )**, and **BitBlt( )**. We will also be using **CreateCompatibleBitmap( )** and **PatBlt( )**, which are described here.

The **CreateCompatibleBitmap( )** function creates a bitmap that is compatible with a specified device context. This bitmap can be used by any memory device context that is compatible with the specified DC. Its prototype is shown here:

HBITMAP CreateCompatibleBitmap(HDC *hdc*, int *width*, int *height*);

Here, *hdc* is the handle for the device context for which the bitmap will be compatible. The dimensions of the bitmap are specified in *width* and *height*. These values are in pixels. The function returns a handle to the compatible bitmap or **NULL** on failure.

The **PatBlt( )** function fills a rectangle with the color and pattern of the currently selected *brush*. A brush is an object that specifies how a window (or region) will be filled. Filling an area using a brush is also commonly referred to as *painting* the region. **PatBlt( )** has this prototype:

BOOL PatBlt(HDC *hdc*, int *X*, int *Y*, int *width*, int *height*, DWORD *dwHow*);

Here, *hdc* is the handle of the device to fill. The coordinates *X* and *Y* specify the upper-left corner of the region to be filled. The width and height of the region are specified in *width* and *height*. The value passed in *dwHow* determines how the brush will be applied. It must be one of these macros:

Macro	Meaning
BLACKNESS	Region is black (brush is ignored).
WHITENESS	Region is white (brush is ignored).
PATCOPY	Brush is copied to region.
PATINVERT	Brush is ORed to region.
DSTINVERT	Region is inverted (brush is ignored).

Therefore, if you wish to apply the current brush unaltered, you would select **PATCOPY** for the value of *dwHow*. The function returns nonzero if successful, zero otherwise.

Creating and Using a Virtual Window

Let's begin by restating the procedure that will be implemented. To create an easy and convenient means of restoring a window after a **WM_PAINT** message has been received, a virtual window will be maintained and all output will be written to that virtual window. Each time a repaint request is received, the contents of that window are copied into the window that is physically on the screen. Now, let's implement this approach.

8

Creating the Virtual Window

First, a virtual device context must be created that is compatible with the physical device context. This will be done only once, when the program begins execution and a **WM_CREATE** message is received. This compatible device context will stay in existence the entire time the program is executing. Here is the code that performs this function.

```
case WM_CREATE:
  /* get screen coordinates */
  maxX = GetSystemMetrics(SM_CXSCREEN);
  maxY = GetSystemMetrics(SM_CYSCREEN);
```

```
/* make a compatible memory image */
hdc = GetDC(hwnd);
memdc = CreateCompatibleDC(hdc);
hbit = CreateCompatibleBitmap(hdc, maxX, maxY);
SelectObject(memdc, hbit);
hbrush = (HBRUSH) GetStockObject(WHITE_BRUSH);
SelectObject(memdc, hbrush);
PatBlt(memdc, 0, 0, maxX, maxY, PATCOPY);
ReleaseDC(hwnd, hdc);
break;
```

Let's examine this code closely. First, the dimensions of the screen are obtained. They will be used to create a compatible bitmap. Then the current device context is obtained. Next, a compatible device context is created in memory, using **CreateCompatibleDC( )**. The handle to this device context is stored in **memdc**, which is a global variable. Then, a compatible bitmap is created. This establishes a one-to-one mapping between the virtual window and the physical window. The dimensions of the bitmap are those of the maximum screen size. This ensures that the bitmap will always be large enough to fully restore the window as long as the window is no larger than the size of the screen. (Actually, slightly smaller values could be used, since the borders aren't repainted, but this minor improvement is left to you, as an exercise.) The handle to the bitmap is stored in the global variable **hbit**. Next, a stock white brush is obtained and its handle is stored in the global variable **hbrush**. This brush is selected into the memory device context and then **PatBlt( )** paints the entire virtual window using the brush. Thus, the virtual window will have a white background, which matches the background of the physical window in the example program that follows. (Remember, these colors are under your control; the colors used here are arbitrary.) Finally, the physical device context is released. However, the memory device context stays in existence until the program ends.

Using the Virtual Window

Once the virtual window has been created, you must make sure that a complete copy of all output is also written to the virtual window. Each time a **WM_PAINT** message is received, you will use the contents of the virtual window to restore the contents of the physical window. You will do this in much the same way that you copied a bitmapped image to the window in Chapter 7: by using the **BitBlt( )** function. For example, here is a reworked version of the **IDM_SHOW** message from the previous program that uses the virtual window.

```
case IDM_SHOW:
  /* set text color to black */
  SetTextColor(memdc, RGB(0, 0, 0));
  /* set background color to turquoise */
  SetBkColor(hdc, RGB(0, 255, 255));

  /* get text metrics */
  GetTextMetrics(memdc, &tm);

  sprintf(str, "The font is %ld pixels high.", tm.tmHeight);
  TextOut(memdc, X, Y, str, strlen(str)); /* output string */
  Y = Y + tm.tmHeight + tm.tmExternalLeading; /* next line */

  strcpy(str, "This is on the next line. ");
  TextOut(memdc, X, Y, str, strlen(str)); /* output string */

  /* compute length of a string */
  GetTextExtentPoint32(memdc, str, strlen(str), &size);
  sprintf(str, "Previous string is %ld units long", size.cx);
  X = size.cx; /* advance to end of previous string */
  TextOut(memdc, X, Y, str, strlen(str));
  Y = Y + tm.tmHeight + tm.tmExternalLeading; /* next line */
  X = 0; /* reset X */

  sprintf(str, "Screen dimensions: %d %d", maxX, maxY);
  TextOut(memdc, X, Y, str, strlen(str));
  Y = Y + tm.tmHeight + tm.tmExternalLeading; /* next line */
  InvalidateRect(hwnd, NULL, 1);
  break;
```

8

This version directs all output to **memdc** and then calls **InvalidateRect( )** to cause the physical window to be updated. Of course, it would also be possible to direct output to both the physical window and the virtual window. In this approach, the virtual window is copied to the physical window only when the window needs to be restored.

Each time a **WM_PAINT** message is received, the contents of the virtual window are copied into the physical device. This is accomplished by the following code.

```
case WM_PAINT: /* process a repaint request */
  hdc = BeginPaint(hwnd, &paintstruct); /* get DC */

  /* now, copy memory image onto screen */
```

```
BitBlt(hdc, 0, 0, maxX, maxY, memdc, 0, 0, SRCCOPY);

EndPaint(hwnd, &paintstruct); /* release DC */
break;
```

As you can see, the **BitBlt( )** function is used to copy the image from **memdc** into **hdc**. Remember, the parameter **SRCCOPY** simply means to copy the image as-is without alteration directly from the source to the target. Because all output has been stored in **memdc**, this statement causes that output to actually be displayed. More importantly, if the window is covered and then uncovered, the **WM_PAINT** message will be received and this code causes the contents of that window to be automatically restored.

The Entire Virtual Window Demonstration Program

Here is the complete program that demonstrates using a virtual window.

```
/* Repaint using a virtual window. */

#include <windows.h>
#include <string.h>
#include <stdio.h>
#include "text.h"

LRESULT CALLBACK WindowFunc(HWND, UINT, WPARAM, LPARAM);

char szWinName[] = "MyWin"; /* name of window class */

char str[255]; /* holds output strings */

int X=0, Y=0; /* current output location */
int maxX, maxY; /* screen dimensions */

HDC memdc; /* store the virtual device handle */
HBITMAP hbit; /* store the virtual bitmap */
HBRUSH hbrush; /* store the brush handle */

int WINAPI WinMain(HINSTANCE hThisInst, HINSTANCE hPrevInst,
                   LPSTR lpszArgs, int nWinMode)
{
  HWND hwnd;
  MSG msg;
  WNDCLASSEX wcl;
  HACCEL hAccel;
```

```
/* Define a window class. */
wcl.cbSize = sizeof(WNDCLASSEX);

wcl.hInstance = hThisInst; /* handle to this instance */
wcl.lpszClassName = szWinName; /* window class name */
wcl.lpfnWndProc = WindowFunc; /* window function */
wcl.style = 0; /* default style */

wcl.hIcon = LoadIcon(NULL, IDI_APPLICATION); /* standard icon */
wcl.hIconSm = LoadIcon(NULL, IDI_APPLICATION); /* small icon */
wcl.hCursor = LoadCursor(NULL, IDC_ARROW); /* cursor style */

wcl.lpszMenuName = "MyMenu"; /* main menu */
wcl.cbClsExtra = 0; /* no extra */
wcl.cbWndExtra = 0; /* information needed */

/* Make the window white. */
wcl.hbrBackground = (HBRUSH) GetStockObject(WHITE_BRUSH);

/* Register the window class. */
if(!RegisterClassEx(&wcl)) return 0;

/* Now that a window class has been registered, a window
   can be created. */
hwnd = CreateWindow(
  szWinName, /* name of window class */
  "Fun with Text", /* title */
  WS_OVERLAPPEDWINDOW, /* window style - normal */
  CW_USEDEFAULT, /* X coordinate - let Windows decide */
  CW_USEDEFAULT, /* Y coordinate - let Windows decide */
  CW_USEDEFAULT, /* width - let Windows decide */
  CW_USEDEFAULT, /* height - let Windows decide */
  HWND_DESKTOP, /* no parent window */
  NULL, /* no override of class menu */
  hThisInst, /* handle of this instance of the program */
  NULL /* no additional arguments */
);

/* Load accelerators. */
hAccel = LoadAccelerators(hThisInst, "MyMenu");

/* Display the window. */
ShowWindow(hwnd, nWinMode);
UpdateWindow(hwnd);
```

```
    /* Create the message loop. */
    while(GetMessage(&msg, NULL, 0, 0))
    {
      if(!TranslateAccelerator(hwnd, hAccel, &msg)) {
        TranslateMessage(&msg); /* translate keyboard messages */
        DispatchMessage(&msg); /* return control to Windows 98 */
      }
    }
    return msg.wParam;
}

/* This function is called by Windows 98 and is passed
   messages from the message queue.
*/
LRESULT CALLBACK WindowFunc(HWND hwnd, UINT message,
                            WPARAM wParam, LPARAM lParam)
{
  HDC hdc;
  PAINTSTRUCT paintstruct;
  TEXTMETRIC tm;
  SIZE size;
  int response;

  switch(message) {
    case WM_CREATE:
      /* get screen coordinates */
      maxX = GetSystemMetrics(SM_CXSCREEN);
      maxY = GetSystemMetrics(SM_CYSCREEN);

      /* make a compatible memory image */
      hdc = GetDC(hwnd);
      memdc = CreateCompatibleDC(hdc);
      hbit = CreateCompatibleBitmap(hdc, maxX, maxY);
      SelectObject(memdc, hbit);
      hbrush = (HBRUSH) GetStockObject(WHITE_BRUSH);
      SelectObject(memdc, hbrush);
      PatBlt(memdc, 0, 0, maxX, maxY, PATCOPY);
      ReleaseDC(hwnd, hdc);
      break;
    case WM_COMMAND:
      switch(LOWORD(wParam)) {
        case IDM_SHOW:
          /* set text color to black */
          SetTextColor(memdc, RGB(0, 0, 0));
```

```
                    /* set background color to turquoise */
                    SetBkColor(hdc, RGB(0, 255, 255));

                    /* get text metrics */
                    GetTextMetrics(memdc, &tm);

                    sprintf(str, "The font is %ld pixels high.",
                            tm.tmHeight);
                    TextOut(memdc, X, Y, str, strlen(str)); /* output string */
                    Y = Y + tm.tmHeight + tm.tmExternalLeading; /* next line */

                    strcpy(str, "This is on the next line. ");
                    TextOut(memdc, X, Y, str, strlen(str)); /* output string */

                    /* compute length of a string */
                    GetTextExtentPoint32(memdc, str, strlen(str), &size);
                    sprintf(str, "Previous string is %ld units long",
                            size.cx);
                    X = size.cx; /* advance to end of previous string */
                    TextOut(memdc, X, Y, str, strlen(str));
                    Y = Y + tm.tmHeight + tm.tmExternalLeading; /* next line */
                    X = 0;  /* reset X */

                    sprintf(str, "Screen dimensions: %d %d", maxX, maxY);
                    TextOut(memdc, X, Y, str, strlen(str));
                    Y = Y + tm.tmHeight + tm.tmExternalLeading; /* next line */
                    InvalidateRect(hwnd, NULL, 1);
                    break;
                case IDM_RESET:
                  X = Y = 0;
                   /* erase by repainting background */
                  PatBlt(memdc, 0, 0, maxX, maxY, PATCOPY);
                  InvalidateRect(hwnd, NULL, 1);
                  break;
                case IDM_EXIT:
                  response = MessageBox(hwnd, "Quit the Program?",
                                        "Exit", MB_YESNO);
                  if(response == IDYES) PostQuitMessage(0);
                  break;
                case IDM_HELP:
```

8

```
            MessageBox(hwnd, "F2: Display\nF3: Reset", "Help",
                    MB_OK);
          break;
      }
      break;
    case WM_PAINT: /* process a repaint request */
      hdc = BeginPaint(hwnd, &paintstruct); /* get DC */

      /* now, copy memory image onto screen */
      BitBlt(hdc, 0, 0, maxX, maxY, memdc, 0, 0, SRCCOPY);
      EndPaint(hwnd, &paintstruct); /* release DC */
      break;
    case WM_DESTROY: /* terminate the program */
      DeleteDC(memdc); /* delete the memory device */
      PostQuitMessage(0);
      break;
    default:
      /* Let Windows 98 process any messages not specified in
      the preceding switch statement. */
      return DefWindowProc(hwnd, message, wParam, lParam);
  }
  return 0;
}
```

When you run this program, you will see two immediate improvements. First, each time you cover and then uncover the window, the contents are restored. Second, when you select Reset, the window is cleared. This occurs because the call to **BitBlt( )** inside the **IDM_RESET** message causes the brush to be used to paint the window, thus erasing any preexisting contents.

Improving Repaint Efficiency

The virtual window method just described shows the general technique for using a virtual window to handle repaint requests. However, it is possible to make a rather significant improvement to the preceding program. As the program is written, it suffers from two inefficiencies. First, the entire virtual window is copied to the physical window no matter how large (or small) the physical window actually is. Since the virtual window is the size of the entire screen, this approach is clearly inefficient. Because output is automatically clipped, no harm is caused by this approach. It just wastes CPU time.

The second problem is that no matter how much of the physical window actually needs to be repainted, the entire window is repainted each time a

WM_PAINT message arrives. This is the way most beginning Windows programmers handle a repaint request. It is, of course, not the best way. The trouble is that often only a corner of a window actually needs to be restored. It is important to understand that restoring a window is expensive in terms of time. The larger the window, the longer it takes to restore it. Repainting parts of a window that don't need it wastes time and can make your application look sluggish.

Both of these inefficiencies are rooted in the fact that the preceding program paints more of the window than it needs to. The solution is to change the program so that it repaints only those portions of the window that actually need to be restored. Using this approach, repaints take less time and your application has a much snappier feel. Frankly, optimizing window repainting is one of the most important performance improvements that you can make to your program.

Fortunately, Windows 98 automatically provides the information we need to implement a more efficient repaint handler, through the **BeginPaint( )** function. To begin, let's review the information obtained by **BeginPaint( )**.

A Closer Look at BeginPaint( )

As you learned in Chapter 3, when a **WM_PAINT** message is processed, you must call **BeginPaint( )** to obtain a device context. In addition to acquiring a device context, **BeginPaint( )** also obtains information about the display state of the window. We will use this information to optimize repainting.

8

Recall the prototype for **BeginPaint( )**, as shown here:

HDC BeginPaint(HWND *hwnd*, PAINTSTRUCT **lpPS*);

BeginPaint( ) returns a device context if successful or **NULL** on failure. Here, *hwnd* is the handle of the window for which the device context is being obtained. The second parameter is a pointer to a structure of type **PAINTSTRUCT**. The structure pointed to by *lpPS* will contain information that your program can use to repaint the window. **PAINTSTRUCT** is defined like this:

```
typedef struct tagPAINTSTRUCT {
  HDC hdc; /* handle to device context */
  BOOL fErase; /* true if background must be erased */
  RECT rcPaint; /* coordinates of region to redraw */
  BOOL fRestore;  /* reserved */
  BOOL fIncUpdate; /* reserved */
```

```
    BYTE rgbReserved[32]; /* reserved */
} PAINTSTRUCT;
```

The field that is of particular interest to us is **rcPaint**. This element contains the coordinates of the region of the window that needs to be repainted. We can take advantage of this information to reduce the time needed to restore a window.

Reducing Virtual Window Repaint Time

The key to decreasing the time it takes to restore a window when a **WM_PAINT** message is received is to restore only the portion of the window defined by **rcPaint**. This is easy to accomplish when using a virtual window. Simply copy the same region from the virtual window to the physical window. Since the two device contexts are identical, so are their coordinate systems. The coordinates that are contained in **rcPaint** can be used for both the physical window and the virtual window. For example, here is a better way to respond to **WM_PAINT**.

```
case WM_PAINT: /* an improved response to a repaint request */
  hdc = BeginPaint(hwnd, &paintstruct); /* get DC */

  /* copy a portion of the virtual window */
  BitBlt(hdc, paintstruct.rcPaint.left, paintstruct.rcPaint.top,
         paintstruct.rcPaint.right-paintstruct.rcPaint.left,
         paintstruct.rcPaint.bottom-paintstruct.rcPaint.top,
         memdc,
         paintstruct.rcPaint.left, paintstruct.rcPaint.top,
         SRCCOPY);

  EndPaint(hwnd, &paintstruct); /* release DC */
  break;
```

To see the effectiveness of this version, substitute it into the program from the preceding section. Because this version copies only the rectangle defined by **rcPaint**, no time is wasted copying information that has not been overwritten or that is outside the current boundaries of the window.

Notice how easy it is to optimize the repainting of a window when using the virtual window method. Almost no additional programming effort is required. The virtual window method of repainting is an elegant solution to many repaint-related operations.

For most of the examples in this book, efficient repaints are not needed. In fact, most programs won't even bother repainting the client area because the extra code will simply clutter the point of the example. However, in real programs that you write, the efficient handling of **WM_PAINT** is a crucial performance issue.

Working with Fonts

Windows in general, and Windows 98 specifically, gives you nearly complete control over the user interface. It provides a rich and varied set of text-based features of which you can take advantage. One such feature is its collection of various type fonts. By taking control of the type fonts used by your application, you can create a unique look that sets your program apart from the crowd. Using Windows 98, you have several built-in type fonts to choose from. You can also create custom fonts. Both of these topics are discussed here. We will begin by defining a few terms.

Fonts, Families, Typefaces, and Styles

A font defines a complete set of characters in a particular size, style, and typeface.

In the most general sense, a *font* describes a set of characters and features common to those characters. As you almost certainly know, there are many different kinds of type fonts in common use. For example, Courier and Times Roman are two of the most popular. A font defines four attributes: a character set, a typeface, a style, and a size. Let's look at each.

8

Windows 98 supports various character sets. The one that we will be using is the standard Windows character set. This set is based upon the ANSI character set and each character is 8 bits. This makes the Windows character set suitable for most Western languages. Other character sets supported by Windows are Unicode, OEM (Original Equipment Manufacturer), and symbol (a set of symbolic characters used for representing mathematical expressions). Custom character sets are also allowed.

A typeface specifies a specific design of type.

A *typeface* defines the precise shape and design of the characters within a font. Thus, the typeface determines the unique visual characteristics of a font.

In general, the *style* of a font determines whether a font is displayed normally, in bold, or in italics. In Windows, you have fine-grained control over the weight (i.e., thickness) of a font, so there are actually several gradients of font thickness.

Type size is measured in *points*, which are 1/72 of an inch.

A serif is a small line found at the endpoints of characters.

The pitch of a font determines its character spacing.

Windows organizes fonts into five *families*, which share basic attributes. These families are Decorative, Modern, Roman, Script, and Swiss. Decorative fonts are specialty fonts. Modern fonts are nonproportional. The Roman family is proportional and includes serifs. (*Serifs* are short lines found at the end points of characters.) Members of the Script family appear somewhat like handwriting. The Swiss family is proportional and sans serif (that is, does not have serifs).

In proportional fonts, the width of each character, or *pitch*, may differ. These are also called *variable-pitch* fonts. In nonproportional fonts, the width of each character is the same. These are called *fixed-pitch*, or *monospaced*, fonts.

Raster, Vector, and TrueType Fonts

A glyph is a character or symbol.

Windows 98 supports three ways in which a font can be stored and displayed. These are called *raster, vector,* and *TrueType*. Raster fonts store bitmaps for each character, or *glyph*, in the font. This makes them easy to display but difficult to scale. Raster fonts are most often used on display monitors and bitmapped printers. Vector fonts store the endpoints to the line segments that make up each glyph. These segments are then drawn to display each character. Vector fonts are best when used on plotters. TrueType fonts store information about the lines and arcs that make up each glyph, as well as instructions on how to draw the character. This approach gives TrueType fonts excellent scalability. They are also the most faithfully translated from screen to printer. For this reason, TrueType fonts are quite popular for desktop publishing applications.

Using Built-in Fonts

Windows 98's built-in fonts are stock objects that are selected using **GetStockObject( )**. At the time of this writing, Windows 98 supports six built-in fonts. The macros associated with these fonts are shown here.

Font	Description
ANSI_FIXED_FONT	Fixed-pitch font
ANSI_VAR_FONT	Variable-pitch font
DEFAULT_GUI_FONT	Font used by Windows
OEM_FIXED_FONT	OEM-defined font
SYSTEM_FONT	Font used by Windows
SYSTEM_FIXED_FONT	Font used by older versions of Windows

The system fonts are those character fonts used by Windows for things like menus and dialog boxes. Older versions of Windows use a fixed-pitch system font, but beginning with Windows 3.0, a variable font is used. Windows 98 also uses the variable font.

Selecting and using a built-in font is easy. To do so, your program must first create a font handle, which is of type **HFONT**. Next, it must load the desired font, using **GetStockObject( )**, which returns a handle to the font. To switch to the font, select it using **SelectObject( )** with the new font as a parameter. **SelectObject( )** will return a handle to the old font, which you may want to save so that you can switch back to it after you are done using the new font.

The following program demonstrates changing fonts. It uses the virtual window technology just developed to handle repainting.

```
/* Demonstrate built-in fonts. */

#include <windows.h>
#include <string.h>
#include <stdio.h>
#include "text.h"

LRESULT CALLBACK WindowFunc(HWND, UINT, WPARAM, LPARAM);

char szWinName[] = "MyWin"; /* name of window class */

char str[255]; /* holds output strings */

int X=0, Y=0; /* current output location */
int maxX, maxY; /* screen dimensions */

HDC memdc; /* store the virtual device handle */
HBITMAP hbit; /* store the virtual bitmap */
HBRUSH hbrush; /* store the brush handle */
HFONT holdf, hnewf; /* store the font handles */

int WINAPI WinMain(HINSTANCE hThisInst, HINSTANCE hPrevInst,
                   LPSTR lpszArgs, int nWinMode)
{
  HWND hwnd;
  MSG msg;
  WNDCLASSEX wcl;
  HACCEL hAccel;

  /* Define a window class. */
```

8

```
wcl.cbSize = sizeof(WNDCLASSEX);

wcl.hInstance = hThisInst; /* handle to this instance */
wcl.lpszClassName = szWinName; /* window class name */
wcl.lpfnWndProc = WindowFunc; /* window function */
wcl.style = 0; /* default style */

wcl.hIcon = LoadIcon(NULL, IDI_APPLICATION); /* standard icon */
wcl.hIconSm = LoadIcon(NULL, IDI_APPLICATION); /* small icon */
wcl.hCursor = LoadCursor(NULL, IDC_ARROW); /* cursor style */

/* specify name of menu resource */
wcl.lpszMenuName = "FontMenu"; /* main menu */

wcl.cbClsExtra = 0; /* no extra */
wcl.cbWndExtra = 0; /* information needed */

/* Make the window white. */
wcl.hbrBackground = (HBRUSH) GetStockObject(WHITE_BRUSH);

/* Register the window class. */
if(!RegisterClassEx(&wcl)) return 0;

/* Now that a window class has been registered, a window
   can be created. */
hwnd = CreateWindow(
  szWinName, /* name of window class */
  "Using Built-in Fonts", /* title */
  WS_OVERLAPPEDWINDOW, /* window style - normal */
  CW_USEDEFAULT, /* X coordinate - let Windows decide */
  CW_USEDEFAULT, /* Y coordinate - let Windows decide */
  CW_USEDEFAULT, /* width - let Windows decide */
  CW_USEDEFAULT, /* height - let Windows decide */
  HWND_DESKTOP, /* no parent window */
  NULL, /* no override of class menu */
  hThisInst, /* handle of this instance of the program */
  NULL /* no additional arguments */
);

/* Load accelerators. */
hAccel = LoadAccelerators(hThisInst, "FontMenu");

/* Display the window. */
ShowWindow(hwnd, nWinMode);
UpdateWindow(hwnd);
```

```
  /* Create the message loop. */
  while(GetMessage(&msg, NULL, 0, 0))
  {
    if(!TranslateAccelerator(hwnd, hAccel, &msg)) {
      TranslateMessage(&msg); /* translate keyboard messages */
      DispatchMessage(&msg); /* return control to Windows 98 */
    }
  }
  return msg.wParam;
}

/* This function is called by Windows 98 and is passed
   messages from the message queue.
*/
LRESULT CALLBACK WindowFunc(HWND hwnd, UINT message,
                            WPARAM wParam, LPARAM lParam)
{
  HDC hdc;
  PAINTSTRUCT paintstruct;
  static TEXTMETRIC tm;
  SIZE size;
  static fontswitch = 0;
  int response;

  switch(message) {
    case WM_CREATE:
      /* get screen coordinates */
      maxX = GetSystemMetrics(SM_CXSCREEN);
      maxY = GetSystemMetrics(SM_CYSCREEN);

      /* create a virtual window */
      hdc = GetDC(hwnd);
      memdc = CreateCompatibleDC(hdc);
      hbit = CreateCompatibleBitmap(hdc, maxX, maxY);
      SelectObject(memdc, hbit);
      hbrush = (HBRUSH) GetStockObject(WHITE_BRUSH);
      SelectObject(memdc, hbrush);
      PatBlt(memdc, 0, 0, maxX, maxY, PATCOPY);

      /* get new font */
      hnewf = (HFONT) GetStockObject(ANSI_VAR_FONT);

      ReleaseDC(hwnd, hdc);
      break;
```

8

```
case WM_COMMAND:
  switch(LOWORD(wParam)) {
    case IDM_SHOW:
      /* get text metrics */
      GetTextMetrics(memdc, &tm);

      sprintf(str, "The font is %ld pixels high.",
              tm.tmHeight);
      TextOut(memdc, X, Y, str, strlen(str));
      Y = Y + tm.tmHeight + tm.tmExternalLeading; /* next line */

      strcpy(str, "This is on the next line. ");
      TextOut(memdc, X, Y, str, strlen(str));

      /* compute length of a string */
      GetTextExtentPoint32(memdc, str, strlen(str), &size);
      sprintf(str, "Previous string is %ld units long",
              size.cx);
      X = size.cx; /* advance to end of previous string */
      TextOut(memdc, X, Y, str, strlen(str));
      Y = Y + tm.tmHeight + tm.tmExternalLeading; /* next line */

      X = 0; /* reset X */

      sprintf(str, "Screen dimensions: %d %d", maxX, maxY);
      TextOut(memdc, X, Y, str, strlen(str));
      Y = Y + tm.tmHeight + tm.tmExternalLeading; /* next line */

      InvalidateRect(hwnd, NULL, 1);
      break;
    case IDM_RESET:
      X = Y = 0;
      /* erase by repainting background */
      PatBlt(memdc, 0, 0, maxX, maxY, PATCOPY);

      InvalidateRect(hwnd, NULL, 1);
      break;
    case IDM_FONT:
      if(!fontswitch) {  /* switch to new font */
        holdf = (HFONT) SelectObject(memdc, hnewf);
        fontswitch = 1;
      }
      else { /* switch to old font */
        SelectObject(memdc, holdf);
```

```
                     fontswitch = 0;
               }
             break;
          case IDM_EXIT:
             response = MessageBox(hwnd, "Quit the Program?",
                                   "Exit", MB_YESNO);
             if(response == IDYES) PostQuitMessage(0);
             break;
          case IDM_HELP:
             MessageBox(hwnd, "F2: Display\nF3: Change Font\nF4: Reset",
                        "Font Fun", MB_OK);
             break;
        }
        break;
     case WM_PAINT: /* process a repaint request */
       hdc = BeginPaint(hwnd, &paintstruct); /* get DC */

       /* copy virtual window onto screen */
       BitBlt(hdc, 0, 0, maxX, maxY, memdc, 0, 0, SRCCOPY);

       EndPaint(hwnd, &paintstruct); /* release DC */
       break;
     case WM_DESTROY: /* terminate the program */
       DeleteDC(memdc);
       PostQuitMessage(0);
       break;
     default:
       /* Let Windows 98 process any messages not specified in
       the preceding switch statement. */
       return DefWindowProc(hwnd, message, wParam, lParam);
   }
   return 0;
}
```

The resource file used by the program is shown here.

```
#include <windows.h>
#include "text.h"

FontMenu MENU
{
  POPUP "&Fonts" {
    MENUITEM "&Display\tF2", IDM_SHOW
```

8

```
      MENUITEM "Change &Font\tF3", IDM_FONT
      MENUITEM "&Reset\tF4", IDM_RESET
      MENUITEM "E&xit\tCtrl+X", IDM_EXIT
    }
  MENUITEM "&Help", IDM_HELP
}


FontMenu ACCELERATORS
{
  VK_F2, IDM_SHOW, VIRTKEY
  VK_F3, IDM_FONT, VIRTKEY
  VK_F4, IDM_RESET, VIRTKEY
  "^X", IDM_EXIT
  VK_F1, IDM_HELP, VIRTKEY
}
```

The TEXT.H header file is shown here.

```
#define IDM_SHOW    100
#define IDM_FONT    101
#define IDM_RESET   102
#define IDM_EXIT    103
#define IDM_HELP    104
```

Sample output produced by this program is shown in Figure 8-2.

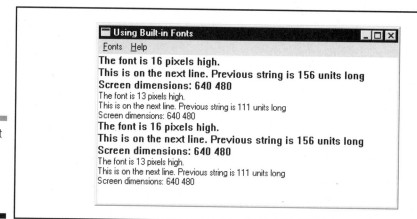

Sample output from the built-in font program

Figure 8-2.

The program works like this. Each time you select Display, text is output using the currently selected font. Each time you select Change Font, the currently selected font is toggled between the ANSI variable font and the default font. You can clear the window by selecting Reset. Notice that this option simply resets the X and Y coordinates to zero and then calls **PatBlt( )** using **PATCOPY** to overpaint the background of the virtual window.

Creating Custom Fonts

Although it may sound complex, it is actually very easy to create a custom font. There are two major advantages to doing this. First, a custom font gives your application a unique look that will set it apart. Second, creating your own font lets you control precisely what occurs when text is output. Before beginning, it is important to understand that you will not be defining a new typeface. Instead, you will be tailoring an existing typeface so that it meets the specifications that you desire. (That is, you don't need to define the shape of each character in the font that you create.)

To create your own font, use the **CreateFont( )** API function, whose prototype is shown here.

```
HFONT CreateFont(int Height, int Width, int Escapement,
                 int Orientation, int Weight,
                 DWORD Ital, DWORD Underline,
                 DWORD StrikeThru, DWORD Charset,
                 DWORD Precision, DWORD ClipPrecision,
                 DWORD Quality, DWORD PitchFam,
                 LPCSTR TypefaceName);
```

8

The escapement specifies the angle of a line of text. Orientation specifies the angle of a character itself.

The height of the font is passed in *Height*. If *Height* is zero, then a default size is used. The width of the font is specified in *Width*. If *Width* is zero, then Windows chooses an appropriate value based upon the current aspect ratio. Both *Height* and *Width* are stated in terms of logical units.

Text can be output at any angle within the window. The angle at which it is displayed is determined by the *Escapement* parameter. For normal, horizontal text, this value should be 0. Otherwise, it specifies the number of 1/10-degree increments through which the text should be rotated in a counterclockwise direction. For example, a value of 900 causes the text to be rotated 90 degrees, causing output to be vertical.

The angle of each individual character can also be specified using the *Orientation* parameter. It too uses 1/10-degree increments to specify the angle of each character relative to horizontal in a counterclockwise direction.

PORTABILITY: For Windows 95 and Windows 98, both the *Escapement* and *Orientation* parameters of **CreateFont( )** must be set to the same angle. However, under Windows NT, these two parameters may differ.

Weight specifies the preferred weight of the font in the range of 0 to 1000. A value of 0 specifies the default weight. To specify a normal weight, use 400. For bold, use 700. You can also use any of these macros to specify the font weight.

FW_DONTCARE

FW_THIN

FW_EXTRALIGHT

FW_LIGHT

FW_NORMAL

FW_MEDIUM

FW_SEMIBOLD

FW_BOLD

FW_EXTRABOLD

FW_HEAVY

To create an italic font, specify *Ital* as nonzero. Otherwise, this parameter should be zero. To create an underlined font, specify *Underline* as nonzero. Otherwise, this parameter should be zero. To create a strike-through font, specify *StrikeThru* as nonzero. Otherwise, this parameter should be zero.

Charset indicates which character set is desired. The example that follows uses **ANSI_CHARSET**. *Precision* specifies the preferred output precision. This determines just how closely the output must match the requested font's characteristics. The examples in this chapter use **OUT_DEFAULT_PRECIS**. *ClipPrecision* specifies the preferred clipping precision. Clipping precision determines how each character that extends beyond the clipping region is to be "clipped." The value used by the example in this chapter is **CLIP_DEFAULT_PRECIS**. (For other valid values for *Charset, Precision,* and *ClipPrecision,* consult an API reference.)

Quality determines how closely the logical font will be matched with the actual physical fonts provided for the requested output device. It can be one of these values.

DEFAULT_QUALITY   DRAFT_QUALITY   PROOF_QUALITY

PitchFam specifies the pitch and family of the font. There are three pitch choices:

DEFAULT_PITCH   FIXED_PITCH   VARIABLE_PITCH

There are six possible font families:

FF_DECORATIVE   FF_DONTCARE   FF_MODERN

FF_ROMAN   FF_SCRIPT   FF_SWISS

8

The **FF_DONTCARE** family is used when you don't care what font family is used. The font family is meaningful only if the typeface you specify is not available on the system. To create the value for *PitchFam*, OR together one pitch value and one font family value.

A pointer to the name of the typeface is passed in *TypefaceName*. This name cannot be longer than 32 characters. The font you specify must be installed in your system. Alternatively, you can specify **NULL** for this parameter and Windows 98 will automatically select a font that is compatible with the characteristics that you specify in the other parameters. (You will see how to obtain a list of available fonts later in this chapter.)

If successful, **CreateFont( )** returns a handle to the font. On failure, **NULL** is returned. Fonts created using **CreateFont( )** must be deleted before your program ends. To delete a font, call **DeleteObject( )**.

Here is a program that demonstrates two custom fonts. The first is based upon the Courier New font, the second upon Century Gothic. Each time you choose the Change Font menu item, a new font is selected and displayed. This program uses the same resource and header files as the program in the preceding section. Sample output is shown in Figure 8-3.

```c
/* Create a custom font. */

#include <windows.h>
#include <string.h>
#include <stdio.h>
#include "text.h"

LRESULT CALLBACK WindowFunc(HWND, UINT, WPARAM, LPARAM);

char szWinName[] = "MyWin"; /* name of window class */

char str[255]; /* holds output strings */
char fname[40] = "Default"; /* name of font */

int X=0, Y=0; /* current output location */
int maxX, maxY; /* screen dimensions */

HDC memdc; /* store the virtual device handle */
HBITMAP hbit; /* store the virtual bitmap */
HBRUSH hbrush; /* store the brush handle */
HFONT holdf, hnewf1, hnewf2; /* store the font handles */

int WINAPI WinMain(HINSTANCE hThisInst, HINSTANCE hPrevInst,
                   LPSTR lpszArgs, int nWinMode)
{
  HWND hwnd;
  MSG msg;
  WNDCLASSEX wcl;
  HACCEL hAccel;

  /* Define a window class. */
  wcl.cbSize = sizeof(WNDCLASSEX);

  /* Define a window class. */
  wcl.hInstance = hThisInst; /* handle to this instance */
  wcl.lpszClassName = szWinName; /* window class name */
  wcl.lpfnWndProc = WindowFunc; /* window function */
  wcl.style = 0; /* default style */

  wcl.hIcon = LoadIcon(NULL, IDI_APPLICATION); /* standard icon */
  wcl.hIconSm = LoadIcon(NULL, IDI_APPLICATION); /* small icon */
```

```
wcl.hCursor = LoadCursor(NULL, IDC_ARROW); /* cursor style */

/* specify name of menu resource */
wcl.lpszMenuName = "FontMenu"; /* main menu */

wcl.cbClsExtra = 0; /* no extra */
wcl.cbWndExtra = 0; /* information needed */

/* Make the window white. */
wcl.hbrBackground = (HBRUSH) GetStockObject(WHITE_BRUSH);

/* Register the window class. */
if(!RegisterClassEx(&wcl)) return 0;

/* Now that a window class has been registered, a window
   can be created. */
hwnd = CreateWindow(
  szWinName, /* name of window class */
  "Using Custom Fonts", /* title */
  WS_OVERLAPPEDWINDOW, /* window style - normal */
  CW_USEDEFAULT, /* X coordinate - let Windows decide */
  CW_USEDEFAULT, /* Y coordinate - let Windows decide */
  CW_USEDEFAULT, /* width - let Windows decide */
  CW_USEDEFAULT, /* height - let Windows decide */
  HWND_DESKTOP, /* no parent window */
  NULL, /* no override of class menu */
  hThisInst, /* handle of this instance of the program */
  NULL /* no additional arguments */
);

/* Load accelerators. */
hAccel = LoadAccelerators(hThisInst, "FontMenu");

/* Display the window. */
ShowWindow(hwnd, nWinMode);
UpdateWindow(hwnd);

/* Create the message loop. */
while(GetMessage(&msg, NULL, 0, 0))
{
  if(!TranslateAccelerator(hwnd, hAccel, &msg)) {
    TranslateMessage(&msg); /* translate keyboard messages */
    DispatchMessage(&msg); /* return control to Windows 98 */
  }
}
```

```
        return msg.wParam;
}

/* This function is called by Windows 98 and is passed
   messages from the message queue.
*/
LRESULT CALLBACK WindowFunc(HWND hwnd, UINT message,
                            WPARAM wParam, LPARAM lParam)
{
  HDC hdc;
  PAINTSTRUCT paintstruct;
  static TEXTMETRIC tm;
  SIZE size;
  static fontswitch = 0;
  int response;

  switch(message) {
    case WM_CREATE:
      /* get screen coordinates */
      maxX = GetSystemMetrics(SM_CXSCREEN);
      maxY = GetSystemMetrics(SM_CYSCREEN);

      /* create a virtual window */
      hdc = GetDC(hwnd);
      memdc = CreateCompatibleDC(hdc);
      hbit = CreateCompatibleBitmap(hdc, maxX, maxY);
      SelectObject(memdc, hbit);
      hbrush = (HBRUSH) GetStockObject(WHITE_BRUSH);
      SelectObject(memdc, hbrush);
      PatBlt(memdc, 0, 0, maxX, maxY, PATCOPY);

      /* create new fonts */
      hnewf1 = CreateFont(14, 0, 0, 0, FW_NORMAL,
                          0, 0, 0, ANSI_CHARSET,
                          OUT_DEFAULT_PRECIS,
                          CLIP_DEFAULT_PRECIS,
                          DEFAULT_QUALITY,
                          DEFAULT_PITCH | FF_DONTCARE,
                          "Courier New");
      hnewf2 = CreateFont(20, 0, 0, 0, FW_SEMIBOLD,
                          0, 0, 0, ANSI_CHARSET,
                          OUT_DEFAULT_PRECIS,
                          CLIP_DEFAULT_PRECIS,
                          DEFAULT_QUALITY,
                          DEFAULT_PITCH | FF_DONTCARE,
                          "Century Gothic");
```

```
      ReleaseDC(hwnd, hdc);
      break;
case WM_COMMAND:
  switch(LOWORD(wParam)) {
    case IDM_SHOW:
      /* get text metrics */
      GetTextMetrics(memdc, &tm);

      sprintf(str, "%s font is %ld pixels high.",
              fname, tm.tmHeight);
      TextOut(memdc, X, Y, str, strlen(str));
      Y = Y + tm.tmHeight + tm.tmExternalLeading; /* next line */

      strcpy(str, "This is on the next line. ");
      TextOut(memdc, X, Y, str, strlen(str));

      /* compute length of a string */
      GetTextExtentPoint32(memdc, str, strlen(str), &size);
      sprintf(str, "Previous string is %ld units long",
              size.cx);
      X = size.cx; /* advance to end of previous string */
      TextOut(memdc, X, Y, str, strlen(str));
      Y = Y + tm.tmHeight + tm.tmExternalLeading; /* next line */
      X = 0; /* reset X */

      sprintf(str, "Screen dimensions: %d %d", maxX, maxY);
      TextOut(memdc, X, Y, str, strlen(str));
      Y = Y + tm.tmHeight + tm.tmExternalLeading; /* next line */

      InvalidateRect(hwnd, NULL, 1);
      break;
    case IDM_RESET:
      X = Y = 0;
      /* erase by repainting background */
      PatBlt(memdc, 0, 0, maxX, maxY, PATCOPY);
      InvalidateRect(hwnd, NULL, 1);
      break;
    case IDM_FONT:
      switch(fontswitch) {
        case 0: /* switch to new font1 */
          holdf = (HFONT) SelectObject(memdc, hnewf1);
          fontswitch = 1;
          strcpy(fname, "Courier New");
```

8

```
            break;
          case 1: /* switch to new font2 */
            SelectObject(memdc, hnewf2);
            fontswitch = 2;
            strcpy(fname, "Century Gothic");
            break;
          default: /* switch to old font */
            SelectObject(memdc, holdf);
            fontswitch = 0;
            strcpy(fname, "Default");
        }
        break;
      case IDM_EXIT:
        response = MessageBox(hwnd, "Quit the Program?",
                            "Exit", MB_YESNO);
        if(response == IDYES) PostQuitMessage(0);
        break;
      case IDM_HELP:
        MessageBox(hwnd, "F2: Display\nF3: Change Font\nF4: Reset",
                 "Custom Fonts", MB_OK);
        break;
    }
    break;
  case WM_PAINT: /* process a repaint request */
    hdc = BeginPaint(hwnd, &paintstruct); /* get DC */

    /* copy virtual window onto screen */
    BitBlt(hdc, 0, 0, maxX, maxY, memdc, 0, 0, SRCCOPY);

    EndPaint(hwnd, &paintstruct); /* release DC */
    break;
  case WM_DESTROY: /* terminate the program */
    DeleteDC(memdc);
    DeleteObject(hnewf1);
    DeleteObject(hnewf2);
    PostQuitMessage(0);
    break;
  default:
    /* Let Windows 98 process any messages not specified in
    the preceding switch statement. */
    return DefWindowProc(hwnd, message, wParam, lParam);
  }
  return 0;
}
```

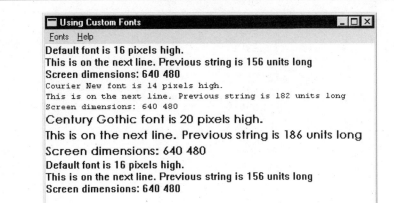

Sample output
from the
custom font
program

Figure 8-3.

Using CreateFontIndirect( )

There is an alternative to **CreateFont( )** that you will find useful in some
situations. It is called **CreateFontIndirect( )**, and it creates a font based
upon the information contained in a **LOGFONT** structure. Its prototype
is shown here:

HFONT CreateFontIndirect(CONST LOGFONT *lpFont);

The function returns a handle to the font that best matches the
information supplied in the structure pointed to by *lpFont*. It returns
NULL on failure. You must delete the font handled, using
DeleteObject( ), before your program ends.

The **LOGFONT** structure encapsulates logical information about a font. It
is defined like this.

```
typedef struct tagLOGFONT
{
  LONG lfHeight; /* height of font */
  LONG lfWidth; /* width of font */
  LONG lfEscapement; /* angle of text */
  LONG lfOrientation; /* angle of character */
```

8

```
  LONG lfWeight; /* darkness */
  BYTE lfItalic; /* 1 if ital */
  BYTE lfUnderline; /* 1 if underline */
  BYTE lfStrikeOut; /* 1 if strike-through */
  BYTE lfCharSet; /* character set */
  BYTE lfOutPrecision; /* output precision */
  BYTE lfClipPrecision; /* clipping precision  */
  BYTE lfQuality; /* display quality */
  BYTE lfPitchAndFamily; /* pitch and family */
  CHAR lfFaceName[LF_FACESIZE]; /* name */
} LOGFONT;
```

The fields in **LOGFONT** have the same meaning and use the same values
as the parameters to **CreateFont( )**, described earlier. For example, here
is the call to **CreateFontIndirect( )** that creates the same Century
Gothic font that was created by calling **CreateFont( )** in the preceding
program.

```
LOGFONT lf;

lf.lfHeight = 20;
lf.lfWidth = 0;
lf.lfEscapement = 0;
lf.lfOrientation = 0;
lf.lfWeight = FW_SEMIBOLD;
lf.lfItalic = 0;
lf.lfUnderline = 0;
lf.lfStrikeOut = 0;
lf.lfCharSet = ANSI_CHARSET;
lf.lfOutPrecision = OUT_DEFAULT_PRECIS;
lf.lfClipPrecision = CLIP_DEFAULT_PRECIS;
lf.lfQuality = DEFAULT_QUALITY;
lf.lfPitchAndFamily = DEFAULT_PITCH | FF_DONTCARE;
strcpy(lf.lfFaceName, "Century Gothic");
hnewf2 = CreateFontIndirect(&lf);
```

While there is no particular benefit in this situation to using
CreateFontIndirect( ) over **CreateFont( )**, there are times when there
will be. For example, when you obtain information about existing fonts,
each font's description is stored in a **LOGFONT** structure. The contents
of this structure can be used in a call to **CreateFontIndirect( )** to create
the font.

Enumerating Fonts

The preceding programs have simply assumed that the desired fonts were available when creating fonts. However, it is usually not a good idea to assume anything when programming for Windows. For example, it is possible to add fonts to or to remove fonts from a system. Fortunately, there is a relatively easy way to determine what fonts are available for use.

To enumerate the available fonts, you will use the **EnumFontFamiliesEx( )** API function, shown here.

```
int EnumFontFamiliesEx(HDC hdc, LPLOGFONT lpFontInfo,
                       FONTENUMPROC EnumFunc,
                       LPARAM lParam, DWORD NotUsed);
```

Here, *hdc* is the device context from which the fonts are being obtained. Different device contexts may support different fonts. Various characteristics that define the type of fonts that you want enumerated are passed in the **LOGFONT** structure pointed to by *lpFontInfo*. (**LOGFONT** is described in the *In Depth* box in this chapter.) *EnumFunc* is a pointer to a callback function that will be called once for each font enumerated. You can use *lParam* to pass any application-dependent information to the callback function pointed to by *EnumProc*. *NotUsed* is unused and must be zero. The function returns the last value returned by *EnumProc*.

Before calling **EnumFontFamiliesEx( )**, you must initialize three fields in the **LOGFONT** structure pointed to by *FontInfo*: **lfCharSet**, **lfPitchAndFamily**, and **lfFaceName**. To enumerate only fonts with a particular character set, specify the name of that set in **lfCharSet**. To enumerate fonts with any type of character set, use **DEFAULT_CHARSET**. To enumerate all fonts of a particular typeface, specify the name of the typeface in **lfFaceName**. To enumerate a representative font for all typefaces, initialize this member using the null string. Finally, for most applications, **lfPitchAndFamily** must be set to zero. (For Hebrew or Arabic, set this field to **MONO_FONT**.)

Each time Windows 98 enumerates a font, it calls the function pointed to by *EnumFunc*. This function processes each enumerated font and then returns nonzero if it wishes to process another font, or zero to stop. This function must have this general form.

```
int CALLBACK EnumFunc(ENUMLOGFONTEX *lpLFInfo,
                      NEWTEXTMETRICEX *lpTMInfo,
                      int type, LPARAM lParam);
```

8

Here, *lpLFInfo* is a pointer to an **ENUMLOGFONTEX** structure that contains logical information about the enumerated font. *lpTMInfo* is a pointer to a **NEWTEXTMETRICEX** structure that contains physical information about the font. Non-TrueType fonts receive a pointer to a **TEXTMETRIC** structure instead. The value of *type* indicates the font type. It can be any of these three:

RASTER_FONTTYPE   TRUETYPE_FONTTYPE   DEVICE_FONTTYPE

lParam receives the value passed by *lParam* by **EnumFontFamiliesEx( )**.

PORTABILITY: Windows 3.1 does not support **EnumFontFamiliesEx( )**. Windows 3.1 programs use either **EnumFonts( )** or **EnumFontFamilies( )**. You will want to upgrade these when porting to Windows 98.

The **ENUMLOGFONTEX** structure is defined as shown here.

```
typedef struct tagENUMLOGFONTEX
{
  LOGFONT elfLogFont;
  BYTE elfFullName[LF_FULLFACESIZE]; /* full name of font */
  BYTE elfStyle[LF_FACESIZE]; /* style of font */
  BYTE elfScript[LF_FACESIZE]; /* script used by font */
} ENUMLOGFONTEX;
```

elfLogFont is a **LOGFONT** structure that contains most of the logical font information. The information used in this structure could be used in a call to **CreateFont( )** or **CreateFontIndirect( )**. The full name of the font is contained in **elfFullName**. The style (i.e., bold, italics, etc.) is contained in **elfStyle**. The name of the script is found in **elfScript**.

A Font Enumeration Program

The following program shows how to enumerate fonts two different ways. First, when you select Available Fonts from the Enumerate menu, you obtain representative fonts for all of the supported typefaces. By choosing Selected Typeface, you will obtain all fonts for the typeface that you specify. Sample output is shown in Figure 8-4.

```c
/* Enumerating Fonts */

#include <windows.h>
#include <string.h>
#include <stdio.h>
#include "font.h"

LRESULT CALLBACK WindowFunc(HWND, UINT, WPARAM, LPARAM);
int CALLBACK FontFunc(ENUMLOGFONTEX *lpLF,
                      NEWTEXTMETRICEX *lpTM,
                      int type, LPARAM lParam);
BOOL CALLBACK FontDialog(HWND hdwnd, UINT message,
                         WPARAM wParam, LPARAM lParam);

char szWinName[] = "MyWin"; /* name of window class */

char str[255]; /* holds output strings */
char fontstr[255]; /* holds user-entered font name */

int X=0, Y=0; /* current output location */
int maxX, maxY; /* screen dimensions */

int linespacing; /* spacing between lines */

HDC memdc; /* store the virtual device handle */
HBITMAP hbit; /* store the virtual bitmap */
HBRUSH hbrush; /* store the brush handle */

HINSTANCE hInst;

int WINAPI WinMain(HINSTANCE hThisInst, HINSTANCE hPrevInst,
                   LPSTR lpszArgs, int nWinMode)
{
  HWND hwnd;
  MSG msg;
  WNDCLASSEX wcl;
  HACCEL hAccel;

  /* Define a window class. */
  wcl.cbSize = sizeof(WNDCLASSEX);

  /* Define a window class. */
  wcl.hInstance = hThisInst; /* handle to this instance */
  wcl.lpszClassName = szWinName; /* window class name */
```

8

```
wcl.lpfnWndProc = WindowFunc; /* window function */
wcl.style = 0; /* default style */

wcl.hIcon = LoadIcon(NULL, IDI_APPLICATION); /* standard icon */
wcl.hIconSm = LoadIcon(NULL, IDI_APPLICATION); /* small icon */
wcl.hCursor = LoadCursor(NULL, IDC_ARROW); /* cursor style */

/* specify name of menu resource */
wcl.lpszMenuName = "FontEnumMenu"; /* main menu */

wcl.cbClsExtra = 0; /* no extra */
wcl.cbWndExtra = 0; /* information needed */

/* Make the window white. */
wcl.hbrBackground = (HBRUSH) GetStockObject(WHITE_BRUSH);

/* Register the window class. */
if(!RegisterClassEx(&wcl)) return 0;

/* Now that a window class has been registered, a window
   can be created. */
hwnd = CreateWindow(
  szWinName, /* name of window class */
  "Enumerating Fonts", /* title */
  WS_OVERLAPPEDWINDOW, /* window style - normal */
  CW_USEDEFAULT, /* X coordinate - let Windows decide */
  CW_USEDEFAULT, /* Y coordinate - let Windows decide */
  CW_USEDEFAULT, /* width - let Windows decide */
  CW_USEDEFAULT, /* height - let Windows decide */
  HWND_DESKTOP, /* no parent window */
  NULL, /* no override of class menu */
  hThisInst, /* handle of this instance of the program */
  NULL /* no additional arguments */
);

hInst = hThisInst;

/* Load accelerators. */
hAccel = LoadAccelerators(hThisInst, "FontEnumMenu");

/* Display the window. */
ShowWindow(hwnd, nWinMode);
UpdateWindow(hwnd);

/* Create the message loop. */
```

```
      while(GetMessage(&msg, NULL, 0, 0))
      {
        if(!TranslateAccelerator(hwnd, hAccel, &msg)) {
          TranslateMessage(&msg); /* translate keyboard messages */
          DispatchMessage(&msg); /* return control to Windows 98 */
        }
      }
      return msg.wParam;
}

/* This function is called by Windows 98 and is passed
   messages from the message queue.
*/
LRESULT CALLBACK WindowFunc(HWND hwnd, UINT message,
                            WPARAM wParam, LPARAM lParam)
{
  HDC hdc;
  static TEXTMETRIC tm;
  PAINTSTRUCT paintstruct;
  LOGFONT lf;
  int result;
  int response;

  switch(message) {
    case WM_CREATE:
      /* get screen coordinates */
      maxX = GetSystemMetrics(SM_CXSCREEN);
      maxY = GetSystemMetrics(SM_CYSCREEN);

      /* create a virtual window */
      hdc = GetDC(hwnd);
      memdc = CreateCompatibleDC(hdc);
      hbit = CreateCompatibleBitmap(hdc, maxX, maxY);
      SelectObject(memdc, hbit);
      hbrush = (HBRUSH) GetStockObject(WHITE_BRUSH);
      SelectObject(memdc, hbrush);
      PatBlt(memdc, 0, 0, maxX, maxY, PATCOPY);

      /* get text metrics */
      GetTextMetrics(memdc, &tm);
      /* compute linespacing */
      linespacing = tm.tmHeight + tm.tmExternalLeading;

      /* display header in bright red/orange */
      SetTextColor(memdc, RGB(255, 100, 0));
```

8

```
      TextOut(memdc, X, 0, "Typeface", strlen("Typeface"));
      TextOut(memdc, X+200, 0, "Style", strlen("Style"));
      TextOut(memdc, X+300, 0, "Script", strlen("Script"));
      SetTextColor(memdc, RGB(0, 0, 0));

      ReleaseDC(hwnd, hdc);
      break;
  case WM_COMMAND:
    switch(LOWORD(wParam)) {
      case IDM_FONTS: /* display fonts */
        Y = linespacing + linespacing/2;
        PatBlt(memdc, 0, linespacing, maxX, maxY, PATCOPY);

        lf.lfCharSet = DEFAULT_CHARSET;
        strcpy(lf.lfFaceName, "");
        lf.lfPitchAndFamily = 0;

        /* enumerate fonts */
        hdc = GetDC(hwnd);
        EnumFontFamiliesEx(hdc, &lf,
            (FONTENUMPROC) FontFunc, (LPARAM)hwnd, 0);
        ReleaseDC(hwnd, hdc);

        break;
      case IDM_TYPEFACE: /* display selected typeface */
        /* get name of font */
        result = DialogBox(hInst, "FontDB", hwnd,
                           (DLGPROC) FontDialog);

        if(!result) break; /* user cancelled */

        Y = linespacing + linespacing/2;
        PatBlt(memdc, 0, linespacing, maxX, maxY, PATCOPY);

        lf.lfCharSet = DEFAULT_CHARSET;
        strcpy(lf.lfFaceName, fontstr);
        lf.lfPitchAndFamily = 0;

        /* enumerate all styles for given font */
        hdc = GetDC(hwnd);
        EnumFontFamiliesEx(hdc, &lf,
            (FONTENUMPROC) FontFunc, (LPARAM) hwnd, 0);
        ReleaseDC(hwnd, hdc);

        break;
```

```
        case IDM_EXIT:
          response = MessageBox(hwnd, "Quit the Program?",
                                "Exit", MB_YESNO);
          if(response == IDYES) PostQuitMessage(0);
          break;
        case IDM_HELP:
          MessageBox(hwnd, "F2: Show Fonts\nF3: Show Typeface\n",
                            "Show Fonts", MB_OK);
          break;
      }
      break;
    case WM_PAINT: /* process a repaint request */
      hdc = BeginPaint(hwnd, &paintstruct); /* get DC */

      /* copy virtual window onto the screen */
      BitBlt(hdc, 0, 0, maxX, maxY, memdc, 0, 0, SRCCOPY);
      EndPaint(hwnd, &paintstruct); /* release DC */
      break;
    case WM_DESTROY: /* terminate the program */
      DeleteDC(memdc);
      PostQuitMessage(0);
      break;
    default:
      /* Let Windows 98 process any messages not specified in
      the preceding switch statement. */
      return DefWindowProc(hwnd, message, wParam, lParam);
  }
  return 0;
}


/* Enumerate Fonts */
int CALLBACK FontFunc(ENUMLOGFONTEX *lpLF,
                      NEWTEXTMETRICEX *lpTM,
                      int type, LPARAM lParam)
{
  int response;
  RECT rect;

  /* display font info */
  TextOut(memdc, X, Y, lpLF->elfLogFont.lfFaceName,
          strlen(lpLF->elfLogFont.lfFaceName)); /* output font name */
  TextOut(memdc, X+200, Y, (char *)lpLF->elfStyle,
          strlen((char *)lpLF->elfStyle)); /* output style */
  TextOut(memdc, X+300, Y, (char *)lpLF->elfScript,
```

8

```
                  strlen((char *)lpLF->elfScript)); /* output script style */


  Y += linespacing;

  InvalidateRect((HWND)lParam, NULL, 0);

  /* get current dimensions of the client area */
  GetClientRect((HWND)lParam, &rect);

  /* pause at bottom of window */
  if( (Y + linespacing) >= rect.bottom) {
    Y = linespacing + linespacing/2; /* reset to top */
    response = MessageBox((HWND)lParam, "More?",
                          "More Fonts?", MB_YESNO);
    if(response == IDNO) return 0;
    PatBlt(memdc, 0, linespacing, maxX, maxY, PATCOPY);
  }

  return 1;
}

/* Enumerate font dialog box */
BOOL CALLBACK FontDialog(HWND hdwnd, UINT message,
                         WPARAM wParam, LPARAM lParam)
{
  switch(message) {
    case WM_COMMAND:
      switch(LOWORD(wParam)) {
        case IDCANCEL:
          EndDialog(hdwnd, 0);
          return 1;
        case IDD_ENUM:
          /* get typeface name */
          GetDlgItemText(hdwnd, IDD_EB1, fontstr, 80);
          EndDialog(hdwnd, 1);
          return 1;
      }
      break;
  }
  return 0;
}
```

This program uses the following resource file.

```
#include <windows.h>
#include "font.h"

FontEnumMenu MENU
{
  POPUP "Enumerate" {
    MENUITEM "Available &Fonts\tF2", IDM_FONTS
    MENUITEM "Selected &Typeface\tF3", IDM_TYPEFACE
    MENUITEM "E&xit\tCtrl+X", IDM_EXIT
  }
  MENUITEM "&Help", IDM_HELP
}


FontEnumMenu ACCELERATORS
{
  VK_F2, IDM_FONTS, VIRTKEY
  VK_F3, IDM_TYPEFACE, VIRTKEY
  "^X", IDM_EXIT
  VK_F1, IDM_HELP, VIRTKEY
}

FontDB DIALOG 10, 10, 100, 60
CAPTION "Enumerate Typeface"
STYLE WS_POPUP | WS_CAPTION | WS_SYSMENU | WS_VISIBLE
{
  CTEXT "Enter Typeface", 300, 10, 10, 80, 12
  EDITTEXT IDD_EB1, 10, 20, 80, 12, ES_LEFT |
           WS_VISIBLE | WS_BORDER | ES_AUTOHSCROLL |
           WS_TABSTOP
  DEFPUSHBUTTON "Enumerate" IDD_ENUM, 30, 40, 40, 14,
           WS_CHILD | WS_VISIBLE | WS_TABSTOP
}
```

The FONT.H header file is shown here.

```
#define IDM_FONTS      100
#define IDM_TYPEFACE   101
#define IDM_EXIT       102
#define IDM_HELP       103

#define IDD_EB1        200
#define IDD_ENUM       201
```

8

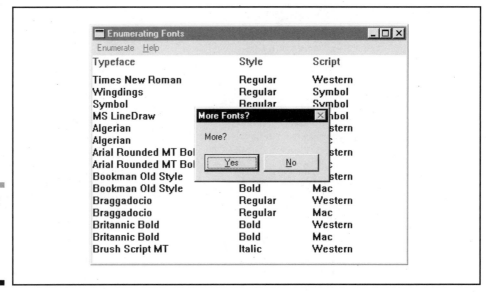

Let's take a closer look at this program. When you select Available fonts,
EnumFontFamiliesEx( ) is called with **lf.lfFaceName** containing a null
string. This causes a representative font from each typeface supported by the
system to be returned. When you choose Selected Typeface, you activate a
small dialog box in which you can enter the name of the desired typeface.
This string is then used for the **lf.lfFaceName** field. This causes all fonts of
only that typeface to be enumerated.

The callback function **FontFunc( )** receives each enumerated font and
displays it. For simplicity, the function displays a window full of fonts and
then pops up a message box, asking if you want to see more. If you do, the
next window's worth is shown. To determine the current size of the window,
FontFunc( ) calls **GetClientRect( )**. **GetClientRect( )** has this prototype:

BOOL GetClientRect(HWND *hwnd*, LPRECT *lpDim*);

Here, *hwnd* is the handle of the window in question, and *lpDim* is a pointer
to a **RECT** structure that will receive the current coordinates of the client

area of the window. The function returns nonzero if successful and zero on failure. This function is useful whenever you need to know the current size of the client area of a window. In this program, the value in **rect.bottom** is used to determine if there is sufficient room to display another line of text within the current height of the window.

Here is a challenge that you might find interesting: Each time a font is enumerated, its logical settings are returned in a **LOGFONT** structure. Use this structure to create a font, using **CreateFontIndirect( )** to actually create each font that is enumerated and then display a string in that font. This makes an easy way to actually see what fonts are available for your use.

Remember, Windows 98 support for fonts and text is quite rich. You will want to investigate this area on your own. In the next chapter, we will continue exploring window output by working with graphics.

8

CHAPTER 9

Working with Graphics

Windows 98 has a rich and flexible set of graphics functions available to the programmer. This is not surprising since it is a graphical operating system. However, what you might find surprising is how tightly integrated graphics are into the Window display system. In fact, much of what you learned in the preceding chapter about text is applicable to graphics. For example, the same brush that is used to paint the window is used to fill an object. This chapter discusses and demonstrates several of Windows' graphics functions.

This chapter also examines several features that control precisely how output is mapped to a window. Specifically, it discusses how to set the current mapping mode, how to change the logical coordinates associated with a window, and how to define a viewport. These factors have a profound effect on how both graphics and text are displayed.

Keep in mind that the discussion of graphics and related topics in this chapter only scratches the surface. For example, there are several other graphics-related API functions available for your use beyond those described here. The Windows 98 graphics system is quite powerful, and you will want to explore it further on your own.

The Graphics Coordinate System

The graphics coordinate system is the same as that used by the text-based functions. This means that, by default, the upper-left corner is location 0,0 and that logical units are equivalent to pixels. Remember, the coordinate system and the mapping of logical units to pixels is under your control and may be changed. (You will see how later in this chapter.)

Windows 98 (and Windows in general) maintains a *current position* that is used and updated by certain graphics functions. When your program begins, the current location is set to 0,0. Keep in mind that the location of the current position is completely invisible. That is, no graphics "cursor" is displayed. Instead, the current position is simply the next place in the window at which certain graphics functions will begin.

Pens and Brushes

The Windows graphics system is based upon two important objects: pens and brushes. You learned about Windows' built-in brushes in Chapter 8. All of that information applies to the graphics functions described here as well. By default, closed graphics shapes, such as rectangles and ellipses, are filled using

Pens draw lines and brushes fill areas.

the currently selected brush. Pens are resources that draw the lines and curves specified by the various graphics functions. The default pen is black and one pixel thick, but you can alter these attributes.

Until now, we have only been working with stock objects. In this chapter you will learn how to create custom brushes and pens. There is one important thing to remember about custom objects: they must be deleted before your program ends. This is accomplished using **DeleteObject( )**.

Setting a Pixel

You can set the color of any specific pixel using the API function **SetPixel( )**, whose prototype is shown here:

COLORREF SetPixel(HDC *hdc*, int *X*, int *Y*, COLORREF *color*);

Here, *hdc* is the handle to the desired device context. The coordinates of the point to set are specified by *X,Y*, and the color is specified in *color*. The function returns the original color of the pixel, or –1 if an error occurs or if the location specified is outside the window.

Drawing a Line

To draw a line, use the **LineTo( )** function. This function draws a line using the currently selected pen. Its prototype is shown here:

BOOL LineTo(HDC *hdc*, int *X*, int *Y*);

9

The handle of the device context in which to draw the line is specified by *hdc*. The line is drawn from the current graphics position to the coordinates specified by *X,Y*. The current position is then changed to *X,Y*. The function returns nonzero if successful (i.e., the line is drawn) and zero on failure.

Some programmers are surprised by the fact that **LineTo( )** uses the current position as its starting location and then sets the current position to the end point of the line that is drawn (instead of leaving it unchanged). However, there is a good reason for this. Many times, when displaying lines, one line will begin at the end of the previous line. When this is the case, **LineTo( )** operates extremely efficiently by avoiding the additional overhead of passing an extra set of coordinates. When this is not the case, you can set the current location to any position you like using the **MoveToEx( )** function, described next, prior to calling **LineTo( )**.

Setting the Current Location

To set the current position, use the **MoveToEx( )** function, whose prototype is shown here:

BOOL MoveToEx(HDC *hdc*, int *X*, int *Y*, LPPOINT *lpCoord*);

The handle to the device context is specified in *hdc*. The coordinates of the new current position are specified by *X,Y*. The previous current position is returned in the **POINT** structure pointed to by *lpCoord*. Recall that **POINT** is defined like this:

```
typedef struct tagPOINT {
  LONG x;
  LONG y;
} POINT;
```

However, if you use **NULL** for the *lpCoord* parameter, then **MoveToEx( )** does not obtain the previous current position. **MoveToEx( )** returns nonzero if successful and zero on failure.

PORTABILITY: In Windows 3.1, the function that moves the current location is called **MoveTo( )**. It has only three parameters, which are the same as the first three parameters of **MoveToEx( )**. It returns the previous location as a double word. This function is not supported by Win32. If you are porting code that uses this function, make appropriate changes. If your program doesn't need the previous location, simply make the *lpCoord* parameter **NULL**.

Drawing an Arc

You can draw an elliptical arc (a portion of an ellipse) in the current pen color using the **Arc( )** function. Its prototype is shown here.

BOOL Arc(HDC *hdc*, int *upX*, int *upY*, int *lowX*, int *lowY*,
         int *startX*, int *startY*, int *endX*, int *endY*);

Here, *hdc* is the handle of the device context in which the arc will be drawn. The arc is defined by two objects. First, the arc is a portion of an ellipse that is bounded by the rectangle whose upper-left corner is at *upX,upY* and whose lower-right corner is at *lowX,lowY*. The portion of the ellipse that is actually drawn (i.e., the arc) starts at the intersection of a line from the center of the rectangle through the point specified by *startX,startY* and ends at the intersection of a line from the center of the rectangle through the point *endX,endY*. The arc is drawn counterclockwise starting from *startX,startY*. Figure 9-1 illustrates how **Arc( )** works.

Arc( ) returns nonzero if successful and zero on failure.

Displaying Rectangles

You can display a rectangle in the current pen using the **Rectangle( )** function, whose prototype is shown here:

BOOL Rectangle(HDC *hdc*, int *upX*, int *upY*, int *lowX*, int *lowY*);

As usual, *hdc* is the handle of the device context. The upper-left corner of the rectangle is specified by *upX,upY*, and the lower-right corner is specified by *lowX,lowY*. The function returns nonzero if successful and zero if an error occurs. The rectangle is automatically filled using the current brush.

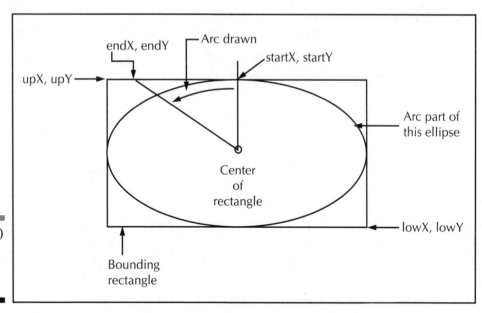

9

How the **Arc( )** function operates

Figure 9-1.

You can display a rounded rectangle using the **RoundRect( )** function. A rounded rectangle has its corners rounded slightly. The prototype for **RoundRect( )** is shown here.

BOOL RoundRect(HDC *hdc*, int *upX*, int *upY*,
　　　　　　int *lowX*, int *lowY*,
　　　　　　int *curveX*, int *curveY*);

The first five parameters are the same as for **Rectangle( )**. How the corners are curved is determined by the values of *curveX* and *curveY*, which define the width and the height of the ellipse that describes the curve. The function returns nonzero if successful and zero if a failure occurs. The rounded rectangle is automatically filled using the current brush.

Drawing Ellipses and Pie Slices

To draw an ellipse or a circle in the current pen, use the **Ellipse( )** function, whose prototype is shown here:

BOOL Ellipse(HDC *hdc*, int *upX*, int *upY*, int *lowX*, int *lowY*);

Here, *hdc* is the handle of the device content in which the ellipse will be drawn. The ellipse is defined by specifying its bounding rectangle. The upper-left corner of the rectangle is specified by *upX,upY,* and the lower-right corner is specified by *lowX,lowY*. To draw a circle, specify a square rectangle.

The function returns nonzero if successful and zero if a failure occurs. The ellipse is filled using the current brush.

Related to the ellipse is the pie slice. A *pie slice* is an object that includes an arc and lines from each end point of the arc to the center. To draw a pie slice, use the **Pie( )** function, whose prototype is shown here.

BOOL Pie(HDC *hdc*, int *upX*, int *upY*,
　　　　int *lowX*, int *lowY*,
　　　　int *startX*, int *startY*,
　　　　int *endX*, int *endY*);

Here, *hdc* is the handle of the device context in which the pie slice will be drawn. The arc of the slice is defined by two objects. First, the arc is a portion of an ellipse that is bounded by the rectangle whose upper-left corner is at *upX,upY* and whose lower-right corner is at *lowX,lowY*. The portion of the ellipse that is actually drawn (i.e., the arc of the slice) starts at the intersection of a line from the center of the rectangle through the point specified by *startX,startY* and ends at the intersection of a line from the center of the rectangle through the point *endX,endY*.

The slice is drawn in the current pen and filled using the current brush. The **Pie( )** function returns nonzero if successful and zero if an error occurs.

Working with Pens

Graphics objects are drawn using the current pen. By default, this is a black pen that is one pixel wide. There are three stock pens: black, white, and null. A handle to each of these can be obtained using **GetStockObject( )**, discussed earlier in this book. The macros for these stock pens are **BLACK_PEN**, **WHITE_PEN**, and **NULL_PEN**, respectively. Pen handles are of type **HPEN**.

Frankly, the stock pens are quite limited, and usually you will want to define your own pens for your application. This is accomplished using the function **CreatePen( )**, whose prototype is shown here:

    HPEN CreatePen(int *Style*, int *width*, COLORREF *color*);

The *Style* parameter determines what type of pen is created. It must be one of these values:

Macro	Pen Style
PS_DASH	Dashed
PS_DASHDOT	Dash-dot
PS_DASHDOTDOT	Dash-dot-dot
PS_DOT	Dotted
PS_INSIDEFRAME	Solid pen that is within a bounded region
PS_NULL	None
PS_SOLID	Solid line

9

The dotted and/or dashed styles may only be applied to pens that are one unit thick. The **PS_INSIDEFRAME** pen is a solid pen that will be completely within the dimensions of any object that is drawn, even when that pen is more than one unit thick. For example, if a pen with **PS_INSIDEFRAME** style and width of three is used to draw a rectangle, then the outside of the line will be within the coordinates of the rectangle. (When a wide pen of a different style is used, the line may be partially outside the dimensions of the object.)

The thickness of a pen is specified by *width*, which is in logical units. The color of the pen is specified by *color*, which is a **COLORREF** value (discussed in Chapter 8). For the examples in this chapter, all colors are specified as RGB values.

Once a pen has been created, it is selected into a device context using **SelectObject( )**. For example, the following fragment creates a red pen and then selects it for use.

```
HPEN hRedpen;
hRedpen = CreatePen(PS_SOLID, 1, RGB(255,0,0));
SelectObject(hdc, hRedpen);
```

Remember, you must delete any custom pens you create by calling **DeleteObject( )** before your program terminates.

Creating Custom Brushes

Custom brushes are created in a way similar to custom pens. There are various styles of brushes. The most common custom brush is a *solid brush*. A solid brush is created using the **CreateSolidBrush( )** API function, whose prototype is shown here:

HBRUSH CreateSolidBrush(COLORREF *color*);

The color of the brush is specified in *color*, and a handle to the brush is returned.

Once a custom brush has been created, it is selected into the device context using **SelectObject( )**. For example, the following fragment creates a green brush and then selects it for use.

```
HBRUSH hGreenbrush

hGreenbrush = CreateSolidBrush(RGB(0, 255 ,0));
SelectObject(hdc, hGreenbrush);
```

Like custom pens, custom brushes must be deleted before your program terminates.

In addition to solid brushes, there are two other types of brushes that you can create: a pattern brush and a hatch brush. A pattern brush fills areas with a bitmapped image. A hatch brush uses some form of hatchwork design. These brushes are created using **CreatePatternBrush( )** and **CreateHatchBrush( )**, respectively. The prototypes for these functions are shown here.

HBRUSH CreatePatternBrush(HBITMAP *hBMap*);

HBRUSH CreateHatchBrush(int *Style*, COLORREF *color*);

For **CreatePatternBrush( )**, *hBMap* is the handle of the bitmap whose pattern will be used as the brush. That is, the specified bitmap will be used to fill areas and paint backgrounds. The function returns a handle to the brush or **NULL** on error.

NOTE: To create a brush using a device-independent bitmap, use **CreateDIBPaternBrushPt( )**.

Brushes created using **CreateHatchBrush( )** have a hatched appearance. The exact nature of the hatching is determined by the value of *Style,* which must be one of those shown here:

9

Style	Hatching
HS_BDIAGONAL	Angled downwards
HS_CROSS	Horizontal and vertical
HS_DIAGCROSS	Angled crosshatch
HS_FDIAGONAL	Angled upwards
HS_HORIZONTAL	Horizontal
HS_VERTICAL	Vertical

The color of the brush is determined by the **COLORREF** value specified in *color*. It returns a handle to the brush or **NULL** on failure.

Deleting Custom Pens and Brushes

You must delete custom pens and brushes before your program terminates.
You do this using the **DeleteObject( )** API function. Remember, you
cannot—and must not—delete stock objects. Also, the object being deleted
must not be currently selected into any device context.

A Graphics Demonstration

The following program demonstrates the various graphics functions just
discussed. The program uses the virtual window technique developed in
Chapter 8. It directs output to a memory device context that is then
copied to the physical window when a **WM_PAINT** message is received.
(Remember, this approach to output allows a window's contents to be
automatically updated each time a **WM_PAINT** message is received.)

```
/* Demonstrate the basic graphics functions. */

#include <windows.h>
#include "graph.h"

LRESULT CALLBACK WindowFunc(HWND, UINT, WPARAM, LPARAM);

char szWinName[] = "MyWin"; /* name of window class */

char str[255]; /* holds output strings */

int maxX, maxY; /* screen dimensions */

HDC memdc; /* handle of memory DC */
HBITMAP hbit; /* handle of compatible bitmap */
HBRUSH hbrush, hOldbrush; /* handles of brushes */

/* create pens */
HPEN hOldpen; /* handle of old pen */
HPEN hRedpen, hGreenpen, hBluepen, hYellowpen;

int WINAPI WinMain(HINSTANCE hThisInst, HINSTANCE hPrevInst,
                   LPSTR lpszArgs, int nWinMode)
{
  HWND hwnd;
  MSG msg;
  WNDCLASSEX wcl;
  HACCEL hAccel;
```

```
/* Define a window class. */
wcl.cbSize = sizeof(WNDCLASSEX);

wcl.hInstance = hThisInst; /* handle to this instance */
wcl.lpszClassName = szWinName; /* window class name */
wcl.lpfnWndProc = WindowFunc; /* window function */
wcl.style = 0; /* default style */

wcl.hIcon = LoadIcon(NULL, IDI_APPLICATION); /* standard icon */
wcl.hIconSm = LoadIcon(NULL, IDI_APPLICATION); /* small icon */
wcl.hCursor = LoadCursor(NULL, IDC_ARROW); /* cursor style */

wcl.lpszMenuName = "MyMenu"; /* main menu */
wcl.cbClsExtra = 0; /* no extra */
wcl.cbWndExtra = 0; /* information needed */

/* Make the window white. */
wcl.hbrBackground = (HBRUSH) GetStockObject(WHITE_BRUSH);

/* Register the window class. */
if(!RegisterClassEx(&wcl)) return 0;

/* Now that a window class has been registered, a window
   can be created. */
hwnd = CreateWindow(
  szWinName, /* name of window class */
  "Fun with Graphics", /* title */
  WS_OVERLAPPEDWINDOW, /* window style - normal */
  CW_USEDEFAULT, /* X coordinate - let Windows decide */
  CW_USEDEFAULT, /* Y coordinate - let Windows decide */
  CW_USEDEFAULT, /* width - let Windows decide */
  CW_USEDEFAULT, /* height - let Windows decide */
  HWND_DESKTOP, /* no parent window */
  NULL, /* no override of class menu */
  hThisInst, /* handle of this instance of the program */
  NULL /* no additional arguments */
);

/* Load accelerators. */
hAccel = LoadAccelerators(hThisInst, "MyMenu");

/* Display the window. */
ShowWindow(hwnd, nWinMode);
UpdateWindow(hwnd);
```

9

```
/* Create the message loop. */
while(GetMessage(&msg, NULL, 0, 0))
{
  if(!TranslateAccelerator(hwnd, hAccel, &msg)) {
    TranslateMessage(&msg); /* translate keyboard messages */
    DispatchMessage(&msg); /* return control to Windows 98 */
  }
}
return msg.wParam;
}

/* This function is called by Windows 98 and is passed
   messages from the message queue.
*/
LRESULT CALLBACK WindowFunc(HWND hwnd, UINT message,
                            WPARAM wParam, LPARAM lParam)
{
  HDC hdc;
  PAINTSTRUCT paintstruct;
  int response;

  switch(message) {
    case WM_CREATE:
      /* get screen coordinates */
      maxX = GetSystemMetrics(SM_CXSCREEN);
      maxY = GetSystemMetrics(SM_CYSCREEN);

      /* make a compatible memory image device */
      hdc = GetDC(hwnd);
      memdc = CreateCompatibleDC(hdc);
      hbit = CreateCompatibleBitmap(hdc, maxX, maxY);
      SelectObject(memdc, hbit);
      hbrush = (HBRUSH) GetStockObject(WHITE_BRUSH);
      SelectObject(memdc, hbrush);
      PatBlt(memdc, 0, 0, maxX, maxY, PATCOPY);

      hRedpen = CreatePen(PS_SOLID, 1, RGB(255,0,0));
      hGreenpen = CreatePen(PS_SOLID, 2, RGB(0,255,0));
      hBluepen = CreatePen(PS_SOLID, 3, RGB(0,0,255));
      hYellowpen = CreatePen(PS_SOLID, 4, RGB(255, 255, 0));

      /* save default pen */
      hOldpen = (HPEN) SelectObject(memdc, hRedpen);
      SelectObject(memdc, hOldpen);
```

```
        ReleaseDC(hwnd, hdc);
        break;
case WM_COMMAND:
    switch(LOWORD(wParam)) {
      case IDM_LINES:
        /* set 2 pixels */
        SetPixel(memdc, 40, 14, RGB(0, 0, 0));
        SetPixel(memdc, 40, 15, RGB(0, 0, 0));

        LineTo(memdc, 100, 50);
        MoveToEx(memdc, 100, 50, NULL);

        /* change to green pen */
        hOldpen = (HPEN) SelectObject(memdc, hGreenpen);
        LineTo(memdc, 200, 100);

        /* change to yellow pen */
        SelectObject(memdc, hYellowpen);
        LineTo(memdc, 0, 200);

        /* change to blue pen */
        SelectObject(memdc, hBluepen);
        LineTo(memdc, 200, 200);

        /* change to red pen */
        SelectObject(memdc, hRedpen);
        LineTo(memdc, 0, 0);

        /* return to default pen */
        SelectObject(memdc, hOldpen);

        Arc(memdc, 0, 0, 300, 300, 0, 50, 200, 50);
        /* show intersecting lines that define arc */
        MoveToEx(memdc, 150, 150, NULL);
        LineTo(memdc, 0, 50);
        MoveToEx(memdc, 150, 150, NULL);
        LineTo(memdc, 200, 50);

        InvalidateRect(hwnd, NULL, 1);
        break;
      case IDM_RECTANGLES:
        /* display, but don't fill */
        hOldbrush = (HBRUSH) SelectObject(memdc,
                           GetStockObject(HOLLOW_BRUSH));
```

9

```
/* draw some rectangles */
Rectangle(memdc, 50, 50, 300, 300);
RoundRect(memdc, 125, 125, 220, 240, 15, 13);

/* use a red pen */
SelectObject(memdc, hRedpen);
Rectangle(memdc, 100, 100, 200, 200);
SelectObject(memdc, hOldpen); /* return to default pen */

/* restore default brush */
SelectObject(memdc, hOldbrush);

InvalidateRect(hwnd, NULL, 1);
break;
case IDM_ELLIPSES:
/* make blue brush */
hbrush = CreateSolidBrush(RGB(0, 0, 255));
hOldbrush = (HBRUSH) SelectObject(memdc, hbrush);

/* fill these ellipses with blue */
Ellipse(memdc, 50, 200, 100, 280);
Ellipse(memdc, 75, 25, 280, 100);

/* use a red pen and fill with green */
SelectObject(memdc, hRedpen);
DeleteObject(hbrush); /* delete brush */
/* create green brush */
hbrush = CreateSolidBrush(RGB(0, 255, 0));
SelectObject(memdc, hbrush); /* select green brush */
Ellipse(memdc, 100, 100, 200, 200);

/* draw a pie slice */
Pie(memdc, 200, 200, 340, 340, 225, 200, 200, 250);

SelectObject(memdc, hOldpen); /* return to default pen */

SelectObject(memdc, hOldbrush); /* select default brush */
DeleteObject(hbrush); /* delete green brush */

InvalidateRect(hwnd, NULL, 1);
break;
```

```
      case IDM_RESET:
        /* reset current position to 0,0 */
        MoveToEx(memdc, 0, 0, NULL);
        /* erase by repainting background */
        PatBlt(memdc, 0, 0, maxX, maxY, PATCOPY);
        InvalidateRect(hwnd, NULL, 1);
        break;
      case IDM_EXIT:
        response = MessageBox(hwnd, "Quit the Program?",
                              "Exit", MB_YESNO);
        if(response == IDYES) PostQuitMessage(0);
        break;
      case IDM_HELP:
        MessageBox(hwnd, "F2: Lines\nF3: Rectangles\n"
                   "F4: Ellipses\nF5: Reset",
                   "Graphics Fun", MB_OK);
        break;
    }
    break;
  case WM_PAINT: /* process a repaint request */
    hdc = BeginPaint(hwnd, &paintstruct); /* get DC */

    /* now, copy memory image onto screen */
    BitBlt(hdc, 0, 0, maxX, maxY, memdc, 0, 0, SRCCOPY);

    EndPaint(hwnd, &paintstruct); /* release DC */
    break;
  case WM_DESTROY: /* terminate the program */
    DeleteObject(hRedpen); /* delete pens */
    DeleteObject(hGreenpen);
    DeleteObject(hBluepen);
    DeleteObject(hYellowpen);

    DeleteDC(memdc);
    PostQuitMessage(0);
    break;
  default:
    /* Let Windows 98 process any messages not specified in
       the preceding switch statement. */
    return DefWindowProc(hwnd, message, wParam, lParam);
  }
  return 0;
}
```

9

This program requires the resource file shown here:

```
#include <windows.h>
#include "graph.h"

MyMenu MENU
{
  POPUP "&Graphics" {
    MENUITEM "&Lines\tF2", IDM_LINES
    MENUITEM "&Rectangles\tF3", IDM_RECTANGLES
    MENUITEM "&Ellipses\tF4", IDM_ELLIPSES
    MENUITEM "&Reset", IDM_RESET
    MENUITEM "E&xit\tCtrl+X", IDM_EXIT
  }
  MENUITEM "&Help", IDM_HELP
}

MyMenu ACCELERATORS
{
  VK_F2, IDM_LINES, VIRTKEY
  VK_F3, IDM_RECTANGLES, VIRTKEY
  VK_F4, IDM_ELLIPSES, VIRTKEY
  VK_F5, IDM_RESET, VIRTKEY
  "^X", IDM_EXIT
  VK_F1, IDM_HELP, VIRTKEY
}
```

It also requires the header file GRAPH.H shown here:

```
#define IDM_LINES       100
#define IDM_RECTANGLES 101
#define IDM_ELLIPSES    102
#define IDM_RESET       103
#define IDM_EXIT        104
#define IDM_HELP        105
```

The program displays a main menu that lets you display lines (plus two pixels), rectangles, and ellipses. It also lets you reset the window, which erases its contents and resets the current position, and start over. Sample output is shown in Figure 9-2.

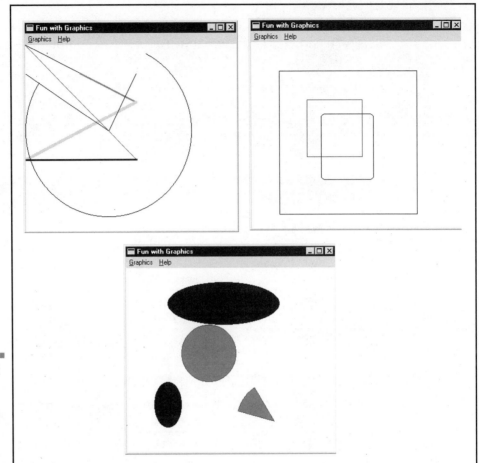

Sample output
from the
graphics
demonstration
program

Figure 9-2.

9

Setting the Output Mode

Whenever your program outputs graphics to a window, how that output
is actually copied to the window is determined by the output mode in
effect at the time. By default, information is copied as-is to the window,
overwriting any previous contents. However, other output modes can be

used. For example, output can be ANDed, ORed, or XORed with the current contents of the window. To specify the output mode, use the **SetROP2( )** function. Its prototype is shown here:

   int SetROP2(HDC *hdc*, int *Mode*);

Here, *hdc* is the handle of the device context being affected, and *Mode* specifies the new drawing mode. **SetROP2( )** returns the previous drawing mode or zero on failure. *Mode* must be one of the values shown here.

Macro	Drawing Mode
R2_BLACK	Result is black.
R2_COPYPEN	Output is copied to the window, overwriting current contents.
R2_MASKPEN	Output is ANDed with the current screen color.
R2_MASKNOTPEN	Inverse of output is ANDed with the current screen color.
R2_MASKPENNOT	Output is ANDed with the inverse of the current screen color.
R2_MERGEPEN	Output is ORed with the current screen color.
R2_MERGENOTPEN	Inverse of output is ORed with the current screen color.
R2_MERGEPENNOT	Output is ORed with the inverse current screen color.
R2_NOP	No effect.
R2_NOT	Result is the inverse of the current screen color.
R2_NOTCOPYPEN	Inverse of the output color is copied to the window.
R2_NOTMASKPEN	Resulting color is the inverse of R2_MASKPEN.
R2_NOTMERGEPEN	Resulting color is the inverse of R2_MERGEPEN.

Macro	Drawing Mode
R2_NOTXORPEN	Resulting color is the inverse of R2_XORPEN.
R2_WHITE	Result is white.
R2_XORPEN	Output is exclusive-ORed with the current screen color.

The **R2_XORPEN** is especially interesting because it allows output to be temporarily displayed without losing the information that is already on the screen. The reason for this has to do with a special property of the XOR operation. Consider the following. When one value, called A, is XORed with another, called B, it produces a result which, when XORed with B a second time, produces the original value, A. Thus, if you XOR output to the screen and then XOR the same output to the screen a second time, the original contents of the screen will be restored. This means that you can XOR output to the screen to display something temporarily and then simply XOR it to the screen again to restore the screen's original contents. This technique was briefly discussed in Chapter 7 as it related to the displaying of bitmaps. You might find it interesting to experiment with **R2_XORPEN** and the other output mode on your own.

One final point: The ROP in the name of the function stands for Raster OPerations. This function applies only to raster devices, such as monitors.

9

Understanding Mapping Modes and Viewports

The mapping mode determines how logical units are converted into physical units.

Before concluding, we will examine two more aspects of Windows 98's graphics system: mapping modes and viewports. As you know, the Windows text and graphics functions operate on logical units. These logical units are then translated by Windows into physical units (i.e., pixels) when an object is displayed. How the translation from logical units to physical units is made is determined by the current *mapping mode*. By default, logical units are the same as pixels. However, you can change the ratio of logical units to physical units by changing the mapping mode.

A viewport is a rectangular region defined in device space.

In addition to changing the mapping mode, for certain mapping modes you can also set two other attributes that affect the translation of logical to physical units. First, you can define the length and width of a window in terms of logical units that you select. Second, you can set the physical extents of the viewport. The *viewport* is a rectangular region defined within a device space. The dimensions of the viewport help determine the ratio of logical units to physical units. Output is mapped so that it fits within the viewport's boundaries. For most mapping modes, the size of the viewport is predetermined and cannot be altered. But there are two mapping modes in which the size of the viewport is under your control. You can also set the origin of the viewport.

Setting the Mapping Mode

By default, logical units are the same as pixels. Thus, the default ratio of logical units to pixels is one to one. You can change this ratio by changing the mapping mode. To set the current mapping mode, use **SetMapMode( )**. It has this prototype:

    int SetMapMode(HDC *hdc*, int *mode*);

The handle to the device context is specified by *hdc*. *mode* specifies the new mapping mode, and it can be any one of the following constants.

Mapping Mode	Meaning
MM_ANISOTROPIC	Maps logical units to programmer-defined units with arbitrarily scaled axes.
MM_HIENGLISH	Maps each logical unit to 0.001 inch.
MM_HIMETRIC	Maps each logical unit to 0.01 millimeter.
MM_ISOTROPIC	Maps logical units to programmer-defined units with equally scaled axes (this establishes a one-to-one aspect ratio).
MM_LOENGLISH	Maps each logical unit to 0.01 inch.
MM_LOMETRIC	Maps each logical unit to 0.1 millimeter.
MM_TEXT	Maps each logical unit to one device pixel.
MM_TWIPS	Maps each logical unit to 1/20 of a printer's point, or approximately 1/1440 inch.

SetMapMode( ) returns the previous mapping mode or zero if an error occurs.

For **MM_TEXT**, positive *X* values move right and positive *Y* values move down. For **MM_ANISOTROPIC** and **MM_ISOTROPIC**, the positive direction of the *X* and *Y* coordinates are user definable. For the remaining modes, positive *X* values move right and positive *Y* values move up as in the normal, Cartesian coordinate plane.

The default mapping mode is **MM_TEXT**. There are several reasons why you might want to change the current mapping mode. First, if you want your program's output to be displayed in physical units, you can select one of the real-world modes, such as **MM_LOMETRIC**. Second, you might want to define units for your program that best fit the nature of what you are displaying. Third, you might want to change the scale of what is displayed. (That is, you might want to enlarge or shrink the size of what is output.) Finally, you may want to establish a one-to-one aspect ratio between the *X* and *Y* axes. When this is done, each *X* unit represents the same physical distance as each *Y* unit.

REMEMBER: Changing the mapping mode changes the way logical units are translated into physical units (pixels).

Defining the Window Extents

9

Selecting either the **MM_ISOTROPIC** or **MM_ANISOTROPIC** mapping modes allows you to define the size of the window in terms of logical units. In fact, if you select either of these mapping modes, you must define the dimensions of the window. (Since **MM_ISOTROPIC** and **MM_ANISOTROPIC** operate on programmer-defined units, the limits are technically undefined until you define them.) To define the *X* and *Y* extents of a window, use the **SetWindowExtEx( )** function, shown here.

  BOOL SetWindowExtEx(HDC *hdc*, int *Xextent*, int *Yextent*, LPSIZE *size*);

The handle of the device context is specified in *hdc*. *Xextent* and *Yextent* specify the new horizontal and vertical extents measured in logical units. The previous window extents are copied into the **SIZE** structure pointed to by *size*. However, if *size* is **NULL**, then the previous extents are ignored. The function returns nonzero if successful, and zero on failure.

SetWindowExtEx( ) has an effect only when the mapping mode is **MM_ANISOTROPIC** or **MM_ISOTROPIC**.

Recall that the **SIZE** structure is defined like this:

```
typedef struct tagSIZE {
  LONG cx;
  LONG cy;
} SIZE;
```

When you change the logical dimensions of a window, you are not changing the physical size of the window on the screen; you are simply defining the size of the window in terms of logical units that you choose. (Or, more precisely, you are defining the relationship between the logical units used by the window and the physical units—pixels—used by the device.) For example, the same window could be given logical dimensions of 100×100 or 50×75. The only difference is the ratio of logical units to pixels when an image is displayed.

PORTABILITY: **SetWindowExtEx( )** replaces the older **SetWindowExt( )** function. Be aware of this when porting older code.

Defining a Viewport

As mentioned, a viewport is a region within a device space that determines how logical units are mapped to the physical device. The viewport dimensions define the physical part of the ratio used to convert logical units into pixels. (The window extents define the logical part.) For most mapping modes, the size of the viewport is fixed and cannot be altered by your program. However, for **MM_ISOTROPIC** and **MM_ANISOTROPIC**, the size of the viewport can be defined. This means that in these mapping modes, the ratio of logical units to pixels is under your control.

A viewport is defined using the **SetViewportExtEx( )** function. Its prototype is shown here:

BOOL SetViewportExtEx(HDC *hdc*, int *Xextent*, int *Yextent*, LPSIZE *size*);

The handle of the device context is specified in *hdc*. *Xextent* and *Yextent* specify the new horizontal and vertical viewport extents, in pixels. The function returns nonzero if successful and zero on failure. The previous viewport extents are returned in the **SIZE** structure pointed to by size. However, if *size* is **NULL**, then the previous extents are ignored. **SetViewportExtEx( )** has an effect only when the mapping mode is **MM_ANISOTROPIC** or **MM_ISOTROPIC**.

A viewport may be any size you desire—that is, it may encompass the entire window or simply a part thereof.

Output is automatically mapped from the window device context (logical units) to the viewport (pixels) and scaled accordingly. Therefore, by changing the *X* and *Y* extents of the viewport, you are changing the ratio of logical units to pixels. This, in effect, changes the size of anything displayed within it. Thus, if you make the viewport extents larger, the contents of the viewport will get larger. Conversely, if you make the extents smaller, the contents of the viewport will shrink. This fact can be used as a means of enlarging or shrinking an image, as the following program demonstrates.

PORTABILITY: **SetViewportExtEx( )** replaces the older **SetViewportExt( )** function. Be sure to make this change when porting code.

9

Setting the Viewport Origin

By default, the origin of the viewport is at 0,0 within the window. However, you can change this using **SetViewportOrgEx( )**, shown here.

    BOOL SetViewportOrgEx(HDC *hdc*, int *X*, int *Y*, LPPOINT *OldOrg*);

The handle of the device context is passed in *hdc*. The new origin, specified in pixels, for the viewport is passed in *X,Y*. The previous origin is returned in the **POINT** structure pointed to by *OldOrg*. If this parameter is **NULL**, the previous origin is ignored.

Changing the origin of the viewport changes where images are drawn in the window. You will see the effect of this in the sample program that follows.

PORTABILITY: **SetViewportOrgEx( )** replaces the older **SetViewportOrg( )** function.

A Sample Mapping Mode Program

The following program is an expanded version of the preceding graphics program that sets the mapping mode, the window extents, and the viewport extents. Sample output from this program is shown in Figure 9-3. It sets the mapping mode to **MM_ANISOTROPIC**, sets the window extents to 200×200, and sets the initial viewport extents to 10×10. When you run this program, each time you select the Magnify option, the viewport extents will be increased by 10 units in each dimension, causing the image to become larger within the window. Selecting the Origin option will cause the viewport origin to be moved 50 pixels in both the X and Y direction.

```
/* Set the mapping mode, the window and the viewport
   extents. */

#include <windows.h>
#include "graph.h"

LRESULT CALLBACK WindowFunc(HWND, UINT, WPARAM, LPARAM);

char szWinName[] = "MyWin"; /* name of window class */

char str[255]; /* holds output strings */

int maxX, maxY; /* screen dimensions */

int X = 10, Y = 10; /* viewport extents */
int orgX=0, orgY=0; /* viewport orgin */

HDC memdc; /* handle of memory DC */
HBITMAP hbit; /* handle of compatible bitmap */
HBRUSH hbrush, hOldbrush; /* handles of brushes */

/* create pens */
HPEN hOldpen; /* handle of old pen */
HPEN hRedpen, hGreenpen, hBluepen, hYellowpen;
```

```
int WINAPI WinMain(HINSTANCE hThisInst, HINSTANCE hPrevInst,
                   LPSTR lpszArgs, int nWinMode)
{
  HWND hwnd;
  MSG msg;
  WNDCLASSEX wcl;
  HACCEL hAccel;

  /* Define a window class. */
  wcl.cbSize = sizeof(WNDCLASSEX);

  wcl.hInstance = hThisInst; /* handle to this instance */
  wcl.lpszClassName = szWinName; /* window class name */
  wcl.lpfnWndProc = WindowFunc; /* window function */
  wcl.style = 0; /* default style */

  wcl.hIcon = LoadIcon(NULL, IDI_APPLICATION); /* standard icon */
  wcl.hIconSm = LoadIcon(NULL, IDI_APPLICATION); /* small icon */
  wcl.hCursor = LoadCursor(NULL, IDC_ARROW); /* cursor style */

  wcl.lpszMenuName = "MyMenu"; /* main menu */
  wcl.cbClsExtra = 0; /* no extra */
  wcl.cbWndExtra = 0; /* information needed */

  /* Make the window white. */
  wcl.hbrBackground = (HBRUSH) GetStockObject(WHITE_BRUSH);

  /* Register the window class. */
  if(!RegisterClassEx(&wcl)) return 0;

  /* Now that a window class has been registered, a window
     can be created. */
  hwnd = CreateWindow(
    szWinName, /* name of window class */
    "Changing Mapping Modes", /* title */
    WS_OVERLAPPEDWINDOW, /* window style - normal */
    CW_USEDEFAULT, /* X coordinate - let Windows decide */
    CW_USEDEFAULT, /* Y coordinate - let Windows decide */
    CW_USEDEFAULT, /* width - let Windows decide */
    CW_USEDEFAULT, /* height - let Windows decide */
    HWND_DESKTOP, /* no parent window */
    NULL, /* no override of class menu */
    hThisInst, /* handle of this instance of the program */
    NULL /* no additional arguments */
  );
```

9

```
    /* Load accelerators. */
    hAccel = LoadAccelerators(hThisInst, "MyMenu");

    /* Display the window. */
    ShowWindow(hwnd, nWinMode);
    UpdateWindow(hwnd);

    /* Create the message loop. */
    while(GetMessage(&msg, NULL, 0, 0))
    {
      if(!TranslateAccelerator(hwnd, hAccel, &msg)) {
        TranslateMessage(&msg); /* translate keyboard messages */
        DispatchMessage(&msg); /* return control to Windows 98 */
      }
    }
    return msg.wParam;
}

/* This function is called by Windows 98 and is passed
   messages from the message queue.
*/
LRESULT CALLBACK WindowFunc(HWND hwnd, UINT message,
                            WPARAM wParam, LPARAM lParam)
{
  HDC hdc;
  PAINTSTRUCT paintstruct;
  int response;

  switch(message) {
    case WM_CREATE:
      /* get screen coordinates */
      maxX = GetSystemMetrics(SM_CXSCREEN);
      maxY = GetSystemMetrics(SM_CYSCREEN);

      /* make a compatible memory image device */
      hdc = GetDC(hwnd);
      memdc = CreateCompatibleDC(hdc);
      hbit = CreateCompatibleBitmap(hdc, maxX, maxY);
      SelectObject(memdc, hbit);
      hbrush = (HBRUSH) GetStockObject(WHITE_BRUSH);
      SelectObject(memdc, hbrush);
      PatBlt(memdc, 0, 0, maxX, maxY, PATCOPY);

      hRedpen = CreatePen(PS_SOLID, 1, RGB(255,0,0));
```

```
    hGreenpen = CreatePen(PS_SOLID, 2, RGB(0,255,0));
    hBluepen = CreatePen(PS_SOLID, 3, RGB(0,0,255));
    hYellowpen = CreatePen(PS_SOLID, 4, RGB(255, 255, 0));

    /* save default pen */
    hOldpen = (HPEN) SelectObject(memdc, hRedpen);
    SelectObject(memdc, hOldpen);

    ReleaseDC(hwnd, hdc);
    break;
case WM_COMMAND:
  switch(LOWORD(wParam)) {
    case IDM_LINES:
      /* set 2 pixels */
      SetPixel(memdc, 40, 14, RGB(0, 0, 0));
      SetPixel(memdc, 40, 15, RGB(0, 0, 0));

      LineTo(memdc, 100, 50);
      MoveToEx(memdc, 100, 50, NULL);

      /* change to green pen */
      hOldpen = (HPEN) SelectObject(memdc, hGreenpen);
      LineTo(memdc, 200, 100);

      /* change to yellow pen */
      SelectObject(memdc, hYellowpen);
      LineTo(memdc, 0, 200);

      /* change to blue pen */
      SelectObject(memdc, hBluepen);
      LineTo(memdc, 200, 200);

      /* change to red pen */
      SelectObject(memdc, hRedpen);
      LineTo(memdc, 0, 0);

      /* return to default pen */
      SelectObject(memdc, hOldpen);

      Arc(memdc, 0, 0, 300, 300, 0, 50, 200, 50);
      /* show intersecting lines that define arc */
      MoveToEx(memdc, 150, 150, NULL);
      LineTo(memdc, 0, 50);
      MoveToEx(memdc, 150, 150, NULL);
      LineTo(memdc, 200, 50);
```

9

```
        InvalidateRect(hwnd, NULL, 1);
        break;
    case IDM_RECTANGLES:
      /* display, but don't fill */
      hOldbrush = (HBRUSH) SelectObject(memdc,
                            GetStockObject(HOLLOW_BRUSH));

      /* draw some rectangles */
      Rectangle(memdc, 50, 50, 300, 300);
      RoundRect(memdc, 125, 125, 220, 240, 15, 13);

      /* use a red pen */
      SelectObject(memdc, hRedpen);
      Rectangle(memdc, 100, 100, 200, 200);
      SelectObject(memdc, hOldpen); /* return to default pen */

      /* restore default brush */
      SelectObject(memdc, hOldbrush);

      InvalidateRect(hwnd, NULL, 1);
      break;
    case IDM_ELLIPSES:
      /* make blue brush */
      hbrush = CreateSolidBrush(RGB(0, 0, 255));
      hOldbrush = (HBRUSH) SelectObject(memdc, hbrush);

      /* fill these ellipses with blue */
      Ellipse(memdc, 50, 200, 100, 280);
      Ellipse(memdc, 75, 25, 280, 100);

      /* use a red pen and fill with green */
      SelectObject(memdc, hRedpen);
      DeleteObject(hbrush); /* delete brush */
      /* create green brush */
      hbrush = CreateSolidBrush(RGB(0, 255, 0));
      SelectObject(memdc, hbrush); /* select green brush */
      Ellipse(memdc, 100, 100, 200, 200);

      /* draw a pie slice */
      Pie(memdc, 200, 200, 340, 340, 225, 200, 200, 250);

      SelectObject(memdc, hOldpen); /* return to default pen */

      SelectObject(memdc, hOldbrush); /* select default brush */
      DeleteObject(hbrush); /* delete green brush */
```

```
            InvalidateRect(hwnd, NULL, 1);
            break;
        case IDM_SIZE: /* increment size by 10 each time */
            /* reset current position to 0,0 */
            X += 10;
            Y += 10;
            InvalidateRect(hwnd, NULL, 1);
            break;
        case IDM_ORG: /* change viewport origin */
            orgX += 50;
            orgY += 50;
            InvalidateRect(hwnd, NULL, 1);
            break;
        case IDM_RESET:
            /* reset current position to 0,0 */
            MoveToEx(memdc, 0, 0, NULL);
            /* erase by repainting background */
            PatBlt(memdc, 0, 0, maxX, maxY, PATCOPY);
            InvalidateRect(hwnd, NULL, 1);
            break;
        case IDM_EXIT:
            response = MessageBox(hwnd, "Quit the Program?",
                                  "Exit", MB_YESNO);
            if(response == IDYES) PostQuitMessage(0);
            break;
        case IDM_HELP:
            MessageBox(hwnd, "F2: Lines\nF3: Rectangles\n"
                       "F4: Ellipses\nF5: Magnify\n"
                       "F6: Orign\nF7: Reset",
                       "Graphics Fun", MB_OK);
            break;
    }
    break;
case WM_PAINT: /* process a repaint request */
    hdc = BeginPaint(hwnd, &paintstruct); /* get DC */

    /* set mapping mode, window and viewport extents */
    SetMapMode(hdc, MM_ANISOTROPIC);
    SetWindowExtEx(hdc, 200, 200, NULL);
    SetViewportExtEx(hdc, X, Y, NULL);
    SetViewportOrgEx(hdc, orgX, orgY, NULL);

    /* now, copy memory image onto screen */
    BitBlt(hdc, 0, 0, maxX, maxY, memdc, 0, 0, SRCCOPY);

    EndPaint(hwnd, &paintstruct); /* release DC */
    break;
```

9

```
      case WM_DESTROY: /* terminate the program */
        DeleteObject(hRedpen); /* delete pens */
        DeleteObject(hGreenpen);
        DeleteObject(hBluepen);
        DeleteObject(hYellowpen);

        DeleteDC(memdc);
        PostQuitMessage(0);
        break;
      default:
        /* Let Windows 98 process any messages not specified in
           the preceding switch statement. */
        return DefWindowProc(hwnd, message, wParam, lParam);
  }
  return 0;
}
```

This program uses the following resource file.

```
#include <windows.h>
#include "graph.h"

MyMenu MENU
{
  POPUP "&Viewport" {
    MENUITEM "&Lines\tF2", IDM_LINES
    MENUITEM "&Rectangles\tF3", IDM_RECTANGLES
    MENUITEM "&Ellipses\tF4", IDM_ELLIPSES
    MENUITEM "&Magnify\tF5", IDM_SIZE
    MENUITEM "&Orgin\tF6", IDM_ORG
    MENUITEM "&Reset\tF7", IDM_RESET
    MENUITEM "E&xit\tCtrl+X", IDM_EXIT
  }
  MENUITEM "&Help", IDM_HELP
}


MyMenu ACCELERATORS
{
  VK_F2, IDM_LINES, VIRTKEY
  VK_F3, IDM_RECTANGLES, VIRTKEY
  VK_F4, IDM_ELLIPSES, VIRTKEY
  VK_F5, IDM_SIZE, VIRTKEY
  VK_F6, IDM_ORG, VIRTKEY
  VK_F7, IDM_RESET, VIRTKEY
  "^X", IDM_EXIT
  VK_F1, IDM_HELP, VIRTKEY
}
```

The header file GRAPH.H must be modified so that it now looks like this:

```
#define IDM_LINES       100
#define IDM_RECTANGLES 101
#define IDM_ELLIPSES   102
#define IDM_SIZE        103
#define IDM_ORG         104
#define IDM_RESET       105
#define IDM_EXIT        106
#define IDM_HELP        107
```

In the next chapter we will again take up the subject of controls by beginning our examination of the Windows 98 common controls.

9

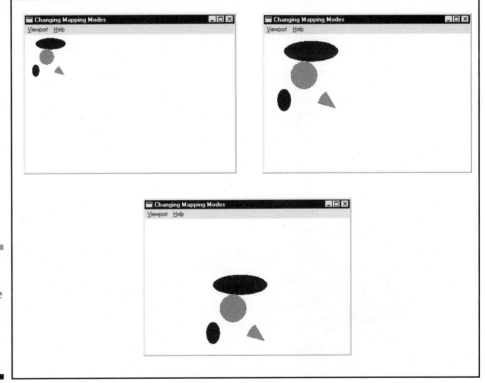

Sample output from the mapping mode program at various magnifications

Figure 9-9.

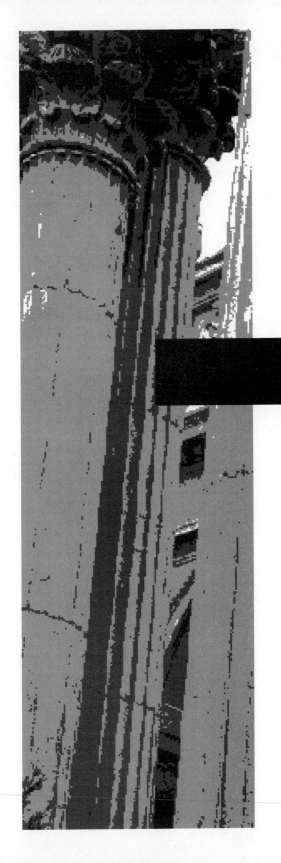

CHAPTER 10

Introducing
Common Controls

This chapter introduces one of the most exciting features of the Windows 98 user interface: common controls. In the preceding chapters you have learned about the standard controls, such as push buttons and scroll bars. However, Windows 98 defines several additional controls that add sophistication to your application and greatly enhance the interface to any Windows program. The common controls give you added power and flexibility. They also help give your application a crisp, modern look.

The following common controls are supported by Windows 98:

Control	Description
Animation Control	Displays an AVI file.
ComboBoxEx Control	Combo box with extended capabilities.
Date and Time Picker Controls	Updates date and time.
Drag List Box	A list box that allows items to be dragged.
Flat Scroll Bars	Flat rather than three-dimensional scroll bars.
Header Control	A column heading.
Hot Key Control	Supports user-created hot keys.
Image List	A list of graphical images.
IP Control	Supports user-entered Internet Protocol (IP) addresses.
List View Control	A list of icons and labels.
Month Calendar Control	A calendar-based control used for dates.
Pager Control	Scrollable control that contains other controls.
Progress Bar	A visual gauge used to indicate the degree to which a task is completed.
Property Sheet	A properties dialog box.
Rebar Control	A bar that contains other controls.
Rich Edit Control	A sophisticated edit box.
Status Window	A bar that displays information related to an application.

Control	Description
Tab Control	A tab-based menu (this control looks like the tabs on file folders).
Toolbar	A graphics-based menu.
Tooltip	Small pop-up text boxes; typically used to describe toolbar buttons or other control elements.
Trackbar	A slider-based control (similar in concept to a scroll bar, but looks like a fader control on a stereo).
Tree View Control	A tree-structured display.
Up-Down (Spin) Control	Up and down arrows; called a spin control when linked with an edit box.

Common controls are sophisticated interface components.

These controls are called *common controls* because they represent an extended set of controls that will be used by many applications. You have certainly encountered several of these controls if you have been using Windows for very long. While it won't be possible to discuss all of the common controls in this book, we will look at several of the most important and representative.

This chapter discusses the theory and general procedure for using a common control in your program. It then explores toolbars and tooltips. More common controls are examined in the following chapters.

PORTABILITY: Windows 95/NT 4 supports most of the common controls. None are available for Windows 3.1. (A few of the common controls are supported for Windows 3.1 if you are using the Microsoft Foundation Classes, but they are not part of Win16.)

10

Including and Initializing the Common Controls

Before you can use the common controls, you must include the standard header file COMMCTRL.H in your program. You must also make sure that the common controls library is linked into your program. For Microsoft Visual C++, the common controls library is called COMCTL32.LIB. This library is not automatically included, so you will need to add it to your project's linker options. Borland C++ links the appropriate library automatically. For other compilers, consult your user manual.

Applications that use one or more common controls must call **InitCommonControlsEx( )** prior to using the first common control. **InitCommonControlsEx( )** ensures that the appropriate components found in the common controls dynamic link library (DLL) are loaded and that the common controls subsystem is initialized. The prototype for **InitCommonControlsEx( )** is shown here.

    BOOL InitCommonControlsEx(LPINITCOMMONCONTROLSEX *lpcc*);

Here, *lpcc* is a pointer to an **INITCOMMONCONTROLSEX** structure that determines which controls are loaded and initialized. The function returns nonzero if successful and zero on failure.

The **INITCOMMONCONTROLSEX** structure is defined like this:

```
typedef struct tagINITCOMMONCONTROLSEX {
  DWORD dwSize;
  DWORD dwICC;
} INITCOMMONCONTROLSEX;
```

The **dwSize** member must contain the size of the **INITCOMMONCONT-ROLSEX** structure. The **dwICC** member specifies which control or set of controls is loaded. It must be one or more the following values.

Macro	Loads
ICC_ANIMATE_CLASS	Animation control.
ICC_BAR_CLASSES	Status bar, toolbar, tooltip, and trackbar controls.
ICC_COOL_CLASSES	Rebar control.
ICC_DATE_CLASSES	Date and time picker control.
ICC_HOTKEY_CLASS	Hot key control.
ICC_INTERNET_CLASSES	Internet address control.

Macro	Loads
ICC_LISTVIEW_CLASSES	Listview and header controls.
ICC_PAGESCROLLER_CLASS	Page scrolling control.
ICC_PROGRESS_CLASS	Progress bar.
ICC_TAB_CLASSES	Tab and tooltip controls.
ICC_TREEVIEW_CLASSES	Treeview and tooltip controls.
ICC_UPDOWN_CLASSES	Up-down controls.
ICC_USEREX_CLASSES	ComboBoxEx control.
ICC_WIN95_CLASSES	Common controls supported by Windows 95.

For example, the following code ensures that the toolbar control classes are loaded and initialized.

```
INITCOMMONCONTROLSEX cc;

cc.dwSize = sizeof(INITCOMMONCONTROLSEX);
cc.dwICC = ICC_BAR_CLASSES;
InitCommonControlsEx(&cc);
```

A good place to call **InitCommonControlsEx( )** is after your main window class has been registered.

PORTABILITY: **InitCommonControlsEx( )** replaces the older **InitCommonControls( )** function.

10

Common Controls Are Windows

Before continuing, it is important to understand that all of the common controls are child windows. They will be created by calling one of three functions: **CreateWindow( )**, **CreateWindowEx( )**, or a control-specific API function. (The **CreateWindowEx( )** function allows extended style attributes to be specified.) Because the common controls are windows, they can be managed in more or less the same way as you manage other windows used by your program.

Many common controls send your program either **WM_COMMAND** or **WM_NOTIFY** messages when they are accessed by the user. For many common controls, your program communicates by sending the control a message using the **SendMessage( )** API function, whose prototype is shown here.

```
LRESULT SendMessage(HWND hwnd, UINT Msg, WPARAM wParam,
                    LPARAM lParam);
```

Here, *hwnd* is the handle of the control, *Msg* is the message that you want to send to the control, and *wParam* and *lParam* contain any additional information associated with the message. The function returns the control's response, if any.

Using a Toolbar

Perhaps the most sought after of the common controls is the *toolbar*. A toolbar is essentially a graphical menu. In the toolbar, menu items are represented by icons, which form graphical buttons. Often, a toolbar is used in conjunction with a standard menu. As such, it provides an alternative means of making a menu selection. In a sense, a toolbar is a menu accelerator for the mouse.

To create a toolbar, use the **CreateToolbarEx( )** function, which is shown here.

```
HWND CreateToolbarEx(HWND hwnd, DWORD dwStyle, UINT ID,
                     int NumBitmaps, HINSTANCE hInst,
                     UINT BmpID, LPCTBBUTTON Buttons,
                     int NumButtons,
                     int ButtonWidth, int ButtonHeight,
                     int BmpWidth, int BmpHeight,
                     UINT Size);
```

Here, *hwnd* is the handle of the parent window that owns the toolbar.

The style of the toolbar is passed in *dwStyle*. The toolbar style must include **WS_CHILD**. It can also include other standard styles, such as **WS_BORDER** or **WS_VISIBLE**. Several toolbar style options are available. Here are some of the most popular.

TBSTYLE_TOOLTIPS	Include tooltips.
TBSTYLE_WRAPABLE	Wrap a long toolbar to the next line.
TBSTYLE_FLAT	Toolbar is flat.
TBSTYLE_TRANSPARENT	Toolbar is transparent.

The identifier associated with the toolbar is passed in *ID*. The identifier of the bitmap resource that forms the toolbar is passed in *BmpID*. This bitmap contains all of the images displayed within the individual toolbar buttons. The number of individual bitmap images contained in the bitmap specified by *BmpID* is passed in *NumBitmaps*. The instance handle of the application is passed in *hInst*. If you prefer, you can pass the handle to a bitmap in *BmpID* instead of its resource ID. In this case, you must specify *hInst* as **NULL**.

Information about each button is passed in an array of **TBBUTTON** structures pointed to by *Buttons*. The number of buttons in the toolbar is specified in *NumButtons*. The width and height of the buttons are passed in *ButtonWidth* and *ButtonHeight*. The width and height of the images within each button are passed in *BmpWidth* and *BmpHeight*. These dimensions are specified in terms of pixels. If *ButtonWidth* and *ButtonHeight* are zero, then appropriate button dimensions that fit the bitmap size are supplied automatically. The size of the **TBBUTTON** structure is passed in *Size*.

CreateToolbarEx( ) returns a handle to the toolbar window. It returns **NULL** on failure.

Each button has a **TBBUTTON** structure associated with it that defines its various characteristics. The **TBBUTTON** structure is shown here.

```
typedef struct _TBBUTTON {
  int iBitmap;
  int idCommand;
  BYTE fsState;
  BYTE fsStyle;
  DWORD dwData;
  int iString;
} TBBUTTON;
```

10

The index of the bitmap image associated with the button is contained in **iBitmap**. The buttons begin their indexing at zero and are displayed left to right.

The ID associated with the button is stored in **idCommand**. Each time the button is pressed, a **WM_COMMAND** message will be generated and sent to the parent window. The value of **idCommand** will be contained in the low-order word of **wParam**.

The initial state of the button is stored in **fsState**. It can be one (or more) of the following values.

State	Meaning
TBSTATE_CHECKED	Button is pressed.
TBSTATE_ELLIPSES	Ellipsis is shown when button text is truncated.
TBSTATE_ENABLE	Button may be pressed.
TBSTATE_HIDDEN	Button is hidden and inactive.
TBSTATE_INDETERMINATE	Button is gray and inactive.
TBSTATE_MARKED	Button is marked (this differs from checked).
TBSTATE_PRESSED	Button is pressed.
TBSTATE_WRAP	Following buttons are on new line.

The style of the button is contained in **fsStyle**. It can be any valid combination of the following values.

Style	Meaning
BSTYLE_AUTOSIZE	The text in a button determines its size.
TBSTYLE_BUTTON	Standard button.
TBSTYLE_CHECK	Button toggles between checked and unchecked each time it is pressed.
TBSTYLE_CHECKGROUP	A check button that is part of a mutually exclusive group.
TBSTYLE_DROPDOWN	Button is a drop-down list.
TBSTYLE_GROUP	A standard button that is part of a mutually exclusive group.

Style	Meaning
TBSTYLE_NOPREFIX	No accelerator prefix is shown.
TBSTYLE_SEP	Separates buttons (**idCommand** must be zero when this style is used).

Notice the **TBSTYLE_SEP** style. This style is used to provide a gap between buttons on the toolbar. This allows you to visually group buttons into clusters.

The **dwData** field contains user-defined data. The **iString** field is the index of an optional string associated with the button. These fields should be zero if they are unused.

In their default configuration, toolbars are fully automated controls and require virtually no management by your program in order to use them. However, you can manually manage a toolbar if you like by sending it explicit control messages. These messages are sent to the toolbar using **SendMessage( )**. Three common toolbar messages are shown here. (You will want to explore the other toolbar messages on your own.)

Message	Meaning
TB_CHECKBUTTON	Presses or clears a toolbar button. *wParam* must contain the ID of the button. *lParam* must be nonzero to press or 0 to clear.
TB_ENABLEBUTTON	Enables or disables a toolbar button. *wParam* must contain the ID of the button. *lParam* must be nonzero to enable or 0 to disable.
TB_HIDEBUTTON	Hides or shows a toolbar button. *wParam* must contain the ID of the button. *lParam* must be nonzero to hide or zero to show.

10

Toolbars can also generate notification messages that inform your program about various activities related to the toolbar. For simple toolbars, you won't need to worry about these messages. (The notification messages all begin with **TBN_**, and you can find information on them by examining the COMMCTRL.H header file or your API library reference.)

Creating the Toolbar Bitmap

Before you can use a toolbar, you must create the icons that form the graphics images inside each button. To do this, you must use an image editor. The process is similar to creating a single icon (the way you did when working with custom icons in Chapter 7). However, there is one important point to remember: there is only one bitmap associated with the toolbar, and this bitmap must contain all of the button images. Thus, if your toolbar will have six buttons, then the bitmap associated with your toolbar must define six images. For example, if your toolbar images are each 16 × 16 bits and your toolbar has six buttons, then your toolbar bitmap will have to be 16 bits high × 96 (6 times 16) bits long.

For the toolbar examples presented in this chapter, you will need five images. Each image must be 16 × 16 bits. This means that you will need to create a bitmap that is 16 × 80. Figure 10-1 shows how the toolbar bitmap used by the sample programs in this chapter looks inside the image editor. The toolbar will be used as an alternative menu for the graphics program developed in the preceding chapter. Store your bitmap in a file called TOOLBAR.BMP.

A Simple Toolbar Sample Program

The following program adds a toolbar to the graphics program developed in the preceding chapter. The toolbar duplicates the menu options. It allows you to displays lines, rectangles, and ellipses. You can also reset the window and choose Help.

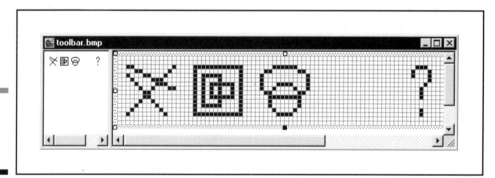

The toolbar bitmap while being edited

Figure 10-1.

```
/* Demonstrate a toolbar. */

#include <windows.h>
#include <commctrl.h>
#include "tb.h"

#define NUMBUTTONS 6

void InitToolbar(); /* initialize the tool bar */

LRESULT CALLBACK WindowFunc(HWND, UINT, WPARAM, LPARAM);

char szWinName[] = "MyWin"; /* name of window class */

int maxX, maxY; /* screen dimensions */

HDC memdc; /* handle of memory DC */
HBITMAP hbit; /* handle of compatible bitmap */
HBRUSH hbrush, hOldbrush; /* handles of brushes */

/* create pens */
HPEN hOldpen; /* handle of old pen */
HPEN hRedpen, hGreenpen, hBluepen, hYellowpen;

TBBUTTON tbButtons[NUMBUTTONS];

HWND tbwnd; /* toolbar handle */

int WINAPI WinMain(HINSTANCE hThisInst, HINSTANCE hPrevInst,
                   LPSTR lpszArgs, int nWinMode)
{
  HWND hwnd;
  MSG msg;
  WNDCLASSEX wcl;
  HACCEL hAccel;
  INITCOMMONCONTROLSEX cc;

  /* Define a window class. */
  wcl.cbSize = sizeof(WNDCLASSEX);

  wcl.hInstance = hThisInst; /* handle to this instance */
  wcl.lpszClassName = szWinName; /* window class name */
```

```
wcl.lpfnWndProc = WindowFunc; /* window function */
wcl.style = 0; /* default style */

wcl.hIcon = LoadIcon(NULL, IDI_APPLICATION); /* standard icon */
wcl.hIconSm = LoadIcon(NULL, IDI_APPLICATION); /* small icon */
wcl.hCursor = LoadCursor(NULL, IDC_ARROW); /* cursor style */

wcl.lpszMenuName = "MyMenu"; /* main menu */
wcl.cbClsExtra = 0; /* no extra */
wcl.cbWndExtra = 0; /* information needed */

/* Make the window white. */
wcl.hbrBackground = (HBRUSH) GetStockObject(WHITE_BRUSH);

/* Register the window class. */
if(!RegisterClassEx(&wcl)) return 0;

/* Now that a window class has been registered, a window
   can be created. */
hwnd = CreateWindow(
  szWinName, /* name of window class */
  "Using a Toolbar", /* title */
  WS_OVERLAPPEDWINDOW, /* window style - normal */
  CW_USEDEFAULT, /* X coordinate - let Windows decide */
  CW_USEDEFAULT, /* Y coordinate - let Windows decide */
  CW_USEDEFAULT, /* width - let Windows decide */
  CW_USEDEFAULT, /* height - let Windows decide */
  HWND_DESKTOP, /* no parent window */
  NULL, /* no override of class menu */
  hThisInst, /* handle of this instance of the program */
  NULL /* no additional arguments */
);

/* Load accelerators. */
hAccel = LoadAccelerators(hThisInst, "MyMenu");

/* Initialize the common controls. */
cc.dwSize = sizeof(INITCOMMONCONTROLSEX);
cc.dwICC = ICC_BAR_CLASSES;
InitCommonControlsEx(&cc);

InitToolbar(); /* initialize the toolbar structures */

tbwnd = CreateToolbarEx(hwnd,
                WS_VISIBLE | WS_CHILD | WS_BORDER,
```

```
                                IDM_TOOLBAR,
                                NUMBUTTONS,
                                hThisInst,
                                IDTB_BMP,
                                tbButtons,
                                NUMBUTTONS,
                                16, 16, 16, 16,
                                sizeof(TBBUTTON));

  /* Display the window. */
  ShowWindow(hwnd, nWinMode);
  UpdateWindow(hwnd);

  /* Create the message loop. */
  while(GetMessage(&msg, NULL, 0, 0))
  {
    if(!TranslateAccelerator(hwnd, hAccel, &msg)) {
      TranslateMessage(&msg); /* translate keyboard messages */
      DispatchMessage(&msg); /* return control to Windows 98 */
    }
  }
  return msg.wParam;
}

/* This function is called by Windows 98 and is passed
   messages from the message queue.
*/
LRESULT CALLBACK WindowFunc(HWND hwnd, UINT message,
                            WPARAM wParam, LPARAM lParam)
{
  HDC hdc;
  PAINTSTRUCT paintstruct;
  int response;

  switch(message) {
    case WM_CREATE:
      /* get screen coordinates */
      maxX = GetSystemMetrics(SM_CXSCREEN);
      maxY = GetSystemMetrics(SM_CYSCREEN);

      /* make a compatible memory image device */
      hdc = GetDC(hwnd);
      memdc = CreateCompatibleDC(hdc);
      hbit = CreateCompatibleBitmap(hdc, maxX, maxY);
      SelectObject(memdc, hbit);
```

10

```
    hbrush = (HBRUSH) GetStockObject(WHITE_BRUSH);
    SelectObject(memdc, hbrush);
    PatBlt(memdc, 0, 0, maxX, maxY, PATCOPY);

    hRedpen = CreatePen(PS_SOLID, 1, RGB(255,0,0));
    hGreenpen = CreatePen(PS_SOLID, 2, RGB(0,255,0));
    hBluepen = CreatePen(PS_SOLID, 3, RGB(0,0,255));
    hYellowpen = CreatePen(PS_SOLID, 4, RGB(255, 255, 0));

    /* save default pen */
    hOldpen = (HPEN) SelectObject(memdc, hRedpen);
    SelectObject(memdc, hOldpen);

    ReleaseDC(hwnd, hdc);
    break;
case WM_COMMAND:
  switch(LOWORD(wParam)) {
    case IDM_LINES:
      /* set 2 pixels */
      SetPixel(memdc, 40, 14, RGB(0, 0, 0));
      SetPixel(memdc, 40, 15, RGB(0, 0, 0));

      LineTo(memdc, 100, 50);
      MoveToEx(memdc, 100, 50, NULL);

      /* change to green pen */
      hOldpen = (HPEN) SelectObject(memdc, hGreenpen);
      LineTo(memdc, 200, 100);

      /* change to yellow pen */
      SelectObject(memdc, hYellowpen);
      LineTo(memdc, 0, 200);

      /* change to blue pen */
      SelectObject(memdc, hBluepen);
      LineTo(memdc, 200, 200);

      /* change to red pen */
      SelectObject(memdc, hRedpen);
      LineTo(memdc, 0, 0);

      /* return to default pen */
      SelectObject(memdc, hOldpen);

      Arc(memdc, 0, 0, 300, 300, 0, 50, 200, 50);
```

```
                    /* show intersecting lines that define arc */
                    MoveToEx(memdc, 150, 150, NULL);
                    LineTo(memdc, 0, 50);
                    MoveToEx(memdc, 150, 150, NULL);
                    LineTo(memdc, 200, 50);

                    InvalidateRect(hwnd, NULL, 1);
                    break;
                case IDM_RECTANGLES:
                    /* display, but don't fill */
                    hOldbrush = (HBRUSH) SelectObject(memdc,
                                        GetStockObject(HOLLOW_BRUSH));

                    /* draw some rectangles */
                    Rectangle(memdc, 50, 50, 300, 300);
                    RoundRect(memdc, 125, 125, 220, 240, 15, 13);

                    /* use a red pen */
                    SelectObject(memdc, hRedpen);
                    Rectangle(memdc, 100, 100, 200, 200);
                    SelectObject(memdc, hOldpen); /* return to default pen */

                    /* restore default brush */
                    SelectObject(memdc, hOldbrush);

                    InvalidateRect(hwnd, NULL, 1);
                    break;
                case IDM_ELLIPSES:
                    /* make blue brush */
                    hbrush = CreateSolidBrush(RGB(0, 0, 255));
                    hOldbrush = (HBRUSH) SelectObject(memdc, hbrush);

                    /* fill these ellipses with blue */
                    Ellipse(memdc, 50, 200, 100, 280);
                    Ellipse(memdc, 75, 25, 280, 100);

                    /* use a red pen and fill with green */
                    SelectObject(memdc, hRedpen);
                    DeleteObject(hbrush); /* delete brush */
                    /* create green brush */
                    hbrush = CreateSolidBrush(RGB(0, 255, 0));
                    SelectObject(memdc, hbrush); /* select green brush */
                    Ellipse(memdc, 100, 100, 200, 200);

                    /* draw a pie slice */
```

10

```
              Pie(memdc, 200, 200, 340, 340, 225, 200, 200, 250);

              SelectObject(memdc, hOldpen); /* return to default pen */

              SelectObject(memdc, hOldbrush); /* select default brush */
              DeleteObject(hbrush); /* delete green brush */

              InvalidateRect(hwnd, NULL, 1);
              break;
            case IDM_RESET:
              /* reset current position to 0,0 */
              MoveToEx(memdc, 0, 0, NULL);
              /* erase by repainting background */
              PatBlt(memdc, 0, 0, maxX, maxY, PATCOPY);
              InvalidateRect(hwnd, NULL, 1);
              break;
            case IDM_SHOW: /* show toolbar */
              ShowWindow(tbwnd, SW_RESTORE);
              break;
            case IDM_HIDE: /* hide toolbar */
              ShowWindow(tbwnd, SW_HIDE);
              break;
            case IDM_EXIT:
              response = MessageBox(hwnd, "Quit the Program?",
                                    "Exit", MB_YESNO);
              if(response == IDYES) PostQuitMessage(0);
              break;
            case IDM_HELP:
              /* show help button as pressed */
              SendMessage(tbwnd, TB_CHECKBUTTON,
                          (LPARAM) IDM_HELP, (WPARAM) 1);

              MessageBox(hwnd, "F2: Lines\nF3: Rectangles\n"
                          "F4: Ellipses\nF5: Reset\n"
                          "F6: Show Toolbar\n"
                          "F7: Hide Toolbar",
                          "Graphics Fun", MB_OK);

              /* reset the help button */
              SendMessage(tbwnd, TB_CHECKBUTTON,
                          (LPARAM) IDM_HELP, (WPARAM) 0);
              break;
          }
        break;
```

```
     case WM_PAINT: /* process a repaint request */
       hdc = BeginPaint(hwnd, &paintstruct); /* get DC */

       /* now, copy memory image onto screen */
       BitBlt(hdc, 0, 0, maxX, maxY, memdc, 0, 0, SRCCOPY);

       EndPaint(hwnd, &paintstruct); /* release DC */
       break;
     case WM_DESTROY: /* terminate the program */
       DeleteObject(hRedpen); /* delete pens */
       DeleteObject(hGreenpen);
       DeleteObject(hBluepen);
       DeleteObject(hYellowpen);

       DeleteDC(memdc);
       PostQuitMessage(0);
       break;
     default:
       /* Let Windows 98 process any messages not specified in
       the preceding switch statement. */
       return DefWindowProc(hwnd, message, wParam, lParam);
   }
   return 0;
}

/* Initialize the toolbar structures. */
void InitToolbar()
{
  tbButtons[1].iBitmap = 0;
  tbButtons[0].idCommand = IDM_LINES;
  tbButtons[0].fsState = TBSTATE_ENABLED;
  tbButtons[0].fsStyle = TBSTYLE_BUTTON;
  tbButtons[0].dwData = 0L;
  tbButtons[0].iBitmap = 0;
  tbButtons[0].iString = 0;

  tbButtons[1].iBitmap = 1;
  tbButtons[1].idCommand = IDM_RECTANGLES;
  tbButtons[1].fsState = TBSTATE_ENABLED;
  tbButtons[1].fsStyle = TBSTYLE_BUTTON;
  tbButtons[1].dwData = 0L;
  tbButtons[1].iString = 0;

  tbButtons[2].iBitmap = 2;
  tbButtons[2].idCommand = IDM_ELLIPSES;
```

10

```
  tbButtons[2].fsState = TBSTATE_ENABLED;
  tbButtons[2].fsStyle = TBSTYLE_BUTTON;
  tbButtons[2].dwData = 0L;
  tbButtons[2].iString = 0;

  tbButtons[3].iBitmap = 3;
  tbButtons[3].idCommand = IDM_RESET;
  tbButtons[3].fsState = TBSTATE_ENABLED;
  tbButtons[3].fsStyle = TBSTYLE_BUTTON;
  tbButtons[3].dwData = 0L;
  tbButtons[3].iString = 0;

  /* button separator */
  tbButtons[4].iBitmap = 0;
  tbButtons[4].idCommand = 0;
  tbButtons[4].fsState = TBSTATE_ENABLED;
  tbButtons[4].fsStyle = TBSTYLE_SEP;
  tbButtons[4].dwData = 0L;
  tbButtons[4].iString = 0;

  tbButtons[5].iBitmap = 4;
  tbButtons[5].idCommand = IDM_HELP;
  tbButtons[5].fsState = TBSTATE_ENABLED;
  tbButtons[5].fsStyle = TBSTYLE_BUTTON;
  tbButtons[5].dwData = 0L;
  tbButtons[5].iString = 0;
}
```

This program requires the following resource file.

```
#include <windows.h>
#include "tb.h"

IDTB_BMP BITMAP "toolbar.bmp"

MyMenu MENU
{
  POPUP "&Draw"
  {
    MENUITEM "&Lines\tF2", IDM_LINES
    MENUITEM "&Rectangles\tF3", IDM_RECTANGLES
    MENUITEM "&Ellipses\tF4", IDM_ELLIPSES
    MENUITEM "E&xit\tCtrl+X", IDM_EXIT
  }
```

```
    POPUP "&Options"
    {
      MENUITEM "&Reset\tF5", IDM_RESET
      MENUITEM "&Show Toolbar\tF6", IDM_SHOW
      MENUITEM "&Hide Toolbar\tF7", IDM_HIDE
    }
    MENUITEM "&Help", IDM_HELP
}

MyMenu ACCELERATORS
{
  VK_F2, IDM_LINES, VIRTKEY
  VK_F3, IDM_RECTANGLES, VIRTKEY
  VK_F4, IDM_ELLIPSES, VIRTKEY
  VK_F5, IDM_RESET, VIRTKEY
  VK_F6, IDM_SHOW, VIRTKEY
  VK_F7, IDM_HIDE, VIRTKEY
  "^X", IDM_EXIT
  VK_F1, IDM_HELP, VIRTKEY
}
```

The TB.H header file is shown here.

```
#define IDM_LINES        100
#define IDM_RECTANGLES 101
#define IDM_ELLIPSES    102
#define IDM_SHOW        103
#define IDM_HIDE        104
#define IDM_RESET       105
#define IDM_EXIT        106
#define IDM_HELP        107


#define IDM_TOOLBAR     200


#define IDTB_BMP        300
```

10

Most of the code in this program is straightforward. Here is a brief description. (Remember, the non-toolbar-related code was discussed in the preceding chapter.) The toolbar information is held in the **tbButtons** array. This array is initialized in **InitToolBar( )**. Notice that the fifth structure is simply a button separator. In **WinMain( )**, the **InitCommonControlsEx( )** function is called. Next, the toolbar is created and a handle to it is assigned to **tbwnd**.

Each button in the toolbar corresponds to a menu entry in the main menu. Specifically, each of the buttons (other than the separator) is associated with a menu ID. When a button is pressed, its associated ID will be sent to the program as part of a **WM_COMMAND** message in just the same way as if a menu item had been selected. In fact, the same **case** statement handles both toolbar button presses and menu selections.

Since a toolbar is a window, it may be displayed or hidden like any other window using the **ShowWindow( )** function. To hide the toolbar, select Hide Toolbar in the Options menu. To redisplay the toolbar, select Show Toolbar. Since the toolbar overlays part of the client area of the main window, you should always allow the user to remove the toolbar if it is not needed. As the program illustrates, this is very easy to do.

There is one other point of interest in the program. Notice the code inside the **IDM_HELP** case. When Help is selected (either through the main menu or by pressing the Help button), the Help toolbar button is manually pressed by sending it a **TB_CHECKBUTTON** message. After the user closes the Help message box, the button is manually released. Thus, the Help button remains pressed while the Help message box is displayed. This is an example of how a toolbar can be manually managed by your program when necessary.

Sample output from the toolbar program is shown in Figure 10-2.

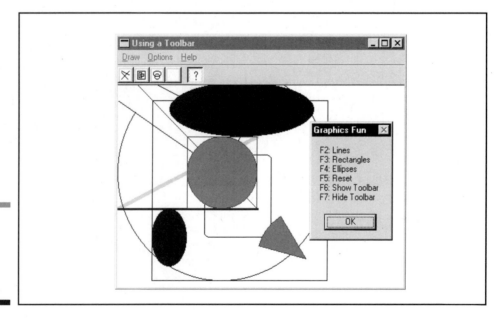

Sample output from the toolbar program

Figure 10-2.

Passing Along WM_SIZE Messages

Try the following experiment with the toolbar program. Execute the program and then increase its horizontal size. As you will see, the toolbar is *not* automatically expanded to the new size. The reason for this is that a toolbar is a child window of the program's main window. It does not automatically receive resize messages when its parent window changes size. Instead, if you want a child window (in this case, a toolbar) to receive resize messages, you must pass that message along to it. For example, to do this in the toolbar program, add the following **case** to **WindowFunc( )**.

```
case WM_SIZE:
  /* pass resize message along to toolbar */
  SendMessage(tbwnd, WM_SIZE, wParam, lParam);
  break;
```

After adding this code, when you expand the main window, the toolbar will automatically be resized appropriately.

In general, each time your main window is resized, it receives a **WM_SIZE** message. In **LOWORD(lParam)** is the new width of the window. The new height of the window is in **HIWORD(lParam)**. The value in **wParam** will be one of those shown here.

wParam	Meaning
SIZE_RESTORED	Window resized.
SIZE_MAXIMIZED	Window maximized.
SIZE_MINIMIZED	Window minimized.
SIZE_MAXHIDE	Another window has been maximized.
SIZE_MAXSHOW	Another window has been restored.

As a rule, if your program contains a child window, your main window function will need to pass sizing messages along to the child window when appropriate.

10

Adding Tooltips

As you have probably already seen when using Windows 98, some toolbars automatically pop up small text windows after the mouse pointer has paused for about one second over a toolbar button. These small text windows are called *tooltips*. Although not technically required, tooltips should be included with most toolbars because users will expect to see them. In this section, we will add tooltips to the toolbar developed in the preceding section.

Tooltips are small text messages that appear when the mouse pauses over a control.

To add tooltips to a toolbar, you must first include the **TBSTYLE_ TOOLTIPS** style when you create the toolbar. This enables the toolbar to send a **WM_NOTIFY** message when the mouse pointer lingers over a button for more than about one second. In general, **WM_NOTIFY** messages are generated by controls when some event occurs. In the case of tooltips, one is sent when the tooltip text needs to be displayed. When this occurs, **lParam** will point to a **NMTTDISPINFO** structure, which is defined like this:

```
typedef struct {
  NMHDR hdr;
  LPSTR lpszText;
  char szText[80];
  HINSTANCE hinst;
  UINT uFlags;
  LPARAM lParam;
} NMTTDISPINFO;
```

The first member of **NMTTDISPINFO** is an **NMHDR** structure, which is defined like this:

```
typedef struct tagNMHDR
{
  HWND  hwndFrom; /* handle of control */
  UINT  idFrom; /* control ID */
  UINT  code; /* notification code */
} NMHDR;
```

If a tooltip is being requested, then **code** will contain the notification message **TTN_GETDISPINFO** and **idFrom** will contain the ID of the button for which the tip is needed. Since other controls can generate **WM_NOTIFY** messages and toolbars can generate other types of notification messages, you will need to check these fields to determine precisely what event has occurred.

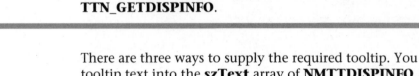

PORTABILITY: The **NMTTDISPINFO** structure used to be called **TOOLTIPTEXT**, and this old name is still valid. However, new code should use **NMTTDISPINFO**. The **TTN_GETDISPINFO** message used to be called **TTN_NEEDTEXT**, and this name is still valid. But for new code, use **TTN_GETDISPINFO**.

There are three ways to supply the required tooltip. You must either copy the tooltip text into the **szText** array of **NMTTDISPINFO**, point **lpszText** to the text, or supply the resource ID of a string resource. When using a string resource, the string ID is assigned to **lpszText** and **hinst** must be the handle of the instance that contains the string resource (which is usually the instance handle of your program). By far the easiest way to supply the tooltip is to simply point **lpszText** to a string supplied by your program. For example, the following case responds to tooltip requests for the graphics program.

```
LPNMTTDISPINFO TTtext;
// ...
case WM_NOTIFY: /* respond to tooltip request */
  TTtext = (LPNMTTDISPINFO) lParam;
  if(TTtext->hdr.code == TTN_GETDISPINFO)
    switch(TTtext->hdr.idFrom) {
      case IDM_LINES: TTtext->lpszText = "Lines";
        break;
      case IDM_RECTANGLES: TTtext->lpszText = "Rectangles";
        break;
      case IDM_ELLIPSES: TTtext->lpszText = "Ellipses";
        break;
      case IDM_RESET: TTtext->lpszText = "Reset and Clear";
        break;
      case IDM_HELP: TTtext->lpszText = "Help";
        break;
    }
  break;
```

10

Once the tooltip text has been set and control passes back to Windows, the tooltip will automatically be displayed. Your program need perform no further action. As you can see, tooltips are largely automated and easy to add to your application.

The Entire Toolbar Program Including Tooltips

The entire toolbar with tooltips program is shown here. It uses the same resource file and header file as the preceding version. Sample output from this program is shown in Figure 10-3.

```c
/* Add tooltips to the toolbar. */

#include <windows.h>
#include <commctrl.h>
#include "tb.h"

#define NUMBUTTONS 6

void InitToolbar(); /* initialize the tool bar */

LRESULT CALLBACK WindowFunc(HWND, UINT, WPARAM, LPARAM);

char szWinName[] = "MyWin"; /* name of window class */

int maxX, maxY; /* screen dimensions */

HDC memdc; /* handle of memory DC */
HBITMAP hbit; /* handle of compatible bitmap */
HBRUSH hbrush, hOldbrush; /* handles of brushes */

/* create pens */
HPEN hOldpen; /* handle of old pen */
HPEN hRedpen, hGreenpen, hBluepen, hYellowpen;

TBBUTTON tbButtons[NUMBUTTONS];

HWND tbwnd; /* toolbar handle */

int WINAPI WinMain(HINSTANCE hThisInst, HINSTANCE hPrevInst,
                   LPSTR lpszArgs, int nWinMode)
{
  HWND hwnd;
  MSG msg;
  WNDCLASSEX wcl;
  HACCEL hAccel;
  INITCOMMONCONTROLSEX cc;

  /* Define a window class. */
  wcl.cbSize = sizeof(WNDCLASSEX);
```

```
wcl.hInstance = hThisInst; /* handle to this instance */
wcl.lpszClassName = szWinName; /* window class name */
wcl.lpfnWndProc = WindowFunc; /* window function */
wcl.style = 0; /* default style */

wcl.hIcon = LoadIcon(NULL, IDI_APPLICATION); /* standard icon */
wcl.hIconSm = LoadIcon(NULL, IDI_APPLICATION); /* small icon */
wcl.hCursor = LoadCursor(NULL, IDC_ARROW); /* cursor style */

wcl.lpszMenuName = "MyMenu"; /* main menu */
wcl.cbClsExtra = 0; /* no extra */
wcl.cbWndExtra = 0; /* information needed */

/* Make the window white. */
wcl.hbrBackground = (HBRUSH) GetStockObject(WHITE_BRUSH);

/* Register the window class. */
if(!RegisterClassEx(&wcl)) return 0;

/* Now that a window class has been registered, a window
   can be created. */
hwnd = CreateWindow(
  szWinName, /* name of window class */
  "Using a Toolbar", /* title */
  WS_OVERLAPPEDWINDOW, /* window style - normal */
  CW_USEDEFAULT, /* X coordinate - let Windows decide */
  CW_USEDEFAULT, /* Y coordinate - let Windows decide */
  CW_USEDEFAULT, /* width - let Windows decide */
  CW_USEDEFAULT, /* height - let Windows decide */
  HWND_DESKTOP, /* no parent window */
  NULL, /* no override of class menu */
  hThisInst, /* handle of this instance of the program */
  NULL /* no additional arguments */
);

/* load accelerators */
hAccel = LoadAccelerators(hThisInst, "MyMenu");

/* Initialize the common controls. */
cc.dwSize = sizeof(INITCOMMONCONTROLSEX);
cc.dwICC = ICC_BAR_CLASSES;
InitCommonControlsEx(&cc);

InitToolbar(); /* initialize the toolbar structures */
```

10

```
/* create the toolbar */
tbwnd = CreateToolbarEx(hwnd,
                        WS_VISIBLE | WS_CHILD |
                        WS_BORDER | TBSTYLE_TOOLTIPS,
                        IDM_TOOLBAR,
                        NUMBUTTONS,
                        hThisInst,
                        IDTB_BMP,
                        tbButtons,
                        NUMBUTTONS,
                        16, 16, 16, 16,
                        sizeof(TBBUTTON));

/* Display the window. */
ShowWindow(hwnd, nWinMode);
UpdateWindow(hwnd);

/* Create the message loop. */
while(GetMessage(&msg, NULL, 0, 0))
{
  if(!TranslateAccelerator(hwnd, hAccel, &msg)) {
    TranslateMessage(&msg); /* translate keyboard messages */
    DispatchMessage(&msg); /* return control to Windows 98 */
  }
}
return msg.wParam;
}

/* This function is called by Windows 98 and is passed
   messages from the message queue.
*/
LRESULT CALLBACK WindowFunc(HWND hwnd, UINT message,
                            WPARAM wParam, LPARAM lParam)
{
  HDC hdc;
  PAINTSTRUCT paintstruct;
  LPNMTTDISPINFO TTtext;
  int response;

  switch(message) {
    case WM_CREATE:
      /* get screen coordinates */
      maxX = GetSystemMetrics(SM_CXSCREEN);
      maxY = GetSystemMetrics(SM_CYSCREEN);
```

```
      /* make a compatible memory image device */
      hdc = GetDC(hwnd);
      memdc = CreateCompatibleDC(hdc);
      hbit = CreateCompatibleBitmap(hdc, maxX, maxY);
      SelectObject(memdc, hbit);
      hbrush = (HBRUSH) GetStockObject(WHITE_BRUSH);
      SelectObject(memdc, hbrush);
      PatBlt(memdc, 0, 0, maxX, maxY, PATCOPY);

      hRedpen = CreatePen(PS_SOLID, 1, RGB(255,0,0));
      hGreenpen = CreatePen(PS_SOLID, 2, RGB(0,255,0));
      hBluepen = CreatePen(PS_SOLID, 3, RGB(0,0,255));
      hYellowpen = CreatePen(PS_SOLID, 4, RGB(255, 255, 0));

      /* save default pen */
      hOldpen = (HPEN) SelectObject(memdc, hRedpen);
      SelectObject(memdc, hOldpen);

      ReleaseDC(hwnd, hdc);
      break;
    case WM_NOTIFY: /* respond to tooltip request */
      TTtext = (LPNMTTDISPINFO) lParam;
      if(TTtext->hdr.code == TTN_GETDISPINFO)
        switch(TTtext->hdr.idFrom) {
          case IDM_LINES: TTtext->lpszText = "Lines";
            break;
          case IDM_RECTANGLES: TTtext->lpszText = "Rectangles";
            break;
          case IDM_ELLIPSES: TTtext->lpszText = "Ellipses";
            break;
          case IDM_RESET: TTtext->lpszText = "Reset and Clear";
            break;
          case IDM_HELP: TTtext->lpszText = "Help";
            break;
        }
      break;
    case WM_COMMAND:
      switch(LOWORD(wParam)) {
        case IDM_LINES:
          /* set 2 pixels */
          SetPixel(memdc, 40, 14, RGB(0, 0, 0));
          SetPixel(memdc, 40, 15, RGB(0, 0, 0));

          LineTo(memdc, 100, 50);
```

10

```
    MoveToEx(memdc, 100, 50, NULL);

    /* change to green pen */
    hOldpen = (HPEN) SelectObject(memdc, hGreenpen);
    LineTo(memdc, 200, 100);

    /* change to yellow pen */
    SelectObject(memdc, hYellowpen);
    LineTo(memdc, 0, 200);

    /* change to blue pen */
    SelectObject(memdc, hBluepen);
    LineTo(memdc, 200, 200);

    /* change to red pen */
    SelectObject(memdc, hRedpen);
    LineTo(memdc, 0, 0);

    /* return to default pen */
    SelectObject(memdc, hOldpen);

    Arc(memdc, 0, 0, 300, 300, 0, 50, 200, 50);
    /* show intersecting lines that define arc */
    MoveToEx(memdc, 150, 150, NULL);
    LineTo(memdc, 0, 50);
    MoveToEx(memdc, 150, 150, NULL);
    LineTo(memdc, 200, 50);

    InvalidateRect(hwnd, NULL, 1);
    break;
  case IDM_RECTANGLES:
    /* display, but don't fill */
    hOldbrush = (HBRUSH) SelectObject(memdc,
                            GetStockObject(HOLLOW_BRUSH));

    /* draw some rectangles */
    Rectangle(memdc, 50, 50, 300, 300);
    RoundRect(memdc, 125, 125, 220, 240, 15, 13);

    /* use a red pen */
    SelectObject(memdc, hRedpen);
    Rectangle(memdc, 100, 100, 200, 200);
    SelectObject(memdc, hOldpen); /* return to default pen */

    /* restore default brush */
```

```
        SelectObject(memdc, hOldbrush);

        InvalidateRect(hwnd, NULL, 1);
        break;
    case IDM_ELLIPSES:
        /* make blue brush */
        hbrush = CreateSolidBrush(RGB(0, 0, 255));
        hOldbrush = (HBRUSH) SelectObject(memdc, hbrush);

        /* fill these ellipses with blue */
        Ellipse(memdc, 50, 200, 100, 280);
        Ellipse(memdc, 75, 25, 280, 100);

        /* use a red pen and fill with green */
        SelectObject(memdc, hRedpen);
        DeleteObject(hbrush); /* delete brush */
        /* create green brush */
        hbrush = CreateSolidBrush(RGB(0, 255, 0));
        SelectObject(memdc, hbrush); /* select green brush */
        Ellipse(memdc, 100, 100, 200, 200);

        /* draw a pie slice */
        Pie(memdc, 200, 200, 340, 340, 225, 200, 200, 250);

        SelectObject(memdc, hOldpen); /* return to default pen */
        SelectObject(memdc, hOldbrush); /* select default brush */
        DeleteObject(hbrush); /* delete green brush */

        InvalidateRect(hwnd, NULL, 1);
        break;
    case IDM_SHOW: /* show toolbar */
        ShowWindow(tbwnd, SW_RESTORE);
        break;
    case IDM_HIDE: /* hide toolbar */
        ShowWindow(tbwnd, SW_HIDE);
        break;
    case IDM_RESET:
        /* reset current position to 0,0 */
        MoveToEx(memdc, 0, 0, NULL);
        /* erase by repainting background */
        PatBlt(memdc, 0, 0, maxX, maxY, PATCOPY);
        InvalidateRect(hwnd, NULL, 1);
        break;
```

10

```
      case IDM_EXIT:
        response = MessageBox(hwnd, "Quit the Program?",
                             "Exit", MB_YESNO);
        if(response == IDYES) PostQuitMessage(0);
        break;
      case IDM_HELP:
        /* show help button as pressed */
        SendMessage(tbwnd, TB_CHECKBUTTON,
                    (LPARAM) IDM_HELP, (WPARAM) 1);

        MessageBox(hwnd, "F2: Lines\nF3: Rectangles\n"
                   "F4: Ellipses\nF5: Reset\n"
                   "F6: Show Toolbar\n"
                   "F7: Hide Toolbar",
                   "Graphics Fun", MB_OK);

        /* reset the help button */
        SendMessage(tbwnd, TB_CHECKBUTTON,
                    (LPARAM) IDM_HELP, (WPARAM) 0);
        break;
    }
    break;
  case WM_PAINT: /* process a repaint request */
    hdc = BeginPaint(hwnd, &paintstruct); /* get DC */

    /* now, copy memory image onto screen */
    BitBlt(hdc, 0, 0, maxX, maxY, memdc, 0, 0, SRCCOPY);

    EndPaint(hwnd, &paintstruct); /* release DC */
    break;
  case WM_DESTROY: /* terminate the program */
    DeleteObject(hRedpen); /* delete pens */
    DeleteObject(hGreenpen);
    DeleteObject(hBluepen);
    DeleteObject(hYellowpen);

    DeleteDC(memdc);
    PostQuitMessage(0);
    break;
  default:
    /* Let Windows 98 process any messages not specified in
    the preceding switch statement. */
    return DefWindowProc(hwnd, message, wParam, lParam);
```

```
    }
    return 0;
}

/* Initialize the toolbar structures. */
void InitToolbar()
{
  tbButtons[1].iBitmap = 0;
  tbButtons[0].idCommand = IDM_LINES;
  tbButtons[0].fsState = TBSTATE_ENABLED;
  tbButtons[0].fsStyle = TBSTYLE_BUTTON;
  tbButtons[0].dwData = 0L;
  tbButtons[0].iBitmap = 0;
  tbButtons[0].iString = 0;

  tbButtons[1].iBitmap = 1;
  tbButtons[1].idCommand = IDM_RECTANGLES;
  tbButtons[1].fsState = TBSTATE_ENABLED;
  tbButtons[1].fsStyle = TBSTYLE_BUTTON;
  tbButtons[1].dwData = 0L;
  tbButtons[1].iString = 0;

  tbButtons[2].iBitmap = 2;
  tbButtons[2].idCommand = IDM_ELLIPSES;
  tbButtons[2].fsState = TBSTATE_ENABLED;
  tbButtons[2].fsStyle = TBSTYLE_BUTTON;
  tbButtons[2].dwData = 0L;
  tbButtons[2].iString = 0;

  tbButtons[3].iBitmap = 3;
  tbButtons[3].idCommand = IDM_RESET;
  tbButtons[3].fsState = TBSTATE_ENABLED;
  tbButtons[3].fsStyle = TBSTYLE_BUTTON;
  tbButtons[3].dwData = 0L;
  tbButtons[3].iString = 0;

  /* button separator */
  tbButtons[4].iBitmap = 0;
  tbButtons[4].idCommand = 0;
  tbButtons[4].fsState = TBSTATE_ENABLED;
  tbButtons[4].fsStyle = TBSTYLE_SEP;
  tbButtons[4].dwData = 0L;
  tbButtons[4].iString = 0;
```

10

```
  tbButtons[5].iBitmap = 4;
  tbButtons[5].idCommand = IDM_HELP;
  tbButtons[5].fsState = TBSTATE_ENABLED;
  tbButtons[5].fsStyle = TBSTYLE_BUTTON;
  tbButtons[5].dwData = 0L;
  tbButtons[5].iString = 0;
}
```

In the next chapter we will continue to explore the common controls, examining up-down controls (also called spin controls), trackbars, and progress bars.

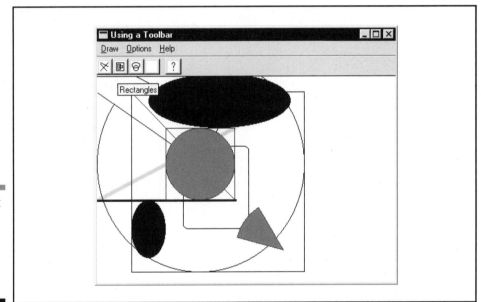

Sample output
from the
toolbar with
tooltips
program
Figure 10-3.

CHAPTER 11

More Common Controls

This chapter continues our look at the Windows 98 common controls. Here we will examine the up-down control, the trackbar, and the progress bar.

Using Up-Down Controls

An up-down control is essentially a scroll bar control without the bar.

A spin control is a combination of an up-down control and an edit box.

One control that you will find useful in a number of situations is the up-down control. An up-down control is essentially a scroll bar without the bar! That is, it consists only of the arrows found on the ends of a scroll bar; there is no bar between them. As you may have seen while using various Windows applications, some scrollbars are so small that the bar is essentially pointless. Also, some situations don't lend themselves to the concept of the bar, but benefit from the use of the up and down arrows. To accommodate these situations, the designers of Windows decided to define the up-down control. As you will see, using an up-down control is much like using a scroll bar.

An up-down control may be used two different ways. First, it may be used more or less like a stand-alone scroll bar. Second, it can be used in conjunction with another control, called its *buddy window*. The most common buddy window is an edit box. When this is the case, a *spin control* (or spinner) is created. When using a spin control, almost all of the overhead required to manage the control is provided automatically. This makes the spin control easy to add to your application. This chapter presents two up-down examples. The first creates a stand-alone up-down control. The second example uses a buddy window to create a spin control.

Creating an Up-Down Control

To create an up-down control, use the **CreateUpDownControl( )** function, shown here.

HWND CreateUpDownControl(DWORD *Style*, int *X*, int *Y*,
        int *Width*, int *Height*, HWND *hParent*,
        int *ID*, HINSTANCE *hInst*,
        HWND *hBuddy*, int *Max*, int *Min*, int *StartPos*);

Here, *Style* specifies the style of the up-down control. This parameter must include the standard styles **WS_CHILD**, **WS_VISIBLE**, and **WS_BORDER**. It may also include one or more of the up-down styles shown in Table 11-1.

Style	Meaning
UDS_ALIGNLEFT	Aligns up-down control to the left of its buddy window.
UDS_ALIGNRIGHT	Aligns up-down control to the right of its buddy window.
UDS_ARROWKEYS	Enables arrow keys. (That is, arrow keys may be used to move the control.)
TBS_AUTOBUDDY	Buddy window is previous window in z-order.
UDS_HORZ	Up-down control is horizontal. Up-down controls are vertical by default.
UDS_NOTHOUSANDS	Commas not used in large values when displayed in buddy window. (Applies to spin controls only.)
UDS_SETBUDDYINT	Automatically sets the text within the buddy window when the control position is changed. This allows the buddy window to show the current position of the up-down control.
UDS_WRAP	Position of up-down control will "wrap around" when moved past an end.

The Up-Down
Control Styles
Table 11-1.

The location of the upper-left corner of the up-down control is passed in *X* and *Y*. The width and height of the control are specified in *Width* and *Height*.

The handle of the parent window is passed in *hParent*. The ID associated with the up-down control is specified in *ID*. The instance handle of the application is passed in *hInst*. The handle of the buddy window is passed in *hBuddy*. If there is no buddy window, then this parameter must be **NULL**.

The range of the control is passed in *Max* and *Min*. If *Max* is less then *Min*, then the control runs backwards. The initial position of the control (which must be within the specified range) is passed in *StartPos*. This value determines the control's initial value. It is important to understand that an up-down control maintains an internal counter that is incremented or decremented each time one of the arrows is pressed. This internal value will always be within the range specified with the control is created.

11

The function returns a handle to the control. It returns **NULL** on failure.

Receiving Up-Down Control Messages

When one of the arrows of an up-down control is pressed, it sends either a **WM_VSCROLL** or a **WM_HSCROLL** message to its parent window, depending upon whether the up-down control is vertical (the default) or horizontal. The handle of the up-down control will be in *lParam*. Since there may be more than one control that generates **WM_VSCROLL** or **WM_HSCROLL** messages, you will need to check this handle to determine if it is that of the up-down control.

Sending Up-Down Control Messages

Up-down controls respond to a variety of messages. Several commonly used ones are shown in Table 11-2. For example, to obtain the value of the control (i.e., its position), send the control a **UDM_GETPOS** message. The current

Message	Meaning
UDM_GETBUDDY	Obtains handle of buddy window. The handle is returned. *wParam* is 0. *lParam* is 0.
UDM_GETPOS	Obtains the current position. The current position is in the low-order word of the return value. If an error occurs, the high-order word of the return value is nonzero. *wParam* is 0. *lParam* is 0.
UDM_GETRANGE	Obtains the current range. The maximum value is in the low-order word of the return value and the minimum value is in the high-order word of the return value. *wParam* is 0. *lParam* is 0.
UDM_SETBUDDY	Specifies a new buddy window. The handle of the old buddy window is returned. *wParam* is the handle of new buddy window. *lParam* is 0.
UDM_SETPOS	Sets the current position. *wParam* is 0. *lParam* is new current position.
UDM_SETRANGE	Sets the current range. *wParam* is 0. *lParam* is the range. Its low-order word contains maximum, high-order word contains minimum.

Common
Up-Down
Messages
Table 11-2.

position of the control is returned. To set the position of an up-down control, use the **UDM_SETPOS** message. You send the control messages using **SendMessage( )**.

Using an Up-Down Control

The following program creates a stand-alone up-down control within a dialog box. In this example, the up-down control is not linked to a buddy window. The up-down control has a range of 0 to 100, with an initial position of 50. Each time the position of the control is changed (by pressing an arrow), the new position is displayed in the client area of the dialog box. Sample output from the program is shown in Figure 11-1.

```
/* Demonstrate up-down basics. */

#include <windows.h>
#include <commctrl.h>
#include <stdio.h>
#include "updown.h"

LRESULT CALLBACK WindowFunc(HWND, UINT, WPARAM, LPARAM);
BOOL CALLBACK DialogFunc(HWND, UINT, WPARAM, LPARAM);

char szWinName[] = "MyWin"; /* name of window class */

HINSTANCE hInst;

int WINAPI WinMain(HINSTANCE hThisInst, HINSTANCE hPrevInst,
                   LPSTR lpszArgs, int nWinMode)
{
  HWND hwnd;
  MSG msg;
  WNDCLASSEX wcl;
  HACCEL hAccel;
  INITCOMMONCONTROLSEX cc;

  /* Define a window class. */
  wcl.cbSize = sizeof(WNDCLASSEX);

  wcl.hInstance = hThisInst; /* handle to this instance */
  wcl.lpszClassName = szWinName; /* window class name */
  wcl.lpfnWndProc = WindowFunc; /* window function */
  wcl.style = 0; /* default style */
```

11

```
wcl.hIcon = LoadIcon(NULL, IDI_APPLICATION); /* standard icon */
wcl.hIconSm = LoadIcon(NULL, IDI_APPLICATION); /* small icon */
wcl.hCursor = LoadCursor(NULL, IDC_ARROW); /* cursor style */

wcl.lpszMenuName = "MyMenu"; /* main menu */
wcl.cbClsExtra = 0; /* no extra */
wcl.cbWndExtra = 0; /* information needed */

/* Make the window white. */
wcl.hbrBackground = (HBRUSH) GetStockObject(WHITE_BRUSH);

/* Register the window class. */
if(!RegisterClassEx(&wcl)) return 0;

/* Now that a window class has been registered, a window
   can be created. */
hwnd = CreateWindow(
  szWinName, /* name of window class */
  "Using an Up-Down Control", /* title */
  WS_OVERLAPPEDWINDOW, /* window style - normal */
  CW_USEDEFAULT, /* X coordinate - let Windows decide */
  CW_USEDEFAULT, /* Y coordinate - let Windows decide */
  CW_USEDEFAULT, /* width - let Windows decide */
  CW_USEDEFAULT, /* height - let Windows decide */
  HWND_DESKTOP, /* no parent window */
  NULL, /* no override of class menu */
  hThisInst, /* handle of this instance of the program */
  NULL /* no additional arguments */
);

hInst = hThisInst; /* save the current instance handle */

/* Load accelerators. */
hAccel = LoadAccelerators(hThisInst, "MyMenu");

/* Initialize the common controls. */
cc.dwSize = sizeof(INITCOMMONCONTROLSEX);
cc.dwICC = ICC_UPDOWN_CLASS;
InitCommonControlsEx(&cc);

/* Display the window. */
ShowWindow(hwnd, nWinMode);
UpdateWindow(hwnd);

/* Create the message loop. */
```

```
   while(GetMessage(&msg, NULL, 0, 0))
   {
     if(!TranslateAccelerator(hwnd, hAccel, &msg)) {
       TranslateMessage(&msg); /* translate keyboard messsages */
       DispatchMessage(&msg); /* return control to Windows 98 */
     }
   }
   return msg.wParam;
}

/* This function is called by Windows 98 and is passed
   messages from the message queue.
*/
LRESULT CALLBACK WindowFunc(HWND hwnd, UINT message,
                            WPARAM wParam, LPARAM lParam)
{
  int response;

  switch(message) {
    case WM_COMMAND:
      switch(LOWORD(wParam)) {
        case IDM_DIALOG:
          DialogBox(hInst, "MyDB", hwnd, (DLGPROC) DialogFunc);
          break;
        case IDM_EXIT:
          response = MessageBox(hwnd, "Quit the Program?",
                                "Exit", MB_YESNO);
          if(response == IDYES) PostQuitMessage(0);
          break;
        case IDM_HELP:
          MessageBox(hwnd, "Try the up-down control.", "Help",
                     MB_OK);
          break;
      }
      break;
    case WM_DESTROY: /* terminate the program */
      PostQuitMessage(0);
      break;
    default:
      /* Let Windows 98 process any messages not specified in
         the preceding switch statement. */
      return DefWindowProc(hwnd, message, wParam, lParam);
  }
  return 0;
}
```

11

```
/* Dialog function. */
BOOL CALLBACK DialogFunc(HWND hdwnd, UINT message,
                         WPARAM wParam, LPARAM lParam)
{
  char str[80];
  long udpos = 0;
  HDC hdc;
  static HWND udWnd;

  switch(message) {
    case WM_INITDIALOG:
      udWnd = CreateUpDownControl(
                  WS_CHILD | WS_BORDER | WS_VISIBLE,
                  10, 10, 50, 50,
                  hdwnd,
                  ID_UPDOWN,
                  hInst,
                  NULL,
                  100, 0, 50);
      return 1;
    case WM_COMMAND:
      switch(LOWORD(wParam)) {
        case IDCANCEL:
          EndDialog(hdwnd, 0);
          return 1;
      }
    case WM_VSCROLL:  /* manually process an up-down control */
      if(udWnd==(HWND)lParam) {
        udpos = SendMessage(udWnd, UDM_GETPOS, 0, 0);
        sprintf(str, "%d", LOWORD(udpos));
        hdc = GetDC(hdwnd);
        TextOut(hdc, 55, 30, "     ", 6);
        TextOut(hdc, 55, 30, str, strlen(str));
        ReleaseDC(hdwnd, hdc);
        return 1;
      }
  }
  return 0;
}
```

The program also requires the following resource file.

```
#include <windows.h>
#include "updown.h"
```

```
MyMenu MENU
{
  POPUP "&Dialog" {
    MENUITEM "&Dialog\tF2", IDM_DIALOG
    MENUITEM "E&xit\tCtrl+X", IDM_EXIT
  }
  MENUITEM "&Help", IDM_HELP
}

MyMenu ACCELERATORS
{
  VK_F2, IDM_DIALOG, VIRTKEY
  "^X", IDM_EXIT
  VK_F1, IDM_HELP, VIRTKEY
}

MyDB DIALOG 18, 18, 142, 92
CAPTION "Demonstrate Up-Down Control"
STYLE DS_MODALFRAME | WS_POPUP | WS_CAPTION | WS_SYSMENU
{
  PUSHBUTTON "Cancel", IDCANCEL, 52, 65, 37, 14,
             WS_CHILD | WS_VISIBLE | WS_TABSTOP
}
```

You will also need the header file UPDOWN.H shown here. (The value **ID_EB1** will be used by the next example.)

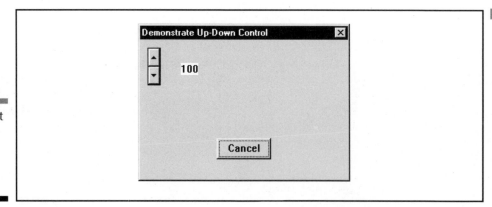

Sample output
from the first
up-down
example

Figure 11-1.

11

```
#define IDM_DIALOG   100
#define IDM_EXIT     101
#define IDM_HELP     102

#define ID_UPDOWN    201
#define ID_EB1       202
```

In the program, the up-down control is contained within the dialog box. The control is created when the dialog box is initialized using the following code.

```
case WM_INITDIALOG:
  udWnd = CreateUpDownControl(
                WS_CHILD | WS_BORDER | WS_VISIBLE,
                10, 10, 50, 50,
                hdwnd,
                ID_UPDOWN,
                hInst,
                NULL,
                100, 0, 50);
    return 1;
```

This call to **CreateUpDownControl( )** creates an up-down control that is at location 10,10 within the dialog box. The control is 50 pixels wide and 50 pixels tall. Because the control is a child window of the dialog box, the dialog box's handle (**hdwnd**) is passed as the parent handle. The ID of the up-down control is **ID_UPDOWN**. Although this value is not required by this simple example, other programs will make use of it. **hInst** is the instance handle of the program. Because there is no buddy window, **NULL** is passed for the buddy parameter. The range of the up-down control is 0 to 100 and the initial position is 50.

Each time the up-down control is accessed, a **WM_VSCROLL** message is sent to the dialog box. The code that processes this message is shown here. The handle of the up-down control is contained in **lParam**. This handle is tested against that returned by **CreateUpDownControl( )** to confirm that it is the up-down control that generated the message. While there is only one control in this example, real-world applications may have several controls capable of generating a **WM_VSCROLL** message, so you should always confirm which control has been accessed.

```
case WM_VSCROLL:  /* manually process an up-down control */
  if(udWnd==(HWND)lParam) {
```

```
udpos = SendMessage(udWnd, UDM_GETPOS, 0, 0);
sprintf(str, "%d", LOWORD(udpos));
hdc = GetDC(hdwnd);
TextOut(hdc, 55, 30, "        ", 6);
TextOut(hdc, 55, 30, str, strlen(str));
ReleaseDC(hdwnd, hdc);
return 1;
}
```

To obtain the new up-down position, the **UDM_GETPOS** message is sent
using **SendMessage( )**. The position is found in the low-order word of the
return value. This value is then displayed in the client area of the dialog box.

PORTABILITY: Remember, up-down controls were not supported
by Windows 3.1. Therefore, you must be careful when adding one to an
older program. It is not uncommon for older programs to assume that a
WM_VSCROLL is generated by a standard scroll bar. When adding an
up-down control, you will frequently need to add a test to the portion of the
program that processes scroll bar messages to confirm that it was actually the
scroll bar and not an up-down control that generated the **WM_VSCROLL**
message.

Creating a Spin Control

While there is nothing whatsoever wrong with creating and using a
stand-alone up-down control, the up-down control is most often linked with
an edit box. As mentioned, this combination is called a spin control. Because
the spin control is such a common use of an up-down control, Windows 98
provides special support for it. In fact, a spin control is a completely
automated control—your program incurs virtually no management overhead
itself.

11

To create a spin control, you must specify an edit control as a buddy window
to an up-down control. After you have done this, each time the up-down
control is changed, its new position is automatically displayed in the edit
box. Further, if you manually change the value in the edit box, the up-down
control is automatically set to reflect that value.

A Spin Control Sample Program

Creating a spin control is an easy, two-step process. First, add an edit box
to your program's resource file. Second, pass the handle of that box as the
buddy window when the up-down control is created. The following program
applies these steps.

```c
/* Demonstrate a spin control. */

#include <windows.h>
#include <commctrl.h>
#include <stdio.h>
#include "updown.h"

LRESULT CALLBACK WindowFunc(HWND, UINT, WPARAM, LPARAM);
BOOL CALLBACK DialogFunc(HWND, UINT, WPARAM, LPARAM);

char szWinName[] = "MyWin"; /* name of window class */

HINSTANCE hInst;

int WINAPI WinMain(HINSTANCE hThisInst, HINSTANCE hPrevInst,
                   LPSTR lpszArgs, int nWinMode)
{
  HWND hwnd;
  MSG msg;
  WNDCLASSEX wcl;
  HACCEL hAccel;
  INITCOMMONCONTROLSEX cc;

  /* Define a window class. */
  wcl.cbSize = sizeof(WNDCLASSEX);

  wcl.hInstance = hThisInst; /* handle to this instance */
  wcl.lpszClassName = szWinName; /* window class name */
  wcl.lpfnWndProc = WindowFunc; /* window function */
  wcl.style = 0; /* default style */

  wcl.hIcon = LoadIcon(NULL, IDI_APPLICATION); /* standard icon */
  wcl.hIconSm = LoadIcon(NULL, IDI_APPLICATION); /* small icon */
  wcl.hCursor = LoadCursor(NULL, IDC_ARROW); /* cursor style */

  wcl.lpszMenuName = "MyMenu"; /* main menu */
  wcl.cbClsExtra = 0; /* no extra */
  wcl.cbWndExtra = 0; /* information needed */
```

```
/* Make the window white. */
wcl.hbrBackground = (HBRUSH) GetStockObject(WHITE_BRUSH);

/* Register the window class. */
if(!RegisterClassEx(&wcl)) return 0;

/* Now that a window class has been registered, a window
   can be created. */
hwnd = CreateWindow(
  szWinName, /* name of window class */
  "Using a Spin Control", /* title */
  WS_OVERLAPPEDWINDOW, /* window style - normal */
  CW_USEDEFAULT, /* X coordinate - let Windows decide */
  CW_USEDEFAULT, /* Y coordinate - let Windows decide */
  CW_USEDEFAULT, /* width - let Windows decide */
  CW_USEDEFAULT, /* height - let Windows decide */
  HWND_DESKTOP, /* no parent window */
  NULL, /* no override of class menu */
  hThisInst, /* handle of this instance of the program */
  NULL /* no additional arguments */
);

hInst = hThisInst; /* save the current instance handle */

/* Load accelerators. */
hAccel = LoadAccelerators(hThisInst, "MyMenu");

/* Initialize the common controls. */
cc.dwSize = sizeof(INITCOMMONCONTROLSEX);
cc.dwICC = ICC_UPDOWN_CLASS;
InitCommonControlsEx(&cc);

/* Display the window. */
ShowWindow(hwnd, nWinMode);
UpdateWindow(hwnd);

/* Create the message loop. */
while(GetMessage(&msg, NULL, 0, 0))
{
  if(!TranslateAccelerator(hwnd, hAccel, &msg)) {
    TranslateMessage(&msg); /* translate keyboard messages */
    DispatchMessage(&msg); /* return control to Windows 98 */
  }
}
```

11

```
      return msg.wParam;
}

/* This function is called by Windows 98 and is passed
   messages from the message queue.
*/
LRESULT CALLBACK WindowFunc(HWND hwnd, UINT message,
                            WPARAM wParam, LPARAM lParam)
{
  int response;

  switch(message) {
    case WM_COMMAND:
      switch(LOWORD(wParam)) {
        case IDM_DIALOG:
          DialogBox(hInst, "MyDB", hwnd, (DLGPROC) DialogFunc);
          break;
        case IDM_EXIT:
          response = MessageBox(hwnd, "Quit the Program?",
                                "Exit", MB_YESNO);
          if(response == IDYES) PostQuitMessage(0);
          break;
        case IDM_HELP:
          MessageBox(hwnd, "Try the spin control.", "Help", MB_OK);
          break;
      }
      break;
    case WM_DESTROY: /* terminate the program */
      PostQuitMessage(0);
      break;
    default:
      /* Let Windows 98 process any messages not specified in
         the preceding switch statement. */
      return DefWindowProc(hwnd, message, wParam, lParam);
  }
  return 0;
}

/* Dialog function. */
BOOL CALLBACK DialogFunc(HWND hdwnd, UINT message,
                         WPARAM wParam, LPARAM lParam)
{
  static HWND hEboxWnd;
  static HWND udWnd;
```

```
      switch(message) {
        case WM_INITDIALOG:
          hEboxWnd = GetDlgItem(hdwnd, ID_EB1);
          udWnd = CreateUpDownControl(
                        WS_CHILD | WS_BORDER | WS_VISIBLE |
                        UDS_SETBUDDYINT | UDS_ALIGNRIGHT,
                        10, 10, 50, 50,
                        hdwnd,
                        ID_UPDOWN,
                        hInst,
                        hEboxWnd,
                        100, 0, 50);
          return 1;
        case WM_COMMAND:
          switch(LOWORD(wParam)) {
            case IDCANCEL:
              EndDialog(hdwnd, 0);
              return 1;
          }
      }
      return 0;
}
```

This program uses the following resource file. Notice that an edit box has been included in the dialog box's definition.

```
#include <windows.h>
#include "updown.h"

MyMenu MENU
{
  POPUP "&Dialog" {
    MENUITEM "&Dialog\tF2", IDM_DIALOG
    MENUITEM "E&xit\tCtrl+X", IDM_EXIT
  }
  MENUITEM "&Help", IDM_HELP
}

MyMenu ACCELERATORS
{
  VK_F2, IDM_DIALOG, VIRTKEY
  "^X", IDM_EXIT
  VK_F1, IDM_HELP, VIRTKEY
}
```

11

```
MyDB DIALOG 18, 18, 142, 92
CAPTION "Demonstrate Spin Control"
STYLE DS_MODALFRAME | WS_POPUP | WS_CAPTION | WS_SYSMENU
{
  PUSHBUTTON "Cancel", IDCANCEL, 52, 65, 37, 14,
             WS_CHILD | WS_VISIBLE | WS_TABSTOP
  EDITTEXT ID_EB1, 10, 10, 30, 12, ES_LEFT | WS_CHILD |
           WS_VISIBLE | WS_BORDER
}
```

Sample output from the program is shown in Figure 11-2.

To understand how the spin control is created, look at the
WM_INITDIALOG case code, shown here.

```
case WM_INITDIALOG:
  hEboxWnd = GetDlgItem(hdwnd, ID_EB1);
  udWnd = CreateUpDownControl(
             WS_CHILD | WS_BORDER | WS_VISIBLE |
             UDS_SETBUDDYINT | UDS_ALIGNRIGHT,
             10, 10, 50, 50,
             hdwnd,
             ID_UPDOWN,
             hInst,
             hEboxWnd,
             100, 0, 50);
  return 1;
```

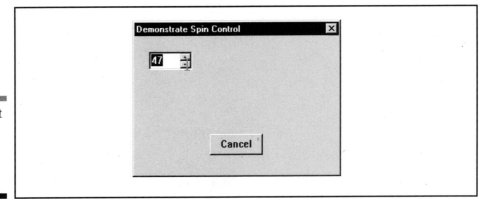

Sample output
from the spin
control
program
Figure 11-2.

Since the dialog box is defined in the resource file, the program must call **GetDlgItem( )** to obtain its handle. **GetDlgItem( )** is defined like this:

HWND GetDlgItem(HWND *hDialog*, int *ID*);

GetDlgItem( ) returns a handle to the specified control. The handle of the dialog box that contains the control is specified in *hDialog*. The ID of the control is passed in *ID*. The function returns **NULL** if an error occurs.

Once the handle of the dialog box has been obtained, it is passed as the buddy window to the **CreateUpDownControl( )** function. Once the up-down control has been created with an edit box as its buddy window, the two controls are automatically linked together, forming the spin control.

Using a Trackbar

A trackbar is a special type of scroll bar that resembles a slider control found on stereos, etc.

One of the most visually appealing of the common controls is the trackbar (sometimes called a *slider control*). A trackbar is visually similar to a slide control found on various types of electronic equipment, such as stereos. It consists of a pointer that moves within a track. Although it looks quite different, a trackbar is handled like a scroll bar by your program.

Trackbars are particularly useful when your program is emulating a real device. For example, if your program is controlling a graphic equalizer, then trackbars are an excellent choice for representing and setting the frequency curve.

To create a trackbar, use either **CreateWindow( )** or **CreateWindowEx( )**. The window class of a trackbar is **TRACKBAR_CLASS**.

Trackbar Styles

11

When creating the trackbar, you can specify various style options. Several common ones are shown in Table 11-3. You will almost always want to include **TBS_AUTOTICKS** because this style causes small "tick" marks to be automatically shown on the bar. The tick marks provide a scale for the bar. Another useful style is **TBS_TOOLTIPS**. This causes a tooltip to be displayed that contains the current position of the slider.

Style	Effect
TBS_AUTOTICKS	Automatically adds tick marks to the trackbar.
TBS_HORZ	Trackbar is horizontal. (This is the default.)
TBS_VERT	Trackbar is vertical.
TBS_BOTTOM	Tick marks on bottom of bar. (This is the default for horizontal trackbars.)
TBS_TOP	Tick marks on top of bar.
TBS_LEFT	Tick marks on left of bar.
TBS_RIGHT	Tick marks on right of bar. (This is the default for vertical trackbars.)
TBS_BOTH	Tick marks on both sides of bar.
TBS_TOOLTIPS	Trackbar includes a tooltip. By default, the tooltip displays the current position of the slider.

Common
Trackbar Style
Options
Table 11-3.

PORTABILITY: Early versions of the trackbar did not support tooltips. This is a feature you will want to add when updating older code.

Sending Trackbar Messages

Like the other common controls we have examined, you send a trackbar a message using the **SendMessage( )** function. Common trackbar messages are shown in Table 11-4. Two messages that you will almost always need to send to a trackbar are **TBM_SETRANGE** and **TBM_SETPOS**. These set the range of the trackbar and establish its initial position, respectively. These items cannot be set when the trackbar is created. If your trackbar includes tooltips, you can change the position of the tooltip by sending the trackbar a **TBM_SETTIPSIDE** message.

Processing Trackbar Notification Messages

When a trackbar is accessed, it generates either a **WM_HSCROLL** or a **WM_VSCROLL** scroll message, depending upon whether the trackbar is

Message	Meaning
TBM_GETPOS	Obtains the current position. *wParam* is 0. *lParam* is 0.
TBM_GETRANGEMAX	Gets the maximum trackbar range. *wParam* is 0. *lParam* is 0.
TBM_GETRANGEMIN	Gets the minimum trackbar range. *wParam* is 0. *lParam* is 0.
TBM_SETPOS	Sets the current position. *wParam* is nonzero to redraw the trackbar and zero otherwise. *lParam* contains the new position.
TBM_SETRANGE	Sets the trackbar range. *wParam* is nonzero to redraw trackbar and 0 otherwise. *lParam* contains the range. The minimum value is in the low-order word. The maximum value is in the high-order word.
TBM_SETRANGEMAX	Sets the maximum range. *wParam* is nonzero to redraw trackbar and 0 otherwise. *lParam* contains the maximum range value.
TBM_SETRANGEMIN	Sets the minimum range. *wParam* is nonzero to redraw trackbar and 0 otherwise. *lParam* contains the minimum range value.
TBM_SETTIPSIDE	Sets the location in which the tooltip for a trackbar is displayed. *wParam* must be either TBTS_TOP, TBTS_BOTTOM, TBTS_LEFT, or TBTS_RIGHT. *lParam* is 0.

Common
Trackbar
Messages
Table 11-4.

11

horizontal or vertical. A notification message describing the nature of the activity is passed in the low-order word of *wParam*. The handle of the trackbar that generated the message is in *lParam*. Common trackbar notification messages are shown in Table 11-5.

Trackbars are fully automated. For example, the trackbar will move itself when its position is changed by the user. Your program does not need to do this manually.

Message	Meaning
TB_BOTTOM	END key is pressed. Slider is moved to minimum value.
TB_ENDTRACK	End of trackbar activity.
TB_LINEDOWN	Right or down arrow key pressed.
TB_LINEUP	Left or up arrow key pressed.
TB_PAGEDOWN	PAGE DOWN key pressed or mouse click before slider.
TB_PAGEUP	PAGE UP pressed or mouse click after slider.
TB_THUMBPOSITION	Slider moved using the mouse.
TB_THUMBTRACK	Slider dragged using the mouse.
TB_TOP	HOME key pressed. Slider is moved to maximum value.

Common Trackbar Notification Messages
Table 11-5.

NOTE: When a **WM_VSCROLL** or **WM_HSCROLL** message is received from a trackbar, the value in **HIWORD(wParam)** will be zero unless the notification message is either **TB_THUMBPOSITION** or **TB_THUMBTRACK**. In this case it will contain the current position of the bar. In general, to obtain the current trackbar position, you can always send a **TBM_GETPOS** message.

A Trackbar Demonstration Program

The following program demonstrates the trackbar by adding one to the previous spin control program. As you will see when you run the program, whenever you change the trackbar, the spin control is updated. If you change the spin control, the trackbar is changed. Thus, both the sending of messages to the trackbar and the receipt of messages from the trackbar are illustrated. Notice that a default tooltip is included for the trackbar. Sample output is shown in Figure 11-3.

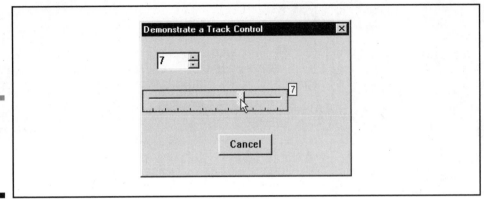

Sample output
from the
trackbar
program
Figure 11-3.

```
/* Demonstrate a trackbar. */

#include <windows.h>
#include <commctrl.h>
#include "track.h"

LRESULT CALLBACK WindowFunc(HWND, UINT, WPARAM, LPARAM);
BOOL CALLBACK DialogFunc(HWND, UINT, WPARAM, LPARAM);

char szWinName[] = "MyWin"; /* name of window class */

HINSTANCE hInst;

int WINAPI WinMain(HINSTANCE hThisInst, HINSTANCE hPrevInst,
                   LPSTR lpszArgs, int nWinMode)
{
  HWND hwnd;
  MSG msg;
  WNDCLASSEX wcl;
  HACCEL hAccel;
  INITCOMMONCONTROLSEX cc;

  /* Define a window class. */
  wcl.cbSize = sizeof(WNDCLASSEX);

  wcl.hInstance = hThisInst; /* handle to this instance */
  wcl.lpszClassName = szWinName; /* window class name */
```

11

```
wcl.lpfnWndProc = WindowFunc; /* window function */
wcl.style = 0; /* default style */

wcl.hIcon = LoadIcon(NULL, IDI_APPLICATION); /* standard icon */
wcl.hIconSm = LoadIcon(NULL, IDI_APPLICATION); /* small icon */
wcl.hCursor = LoadCursor(NULL, IDC_ARROW); /* cursor style */

wcl.lpszMenuName = "MyMenu"; /* main menu */
wcl.cbClsExtra = 0; /* no extra */
wcl.cbWndExtra = 0; /* information needed */

/* Make the window white. */
wcl.hbrBackground = (HBRUSH) GetStockObject(WHITE_BRUSH);

/* Register the window class. */
if(!RegisterClassEx(&wcl)) return 0;

/* Now that a window class has been registered, a window
   can be created. */
hwnd = CreateWindow(
  szWinName, /* name of window class */
  "Using a Track Bar", /* title */
  WS_OVERLAPPEDWINDOW, /* window style - normal */
  CW_USEDEFAULT, /* X coordinate - let Windows decide */
  CW_USEDEFAULT, /* Y coordinate - let Windows decide */
  CW_USEDEFAULT, /* width - let Windows decide */
  CW_USEDEFAULT, /* height - let Windows decide */
  HWND_DESKTOP, /* no parent window */
  NULL, /* no override of class menu */
  hThisInst, /* handle of this instance of the program */
  NULL /* no additional arguments */
);

hInst = hThisInst; /* save the current instance handle */

/* Load accelerators. */
hAccel = LoadAccelerators(hThisInst, "MyMenu");

/* Initialize the common controls. */
cc.dwSize = sizeof(INITCOMMONCONTROLSEX);
cc.dwICC = ICC_BAR_CLASSES | ICC_UPDOWN_CLASS;
InitCommonControlsEx(&cc);

/* Display the window. */
ShowWindow(hwnd, nWinMode);
```

```
      UpdateWindow(hwnd);

      /* Create the message loop. */
      while(GetMessage(&msg, NULL, 0, 0))
      {
        if(!TranslateAccelerator(hwnd, hAccel, &msg)) {
          TranslateMessage(&msg); /* translate keyboard messages */
          DispatchMessage(&msg); /* return control to Windows 98 */
        }
      }
      return msg.wParam;
}

/* This function is called by Windows 98 and is passed
   messages from the message queue.
*/
LRESULT CALLBACK WindowFunc(HWND hwnd, UINT message,
                            WPARAM wParam, LPARAM lParam)
{
  int response;
  switch(message) {
    case WM_COMMAND:
      switch(LOWORD(wParam)) {
        case IDM_DIALOG:
          DialogBox(hInst, "MyDB", hwnd, (DLGPROC) DialogFunc);
          break;
        case IDM_EXIT:
          response = MessageBox(hwnd, "Quit the Program?",
                                "Exit", MB_YESNO);
          if(response == IDYES) PostQuitMessage(0);
          break;
        case IDM_HELP:
          MessageBox(hwnd, "Try the trackbar.", "Help", MB_OK);
          break;
      }
      break;
    case WM_DESTROY: /* terminate the program */
      PostQuitMessage(0);
      break;
    default:
      /* Let Windows 98 process any messages not specified in
         the preceding switch statement. */
      return DefWindowProc(hwnd, message, wParam, lParam);
  }
  return 0;
```

11

```
}

/* Dialog function. */
BOOL CALLBACK DialogFunc(HWND hdwnd, UINT message,
                         WPARAM wParam, LPARAM lParam)
{
  static long udpos = 0;
  static long trackpos = 0;
  static HWND hEboxWnd;
  static HWND hTrackWnd;
  static HWND udWnd;
  int low=0, high=10;

  switch(message) {
    case WM_INITDIALOG:
      hEboxWnd = GetDlgItem(hdwnd, ID_EB1);
      udWnd = CreateUpDownControl(
                  WS_CHILD | WS_BORDER | WS_VISIBLE |
                  UDS_SETBUDDYINT | UDS_ALIGNRIGHT,
                  10, 10, 50, 50,
                  hdwnd,
                  ID_UPDOWN,
                  hInst,
                  hEboxWnd,
                  high, low, high/2);

      /* Create a track bar */
      hTrackWnd = CreateWindow(TRACKBAR_CLASS,
                  "Track Bar", /* not used in this example */
                  WS_CHILD | WS_VISIBLE | WS_TABSTOP |
                  TBS_AUTOTICKS | TBS_TOOLTIPS | WS_BORDER,
                  0, 70,
                  200, 30,
                  hdwnd,
                  NULL,
                  hInst,
                  NULL
      );
      SendMessage(hTrackWnd, TBM_SETRANGE,
                  (WPARAM) 1, (LPARAM) MAKELONG(low, high));
      SendMessage(hTrackWnd, TBM_SETPOS,
                  (WPARAM) 1, (LPARAM) high/2);
      return 1;
    case WM_VSCROLL: /* process up-down control */
      if(udWnd==(HWND)lParam) {
```

```
              trackpos = GetDlgItemInt(hdwnd, ID_EB1, NULL, 1);
              SendMessage(hTrackWnd, TBM_SETPOS,
                          (WPARAM) 1, (LPARAM) trackpos);
           }
           return 1;
         case WM_HSCROLL: /* track bar was activated */
           if(hTrackWnd != (HWND)lParam) break; /* not track bar */

           switch(LOWORD(wParam)) {
             case TB_TOP:
             case TB_BOTTOM:           /* For this example */
             case TB_LINEDOWN:         /* all messages will be */
             case TB_LINEUP:           /* processed in the same */
             case TB_THUMBPOSITION:    /* way. */
             case TB_THUMBTRACK:
             case TB_PAGEUP:
             case TB_PAGEDOWN:
                trackpos = SendMessage(hTrackWnd, TBM_GETPOS,
                                       0, 0);
                SetDlgItemInt(hdwnd, ID_EB1, trackpos, 1);
                return 1;
           }
           break;
         case WM_COMMAND:
           switch(LOWORD(wParam)) {
             case IDCANCEL:
               EndDialog(hdwnd, 0);
               return 1;
           }
      }
      return 0;
}
```

This program uses the following resource file.

11

```
#include <windows.h>
#include "track.h"

MyMenu MENU
{
  POPUP "&Dialog" {
    MENUITEM "&Dialog\tF2", IDM_DIALOG
    MENUITEM "E&xit\tCtrl+X", IDM_EXIT
  }
  MENUITEM "&Help", IDM_HELP
```

```
}

MyMenu ACCELERATORS
{
  VK_F2, IDM_DIALOG, VIRTKEY
  "^X", IDM_EXIT
  VK_F1, IDM_HELP, VIRTKEY
}

MyDB DIALOG 18, 18, 142, 92
CAPTION "Demonstrate a Track Control"
STYLE DS_MODALFRAME | WS_POPUP | WS_CAPTION | WS_SYSMENU
{
  PUSHBUTTON "Cancel", IDCANCEL, 52, 65, 37, 14,
            WS_CHILD | WS_VISIBLE | WS_TABSTOP
  EDITTEXT ID_EB1, 10, 10, 30, 12, ES_LEFT | WS_CHILD |
          WS_VISIBLE | WS_BORDER
}
```

The header file TRACK.H is shown here. (It is the same as UPDOWN.H used
by the previous program.)

```
#define IDM_DIALOG  100
#define IDM_EXIT    101
#define IDM_HELP    102

#define ID_UPDOWN   201
#define ID_EB1      202
```

Inside the program, both a trackbar and a spin control are created when the
dialog box is first displayed. After the trackbar is created, its range is set to 0
through 10. Its initial position is set at 5. (The same range and initial value
are also given to the spin control.) Notice that the range is set using the
macro **MAKELONG( )**. This macro assembles two integers into a long
integer. It has this general form:

DWORD MAKELONG(WORD *low*, WORD *high*);

The low-order part of the double word value is specified in *low* and the
high-order portion is specified in *high*. **MAKELONG( )** is quite useful when
you need to encode two word values into a long integer.

Whenever the spin control is changed, a **WM_VSCROLL** message is received and the position of the trackbar is adjusted accordingly, as shown here.

```
case WM_VSCROLL: /* process up-down control */
  if(udWnd==(HWND)lParam) {
    trackpos = GetDlgItemInt(hdwnd, ID_EB1, NULL, 1);
    SendMessage(hTrackWnd, TBM_SETPOS,
                (WPARAM) 1, (LPARAM) trackpos);
  }
  return 1;
```

This fragment obtains the new value from the edit box by calling **GetDlgItemInt( )**. This function is similar to **GetDlgItemText( )**, which you learned about in Chapter 5. However, instead of obtaining the text from an edit box, **GetDlgItemInt( )** returns the integer equivalent of the contents of the box. For example, if the box contains the string 102, then **GetDlgItemInt( )** will return the value 102. For obvious reasons, this function applies only to edit boxes that contain numeric values. The prototype for **GetDlgItemInt( )** is shown here.

UINT GetDlgItemInt(HWND *hDialog*, int *ID*, BOOL **error*, BOOL *signed*);

The handle of the dialog box that contains the edit control is passed in *hDialog*. The ID of the dialog box is passed in *ID*. If the edit box does not contain a valid numeric string, zero is returned. However, zero is also a valid value. For this reason, the success or failure of the function is returned in the variable pointed to by *error*. After the call, the variable pointed to by *error* will be nonzero if the return value is valid. It will be zero if an error occurred. If you don't care about errors, you can use **NULL** for this parameter. If *signed* is a nonzero value, then a leading minus sign is allowed and a signed value will be returned by **GetDlgItemInt( )**. Otherwise, an unsigned value will be assumed and returned.

After the setting in the edit box has been obtained, it is passed to the trackbar using the **SendMessage( )** function. In this way, if you change the value of the spin control, the trackbar will be automatically moved to reflect the new value.

Whenever the trackbar is moved, a **WM_HSCROLL** message is received and processed by the following code.

11

```
case WM_HSCROLL: /* track bar was activated */
  if(hTrackWnd != (HWND)lParam) break; /* not track bar */

  switch(LOWORD(wParam)) {
    case TB_TOP:
    case TB_BOTTOM:         /* For this example */
    case TB_LINEDOWN:       /* all messages will be */
    case TB_LINEUP:         /* processed in the same */
    case TB_THUMBPOSITION: /* way. */
    case TB_THUMBTRACK:
    case TB_PAGEUP:
    case TB_PAGEDOWN:
      trackpos = SendMessage(hTrackWnd, TBM_GETPOS,
                             0, 0);
      SetDlgItemInt(hdwnd, ID_EB1, trackpos, 1);
      return 1;
  }
  break;
```

When the user moves the slider within the trackbar, the trackbar's position is automatically updated—your program does not have to do this itself. After the trackbar has been moved, the program obtains its new value and then uses this value to update the spin control. The value within the spin control's edit box is set using **SetDlgItemInt( )**. This function is essentially the reverse of **GetDlgItemInt( )** just discussed. It has the following prototype:

BOOL SetDlgItemInt(HWND *hDialog*, int *ID*, UINT *value*, BOOL *signed*);

The handle of the dialog box that contains the edit control is passed in *hDialog*. The ID of the dialog box is passed in *ID*. The value to put into the edit box is passed in *value*. If *signed* is a nonzero value, then negative values are allowed. Otherwise, an unsigned value is assumed. The function returns nonzero if successful and zero on failure.

In this example, the trackbar may be moved using either the mouse or the keyboard. In fact, the reason that so many **TB_** messages are included is to support the keyboard interface. You might want to try taking some of these messages out and observe the results.

Remember, the linkage of the trackbar with the spin control within this program is purely arbitrary and for the sake of illustration. Trackbars can be used entirely on their own.

Using Buddy Windows with Trackbars

You can add a buddy window to a trackbar. As is the case with up-down controls, trackbar buddy windows are usually edit boxes. To add a buddy window to a trackbar, send the trackbar a **TBM_SETBUDDY** message after it has been created. In *lParam,* specify the handle of the buddy. In *wParam,* specify its position. To position the buddy window on the right side of a horizontal bar or the bottom of a vertical bar, pass 0 in *wParam.* To position the buddy window on the left side of a horizontal bar or the top of a vertical bar, pass nonzero. Trackbars may have one or two buddy windows. When two are used, one is on each side.

If you want to try using a buddy window with a trackbar, just change the trackbar example in this chapter so that it uses the edit control as a buddy window for the trackbar rather than the up-down control. First, pass **NULL** in the buddy window parameter for the up-down control so that it no longer uses the edit box for a buddy window. Next, send this **TBM_SETBUDDY** message to the trackbar after it has been created.

```
SendMessage(hTrackWnd, TBM_SETBUDDY, (WPARAM) 0,
            (LPARAM) hEboxWnd);
```

Also, you will need to shorten the width of the edit box a bit within the resource file. After making these changes, the trackbar will look like the one shown here.

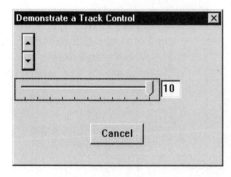

11

Using a Progress Bar

A progress bar indicates the degree to which a task has been completed.

One of the simpler of the common controls is the *progress bar*. You have probably seen progress bars in action. They are small windows in which the degree of completion of a long task is depicted. For example, progress bars are commonly used by installation programs, sorts, and file transfer programs.

Progress bars are created using either **CreateWindow( )** or **CreateWindowEx( )** by specifying the **PROGRESS_CLASS** window class.

Sending Progress Bar Messages

Your program sends a progress bar a message using the standard **SendMessage( )** function. (Progress bars do not generate messages.) Generally, you will send messages to set a progress bar's range and increment its progress. Common progress bar messages are shown in Table 11-6.

By default, a progress bar has the range 0 through 100. However, you can set it to any value between 0 through 65,535. Typically, you will advance the bar by sending it a **PBM_STEPIT** message. This causes the bar's current position to advance by a predetermined increment called a *step*. By default, the step increment is 10, but it may be any value you like. As you increment the bar's

Message	Meaning
PBM_SETPOS	Sets the progress bar's position. The old position is returned. *wParam* contains the new position. *lParam* is 0.
PBM_SETRANGE	Sets the progress bar's range. The old range is returned with the maximum in the high-order word and the minimum in the low-order word. *wParam* is 0. *lParam* contains the range. The maximum value is in the high-order word. The minimum value is in the low-order word.
PBM_SETSTEP	Sets the increment (or step) value. The old increment is returned. *wParam* contains the new increment. *lParam* is 0.
PBM_STEPIT	Advances the bar's progress by the step value. *wParam* is 0. *lParam* is 0.

Common Progress Bar Messages
Table 11-6.

position, more of the bar is filled. Since a progress bar is used to display the degree of completion of a long task, the task should end when the bar is fully filled.

A Simple Progress Bar Program

The following short program illustrates how to use a progress bar. It creates a dialog box that contains a progress bar and a push button named Progress. The progress bar has a range of 0 to 50 and a step increment of 5. Each time you press the Progress push button, the progress bar is incremented another step. When the bar is filled, the dialog box automatically removes itself. Sample output is shown in Figure 11-4.

```c
/* Demonstrate a progress bar. */

#include <windows.h>
#include <commctrl.h>
#include "prog.h"

#define MAX 50

LRESULT CALLBACK WindowFunc(HWND, UINT, WPARAM, LPARAM);
BOOL CALLBACK DialogFunc(HWND, UINT, WPARAM, LPARAM);

char szWinName[] = "MyWin"; /* name of window class */

HINSTANCE hInst;

int WINAPI WinMain(HINSTANCE hThisInst, HINSTANCE hPrevInst,
                   LPSTR lpszArgs, int nWinMode)
{
  HWND hwnd;
  MSG msg;
  WNDCLASSEX wcl;
  HACCEL hAccel;
  INITCOMMONCONTROLSEX cc;

  /* Define a window class. */
  wcl.cbSize = sizeof(WNDCLASSEX);

  wcl.hInstance = hThisInst; /* handle to this instance */
  wcl.lpszClassName = szWinName; /* window class name */
  wcl.lpfnWndProc = WindowFunc; /* window function */
  wcl.style = 0; /* default style */
```

11

```
wcl.hIcon = LoadIcon(NULL, IDI_APPLICATION); /* standard icon */
wcl.hIconSm = LoadIcon(NULL, IDI_APPLICATION); /* small icon */
wcl.hCursor = LoadCursor(NULL, IDC_ARROW); /* cursor style */

wcl.lpszMenuName = "MyMenu"; /* main menu */
wcl.cbClsExtra = 0; /* no extra */
wcl.cbWndExtra = 0; /* information needed */

/* Make the window white. */
wcl.hbrBackground = (HBRUSH) GetStockObject(WHITE_BRUSH);

/* Register the window class. */
if(!RegisterClassEx(&wcl)) return 0;

/* Now that a window class has been registered, a window
   can be created. */
hwnd = CreateWindow(
  szWinName, /* name of window class */
  "Using a Progess Bar", /* title */
  WS_OVERLAPPEDWINDOW, /* window style - normal */
  CW_USEDEFAULT, /* X coordinate - let Windows decide */
  CW_USEDEFAULT, /* Y coordinate - let Windows decide */
  CW_USEDEFAULT, /* width - let Windows decide */
  CW_USEDEFAULT, /* height - let Windows decide */
  HWND_DESKTOP, /* no parent window */
  NULL, /* no override of class menu */
  hThisInst, /* handle of this instance of the program */
  NULL /* no additional arguments */
);

hInst = hThisInst; /* save the current instance handle */

/* Load accelerators. */
hAccel = LoadAccelerators(hThisInst, "MyMenu");

/* Initialize the common controls. */
cc.dwSize = sizeof(INITCOMMONCONTROLSEX);
cc.dwICC = ICC_PROGRESS_CLASS;
InitCommonControlsEx(&cc);

/* Display the window. */
ShowWindow(hwnd, nWinMode);
UpdateWindow(hwnd);
```

```
      /* Create the message loop. */
      while(GetMessage(&msg, NULL, 0, 0))
      {
        if(!TranslateAccelerator(hwnd, hAccel, &msg)) {
          TranslateMessage(&msg); /* translate keyboard messages */
          DispatchMessage(&msg); /* return control to Windows 98 */
        }
      }
      return msg.wParam;
    }


    /* This function is called by Windows 98 and is passed
       messages from the message queue.
    */
    LRESULT CALLBACK WindowFunc(HWND hwnd, UINT message,
                                WPARAM wParam, LPARAM lParam)
    {
      int response;

      switch(message) {
        case WM_COMMAND:
          switch(LOWORD(wParam)) {
            case IDM_DIALOG:
              DialogBox(hInst, "MyDB", hwnd, (DLGPROC) DialogFunc);
              break;
            case IDM_EXIT:
              response = MessageBox(hwnd, "Quit the Program?",
                                    "Exit", MB_YESNO);
              if(response == IDYES) PostQuitMessage(0);
              break;
            case IDM_HELP:
              MessageBox(hwnd, "Try the progress bar.", "Help", MB_OK);
              break;
          }
          break;
        case WM_DESTROY: /* terminate the program */
          PostQuitMessage(0);
          break;
        default:
          /* Let Windows 98 process any messages not specified in
             the preceding switch statement. */
          return DefWindowProc(hwnd, message, wParam, lParam);
      }
      return 0;
    }
```

11

```
/* Dialog function. */
BOOL CALLBACK DialogFunc(HWND hdwnd, UINT message,
                         WPARAM wParam, LPARAM lParam)
{
  static HWND hProgWnd;
  static int pos = 0;

  switch(message) {
    case WM_INITDIALOG:
      pos = 0;
      hProgWnd = CreateWindowEx(0, /* no extended style */
                    PROGRESS_CLASS,
                    "Progress Bar", /* not used in this example */
                    WS_CHILD | WS_VISIBLE | WS_BORDER,
                    0, 70,
                    110, 20,
                    hdwnd,
                    NULL,
                    hInst,
                    NULL);

      /* set range and increment */
      SendMessage(hProgWnd, PBM_SETRANGE, 0,
                  (LPARAM) MAKELONG(0, 50));
      SendMessage(hProgWnd, PBM_SETSTEP, (WPARAM) 5, 0);
      return 1;
    case WM_COMMAND:
      switch(LOWORD(wParam)) {
        case IDCANCEL:
          EndDialog(hdwnd, 0);
          return 1;
        case ID_PROG:
          SendMessage(hProgWnd, PBM_STEPIT, 0, 0);
          pos += 5; /* step unit is 5 */
          if(pos==50) EndDialog(hdwnd, 0);
          return 1;
      }
  }
  return 0;
}
```

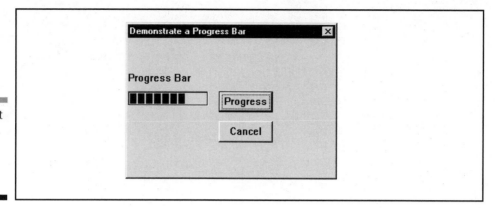

Sample output
from the
progress bar
program

Figure 11-4.

The program requires the following resource file.

```
#include <windows.h>
#include "prog.h"

MyMenu MENU
{
  POPUP "&Dialog" {
    MENUITEM "&Dialog\tF2", IDM_DIALOG
    MENUITEM "E&xit\tCtrl+X", IDM_EXIT
  }
  MENUITEM "&Help", IDM_HELP
}

MyMenu ACCELERATORS
{
  VK_F2, IDM_DIALOG, VIRTKEY
  "^X", IDM_EXIT
  VK_F1, IDM_HELP, VIRTKEY
}

MyDB DIALOG 18, 18, 142, 92
CAPTION "Demonstrate a Progress Bar"
STYLE DS_MODALFRAME | WS_POPUP | WS_CAPTION | WS_SYSMENU
{
```

11

```
DEFPUSHBUTTON "Progress", ID_PROG, 62, 35, 37, 14,
          WS_CHILD | WS_VISIBLE | WS_TABSTOP
PUSHBUTTON "Cancel", IDCANCEL, 62, 55, 37, 14,
          WS_CHILD | WS_VISIBLE | WS_TABSTOP
LTEXT "Progress Bar",
     ID_STATIC, 0, 22, 100, 10
}
```

The header file PROG.H is shown here.

```
#define IDM_DIALOG  100
#define IDM_EXIT    101
#define IDM_HELP    102

#define ID_PROG     201
#define ID_STATIC   202
```

When using a progress bar, remember that one reason it exists is to reassure the user that the program is still proceeding normally. Therefore, you will want to increment the bar frequently. Remember, the user will be relying upon its progress as feedback that the program is still running. If you change it too slowly, a nervous user may reset the computer, thinking that the program has crashed!

In the next chapter we will continue to explore the common controls by examining the status bar, the tab control, and the tree view control.

IN DEPTH

Creating Smooth and Vertical Progress Bars

Originally, progress bars did not offer any style options, but two new styles have recently been added. The first is **PBS_SMOOTH**. By default, progress bars display their progress in steps. By specifying **PBS_SMOOTH**, the progress is shown in a smooth, continuous fashion. The second is

PBS_VERTICAL. It creates a vertical progress bar. Normally, progress bars advance from left to right. A vertical progress bar advances from bottom to top.

Here is how the example progress bar appears with the **PBS_SMOOTH** style.

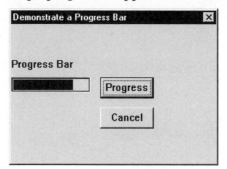

Here is the same bar with the **PBS_VERTICAL** style added.

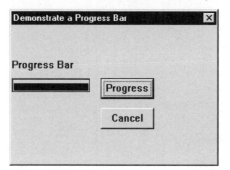

The addition of smooth and vertical progress styles gives you the ability to tailor a progress bar to the precise needs of your program. For example, using a small vertical progress bar saves a significant amount of screen space. A smooth progress bar is especially pleasing when the bar advances at a fairly rapid, fixed rate. Although the progress bar is one of Windows 98's simplest common controls, its use is an important factor in inspiring confidence in your applications.

11

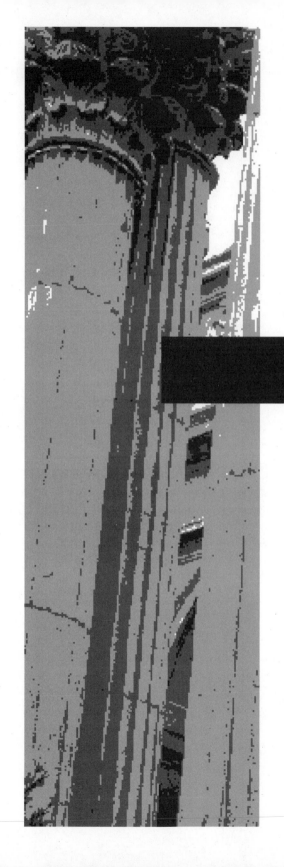

CHAPTER 12

Status Windows, Tab Controls, and Tree Views

This chapter examines three more common controls: the status window, the tab control, and the tree view.

Using a Status Window

A status window or bar is a small horizontal window located at the bottom of its parent. It is typically used to display status information.

Frequently an application will need to keep the user apprised of the status of certain program variables, attributes, or parameters. In the past, each program had to define its own way of accomplishing this. However, Windows 98 includes a standard control for this purpose, called the *status window* or *status bar*. A status window is a bar that (typically) is displayed along the bottom of a window. It is used to display information related to the program.

As you will see, status bars are easy to implement. If you make a status bar a standard feature of each application that you write, you will be providing status information in a consistent and easily recognizable manner.

Creating a Status Window

To create a status window, you can use **CreateStatusWindow( )**, shown here.

HWND CreateStatusWindow(LONG *WinStyle*, LPCSTR *lpszFirstPart*,
HWND *hParent*, UINT *ID*);

Here, *WinStyle* specifies the style of the status bar. It must include **WS_CHILD**. It is also usually created using the **WS_VISIBLE** style, so that it is automatically displayed. A status window can consist of two or more partitions in which text is displayed. A pointer to the string that will be displayed in the first part of the status bar is passed in *lpszFirstPart*. This parameter can be null if this text will be set later. The handle of the parent window is passed in *hParent,* and the ID of the status bar is passed in *ID*. The handle to the status bar is returned. **NULL** is returned on failure.

Notice that you don't pass the dimensions or location of the status window when it is created. The reason for this is that it is automatically sized to fit its parent window and positioned along the bottom of the parent window. If you want to display the status bar at the top of the parent window, include the **CCS_TOP** style in the *WinStyle* parameter.

NOTE: You can also create a status bar by using either
CreateWindow( ) or **CreateWindowEx( )** and specifying the window
class **STATUSCLASSNAME**. But **CreateStatusWindow( )** is easier.

A status window is generally divided into two or more parts. (However, a single-part status window is perfectly acceptable.) Once the parts have been established, you may write text to each part individually. Each part is referred to by its index. The first part has an index value of 0. As just described, you can set the text in the first part when the status bar is created.

Status Window Messages

Your program will send the status bar messages using the standard **SendMessage( )** function. Common status window messages are shown in Table 12-1.

Almost all applications will send **SB_SETPARTS**, which sets the number of parts to the status bar, and **SB_SETTEXT**, which writes text to a part. The general procedure when creating a status bar is shown here.

1. Create the status window.
2. Set the number of parts by sending an **SB_SETPARTS** message.
3. Set the text in each part by sending an **SB_SETTEXT** message.

Message	Meaning
SB_GETPARTS	Obtains the *X* coordinate of the right edge of the parts in a status bar. The number of parts in the status bar is returned. (Zero is returned on failure.) *wParam* specifies the number of parts to obtain. *lParam* is a pointer to an integer array that will receive the *X* coordinate of the right edge of each part. The array must be at least as large as the number of parts requested. If an edge is bounded by the border of the window, its *X* coordinate will be -1.

Commonly
Used Status
Bar Messages
Table 12-1.

12

Message	Meaning
SB_GETTEXT	Obtains the text from the specified part. The low-order word of the return value contains the number of characters in the text. The high-order word contains a value that describes how the text is displayed. If it is 0, the text appears beneath the level of the window. If it is **SBT_POPOUT**, the text appears above the level of the window. If it is **SBT_NOBORDERS**, the text is displayed without a border. If it is **SBT_RTLREADING**, the text is displayed right to left. *wParam* specifies the index of the desired part. *lParam* points to a character array that will receive the text. (Make sure this array is large enough to hold the text contained in the part.)
SB_SETPARTS	Specifies the number of parts in a status bar. It returns nonzero if successful and zero on failure. *wParam* specifies the number of parts. *lParam* is a pointer to an array of integers that contains the *X* coordinate of the right edge of each part. A value of -1 specifies the right boundary of the parent window.
SB_SETTEXT	Outputs text to a part. It returns nonzero if successful and zero on failure. *wParam* specifies the index of the part that will receive the text ORed a value that determines how the text will be displayed. If the display value is zero, then the text appears beneath the level of the window. (This is the default.) If the display value is **SBT_POPOUT**, the text appears above the level of the window. If it is **SBT_NOBORDERS**, the text is displayed without a border. If the display value is **SBT_OWNERDRAW**, the parent window displays the text. If it is **SBT_RTLREADING**, the text is displayed right to left. *lParam* is a pointer to the string to be displayed.

Commonly
Used Status
Bar Messages
(*continued*)

Table 12-1.

Once a status bar has been initialized, you can update each part as needed by sending an **SB_SETTEXT** message.

Using a Status Bar

The following program uses a status bar to report the settings within a dialog
box. The dialog box contains a spin control and two check boxes. In the
status bar, the status of each control is updated whenever the control is
changed. The status bar program is shown here. Sample output from the
program is shown in Figure 12-1.

```
/* Demonstrate a status bar. */

#include <windows.h>
#include <commctrl.h>
#include <stdio.h>
#include "status.h"

#define NUMPARTS 3

LRESULT CALLBACK WindowFunc(HWND, UINT, WPARAM, LPARAM);
BOOL CALLBACK DialogFunc(HWND, UINT, WPARAM, LPARAM);
void InitStatus(HWND hwnd);

char szWinName[] = "MyWin"; /* name of window class */

HINSTANCE hInst;
HWND hwnd;
HWND hStatusWnd;

int parts[NUMPARTS];

int WINAPI WinMain(HINSTANCE hThisInst, HINSTANCE hPrevInst,
                   LPSTR lpszArgs, int nWinMode)
{
  MSG msg;
  WNDCLASSEX wcl;
  HACCEL hAccel;
  INITCOMMONCONTROLSEX cc;

  /* Define a window class. */
  wcl.cbSize = sizeof(WNDCLASSEX);
```

12

```
wcl.hInstance = hThisInst; /* handle to this instance */
wcl.lpszClassName = szWinName; /* window class name */
wcl.lpfnWndProc = WindowFunc; /* window function */
wcl.style = 0; /* default style */

wcl.hIcon = LoadIcon(NULL, IDI_APPLICATION); /* standard icon */
wcl.hIconSm = LoadIcon(NULL, IDI_APPLICATION); /* small icon */
wcl.hCursor = LoadCursor(NULL, IDC_ARROW); /* cursor style */

wcl.lpszMenuName = "MyMenu"; /* main menu */
wcl.cbClsExtra = 0; /* no extra */
wcl.cbWndExtra = 0; /* information needed */

/* Make the window white. */
wcl.hbrBackground = (HBRUSH) GetStockObject(WHITE_BRUSH);

/* Register the window class. */
if(!RegisterClassEx(&wcl)) return 0;

/* Now that a window class has been registered, a window
   can be created. */
hwnd = CreateWindow(
  szWinName, /* name of window class */
  "Using a Status Bar", /* title */
  WS_OVERLAPPEDWINDOW, /* window style - normal */
  CW_USEDEFAULT, /* X coordinate - let Windows decide */
  CW_USEDEFAULT, /* Y coordinate - let Windows decide */
  CW_USEDEFAULT, /* width - let Windows decide */
  CW_USEDEFAULT, /* height - let Windows decide */
  HWND_DESKTOP, /* no parent window */
  NULL, /* no override of class menu */
  hThisInst, /* handle of this instance of the program */
  NULL /* no additional arguments */
);

/* Initialize the common controls. */
cc.dwSize = sizeof(INITCOMMONCONTROLSEX);
cc.dwICC = ICC_UPDOWN_CLASS | ICC_BAR_CLASSES;
InitCommonControlsEx(&cc);

hInst = hThisInst; /* save the current instance handle */

/* Load accelerators. */
hAccel = LoadAccelerators(hThisInst, "MyMenu");
```

```
      /* Display the window. */
      ShowWindow(hwnd, nWinMode);
      UpdateWindow(hwnd);

      /* Create the message loop. */
      while(GetMessage(&msg, NULL, 0, 0))
      {
        if(!TranslateAccelerator(hwnd, hAccel, &msg)) {
          TranslateMessage(&msg); /* Translate keyboard messages */
          DispatchMessage(&msg); /* return control to Windows 98 */
        }
      }
      return msg.wParam;
}

/* This function is called by Windows 98 and is passed
   messages from the message queue.
*/
LRESULT CALLBACK WindowFunc(HWND hwnd, UINT message,
                            WPARAM wParam, LPARAM lParam)
{
  int response;

  switch(message) {
    case WM_COMMAND:
      switch(LOWORD(wParam)) {
        case IDM_DIALOG:
          DialogBox(hInst, "MyDB", hwnd, (DLGPROC) DialogFunc);
          break;
        case IDM_EXIT:
          response = MessageBox(hwnd, "Quit the Program?",
                                "Exit", MB_YESNO);
          if(response == IDYES) PostQuitMessage(0);
          break;
        case IDM_HELP:
          MessageBox(hwnd, "Try the status bar.", "Help", MB_OK);
          break;
      }
      break;
    case WM_DESTROY: /* terminate the program */
      PostQuitMessage(0);
      break;
    default:
      /* Let Windows 98 process any messages not specified in
         the preceding switch statement. */
```

12

```
      return DefWindowProc(hwnd, message, wParam, lParam);
  }
  return 0;
}

/* Dialog function. */
BOOL CALLBACK DialogFunc(HWND hdwnd, UINT message,
                         WPARAM wParam, LPARAM lParam)
{
  static long udpos = 0;
  static char str[80];
  static HWND hEboxWnd;
  static HWND udWnd;
  static statusCB1, statusCB2;
  int low=0, high=20;

  switch(message) {
    case WM_INITDIALOG:
      InitStatus(hdwnd); /* initialize the status bar */

      hEboxWnd = GetDlgItem(hdwnd, ID_EB1);
      udWnd = CreateUpDownControl(
                    WS_CHILD | WS_BORDER | WS_VISIBLE |
                    UDS_SETBUDDYINT | UDS_ALIGNRIGHT,
                    10, 10, 50, 50,
                    hdwnd,
                    ID_UPDOWN,
                    hInst,
                    hEboxWnd,
                    high, low, high/2);
      return 1;
    case WM_VSCROLL: /* process up-down control */
      if(udWnd==(HWND)lParam) {
        udpos = GetDlgItemInt(hdwnd, ID_EB1, NULL, 1);
        sprintf(str, "Up-down: %d", udpos);
        SendMessage(hStatusWnd, SB_SETTEXT,
                    (WPARAM) 0, (LPARAM) str);
      }
      return 1;
    case WM_COMMAND:
      switch(LOWORD(wParam)) {
        case ID_CB1: /* process checkbox 1 */
          statusCB1 = SendDlgItemMessage(hdwnd, ID_CB1,
                    BM_GETCHECK, 0, 0);
          if(statusCB1) sprintf(str, "Option 1 ON");
          else sprintf(str, "Option 1 OFF");
```

```
            SendMessage(hStatusWnd, SB_SETTEXT,
                    (WPARAM) 1, (LPARAM) str);
          return 1;
        case ID_CB2: /* process checkbox 2 */
          statusCB2 = SendDlgItemMessage(hdwnd, ID_CB2,
                    BM_GETCHECK, 0, 0);
          if(statusCB2) sprintf(str, "Option 2 ON");
          else sprintf(str, "Option 2 OFF");
          SendMessage(hStatusWnd, SB_SETTEXT,
                    (WPARAM) 2, (LPARAM) str);
          return 1;
        case ID_RESET: /* reset options */
          SendMessage(udWnd, UDM_SETPOS, 0, (LPARAM) high /2);
          SendMessage(hStatusWnd, SB_SETTEXT, (WPARAM) 0,
                    (LPARAM) "Up-down: 10");
          SendDlgItemMessage(hdwnd, ID_CB1,
                    BM_SETCHECK, 0, 0);
          SendDlgItemMessage(hdwnd, ID_CB2,
                    BM_SETCHECK, 0, 0);
          SendMessage(hStatusWnd, SB_SETTEXT, (WPARAM) 1,
                    (LPARAM) "Option 1: OFF");
          SendMessage(hStatusWnd, SB_SETTEXT, (WPARAM) 2,
                    (LPARAM) "Option 2: OFF");
          return 1;
        case IDCANCEL:
        case IDOK:
          EndDialog(hdwnd, 0);
          return 1;
      }
  }
  return 0;
}

/* Initialize the status bar. */
void InitStatus(HWND hwnd)
{
  RECT WinDim;
  int i;

  GetClientRect(hwnd, &WinDim);

  for(i=1; i<=NUMPARTS; i++)
    parts[i-1] = WinDim.right/NUMPARTS * i;

  /* Create a status bar */
  hStatusWnd = CreateWindow(STATUSCLASSNAME,
```

12

```
                 "", /* not used in this example */
                 WS_CHILD | WS_VISIBLE,
                 0, 0, 0, 0,
                 hwnd,
                 NULL,
                 hInst,
                 NULL
         );

  SendMessage(hStatusWnd, SB_SETPARTS,
              (WPARAM) NUMPARTS, (LPARAM) parts);

  SendMessage(hStatusWnd, SB_SETTEXT, (WPARAM) 0,
              (LPARAM) "Up-down: 10");
  SendMessage(hStatusWnd, SB_SETTEXT, (WPARAM) 1,
              (LPARAM) "Option 1: OFF");
  SendMessage(hStatusWnd, SB_SETTEXT, (WPARAM) 2,
              (LPARAM) "Option 2: OFF");
}
```

This program requires the following resource file.

```
#include <windows.h>
#include "status.h"

MyMenu MENU
{
  POPUP "&Dialog" {
    MENUITEM "&Dialog\tF2", IDM_DIALOG
    MENUITEM "E&xit\tCtrl+X", IDM_EXIT
  }
  MENUITEM "&Help", IDM_HELP
}

MyMenu ACCELERATORS
{
  VK_F2, IDM_DIALOG, VIRTKEY
  "^X", IDM_EXIT
  VK_F1, IDM_HELP, VIRTKEY
}

MyDB DIALOG 18, 18, 150, 92
CAPTION "Demonstrate a Status Bar"
STYLE DS_MODALFRAME | WS_POPUP | WS_CAPTION | WS_SYSMENU
{
  PUSHBUTTON "Reset", ID_RESET, 92, 34, 37, 14,
             WS_CHILD | WS_VISIBLE | WS_TABSTOP
```

```
PUSHBUTTON "OK", IDOK, 92, 53, 37, 14,
          WS_CHILD | WS_VISIBLE | WS_TABSTOP
EDITTEXT ID_EB1, 10, 10, 30, 12, ES_LEFT | WS_CHILD |
        WS_VISIBLE | WS_BORDER
AUTOCHECKBOX "Option 1", ID_CB1, 10, 40, 48, 12
AUTOCHECKBOX "Option 2", ID_CB2, 10, 60, 48, 12
}
```

The header file STATUS.H is shown here.

```
#define IDM_DIALOG   100
#define IDM_EXIT     101
#define IDM_HELP     102

#define ID_UPDOWN    201
#define ID_EB1       202
#define ID_CB1       203
#define ID_CB2       204
#define ID_RESET     205
```

Inside the program, the function **InitStatus( )** creates and initializes the status window. First, the status bar is divided into three equal parts. The division of the status bar is aided by the **GetClientRect( )** API function, which was described in Chapter 8. Recall that this function obtains the current size of the client area of the specified window.

Since there are three parts to the status bar, the width of the dialog box (as obtained by **GetClientRect( )**) is divided into three parts and these become the end points for the status bar parts and are put into the **parts** array. Remember, the end point—not the width—of each part must be passed to

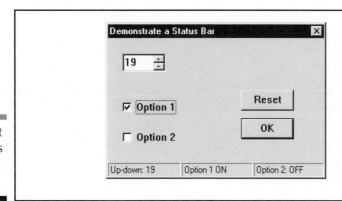

Sample output
from the status
bar program
Figure 12-1.

the status window. Once the parts have been set, the initial text in each part is displayed.

Within **DialogFunc( )**, the text within each part of the status bar is updated each time a control is changed. This is accomplished by sending an **SB_SETTEXT** message to the part associated with the control that has changed its state.

Resizing a Status Bar

Although a status bar will initially size itself to fit its parent window, it will not automatically change its size when the parent window does. Recall that a window receives a **WM_SIZE** message after its size has been changed. To allow a child status window to be resized with its parent, you must pass the **WM_SIZE** message received by the parent window to the status window using the **SendMessage( )** function. (This process is similar to that used to resize a toolbar, as described in Chapter 10.)

For example, to allow the status window in the preceding example to be automatically resized when the size of its parent dialog box is changed, add this case to **DialogFunc( )**. It passes along the **WM_SIZE** message and then resets the dimensions of the status bar partitions.

```
case WM_SIZE:
  SendMessage(hStatusWnd, WM_SIZE, wParam, lParam);
  GetClientRect(hdwnd, &WinDim);
  for(i=1; i<=NUMPARTS; i++)
    parts[i-1] = WinDim.right/NUMPARTS * i;
  SendMessage(hStatusWnd, SB_SETPARTS,
              (WPARAM) NUMPARTS, (LPARAM) parts);
  return 1;
```

You must also add

```
RECT WinDim;
int i;
```

to **DialogFunc( )**. Finally, in order for the dialog box to be capable of being resized, it must be created with the **WS_SIZEBOX** style also included.

Once you have made these modifications, execute the status bar program and then try resizing the status dialog box. As you will see, the status bar is automatically resized, too. For example, Figure 12-2 shows the dialog box after it has been lengthened.

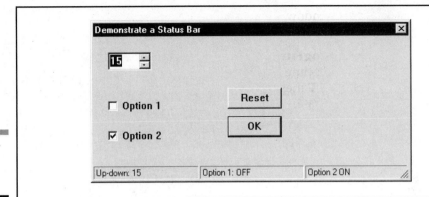

The status bar
after resizing
Figure 12-2.

IN DEPTH

Adding Tooltips to a Status Window

You can easily add tooltips to a status bar. Just include the
SBT_TOOLTIPS style when you create the status window. These tips
will only be shown when the status text cannot be fully displayed
because the size of a part is too small.

To set the tooltip text for each part, send an **SB_SETTIPTEXT** message.
In *wParam,* specify the index of the part for which the tooltip text is
being set. In *lParam,* pass a pointer to the text. In general, you will set the
tooltip text to the same string as would be displayed in the status window
if the window were wide enough to accept it. For example, the following
fragment enhances the status window demonstration program so that it
updates the tooltip text each time the up-down control is changed.

```
case WM_VSCROLL: /* process up-down control */
  if(udWnd==(HWND)lParam) {
    udpos = GetDlgItemInt(hdwnd, ID_EB1, NULL, 1);
    sprintf(str, "Up-down: %d", udpos);
    SendMessage(hStatusWnd, SB_SETTEXT,
              (WPARAM) 0, (LPARAM) str);


    /* update tooltip text */
    SendMessage(hStatusWnd, SB_SETTIPTEXT,
              (WPARAM) 0, (LPARAM)str);
```

12

```
    }
    return 1;
```

To try this fragment, make sure that you create the status window using **SBT_TOOLTIPS**. Also remember that the tooltip will not be shown unless the status window cannot display the entire status message. Therefore you will need to resize the dialog box so that the status messages don't fully fit. Here is how the tooltip will look.

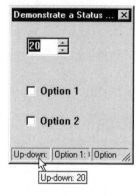

Adding tooltips to your status windows gives them that extra polish and "mark of distinction" that helps put your application into a class of its own.

Introducing Tab Controls

One of the more visually interesting common controls is the tab control. A tab control emulates the tabs on a set of file folders. Each time a tab is selected, its associated folder comes to the surface. While tab controls are easy to use, they are a bit complicated to program for. In this section, tab control basics are introduced. In the next section, additional tab control features are discussed.

A tab control creates a window that looks like a set of file folders.

Creating a Tab Control

To create a tab control, you use either **CreateWindow( )** or **CreateWindowEx( )**, specifying the window class **WC_TABCONTROL**. Typically, a tab control will be a child window. It is also usually created using the **WS_VISIBLE** style, so that it is automatically displayed. For example, the following creates a tab control.

```
hTabWnd = CreateWindow(
            WC_TABCONTROL,
            "",
            WS_VISIBLE | WS_TABSTOP | WS_CHILD,
            0, 0, 100, 100,
            hwnd, /* handle of parent */
            NULL,
            hInst, /* instance handle */
            NULL
        );
```

Once created, a tab control can be sent messages by your application or generate messages when it is accessed.

After a tab control has been created, it is empty. Before it can be used, you must insert tabs into it. Each tab is defined by a **TCITEM** structure, which is shown here.

```
typedef struct tagTCITEM
{
  UINT mask;
  DWORD dwState;
  DWORD dwStateMask
  LPSTR pszText;
  int cchTextMax;
  int iImage;
  LPARAM lParam;
} TCITEM;
```

In this structure, the value contained in **mask** determines whether the **dwState**, **pszText**, **iImage**, or **lParam** members of the structure contain valid data. **mask** can contain one or more of the following values:

Value in mask	Meaning
TCIF_IMAGE	**iImage** contains data.
TCIF_PARAM	**lParam** contains data.
TCIF_STATE	**dwState** contains data.
TCIF_TEXT	**pszText** contains data.

12

mask may also contain the value **TCIF_RTLREADING**, which means that the text should be displayed right to left.

When a tab is being created, the value of **dwState** is not used. When information is being obtained about an existing tab, **dwState** indicates its state. It will be either zero, **TCIS_BUTTONPRESSED** (the tab is selected), or **TCIS_HIGHLIGHTED** (the tab is highlighted). The value of **dwStateMask** determines which bits in **dwState** are valid. This field is not used when inserting items.

When a tab is being set, **pszText** points to the string that will be displayed within the tab. When information about a tab is being obtained, **pszText** must point to an array that will receive the text. In this case, the value of **cchTextMax** specifies the size of the array pointed to by **pszText**.

If there is an image list associated with the tab control, then **iImage** will contain the index of the image associated with the specified tab. If there is no image list associated with the tab control, **iImage** should be -1. We won't be using images in the tab control examples shown in this chapter, but you might find them useful for your applications.

lParam contains application-defined data.

PORTABILITY: The **TCITEM** structure replaces the older **TC_ITEM** structure. In **TC_ITEM**, **dwState** and **dwStateMask** were reserved fields.

Sending Tab Control Messages

You can send a tab control several different types of messages using the **SendMessage( )** function. Several commonly used tab control messages are shown in Table 12-2. As an alternative to using **SendMessage( )**, special macros were created that simplify the process of sending messages to tab controls. The tab control macros corresponding to the messages in Table 12-2 are shown here. In all cases, *hTabWnd* is the handle of the tab control.

```
VOID TabCtrl_AdjustRect(HWND hTabWnd, BOOL operation, RECT *lpRect);
BOOL TabCtrl_DeleteAllItems(HWND hTabWnd);
BOOL TabCtrl_DeleteItem(HWND hTabWnd, int index);
int TabCtrl_GetCurSel(HWND hTabWnd);
BOOL TabCtrl_GetItem(HWND hTabWnd, int index, TCITEM *lpitem);
```

```
int TabCtrl_GetItemCount(HWND hTabWnd);
int TabCtrl_InsertItem(HWND hTabWnd, int index, CONST TCITEM *lpitem);
int TabCtrl_SetCurSel(HWND hTabWnd, int index);
BOOL TabCtrl_SetItem(HWND hTabWnd, int index, TCITEM *lpitem);
```

In general, the macros are easier to use than the equivalent calls to
SendMessage( ).

Message	Meaning
TCM_ADJUSTRECT	Translates between the dimensions of the tab control's display area and its window. *wParam* specifies the operation. If it is nonzero, then given the dimensions of a tab control's display area, the dimensions of the window rectangle are obtained. If it is zero, then given the dimensions of the window rectangle, the display area of the tab control is obtained. *lParam* points to a **RECT** structure that contains the coordinates of the region to be translated. (That is, either the window or the tab control's display area.) On return, this structure will contain the translated coordinates.
TCM_DELETEALLITEMS	Deletes all tabs in the control. Returns nonzero if successful and zero on failure. *wParam* is 0. *lParam* is 0.
TCM_DELETEITEM	Deletes a specified tab. Returns nonzero if successful and zero on failure. *wParam* specifies the index of the tab to remove. *lParam* is 0.
TCM_GETCURSEL	Returns the index of the currently selected tab or −1 if no tab is selected. *wParam* is 0. *lParam* is 0.
TCM_GETITEM	Obtains information about the specified tab. Returns nonzero if successful and zero on failure. *wParam* specifies the index of the tab. *lParam* is a pointer to a **TCITEM** structure that receives the information about the item.
TCM_GETITEMCOUNT	Returns the number of tabs. *wParam* is 0. *lParam* is 0.

Commonly
Used Tab
Control
Messages
Table 12-2.

12

Message	Meaning
TCM_INSERTITEM	Creates (i.e., inserts) a new tab. Returns the index of the item being inserted or −1 on failure. *wParam* specifies the index of the tab. *lParam* is a pointer to a **TCITEM** structure that describes the tab.
TCM_SETCURSEL	Selects a tab. Returns the index of the previously selected tab or −1 if no tab was previously selected. *wParam* specifies the index of the tab being selected. *lParam* is 0.
TCM_SETITEM	Sets information about the specified tab. Returns nonzero if successful and zero on failure. *wParam* specifies the index of the tab. *lParam* is a pointer to a **TCITEM** structure that contains the information about the item.

Commonly
Used Tab
Control
Messages
(*continued*)
Table 12-2.

When a tab control is created, it has no tabs. Therefore, your program will always send at least one **TCM_INSERTITEM** message to it. Although neither of the examples in this chapter requires its use, one message that your real-world applications will probably employ is **TCM_ADJUSTRECT**. This message is used to obtain the dimensions of the display area of a tab control. Remember, when you create a tab control, its window contains both the tabs themselves and the area in which you will display information or pop up a dialog box. The display area is the part of a tab control window that excludes the tabs. (That is, the display area is the part of the tab control window that you may use to display other items.) Since it is the display area that will contain the information associated with the tab, you will often need to know its dimensions.

Tab Notification Messages

When a tab control is accessed by the user, a **WM_NOTIFY** message is generated. Tab controls can generate two selection-change notification codes: **TCN_SELCHANGE** and **TCN_SELCHANGING**. **TCN_SELCHANGING** is sent when a tab selection is about to change. **TCN_SELCHANGE** is sent after a new tab is selected.

When a **WM_NOTIFY** message is received, *lParam* will point to a **NMHDR** structure (discussed in Chapter 10). The notification code will be contained in the **code** field of the **NMHDR** structure. The handle of the tab control that generates the message is found in the **hwndFrom** field.

A Simple Tab Demonstration Program

The following short program demonstrates the tab control. It creates a tab control and then creates three tabs, labeled One, Two, and Three. Each time a new tab is selected, a message is displayed reporting this fact. Sample output is shown in Figure 12-3.

```
/* Demonstrate a tab control. */

#include <windows.h>
#include <commctrl.h>
#include <stdio.h>

LRESULT CALLBACK WindowFunc(HWND, UINT, WPARAM, LPARAM);

char szWinName[] = "MyWin"; /* name of window class */

HINSTANCE hInst;
HWND hwnd;
HWND hTabWnd;

int WINAPI WinMain(HINSTANCE hThisInst, HINSTANCE hPrevInst,
                   LPSTR lpszArgs, int nWinMode)
{
  MSG msg;
  WNDCLASSEX wcl;
  INITCOMMONCONTROLSEX cc;

  /* Define a window class. */
  wcl.cbSize = sizeof(WNDCLASSEX);

  wcl.hInstance = hThisInst; /* handle to this instance */
  wcl.lpszClassName = szWinName; /* window class name */
  wcl.lpfnWndProc = WindowFunc; /* window function */
  wcl.style = 0; /* default style */

  wcl.hIcon = LoadIcon(NULL, IDI_APPLICATION); /* standard icon */
  wcl.hIconSm = LoadIcon(NULL, IDI_APPLICATION); /* small icon */
  wcl.hCursor = LoadCursor(NULL, IDC_ARROW); /* cursor style */

  wcl.lpszMenuName = NULL; /* no main menu */
```

12

```
wcl.cbClsExtra = 0; /* no extra */
wcl.cbWndExtra = 0; /* information needed */

/* Make the window white. */
wcl.hbrBackground = (HBRUSH) GetStockObject(WHITE_BRUSH);

/* Register the window class. */
if(!RegisterClassEx(&wcl)) return 0;

/* Now that a window class has been registered, a window
   can be created. */
hwnd = CreateWindow(
  szWinName, /* name of window class */
  "Using a Tab Control", /* title */
  WS_OVERLAPPEDWINDOW, /* window style - normal */
  CW_USEDEFAULT, /* X coordinate - let Windows decide */
  CW_USEDEFAULT, /* Y coordinate - let Windows decide */
  CW_USEDEFAULT, /* width - let Windows decide */
  CW_USEDEFAULT, /* height - let Windows decide */
  HWND_DESKTOP, /* no parent window */
  NULL, /* no override of class menu */
  hThisInst, /* handle of this instance of the program */
  NULL /* no additional arguments */
);

/* Initialize the common controls. */
cc.dwSize = sizeof(INITCOMMONCONTROLSEX);
cc.dwICC = ICC_TAB_CLASSES;
InitCommonControlsEx(&cc);

hInst = hThisInst; /* save the current instance handle */

/* Display the window. */
ShowWindow(hwnd, nWinMode);
UpdateWindow(hwnd);

/* Create the message loop. */
while(GetMessage(&msg, NULL, 0, 0))
{
  TranslateMessage(&msg); /* translate keyboard messages */
  DispatchMessage(&msg); /* return control to Windows 98 */
}
return msg.wParam;
}
```

```
/* This function is called by Windows 98 and is passed
   messages from the message queue.
*/
LRESULT CALLBACK WindowFunc(HWND hwnd, UINT message,
                            WPARAM wParam, LPARAM lParam)
{
  NMHDR *nmptr;
  int tabnumber;
  HDC hdc;
  char str[80];
  TCITEM tci;
  RECT WinDim;

  switch(message) {
    case WM_CREATE:
      GetClientRect(hwnd, &WinDim);  /* get size of parent window */

      /* create a tab control */
      hTabWnd = CreateWindow(
                  WC_TABCONTROL,
                  "",
                  WS_VISIBLE | WS_TABSTOP | WS_CHILD,
                  0, 0, WinDim.right, WinDim.bottom,
                  hwnd,
                  NULL,
                  hInst,
                  NULL
                );

      tci.mask = TCIF_TEXT;
      tci.iImage = -1;

      tci.pszText = "One";
      TabCtrl_InsertItem(hTabWnd, 0, &tci);

      tci.pszText = "Two";
      TabCtrl_InsertItem(hTabWnd, 1, &tci);

      tci.pszText = "Three";
      TabCtrl_InsertItem(hTabWnd, 2, &tci);
      break;
    case WM_NOTIFY: /* process a tab change */
      nmptr = (LPNMHDR) lParam;
      if(nmptr->code == TCN_SELCHANGE) {
```

12

```
        tabnumber = TabCtrl_GetCurSel((HWND)nmptr->hwndFrom);
        hdc = GetDC(hTabWnd);
        sprintf(str, "Changed to Tab %d", tabnumber+1);
        SetBkColor(hdc, RGB(200, 200, 200));
        TextOut(hdc, 40, 100, str, strlen(str));
        ReleaseDC(hTabWnd, hdc);
      }
      break;
    case WM_DESTROY: /* terminate the program */
      PostQuitMessage(0);
      break;
    default:
     /* Let Windows 98 process any messages not specified in
         the preceding switch statement. */
      return DefWindowProc(hwnd, message, wParam, lParam);
  }
  return 0;
}
```

In the program, just before the tab control is created, a call is made to **GetClientRect( )** to obtain the size of the main window. When the tab control is created, it is sized to fill the entire client area of its parent window. While this is arbitrary, it is not uncommon. After the tab control has been created, three tabs are inserted.

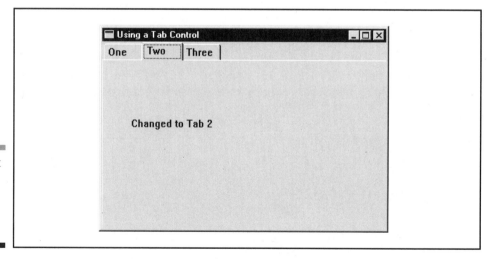

Sample output from the first tab control program

Figure 12-3.

Inside **WindowFunc( )**, each time a **WM_NOTIFY** message contains the **TCN_SELCHANGE** code, a message is displayed within the tab control display area, indicating that the selection has changed to the specified tab.

Using Tab Controls

While tab controls are quite easy to create, they are a bit tricky to use. The reason for this is that each tab will typically have associated with it a dialog box. Each time a new tab is selected, the currently displayed dialog box must be removed and the new dialog box displayed. Also, in general, you will want to fit each dialog box to the display area of the tab control. Frankly, there are many other subtle issues associated with tab controls and their dialog boxes that are simply beyond the scope of this book. However, in this section you will learn the general method of applying a tab control to your application. Once you understand the basics, you will be able to add other features to your tab controls on your own.

Tab control dialog boxes must be modeless.

Since a new tab may be selected at any time, this implies that modeless (rather than modal) dialog boxes must be used. As you should recall, a modeless dialog box allows other parts of your application to be activated without deactivating the dialog box. (This differs from modal dialog boxes, which must be closed by the user before other parts of the program can be used.) Typically, when a new tab is selected, your application will close the currently displayed dialog box and then activate the next one. Because a dialog box may be closed at any time, your program must take appropriate action (such as saving its settings) before displaying the new box.

To demonstrate a tab control, the following program creates a tab control that has three tabs, called Options, Pitch, and Page Size. Each tab is associated with its own modeless dialog box. The first dialog box is the one created for the status bar example earlier in this chapter. The other two are simply placeholders used for the sake of illustration. Sample output from this program is shown in Figure 12-4.

```
/* Demonstrate a tab control. */

#include <windows.h>
#include <commctrl.h>
#include <stdio.h>
#include "tab.h"

#define NUMPARTS 3
```

12

```
LRESULT CALLBACK WindowFunc(HWND, UINT, WPARAM, LPARAM);
BOOL CALLBACK DialogFunc1(HWND, UINT, WPARAM, LPARAM);
BOOL CALLBACK DialogFunc2(HWND, UINT, WPARAM, LPARAM);
BOOL CALLBACK DialogFunc3(HWND, UINT, WPARAM, LPARAM);
void InitStatus(HWND hwnd);

char szWinName[] = "MyWin"; /* name of window class */

HINSTANCE hInst;
HWND hwnd;
HWND hStatusWnd;
HWND hTabWnd;

int parts[NUMPARTS];

HWND hDlg = (HWND) NULL;

int WINAPI WinMain(HINSTANCE hThisInst, HINSTANCE hPrevInst,
                   LPSTR lpszArgs, int nWinMode)
{
  MSG msg;
  WNDCLASSEX wcl;
  INITCOMMONCONTROLSEX cc;

  /* Define a window class. */
  wcl.cbSize = sizeof(WNDCLASSEX);

  wcl.hInstance = hThisInst; /* handle to this instance */
  wcl.lpszClassName = szWinName; /* window class name */
  wcl.lpfnWndProc = WindowFunc; /* window function */
  wcl.style = 0; /* default style */

  wcl.hIcon = LoadIcon(NULL, IDI_APPLICATION); /* standard icon */
  wcl.hIconSm = LoadIcon(NULL, IDI_APPLICATION); /* small icon */
  wcl.hCursor = LoadCursor(NULL, IDC_ARROW); /* cursor style */

  wcl.lpszMenuName = NULL; /* no main menu */
  wcl.cbClsExtra = 0; /* no extra */
  wcl.cbWndExtra = 0; /* information needed */

  /* Make the window white. */
  wcl.hbrBackground = (HBRUSH) GetStockObject(WHITE_BRUSH);

  /* Register the window class. */
  if(!RegisterClassEx(&wcl)) return 0;
```

```
      /* Now that a window class has been registered, a window
         can be created. */
      hwnd = CreateWindow(
        szWinName, /* name of window class */
        "Using a Tab Control", /* title */
        WS_OVERLAPPEDWINDOW, /* window style - normal */
        CW_USEDEFAULT, /* X coordinate - let Windows decide */
        CW_USEDEFAULT, /* Y coordinate - let Windows decide */
        CW_USEDEFAULT, /* width - let Windows decide */
        CW_USEDEFAULT, /* height - let Windows decide */
        HWND_DESKTOP, /* no parent window */
        NULL, /* no override of class menu */
        hThisInst, /* handle of this instance of the program */
        NULL /* no additional arguments */
      );

      /* Initialize the common controls. */
      cc.dwSize = sizeof(INITCOMMONCONTROLSEX);
      cc.dwICC = ICC_UPDOWN_CLASS | ICC_TAB_CLASSES;
      InitCommonControlsEx(&cc);

      hInst = hThisInst; /* save the current instance handle */

      /* Display the window. */
      ShowWindow(hwnd, nWinMode);
      UpdateWindow(hwnd);

      /* Create the message loop. */
      while(GetMessage(&msg, NULL, 0, 0))
      {
        if(!IsDialogMessage(hDlg, &msg)) {
          TranslateMessage(&msg); /* translate keyboard messages */
          DispatchMessage(&msg); /* return control to Windows 98 */
        }
      }
      return msg.wParam;
    }

/* This function is called by Windows 98 and is passed
   messages from the message queue.
*/
LRESULT CALLBACK WindowFunc(HWND hwnd, UINT message,
                              WPARAM wParam, LPARAM lParam)
{
```

12

```
NMHDR *nmptr;
int tabnumber = 0;
TCITEM tci;

switch(message) {
  case WM_CREATE:
    hTabWnd = CreateWindow(
               WC_TABCONTROL,
               "",
               WS_VISIBLE | WS_TABSTOP | WS_CHILD,
               20, 20, 325, 250,
               hwnd,
               NULL,
               hInst,
               NULL
             );

    tci.mask = TCIF_TEXT;
    tci.iImage = -1;

    tci.pszText = "Options";
    TabCtrl_InsertItem(hTabWnd, 0, &tci);

    tci.pszText = "Pitch";
    TabCtrl_InsertItem(hTabWnd, 1, &tci);

    tci.pszText = "Page Size";
    TabCtrl_InsertItem(hTabWnd, 2, &tci);

    hDlg = CreateDialog(hInst, "MyDB1", hTabWnd,
                        (DLGPROC) DialogFunc1);
    break;
  case WM_NOTIFY:
    nmptr = (LPNMHDR) lParam;
    if(nmptr->code == TCN_SELCHANGE) {
      if(hDlg) DestroyWindow(hDlg);
      tabnumber = TabCtrl_GetCurSel((HWND)nmptr->hwndFrom);
      switch(tabnumber) {
        case 0:
          hDlg = CreateDialog(hInst, "MyDB1",
                              hTabWnd, (DLGPROC) DialogFunc1);
          break;
        case 1:
          hDlg = CreateDialog(hInst, "MyDB2",
                              hTabWnd, (DLGPROC) DialogFunc2);
```

```
            break;
          case 2:
            hDlg = CreateDialog(hInst, "MyDB3",
                                hTabWnd, (DLGPROC) DialogFunc3);
            break;
        }
      }
      break;
    case WM_DESTROY: /* terminate the program */
      if(hDlg) DestroyWindow(hDlg);
      PostQuitMessage(0);
      break;
    default:
      /* Let Windows 98 process any messages not specified in
         the preceding switch statement. */
      return DefWindowProc(hwnd, message, wParam, lParam);
  }
  return 0;
}


/* First dialog function. */
BOOL CALLBACK DialogFunc1(HWND hdwnd, UINT message,
                          WPARAM wParam, LPARAM lParam)
{
  static long udpos = 0;
  static char str[80];
  static HWND hEboxWnd;
  static HWND udWnd;
  static statusCB1, statusCB2;
  int low=0, high=20;

  switch(message) {
    case WM_INITDIALOG:
      InitStatus(hdwnd);

      hEboxWnd = GetDlgItem(hdwnd, ID_EB1);
      udWnd = CreateUpDownControl(
                    WS_CHILD | WS_BORDER | WS_VISIBLE |
                    UDS_SETBUDDYINT | UDS_ALIGNRIGHT,
                    10, 10, 50, 50,
                    hdwnd,
                    ID_UPDOWN,
                    hInst,
                    hEboxWnd,
                    high, low, high/2);
```

12

```
          return 1;
      case WM_VSCROLL: /* process up-down control */
        if(udWnd==(HWND)lParam) {
          udpos = GetDlgItemInt(hdwnd, ID_EB1, NULL, 1);
          sprintf(str, "Up-down: %d", udpos);
          SendMessage(hStatusWnd, SB_SETTEXT,
                      (WPARAM) 0, (LPARAM) str);
        }
        return 1;
      case WM_COMMAND:
        switch(LOWORD(wParam)) {
          case ID_CB1: /* process checkbox 1 */
            statusCB1 = SendDlgItemMessage(hdwnd, ID_CB1,
                        BM_GETCHECK, 0, 0);
            if(statusCB1) sprintf(str, "Option 1: ON");
            else sprintf(str, "Option 1: OFF");
            SendMessage(hStatusWnd, SB_SETTEXT,
                        (WPARAM) 1, (LPARAM) str);

            return 1;
          case ID_CB2: /* process checkbox 2 */
            statusCB2 = SendDlgItemMessage(hdwnd, ID_CB2,
                        BM_GETCHECK, 0, 0);
            if(statusCB2) sprintf(str, "Option 2: ON");
            else sprintf(str, "Option 2: OFF");
            SendMessage(hStatusWnd, SB_SETTEXT,
                        (WPARAM) 2, (LPARAM) str);
            return 1;
          case ID_RESET: /* reset options */
            SendMessage(udWnd, UDM_SETPOS, 0, (LPARAM) high /2);
            SendMessage(hStatusWnd, SB_SETTEXT, (WPARAM) 0,
                (LPARAM) "Up-down: 10");
            SendDlgItemMessage(hdwnd, ID_CB1,
                        BM_SETCHECK, 0, 0);
            SendDlgItemMessage(hdwnd, ID_CB2,
                        BM_SETCHECK, 0, 0);
            SendMessage(hStatusWnd, SB_SETTEXT, (WPARAM) 1,
                (LPARAM) "Option 1: OFF");
            SendMessage(hStatusWnd, SB_SETTEXT, (WPARAM) 2,
                (LPARAM) "Option 2: OFF");
            return 1;
          case IDCANCEL:
          case IDOK:
```

```
                    PostQuitMessage(0);
                    return 1;
            }
        }
        return 0;
}


/* Second dialog function. This is just a placeholder. */
BOOL CALLBACK DialogFunc2(HWND hdwnd, UINT message,
                            WPARAM wParam, LPARAM lParam)
{
    switch(message) {
      case WM_COMMAND:
        switch(LOWORD(wParam)) {
          case IDOK:
            PostQuitMessage(0);
            return 1;
        }
    }
    return 0;
}


/* Third dialog function. This is just a placeholder. */
BOOL CALLBACK DialogFunc3(HWND hdwnd, UINT message,
                            WPARAM wParam, LPARAM lParam)
{
    switch(message) {
      case WM_COMMAND:
        switch(LOWORD(wParam)) {
          case IDOK:
            PostQuitMessage(0);
            return 1;
        }
    }
    return 0;
}


/* Initialize the status bar. */
void InitStatus(HWND hwnd)
{
    RECT WinDim;
    int i;

    GetClientRect(hwnd, &WinDim);
```

12

```
  for(i=1; i<=NUMPARTS; i++)
    parts[i-1] = WinDim.right/NUMPARTS * i;

  /* Create a status bar */
  hStatusWnd = CreateWindow(STATUSCLASSNAME,
                "", /* not used in this example */
                WS_CHILD | WS_VISIBLE,
                0, 0, 0, 0,
                hwnd,
                NULL,
                hInst,
                NULL
          );

  SendMessage(hStatusWnd, SB_SETPARTS,
                (WPARAM) NUMPARTS, (LPARAM) parts);

  SendMessage(hStatusWnd, SB_SETTEXT, (WPARAM) 0,
                (LPARAM) "Up-down: 10");
  SendMessage(hStatusWnd, SB_SETTEXT, (WPARAM) 1,
                (LPARAM) "Option 1: OFF");
  SendMessage(hStatusWnd, SB_SETTEXT, (WPARAM) 2,
                (LPARAM) "Option 2: OFF");
}
```

This program requires the following resource file.

```
#include <windows.h>
#include "tab.h"

MyDB1 DIALOG 2, 16, 158, 106
STYLE WS_CHILD | WS_VISIBLE | WS_BORDER
{
  PUSHBUTTON "Reset", ID_RESET, 92, 34, 37, 14,
            WS_CHILD | WS_VISIBLE | WS_TABSTOP
  PUSHBUTTON "OK", IDOK, 92, 53, 37, 14,
            WS_CHILD | WS_VISIBLE | WS_TABSTOP
  EDITTEXT ID_EB1, 10, 10, 30, 12, ES_LEFT | WS_CHILD |
          WS_VISIBLE | WS_BORDER
  AUTOCHECKBOX "Option 1", ID_CB1, 10, 40, 48, 12
  AUTOCHECKBOX "Option 2", ID_CB2, 10, 60, 48, 12
}
```

```
MyDB2 DIALOG 2, 16, 158, 106
STYLE WS_CHILD | WS_VISIBLE | WS_BORDER
{
  PUSHBUTTON "OK", IDOK, 92, 53, 37, 14,
            WS_CHILD | WS_VISIBLE | WS_TABSTOP
  LTEXT "Choose Pitch", ID_LTEXT1, 10, 10, 60, 12
  AUTORADIOBUTTON "High Pitch", ID_RB1, 10, 40, 48, 12
  AUTORADIOBUTTON "Medium Pitch", ID_RB2, 10, 60, 60, 12
  AUTORADIOBUTTON "Low Pitch", ID_RB3, 10, 80, 48, 12
}

MyDB3 DIALOG  2, 16, 158, 106
STYLE WS_CHILD | WS_VISIBLE | WS_BORDER
{
  PUSHBUTTON "OK", IDOK, 92, 53, 37, 14,
            WS_CHILD | WS_VISIBLE | WS_TABSTOP
  LTEXT "Choose  Page Size", ID_LTEXT2, 10, 10, 70, 12
  AUTORADIOBUTTON "Small", ID_RB4, 10, 40, 48, 12
  AUTORADIOBUTTON "Medium", ID_RB5, 10, 60, 48, 12
  AUTORADIOBUTTON "Large", ID_RB6, 10, 80, 48, 12
}
```

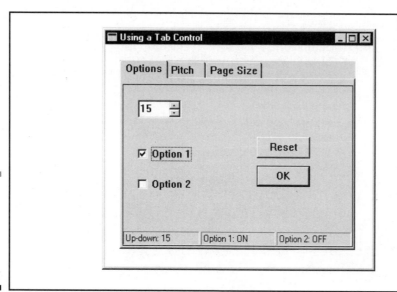

Sample output
from the
second tab
control
program

Figure 12-4.

12

The header file TAB.H is shown here.

```
#define IDM_DIALOG   100
#define IDM_HELP     101

#define ID_UPDOWN    201
#define ID_EB1       202
#define ID_CB1       203
#define ID_CB2       204
#define ID_RESET     205
#define ID_RB1       206
#define ID_RB2       207
#define ID_RB3       208
#define ID_RB4       209
#define ID_RB5       210
#define ID_RB6       211
#define ID_LTEXT1    212
#define ID_LTEXT2    213
```

The interesting portion of this program occurs inside the **WM_NOTIFY** case
of **WindowFunc( )**. It is shown here for your convenience.

```
case WM_NOTIFY:
  nmptr = (LPNMHDR) lParam;
  if(nmptr->code == TCN_SELCHANGE) {
    if(hDlg) DestroyWindow(hDlg);
    tabnumber = TabCtrl_GetCurSel((HWND)nmptr->hwndFrom);
    switch(tabnumber) {
      case 0:
        hDlg = CreateDialog(hInst, "MyDB1",
                    hTabWnd, (DLGPROC) DialogFunc1);
        break;
      case 1:
        hDlg = CreateDialog(hInst, "MyDB2",
                    hTabWnd, (DLGPROC) DialogFunc2);
        break;
      case 2:
        hDlg = CreateDialog(hInst, "MyDB3",
                    hTabWnd, (DLGPROC) DialogFunc3);
        break;
    }
  }
  break;
```

Each time a new tab is selected, two events occur. First, the dialog box associated with the currently selected tab is removed by calling **DestroyWindow( )**. (As you should recall, to close a modeless dialog box, you must call **DestroyWindow( )** rather than **EndDialog( )**, which is used for modal dialog boxes.) Next, the current tab selection is obtained and its dialog box is created using **CreateDialog( )**. (Remember, **CreateDialog( )** creates modeless dialog boxes.) This is the general procedure that you should follow with your own tab control dialog boxes.

Before moving on, you should experiment with this program. Try making changes to the dialog boxes or to the tab control. In addition, tab controls may also have tooltips associated with them. As a challenge, you might want to try adding them to the preceding example.

Tree View Controls

The next control that we will look at is the tree view control. Tree view controls are used to display information using a tree structure. For example, the directory list used by Windows 98's Explorer is an example of a tree view control. Because trees imply a hierarchy, tree view controls should only be used to display hierarchical information. Tree view controls are very powerful and support a large number of different options. In fact, one could nearly write a book about tree view controls alone! For this reason, this section only discusses tree view fundamentals. Once you understand the basics, you will be able to easily incorporate the other tree view features on your own.

Create a Tree View Control

A tree view control is a window that is created using either **CreateWindow( )** or **CreateWindowEx( )** and specifying the **WC_TREEVIEW** class. Typically, a tree view control will be a child window, so the **WS_CHILD** style is needed. It is usually created using the **WS_VISIBLE** style, so that it is automatically displayed. **WS_TABSTOP** is also commonly included. Tree view controls also allow additional tree-related styles to be specified when they are created, including:

12

Style	Meaning
TVS_HASLINES	Lines link branches in the tree.
TVS_LINESATROOT	Lines link root to the branches.
TVS_HASBUTTONS	Expand/Collapse buttons are included to the left of each branch.

Including the **TVS_HASLINES** and **TVS_LINESATROOT** styles causes lines to be drawn to each item in the tree. This gives the tree view control its "tree-like" look. Including **TVS_HASBUTTONS** causes the standard expand/collapse buttons to be added. These buttons contain a + if the branch may be expanded at least one more level and a – if the branch is fully expanded. You may also click on these buttons to expand or collapse a branch. Typically, all three of these styles are included when a tree view control is created. For example, the following creates a standard tree view window.

```
hTreeWndCtrl = CreateWindow(
          WC_TREEVIEW,
          "",
          WS_VISIBLE | WS_TABSTOP | WS_CHILD |
          TVS_HASLINES | TVS_HASBUTTONS |
          TVS_LINESATROOT,
          0, 0, 120, 120,
          hwnd, /* handle of parent */
          NULL,
          hInst, /* instance handle */
          NULL
      );
```

When the tree view control is first created, it is empty. You must add each item in the tree, as described in the next section.

A tree view will automatically add a scroll bar when the tree expands to a point at which it can no longer be displayed with the space allotted for it. In Windows 98, tree view controls will also automatically display a tooltip when the mouse is over a tree item for which the text is not fully shown. The tooltip will contain the full text of the item. If you do not want tooltips to be displayed, include the **TVS_NOTOOLTIPS** style.

Sending Tree View Messages

Tree view controls respond to several messages. Some commonly used tree view control messages are shown in Table 12-3. You can send these messages using either **SendMessage( )** or special macros created expressly for this purpose. Tree view control macros corresponding to the messages in Table 12-3 are shown here. In all cases, *hTreeWnd* is the handle of the tree view control.

BOOL TreeView_DeleteItem(HWND *hTreeWnd*, HTREEITEM *hItem*)

BOOL TreeView_Expand(HWND *hTreeWnd*, HTREEITEM *hItem*,
                UINT *action*)

BOOL TreeView_GetItem(HWND *hTreeWnd*, TVITEM **lpItem*)

HTREEVIEW TreeView_InsertItem(HWND *hwnd*,
                                TVINSERTSTRUCT **lpitem*)

BOOL TreeView_Select(HWND *hTreeWnd*, HTREEITEM *hItem*,
                UINT *action*)

Message	Meaning
TVM_DELETEITEM	Deletes an item from the tree list. Returns nonzero if successful and zero on failure. *wParam* is 0. *lParam* specifies the handle of the item to delete.
TVM_EXPAND	Expands or collapses the tree list one level. Returns nonzero if successful and zero on failure. *wParam* specifies the operation. It must be **TVE_COLLAPSE** (collapses tree), **TVE_COLLAPSERESET** (collapses tree and deletes child items), **TVE_EXPAND** (expands a tree), **TVE_EXPANDPARTIAL** (partially expands a tree), or **TVE_TOGGLE** (toggles state). **TVE_COLLAPSERESET** must be used in conjunction with **TVE_COLLAPSE**. **TVE_EXPANDPARTIAL** must be used with **TVE_EXPAND**. *lParam* specifies the handle of the parent of the branch.
TVM_GETITEM	Obtains an item's attributes. Returns nonzero if successful and zero on failure. *wParam* is 0. *lParam* specifies a pointer to a **TVITEM** structure that receives information about the item.
TVM_INSERTITEM	Inserts an item into the tree. Returns a handle to the item being inserted or **NULL** on failure. *wParam* is 0. *lParam* specifies a pointer to a **TVINSERTSTRUCT** that contains information about the item.

Commonly
Used Tree
View Control
Messages
Table 12-3.

12

Message	Meaning
TVM_SELECTITEM	Selects a tree view item. Returns nonzero if successful and zero on failure. *wParam* specifies the specific action. If it is **TVGN_CARET**, the item is selected. If it is **TVGN_DROPHILITE**, the item is highlighted for a drag/drop operation. If it is **TVGN_FIRSTVISIBLE**, the tree view is scrolled so that the specified item is the first visible item. *lParam* specifies the handle of the item.

Commonly
Used Tree
View Control
Messages
(*continued*)
Table 12-3.

The only messages used by the example in this chapter are **TVM_INSERTITEM** and **TVM_EXPAND**. Your application will probably use others.

When an item is inserted, the item's information is contained in a **TVINSERTSTRUCT** structure, which is shown here.

```
typedef struct tagTVINSERTSTRUCT {
  HTREEITEM hParent;
  HTREEITEM hInsertAfter;
  union {
    TVITEMEX item;
    TVITEM item;
  }
} TVINSERTSTRUCT;
```

Here, **hParent** is the handle to the parent of the item. If the item has no parent, then this field should contain **TVI_ROOT**. The value in **hInsertAfter** determines how the new item will be inserted into the tree. If it contains the handle of an item, the new item will be inserted after that item. Otherwise, **hInsertAfter** can be one of the following values.

TVI_FIRST	Insert at beginning of list.
TVI_LAST	Insert at end of list.
TVI_SORT	Insert in alphabetical order.

The contents of **item** describe the item. This field must be either a **TVITEM** or a **TVITEMEX** structure. **TVITEMEX** is an expanded version of **TVITEM,** which provides some special-use capabilities not required by the examples in this chapter. **TVITEM** is shown here.

```
typedef struct tagTVITEM {
  UINT mask;
  HTREEITEM hItem;
  UINT state;
  UINT stateMask;
  LPSTR pszText;
  int cchTextMax;
  int iImage;
  int iSelectedImage;
  int cChildren;
  LPARAM lParam;
} TVITEM;
```

Here, the values in **mask** determine which of the other members of **TVITEM** contain valid data when this structure receives information from the tree view control. The values that it may contain are shown here.

Value in mask	Meaning
TVIF_HANDLE	**hItem** contains data.
TVIF_STATE	**state** and **stateMask** contain data.
TVIF_TEXT	**pszText** and **cchTextMax** contain data.
TVIF_IMAGE	**iImage** contains data.
TVIF_SELECTEDIMAGE	**iSelectedImage** contains data.
TVIF_CHILDREN	**cChildren** contains data.
TVIF_LPARAM	**lParam** contains data.

The **hItem** field contains the handle of the item.

The **state** member contains the state of the tree view control. Here are some common tree state values:

12

State	Meaning
TVIS_DROPHILITED	Item is highlighted as the target of drag/drop operation.
TVIS_EXPANDED	Branch descending from item is fully expanded. (Applies to parent items only.)
TVIS_EXPANDEDONCE	Branch descending from item is expanded one (or more) levels. (Applies to parent items only.)
TVIS_EXPANDPARTIAL	Branch descending from item is partially expanded.
TVIS_SELECTED	Item is selected.

The **stateMask** determines which state to set or obtain. It will also be one or more of the preceding values.

When an item is being inserted into the tree, **pszText** points to the string that will be displayed in the tree. When information about an item is being obtained, **pszText** must point to an array that will receive its text. In this case, the value of **cchTextMax** specifies the size of the array pointed to by **pszText**. Otherwise, **cchTextMax** is ignored.

If there is an image list associated with the tree view control, then **iImage** will contain the index of the image associated with the item when it is not selected. **iImageSelected** contains the index of the image used by the item when it is selected. (We won't be using images in the tree view created in this chapter.)

cChildren will contain 1 if the item has child items and zero if it does not. **lParam** contains application-defined data.

Tree View Notification Messages

When a tree view control is accessed, it generates a **WM_NOTIFY** message. There are several notification messages associated with tree view controls. Some commonly used ones are shown here.

Notification Message	Meaning
TVN_DELETEITEM	An item has been deleted.
TVN_ITEMEXPANDING	A branch is about to expand or collapse.

Notification Message	Meaning
TVN_ITEMEXPANDED	A branch has expanded or collapsed.
TVN_SELCHANGING	A new item is about to be selected.
TVN_SELCHANGED	A new item has been selected.

For these notification messages, when the **WM_NOTIFY** message is received, *lParam* will point to an **NMTREEVIEW** structure. This structure is shown here.

```
typedef struct tagNMTREEVIEW {
  NMHDR hdr;
  UINT action;
  TVITEM itemOld;
  TVITEM itemNew;
  POINT ptDrag;
} NMTREEVIEW;
```

The first field in **NMTREEVIEW** is the standard **NMHDR** structure. The notification code will be contained in the **hdr.code**. The handle of the tree control that generates the message is found in the **hdr.hwndFrom** field.

The **action** field contains notification-specific information. The structures **itemOld** and **itemNew** contain information about the previously selected item (if applicable) and the newly selected item (again, if applicable). The location of the mouse at the time the message was generated is contained in **ptDrag**.

For the **TVN_SELCHANGING** and **TVN_SELCHANGED**, **itemOld** describes the previously selected item and **itemNew** describes the newly selected item. For **TVN_ITEMEXPANDING** and **TVN_ITEMEXPANDED**, **itemNew** describes the item that is the parent of the branch that is expanding. For **TVN_DELETEITEM**, **itemOld** describes the item that was deleted.

12

PORTABILITY: The structures associated with a tree view control have undergone a name change. The following table lists the old and new names of the tree view structures used in this chapter. At the time of this writinig, the old names are still valid. However, you should use the new names for new programs or when updating old ones.

Old Name	New Name
TV_ITEM	TVITEM
TV_INSERTSTRUCT	TVINSERTSTRUCT
NM_TREEVIEW	NMTREEVIEW
NM_DISPINO	NMTVDISPINFO

A Tree View Demonstration Program

The following program demonstrates a tree view control. It creates a tree view control and then inserts five items into it. The program also includes a menu that can expand one branch, expand the entire tree, or collapse a branch. Each time a new tree view item is selected, the selection is displayed in the program's window. Sample output from the program is shown in Figure 12-5.

```
/* Demonstrate a tree control. */

#include <windows.h>
#include <commctrl.h>
#include <string.h>
#include "tree.h"

#define NUM 5

LRESULT CALLBACK WindowFunc(HWND, UINT, WPARAM, LPARAM);
void InitTree(void);
void report(HDC hdc, char *s);

char szWinName[] = "MyWin"; /* name of window class */

HINSTANCE hInst;
HWND hwnd;
HWND hTreeWndCtrl;
HTREEITEM hTreeWnd[NUM];
HTREEITEM hTreeCurrent;

int WINAPI WinMain(HINSTANCE hThisInst, HINSTANCE hPrevInst,
                   LPSTR lpszArgs, int nWinMode)
{
  MSG msg;
```

```
WNDCLASSEX wcl;
HACCEL hAccel;
INITCOMMONCONTROLSEX cc;

/* Define a window class. */
wcl.cbSize = sizeof(WNDCLASSEX);

wcl.hInstance = hThisInst; /* handle to this instance */
wcl.lpszClassName = szWinName; /* window class name */
wcl.lpfnWndProc = WindowFunc; /* window function */
wcl.style = 0; /* default style */

wcl.hIcon = LoadIcon(NULL, IDI_APPLICATION); /* standard icon */
wcl.hIconSm = LoadIcon(NULL, IDI_APPLICATION); /* small icon */
wcl.hCursor = LoadCursor(NULL, IDC_ARROW); /* cursor style */

wcl.lpszMenuName = "MyMenu"; /* main menu */
wcl.cbClsExtra = 0; /* no extra */
wcl.cbWndExtra = 0; /* information needed */

/* Make the window white. */
wcl.hbrBackground = (HBRUSH) GetStockObject(WHITE_BRUSH);

/* Register the window class. */
if(!RegisterClassEx(&wcl)) return 0;

/* Now that a window class has been registered, a window
   can be created. */
hwnd = CreateWindow(
  szWinName, /* name of window class */
  "Using a Tree Control", /* title */
  WS_OVERLAPPEDWINDOW, /* window style - normal */
  CW_USEDEFAULT, /* X coordinate - let Windows decide */
  CW_USEDEFAULT, /* Y coordinate - let Windows decide */
  CW_USEDEFAULT, /* width - let Windows decide */
  CW_USEDEFAULT, /* height - let Windows decide */
  HWND_DESKTOP, /* no parent window */
  NULL, /* no override of class menu */
  hThisInst, /* handle of this instance of the program */
  NULL /* no additional arguments */
);

/* Initialize the common controls. */
cc.dwSize = sizeof(INITCOMMONCONTROLSEX);
cc.dwICC = ICC_TREEVIEW_CLASSES;
InitCommonControlsEx(&cc);
```

12

```
    hInst = hThisInst; /* save the current instance handle */

    /* Load accelerators. */
    hAccel = LoadAccelerators(hThisInst, "MyMenu");

    /* Display the window. */
    ShowWindow(hwnd, nWinMode);
    UpdateWindow(hwnd);

    /* Create the message loop. */
    while(GetMessage(&msg, NULL, 0, 0))
    {
      if(!TranslateAccelerator(hwnd, hAccel, &msg)) {
        TranslateMessage(&msg); /* translate keyboard messages */
        DispatchMessage(&msg); /* return control to Windows 98 */
      }
    }
    return msg.wParam;
}

/* This function is called by Windows 98 and is passed
   messages from the message queue.
*/
LRESULT CALLBACK WindowFunc(HWND hwnd, UINT message,
                            WPARAM wParam, LPARAM lParam)
{
  HDC hdc;
  static char selection[80] = "";
  NMTREEVIEW *nmptr;
  PAINTSTRUCT paintstruct;
  int response, i;

  switch(message) {
    case WM_CREATE:
      /* create a tree view */
      hTreeWndCtrl = CreateWindow(
                       WC_TREEVIEW,
                       "",
                       WS_VISIBLE | WS_TABSTOP | WS_CHILD |
                       TVS_HASLINES | TVS_HASBUTTONS |
                       TVS_LINESATROOT,
                       0, 0, 120, 120,
                       hwnd,
                       NULL,
```

```
                              hInst,
                              NULL
                    );

        InitTree();
        break;
    case WM_COMMAND:
        switch(LOWORD(wParam)) {
            case IDM_EXPAND:
                TreeView_Expand(hTreeWndCtrl, hTreeCurrent, TVE_EXPAND);
                break;
            case IDM_EXPANDALL:
                for(i=0; i<NUM; i++)
                    TreeView_Expand(hTreeWndCtrl, hTreeWnd[i], TVE_EXPAND);
                break;
            case IDM_COLLAPSE:
                TreeView_Expand(hTreeWndCtrl, hTreeCurrent,
                                TVE_COLLAPSE);
                break;
            case IDM_EXIT:
                response = MessageBox(hwnd, "Quit the Program?",
                                      "Exit", MB_YESNO);
                if(response == IDYES) PostQuitMessage(0);
                break;
            case IDM_HELP:
                MessageBox(hwnd, "Try the tree view.", "Help", MB_OK);
                break;
        }
        break;
    case WM_NOTIFY:
        nmptr = (LPNMTREEVIEW) lParam;
        if(nmptr->hdr.code == TVN_SELCHANGED) {
            InvalidateRect(hwnd, NULL, 1);
            if(nmptr->itemNew.hItem == hTreeWnd[0])
                strcpy(selection, "One.");
            else if(nmptr->itemNew.hItem == hTreeWnd[1])
                strcpy(selection, "Two.");
            if(nmptr->itemNew.hItem == hTreeWnd[2])
                strcpy(selection, "Three.");
            if(nmptr->itemNew.hItem == hTreeWnd[3])
                strcpy(selection, "Four.");
            if(nmptr->itemNew.hItem == hTreeWnd[4])
                strcpy(selection, "Five.");

            hTreeCurrent = nmptr->itemNew.hItem;
```

12

```
        }
      break;
    case WM_PAINT:
      hdc = BeginPaint(hwnd, &paintstruct);
      report(hdc, selection);
      EndPaint(hwnd, &paintstruct);
      break;
    case WM_DESTROY: /* terminate the program */
      PostQuitMessage(0);
      break;
    default:
      /* Let Windows 98 process any messages not specified in
         the preceding switch statement. */
      return DefWindowProc(hwnd, message, wParam, lParam);
  }
  return 0;
}

/* Report Selection */
void report(HDC hdc, char *s)
{
  char str[80];

  if(*s) {
    strcpy(str, "Selection is ");
    strcat(str, s);
  }
  else strcpy(str, "No selection has been made.");
  TextOut(hdc, 0, 200, str, strlen(str));
}

/* Initialize the tree list. */
void InitTree(void)
{
  TVINSERTSTRUCT tvs;
  TVITEM tvi;

  tvs.hInsertAfter = TVI_LAST; /* make tree in order given */
  tvi.mask = TVIF_TEXT;

  tvi.pszText = "One";
  tvs.hParent = TVI_ROOT;
  tvs.item = tvi;
  hTreeWnd[0] = TreeView_InsertItem(hTreeWndCtrl, &tvs);
  hTreeCurrent = hTreeWnd[0];
```

```
    tvi.pszText = "Two";
    tvs.hParent = hTreeWnd[0];
    tvs.item = tvi;
    hTreeWnd[1] = TreeView_InsertItem(hTreeWndCtrl, &tvs);

    tvi.pszText = "Three";
    tvs.item = tvi;
    tvs.hParent = hTreeWnd[1];
    hTreeWnd[2] = TreeView_InsertItem(hTreeWndCtrl, &tvs);

    tvi.pszText = "Four";
    tvs.item = tvi;
    tvs.hParent = hTreeWnd[2];
    hTreeWnd[3] = TreeView_InsertItem(hTreeWndCtrl, &tvs);

    tvi.pszText = "Five";
    tvs.item = tvi;
    tvs.hParent = hTreeWnd[2];
    hTreeWnd[4] = TreeView_InsertItem(hTreeWndCtrl, &tvs);
}
```

The program requires the following resource file.

```
#include <windows.h>
#include "tree.h"

MyMenu MENU
{
  POPUP "&Treeview" {
    MENUITEM "&Expand One\tF2", IDM_EXPAND
    MENUITEM "Expand &All\tF3", IDM_EXPANDALL
    MENUITEM "&Collapse\tF4", IDM_COLLAPSE
    MENUITEM "E&xit\tCtrl+X", IDM_EXIT
  }
  MENUITEM "&Help", IDM_HELP
}

MyMenu ACCELERATORS
{
  VK_F2, IDM_EXPAND, VIRTKEY
  VK_F3, IDM_EXPANDALL, VIRTKEY
  VK_F4, IDM_COLLAPSE, VIRTKEY
  "^X", IDM_EXIT
```

12

```
   VK_F1, IDM_HELP, VIRTKEY
}
```

The TREE.H header file is shown here.

```
#define IDM_EXPAND    100
#define IDM_EXPANDALL 101
#define IDM_COLLAPSE  102
#define IDM_EXIT      103
#define IDM_HELP      104
```

In the program, the function **InitTree( )** initializes the tree view control. Notice that the handle of each item is stored in the **hTreeWnd** array. These handles are used to identify items when they are selected in the tree list. **hTreeCurrent** identifies the currently selected item. This handle is used when the user expands or collapses a branch using the menu.

Inside **WindowFunc( )**, each time a new item is selected, a **WM_NOTIFY** message is received and processed. The value of **itemNew** is checked against the list of item handles stored in the **hTreeWnd** array. When the matching handle is found, the new selection is reported.

While this example illustrates the most important and fundamental aspects of tree view controls, it just scratches the surface of their power. For example, using a tree view, you can drag and drop an item from one tree to another.

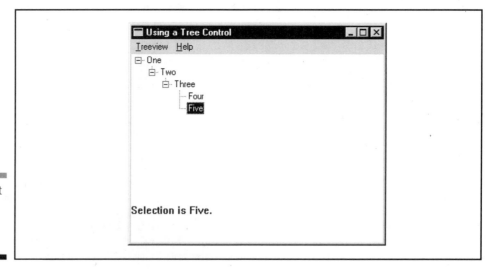

Sample output from the tree view program

Figure 12-5.

You can also allow the tree view labels to be edited (see the In Depth box). The tree view is one control that you will definitely want to explore further on your own.

In the next chapter, we will examine two of Windows 98's most sophisticated controls: property sheets and wizards.

IN DEPTH

Editing Tree View Labels

It is possible to create a tree view that allows the user to modify the labels in the tree. To do so, you must include the **TVS_EDITLABELS** style when you create the control. You must also handle these two notification messages: **TVN_BEGINLABELEDIT** and **TVN_ENDLABELEDIT**. (Remember, notification messages are sent via the **WM_NOTIFY** message.) For both messages, *lParam* points to a **NMTVDISPINFO** structure, shown here.

```
typedef struct tagNMTVDISPINFO {
  NMHDR hdr;
  TVITEM item;
} NMTVDISPINFO;
```

When the user begins editing a label, your program will receive a **TVN_BEGINLABELEDIT** notification message. To allow the user to edit the label, your program must return zero. To disallow editing, return nonzero.

When the user finishes editing, your program receives a **TVN_ENDLABELEDIT** notification message. If the editing was canceled by the user, then the **pszText** field of **item** will be null. Otherwise, it will contain the new label. If editing was cancelled, your program should return zero. This causes the original label to remain. Otherwise, have the program return nonzero to cause the new label to be used.

To experiment with editing tree view labels, add **TVS_EDITLABELS** to the tree view control created in the example program and then substitute the following **WM_NOTIFY** case into **WindowFunc( )**.

12

```
case WM_NOTIFY:
  nmptr = (LPNMTREEVIEW) lParam;
  switch(nmptr->hdr.code) {
    case TVN_BEGINLABELEDIT:
      return 0;
    case TVN_ENDLABELEDIT:
      if(((NMTVDISPINFO *) nmptr)->item.pszText)
        return 1; /* label was edited */
      else
        return 0;  /* user cancelled */
  }
  break;
```

After making these changes, you can alter the contents of a tree view label.

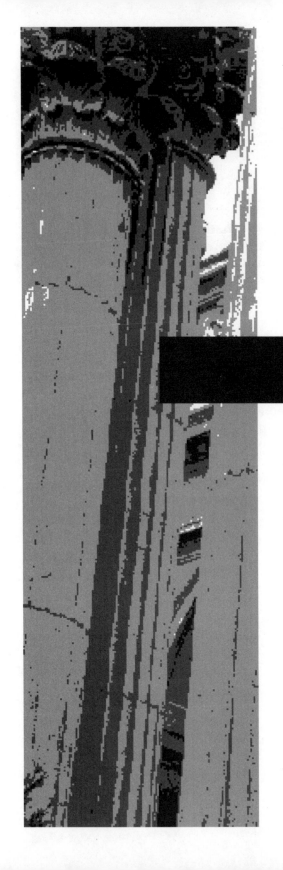

CHAPTER 13

Property Sheets and Wizards

417

This chapter describes how to create one of Windows 98's most sophisticated controls: the *wizard*. As you probably know, a wizard is a sequenced set of dialog boxes that guide the user through a complex group of selections. The dialog boxes that constitute the wizard must be accessed in the order in which they are presented by the wizard. Wizards are used frequently in Windows 98. For example, when you install a new printer, the printer installation wizard is activated.

Wizards are built upon another common control element: the *property sheet*. A property sheet is typically used to view and set various properties associated with some item. Although they look like the tab control described in the preceding chapter, property sheets are much more powerful.

Since property sheets underpin wizards, we will begin there.

Property Sheet Basics

Property sheets allow the user to examine or alter various properties associated with some item. For example, a property sheet is typically used to set printer options or a modem configuration. From the user's perspective, a property sheet consists of one or more *pages*. Each page has a tab associated with it. A page is activated by selecting its tab. A sample property sheet is shown in Figure 13-1.

A property sheet provides a convenient way of managing the properties associated with some item.

From the programmer's perspective, a property sheet is a collection of one or more modeless dialog boxes. That is, each page in a property sheet is defined by a dialog box template, and interaction with the page is handled by a dialog function. Most commonly, each dialog box template is specified in your application's resource file.

All property sheets contain two buttons, OK and Cancel, and usually a third called Apply. It is also possible to include a Help button. It is important to understand that although the dialog functions associated with each page provide the mechanism by which the user sets or views the properties, only the property sheet control itself can accept or cancel the user's changes. Put differently, no page dialog function should include an OK or Cancel button. These two operations are provided by the property sheet control.

The dialog boxes that constitute the property sheet are enclosed within the property sheet control. The property sheet control manages interaction with and between the individual pages. As a general rule, each dialog box function responds to its own controls in the normal fashion. That is, the individual controls that make up each page are handled in the standard way by the page's dialog box function. However, each page must also respond to messages generated by the enclosing property sheet. When the property sheet

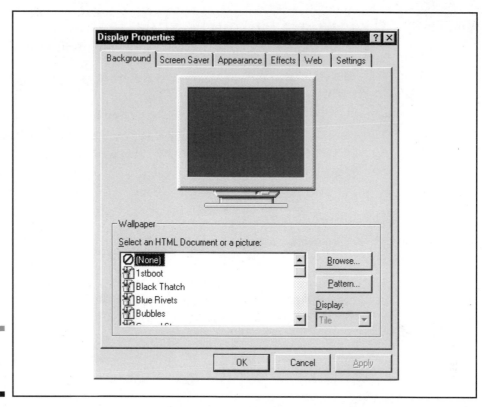

A sample
property sheet
Figure 13-1.

needs to communicate with a page, it does so by sending it a **WM_NOTIFY**
message. Each page in a property sheet must be able to respond to this
message. (The details of this are discussed shortly.)

There is one very important requirement that you must follow when creating
a property sheet: The modeless dialog box function associated with each page
must *not* close its dialog box. That is, it must not call **DestroyWindow( )**.
Instead, the enclosing property sheet control itself will take care of this. (If
you do close one of the page dialog boxes, that dialog box will then be
empty. This is a violation of Windows 98 style rules, to say the least!)

13

REMEMBER: Since a property sheet is a common control, you must
include the header file COMMCTRL.H in your program and link in the
necessary common control library.

Creating a Property Sheet

There are four steps required to create a property sheet. They are

1. Information about each page in the control must be stored in a **PROPSHEETPAGE** structure.
2. Each page must be created by calling **CreatePropertySheetPage( )**.
3. Information about the property sheet itself must be stored in a **PROPSHEETHEADER** structure.
4. The property sheet control is created and displayed by calling **PropertySheet( )**.

Let's look at each step now.

Defining a Property Sheet Page

Each page in a property sheet must be defined in a **PROPSHEETPAGE** structure. **PROPSHEETPAGE** is defined like this.

```
typedef struct _PROPSHEETPAGE {
  DWORD dwSize;
  DWORD dwFlags;
  HINSTANCE hInstance;
  union {
    LPCSTR pszTemplate;
    LPCDLGTEMPLATE pResource;
  };
  union {
    HICON hIcon;
    LPCSTR pszIcon;
  };
  LPCSTR pszTitle;
  DLGPROC pfnDlgProc;
  LPARAM lParam;
  LPFNPSPCALLBACK pfnCallback;
  UINT FAR *pcRefParent;
  LPCSTR pszHeaderTitle;
  LPCSTR pszHeaderSubTitle;
} PROPSHEETPAGE;
```

Here, **dwSize** must contain the size, in bytes, of the **PROPSHEETPAGE** structure.

The value of **dwFlags** determines which of the remaining members contain valid information. It must be a combination of one or more of the flags shown in Table 13-1. The flags can be combined by ORing them together.

hInstance specifies the instance handle of the application.

pszTemplate specifies the name or ID of the dialog box template associated with this page. However, if the **PSP_DLGINDIRECT** flag is included, then **pszTemplate** is ignored and the dialog box described by **pResource** is used.

If you wish to include a small icon in the tab associated with a page, it must be specified in either the **hIcon** or the **pszIcon** member. You must also

The Valid
Values for the
dwFlags
Member of
PROPSHEET-PAGE
Table 13-1.

Flag	Meaning
PSP_DEFAULT	Use defaults.
PSP_DLGINDIRECT	Use **pResource**, not **pszTemplate**.
PSP_HASHELP	Displays Help button.
PSP_HIDEHEADER	The header is not displayed.
PSP_PREMATURE	Page created when property sheet control is created. Normally, the page is not created until it is first activated.
PSP_RTLREADING	Text is displayed right-to-left. (Provides support for Hebrew or Arabic.)
PSP_USECALLBACK	Enables **pfnCallback**.
PSP_USEHEADERTITLE	Enables **pszHeaderTitle**.
PSP_USEHEADERSUBTITLE	Enables **pszHeaderSubTitle**.
PSP_USEHICON	Enables **hIcon**.
PSP_USEICONID	Enables **pszIcon**.
PSP_USEREFPARENT	Enables reference counting.
PSP_USETITLE	Uses title specified by **pszTitle** rather than the one defined by the page's dialog box template.

13

include the appropriate flag. **hIcon** specifies an icon handle. **pszIcon** specifes the name or ID of the icon as specified in a resource file.

Normally, the title of the dialog box associated with a page becomes the title of the page. This title is displayed in the tab associated with the page. However, you can specify a different title by storing a pointer to the new title in **pszTitle**. Of course, you must also include the **PSP_USETITLE** flag.

The address of the modeless dialog box function that is associated with the page must be stored in **pfnDlgProc**.

lParam is used for application-specific data.

When **pfnCallback** is enabled, it specifies a callback function that is called whenever the page is created or destroyed. This function is not needed by the examples in this chapter. However, if your application requires this function, it must have the following prototype:

UINT CALLBACK PropPageFunc(HWND *hwnd*, UINT *message*,
  LPPROPSHEETPAGE *lpPropSheet*);

When called, *hwnd* will be **NULL**. The value of *message* will be either **PSPCB_CREATE** or **PSPCB_RELEASE**, which indicate whether the page is being created or destroyed, respectively. *lpPropSheet* points to the **PROPSHEETPAGE** structure of the page being affected. If *message* is **PSPCB_CREATE**, the function must return nonzero to enable page creation or zero to cancel the creation of the page. If *message* is **PSPCB_RELEASE**, the return value is not used.

pcRefParent specifies the address of a reference count variable. This member is only active if **PSP_USEREFPARENT** is specified.

The **pszHeaderTitle** and **pszHeaderSubTitle** fields contain pointers to the strings used as the property sheet's title and subtitle. These are displayed in the header area of a wizard. They are ignored unless **dwFlags** includes **PSP_USEHEADERTITLE** or **PSP_USEHEADERSUBTITLE**, respectively. Also, the property sheet header, described shortly, must include the style **PSH_WIZARD97**. (At the time of this writing, header titles and subtitles apply only to wizards.) The example in this book does make use of these features.

PORTABILITY: The original versions of **PROPSHEETPAGE** did not include the fields **pszHeaderTitle** or **pszHeaderSubTitle** or their associated flags.

Initializing Each Page

After you have loaded a **PROPSHEETPAGE** structure with the necessary information, you must create the page by calling **CreatePropertySheetPage( )**. Its prototype is shown here.

HPROPSHEETPAGE CreatePropertySheetPage
                              (LPCPPROPSHEETPAGE *lpPage*);

Here, *lpPage* is a pointer to a **PROPSHEETPAGE** structure. The function returns a handle to the newly created page. You will usually want to store this handle because it is needed for some property sheet operations. The function returns **NULL** if the page cannot be created.

Initializing the PROPSHEETHEADER Structure

After you have created each page, you must initialize the **PROPSHEETHEADER** structure associated with the property sheet. This structure is defined like this:

```
typedef struct _PROPSHEETHEADER {
  DWORD dwSize;
  DWORD dwFlags;
  HWND  hwndParent;
  HINSTANCE hInstance;
  union {
    HICON hIcon;
    LPCSTR pszIcon;
  };
  LPCSTR pszCaption;
  UINT nPages;
  union {
    UINT nStartPage;
    LPCSTR pStartPage;
  };
  union {
    LPCPROPSHEETPAGE ppsp;
    HPROPSHEETPAGE FAR *phpage;
  };
  PFNPROPSHEETCALLBACK pfnCallback;
  union {
    HBITMAP hbmWatermark;
    LPCSTR pszbmWatermark;
  }
  HPALETTE hplWatermark;
  union {
```

```
    HBITMAP hbmHeader;
    LPCSTR pszbmHeader;
  }
} PROPSHEETHEADER;
```

Here, **dwSize** must contain the size, in bytes, of the **PROPSHEETHEADER** structure.

The value of **dwFlags** determines which of the remaining members contain valid information. It must be a combination of one or more of the flags shown in Table 13-2. The flags can be combined by ORing them together.

Flag	Meaning
PSH_DEFAULT	Use defaults.
PSH_HASHELP	Enable Help button.
PSH_HEADER	Property sheet uses a header bitmap.
PSH_MODELESS	Creates a modeless property sheet control. By default, property sheet controls are modal.
PSH_NOAPPLYNOW	Suppresses the Apply button.
PSH_PROPSHEETPAGE	Enables the **ppsp** member and disables **phpage**.
PSH_PROPTITLE	Appends the word "Properties" to the title specified by **pszCaption**.
PSH_RTLREADING	Text is displayed right-to-left. (Provides support for Hebrew or Arabic.)
PSH_STRETCHWATERMARK	Watermark bitmap is expanded (rather than tiled) to fill the property sheet.
PSH_USECALLBACK	Enables **pfnCallback**.
PSH_USEHBMHEADER	Enables **hbmHeader**; otherwise, **pszbmHeader** is used.

The Valid Values for the **dwFlags** Member of **PROPSHEET-HEADER**

Table 13-2.

Flag	Meaning
PSH_USEHBMWATERMARK	Enables **hbmWaterMark**; otherwise **pszbmWatermark** is used.
PSH_USEHICON	Enables **hIcon**.
PSH_USEICONID	Enables **pszIcon**.
PSH_USEHPLWATERMARK	Enables **hplWatermark**.
PSH_USEPAGELANG	The language is determined by page zero.
PSH_USEPSTARTPAGE	Enables **pStartPage** and disables **nStartPage**.
PSH_WATERMARK	Includes a watermark.
PSH_WIZARD	Creates a wizard.
PSH_WIZARD97	Creates a wizard that may include a header title and subtitle, or a watermark or header bitmap.
PSH_WIZARDCONTEXTHELP	Wizard supports context help.
PSH_WIZARDHASFINISH	Finish button included on all wizard pages.

The Valid Values for the **dwFlags** Member of **PROPSHEET-HEADER** (*continued*)
Table 13-2.

hwndParent specifies the handle of the parent window, which is usually the window that activates the property sheet.

hInstance specifies the instance handle of the application.

If you wish to include a small icon in the title bar of the property sheet, it must be specified in either the **hIcon** or the **pszIcon** member. You must also include the appropriate flag. **hIcon** specifies an icon handle. **pszIcon** specifies the name or ID of the icon as specified in a resource file.

The title of the property sheet control window is pointed to by **pszCaption**.

The number of pages in the property sheet is specified by **nPages**.

13

The first page to be displayed when the property sheet control is activated is specified by either **nStartPage** or **pStartPage**. By default, **nStartPage** is used. **nStartPage** specifies the index of the first page. All page indexes begin at zero. If you include the flag **PSH_USEPSTARTPAGE**, then you must specify the name or the ID of the page in **pStartPage**.

phpage must contain a pointer to an array of property sheet page handles. These handles are created by calling **CreatePropertySheetPage( )**, described earlier. However, if you specify the **PSH_PROPSHEETPAGE** flag, you can specify the address of an array of **PROPSHEETPAGE** structures in the **ppsp** member instead. In this case, the handles will be created automatically and there is no need to call **CreatePropertySheetPage( )**. However, since the page handles are useful for some other operations, you will usually want to create them explicitly.

When **pfnCallback** is enabled, it specifies a callback function that is called whenever the property sheet is created. Although not used by the examples in this chapter, your application may need to create such a function. If so, it must have the following prototype.

> int CALLBACK PropSheetFunc(HWND *hdwnd*, UINT *message*,
>   LPARAM *lParam*);

When called, *hdwnd* will contain the handle of the property sheet control. The value of *message* will be either **PSCB_INITIALIZED**, which means that the property sheet is being initialized, or **PSCB_PRECREATE**, which means that the property sheet is about to be initialized. For **PSCB_INITIALIZED**, *lParam* will be zero. For **PSCB_PRECREATE**, *lParam* points to the dialog box template and *hdwnd* is **NULL**. In either case, the function must return zero.

A recent addition to wizards is the ability to specify a watermark and a header bitmap. For these fields to be active, their respective flags must be set and you must include the **PSH_WIZARD97** flag. The example in this chapter does not use these features, but here is a brief description.

hbmWatermark specifies the handle of the bitmap to be used as a watermark. Alternatively, you can specify the name of this bitmap using **pszbmWatermark**. Normally, the default palette is used to draw the watermark, but you can specify the handle to a palette in the **hplWatermark** field. In each case the appropriate flags must be set.

The handle to the bitmap used for a header is passed in **hbmHeader**. Alternatively, you can specify the resource name of the header in **pszbmHeader**. Of course, the appropriate flags must be set.

PORTABILITY: The original versions of **PROPSHEETHEADER** did not include the fields **hbmWatermark**, **pszbmWatermark**, **hplWatermark**, **bhmHeader**, or **pszbmHeader**. Also, the flags that enable or affect these fields were not defined.

Creating the Property Sheet Control

After the property sheet pages have been defined and the **PROPSHEETHEADER** structure has been initialized, the property sheet control can be created. This is done by calling **PropertySheet( )**, whose prototype is shown here.

    int PropertySheet(LPCPPROPSHEETHEADER *lpHeader*);

Here, *lpHeader* is a pointer to the property sheet header structure. The function returns –1 if an error occurs or a positive value if successful. When creating a modeless property sheet control (that is, one in which you have included the **PSH_MODELESS** flag), then a handle to the property sheet is returned.

Processing Property Sheet Messages

As mentioned, a property sheet control sends messages to the page dialog box functions using the **WM_NOTIFY** message. The value of **lParam** is a pointer to a **NMHDR** structure. Recall that the **NMHDR** structure is defined like this:

```
typedef struct tagNMHDR
{
  HWND hwndFrom;
  UINT idFrom;
  UINT code;
} NMHDR;
```

For **WM_NOTIFY** messages associated with property sheets, **hwndFrom** is the handle of the property sheet control. **idFrom** is not used with property sheets. The value of **code** contains the *notification code*, which describes what action has taken place.

13

The property sheet control uses the notification messages to inform individual dialog boxes about various events. For example, notification messages are sent when a page is selected, when the user presses one of the property sheet buttons, or when the page is being deselected. The notification code specifies the precise nature of the event. Commonly used notification codes are shown in Table 13-3.

In some cases, your dialog box function must respond to a notification message by returning a value to the property sheet control. To accomplish this, you will need to use the **SetWindowLong( )** function. This function sets various attributes associated with a window. The prototype for **SetWindowLong( )** is shown here:

LONG SetWindowLong(HWND *hwnd*, int *index*, LONG *value*);

Notification Code	Meaning	Expected Return Value
PSN_APPLY	Sent when user presses the Apply or OK button.	**PSNRET_NOERROR** (zero) to apply changes; **PSNRET_INVALID_ NOCHANGEPAGE** to prevent changes.
PSN_HELP	Sent when user presses the Help button.	None.
PSN_KILLACTIVE	Sent when a page is losing focus or the OK button has been pressed.	Zero to allow deactivation; nonzero to prevent deactivation.
PSN_QUERYCANCEL	Sent when user presses the Cancel button.	Zero to allow cancellation; nonzero to prevent cancellation.
PSN_RESET	Sent when user presses the Cancel button.	None.
PSN_SETACTIVE	Sent when page gains focus (i.e., when activated).	Zero to allow activation; otherwise, return index of page to activate.
PSN_WIZBACK	Sent when user presses the Back button (wizards only).	Zero to activate previous page; –1 to prevent activation of previous page.

Common Property Sheet Notification Codes

Table 13-3.

Notification Code	Meaning	Expected Return Value
PSN_WIZFINISH	Sent when user presses the Finish button (wizards only).	Zero to terminate wizard; nonzero otherwise.
PSN_WIZNEXT	Sent when user presses the Next button (wizards only).	Zero to activate next page; –1 to prevent activation of next page.

Here, *hwnd* is the handle of the dialog box. *index* specifies the attribute to set. To return a value to a property sheet, the value of *index* will be **DWL_MSGRESULT**. The value to return is passed in *value*. Remember, your dialog box function must still return true if it processes a message and false if it does not. The return value specified using **SetWindowLong( )** specifies the outcome of a **WM_NOTIFY** message only.

Sending Messages to the Property Sheet

In addition to receiving messages, your application may send messages to the property sheet control. This can be accomplished using the **SendMessage( )** function, specifying the handle of the property sheet control as the recipient of the message. All property sheet messages begin with the prefix **PSM_**. Some of the most common ones are shown in Table 13-4.

Message Macro	Meaning
PSM_APPLY	Sends **PSN_APPLY** message. *lParam* is zero. *wParam* is zero. Returns zero if successful and nonzero on failure.
PSM_CHANGED	Enables Apply button. *lParam* is zero. *wParam* contains the handle of page dialog box. No return value.
PSM_SETCURSEL	Changes page. *lParam* contains the handle of the new page. *wParam* contains the index of new page. Returns zero if successful and nonzero on failure.

13

Message Macro	Meaning
PSM_SETWIZBUTTONS	Enables wizard buttons (applies only to wizards). *lParam* must contain one or more of the following flags: **PSWIZB_BACK**, **PSWIZB_NEXT**, **PSWIZB_FINISH**, or **PSWIZB_DISABLEDFINISH**. *wParam* is zero. No return value.
PSM_UNCHANGED	Disables Apply button. *lParam* is zero. *wParam* contains the handle of page dialog box. No return value.

Common Property Sheet Messages (*continued*)
Table 13-4.

Windows 98 also provides a set of macros to facilitate the sending of property sheet messages. The macros for the messages in Table 13-4 are shown here.

BOOL PropSheet_Apply(HWND *hPropSheet*);

BOOL PropSheet_Changed(HWND *hPropSheet*, HWND *hPageDialog*);

BOOL PropSheet_SetCurSel(HWND *hPropSheet*, HPROPSHEETPAGE *hPage*, int *Index*);

VOID PropSheet_SetWizButtons(HWND *hPropSheet*, DWORD *Flags*);

VOID PropSheet_Unchanged(HWND *hPropSheet*, HWND *hPageDialog*);

Here, *hPropSheet* is the handle of the property sheet control being sent the message. *hPageDialog* is the handle of the page dialog function sending the message. *Index* is the zero-based index of the next page to select. *hPage* specifies the handle of a page. *Flags* specify which wizard buttons will be enabled. The **PropSheet_SetWizButtons( )** macro applies only to wizards and is discussed in detail later in this chapter.

Your application should send a PSM_CHANGED *message whenever a property changes.*

The **PSM_CHANGED** message is particularly important because it enables the Apply button. Your application should send this message whenever the user changes anything within a property sheet.

It is best to use
standard-size
property
sheets.

Property Sheet Dialog Dimensions

The dialog box that underlies a property sheet can be of any size. However, it is recommended that your property sheets be of one of the standard sizes defined by Windows 98 and shown here.

Size	Width	Height
Small	PROP_SM_CXDLG	PROP_SM_CYDLG
Medium	PROP_MED_CXDLG	PROP_MED_CYDLG
Large	PROP_LG_CXDLG	PROP_LG_CYDLG

These macros are defined by including COMMCTRL.H. They are specified in terms of dialog box units and should be used in the DIALOG descriptions within your application's resource file.

A Property Sheet Demonstration Program

The following program displays a property sheet that contains three pages. Although the property sheet does not actually set any real properties, it does demonstrate the necessary procedures required to create and display a property sheet. Sample output is shown in Figure 13-2.

```
/* Demonstrate a Property Sheet */

#include <windows.h>
#include <stdio.h>
#include <commctrl.h>
#include "prop.h"

#define NUMSTRINGS 5
#define NUMPAGES 3

LRESULT CALLBACK WindowFunc(HWND, UINT, WPARAM, LPARAM);
BOOL CALLBACK DialogFunc(HWND, UINT, WPARAM, LPARAM);
BOOL CALLBACK DialogFunc2(HWND, UINT, WPARAM, LPARAM);
BOOL CALLBACK DialogFunc3(HWND, UINT, WPARAM, LPARAM);

char szWinName[] = "MyWin"; /* name of window class */

HINSTANCE hInst;

HWND hDlg; /* dialog box handle */
```

13

```
HPROPSHEETPAGE hPs[3];
HWND hPropSheet;
HWND hPage[3];

char list[][40] = {
  "Red",
  "Green",
  "Yellow",
  "Black",
  "White"
};

int cb1=0, cb2=0, cb3=0;
int rb1=1, rb2=0, rb3=0;
int lb1sel=0;

int WINAPI WinMain(HINSTANCE hThisInst, HINSTANCE hPrevInst,
                   LPSTR lpszArgs, int nWinMode)
{
  HWND hwnd;
  MSG msg;
  WNDCLASSEX wcl;
  HACCEL hAccel;
  INITCOMMONCONTROLSEX cc;

  /* Define a window class. */
  wcl.cbSize = sizeof(WNDCLASSEX);

  wcl.hInstance = hThisInst; /* handle to this instance */
  wcl.lpszClassName = szWinName; /* window class name */
  wcl.lpfnWndProc = WindowFunc; /* window function */
  wcl.style = 0; /* default style */

  wcl.hIcon = LoadIcon(NULL, IDI_APPLICATION); /* standard icon */
  wcl.hIconSm = LoadIcon(NULL, IDI_APPLICATION); /* small icon */
  wcl.hCursor = LoadCursor(NULL, IDC_ARROW); /* cursor style */

  wcl.lpszMenuName = "MyMenu"; /* main menu */
  wcl.cbClsExtra = 0; /* no extra */
  wcl.cbWndExtra = 0; /* information needed */

  /* Make the window white. */
  wcl.hbrBackground = (HBRUSH) GetStockObject(WHITE_BRUSH);

  /* Register the window class. */
```

```
        if(!RegisterClassEx(&wcl)) return 0;

     /* Now that a window class has been registered, a window
        can be created. */
     hwnd = CreateWindow(
       szWinName, /* name of window class */
       "Demonstrate a Property Sheet", /* title */
       WS_OVERLAPPEDWINDOW, /* standard window */
       CW_USEDEFAULT, /* X coordinate - let Windows decide */
       CW_USEDEFAULT, /* Y coordinate - let Windows decide */
       CW_USEDEFAULT, /* width - let Windows decide */
       CW_USEDEFAULT, /* height - let Windows decide */
       HWND_DESKTOP, /* no parent window */
       NULL, /* no override of class menu */
       hThisInst, /* handle of this instance of the program */
       NULL /* no additional arguments */
     );

     hInst = hThisInst; /* save the current instance handle */

     /* Load accelerators. */
     hAccel = LoadAccelerators(hThisInst, "MyMenu");

     /* Initialize the common controls. */
     cc.dwSize = sizeof(INITCOMMONCONTROLSEX);
     cc.dwICC = ICC_TAB_CLASSES;
     InitCommonControlsEx(&cc);

     /* Display the window. */
     ShowWindow(hwnd, nWinMode);
     UpdateWindow(hwnd);

     /* Create the message loop. */
     while(GetMessage(&msg, NULL, 0, 0))
     {
       if(!TranslateAccelerator(hwnd, hAccel, &msg)) {
         TranslateMessage(&msg); /* translate keyboard messages */
         DispatchMessage(&msg); /* return control to Windows 98 */
       }
     }

     return msg.wParam;
}

/* This function is called by Windows 98 and is passed
```

13

```
    messages from the message queue.
*/
LRESULT CALLBACK WindowFunc(HWND hwnd, UINT message,
                            WPARAM wParam, LPARAM lParam)
{
  int response;
  PROPSHEETPAGE PropSheet[3];
  PROPSHEETHEADER PropHdr;

  switch(message) {
    case WM_COMMAND:
      switch(LOWORD(wParam)) {
        case IDM_DIALOG:
          PropSheet[0].dwSize = sizeof(PROPSHEETPAGE);
          PropSheet[0].dwFlags = PSP_DEFAULT;
          PropSheet[0].hInstance = hInst;
          PropSheet[0].pszTemplate = "MyDB";
          PropSheet[0].pszIcon = NULL;
          PropSheet[0].pfnDlgProc = (DLGPROC) DialogFunc;
          PropSheet[0].pszTitle = "";
          PropSheet[0].lParam = 0;
          PropSheet[0].pfnCallback = NULL;

          PropSheet[1].dwSize = sizeof(PROPSHEETPAGE);
          PropSheet[1].dwFlags = PSP_DEFAULT;
          PropSheet[1].hInstance = hInst;
          PropSheet[1].pszTemplate = "MyDB2";
          PropSheet[1].pszIcon = NULL;
          PropSheet[1].pfnDlgProc = (DLGPROC) DialogFunc2;
          PropSheet[1].pszTitle = "";
          PropSheet[1].lParam = 0;
          PropSheet[1].pfnCallback = NULL;

          PropSheet[2].dwSize = sizeof(PROPSHEETPAGE);
          PropSheet[2].dwFlags = PSP_DEFAULT;
          PropSheet[2].hInstance = hInst;
          PropSheet[2].pszTemplate = "MyDB3";
          PropSheet[2].pszIcon = NULL;
          PropSheet[2].pfnDlgProc = (DLGPROC) DialogFunc3;
          PropSheet[2].pszTitle = "";
          PropSheet[2].lParam = 0;
          PropSheet[2].pfnCallback = NULL;

          hPs[0] = CreatePropertySheetPage(&PropSheet[0]);
          hPs[1] = CreatePropertySheetPage(&PropSheet[1]);
```

```
          hPs[2] = CreatePropertySheetPage(&PropSheet[2]);

          PropHdr.dwSize = sizeof(PROPSHEETHEADER);
          PropHdr.dwFlags = PSH_DEFAULT;
          PropHdr.hwndParent = hwnd;
          PropHdr.hInstance = hInst;
          PropHdr.pszIcon = NULL;
          PropHdr.pszCaption = "Sample Property Sheet";
          PropHdr.nPages = 3;
          PropHdr.nStartPage = 0;
          PropHdr.phpage = hPs;
          PropHdr.pfnCallback = NULL;

          PropertySheet(&PropHdr);
          break;
        case IDM_EXIT:
          response = MessageBox(hwnd, "Quit the Program?",
                                "Exit", MB_YESNO);
          if(response == IDYES) PostQuitMessage(0);
          break;
        case IDM_HELP:
          MessageBox(hwnd, "Try the property sheets.",
                     "Help", MB_OK);
          break;
      }
      break;
    case WM_DESTROY: /* terminate the program */
      PostQuitMessage(0);
      break;
    default:
      /* Let Windows 98 process any messages not specified in
         the preceding switch statement. */
      return DefWindowProc(hwnd, message, wParam, lParam);
  }
  return 0;
}

/* The First dialog function. */
BOOL CALLBACK DialogFunc(HWND hdwnd, UINT message,
                         WPARAM wParam, LPARAM lParam)
{
  static long index;
  int i;
  char str[80];
```

```
      switch(message) {
        case WM_NOTIFY:
          switch(((NMHDR *) lParam)->code) {
            case PSN_SETACTIVE: /* page gaining focus */
              hPropSheet = ((NMHDR *) lParam)->hwndFrom;
              SetWindowLong(hdwnd, DWL_MSGRESULT, 0);
              index = lb1sel;
              return 1;
            case PSN_KILLACTIVE: /* page losing focus */
              lb1sel = index;
              SetWindowLong(hdwnd, DWL_MSGRESULT, 0);
              return 1;
/*          case PSN_RESET: -- add your own Cancel code here */
          }
          break;
        case WM_COMMAND:
          switch(LOWORD(wParam)) {
            case IDD_ONE:
              PropSheet_SetCurSel(hPropSheet, hPs[0], 0);
              return 1;
            case IDD_TWO:
              PropSheet_SetCurSel(hPropSheet, hPs[1], 1);
              return 1;
            case IDD_THREE:
              PropSheet_SetCurSel(hPropSheet, hPs[2], 2);
              return 1;
            case IDD_LB1: /* process a list box LBN_DBLCLK */
              PropSheet_Changed(hPropSheet, hdwnd);
              /* see if user made a selection */
              if(HIWORD(wParam)==LBN_DBLCLK) {
                index = SendDlgItemMessage(hdwnd, IDD_LB1,
                         LB_GETCURSEL, 0, 0);  /* get index */
                sprintf(str, "%s", list[index]);
                MessageBox(hdwnd, str, "Selection Made", MB_OK);
              }
              return 1;
          }
          break;
        case WM_INITDIALOG: /* initialize list box */
          for(i=0; i<NUMSTRINGS; i++)
            SendDlgItemMessage(hdwnd, IDD_LB1,
                     LB_ADDSTRING, 0, (LPARAM)list[i]);

          /* select first item */
          SendDlgItemMessage(hdwnd, IDD_LB1, LB_SETCURSEL,
```

```
                              lb1sel, 0);

        return 1;
    }
    return 0;
}


/* The Second dialog function. */
BOOL CALLBACK DialogFunc2(HWND hdwnd, UINT message,
                          WPARAM wParam, LPARAM lParam)
{
    int status;

    switch(message) {
        case WM_NOTIFY:
            switch(((NMHDR *) lParam)->code) {
                case PSN_SETACTIVE:/* page gaining focus */
                    hPropSheet = ((NMHDR *) lParam)->hwndFrom;
                    SetWindowLong(hdwnd, DWL_MSGRESULT, 0);
                    return 1;
                case PSN_KILLACTIVE: /* page losing focus */
                    cb1 = SendDlgItemMessage(hdwnd, IDD_CB1,
                                           BM_GETCHECK, 0, 0);
                    cb2 = SendDlgItemMessage(hdwnd, IDD_CB2,
                                           BM_GETCHECK, 0, 0);
                    cb3 = SendDlgItemMessage(hdwnd, IDD_CB3,
                                           BM_GETCHECK, 0, 0);
                    SetWindowLong(hdwnd, DWL_MSGRESULT, 0);
                    return 1;
/*              case PSN_RESET: -- add your own Cancel code here */
            }
            break;
        case WM_COMMAND:
            switch(LOWORD(wParam)) {
                case IDD_CB1:
                case IDD_CB2:
                case IDD_CB3:
                    PropSheet_Changed(hPropSheet, hdwnd);
                    return 1;
                case IDD_INVERT:
                    PropSheet_Changed(hPropSheet, hdwnd);
                    status = SendDlgItemMessage(hdwnd, IDD_CB1,
                                           BM_GETCHECK, 0, 0);
                    SendDlgItemMessage(hdwnd, IDD_CB1, BM_SETCHECK,
                                    !status, 0);
```

13

```
        status = SendDlgItemMessage(hdwnd, IDD_CB2,
                                   BM_GETCHECK, 0, 0);
        SendDlgItemMessage(hdwnd, IDD_CB2, BM_SETCHECK,
                           !status, 0);

        status = SendDlgItemMessage(hdwnd, IDD_CB3,
                                   BM_GETCHECK, 0, 0);
        SendDlgItemMessage(hdwnd, IDD_CB3, BM_SETCHECK,
                           !status, 0);

        return 1;
      }
      break;
    case WM_INITDIALOG: /* initialize list box */
      SendDlgItemMessage(hdwnd, IDD_CB1, BM_SETCHECK,
                         cb1, 0);
      SendDlgItemMessage(hdwnd, IDD_CB2, BM_SETCHECK,
                         cb2, 0);
      SendDlgItemMessage(hdwnd, IDD_CB3, BM_SETCHECK,
                         cb3, 0);
      return 1;
  }
  return 0;
}

/* The Third dialog function. */
BOOL CALLBACK DialogFunc3(HWND hdwnd, UINT message,
                          WPARAM wParam, LPARAM lParam)
{
  switch(message) {
    case WM_NOTIFY:
      switch(((NMHDR *) lParam)->code) {
        case PSN_SETACTIVE: /* page gaining focus */
          hPropSheet = ((NMHDR *) lParam)->hwndFrom;
          SetWindowLong(hdwnd, DWL_MSGRESULT, 0);
          return 1;
        case PSN_KILLACTIVE: /* page losing focus */
          rb1 = SendDlgItemMessage(hdwnd, IDD_RB1, BM_GETCHECK,
                                   0, 0);
          rb2 = SendDlgItemMessage(hdwnd, IDD_RB2, BM_GETCHECK,
                                   0, 0);
          rb3 = SendDlgItemMessage(hdwnd, IDD_RB3, BM_GETCHECK,
                                   0, 0);
          SetWindowLong(hdwnd, DWL_MSGRESULT, 0);
```

```
                       return 1;
       /*      case PSN_RESET: -- add your own Cancel code here */
              }
            break;
         case WM_COMMAND:
           switch(LOWORD(wParam)) {
             case IDD_RB1:
             case IDD_RB2:
             case IDD_RB3:
               PropSheet_Changed(hPropSheet, hdwnd);
               return 1;
             case IDD_TOP:
               PropSheet_Changed(hPropSheet, hdwnd);
               SendDlgItemMessage(hdwnd, IDD_RB2, BM_SETCHECK,
                              0, 0);
               SendDlgItemMessage(hdwnd, IDD_RB3, BM_SETCHECK,
                              0, 0);
               SendDlgItemMessage(hdwnd, IDD_RB1, BM_SETCHECK,
                              1, 0);
               return 1;
             case IDD_BOTTOM:
               PropSheet_Changed(hPropSheet, hdwnd);
               SendDlgItemMessage(hdwnd, IDD_RB1, BM_SETCHECK,
                              0, 0);
               SendDlgItemMessage(hdwnd, IDD_RB2, BM_SETCHECK,
                              0, 0);
               SendDlgItemMessage(hdwnd, IDD_RB3, BM_SETCHECK,
                              1, 0);
               return 1;
           }
           break;
         case WM_INITDIALOG: /* initialize list box */
           SendDlgItemMessage(hdwnd, IDD_RB1, BM_SETCHECK,
                          rb1, 0);
           SendDlgItemMessage(hdwnd, IDD_RB2, BM_SETCHECK,
                          rb2, 0);
           SendDlgItemMessage(hdwnd, IDD_RB3, BM_SETCHECK,
                          rb3, 0);
           return 1;
       }
     return 0;
   }
```

13

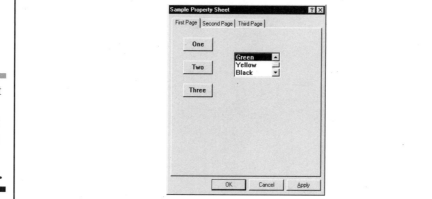

Sample output
from the
property sheet
demonstration
program
Figure 13-2a.

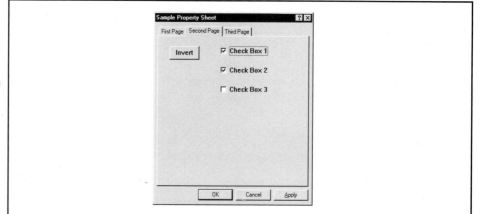

Sample output
from the
property sheet
demonstration
program
Figure 13-2b.

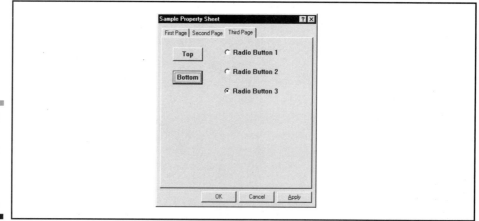

Sample output
from the
property sheet
demonstration
program
Figure 13-2c.

The program requires the following resource file.

```
#include <windows.h>
#include <commctrl.h>
#include "prop.h"

MyMenu MENU
{
  POPUP "&Property Sheet"
  {
    MENUITEM "&Activate\tF2", IDM_DIALOG
    MENUITEM "&Exit\tCtrl+X", IDM_EXIT
  }
  MENUITEM "&Help", IDM_HELP
}

MyMenu ACCELERATORS
{
  VK_F2, IDM_DIALOG, VIRTKEY
  "^X", IDM_EXIT
  VK_F1, IDM_HELP, VIRTKEY
}

MyDB DIALOG 0, 0, PROP_SM_CXDLG, PROP_SM_CYDLG
CAPTION "First Page"
STYLE WS_POPUP | WS_CAPTION | WS_SYSMENU | WS_VISIBLE
{
  DEFPUSHBUTTON "One", IDD_ONE, 11, 10, 32, 14,
            WS_CHILD | WS_VISIBLE | WS_TABSTOP
  PUSHBUTTON "Two", IDD_TWO, 11, 34, 32, 14,
            WS_CHILD | WS_VISIBLE | WS_TABSTOP
  PUSHBUTTON "Three", IDD_THREE, 11, 58, 32, 14,
            WS_CHILD | WS_VISIBLE | WS_TABSTOP
  LISTBOX IDD_LB1, 66, 25, 50, 33, LBS_NOTIFY |
            WS_VISIBLE | WS_BORDER | WS_VSCROLL | WS_TABSTOP
}

MyDB2 DIALOG 0, 0, PROP_SM_CXDLG, PROP_SM_CYDLG
CAPTION "Second Page"
STYLE WS_POPUP | WS_CAPTION | WS_SYSMENU | WS_VISIBLE
{
  DEFPUSHBUTTON "Invert", IDD_INVERT, 11, 10, 32, 14,
            WS_CHILD | WS_VISIBLE | WS_TABSTOP
  AUTOCHECKBOX "Check Box 1", IDD_CB1, 66, 10, 70, 10
  AUTOCHECKBOX "Check Box 2", IDD_CB2, 66, 30, 70, 10
  AUTOCHECKBOX "Check Box 3", IDD_CB3, 66, 50, 70, 10
}
```

13

```
MyDB3 DIALOG 0, 0, PROP_SM_CXDLG, PROP_SM_CYDLG
CAPTION "Third Page"
STYLE WS_POPUP | WS_CAPTION | WS_SYSMENU | WS_VISIBLE
{
  DEFPUSHBUTTON "Top", IDD_TOP, 11, 10, 32, 14,
              WS_CHILD | WS_VISIBLE | WS_TABSTOP
  PUSHBUTTON "Bottom", IDD_BOTTOM, 11, 34, 32, 14,
              WS_CHILD | WS_VISIBLE | WS_TABSTOP
  AUTORADIOBUTTON "Radio Button 1", IDD_RB1, 66, 10, 70, 10
  AUTORADIOBUTTON "Radio Button 2", IDD_RB2, 66, 30, 70, 10
  AUTORADIOBUTTON "Radio Button 3", IDD_RB3, 66, 50, 70, 10

}
```

The header file PROP.H is shown here.

```
#define IDM_DIALOG     100
#define IDM_EXIT       101
#define IDM_HELP       102

#define IDD_ONE        200
#define IDD_TWO        201
#define IDD_THREE      202
#define IDD_TOP        204
#define IDD_BOTTOM     205
#define IDD_INVERT     207

#define IDD_LB1        301

#define IDD_EB1        401

#define IDD_CB1        501
#define IDD_CB2        502
#define IDD_CB3        503

#define IDD_RB1        601
#define IDD_RB2        602
#define IDD_RB3        603
```

In all three page dialog boxes, there is one important thing to notice: each time one is changed by the user, a **PSM_CHANGED** message is sent. For example, when the user alters the state of a check box in the second dialog box, **PropSheet_Changed( )** is called. Once a **PSM_CHANGED** message has been sent, the Apply button will change from inactive to active. In general, you must notify the property sheet control whenever a property changes.

On the first page of the property sheet, the push buttons One, Two, and Three demonstrate how various pages can be selected under program control. That is, pressing Two selects the second page, and pressing Three selects the third page. Of course, pressing One simply reselects the first page. While there is no need for these push buttons in this example (since you can simply click on a page's tab to select it), these buttons illustrate the **PSM_SET-CURSEL** message.

While the dialog boxes in this example are only placeholders, they illustrate the effect of using a property sheet. For example, if the user presses OK or moves to another page, then a **PSN_KILLACTIVE** message is received and any changes made by the user are saved. However, if the user presses Cancel, any changes made to the current page are ignored. As the program is written, pressing Cancel does not undo any changes made to other pages. You might want to try adding this feature on your own by handling the **PSN_RESET** message. You should also try handling the **PSN_APPLY** message.

IN DEPTH

Responding to PSN_HELP

If you include the **PSP_HASHELP** flag when you create a property sheet page, the Help button will be included in the property sheet control whenever that page is active. Pressing this button causes the **PSN_HELP** notification message to be sent. For most applications, you will want to activate the Windows help system (described in Chapter 17) to provide online help relating to the property sheet control. However, the Windows help system is as sophisticated as it is complex. Fortunately, for very limited property sheets, you can respond to a **PSN_HELP** message by simply displaying a message box.

To try handling help requests, add the **PSP_HASHELP** to each property sheet page. For example, here it is added to the first page.

```
PropSheet[0].dwFlags = PSP_DEFAULT | PSP_HASHELP;
```

13

Next, add a handler for **PSN_HELP** to each property page dialog box function under the **WM_NOTIFY** case. For example, here is the handler for the first dialog box.

```
case PSN_HELP:
  MessageBox(hdwnd,
          "This is help for the first property sheet.\n",
          "Page One Help",
          MB_OK);
  return 1;
```

Here is the way the first page looks with the addition of the Help button.

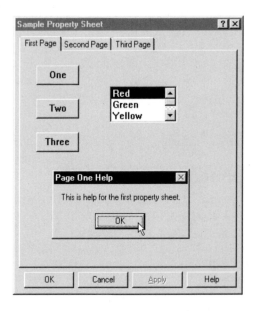

Creating a Wizard

A wizard is a sequenced set of property sheets.

From the programmer's point of view, a wizard is a set of sequenced property sheets. It is defined using the **PROPSHEETPAGE** and **PROPSHEETHEADER** structures defined earlier and created using the

CreatePropertySheetPage( ) and **PropertySheet( )** functions. However, to create a wizard, you must specify the **PSH_WIZARD** flag in the **dwFlags** field of the **PROPSHEETHEADER** structure. When this is done, the dialog boxes will automatically be sequenced from first to last, forming a wizard. If you wish to use a watermark, a header bitmap, or a header title, you will need to specify the **PSH_WIZARD97** flag. However, most wizards do not include these items and they are not used in the example that follows.

Enabling Wizard Buttons

Although including **PSH_WIZARD** automatically transforms your property sheet into a wizard, there are a few more steps that you will need to take in order for your wizard to perform correctly. First, you will need to enable and disable certain buttons manually. For example, on the first page, you will need to enable the Next button but disable the Back button. On the last page, you will need to enable the Back button and the Finish button. On the pages between the first and last, the Next and Back buttons will have to be enabled. To accomplish this, either send a **PSM_SETWIZBUTTONS** message or use the **PropSheet_SetWizButtons( )** macro. As shown earlier, **PropSheet_SetWizButtons( )** has this general form:

VOID PropSheet_SetWizButtons(HWND *hPropSheet*, DWORD *Flags*);

Here, *hPropSheet* is the handle of the property sheet control. In the *Flags* parameter, specify the button or buttons that you want to enable. Only those buttons that you specify will be enabled; the others will be disabled. The button macros are shown here.

PSWIZB_BACK

PSWIZB_NEXT

PSWIZB_FINISH

PSWIZB_DISABLEDFINISH

PSWIZB_DISABLEDFINISH creates a disabled Finish button. You can OR together two or more buttons. Therefore, to enable the Back and Finish buttons, you would use this statement:

```
PropSheet_SetWizButtons(PSWIZB_BACK | PSWIZB_FINISH);
```

13

Using a Bitmap

As you know from using Windows 98, most wizards specify a large bitmap on the left side of the first page. It may also be specified on subsequent pages as well. This bitmap serves to identify the wizard. While not technically required, it is highly recommended that at least the first page of any wizard that you create include such a bitmap.

Style Macros

Windows 98 defines several values that help you create wizards that conform to Microsoft's style rules. These values are shown here.

Value	Meaning
WIZ_CXDLG	Width of page.
WIZ_CYDLG	Height of page.
WIZ_CXBMP	Width of bitmap.
WIZ_BODYX	*X* coordinate of the left side of the body of the page.
WIZ_BODYCX	Width of body, excluding the bitmap area.

These values are in terms of dialog box units.

These style macros can be used to create wizards that are the same size and shape those used by Windows 98. They also help you position each page's controls relative to the area reserved for the bitmap. Keep in mind, however, that if a page does not require a bitmap, you can use the entire page area. In the example that follows, the first two pages display a bitmap and the third page does not.

A Wizard Demonstration Program

The following program demonstrates a wizard. It does so by converting the previous property sheet example into a wizard. Sample output is shown in Figure 13-3.

```
/* Demonstrate a Wizard */

#include <windows.h>
#include <string.h>
```

```
#include <stdio.h>
#include <commctrl.h>
#include "prop.h"

#define NUMSTRINGS 5
#define NUMPAGES 3

#define BITMAPSIZEX 120
#define BITMAPSIZEY 226

LRESULT CALLBACK WindowFunc(HWND, UINT, WPARAM, LPARAM);
BOOL CALLBACK DialogFunc(HWND, UINT, WPARAM, LPARAM);
BOOL CALLBACK DialogFunc2(HWND, UINT, WPARAM, LPARAM);
BOOL CALLBACK DialogFunc3(HWND, UINT, WPARAM, LPARAM);

char szWinName[] = "MyWin"; /* name of window class */

HINSTANCE hInst;

HWND hDlg; /* dialog box handle */
HPROPSHEETPAGE hPs[3];
HWND hPropSheet;
HWND hPage[3];

char list[][40] = {
  "Red",
  "Green",
  "Yellow",
  "Black",
  "White"
};

int cb1=0, cb2=0, cb3=0;
int rb1=1, rb2=0, rb3=0;
int lb1sel=0;

HBITMAP hBit;

int WINAPI WinMain(HINSTANCE hThisInst, HINSTANCE hPrevInst,
                   LPSTR lpszArgs, int nWinMode)
{
  HWND hwnd;
  MSG msg;
  WNDCLASSEX wcl;
  HACCEL hAccel;
  INITCOMMONCONTROLSEX cc;
```

13

```
/* Define a window class. */
wcl.cbSize = sizeof(WNDCLASSEX);

wcl.hInstance = hThisInst; /* handle to this instance */
wcl.lpszClassName = szWinName; /* window class name */
wcl.lpfnWndProc = WindowFunc; /* window function */
wcl.style = 0; /* default style */

wcl.hIcon = LoadIcon(NULL, IDI_APPLICATION); /* standard icon */
wcl.hIconSm = LoadIcon(NULL, IDI_APPLICATION); /* small icon */
wcl.hCursor = LoadCursor(NULL, IDC_ARROW); /* cursor style */

wcl.lpszMenuName = "MyMenu"; /* main menu */
wcl.cbClsExtra = 0; /* no extra */
wcl.cbWndExtra = 0; /* information needed */

/* Make the window white. */
wcl.hbrBackground = (HBRUSH) GetStockObject(WHITE_BRUSH);

/* Register the window class. */
if(!RegisterClassEx(&wcl)) return 0;

/* Now that a window class has been registered, a window
   can be created. */
hwnd = CreateWindow(
  szWinName, /* name of window class */
  "Demonstrate a Wizard", /* title */
  WS_OVERLAPPEDWINDOW, /* standard window */
  CW_USEDEFAULT, /* X coordinate - let Windows decide */
  CW_USEDEFAULT, /* Y coordinate - let Windows decide */
  CW_USEDEFAULT, /* width - let Windows decide */
  CW_USEDEFAULT, /* height - let Windows decide */
  HWND_DESKTOP, /* no parent window */
  NULL, /* no override of class menu */
  hThisInst, /* handle of this instance of the program */
  NULL /* no additional arguments */
);

hInst = hThisInst; /* save the current instance handle */

/* Load accelerators. */
hAccel = LoadAccelerators(hThisInst, "MyMenu");

/* Load bitmap. */
hBit = LoadBitmap(hThisInst, "wizbmp");
```

```
    /* Initialize the common controls. */
    cc.dwSize = sizeof(INITCOMMONCONTROLSEX);
    cc.dwICC = ICC_TAB_CLASSES;
    InitCommonControlsEx(&cc);

    /* Display the window. */
    ShowWindow(hwnd, nWinMode);
    UpdateWindow(hwnd);

    /* Create the message loop. */
    while(GetMessage(&msg, NULL, 0, 0))
    {
      if(!TranslateAccelerator(hwnd, hAccel, &msg)) {
        TranslateMessage(&msg); /* translate keyboard messages */
        DispatchMessage(&msg); /* return control to Windows 98 */
      }
    }

    return msg.wParam;
}

/* This function is called by Windows 98 and is passed
   messages from the message queue.
*/
LRESULT CALLBACK WindowFunc(HWND hwnd, UINT message,
                            WPARAM wParam, LPARAM lParam)
{
  int response;
  PROPSHEETPAGE PropSheet[3];
  PROPSHEETHEADER PropHdr;

  switch(message) {
    case WM_COMMAND:
      switch(LOWORD(wParam)) {
        case IDM_DIALOG:
          PropSheet[0].dwSize = sizeof(PROPSHEETPAGE);
          PropSheet[0].dwFlags = PSP_DEFAULT;
          PropSheet[0].hInstance = hInst;
          PropSheet[0].pszTemplate = "MyDB";
          PropSheet[0].pszIcon = NULL;
          PropSheet[0].pfnDlgProc = (DLGPROC) DialogFunc;
          PropSheet[0].pszTitle = "";
          PropSheet[0].lParam = 0;
          PropSheet[0].pfnCallback = NULL;
```

13

```
    PropSheet[1].dwSize = sizeof(PROPSHEETPAGE);
    PropSheet[1].dwFlags = PSP_DEFAULT;
    PropSheet[1].hInstance = hInst;
    PropSheet[1].pszTemplate = "MyDB2";
    PropSheet[1].pszIcon = NULL;
    PropSheet[1].pfnDlgProc = (DLGPROC) DialogFunc2;
    PropSheet[1].pszTitle = "";
    PropSheet[1].lParam = 0;
    PropSheet[1].pfnCallback = NULL;

    PropSheet[2].dwSize = sizeof(PROPSHEETPAGE);
    PropSheet[2].dwFlags = PSP_DEFAULT;
    PropSheet[2].hInstance = hInst;
    PropSheet[2].pszTemplate = "MyDB3";
    PropSheet[2].pszIcon = NULL;
    PropSheet[2].pfnDlgProc = (DLGPROC) DialogFunc3;
    PropSheet[2].pszTitle = "";
    PropSheet[2].lParam = 0;
    PropSheet[2].pfnCallback = NULL;

    hPs[0] = CreatePropertySheetPage(&PropSheet[0]);
    hPs[1] = CreatePropertySheetPage(&PropSheet[1]);
    hPs[2] = CreatePropertySheetPage(&PropSheet[2]);

    PropHdr.dwSize = sizeof(PROPSHEETHEADER);
    PropHdr.dwFlags = PSH_WIZARD;
    PropHdr.hwndParent = hwnd;
    PropHdr.hInstance = hInst;
    PropHdr.pszIcon = NULL;
    PropHdr.pszCaption = "";
    PropHdr.nPages = 3;
    PropHdr.nStartPage = 0;
    PropHdr.phpage = hPs;
    PropHdr.pfnCallback = NULL;

    PropertySheet(&PropHdr);
    break;
  case IDM_EXIT:
    response = MessageBox(hwnd, "Quit the Program?",
                          "Exit", MB_YESNO);
    if(response == IDYES) PostQuitMessage(0);
    break;
  case IDM_HELP:
    MessageBox(hwnd, "Try the wizard.",
               "Help", MB_OK);
```

```
            break;
        }
        break;
    case WM_DESTROY: /* terminate the program */
        PostQuitMessage(0);
        break;
    default:
        /* Let Windows 98 process any messages not specified in
           the preceding switch statement. */
        return DefWindowProc(hwnd, message, wParam, lParam);
    }
    return 0;
}


/* The first dialog function. */
BOOL CALLBACK DialogFunc(HWND hdwnd, UINT message,
                         WPARAM wParam, LPARAM lParam)
{
    static long index;
    int i;
    char str[80];
    PAINTSTRUCT ps;
    HDC DC, memDC;

    switch(message) {
        case WM_PAINT: /* display icon */
            DC = BeginPaint(hdwnd, &ps);
            memDC = CreateCompatibleDC(DC);
            SelectObject(memDC, hBit);
            BitBlt(DC, 0, 0, BITMAPSIZEX, BITMAPSIZEY,
                    memDC, 0, 0, SRCCOPY);
            EndPaint(hdwnd, &ps);
            DeleteDC(memDC);
            return 1;
        case WM_NOTIFY:
            switch(((NMHDR *) lParam)->code) {
                case PSN_SETACTIVE: /* page gaining focus */
                    hPropSheet = ((NMHDR *) lParam)->hwndFrom;
                    index = lb1sel;
                    PropSheet_SetWizButtons(hPropSheet, PSWIZB_NEXT);
                    SetWindowLong(hdwnd, DWL_MSGRESULT, 0);
                    return 1;
                case PSN_KILLACTIVE: /* page losing focus */
                    lb1sel = index;
                    SetWindowLong(hdwnd, DWL_MSGRESULT, 0);
```

13

```
          return 0;
/*      case PSN_RESET: -- add your own Cancel code here */
        }
      break;
    case WM_COMMAND:
      switch(LOWORD(wParam)) {
        case IDD_ONE:
        case IDD_TWO:
        case IDD_THREE:
          PropSheet_Changed(hPropSheet, hdwnd);
          return 1;
        case IDD_LB1: /* process a list box LBN_DBLCLK */
          PropSheet_Changed(hPropSheet, hdwnd);
          /* see if user made a selection */
          if(HIWORD(wParam)==LBN_DBLCLK) {
            index = SendDlgItemMessage(hdwnd, IDD_LB1,
                    LB_GETCURSEL, 0, 0);  /* get index */
            sprintf(str, "%s", list[index]);

            MessageBox(hdwnd, str, "Selection Made", MB_OK);
          }
          return 1;
      }
      break;
    case WM_INITDIALOG: /* initialize list box */
      for(i=0; i<NUMSTRINGS; i++)
        SendDlgItemMessage(hdwnd, IDD_LB1,
                    LB_ADDSTRING, 0, (LPARAM)list[i]);

      /* select first item */
      SendDlgItemMessage(hdwnd, IDD_LB1, LB_SETCURSEL,
                          lb1sel, 0);

      return 1;
  }
  return 0;
}

/* The Second dialog function. */
BOOL CALLBACK DialogFunc2(HWND hdwnd, UINT message,
                          WPARAM wParam, LPARAM lParam)
{
  int status;
  PAINTSTRUCT ps;
  HDC DC, memDC;
```

```
    switch(message) {
      case WM_PAINT: /* display icon */
        DC = BeginPaint(hdwnd, &ps);
        memDC = CreateCompatibleDC(DC);
        SelectObject(memDC, hBit);
        BitBlt(DC, 0, 0, BITMAPSIZEX, BITMAPSIZEY,
               memDC, 0, 0, SRCCOPY);
        EndPaint(hdwnd, &ps);
        DeleteDC(memDC);
        return 1;
      case WM_NOTIFY:
        switch(((NMHDR *) lParam)->code) {
          case PSN_SETACTIVE:/* page gaining focus */
            hPropSheet = ((NMHDR *) lParam)->hwndFrom;
            PropSheet_SetWizButtons(hPropSheet,
                         PSWIZB_NEXT | PSWIZB_BACK);
            SetWindowLong(hdwnd, DWL_MSGRESULT, 0);
            return 1;
          case PSN_KILLACTIVE: /* page losing focus */
            cb1 = SendDlgItemMessage(hdwnd, IDD_CB1,
                                BM_GETCHECK, 0, 0);
            cb2 = SendDlgItemMessage(hdwnd, IDD_CB2,
                                BM_GETCHECK, 0, 0);
            cb3 = SendDlgItemMessage(hdwnd, IDD_CB3,
                                BM_GETCHECK, 0, 0);
            SetWindowLong(hdwnd, DWL_MSGRESULT, 0);
            return 1;
/*        case PSN_RESET: -- add your own Cancel code here */
        }
        break;
      case WM_COMMAND:
        switch(LOWORD(wParam)) {
          case IDD_CB1:
          case IDD_CB2:
          case IDD_CB3:
            PropSheet_Changed(hPropSheet, hdwnd);
            return 1;
          case IDD_INVERT:
            PropSheet_Changed(hPropSheet, hdwnd);
            status = SendDlgItemMessage(hdwnd, IDD_CB1,
                            BM_GETCHECK, 0, 0);
            SendDlgItemMessage(hdwnd, IDD_CB1, BM_SETCHECK,
                            !status, 0);

            status = SendDlgItemMessage(hdwnd, IDD_CB2,
```

13

```
                                   BM_GETCHECK, 0, 0);
            SendDlgItemMessage(hdwnd, IDD_CB2, BM_SETCHECK,
                              !status, 0);

            status = SendDlgItemMessage(hdwnd, IDD_CB3,
                                    BM_GETCHECK, 0, 0);
            SendDlgItemMessage(hdwnd, IDD_CB3, BM_SETCHECK,
                              !status, 0);

            return 1;
        }
        break;
      case WM_INITDIALOG: /* initialize list box */
        SendDlgItemMessage(hdwnd, IDD_CB1, BM_SETCHECK,
                          cb1, 0);
        SendDlgItemMessage(hdwnd, IDD_CB2, BM_SETCHECK,
                          cb2, 0);
        SendDlgItemMessage(hdwnd, IDD_CB3, BM_SETCHECK,
                          cb3, 0);

        return 1;
  }
  return 0;
}


/* The Third dialog function. */
BOOL CALLBACK DialogFunc3(HWND hdwnd, UINT message,
                          WPARAM wParam, LPARAM lParam)
{
  switch(message) {
    case WM_NOTIFY:
      switch(((NMHDR *) lParam)->code) {
        case PSN_SETACTIVE: /* page gaining focus */
          hPropSheet = ((NMHDR *) lParam)->hwndFrom;
          PropSheet_SetWizButtons(hPropSheet,
                          PSWIZB_FINISH | PSWIZB_BACK);
          SetWindowLong(hdwnd, DWL_MSGRESULT, 0);
          return 1;
        case PSN_WIZFINISH: /* Finish button pressed */
        case PSN_KILLACTIVE: /* page losing focus */
          rb1 = SendDlgItemMessage(hdwnd, IDD_RB1,
                                  BM_GETCHECK, 0, 0);
          rb2 = SendDlgItemMessage(hdwnd, IDD_RB2,
                                  BM_GETCHECK, 0, 0);
          rb3 = SendDlgItemMessage(hdwnd, IDD_RB3,
                                  BM_GETCHECK, 0, 0);
```

```
                  SetWindowLong(hdwnd, DWL_MSGRESULT, 0);
                  return 1;
/*        case PSN_RESET: -- add your own Cancel code here */
        }
        break;
    case WM_COMMAND:
        switch(LOWORD(wParam)) {
            case IDD_RB1:
            case IDD_RB2:
            case IDD_RB3:
                PropSheet_Changed(hPropSheet, hdwnd);
                return 1;
            case IDD_TOP:
                PropSheet_Changed(hPropSheet, hdwnd);
                SendDlgItemMessage(hdwnd, IDD_RB2, BM_SETCHECK,
                                     0, 0);
                SendDlgItemMessage(hdwnd, IDD_RB3, BM_SETCHECK,
                                     0, 0);
                SendDlgItemMessage(hdwnd, IDD_RB1, BM_SETCHECK,
                                     1, 0);
                return 1;
            case IDD_BOTTOM:
                PropSheet_Changed(hPropSheet, hdwnd);
                SendDlgItemMessage(hdwnd, IDD_RB1, BM_SETCHECK, 0, 0);
                SendDlgItemMessage(hdwnd, IDD_RB2, BM_SETCHECK, 0, 0);
                SendDlgItemMessage(hdwnd, IDD_RB3, BM_SETCHECK, 1, 0);
                return 1;
        }
        break;
    case WM_INITDIALOG: /* initialize list box */
        SendDlgItemMessage(hdwnd, IDD_RB1, BM_SETCHECK,
                             rb1, 0);
        SendDlgItemMessage(hdwnd, IDD_RB2, BM_SETCHECK,
                             rb2, 0);
        SendDlgItemMessage(hdwnd, IDD_RB3, BM_SETCHECK,
                             rb3, 0);
        return 1;
    }
    return 0;
}
```

13

This program uses the same PROP.H file as the preceding property sheet program. However, it requires this resource file.

```
#include <windows.h>
#include <commctrl.h>
#include "prop.h"

wizbmp BITMAP bp1.bmp

MyMenu MENU
{
  POPUP "&Wizard Demo"
  {
    MENUITEM "&Start Wizard\tF2", IDM_DIALOG
    MENUITEM "&Exit\tCtrl+X", IDM_EXIT
  }
  MENUITEM "&Help", IDM_HELP
}

MyMenu ACCELERATORS
{
  VK_F2, IDM_DIALOG, VIRTKEY
  "^X", IDM_EXIT
  VK_F1, IDM_HELP, VIRTKEY
}

MyDB DIALOG 0, 0, WIZ_CXDLG, WIZ_CYDLG
CAPTION "Wizard Demo - First Page"
STYLE WS_POPUP | WS_CAPTION | WS_SYSMENU | WS_VISIBLE
{
  DEFPUSHBUTTON "One", IDD_ONE, WIZ_BODYX, 10, 32, 14,
            WS_CHILD | WS_VISIBLE | WS_TABSTOP
  PUSHBUTTON "Two", IDD_TWO, WIZ_BODYX, 34, 32, 14,
            WS_CHILD | WS_VISIBLE | WS_TABSTOP
  PUSHBUTTON "Three", IDD_THREE, WIZ_BODYX, 58, 32, 14,
            WS_CHILD | WS_VISIBLE | WS_TABSTOP
  LISTBOX IDD_LB1, 56+WIZ_BODYX, 25, 50, 33, LBS_NOTIFY |
            WS_VISIBLE | WS_BORDER | WS_VSCROLL | WS_TABSTOP
}

MyDB2 DIALOG 0, 0, WIZ_CXDLG, WIZ_CYDLG
CAPTION "Wizard Demo - Second Page"
STYLE WS_POPUP | WS_CAPTION | WS_SYSMENU | WS_VISIBLE
{
  DEFPUSHBUTTON "Invert", IDD_INVERT, WIZ_BODYX, 10, 32, 14,
            WS_CHILD | WS_VISIBLE | WS_TABSTOP
```

```
    AUTOCHECKBOX "Check Box 1", IDD_CB1,
                56+WIZ_BODYX, 10, 70, 10
    AUTOCHECKBOX "Check Box 2", IDD_CB2,
                56+WIZ_BODYX, 30, 70, 10
    AUTOCHECKBOX "Check Box 3", IDD_CB3,
                56+WIZ_BODYX, 50, 70, 10
}

MyDB3 DIALOG 0, 0, WIZ_CXDLG, WIZ_CYDLG
CAPTION "Wizard Demo - Third Page"
STYLE WS_POPUP | WS_CAPTION | WS_SYSMENU | WS_VISIBLE
{
    DEFPUSHBUTTON "Top", IDD_TOP, 0, 10, 32, 14,
            WS_CHILD | WS_VISIBLE | WS_TABSTOP
    PUSHBUTTON "Bottom", IDD_BOTTOM, 0, 34, 32, 14,
            WS_CHILD | WS_VISIBLE | WS_TABSTOP
    AUTORADIOBUTTON "Radio Button 1", IDD_RB1,
                56, 10, 70, 10
    AUTORADIOBUTTON "Radio Button 2", IDD_RB2,
                56, 30, 70, 10
    AUTORADIOBUTTON "Radio Button 3", IDD_RB3,
                56, 50, 70, 10
}
```

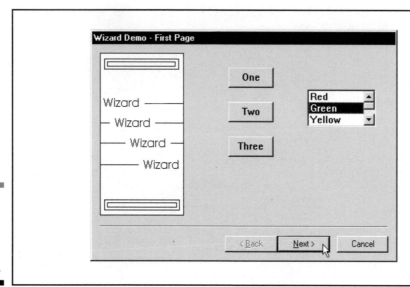

Sample output
from the
wizard
program
Figure 13-3a.

13

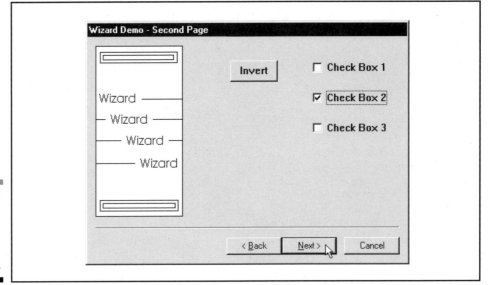

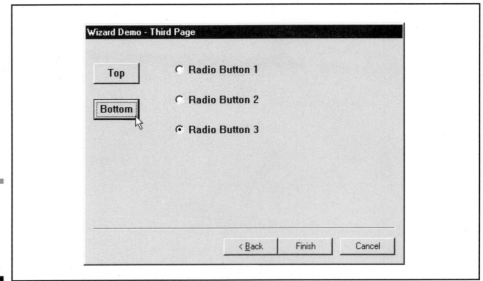

As you can see, very few changes are required to transform a property sheet control into a wizard. Notice, however, that you must enable the appropriate buttons each time a new page is activated. That is, your program must manually enable the Back, Next, and Finish buttons, as needed.

Since wizards are activated in a strictly linear sequence, the One, Two, and Three push buttons on the first page no longer perform any function. That is, it is not proper to activate pages out of sequence when using a wizard.

One final point. Notice that the last page does not display a bitmap. In this case, the controls are not positioned relative to **WIZ_BODYX** but relative to zero. If a page does not contain a bitmap, you may use the entire page for your controls.

Worth the Effort

Property sheets and wizards are two of Windows 98's more sophisticated controls. Although they require a bit of work to set up, they are worth the effort because they help you handle complex input situations. In particular, wizards solve a long-standing problem in the Windows interface: how to guide a user through a complex set of options and selections that require more than one screen full of controls. Now that you know how to handle wizards, you should use one whenever a complicated input operation is required.

CHAPTER 14

Exploring the Header, Month Calendar, and IP Address Controls

This chapter concludes our exploration of Windows 98's common controls by examining the header, the month calendar, and the IP address control. A *header control* is a bar that consists of column headings. The *month calendar* is a new control that displays a full month in calendar format and allows the user to pick a date. The month calendar control is as visually appealing as it is practical. The *IP address control* allows the user to enter an Internet Protocol address. It is one of the simpler common controls, but it is especially useful in today's online environment.

Header Controls

A header control helps you organize and manage columns of information.

You have undoubtedly seen header controls when using Windows 98. For example, when using the Explorer, the detailed view of files is presented using a header control. A header control is not just a set of passive column headings; it allows the user to adjust the width of each column. It is also possible to make the header control respond to mouse clicks. As you will see, the header control is one of the more useful of the common controls because it gives you a standardized way of displaying and managing columns of information.

A header control is created using **CreateWindow( )** or **CreateWindowEx( )**, specifying the **WC_HEADER** window class. A header control should also include the **WS_CHILD** style. Generally, a header control is created with zero width and height. The reason for this is that the control will need to be sized to fit the client area of its parent window. It must also be sized appropriately for the currently selected font. Fortunately, the header control has a mechanism that will determine its correct dimensions after it has been created, making it unnecessary for you to handle these matters manually.

Since a header control will be resized after it is created, you can use the following call to **CreateWindow( )** to create nearly any type of header control.

```
hHeadWnd = CreateWindow(WC_HEADER, NULL,
              WS_CHILD | WS_BORDER,
              CW_USEDEFAULT, CW_USEDEFAULT,
              0, 0, hParent,
              (HMENU) ID_HEADCONTROL,
              hInst, NULL);
```

Here, **hParent** is the handle of the parent window and **hInst** is the instance handle of the application. The ID of the header control is specified by

ID_HEADCONTROL. The dimensions of the control are irrelevant, and the control is not initially visible.

By default, the header control contains only labels and dividers. However, if you include the **HDS_BUTTONS** style when you create the control, then each heading will consist of a push button that is capable of responding to mouse events. It also retains all other attributes of a standard heading. For example, you can still resize a header button by dragging its divider.

A header control is empty when it is first created. Each heading must be added individually. As just mentioned, the control must also be sized to fit the parent window. For these reasons, the header control should initially be invisible. It should be displayed only after it has been given headings and its size has been adjusted. Thus, you must follow these steps when using a header control.

1. Obtain the proper dimensions for the header control and resize the control.
2. Add each heading to the control.
3. Make the header control visible.

To accomplish these steps, you will send various messages to the control.

Sending Messages to a Header Control

A header control responds to various messages. Some of the most frequently used messages are shown in Table 14-1. You can send a header control a message using **SendMessage( )**, specifying the handle of the control as the target. However, for most of these messages, Windows 98 defines macros, which are more convenient to use. Here are the header control message macros for the messages shown in Table 14-1:

```
BOOL Header_DeleteItem(HWND hHeadWnd, int index);

BOOL Header_GetItem(HWND hHeadWnd, int index,
            HDITEM *HdItemPtr);

int Header_GetItemCount(HWND hHeadWnd);

int Header_InsertItem(HWND hHeadWnd, int index,
            HDITEM * HdItemPtr);
```

14

BOOL Header_Layout(HWND *hHeadWnd*, HDLAYOUT *LayoutPtr*);

BOOL Header_SetItem(HWND *hHeadWnd*, int *index*,
HDITEM * *HdItemPtr*);

In all cases, *hHeadWnd* is the handle of the header control, and *index* is the index of the specific heading being affected. *HdItemPtr* is a pointer to an **HDITEM** structure. *LayoutPtr* is a pointer to an **HDLAYOUT** structure. Since these structures are crucial to creating and using a header control, let's examine them now.

Message	Meaning
HDM_DELETEITEM	Deletes a heading. Returns nonzero if successful and zero on failure. *wParam* specifies the index of the heading. *lParam* is zero.
HDM_GETITEM	Obtains heading information. Returns nonzero if successful and zero on failure. *wParam* specifies the index of the heading. *lParam* is a pointer to an **HDITEM** structure that receives the information. The value of the **mask** member of **HDITEM** specifies what information is obtained.
HDM_GETITEMCOUNT	Returns the number of headings or –1 on failure. *wParam* is zero. *lParam* is zero.
HDM_INSERTITEM	Inserts a heading. Returns index of item being inserted if successful and –1 on failure. *wParam* specifies the index after which the new heading is inserted. To insert the first heading, use zero for the index. To insert a heading at the end, specify an index that is greater than the number of headings currently in the header control. *lParam* is a pointer to an **HDITEM** structure that contains the heading being inserted.

Frequently Used Header Control Messages

Table 14-1.

Message	Meaning
HDM_LAYOUT	Obtains appropriate dimensions for the header control given the dimensions of its parent window's client area. Returns nonzero if successful and zero on failure. *wParam* is zero. *lParam* is a pointer to an **HDLAYOUT** structure. Its **prc** member contains the dimensions of the parent window's client area when sent. On return, its **pwpos** member contains the suggested dimensions for the header control.
HDM_SETITEM	Sets heading information. Returns nonzero if successful and zero on failure. *wParam* specifies the index of the heading. *lParam* is a pointer to an **HDITEM** structure that contains the heading's information. The value of the **mask** member of **HDITEM** specifies what information is set.

Frequently Used Header Control Messages (*continued*)

Table 14-1.

The HDITEM Structure

Each header item (i.e., heading) in a header control is defined by an **HDITEM** structure. This structure is shown here.

```
typedef struct _HDITEM
{
  UINT mask;
  int cxy;
  LPSTR pszText;
  HBITMAP hbm;
  int cchTextMax;
  int fmt;
  LPARAM lParam;
  int iImage;
  int iOrder;
} HDITEM;
```

The value of **mask** determines which of the other members of **HDITEM** contain information. It can be any combination of the following values.

14

Value	Meaning
HDI_BITMAP	**hbm** contains the handle of a bitmap.
HDI_FORMAT	**fmt** contains format flags.
HDI_HEIGHT	**cxy** contains the height of the header.
HDI_WIDTH	**cxy** contains the width of the header.
HDI_LPARAM	**lParam** contains information.
HDI_TEXT	**pszText** and **cchTextMax** contain information.
HDI_IMAGE	**iImage** contains information
HDI_ORDER	**iOrder** contains information.

The **cxy** member contains the width or height of the heading, depending upon whether **HDI_WIDTH** or **HDI_HEIGHT** is specified in **mask**.

pszText points to a string that acts as a column label. **cchTextMax** specifies the length of the string.

If a bitmap will be displayed in the heading, then the handle of the bitmap must be specified in **hbm**.

The value contained in **fmt** determines how the header is displayed. It consists of a combination of one justification value and one content value. The content values are as follows.

HDF_STRING	Header displays a string.
HDF_ BITMAP	Header displays a bitmap.
HDF_BITMAP_ON_RIGHT	Bitmap goes to right of text.
HDF_IMAGE	Header uses an image list.
HDF_OWNERDRAW	Owner draws.

The justification values are as follows.

HDF_LEFT	Left justify.
HDF_CENTER	Center.
HDF_RIGHT	Right justify.
HDF_RTLREADING	Text is displayed right-to-left.

The value in **lParam** is application dependent.

If the header includes an image list, then the contents of **iImage** specify the index of an image. The example in this chapter will not use an image list.

When obtaining information about an item, the position of the item, beginning at zero and moving from left to right, is contained in the **iOrder** field.

PORTABILITY: The **HDITEM** structure was formally called **HD_ITEM.** Some compilers may require the old name.

The HDLAYOUT Structure

The **HDLAYOUT** structure is used by the **HDM_LAYOUT** message to obtain appropriate dimensions for a header control given the dimensions of a bounding rectangle, which is usually the client area of the header control's parent window. **HDLAYOUT** is defined like this.

```
typedef struct _HDLAYOUT
{
  RECT *prc;
  WINDOWPOS *pwpos;
} HDLAYOUT;
```

Here, **prc** is a pointer to a **RECT** structure that specifies the size of the area in which the header control will be used. These dimensions are processed by the header control, which determines what its size must be to fit within the specified region. The adjusted dimensions are returned in the **WINDOWPOS** structure pointed to by **pwpos**.

You are already familiar with the **RECT** structure. The **WINDOWPOS** structure is defined like this:

```
typedef struct tagWINDOWPOS {
  HWND hwnd;
  HWND hwndInsertAfter;
  int x;
  int y;
  int cx;
  int cy;
```

14

```
  UINT flags;
} WINDOWPOS;
```

Here, **hwnd** is the handle of the header control. **hwndInsertAfter** is the
handle of the previous window in the Z-order. The upper-left corner of the
window is specified by **x** and **y**. The width is contained in **cx**, and the height
is contained in **cy**. The value in **flags** specifies various attributes associated
with the window. For our purposes, the **WINDOWPOS** structure is
initialized by the header control. There is no reason to alter the contents
of this structure.

PORTABILITY: The **HDLAYOUT** structure was formerly called
HD_LAYOUT. Some compilers may require the old name.

Sizing the Header

To resize a header control after it has been initialized, you must send the
control an **HDM_LAYOUT** message (or use the **Header_Layout( )** macro).
You must then use the dimensions and coordinates returned by this message
to adjust the size of the header control. For example, here is one way to
accomplish this.

```
RECT rect;
HDLAYOUT layout;
WINDOWPOS winpos;

/* get size of parent window */
GetClientRect(hParent, &rect);

/* get header control layout that will fit client area */
layout.pwpos = &winpos;
layout.prc = &rect;
Header_Layout(hHeadWnd, &layout);

/* dimension header to fit current size of client area */
MoveWindow(hHeadWnd, winpos.x, winpos.y,
           winpos.cx, winpos.cy, 0);
```

First, the size of the window in which the header control must fit is obtained by calling **GetClientRect( )**. Then these dimensions are passed to the header control using **Header_Layout( )**. On return, the **pwpos** member will contain the appropriate dimensions for the header control. These dimensions are then used in a call to the **MoveWindow( )** API function, which resizes and positions the header control as specified.

The prototype for **MoveWindow( )** is shown here:

BOOL MoveWindow(HWND *hwnd*, int *NewX*, int *NewY*, int *NewWidth*,
int *NewHeight*, BOOL *Repaint*);

Here, *hwnd* is the handle of the window being affected. The desired location of its upper-left corner is passed in *NewX* and *NewY*. The new width and height are specified in *NewWidth* and *NewHeight*. If *Repaint* is nonzero, the window will be repainted immediately after it has been resized. Otherwise, a repainting request will be put in the window's message queue for later processing. **MoveWindow( )** returns nonzero if successful and zero on failure.

As mentioned earlier, at this point the header control is still not visible. It should not be made visible until after the actual headings have been inserted in the control.

Inserting Headings into the Header Control

After the header control has been appropriately sized, you may insert headings into it. Each heading defines one column. To insert a heading, you must first load an **HDITEM** structure with information about the heading and then call **HeaderInsertItem( )**. For example, the following fragment inserts the first column's heading into a header control.

```
HDITEM hditem;

hditem.mask = HDI_FORMAT | HDI_WIDTH | HDI_TEXT;
hditem.pszText = "Heading #1";
hditem.cchTextMax = strlen(hditem.pszText);
hditem.cxy = 100;
hditem.fmt = HDF_STRING | HDF_LEFT;
Header_InsertItem(hHeadWnd, 0, &hditem);
```

14

In this example, the header displays a string which, in this case, is "Heading #1". The string is left justified. The width of the item is specified as 100, which is arbitrary in this case.

Remember, each time you insert an item, you must specify the index of the item that the new header will follow.

Displaying the Header Control

Once you have inserted all the headings, you can finally display the header control by calling **ShowWindow( )**. For example, to display the header control whose handle is **hHeadWnd**, use the following call.

Header controls are usually invisible when created and must be shown after they are sized and initialized.

```
ShowWindow(hHeadWnd, SW_SHOW); /* display the header control */
```

Keep in mind that, at this point, you have only created the header control, which defines headings for columns of data. You have not displayed any data. This will be done by other parts of your program. However, before you can use the header control, you will need to learn about the various notification messages that it can generate.

Header Notification Messages

Header controls are active rather than passive. That is, they generate messages when they are accessed by the user. For example, when the user resizes a heading, your program will be sent a message describing this event and it will need to respond appropriately. The header control generates several different messages. Which messages your program responds to is determined by how you utilize the control.

A header control sends a message to your program using the **WM_NOTIFY** message. When **WM_NOTIFY** is received, **wParam** contains the ID of the control generating the message. For most header control notification messages, **lParam** points to an **NMHEADER** structure, which is defined like this:

```
typedef struct tagNMHEADER
{
  NMHDR hdr;
  int iItem;
  int iButton;
  HDITEM *pitem;
} NMHEADER;
```

The **hdr** member is the standard **NMHDR** structure that we have been using. For **WM_NOTIFY** messages associated with header controls, **hdr.hwndFrom** is the handle of the header control that generated the message. **hdr.idFrom** is the header control's ID. The value of **hdr.code** contains the notification code, which describes what action has taken place. The header control notification codes are shown in Table 14-2.

The **iItem** member of **NMHEADER** specifies the index of the heading that was accessed. **iButton** specifies which mouse button was pressed. (0 for left, 1 for right, 2 for middle.) For most applications, this is not of interest because it will always be the left mouse button.

The **pitem** member points to an **HDITEM** structure that describes the heading that was accessed. However, when an **HDN_ITEMCLICK** notification is received, **pitem** is **NULL**.

When a header control is single-clicked, the **pitem** *member of* **HDITEM** *will be* **NULL**.

PORTABILITY: The **NMHEADER** structure was formerly called **HD_NOTIFY**.

Pay special attention to the "track" messages. When the user first begins to resize a heading, the header control sends an **HDN_BEGINTRACK** message. When the user finishes resizing, the control sends **HDN_ENDTRACK**. During the resizing, the control sends a stream of **HDN_TRACK** messages.

The Header Control Notification Codes
Table 14-2.

Code	Meaning
HDN_BEGINTRACK	User has started to resize a column heading. Your handler must return zero to enable tracking or nonzero to disable it.
HDN_DIVIDERDBLCLICK	User double-clicked on divider.
HDN_ENDTRACK	User has finished resizing a column heading.
HDN_ITEMCHANGED	A heading has been changed.
HDN_ITEMCHANGING	A heading is going to change. Your handler must return zero to allow a change to occur or nonzero to disallow the change.

14

Code	Meaning
HDN_ITEMCLICK	User clicked on a heading. Applies only to button-style headers.
HDN_ITEMDBLCLICK	User double-clicked on a heading. Applies only to button-style headers.
HDN_TRACK	User is in the process of resizing a column heading. Your handler must return zero to allow tracking to proceed or nonzero to stop tracking.

The Header
Control
Notification
Codes
(*continued*)
Table 14-3.

These messages can be used by your program to continually update the information displayed in the column that is being resized. Doing so allows the user to immediately see the effects of the changes being made. The example that follows demonstrates this procedure.

A Header Control Example

Now that you have seen all the pieces, a header control example can be assembled. The following program creates a header control that has four columns. The control is used to manage a database of books that contains the title of a book, the author, the publisher, and the copyright date. The entire header control program is shown here. Sample output is shown in Figure 14-1.

```
/* A simple header control example. */

#include <windows.h>
#include <commctrl.h>
#include <string.h>
#include <stdio.h>
#include "head.h"

#define NUMCOLS 4
#define DEFWIDTH 100
#define MINWIDTH 10
#define SPACING 8
#define NUMENTRIES 6

LRESULT CALLBACK WindowFunc(HWND, UINT, WPARAM, LPARAM);
```

```
HWND InitHeader(HWND hParent);
void InitDatabase(void);

char szWinName[] = "MyWin"; /* name of window class */

HINSTANCE hInst;
HWND hHeadWnd;

int HeaderHeight;

int columns[NUMCOLS] = {DEFWIDTH, DEFWIDTH,
                        DEFWIDTH, DEFWIDTH};

struct BookDatabase {
  char title[80];
  char author[80];
  char publisher[80];
  char date[20];
} data[NUMENTRIES];

int WINAPI WinMain(HINSTANCE hThisInst, HINSTANCE hPrevInst,
                   LPSTR lpszArgs, int nWinMode)
{
  MSG msg;
  WNDCLASSEX wcl;
  HACCEL hAccel;
  HWND hwnd;
  INITCOMMONCONTROLSEX cc;

  /* Define a window class. */
  wcl.cbSize = sizeof(WNDCLASSEX);

  wcl.hInstance = hThisInst; /* handle to this instance */
  wcl.lpszClassName = szWinName; /* window class name */
  wcl.lpfnWndProc = WindowFunc; /* window function */
  wcl.style = 0; /* default style */

  wcl.hIcon = LoadIcon(NULL, IDI_APPLICATION); /* standard icon */
  wcl.hIconSm = LoadIcon(NULL, IDI_APPLICATION); /* small icon */
  wcl.hCursor = LoadCursor(NULL, IDC_ARROW); /* cursor style */

  wcl.lpszMenuName = "MyMenu"; /* main menu */
  wcl.cbClsExtra = 0; /* no extra */
  wcl.cbWndExtra = 0; /* information needed */
```

14

```
/* Make the window white. */
wcl.hbrBackground = (HBRUSH) GetStockObject(WHITE_BRUSH);

/* Register the window class. */
if(!RegisterClassEx(&wcl)) return 0;

/* Now that a window class has been registered, a window
   can be created. */
hwnd = CreateWindow(
  szWinName, /* name of window class */
  "Using a Header Control", /* title */
  WS_OVERLAPPEDWINDOW, /* standard window */
  CW_USEDEFAULT, /* X coordinate - let Windows decide */
  CW_USEDEFAULT, /* Y coordinate - let Windows decide */
  CW_USEDEFAULT, /* width - let Windows decide */
  CW_USEDEFAULT, /* height - let Windows decide */
  HWND_DESKTOP, /* no parent window */
  NULL, /* no override of class menu */
  hThisInst, /* handle of this instance of the program */
  NULL /* no additional arguments */
);

hInst = hThisInst; /* save the current instance handle */

/* Load accelerators. */
hAccel = LoadAccelerators(hThisInst, "MyMenu");

/* Initialize the common controls. */
cc.dwSize = sizeof(INITCOMMONCONTROLSEX);
cc.dwICC = ICC_LISTVIEW_CLASSES;
InitCommonControlsEx(&cc);

/* Display the window. */
ShowWindow(hwnd, nWinMode);
UpdateWindow(hwnd);

/* Create the message loop. */
while(GetMessage(&msg, NULL, 0, 0))
{
  if(!TranslateAccelerator(hwnd, hAccel, &msg)) {
    TranslateMessage(&msg); /* translate keyboard message */
    DispatchMessage(&msg); /* return control to Windows 98 */
  }
}
return msg.wParam;
```

```
}

/* This function is called by Windows 98 and is passed
   messages from the message queue.
*/
LRESULT CALLBACK WindowFunc(HWND hwnd, UINT message,
                            WPARAM wParam, LPARAM lParam)
{
  int response;
  RECT rect;
  HDLAYOUT layout;
  WINDOWPOS winpos;
  NMHEADER *hdnptr;
  HDITEM *hdiptr;
  PAINTSTRUCT ps;
  TEXTMETRIC tm;
  SIZE size;

  char str[80];
  int i, j, ColStart, chrs;
  int entry;
  int linespacing;

  HDC hdc;

  switch(message) {
    case WM_CREATE:
      hHeadWnd = InitHeader(hwnd);
      InitDatabase();
      break;
    case WM_COMMAND:
      switch(LOWORD(wParam)) {
        case IDM_EXIT:
          response = MessageBox(hwnd, "Quit the Program?",
                                "Exit", MB_YESNO);
          if(response == IDYES) PostQuitMessage(0);
          break;
        case IDM_HELP:
          MessageBox(hwnd, "Try resizing the header.",
                     "Help", MB_OK);
          break;
      }
      break;
    case WM_SIZE:
      /* Resize the header control when its parent window
```

14

```
      changes size. */
   GetClientRect(hwnd, &rect);
   layout.prc = &rect;
   layout.pwpos = &winpos;
   Header_Layout(hHeadWnd, &layout);

   MoveWindow(hHeadWnd, winpos.x, winpos.y,
             winpos.cx, winpos.cy, 1);
   break;
case WM_NOTIFY:
   if(LOWORD(wParam) == ID_HEADCONTROL) {
     hdnptr = (NMHEADER *) lParam;
     hdiptr = (HDITEM *) hdnptr->pitem;
     switch(hdnptr->hdr.code) {
       case HDN_TRACK: /* user changing column width */
         GetClientRect(hwnd, &rect);
         if(hdiptr->cxy < MINWIDTH) {
           hdiptr->cxy = MINWIDTH;
           columns[hdnptr->iItem] = MINWIDTH;
         }
         else
           columns[hdnptr->iItem] = hdiptr->cxy;
         rect.top = HeaderHeight;
         InvalidateRect(hwnd, &rect, 1);
         break;
       /* try handling other header control messages here */
     }
   }
   break;
case WM_PAINT:
   hdc = BeginPaint(hwnd, &ps);

   GetTextMetrics(hdc, &tm);
   linespacing = tm.tmHeight + tm.tmInternalLeading;

   for(entry = 0; entry < NUMENTRIES; entry++) {
     ColStart = 0;
     for(i=0; i<NUMCOLS; i++) {
       switch(i) {
         case 0: strcpy(str, data[entry].title);
           break;
         case 1: strcpy(str, data[entry].author);
           break;
         case 2: strcpy(str, data[entry].publisher);
           break;
```

```
         case 3: strcpy(str, data[entry].date);
           break;
       }

       GetTextExtentPoint32(hdc, str, strlen(str), &size);
       j = 2;
       while((columns[i]-SPACING) < size.cx) {
         chrs = columns[i] / tm.tmAveCharWidth;
         strcpy(&str[chrs-j], "...");
         GetTextExtentPoint32(hdc, str, strlen(str), &size);
         j++;
       }

       TextOut(hdc, ColStart+SPACING,
               HeaderHeight+(entry*linespacing),
               str, strlen(str));

       ColStart += columns[i];
     }
   }
   EndPaint(hwnd, &ps);
   break;
 case WM_DESTROY: /* terminate the program */
   PostQuitMessage(0);
   break;
 default:
   /* Let Windows 98 process any messages not specified in
      the preceding switch statement. */
   return DefWindowProc(hwnd, message, wParam, lParam);
 }
 return 0;
}

/* Initialize the header control. */
HWND InitHeader(HWND hParent)
{
 HWND hHeadWnd;
 RECT rect;
 HDLAYOUT layout;
 WINDOWPOS winpos;
 HDITEM hditem;

 GetClientRect(hParent, &rect);

 /* create the header control */
```

```
hHeadWnd = CreateWindow(WC_HEADER, NULL,
                 WS_CHILD | WS_BORDER,
                 CW_USEDEFAULT, CW_USEDEFAULT,
                 0, 0, hParent,
                 (HMENU) ID_HEADCONTROL,
                 hInst, NULL);

/* get header control layout that will fit client area */
layout.pwpos = &winpos;
layout.prc = &rect;
Header_Layout(hHeadWnd, &layout);

/* dimension header to fit current size of client area */
MoveWindow(hHeadWnd, winpos.x, winpos.y,
           winpos.cx, winpos.cy, 0);

HeaderHeight = winpos.cy; /* save height of header */

/* insert items into the header */
hditem.mask = HDI_FORMAT | HDI_WIDTH | HDI_TEXT;
hditem.pszText = "Title";
hditem.cchTextMax = strlen(hditem.pszText);
hditem.cxy = DEFWIDTH;
hditem.fmt = HDF_STRING | HDF_LEFT;
Header_InsertItem(hHeadWnd, 0, &hditem);

hditem.pszText = "Author";
hditem.cchTextMax = strlen(hditem.pszText);
Header_InsertItem(hHeadWnd, 1, &hditem);

hditem.pszText = "Publisher";
hditem.cchTextMax = strlen(hditem.pszText);
Header_InsertItem(hHeadWnd, 2, &hditem);

hditem.pszText = "Copyright";
hditem.cchTextMax = strlen(hditem.pszText);
Header_InsertItem(hHeadWnd, 3, &hditem);

ShowWindow(hHeadWnd, SW_SHOW); /* display the header control */

return hHeadWnd;
}

/* Sample data to illustrate the header control. */
void InitDatabase(void)
```

```
{
  strcpy(data[0].title, "C++ From the Ground Up, 2nd Ed.");
  strcpy(data[0].author, "Herbert Schildt");
  strcpy(data[0].publisher, "Osborne/McGraw-Hill");
  strcpy(data[0].date, "1998");

  strcpy(data[1].title, "The C++ Programming Language, 3rd Ed.");
  strcpy(data[1].author, "Bjarne Stroustrup");
  strcpy(data[1].publisher, "Addison-Wesley");
  strcpy(data[1].date, "1997");

  strcpy(data[2].title,
         "Windows NT 4 Programming From the Ground Up");
  strcpy(data[2].author, "Herbert Schildt");
  strcpy(data[2].publisher, "Osborne/McGraw-Hill");
  strcpy(data[2].date, "1997");

  strcpy(data[3].title, "C++: The Complete Reference, 3rd Ed.");
  strcpy(data[3].author, "Herbert Schildt");
  strcpy(data[3].publisher, "Osborne/McGraw-Hill");
  strcpy(data[3].date, "1998");

  strcpy(data[4].title, "The Standard C++ Library");
  strcpy(data[4].author, "P. J. Plauger");
  strcpy(data[4].publisher, "Prentice Hall");
  strcpy(data[4].date, "1995");

  strcpy(data[5].title,
         "Java Beans Programming From the Ground Up");
  strcpy(data[5].author, "Joe O'Neil");
  strcpy(data[5].publisher, "Osborne/McGraw-Hill");
  strcpy(data[5].date, "1998");

}
```

The program uses the following resource file.

```
#include <windows.h>
#include "head.h"

MyMenu MENU
{
  POPUP "&Options"
  {
    MENUITEM "&Exit\tCtrl+X", IDM_EXIT
```

14

```
  }
  MENUITEM "&Help", IDM_HELP
}

MyMenu ACCELERATORS
{
  "^X", IDM_EXIT
  VK_F1, IDM_HELP, VIRTKEY
}
```

The header file HEAD.H is shown here.

```
#define IDM_EXIT         100
#define IDM_HELP         101
#define IDM_RESET        102

#define ID_HEADCONTROL   500
```

A Closer Look at the Header Control Example

When the program receives the **WM_CREATE** message, two functions are called: **InitHeader( )** and **InitDatabase( )**. The program uses the function **InitHeader( )** to construct and initialize the header control. It is passed the handle of its parent window. It returns a handle to the header control. The

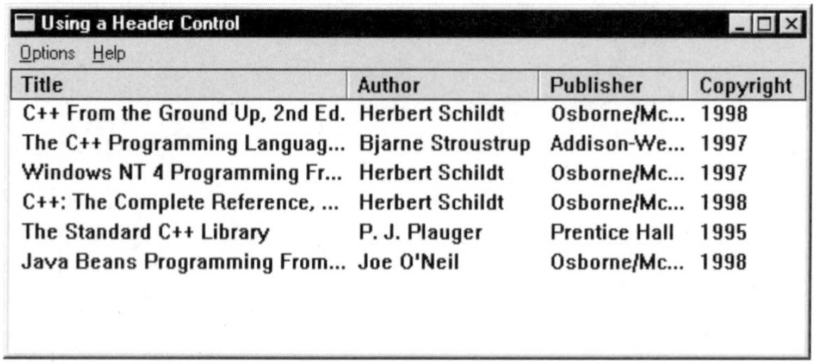

Sample output from the header control example program

Figure 14-1.

header control is given an ID value of **ID_HEADCONTROL**. This value is used to identify the header control when a **WM_NOTIFY** message is received. (Remember, other types of controls also generate **WM_NOTIFY** messages.) Most of the other elements inside the function should be clear because they implement the steps described earlier in this chapter. In this example, all columns are given the same default width, which is 100. Of course, the columns' widths may be adjusted by the user dynamically.

Notice that the height of the header control is saved in the global variable **HeaderHeight**. Since the header control occupies space at the top of the client area of the parent window, **HeaderHeight** is used as an offset when information is displayed in the main window.

Once the header control has been constructed, the database of books is initialized using **InitDatabase( )**. The database is stored in an array of **BookDatabase** structures called **data**. The **BookDatabase** structure contains character arrays that are used to hold information about books. The contents of the **data** array are displayed each time a **WM_PAINT** message is received. Notice how each string is truncated if it is too long to fit within the column. When this is the case, an ellipsis is displayed. The size of each column is stored in the **columns** array.

Each time an **HDN_TRACK** message is received, the program uses the new width of the header to adjust the contents of the information displayed in the columns. It does this by updating the **columns** array with the new column width and then forcing a repaint (by calling **InvalidateRect( )**). Thus, as the user drags the divider, the information in the columns below the header control will be dynamically updated, allowing the user to see the effects of expanding or contracting a column as they are occurring. This makes it much easier for the user to set each column width appropriately because it eliminates guesswork.

There is one other point of interest in this program. Examine the code under the **WM_SIZE** case. As you know, a window receives a **WM_SIZE** message when its size is changed. The program responds to this message by altering the size of the header control so that it continues to fit its parent window. Keep in mind that this step is not technically necessary. In fact, there can be applications of a header control in which you will want its size to remain fixed. However, in this example, the header control is resized to fit the new dimensions of the window.

Before moving on, try experimenting with the header control. For example, observe the effect of using button headers, which are created by including the **HDS_BUTTONS** style. Also try responding to mouse clicks on the button headers.

14

The Month Calendar Control

One very useful new common control is the month calendar. The month calendar control displays one or more months of a calendar and allows you to pick a date. By default, it displays and selects the current date. The user may change the month or year of the calendar. Various pop-up menus, up-down controls, and arrows are automatically supplied making the control exceedingly convenient to use. In fact, the month calendar control is so well designed that although it allows a number of interesting variations, its default mode of operation is what you will usually want. It is also visually appealing and adds professionalism to any application that needs to work with dates.

A month calendar control displays a calendar and allows the user to pick a date.

Creating a Month Calendar

To create a month calendar, you will use either **CreateWindow( )** or **CreateWindowEx( )**, specifying the **MONTHCAL_CLASS** window class. The control should include the **WS_CHILD** style. It will usually include the **WS_VISIBLE** and **WS_BORDER** styles, too. The month calendar is usually created with zero dimensions because its precise size can only be determined at runtime. (Its size is partially determined by the type font, for example.) As you will see, the month calendar provides an easy means of accomplishing this.

The month calendar supports a number of style options that can be specified when it is created. We won't be using any, but they are shown in Table 14-3 for your information.

Style	Effect
MCS_DAYSTATE	Calendar will request information about which days should be marked as special (such as holidays, etc.).
MCS_MULTISELECT	Allows a range of dates to be selected.
MCS_NOTODAY	The current date is not shown.
MCS_NOTODAYCIRCLE	The current date is not circled.
MCS_WEEKNUMBERS	The number of each week is displayed.

Month Calendar Style Options
Table 14-4.

Sending a Month Calendar Messages

A month calendar control responds to various messages. Several commonly used ones are shown in Table 14-4. You can send a month calendar control a message using **SendMessage( )**, specifying the handle of the control as the target. However, Windows 98 defines macros for this purpose, which are more convenient to use. The month calendar control message macros corresponding to the ones in Table 14-4 are shown next.

Message	Meaning
MCM_GETCURSEL	Obtains the currently selected date. Returns nonzero if successful and zero on failure. *wParam* is zero. *lParam* is a pointer to a **SYSTEMTIME** structure that receives the currently selected date.
MCM_GETMINREQRECT	Obtains the dimensions for the smallest window that can hold one month. Returns nonzero if successful and zero on failure. *wParam* is zero. *lParam* points to a **RECT** structure that receives the dimensions.
MCM_GETTODAY	Obtains the current date. Returns nonzero if successful and zero on failure. *wParam* is zero. *lParam* points to a **SYSTEMTIME** structure that receives the current date.
MCM_SETCURSEL	Selects a date. Returns nonzero if successful and zero on failure. *wParam* is zero. *lParam* is a pointer to a **SYSTEMTIME** structure that specifies the desired date.
MCM_SETTODAY	Sets the current date. No return value. *wParam* is zero. *lParam* points to a **SYSTEMTIME** structure that specifies the current date.

Commonly
Used Month
Calendar
Messages
Table 14-5.

14

BOOL MonthCal_GetCurSel(HWND *hCal*, SYSTEMTIME **st*);

BOOL MonthCal_GetMinReqRect(HWND *hCal*, RECT **rect*);

BOOL MonthCal_GetToday(HWND *hCal*, SYSTEMTIME **st*);

BOOL MonthCal_SetCurSel(HWND *hCal*, SYSTEMTIME **st*);

VOID MonthCal_SetToday(HWND *hCal*, SYSTEMTIME **st*);

When setting or getting a date, the date is stored in a **SYSTEMTIME** structure, which is defined like this.

```
typedef struct _SYSTEMTIME {
  WORD wYear; /* year */
  WORD wMonth; /* month (1 through 12) */
  WORD wDayOfWeek; /* day of week (0 through 6) */
  WORD wDay; /* day of month (1 through 31) */
  WORD wHour; /* hour */
  WORD wMinute; /* minutes */
  WORD wSecond; /* seconds */
  WORD wMilliseconds; /* milliseconds */
} SYSTEMTIME;
```

As you can see, **SYSTEMTIME** includes both date and time members. Although the calendar control does not actually deal with times, it will handle them for you. For example, when the control is created, the current time is also stored in the current date.

Month Calendar Notification Messages

A month calendar is mostly a passive control. However, it can generate the following notification messages via **WM_NOTIFY**.

MCN_GETDAYSTATE	Sent to determine how to display a date. For example, holidays may be displayed in bold.
MCN_SELCHANGE	The selected date was changed.
MCN_SELECT	The user selected a date.

We won't be using any of these messages in the following example, but they may be valuable to your own applications.

Sizing the Month Calendar Control

As explained, you will normally create a month calendar with zero
dimensions and then resize it to fit its minimum dimensions. To obtain the
dimensions of the minimal rectangle that can hold one month, send a
MCM_GETMINREQRECT message. Using the dimensions returned by
this message, you can resize the month calendar using a function such as
MoveWindow( ), described earlier. Here is the sequence used to accomplish
these steps by the example program.

```
hCal = CreateWindow(MONTHCAL_CLASS,
          "Month Calendar", /* not used */
          WS_BORDER | WS_VISIBLE | WS_CHILD,
          0, 0, 0, 0,
          hdwnd, NULL, hInst, NULL);

/* now, size the calendar */
MonthCal_GetMinReqRect(hCal, &rect); /* get min size */
MoveWindow(hCal, 0, 0, rect.right, rect.bottom, 1);
```

After this sequence has executed, the control will be precisely large enough to
hold one month's worth of dates, plus all of the menus and controls required
by the calendar.

Demonstrating a Month Calendar Control

The following program demonstrates a month calendar. The main menu
allows you to activate the calendar or display the currently selected date.
The calendar is displayed within a dialog box. In addition to the calendar
itself, the dialog box holds three buttons: Show Date, OK, and Cancel.
Pressing Show Date shows the currently selected date. Pressing OK stores
the currently selected date in the global variable **st**. Pressing Cancel leaves
the previous contents of **st** unchanged. The contents of **st** are used to display
the currently selected date from the main menu. Sample output is shown in
Figure 14-2.

```
/* Demonstrate a month calendar. */

#include <windows.h>
#include <commctrl.h>
#include <stdio.h>
#include "cal.h"
```

14

```c
LRESULT CALLBACK WindowFunc(HWND, UINT, WPARAM, LPARAM);
BOOL CALLBACK DialogFunc(HWND, UINT, WPARAM, LPARAM);

char szWinName[] = "MyWin"; /* name of window class */

HINSTANCE hInst;
HWND hCal;
SYSTEMTIME st;
int dateset = 0;

int WINAPI WinMain(HINSTANCE hThisInst, HINSTANCE hPrevInst,
                   LPSTR lpszArgs, int nWinMode)
{
  MSG msg;
  HWND hwnd;
  WNDCLASSEX wcl;
  HACCEL hAccel;
  INITCOMMONCONTROLSEX cc;

  /* Define a window class. */
  wcl.cbSize = sizeof(WNDCLASSEX);

  wcl.hInstance = hThisInst; /* handle to this instance */
  wcl.lpszClassName = szWinName; /* window class name */
  wcl.lpfnWndProc = WindowFunc; /* window function */
  wcl.style = 0; /* default style */

  wcl.hIcon = LoadIcon(NULL, IDI_APPLICATION); /* standard icon */
  wcl.hIconSm = LoadIcon(NULL, IDI_APPLICATION); /* small icon */
  wcl.hCursor = LoadCursor(NULL, IDC_ARROW); /* cursor style */

  wcl.lpszMenuName = "MyMenu"; /* main menu */
  wcl.cbClsExtra = 0; /* no extra */
  wcl.cbWndExtra = 0; /* information needed */

  /* Make the window white. */
  wcl.hbrBackground = (HBRUSH) GetStockObject(WHITE_BRUSH);

  /* Register the window class. */
  if(!RegisterClassEx(&wcl)) return 0;

  /* Now that a window class has been registered, a window
     can be created. */
  hwnd = CreateWindow(
```

```
    szWinName, /* name of window class */
    "Using a Month Calendar", /* title */
    WS_OVERLAPPEDWINDOW, /* window style - normal */
    CW_USEDEFAULT, /* X coordinate - let Windows decide */
    CW_USEDEFAULT, /* Y coordinate - let Windows decide */
    CW_USEDEFAULT, /* width - let Windows decide */
    CW_USEDEFAULT, /* height - let Windows decide */
    HWND_DESKTOP, /* no parent window */
    NULL, /* no override of class menu */
    hThisInst, /* handle of this instance of the program */
    NULL /* no additional arguments */
  );

  /* Initialize the common controls. */
  cc.dwSize = sizeof(INITCOMMONCONTROLSEX);
  cc.dwICC = ICC_DATE_CLASSES;
  InitCommonControlsEx(&cc);

  hInst = hThisInst; /* save the current instance handle */

  /* Load accelerators. */
  hAccel = LoadAccelerators(hThisInst, "MyMenu");

  /* Display the window. */
  ShowWindow(hwnd, nWinMode);
  UpdateWindow(hwnd);

  /* Create the message loop. */
  while(GetMessage(&msg, NULL, 0, 0))
  {
    if(!TranslateAccelerator(hwnd, hAccel, &msg)) {
      TranslateMessage(&msg); /* Translate keyboard messages */
      DispatchMessage(&msg); /* return control to Windows 98 */
    }
  }
  return msg.wParam;
}

/* This function is called by Windows 98 and is passed
   messages from the message queue.
*/
LRESULT CALLBACK WindowFunc(HWND hwnd, UINT message,
                            WPARAM wParam, LPARAM lParam)
{
  int response;
  char str[255];
```

14

```
switch(message) {
  case WM_COMMAND:
    switch(LOWORD(wParam)) {
      case IDM_DIALOG:
        DialogBox(hInst, "MyDB", hwnd, (DLGPROC) DialogFunc);
        break;
      case IDM_GETDATE:
        if(dateset) {
          sprintf(str, "%d/%d/%d",
                  st.wMonth, st.wDay, st.wYear);
          MessageBox(hwnd, str, "Date Selected", MB_OK);
        } else
          MessageBox(hwnd, "Date not set", "Error", MB_OK);
        break;
      case IDM_EXIT:
        response = MessageBox(hwnd, "Quit the Program?",
                             "Exit", MB_YESNO);
        if(response == IDYES) PostQuitMessage(0);
        break;
      case IDM_HELP:
        MessageBox(hwnd, "Try the calendar.", "Help", MB_OK);
        break;
    }
    break;
  case WM_DESTROY: /* terminate the program */
    PostQuitMessage(0);
    break;
  default:
    /* Let Windows 98 process any messages not specified in
       the preceding switch statement. */
    return DefWindowProc(hwnd, message, wParam, lParam);
}
return 0;
}

/* Dialog function. */
BOOL CALLBACK DialogFunc(HWND hdwnd, UINT message,
                         WPARAM wParam, LPARAM lParam)
{
  static HWND hCal;
  RECT rect;
  char str[255];
  SYSTEMTIME tempst;

  switch(message) {
    case WM_INITDIALOG:
```

```
            hCal = CreateWindow(MONTHCAL_CLASS,
                        "Month Calendar", /* not used */
                        WS_BORDER | WS_VISIBLE | WS_CHILD,
                        0, 0, 0, 0,
                        hdwnd, NULL, hInst, NULL);

          /* now, size the calendar */
          MonthCal_GetMinReqRect(hCal, &rect); /* get min size */
          MoveWindow(hCal, 0, 0, rect.right, rect.bottom, 1);
          return 1;
      case WM_COMMAND:
        switch(LOWORD(wParam)) {
          case ID_GETDATE:
            MonthCal_GetCurSel(hCal, &tempst);
            sprintf(str, "%d/%d/%d", tempst.wMonth,
                    tempst.wDay, tempst.wYear);
            MessageBox(hdwnd, str, "Date Selected", MB_OK);
            return 1;
          case IDOK:
            MonthCal_GetCurSel(hCal, &st);
            dateset = 1;
          case IDCANCEL:
            EndDialog(hdwnd, 0);
            return 1;
        }
  }
  return 0;
}
```

The program uses the following resource file.

```
#include <windows.h>
#include "cal.h"

MyMenu MENU
{
  POPUP "&Calendar" {
    MENUITEM "&Calendar\tF2", IDM_DIALOG
    MENUITEM "&Get Selected Date\tF3", IDM_GETDATE
    MENUITEM "E&xit\tCtrl+X", IDM_EXIT
  }
  MENUITEM "&Help", IDM_HELP
}

MyMenu ACCELERATORS
```

14

```
{
  VK_F2, IDM_DIALOG, VIRTKEY
  VK_F3, IDM_GETDATE, VIRTKEY
  "^X", IDM_EXIT
  VK_F1, IDM_HELP, VIRTKEY
}

MyDB DIALOG 18, 18, 150, 78
CAPTION "Demonstrate a Month Calendar"
STYLE DS_MODALFRAME | WS_POPUP | WS_CAPTION | WS_SYSMENU
{
  DEFPUSHBUTTON "OK", IDOK, 100, 10, 38, 16,
                WS_CHILD | WS_VISIBLE | WS_TABSTOP
  PUSHBUTTON "Show Date", ID_GETDATE, 100, 30, 38, 16,
                WS_CHILD | WS_VISIBLE | WS_TABSTOP
  PUSHBUTTON "Cancel", IDCANCEL, 100, 50, 38, 16,
                WS_CHILD | WS_VISIBLE | WS_TABSTOP

}
```

The header file CAL.H is shown here.

```
#define IDM_DIALOG  100
#define IDM_GETDATE 101
#define IDM_EXIT    102
#define IDM_HELP    103

#define ID_GETDATE  201
```

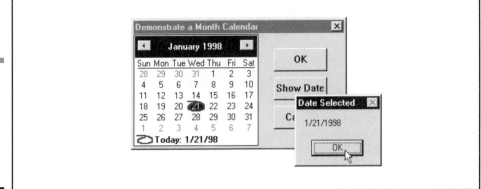

Sample output from the month calendar control program

Figure 14-2.

IN DEPTH

Show More Than One Month

While most applications will display only one month at a time when using a month calendar control, you are not limited to this. To show more than one month, simply size the calendar to some multiple of the dimensions returned by **MCM_GETMINREQRECT**. You will also need to add a little extra space for the gap between each month. For example, the following sequence creates a calendar that shows two months.

```
MonthCal_GetMinReqRect(hCal, &rect);
MoveWindow(hCal, 0, 0, (rect.right*2)+10, rect.bottom, 1);
```

Here is how the calendar control looks:

Using an IP Address Control

The last common control that we will look at is also one of the simplest: the IP address control. This control is essentially a dedicated edit box that supports the entry of a numeric Internet Protocol address of the form

An IP address control supports the entry of an Internet Protocol address.

    nnn . nnn . nnn . nnn

An IP Address control is created using **CreateWindow( )** or **CreateWindowEx( )**, specifying the **WC_IPADDRESS** class. You will usually specify the **WS_VISIBLE** and **WS_CHILD** styles.

14

IP addresses are contained in a four-byte integer, in which the high-order byte contains the leftmost field.

IP Address Control Messages

An IP address control responds to several messages. They are shown in Table 14-5. Most of the time the only message you need to send is **IPM_GETADDRESS**. This obtains the IP address currently held in the control. However, you might want to change the range of addresses accepted by the control. By default, an IP address control restricts the range of each field to 0 through 255. You can change this using **IPM_SETRANGE**.

An IP address control generates only one notification message: **IPN_FIELDCHANGED**. This is sent via a **WM_NOTIFY** message. The value of *lParam* associated with the **WM_NOTIFY** message points to an **NMIPADDRESS** structure, which is defined like this.

```
typedef struct tagNMIPADDRESS {
  NMHDR hdr;
  int iField;
  int iValue;
} NMIPADDRESS;
```

Here, **hdr** is the standard **NMHDR** structure associated with notification messages. The value in **iField** contains the index of the field that was changed. The leftmost field is zero. **iValue** contains the new value of the field. You can override this value by assigning it a different value. This might be useful if an out-of-range value is entered by the user.

Message	Meaning
IPM_CLEARADDRESS	Resets (i.e., zeros) the control. No return value. *wParam* is zero. *lParam* is zero.
IPM_GETADDRESS	Obtains the current address. Returns the number of fields that contain digits. *wParam* is zero. *lParam* points to a **DWORD** variable that will receive the current address.
IPM_ISBLANK	Returns nonzero if the control is empty. Returns zero if at least one field contains digits. *wParam* is zero. *lParam* is zero.
IPM_SETADDRESS	Sets the current address. No return value. *wParam* is zero. *lParam* specifies the address.

IP Address
Control
Messages
Table 14-6.

Message	Meaning
IPM_SETFOCUS	Input focus is set to the IP address control. No return value. *wParam* determines which field will be selected. If this value is zero through three, then the specified field is selected. If *wParam* is four or greater, then the first empty field is selected, or the first field is selected if all fields contain digits. *lParam* is zero.
IPM_SETRANGE	Sets the range of addresses that the control will accept. Returns nonzero if successful and zero on failure. *wParam* contains the index of the field being set. *lParam* specifies the range using a WORD value in which the minimum is in the low-order byte and the maximum is in the high-order byte.

IP Address
Control
Messages
(*continued*)
Table 14-7.

IP Address Macros

The IP address control defines several macros that make it easier to access the fields within an IP address. They are shown here.

BYTE FIRST_IPADDRESS(LPARAM *IPaddr*);

BYTE SECOND_IPADDRESS(LPARAM *IPaddr*);

BYTE THIRD_IPADDRESS(LPARAM *IPaddr*);

BYTE FOURTH_IPADDRESS(LPARAM *IPaddr*);

Each returns the specified field from the specified IP address.

You can construct an IP address using this macro:

LPARAM MAKEIPADDRESS(BYTE *f1*, BYTE *f2*, BYTE *f3*, BYTE *f4*);

Here, *f1* through *f4* specify the values for the address fields.

You can construct a two-byte value that defines a range using this macro:

LPARAM MAKERANGE(BYTE *min*, BYTE *max*);

14

An IP Address Control Example

The following program demonstrates an IP address control. The control is contained in a dialog box. When the dialog box is activated, it displays the

control and allows the user to enter an address. When the user presses the IP
Address button, the current address is obtained and displayed inside a
message box. Sample output is shown in Figure 14-3.

```c
/* Demonstrate an IP address control. */

#include <windows.h>
#include <commctrl.h>
#include <stdio.h>
#include "ip.h"


LRESULT CALLBACK WindowFunc(HWND, UINT, WPARAM, LPARAM);
BOOL CALLBACK DialogFunc(HWND, UINT, WPARAM, LPARAM);

char szWinName[] = "MyWin"; /* name of window class */

HINSTANCE hInst;
HWND hIP;

int WINAPI WinMain(HINSTANCE hThisInst, HINSTANCE hPrevInst,
                   LPSTR lpszArgs, int nWinMode)
{
  MSG msg;
  HWND hwnd;
  WNDCLASSEX wcl;
  HACCEL hAccel;
  INITCOMMONCONTROLSEX cc;

  /* Define a window class. */
  wcl.cbSize = sizeof(WNDCLASSEX);

  wcl.hInstance = hThisInst; /* handle to this instance */
  wcl.lpszClassName = szWinName; /* window class name */
  wcl.lpfnWndProc = WindowFunc; /* window function */
  wcl.style = 0; /* default style */

  wcl.hIcon = LoadIcon(NULL, IDI_APPLICATION); /* standard icon */
  wcl.hIconSm = LoadIcon(NULL, IDI_APPLICATION); /* small icon */
  wcl.hCursor = LoadCursor(NULL, IDC_ARROW); /* cursor style */

  wcl.lpszMenuName = "MyMenu"; /* main menu */
  wcl.cbClsExtra = 0; /* no extra */
  wcl.cbWndExtra = 0; /* information needed */
```

```
/* Make the window white. */
wcl.hbrBackground = (HBRUSH) GetStockObject(WHITE_BRUSH);

/* Register the window class. */
if(!RegisterClassEx(&wcl)) return 0;

/* Now that a window class has been registered, a window
   can be created. */
hwnd = CreateWindow(
  szWinName, /* name of window class */
  "Using an IP Address Control", /* title */
  WS_OVERLAPPEDWINDOW, /* window style - normal */
  CW_USEDEFAULT, /* X coordinate - let Windows decide */
  CW_USEDEFAULT, /* Y coordinate - let Windows decide */
  CW_USEDEFAULT, /* width - let Windows decide */
  CW_USEDEFAULT, /* height - let Windows decide */
  HWND_DESKTOP, /* no parent window */
  NULL, /* no override of class menu */
  hThisInst, /* handle of this instance of the program */
  NULL /* no additional arguments */
);

/* Initialize the common controls. */
cc.dwSize = sizeof(INITCOMMONCONTROLSEX);
cc.dwICC = ICC_INTERNET_CLASSES;
InitCommonControlsEx(&cc);

hInst = hThisInst; /* save the current instance handle */

/* Load accelerators. */
hAccel = LoadAccelerators(hThisInst, "MyMenu");

/* Display the window. */
ShowWindow(hwnd, nWinMode);
UpdateWindow(hwnd);

/* Create the message loop. */
while(GetMessage(&msg, NULL, 0, 0))
{
  if(!TranslateAccelerator(hwnd, hAccel, &msg)) {
    TranslateMessage(&msg); /* Translate keyboard messages */
    DispatchMessage(&msg); /* return control to Windows 98 */
  }
}
return msg.wParam;
```

14

```
}

/* This function is called by Windows 98 and is passed
   messages from the message queue.
*/
LRESULT CALLBACK WindowFunc(HWND hwnd, UINT message,
                              WPARAM wParam, LPARAM lParam)
{
  int response;

  switch(message) {
    case WM_COMMAND:
      switch(LOWORD(wParam)) {
        case IDM_DIALOG:
          DialogBox(hInst, "MyDB", hwnd, (DLGPROC) DialogFunc);
          break;
        case IDM_EXIT:
          response = MessageBox(hwnd, "Quit the Program?",
                                 "Exit", MB_YESNO);
          if(response == IDYES) PostQuitMessage(0);
          break;
        case IDM_HELP:
          MessageBox(hwnd, "Try the IP Address Control.",
                     "Help", MB_OK);
          break;
      }
      break;
    case WM_DESTROY: /* terminate the program */
      PostQuitMessage(0);
      break;
    default:
      /* Let Windows 98 process any messages not specified in
         the preceding switch statement. */
      return DefWindowProc(hwnd, message, wParam, lParam);
  }
  return 0;
}

/* Dialog function. */
BOOL CALLBACK DialogFunc(HWND hdwnd, UINT message,
                           WPARAM wParam, LPARAM lParam)
{
  static HWND hIP;
  char str[255];
  DWORD IPaddr;
```

```
switch(message) {
  case WM_INITDIALOG:
    hIP = CreateWindow(WC_IPADDRESS,
                "IP Address", /* not used */
                WS_BORDER | WS_VISIBLE |
                WS_CHILD | WS_TABSTOP,
                20, 0, 140, 20,
                hdwnd, NULL, hInst, NULL);
    return 1;
  case WM_COMMAND:
    switch(LOWORD(wParam)) {
      case ID_GETADDR:
        SendMessage(hIP, IPM_GETADDRESS, 0, (LPARAM) &IPaddr);
        sprintf(str, "%d.%d.%d.%d",
                FIRST_IPADDRESS(IPaddr),
                SECOND_IPADDRESS(IPaddr),
                THIRD_IPADDRESS(IPaddr),
                FOURTH_IPADDRESS(IPaddr)
              );
        MessageBox(hdwnd, str, "IP Address", MB_OK);
        return 1;
      case IDOK:
      case IDCANCEL:
        EndDialog(hdwnd, 0);
        return 1;
    }
  }
  return 0;
}
```

The resource file for the program is shown here.

```
#include <windows.h>
#include "ip.h"

MyMenu MENU
{
  POPUP "&IP Address" {
    MENUITEM "&Get IP Address\tF2", IDM_DIALOG
    MENUITEM "E&xit\tCtrl+X", IDM_EXIT
  }
  MENUITEM "&Help", IDM_HELP
}
```

14

```
MyMenu ACCELERATORS
{
  VK_F2, IDM_DIALOG, VIRTKEY
  "^X", IDM_EXIT
  VK_F1, IDM_HELP, VIRTKEY
}

MyDB DIALOG 18, 18, 90, 50
CAPTION "Use an IP Address Control"
STYLE DS_MODALFRAME | WS_POPUP | WS_CAPTION | WS_SYSMENU
{
  PUSHBUTTON "OK", IDOK, 2, 20, 40, 16,
              WS_CHILD | WS_VISIBLE | WS_TABSTOP
  PUSHBUTTON "IP Address", ID_GETADDR, 48, 20, 40, 16,
              WS_CHILD | WS_VISIBLE | WS_TABSTOP
}
```

The header file IP.H is shown here.

```
#define IDM_DIALOG   100
#define IDM_EXIT     102
#define IDM_HELP     103

#define ID_GETADDR   201
```

Common Control Wrap-Up

The preceding five chapters have explored the most frequently used common controls. If you can apply these controls, you will have no trouble learning to use the remaining ones on your own. Just remember, in general, using a common control involves these basic mechanisms:

Sample output from the IP address control example

Figure 14-3.

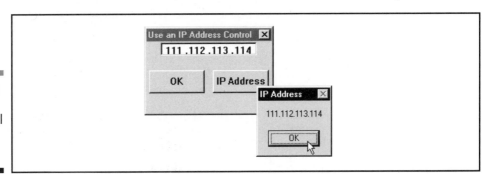

1. Creation and initialization.
2. Sending messages to the control.
3. Handling messages from the control.

As stated in the beginning of Chapter 10, the common controls give your application a sophisticated, modern look. You should take advantage of them whenever you can.

CHAPTER 15

Working with Consoles

A character mode program uses a text-based rather than a window-based interface.

While the Windows graphical user interface (GUI) is excellent for most types of programs, it is cumbersome when all you need is a simple character mode program. A *character mode* program is one that uses mainly the ASCII character set and assumes a character-based device, such as an 80-character × 25-line display system. Thus, a character mode application is the type that is commonly written for DOS. Early versions of Windows, such as Windows 3.1, did not provide any built-in support for writing character mode programs. If you wanted such a program, it had to be written for DOS. Of course, this severely limited the usefulness of a character mode program in a Windows world. (The "marriage" between DOS-style programs and Windows has never been a happy one!) Fortunately, Windows 98 supplies a means of creating a character mode program that is fully integrated into the Windows environment.

A console provides I/O support for character mode programs.

Character mode programs are supported by *consoles*, which provide the basic I/O environment necessary for their execution. Windows 98 (through the Win32 library) provides several console-based API functions. By including support for consoles, Windows 98 makes it easier for a character mode program to coexist with GUI programs. For example, it is now possible to write character mode programs that

◆ respond to Windows-style mouse events

◆ run in their own console session

◆ have access to the (relevant) API functions

◆ allow Windows-based control over keyboard activity, if desired

While GUI programs will always be the most popular type written for Windows 98, a console is a useful alternative. Often, a program is needed that is short, requires little user interaction, and has to be written quickly. For example, file utility programs often fall into this category. For these types of programs, the overhead of implementing them as full-blown GUI applications is difficult to justify. However, as console programs, they are easy to create and are still fully integrated into the Windows 98 environment.

This chapter describes how to write a character mode program and demonstrates several of the console-based API functions.

PORTABILITY: Consoles are not supported by Windows 3.1. They are available in Windows 95 and Windows NT.

Understanding Character Mode

Character mode programs resemble traditional, non-windowed programs that you almost certainly have written. That is, in a character mode program, no window is created. Also, there is no window function. Further, a character mode program begins with a call to **main( )**, not **WinMain( )**. In fact, generally there will not be a function called **WinMain( )** in your program. (If there is, it is treated as just another function with no special meaning.) For the most part, character mode programs do not use most of the Windows features discussed elsewhere in this book.

Given the preceding paragraph, you might be wondering two things. First, what general support does Windows 98 give to a character mode program? Second, since a character mode program is not a Windows program in the usual sense, why not just write a DOS program instead? The answers are interrelated. First, as mentioned, a console-based, character mode program is fully integrated into the Windows 98 environment. For example, mouse support is under the control of Windows 98 when using a character mode program. Second, a character mode program has access to API functions that are unavailable to a DOS program. Finally, DOS is a 16-bit environment. Windows 98 uses 32 bits. For obvious reasons, most modern programs should be written for a 32-bit environment.

If you execute a character mode program from the command prompt, it will inherit that console session. However, as you will soon see, it is possible for each character mode program to allocate its own console. A character mode program can also control several attributes of its console that are generally beyond the control of a DOS program.

All consoles maintain a cursor that marks the place at which the next output to the console will begin. The cursor is automatically updated after each output operation. It is also possible to set the cursor location within a console to any (legal) location you desire.

Allocating a Console

A console's output buffer is called a screen buffer.

In Windows terminology, a console is the interface used by your character mode programs. It contains both input and output buffers. The output buffers are also called *screen buffers*. Each character mode program that you write will operate through a console. In Windows 98, there can be several active consoles, each running its own character mode program.

By default, a character mode program either inherits the current console or is given a console if none exists when it is run. However, often it is better for the program to acquire its own console. The reason for this is simple: Any changes to that console affect only that console and not the inherited console. Therefore, for the cleanest approach to implementing a character mode program, it must create its own console. To do this, use the API function **AllocConsole( )**, whose prototype is shown here:

BOOL AllocConsole(VOID);

This function acquires a new console session for the program that calls it. The function returns nonzero if successful and zero otherwise. An allocated console is freed automatically when the program terminates.

Once a console has been allocated, it creates a window that behaves, more or less, like any other window. It includes a title, a control menu, minimize and maximize boxes, and, if needed, scroll bars. But inside this window, only character-based programs are allowed.

If the character mode program was executed from within a console session, then before a new one can be allocated, the old one inherited by the program must be freed, using **FreeConsole( )**. Its prototype is shown here:

BOOL FreeConsole(VOID);

The function returns nonzero if successful and zero otherwise.

When creating your character mode application, the best approach is to execute this sequence as the first actions taken by **main( )**.

```
FreeConsole();
AllocConsole()
```

Even if no parent console was previously in effect, no harm is done by calling **FreeConsole( )** and, in any case, a new console is allocated.

A console allocated by your program is automatically freed when your program stops running (unless the console is in use by another task, of course). Your program can also free the console explicitly by calling **FreeConsole( )**.

Giving a Title to a Console

You can give a console window a title using the **SetConsoleTitle( )** API function, shown here:

BOOL SetConsoleTitle(LPTSTR *Title*);

Here, the string pointed to by *Title* becomes the title of the console window. The function returns nonzero if successful and zero otherwise.

Acquiring Handles to Standard Input and Output

Many of the console-based API functions require a standard handle to perform I/O. The standard handles are linked to standard input, standard output, and standard error. By default, these handles are linked to the keyboard and the screen, but they may be redirected. When you write to a console, you will write to standard output. When you read from a console, you will read from standard input. Handles to console input and output are of type **HANDLE**.

To acquire a standard handle, use the **GetStdHandle( )** function, whose prototype is shown here:

    HANDLE GetStdHandle(DWORD *StdDev*);

Here, *StdDev* must be one of these macros: **STD_INPUT_HANDLE**, **STD_OUTPUT_HANDLE**, or **STD_ERROR_HANDLE**, which correspond to standard input, standard output, and standard error, respectively. The function returns a handle to the device. On failure, **INVALID_HANDLE_VALUE** is returned.

Outputting Text to the Console

One way to output text to the console is to use the **WriteConsole( )** API function, whose prototype is shown here.

    BOOL WriteConsole(HANDLE *hConOut*, CONST VOID *String*,
                      DWORD *Len*, LPDWORD *NumWritten*,
                      LPVOID *NotUsed*);

Here, *hConOut* is the handle of console output, generally obtained through a call to **GetStdHandle( )**. The string to be output is pointed to by *String*. The number of characters in *String* to output is passed in *Len,* and the actual number of characters written is returned in the long integer pointed to by *NumWritten*. *NotUsed* is reserved for future use and must be **NULL**.

The string is output using the current text and background colors. The output begins at the current cursor location, and the cursor location is automatically updated. The function returns nonzero if successful and zero otherwise.

It is important to understand that **WriteConsole( )** does not provide any formatting capabilities. This means that you will still need to use a function like **sprintf( )** to first construct the string that you want to output if you want to use **WriteConsole( )** to write formatted data.

15

Inputting from the Console

To input information entered at the keyboard, use the **ReadConsole( )** function, shown here.

BOOL ReadConsole(HANDLE *hConIn*, LPVOID *Buf*,
                 DWORD *Len*, LPDWORD *NumRead*,
                 LPVOID *NotUsed*);

Here, *hConIn* is the handle linked to console input. The character array that will receive the characters typed by the user is pointed to by *Buf*. (This string is not automatically null-terminated.) The function will read up to *Len* characters or until ENTER is pressed. The number of characters actually read is returned in the long integer pointed to by *NumRead*. The *NotUsed* parameter is reserved for future use and must be **NULL**. The function returns nonzero if successful and zero otherwise.

IN DEPTH

SetConsoleMode( )

The precise operation of **ReadConsole( )** and **WriteConsole( )** is determined by the current console mode. The console mode can be set using **SetConsoleMode( )**. Its prototype is shown here.

BOOL SetConsoleMode(HANDLE *hCon*, DWORD *NewMode*);

Here, *hCon* is the handle of either the console's input buffer or output buffer, and *NewMode* specifies the new console mode. The function returns nonzero if successful and zero on failure.

The valid values for *NewMode* depend upon whether you are setting the mode of the input buffer or the output buffer. The values for output are **ENABLE_PROCESSED_OUTPUT** and **ENABLE_WRAP_AT_EOL_ OUTPUT**. Both of these are set by default. Enabling processed output allows the console to properly handle carriage return-linefeed sequences, expand tabs, ring the bell, and process backspace characters. **ENABLE_WRAP_AT_EOL_OUTPUT** allows the console window to scroll properly and for output to be wrapped in the expected fashion.

The possible values for input buffers are shown here. You can OR two or more together to obtain the desired mode.

ENABLE_ECHO_INPUT

ENABLE_LINE_INPUT

ENABLE_MOUSE_INPUT

ENABLE_PROCESSED_INPUT

ENABLE_WINDOW_INPUT

By default, all but **ENABLE_WINDOW_INPUT** are on. To receive mouse events, include **ENABLE_MOUSE_INPUT**. When **ENABLE_LINE_INPUT** is included, input obtained using **ReadConsole( )** is line-buffered. To allow the system to process carriage returns, linefeeds, and backspaces when line-buffered input is used, include **ENABLE_PROCESSED_INPUT**. It also prevents controls keys, such as CTRL-C, from being passed to the console. **ENABLE_ECHO_INPUT** causes characters to be echoed to the screen. It must be used in conjunction with **ENABLE_LINE_INPUT**. To receive buffer size events, you must include **ENABLE_WINDOW_INPUT**.

You can obtain the current console mode by calling **GetConsoleMode ( )**, shown here.

BOOL GetConsoleMode(HANDLE *hCon*, LPDWORD *Mode*);

Here, *hCon* is the handle of either the console's input or output buffer. *Mode* is a pointer to a long integer that receives the current console mode. This value will contain one or more of the previously described values. The function returns nonzero if successful and zero on failure.

Setting the Cursor Position

To position the cursor within a console window, use the
SetConsoleCursorPosition( ) function. Its prototype is shown here.

BOOL SetConsoleCursorPosition(HANDLE *hConOut*, COORD *XY*);

Here, *hConOut* is the output handle of the console, and *XY* is a **COORD**
structure that contains the coordinates of the desired cursor location.
COORD is defined like this:

```
typedef struct _COORD {
  SHORT X;
  SHORT Y;
} COORD;
```

The function returns nonzero if successful and zero on failure.

Setting Text and Background Colors

When using a console, by default the text is white and the background is
black. You can change this if you want by using the
SetConsoleTextAttribute( ), whose prototype is shown here:

BOOL SetConsoleTextAttribute(HANDLE *hConOut*, WORD *colors*);

Here, *hConOut* is the handle linked to console output, and *colors* is the value
that determines the text and background colors. The value of *colors* is
constructed by ORing together two or more of the following macros, which
are defined in WINCON.H. (WINCON.H is automatically included when you
include WINDOWS.H.)

Macro	Meaning
FOREGROUND_BLUE	Text includes blue.
FOREGROUND_RED	Text includes red.
FOREGROUND_GREEN	Text includes green.
FOREGROUND_INTENSITY	Text is shown in high intensity.
BACKGROUND_BLUE	Background includes blue.

Macro	Meaning
BACKGROUND_RED	Background includes red.
BACKGROUND_GREEN	Background includes green.
BACKGROUND_INTENSITY	Background is shown in high intensity.

The actual color will be a combination of the color components that you specify. To create white, combine all three colors. For black, specify no color.

SetConsoleTextAttribute( ) returns nonzero if successful and zero on failure.

Console I/O vs. the C/C++ Standard I/O Functions

Once you have obtained a console, it is permissible—indeed, completely valid—to use the C/C++ standard I/O functions and operators with it. However, using the console API functions just described does give your application more control over the console in many situations. Also, in the case of monitoring console events, only the API functions allow full integration with Windows 98. For example, mouse events are not accessible using the standard C/C++ I/O systems. They are accessible, however, by using the console API functions (as you will soon see).

For the example that follows, the standard C/C++ I/O functions are used only to illustrate their validity.

A Console Demonstration Program

The console functions just described are demonstrated by the following program. Its operation should be clear.

```
/* Demonstrate Consoles */

#include <windows.h>
#include <string.h>
#include <stdio.h>

int main()
{
  HANDLE hStdin, hStdout;
  char str[255] = "This is an example of output to a console.";
  DWORD result;
  COORD coord;
```

15

```
int x=0, y=0;
int i;

/* free old console and start fresh with new one */
FreeConsole();
AllocConsole();

/* give console window a title */
SetConsoleTitle("Console Demonstration");

/* get standard handles */
hStdin = GetStdHandle(STD_INPUT_HANDLE);
hStdout = GetStdHandle(STD_OUTPUT_HANDLE);

WriteConsole(hStdout, str, strlen(str), &result, NULL);

/* demonstrate cursor positioning */
for(x=0, y=1; y<10; x+=5, y++) {
  coord.X = x;
  coord.Y = y;
  sprintf(str, "At location %d %d", x, y);
  SetConsoleCursorPosition(hStdout, coord);
  WriteConsole(hStdout, str, strlen(str), &result, NULL);
}

/* change the colors */
coord.X = 0;
coord.Y = 12;
strcpy(str, "This is in blue on green background.");
SetConsoleCursorPosition(hStdout, coord);
SetConsoleTextAttribute(hStdout,
                  FOREGROUND_BLUE | BACKGROUND_GREEN);
WriteConsole(hStdout, str, strlen(str), &result, NULL);

coord.X = 0;
coord.Y = 14;
strcpy(str, "Enter a string: ");
SetConsoleCursorPosition(hStdout, coord);
WriteConsole(hStdout, str, strlen(str), &result, NULL);

/* read input */
ReadConsole(hStdin, str, 80, &result, NULL);
str[result] = '\0'; /* null terminate */
/* display ASCII code of each character in str */
for(i=0; str[i]; i++) printf("%d ", str[i]);
/* now, display as string */
WriteConsole(hStdout, str, strlen(str), &result, NULL);
```

```
/* can use printf(), gets(), etc. */
printf("This is a test.  Enter another string:");
gets(str);
printf("%s\n", str);
printf("Press ENTER: ");

getchar(); /* wait for keypress */

return 0;
}
```

To compile a console program, you will need to use a set of compiler and linker commands different than the ones you have been using to compile Windows-style programs. For example, when using Microsoft Visual C++, you will need to specify Console Application when creating a workspace for your program. For other compilers, check the compiler's user manual for instructions.

Sample output from this program is shown in Figure 15-1.

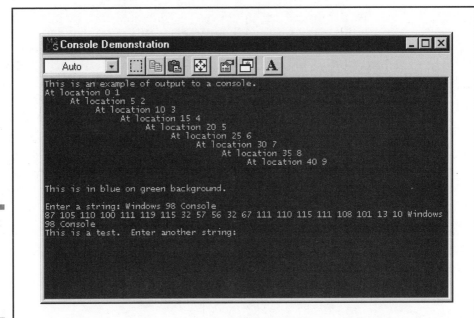

Sample output from the console demonstration program

Figure 15-1.

15

Managing the Mouse

One of the main advantages of using Windows 98 consoles and writing character mode Windows 98 programs over simply letting DOS-style programs execute in a window is that a console gives you access to the mouse. To obtain mouse events (and other information) when using a console, you must use an API console input function called **ReadConsoleInput( )**, whose prototype is shown here.

BOOL ReadConsoleInput(HANDLE *hConIn*,
　　　　　　　　　　PINPUT_RECORD *Buf*,
　　　　　　　　　　DWORD *Num*,
　　　　　　　　　　LPDWORD *NumRead*);

Here, *hConIn* is the handle of the console about which you want information. The parameter *Buf* is a pointer to a structure of type **INPUT_RECORD**, which will receive the information regarding the requested input event or events. The number of event records to input is specified in *Num*, and the amount actually obtained by the function is returned in *NumRead*. The function returns nonzero if successful or zero otherwise.

The **ReadConsoleInput( )** function removes information about one or more input events from the console's input buffer. Each time you strike a key or use the mouse, an input event is generated and the information associated with this event is stored in an **INPUT_RECORD** structure. (Certain other input events may also occur, but only the mouse and keyboard ones are of interest to us in this chapter.) The **ReadConsoleInput( )** function reads one or more of these events and makes the input event information available to your program.

Each event record is returned in a structure of type **INPUT_RECORD**, which is shown here:

```
typedef struct _INPUT_RECORD {
  WORD EventType;
  union {
    KEY_EVENT_RECORD KeyEvent;
    MOUSE_EVENT_RECORD MouseEvent;
    WINDOW_BUFFER_SIZE_RECORD WindowBufferSizeEvent;
    MENU_EVENT_RECORD MenuEvent;
    FOCUS_EVENT_RECORD FocusEvent;
  } Event;
} INPUT_RECORD;
```

The contents of **EventType** determine what type of event has occurred. It can be one of these macros.

Macro	Event
FOCUS_EVENT	Used by Windows 98.
KEY_EVENT	Key pressed.
MENU_EVENT	Used by Windows 98.
MOUSE_EVENT	Mouse event.
WINDOW_BUFFER_SIZE_EVENT	Window resized.

Only mouse and keyboard events are examined in detail here. Focus and menu events are for the internal use of Windows 98 only. A buffer size event may be of interest to your program in some situations, in which case **WindowBufferSizeEvent** contains a **COORD** structure that holds the new dimensions of the screen buffer.

Each time a mouse event occurs, the **EventType** field contains **MOUSE_EVENT** and the **Event** union contains a **MOUSE_EVENT_RECORD** structure that describes the mouse event. This structure is shown here:

```
typedef struct _MOUSE_EVENT_RECORD {
  COORD dwMousePosition;
  DWORD dwButtonState;
  DWORD dwControlKeyState;
  DWORD dwEventFlags;
} MOUSE_EVENT_RECORD;
```

For consoles, mouse coordinates are in terms of characters and rows, not pixels.

The **dwMousePosition** field contains the coordinates of the mouse when the event took place. Since a console is a text-based device, the coordinates are in terms of character position and row, not pixels.

dwButtonState describes the state of the mouse buttons when the event was generated. If bit one is on, then the left mouse button is pressed. If bit two is on, then the right mouse button is pressed. If bit three is on, the middle button (if it exists) is pressed. More than one bit will be set when more than one button is pressed at the same time.

The **dwControlKeyState** field describes the state of the various control keys when the event occurred. It may contain one or more of the following macros.

15

SHIFT_PRESSED

RIGHT_CTRL_PRESSED

LEFT_CTRL_PRESSED

RIGHT_ALT_PRESSED

LEFT_ALT_PRESSED

ENHANCED_KEY

CAPSLOCK_ON

NUMLOCK_ON

SCROLLLOCK_ON

An enhanced key is one of those added to the standard keyboard by the IBM enhanced keyboards. For example, the extra arrow keys are enhanced keys.

dwEventFlags will either be zero, which means that a mouse button has been single-clicked, or it will contain **MOUSE_MOVED** (the mouse has moved), **DOUBLE_CLICK** (a mouse button has been double-clicked), or **MOUSE_WHEELED** (the mouse was physically rolled).

Demonstrating the Console Mouse

The following program illustrates how to manage mouse events when using a console.

```
/* Managing the mouse from a Console. */

#include <windows.h>
#include <string.h>
#include <stdio.h>

int main()
{
  HANDLE hStdin, hStdout;
  char str[80] = "Press a key to stop.";
  DWORD result;
  COORD coord;
  int x=0, y=0;
```

```
          INPUT_RECORD inBuf;

          /* free old console and start fresh with new one */
          FreeConsole();
          AllocConsole();

          /* give console window a title */
          SetConsoleTitle("Mouse with Console Demonstration");

          /* get standard handles */
          hStdin = GetStdHandle(STD_INPUT_HANDLE);
          hStdout = GetStdHandle(STD_OUTPUT_HANDLE);

          WriteConsole(hStdout, str, strlen(str), &result, NULL);

          /* show mouse events until a key is pressed */
          do {
            ReadConsoleInput(hStdin, &inBuf, 1, &result);
            /* if mouse event occurs, report it */
            if(inBuf.EventType==MOUSE_EVENT) {
              sprintf(str, "Button state: %lu, X,Y: %3d,%3d\n",
                      inBuf.Event.MouseEvent.dwButtonState,
                      inBuf.Event.MouseEvent.dwMousePosition.X,
                      inBuf.Event.MouseEvent.dwMousePosition.Y);
              coord.X = 0;
              coord.Y = 1;
              SetConsoleCursorPosition(hStdout, coord);
              WriteConsole(hStdout, str, strlen(str), &result, NULL);

              /* if a double click occurs, report it */
              if(inBuf.Event.MouseEvent.dwEventFlags==DOUBLE_CLICK) {
                sprintf(str, "Double click\a");
                coord.X = inBuf.Event.MouseEvent.dwMousePosition.X;
                coord.Y = inBuf.Event.MouseEvent.dwMousePosition.Y;
                SetConsoleCursorPosition(hStdout, coord);
                WriteConsole(hStdout, str, strlen(str), &result, NULL);
                Sleep(600); /* wait */
                SetConsoleCursorPosition(hStdout, coord);
                strcpy(str, "                 "); /* erase message */
                WriteConsole(hStdout, str, strlen(str), &result, NULL);
              }
            }
          } while(inBuf.EventType!=KEY_EVENT);

          return 0;
        }
```

15

This program displays the current location of the mouse when it is within the console window and the state of the mouse buttons, and it reports when the mouse is double-clicked. The program continues to execute until a key event is generated when you press a key.

The API function **Sleep( )** is used to provide a short delay before the **Double Click** message is erased. This function takes as its argument a value that specifies the number of milliseconds to suspend the execution of the program.

Responding to Keyboard Events

A scan code is a hardware-dependent key code that relates to a key's position on the keyboard.

As you know from your previous programming experience, it is quite common for text-based programs to respond to keypresses in a fashion more subtle than by simply inputting the keystroke. For example, sometimes your program will need to know if a control key is pressed, or the state of the SHIFT key. Also, some applications make use of the *scan code* that corresponds to the key. When you press a key, a scan code (sometimes called a *position code*) is generated that corresponds to the key's position on the keyboard. This code is then translated into an ASCII character. Whatever the need, Windows 98 gives character mode, console-based applications access to all the information associated with a keyboard event. Like mouse events, keyboard events are obtained by calling **ReadConsoleInput( )**, described earlier.

Each time a key is pressed, a keyboard event is generated. When this event is obtained using **ReadConsoleInput( )**, the **EventType** field of the **INPUT_RECORD** structure contains the **KEY_EVENT** value. When this is the case, the **Event** union holds a **KEY_EVENT_RECORD** structure, which describes the event. This structure is shown here.

```
typedef struct _KEY_EVENT_RECORD {
  BOOL bKeyDown;
  WORD wRepeatCount;
  WORD wVirtualKeyCode;
  WORD wVirtualScanCode;
  union {
    WCHAR UnicodeChar;
    CHAR AsciiChar;
  } uChar;
  DWORD dwControlKeyState;
} KEY_EVENT_RECORD;
```

If **bKeyDown** is nonzero, then a key was being pressed when the key event was generated. If it is zero, the key was being released.

The number of times a keystroke is generated when a key is held down and autorepeat takes over is returned in **wRepeatCount**. Even when a key is held down, your program may continue to receive separate events, with **wRepeatCount** containing 1. However, it is permissible for Windows 98 to collapse these events into one event with the number of repeats indicated in **wRepeatCount**.

The virtual key code is returned in **wVirtualKeyCode**.

The scan (position) code of the key is returned in **wVirtualScanCode**.

The union **uChar** contains the ASCII or Unicode code of the key being pressed.

The state of the control keys (and other keys) is returned in **dwControlKeyState**. The values are the same as those described for mouse events.

A Sample Key Event Program

The following program demonstrates keyboard events. This program reports each character typed and the state of the various control keys, when one is pressed. It continues to execute until you click the left mouse button.

```
/* Managing the keyboard from a Console. */

#include <windows.h>
#include <string.h>
#include <stdio.h>

int main()
{
  HANDLE hStdin, hStdout;
  char str[255] = "Press the left mouse button to stop.";
  DWORD result;
  COORD coord;
  int x=0, y=0;
  int i;
  int done = 0;
  INPUT_RECORD inBuf;

  /* free old console and start fresh with new one */
  FreeConsole();
  AllocConsole();

  /* give console window a title */
  SetConsoleTitle("Keyboard Demonstration");
```

15

```
/* get standard handles */
hStdin = GetStdHandle(STD_INPUT_HANDLE);
hStdout = GetStdHandle(STD_OUTPUT_HANDLE);

WriteConsole(hStdout, str, strlen(str), &result, NULL);

/* Show keyboard events until left
   mouse button is pressed. */
do {
  ReadConsoleInput(hStdin, &inBuf, 1, &result);
  /* if key is pressed, report it */
  if(inBuf.EventType==KEY_EVENT) {
    sprintf(str, "Key pressed is: %c\n",
            inBuf.Event.KeyEvent.uChar);
    coord.X = 0;
    coord.Y = 1;
    SetConsoleCursorPosition(hStdout, coord);
    WriteConsole(hStdout, str, strlen(str), &result, NULL);

    /* if a control, alt, etc. key is pressed, report it */
    if(inBuf.Event.KeyEvent.dwControlKeyState &&
       inBuf.Event.KeyEvent.bKeyDown) {
      coord.X = 0;
      coord.Y = 10;
      *str = '\0';
      if(inBuf.Event.KeyEvent.dwControlKeyState
        & RIGHT_ALT_PRESSED)
          strcat(str, "Right alt Key is pressed. ");
      if(inBuf.Event.KeyEvent.dwControlKeyState
        & LEFT_ALT_PRESSED)
          strcat(str, "Left alt Key is pressed. ");
      if(inBuf.Event.KeyEvent.dwControlKeyState
        & RIGHT_CTRL_PRESSED)
          strcat(str, "Right control Key is pressed. ");
      if(inBuf.Event.KeyEvent.dwControlKeyState
        & LEFT_CTRL_PRESSED)
          strcat(str, "Left control Key is pressed. ");
      if(inBuf.Event.KeyEvent.dwControlKeyState
        & SHIFT_PRESSED)
          strcat(str, "Shift key is pressed. ");
      if(inBuf.Event.KeyEvent.dwControlKeyState
        & NUMLOCK_ON)
          strcat(str, "Num lock key on. ");
      if(inBuf.Event.KeyEvent.dwControlKeyState
```

```
            & SCROLLLOCK_ON)
                strcat(str, "Scroll lock key is on. ");
        if(inBuf.Event.KeyEvent.dwControlKeyState
            & CAPSLOCK_ON)
                strcat(str, "Caps lock key is on. ");
        if(inBuf.Event.KeyEvent.dwControlKeyState
            & ENHANCED_KEY)
                strcat(str, "Enhanced key is pressed. ");

        SetConsoleCursorPosition(hStdout, coord);
        strcat(str, "\a");
        WriteConsole(hStdout, str, strlen(str), &result, NULL);
        SetConsoleCursorPosition(hStdout, coord);

        /* wait, then erase the message */
        Sleep(1000);
        coord.X = 0;
        coord.Y = 10;
        i = strlen(str);
        for(*str='\0'; i; i--) strcat(str, " ");
        WriteConsole(hStdout, str, strlen(str), &result, NULL);
      }
    }
    if(inBuf.EventType==MOUSE_EVENT)
      if(inBuf.Event.MouseEvent.dwButtonState==1) done = 1;

  } while(!done);

  return 0;
}
```

As this chapter has shown, creating character mode programs using Windows 98 is quite easy. Therefore, while Windows 98 can execute DOS programs, when creating new character mode applications, you should always use a Windows 98 console and employ its character-mode functions.

In the next chapter, the Windows 98 multitasking system is examined.

15

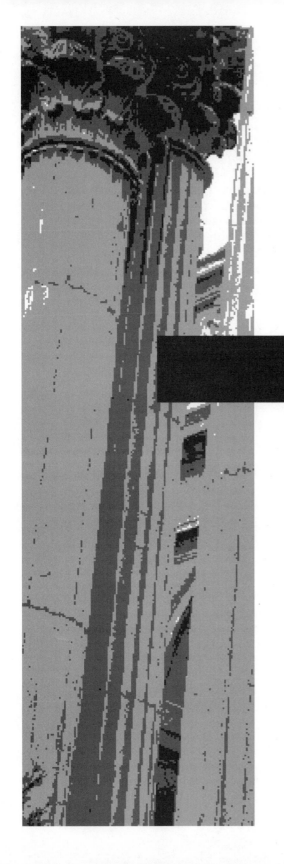

CHAPTER 16

Multitasking

This chapter describes Windows 98's multitasking system. As mentioned at the start of this book, Windows 98 supports two forms of multitasking. The first type is process-based. This is the type of multiprocessing that Windows has supported from its inception. A process is essentially a program that is executing. In process-based multitasking, two or more processes can execute concurrently. The second type of multitasking is thread-based. A thread is a path (or *thread*) of execution within a process. In Windows 98, every process has at least one thread, but it may have two or more. Thread-based multitasking allows two or more parts of a single program to execute concurrently. This added multitasking dimension allows extremely efficient programs to be written because you, the programmer, can define the separate threads of execution and thus manage the way that your program executes. Both process-based and thread-based multitasking are described here, but the emphasis is on the latter since it has the greatest impact on program design and performance.

Thread-based multitasking increased the need for a special type of multitasking feature called *synchronization*, which allows the execution of threads (and processes) to be coordinated in certain well-defined ways. Windows 98 has a complete subsystem devoted to synchronization. Its key features are also discussed in this chapter.

PORTABILITY: Windows 3.1 does not support thread-based multitasking.

Thread Fundamentals

If you have never programmed for a multithreaded environment before, you are in for a pleasant surprise. Multithreaded multitasking adds a new dimension to your programming because it lets you, the programmer, more fully control how pieces of your program execute. This allows you to implement more efficient programs. For example, you could assign one thread of a program the job of sorting a file, another thread the job of gathering information from some remote source, and still another thread the task of performing user input. Because of multithreaded multitasking, each thread could execute concurrently and no CPU time is wasted.

The thread of execution created when a program begins is called its main thread.

It is important to understand that all processes have at least one thread of execution. For the sake of discussion, this is called the *main thread*. However, it is possible to create one or more other threads of execution within the same process. In general, once a new thread is created, it also begins execution. Thus, each process starts with one thread of execution and may create one or more additional threads. In this way, thread-based multitasking is supported.

Creating a Thread

To create a thread, use the API function **CreateThread( )**. Its prototype is shown here:

```
HANDLE CreateThread(LPSECURITY_ATTRIBUTES lpSecAttr,
                    DWORD dwStackSize,
                    LPTHREAD_START_ROUTINE lpThreadFunc,
                    LPVOID lpParam,
                    DWORD dwFlags,
                    LPDWORD lpdwThreadID);
```

Here, *lpSecAttr* is a pointer to a set of security attributes pertaining to the thread. However, security is ignored by Windows 98 and *lpSecAttr* should be **NULL**.

PORTABILITY: In general, security attributes apply only to Windows NT. They are not used by Windows 95 or Windows 98. However, in order for a Windows 98 program to run under Windows NT, the security attributes must be specified as **NULL**. This causes Windows NT to use the default security descriptor.

Each thread has its own stack. You can specify the size of the new thread's stack, in bytes, using the *dwStackSize* parameter. If this value is zero, the thread will be given a stack that is the same size as the main thread of the process that creates it. (Specifying zero is the common approach taken to thread stack size.) The stack will be expanded if necessary.

Each thread of execution begins with a call to a function, called the *thread function*, within the process. Execution of the thread continues until the thread function returns. The address of this function (i.e., the entry point to the thread) is specified in *lpThreadFunc*. All thread functions must have this prototype:

DWORD WINAPI threadfunc(LPVOID *param*);

The thread function is the entry point to a new thread of execution.

Any argument that you need to pass to the new thread is specified in **CreateThread( )**'s *lpParam*. This 32-bit value is received by the thread function in its parameter. This parameter may be used for any purpose. The function returns its exit status.

The *dwFlags* parameter determines the execution state of the thread. If it is zero, the thread begins execution immediately. If it is **CREATE_SUSPEND**, the thread is created in a suspended state, awaiting execution. (It may be started using a call to **ResumeThread( )**, discussed later.)

The identifier associated with a thread is returned in the double word pointed to by *lpdwThreadID*.

The function returns a handle to the thread if successful or **NULL** if a failure occurs. The thread handle can be explicitly destroyed by calling **CloseHandle( )**. Otherwise, it will be destroyed automatically when the parent process ends.

Terminating a Thread

As stated, a thread of execution terminates when its entry function returns. The process may also terminate the thread manually, using either **TerminateThread( )** or **ExitThread( )**, whose prototypes are shown here:

BOOL TerminateThread(HANDLE *hThread*, DWORD *dwStatus*);

VOID ExitThread(DWORD *dwStatus*);

For **TerminateThread( )**, *hThread* is the handle of the thread to be terminated. **ExitThread( )** can only be used to terminate the thread that calls **ExitThread( )**. For both functions, *dwStatus* is the termination status. **TerminateThread( )** returns nonzero if successful and zero otherwise.

Calling **ExitThread( )** is functionally equivalent to allowing a thread function to return normally. This means that the stack is properly reset. When a thread is terminated using **TerminateThread( )**, it is stopped immediately and does not perform any special cleanup activities. Also, **TerminateThread( )** may stop a thread during an important operation. For these reasons, it is usually best (and easiest) to let a thread terminate normally when its entry function returns. This is the approach used by most of the example programs in this chapter.

A Multithreaded Example

The following program creates two threads each time the Demonstrate Threads menu option is selected. Each thread iterates a **for** loop 5,000 times, displaying the number of the iteration each time it repeats. As you will see when you run the program, both threads appear to execute concurrently.

```c
/* A simple multithreaded program. */

#include <windows.h>
#include <string.h>
#include <stdio.h>
#include "thread.h"

#define MAX 5000

LRESULT CALLBACK WindowFunc(HWND, UINT, WPARAM, LPARAM);
DWORD WINAPI MyThread1(LPVOID param);
DWORD WINAPI MyThread2(LPVOID param);

char szWinName[] = "MyWin"; /* name of window class */

char str[255]; /* holds output strings */

DWORD Tid1, Tid2; /* thread IDs */

int WINAPI WinMain(HINSTANCE hThisInst, HINSTANCE hPrevInst,
                   LPSTR lpszArgs, int nWinMode)
{
  HWND hwnd;
  MSG msg;
  WNDCLASSEX wcl;
  HACCEL hAccel;

  /* Define a window class. */
  wcl.cbSize = sizeof(WNDCLASSEX);

  wcl.hInstance = hThisInst; /* handle to this instance */
  wcl.lpszClassName = szWinName; /* window class name */
  wcl.lpfnWndProc = WindowFunc; /* window function */
  wcl.style = 0; /* default style */
```

```
wcl.hIcon = LoadIcon(NULL, IDI_APPLICATION); /* standard icon */
wcl.hIconSm = LoadIcon(NULL, IDI_APPLICATION); /* small icon */
wcl.hCursor = LoadCursor(NULL, IDC_ARROW); /* cursor style */

wcl.lpszMenuName = "ThreadMenu"; /* main menu */
wcl.cbClsExtra = 0; /* no extra */
wcl.cbWndExtra = 0; /* information needed */

/* Make the window white. */
wcl.hbrBackground = (HBRUSH) GetStockObject(WHITE_BRUSH);

/* Register the window class. */
if(!RegisterClassEx(&wcl)) return 0;

/* Now that a window class has been registered, a window
   can be created. */
hwnd = CreateWindow(
  szWinName, /* name of window class */
  "Demonstrate Threads", /* title */
  WS_OVERLAPPEDWINDOW, /* window style - normal */
  CW_USEDEFAULT, /* X coordinate - let Windows decide */
  CW_USEDEFAULT, /* Y coordinate - let Windows decide */
  CW_USEDEFAULT, /* width - let Windows decide */
  CW_USEDEFAULT, /* height - let Windows decide */
  HWND_DESKTOP, /* no parent window */
  NULL, /* no override of class menu */
  hThisInst, /* handle of this instance of the program */
  NULL /* no additional arguments */
);

/* Load accelerators. */
hAccel = LoadAccelerators(hThisInst, "ThreadMenu");

/* Display the window. */
ShowWindow(hwnd, nWinMode);
UpdateWindow(hwnd);

/* Create the message loop. */
while(GetMessage(&msg, NULL, 0, 0))
{
  if(!TranslateAccelerator(hwnd, hAccel, &msg)) {
    TranslateMessage(&msg); /* translate keyboard messages */
    DispatchMessage(&msg); /* return control to Windows 98 */
  }
```

```
      }
    return msg.wParam;
}

/* This function is called by Windows 98 and is passed
   messages from the message queue.
*/
LRESULT CALLBACK WindowFunc(HWND hwnd, UINT message,
                            WPARAM wParam, LPARAM lParam)
{
  int response;

  switch(message) {
    case WM_COMMAND:
      switch(LOWORD(wParam)) {
        case IDM_THREAD: /* create the threads */
          CreateThread(NULL, 0,
                       (LPTHREAD_START_ROUTINE)MyThread1,
                       (LPVOID) hwnd, 0, &Tid1);
          CreateThread(NULL, 0,
                       (LPTHREAD_START_ROUTINE)MyThread2,
                       (LPVOID) hwnd, 0, &Tid2);
          break;
        case IDM_EXIT:
          response = MessageBox(hwnd, "Quit the Program?",
                                "Exit", MB_YESNO);
          if(response == IDYES) PostQuitMessage(0);
          break;
        case IDM_HELP:
          MessageBox(hwnd,
                     "F1: Help\nF2: Demonstrate Threads",
                     "Help", MB_OK);
          break;
      }
      break;
    case WM_DESTROY: /* terminate the program */
      PostQuitMessage(0);
      break;
    default:
      /* Let Windows 98 process any messages not specified in
      the preceding switch statement. */
      return DefWindowProc(hwnd, message, wParam, lParam);
  }
  return 0;
}
```

```
/* A thread of execution within the process. */
DWORD WINAPI MyThread1(LPVOID param)
{
  int i;
  HDC hdc;

  for(i=0; i<MAX; i++) {
    sprintf(str, "Thread 1: loop # %5d ", i);
    hdc = GetDC((HWND) param);
    TextOut(hdc, 1, 1, str, strlen(str));
    ReleaseDC((HWND) param, hdc);
  }
  return 0;
}

/* Another thread of execution within the process. */
DWORD WINAPI MyThread2(LPVOID param)
{
  int i;
  HDC hdc;

  for(i=0; i<MAX; i++) {
    sprintf(str, "Thread 2: loop # %5d ", i);
    hdc = GetDC((HWND) param);
    TextOut(hdc, 1, 20, str, strlen(str));
    ReleaseDC((HWND) param, hdc);
  }
  return 0;
}
```

This program uses the THREAD.H file shown here.

```
#define IDM_THREAD 100
#define IDM_HELP   101
#define IDM_EXIT   102
```

The program also requires this resource file.

```
#include <windows.h>
#include "thread.h"

ThreadMenu MENU
{
  POPUP "&Threads" {
```

```
    MENUITEM "Demonstrate &Threads\tF2", IDM_THREAD
    MENUITEM "E&xit\tCtrl+X", IDM_EXIT
  }
  MENUITEM "&Help", IDM_HELP
}

ThreadMenu ACCELERATORS
{
  VK_F2, IDM_THREAD, VIRTKEY
  "^X", IDM_EXIT
  VK_F1, IDM_HELP, VIRTKEY
}
```

Sample output from the program is shown in Figure 16-1.

A Closer Look at the Multithreaded Program

Each time the Demonstrate Threads option is chosen, the following code
executes.

```
case IDM_THREAD: /* create the threads */
  CreateThread(NULL, 0,
               (LPTHREAD_START_ROUTINE)MyThread1,
               (LPVOID) hwnd, 0, &Tid1);
  CreateThread(NULL, 0,
               (LPTHREAD_START_ROUTINE)MyThread2,
               (LPVOID) hwnd, 0, &Tid2);
  break;
```

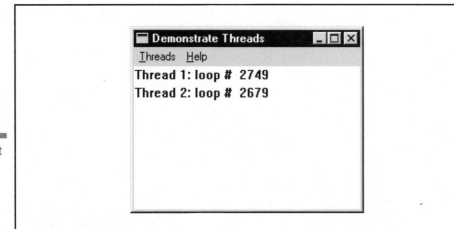

Sample output
from the
multithreaded
program
Figure 16-1.

As you can see, the first call to **CreateThread( )** activates **MyThread1( )** and the second call activates **MyThread2( )**. Notice that the handle of the main window (**hwnd**) is passed as a parameter to each thread function. This handle is used by the threads to obtain a device context so that they may output information to the main window.

Once started, each thread of execution (including the main thread) runs independently. For example, while the threads are executing, you may activate the Help message box, exit the program, or even start another set of threads. If you exit the program, any child threads will be automatically terminated.

Before continuing, you might want to experiment with this program. For example, as it now stands, each thread terminates when its associated function terminates. Try terminating a thread early, using **ExitThread( )**. Also, try starting multiple instances of each thread.

Alternatives to CreateThread( ) and ExitThread( )

A memory leak is the loss of a small amount of memory.

Depending upon what C/C++ compiler you are using and what C standard library functions are employed in your program, you may need to avoid the use of **CreateThread( )** and **ExitThread( )** because they may result in small memory leaks. A *memory leak* is the loss of a small amount of memory. It is usually caused when a portion of memory allocated by a program is not released when the program terminates. For many C/C++ compilers, including Microsoft Visual C++ and Borland C++, if a multithreaded program utilizes standard C library functions and uses **CreateThread( )** and **ExitThread( )**, then small amounts of memory will be lost. (If your program does not use the C standard library, no such losses will occur.) To eliminate this problem, you must use functions defined by the C runtime library to start and stop threads rather than those specified by the Win32 API.

In this section we will examine the alternative thread creation and termination functions provided by Microsoft Visual C++. Similar functions are also provided by Borland C++. If you are using a different compiler, check your user manual to determine if you need to bypass **CreateThread( )** and **ExitThread( )** and how to do so if necessary.

The Visual C++ Thread Functions

The Microsoft Visual C++ alternatives to **CreateThread( )** and **ExitThread( )** are **_beginthreadex( )** and **_endthreadex( )**. You must include the header file PROCESS.H in order to use these functions. Here is the prototype for **_beginthreadex( )**.

```
unsigned long _beginthreadex(void *secAttr, unsigned stackSize,
                             unsigned (_ _stdcall *threadFunc)(void *),
                             void *param, unsigned flags,
                             unsigned *threadID);
```

As you can see, the parameters to **_beginthreadex( )** parallel those of **CreateThread( )**. Furthermore, they have the same meaning as those specified by **CreateThread( )**. *secAttr* is a pointer to a set of security attributes pertaining to the thread. However, for Windows 98, *secAttr* should be **NULL** because the security descriptor is ignored. The size of the new thread's stack, in bytes, is passed in *stackSize* parameter. If this value is zero, the thread will be given a stack that is the same size as the main thread of the process that creates it. The stack will be expanded if necessary.

The address of the thread function (i.e., the entry point to the thread) is specified in *threadFunc*. For **_beginthreadex( )**, a thread function must have this prototype:

```
unsigned_ _stdcall threadfunc(void *param);
```

This prototype is functionally equivalent to the one for **CreateThread( )**, but uses different type names. Any argument that you need to pass to the new thread is specified in **_beginthreadex( )**'s *param* parameter.

The *flags* parameter determines the execution state of the thread. If it is zero, the thread begins execution immediately. If it is **CREATE_SUSPEND**, the thread is created in a suspended state, awaiting execution. (It may be started using a call to **ResumeThread( )**.) The identifier associated with a thread is returned in the variable pointed to by *threadID*.

The function returns a handle to the thread if successful or zero if a failure occurs.

The prototype for **_endthreadex( )** is shown here:

```
void _endthreadex(unsigned status);
```

It functions just like **ExitThread( )** by stopping the thread and returning the exit code specified in *status*.

When using **_beginthreadex( )** and **_endthreadex( )**, you must remember to link in the multithreaded library.

NOTE: Microsoft supplies the functions **_beginthread( )** and **_endthread( )**, which can also be used to create and terminate a thread. However, **_beginthread( )** is a generic thread function that does not provide the detailed level of control available in **CreateThread( )**.

Using the Microsoft C/C++ Thread Functions

To demonstrate the use of the C library thread functions, the preceding thread program will be converted so that it uses Microsoft's **_beginthreadex( )** function. Since the meaning and order of the parameters are the same for both **CreateThread( )** and **_beginthreadex( )**, this is a simple matter. The three changes that need to be made are as follows:

1. PROCESS.H must be included in the program.
2. The prototypes of the thread functions must be changed to reflect the type names used by **_beginthreadex( )**.
3. The calls to **CreateThread( )** need to be replaced by calls to **_beginthreadex( )**.

You must also link your program with the multithreaded library. To do so, select the multithreaded library using the Project/Settings property sheet. The multithreaded library option is under the "C/C++" tab when the category is "Code Generation". The following program reflects these changes.

```
/* Use Microsoft's _beginthreadex() function. */

#include <windows.h>
#include <string.h>
#include <stdio.h>
#include <process.h>
#include "thread.h"

#define MAX 5000

LRESULT CALLBACK WindowFunc(HWND, UINT, WPARAM, LPARAM);

/* use type names required by _beginthreadex() */
unsigned __stdcall MyThread1(void * param);
unsigned __stdcall MyThread2(void * param);

char szWinName[] = "MyWin"; /* name of window class */
```

16

```
char str[255]; /* holds output strings */

DWORD Tid1, Tid2; /* thread IDs */

int WINAPI WinMain(HINSTANCE hThisInst, HINSTANCE hPrevInst,
                   LPSTR lpszArgs, int nWinMode)
{
  HWND hwnd;
  MSG msg;
  WNDCLASSEX wcl;
  HACCEL hAccel;

  /* Define a window class. */
  wcl.cbSize = sizeof(WNDCLASSEX);

  wcl.hInstance = hThisInst; /* handle to this instance */
  wcl.lpszClassName = szWinName; /* window class name */
  wcl.lpfnWndProc = WindowFunc; /* window function */
  wcl.style = 0; /* default style */

  wcl.hIcon = LoadIcon(NULL, IDI_APPLICATION); /* standard icon */
  wcl.hIconSm = LoadIcon(NULL, IDI_APPLICATION); /* small icon */
  wcl.hCursor = LoadCursor(NULL, IDC_ARROW); /* cursor style */

  wcl.lpszMenuName = "ThreadMenu"; /* main menu */
  wcl.cbClsExtra = 0; /* no extra */
  wcl.cbWndExtra = 0; /* information needed */

  /* Make the window white. */
  wcl.hbrBackground = (HBRUSH) GetStockObject(WHITE_BRUSH);

  /* Register the window class. */
  if(!RegisterClassEx(&wcl)) return 0;

  /* Now that a window class has been registered, a window
     can be created. */
  hwnd = CreateWindow(
    szWinName, /* name of window class */
    "Demonstrate Threads", /* title */
    WS_OVERLAPPEDWINDOW, /* window style - normal */
    CW_USEDEFAULT, /* X coordinate - let Windows decide */
    CW_USEDEFAULT, /* Y coordinate - let Windows decide */
    CW_USEDEFAULT, /* width - let Windows decide */
    CW_USEDEFAULT, /* height - let Windows decide */
```

```
    HWND_DESKTOP, /* no parent window */
    NULL, /* no override of class menu */
    hThisInst, /* handle of this instance of the program */
    NULL /* no additional arguments */
  );

  /* Load accelerators. */
  hAccel = LoadAccelerators(hThisInst, "ThreadMenu");

  /* Display the window. */
  ShowWindow(hwnd, nWinMode);
  UpdateWindow(hwnd);

  /* Create the message loop. */
  while(GetMessage(&msg, NULL, 0, 0))
  {
    if(!TranslateAccelerator(hwnd, hAccel, &msg)) {
      TranslateMessage(&msg); /* translate keyboard messages */
      DispatchMessage(&msg); /* return control to Windows 98 */
    }
  }
  return msg.wParam;
}

/* This function is called by Windows 98 and is passed
   messages from the message queue.
*/
LRESULT CALLBACK WindowFunc(HWND hwnd, UINT message,
                            WPARAM wParam, LPARAM lParam)
{
  int response;

  switch(message) {
    case WM_COMMAND:
      switch(LOWORD(wParam)) {
        case IDM_THREAD:
          /* create threads using _beginthreadex() */
          _beginthreadex(NULL, 0, MyThread1,
                         (LPVOID) hwnd, 0,
                         (unsigned *) &Tid1);
          _beginthreadex(NULL, 0, MyThread2,
                         (LPVOID) hwnd, 0,
                         (unsigned *) &Tid2);
          break;
        case IDM_EXIT:
```

```
          response = MessageBox(hwnd, "Quit the Program?",
                                "Exit", MB_YESNO);
          if(response == IDYES) PostQuitMessage(0);
          break;
        case IDM_HELP:
          MessageBox(hwnd,
                     "F1: Help\nF2: Demonstrate Threads",
                     "Help", MB_OK);
          break;
      }
      break;
    case WM_DESTROY: /* terminate the program */
      PostQuitMessage(0);
      break;
    default:
      /* Let Windows 98 process any messages not specified in
      the preceding switch statement. */
      return DefWindowProc(hwnd, message, wParam, lParam);
  }
  return 0;
}

/* A thread of execution within the process. */
unsigned __stdcall MyThread1(void * param)
{
  int i;
  HDC hdc;

  for(i=0; i<MAX; i++) {
    sprintf(str, "Thread 1: loop # %5d ", i);
    hdc = GetDC((HWND) param);
    TextOut(hdc, 1, 1, str, strlen(str));
    ReleaseDC((HWND) param, hdc);
  }
  return 0;
}

/* Another thread of execution within the process. */
unsigned __stdcall MyThread2(void * param)
{
  int i;
  HDC hdc;

  for(i=0; i<MAX; i++) {
    sprintf(str, "Thread 2: loop # %5d ", i);
```

```
      hdc = GetDC((HWND) param);
      TextOut(hdc, 1, 20, str, strlen(str));
      ReleaseDC((HWND) param, hdc);
   }
   return 0;
}
```

Avoiding the C Library Functions

wsprintf( ) and lstrlen( ) are Win32 functions that can be substituted for the standard C functions sprintf( ) and strlen( ).

For many multithreaded programs, it is possible to avoid the use of the C standard library. In this case, you can use **CreateThread( )** and **ExitThread( )** without the potential for incurring memory leaks. For example, many of the programs in this book only use two C library functions: **sprintf( )** and **strlen( )**. Win32 contains substitutes for these functions called **wsprintf( )** and **lstrlen( )**, respectively. These functions contain some additional functionality that allows them to handle Unicode characters, but for the most part they work the same as their C library relatives.

Win32 also contains substitutes for several other C string handling functions, for example, **lstrcat( )**, **lstrcmp( )**, and **lstrcpy( )**. Various character functions are also provided, such as **CharUpper( )**, **CharLower( )**, **IsCharAlpha( )**, and **IsCharAlphaNumeric( )**. In general, if you are using the C standard library only for simple character handling, you can probably bypass it by using the functions built into Win32.

In the remaining examples in this chapter, threads will be created using **CreateThread( )**. The functions **wsprintf( )** and **lstrlen( )** will be substituted for **sprintf( )** and **strlen( )**, to avoid the C standard library. This means that the examples that follow should be able to be compiled and correctly executed by any C/C++ compiler capable of creating Windows 98 programs.

Suspending and Resuming a Thread

A thread of execution may be suspended by calling **SuspendThread( )**. It may be resumed by calling **ResumeThread( )**. The prototypes for these functions are shown here.

DWORD SuspendThread(HANDLE *hThread*);

DWORD ResumeThread(HANDLE *hThread*);

For both functions, the handle to the thread is passed in *hThread*.

A thread will be resumed only after its suspend count reaches zero.

Each thread of execution has associated with it a *suspend count*. If this count is zero, the thread is not suspended. If it is nonzero, the thread is in a suspended state. Each call to **SuspendThread( )** increments the suspend count. Each call to **ResumeThread( )** decrements the suspend count. A suspended thread will resume only after its suspend count has reached zero. Therefore, to resume a suspended thread implies that there must be an equivalent number of calls to **ResumeThread( )** as there have been calls to **SuspendThread( )**.

Both functions return the thread's previous suspend count or –1 if an error occurs.

Sometimes you will want to suspend execution of a thread for only a short period of time and then have it resume. The easiest way to accomplish this is with the **Sleep( )** function, shown here.

VOID Sleep(DWORD *Duration*);

Duration specifies the length of time, in milliseconds, that the calling thread will suspend. When this time has passed, the thread will automatically resume execution.

Sleep( ) has two main uses. First, it can be used to create a short time delay. You saw an example of this use in the preceding chapter. There, it was used to pause execution while a message was briefly displayed on the screen. Its second use is to force a task-switch. When a thread calls **Sleep( )**, the execution of the calling task is suspended and the next ready-to-run thread resumes. You can use **Sleep( )** to give up the remainder of the calling thread's time slice by specifying a zero duration.

Thread Priorities

Each thread has associated with it a priority setting. A thread's priority determines how much CPU time a thread receives. Low-priority threads receive little. High-priority threads receive a lot. Of course, how much CPU time a thread receives has profound impact on its execution characteristics and its interaction with other threads currently executing in the system.

A thread's priority determines how much CPU time it receives.

A thread's priority setting is the combination of two values: the overall priority class of the process and the priority setting of the individual thread relative to that priority class. That is, a thread's actual priority is determined by combining the process's priority class with the thread's individual priority level. Each priority component is examined next.

Priority Classes

You can obtain the current priority class by calling **GetPriorityClass( )**, and you can set the priority class by calling **SetPriorityClass( )**. The prototypes for these functions are shown here.

DWORD GetPriorityClass(HANDLE *hApp*);

BOOL SetPriorityClass(HANDLE *hApp*, DWORD *dwPriority*);

The priority class determines the general priority category for all of the threads in a process.

Here, *hApp* is the handle of the process. **GetPriorityClass( )** returns the priority class of the application or zero on failure. For **SetPriorityClass( )**, *dwPriority* specifies the process's new priority class. The priority class values are shown here, in order of highest to lowest priority.

REALTIME_PRIORITY_CLASS

HIGH_PRIORITY_CLASS

NORMAL_PRIORITY_CLASS

IDLE_PRIORITY_CLASS

Programs are given the **NORMAL_PRIORITY_CLASS** by default. Usually, you won't need to alter the priority class of your program. In fact, changing a process's priority class can have negative consequences on the overall performance of the computer system. For example, if you increase a program's priority class to **REALTIME_PRIORITY_CLASS**, it will dominate the CPU. For some specialized applications, you may need to increase an application's priority class, but usually you won't. For the purposes of this chapter, the default priority setting of a process will be used.

Thread Priorities

A thread's priority setting determines how much CPU time it receives within its process.

For any given priority class, each individual thread's priority determines how much CPU time it receives within its process. When a thread is first created, it is given normal priority. However, you can change a thread's priority—even while it is executing.

You can obtain a thread's priority setting by calling **GetThreadPriority( )**. You can increase or decrease a thread's priority using **SetThreadPriority( )**. The prototypes for these functions are shown here.

BOOL SetThreadPriority(HANDLE *hThread*, int *Priority*);

int GetThreadPriority(HANDLE *hThread*);

For both functions, *hThread* is the handle of the thread. For **SetThreadPriority( )**, *Priority* is the new priority setting. For **GetThreadPriority( )**, the current priority setting is returned. The priority settings are shown here, in order of highest to lowest.

Thread Priority	Value
THREAD_PRIORITY_TIME_CRITICAL	15
THREAD_PRIORITY_HIGHEST	2
THREAD_PRIORITY_ABOVE_NORMAL	1
THREAD_PRIORITY_NORMAL	0
THREAD_PRIORITY_BELOW_NORMAL	−1
THREAD_PRIORITY_LOWEST	−2
THREAD_PRIORITY_IDLE	−15

These values are actually increments or decrements that are applied relative to the priority class of the process. Through the combination of a process's priority class and thread priority, Windows 98 supports 31 different priority settings for application programs.

GetThreadPriority( ) returns **THREAD_PRIORITY_ERROR_RETURN** if an error occurs.

For the most part, if a thread has the normal priority class, you can freely experiment with changing its priority setting without fear of negatively affecting overall system performance. The thread control panel developed in the next section allows you to alter the priority setting of threads within a process (but does not change their priority class).

Creating a Thread Control Panel

When developing multithreaded programs, it is often useful to experiment with various priority settings. It is also useful to be able to dynamically suspend and resume, or even terminate, a thread. As you will see, it is quite easy, using the functions just described, to create a thread control panel that allows you to accomplish these things. Further, you can use the control panel while your multithreaded program is running. The dynamic nature of the thread control panel allows you to easily change the execution profile of a thread and observe the results.

The thread control panel developed in this section is capable of controlling two threads. For the sake of simplicity, the control panel is implemented as a modal dialog box that is executed as part of the program's main thread. It relies upon global thread handles that must be defined by any program that uses the control panel.

The thread control panel is capable of performing the following actions:

◆   Setting a thread's priority

◆   Suspending a thread

◆   Resuming a thread

◆   Terminating a thread

It also displays the current priority setting of each thread.

As stated, the control panel is a modal dialog box. When a modal dialog box is activated, it usually implies that the rest of the application is suspended until the user closes the box. However, in a multithreaded program, it is possible for a modal dialog box to run in its own thread. When this is the case, the other threads in the program remain active. As mentioned, the thread control panel will be executed by the main thread of any program that uses it. Therefore, it will be executing in its own thread of execution. The advantage of this approach is that modal dialog boxes are a little easier to create than are modeless ones. Also, since the dialog box may run in its own thread, there is no particular advantage, in this case, of using a modeless dialog box. As you become more familiar with multithreaded programming, you will find that it simplifies several previously difficult programming situations.

A Thread Control Panel Program

Here is a program that includes the thread control panel and demonstrates its use. It does so by adding the panel to the thread demonstration program shown earlier. Sample output is contained in Figure 16-2. To use the program, first begin execution of the threads (by selecting Start Threads from the Threads menu), and then activate the thread control panel. Once the control panel is active, you can experiment with different priority settings, and so on.

```c
/* Using a thread control panel */

#include <windows.h>
#include "panel.h"

#define MAX 50000

#define NUMPRIORITIES 5
#define OFFSET 2

LRESULT CALLBACK WindowFunc(HWND, UINT, WPARAM, LPARAM);
LRESULT CALLBACK ThreadPanel(HWND, UINT, WPARAM, LPARAM);

DWORD WINAPI MyThread1(LPVOID param);
DWORD WINAPI MyThread2(LPVOID param);

char szWinName[] = "MyWin"; /* name of window class */

char str[255]; /* holds output strings */

DWORD Tid1, Tid2; /* thread IDs */
HANDLE hThread1, hThread2; /* thread handles */

int ThPriority1, ThPriority2; /* thread priorities */
int suspend1 = 0, suspend2 = 0; /* thread states */

char priorities[NUMPRIORITIES][80] = {
  "Lowest",
  "Below Normal",
  "Normal",
  "Above Normal",
  "Highest"
};

HINSTANCE hInst;

int WINAPI WinMain(HINSTANCE hThisInst, HINSTANCE hPrevInst,
                   LPSTR lpszArgs, int nWinMode)
{
  HWND hwnd;
  MSG msg;
  WNDCLASSEX wcl;
```

```
  HACCEL hAccel;

  /* Define a window class. */
  wcl.cbSize = sizeof(WNDCLASSEX);

  wcl.hInstance = hThisInst; /* handle to this instance */
  wcl.lpszClassName = szWinName; /* window class name */
  wcl.lpfnWndProc = WindowFunc; /* window function */
  wcl.style = 0; /* default style */

  wcl.hIcon = LoadIcon(NULL, IDI_APPLICATION); /* standard icon */
  wcl.hIconSm = LoadIcon(NULL, IDI_APPLICATION); /* small icon */
  wcl.hCursor = LoadCursor(NULL, IDC_ARROW);  /* cursor style */

  wcl.lpszMenuName = "ThreadPanelMenu"; /* main menu */
  wcl.cbClsExtra = 0; /* no extra */
  wcl.cbWndExtra = 0; /* information needed */

  /* Make the window white. */
  wcl.hbrBackground = (HBRUSH) GetStockObject(WHITE_BRUSH);

  /* Register the window class. */
  if(!RegisterClassEx(&wcl)) return 0;

  /* Now that a window class has been registered, a window
     can be created. */
  hwnd = CreateWindow(
    szWinName, /* name of window class */
    "Using a Thread Control Panel", /* title */
    WS_OVERLAPPEDWINDOW, /* standard window */
    CW_USEDEFAULT, /* X coordinate - let Windows decide */
    CW_USEDEFAULT, /* Y coordinate - let Windows decide */
    CW_USEDEFAULT, /* width - let Windows decide */
    CW_USEDEFAULT, /* height - let Windows decide */
    HWND_DESKTOP, /* no parent window */
    NULL, /* no override of class menu */
    hThisInst, /* handle of this instance of the program */
    NULL /* no additional arguments */
  );

  hInst = hThisInst; /* save instance handle */

  /* Load accelerators. */
  hAccel = LoadAccelerators(hThisInst, "ThreadPanelMenu");
```

```
      /* Display the window. */
      ShowWindow(hwnd, nWinMode);
      UpdateWindow(hwnd);

      /* Create the message loop. */
      while(GetMessage(&msg, NULL, 0, 0))
      {
        if(!TranslateAccelerator(hwnd, hAccel, &msg)) {
          TranslateMessage(&msg);
          DispatchMessage(&msg);
        }
      }
      return msg.wParam;
}

/* This function is called by Windows 98 and is passed
   messages from the message queue.
*/
LRESULT CALLBACK WindowFunc(HWND hwnd, UINT message,
                            WPARAM wParam, LPARAM lParam)
{
  int response;

  switch(message) {
    case WM_COMMAND:
      switch(LOWORD(wParam)) {
        case IDM_THREAD: /* create the threads */
          suspend1 = suspend2 = 0;
          hThread1 = CreateThread(NULL, 0,
                          (LPTHREAD_START_ROUTINE)MyThread1,
                          (LPVOID) hwnd, 0, &Tid1);
          hThread2 = CreateThread(NULL, 0,
                          (LPTHREAD_START_ROUTINE)MyThread2,
                          (LPVOID) hwnd, 0, &Tid2);
          break;
        case IDM_PANEL: /* activate control panel */
          DialogBox(hInst, "ThreadPanelDB", hwnd, (DLGPROC) ThreadPanel);
          break;
        case IDM_EXIT:
          response = MessageBox(hwnd, "Quit the Program?",
                                "Exit", MB_YESNO);
          if(response == IDYES) PostQuitMessage(0);
          break;
        case IDM_HELP:
          MessageBox(hwnd,
```

```
                          "F1: Help\nF2: Start Threads\nF3: Panel",
                          "Help", MB_OK);
              break;
          }
          break;
        case WM_DESTROY: /* terminate the program */
          PostQuitMessage(0);
          break;
        default:
          /* Let Windows 98 process any messages not specified in
             the preceding switch statement. */
          return DefWindowProc(hwnd, message, wParam, lParam);
    }
    return 0;
}


/* A thread of execution within the process. */
DWORD WINAPI MyThread1(LPVOID param)
{
    int i;
    HDC hdc;

    for(i=0; i<MAX; i++) {
      wsprintf(str, "Thread 1: loop # %5d ", i);
      hdc = GetDC((HWND) param);
      TextOut(hdc, 1, 1, str, lstrlen(str));
      ReleaseDC((HWND) param, hdc);
    }
    return 0;
}


/* Another thread of execution within the process. */
DWORD WINAPI MyThread2(LPVOID param)
{
    int i;
    HDC hdc;

    for(i=0; i<MAX; i++) {
      wsprintf(str, "Thread 2: loop # %5d ", i);
      hdc = GetDC((HWND) param);
      TextOut(hdc, 1, 20, str, lstrlen(str));
      ReleaseDC((HWND) param, hdc);
    }
    return 0;
}
```

```
/* Thread control panel dialog box. */
LRESULT CALLBACK ThreadPanel(HWND hdwnd, UINT message,
                             WPARAM wParam, LPARAM lParam)
{
  long i;
  HWND hpbRes, hpbSus;

  switch(message) {
    case WM_INITDIALOG:
      /* initialize list boxes */
      for(i=0; i<NUMPRIORITIES; i++) {
        SendDlgItemMessage(hdwnd, IDD_LB1,
            LB_ADDSTRING, 0, (LPARAM) priorities[i]);
        SendDlgItemMessage(hdwnd, IDD_LB2,
            LB_ADDSTRING, 0, (LPARAM) priorities[i]);
      }

      /* get current priority */
      ThPriority1 = GetThreadPriority(hThread1) + OFFSET;
      ThPriority2 = GetThreadPriority(hThread2) + OFFSET;

      /* update list box */
      SendDlgItemMessage(hdwnd, IDD_LB1, LB_SETCURSEL,
                         (WPARAM) ThPriority1, 0);
      SendDlgItemMessage(hdwnd, IDD_LB2, LB_SETCURSEL,
                         (WPARAM) ThPriority2, 0);

      /* set suspend and resume buttons for first thread */
      hpbSus = GetDlgItem(hdwnd, IDD_SUSPEND1);
      hpbRes = GetDlgItem(hdwnd, IDD_RESUME1);
      if(suspend1) {
        EnableWindow(hpbSus, 0); /* disable Suspend */
        EnableWindow(hpbRes, 1); /* enable Resume */
      }
      else {
        EnableWindow(hpbSus, 1); /* enable Suspend */
        EnableWindow(hpbRes, 0); /* disable Resume */
      }

      /* set suspend and resume buttons for second thread */
      hpbSus = GetDlgItem(hdwnd, IDD_SUSPEND2);
      hpbRes = GetDlgItem(hdwnd, IDD_RESUME2);
      if(suspend2) {
        EnableWindow(hpbSus, 0); /* disable Suspend */
```

```
      EnableWindow(hpbRes, 1); /* enable Resume */
    }
    else {
      EnableWindow(hpbSus, 1); /* enable Suspend */
      EnableWindow(hpbRes, 0); /* disable Resume */
    }

    return 1;
  case WM_COMMAND:
    switch(wParam) {
      case IDD_TERMINATE1:
        TerminateThread(hThread1, 0);
        return 1;
      case IDD_TERMINATE2:
        TerminateThread(hThread2, 0);
        return 1;
      case IDD_SUSPEND1:
        SuspendThread(hThread1);
        hpbSus = GetDlgItem(hdwnd, IDD_SUSPEND1);
        hpbRes = GetDlgItem(hdwnd, IDD_RESUME1);
        EnableWindow(hpbSus, 0); /* disable Suspend */
        EnableWindow(hpbRes, 1); /* enable Resume */
        suspend1 = 1;
        return 1;
      case IDD_RESUME1:
        ResumeThread(hThread1);
        hpbSus = GetDlgItem(hdwnd, IDD_SUSPEND1);
        hpbRes = GetDlgItem(hdwnd, IDD_RESUME1);
        EnableWindow(hpbSus, 1); /* enable Suspend */
        EnableWindow(hpbRes, 0); /* disable Resume */
        suspend1 = 0;
        return 1;
      case IDD_SUSPEND2:
        SuspendThread(hThread2);
        hpbSus = GetDlgItem(hdwnd, IDD_SUSPEND2);
        hpbRes = GetDlgItem(hdwnd, IDD_RESUME2);
        EnableWindow(hpbSus, 0); /* disable Suspend */
        EnableWindow(hpbRes, 1); /* enable Resume */
        suspend2 = 1;
        return 1;
      case IDD_RESUME2:
        ResumeThread(hThread2);
        hpbSus = GetDlgItem(hdwnd, IDD_SUSPEND2);
        hpbRes = GetDlgItem(hdwnd, IDD_RESUME2);
        EnableWindow(hpbSus, 1); /* enable Suspend */
```

16

```
            EnableWindow(hpbRes, 0); /* disable Resume */
            suspend2 = 0;
            return 1;
        case IDOK: /* actually change priorities */
            ThPriority1 = SendDlgItemMessage(hdwnd, IDD_LB1,
                            LB_GETCURSEL, 0, 0);
            ThPriority2 = SendDlgItemMessage(hdwnd, IDD_LB2,
                            LB_GETCURSEL, 0, 0);
            SetThreadPriority(hThread1, ThPriority1-OFFSET);
            SetThreadPriority(hThread2, ThPriority2-OFFSET);
            return 1;
        case IDCANCEL:
            EndDialog(hdwnd, 0);
            return 1;
        }
    }
    return 0;
}
```

This program requires the header file PANEL.H, shown here.

```
#define IDM_THREAD      100
#define IDM_HELP        101
#define IDM_PANEL       102
#define IDM_EXIT        103

#define IDD_LB1         200
#define IDD_LB2         201
#define IDD_TERMINATE1  202
#define IDD_TERMINATE2  203
#define IDD_SUSPEND1    204
#define IDD_SUSPEND2    205
#define IDD_RESUME1     206
#define IDD_RESUME2     207
#define IDD_TEXT1       208
#define IDD_TEXT2       209
#define IDD_TEXT3       210
```

The resource file required by the program is shown here.

```
#include <windows.h>
#include "panel.h"

ThreadPanelMenu MENU
```

```
{
  POPUP "&Threads" {
    MENUITEM "&Start Threads\tF2", IDM_THREAD
    MENUITEM "&Control Panel\tF3", IDM_PANEL
    MENUITEM "E&xit\tCtrl+X", IDM_EXIT
  }
  MENUITEM "&Help", IDM_HELP
}


ThreadPanelDB DIALOG 20, 20, 170, 140
CAPTION "Thread Control Panel"
STYLE DS_MODALFRAME | WS_POPUP | WS_CAPTION | WS_SYSMENU
{
  DEFPUSHBUTTON "Change", IDOK, 80, 105, 33, 14,
                WS_CHILD | WS_VISIBLE | WS_TABSTOP
  PUSHBUTTON "Done", IDCANCEL, 15, 120, 33, 14,
                WS_CHILD | WS_VISIBLE | WS_TABSTOP
  PUSHBUTTON "Terminate 1", IDD_TERMINATE1, 10, 10, 42, 12,
                WS_CHILD | WS_VISIBLE | WS_TABSTOP
  PUSHBUTTON "Terminate 2", IDD_TERMINATE2, 10, 60, 42, 12,
                WS_CHILD | WS_VISIBLE | WS_TABSTOP
  PUSHBUTTON "Suspend 1", IDD_SUSPEND1, 10, 25, 42, 12,
                WS_CHILD | WS_VISIBLE | WS_TABSTOP
  PUSHBUTTON "Resume 1", IDD_RESUME1, 10, 40, 42, 12,
                WS_CHILD | WS_VISIBLE | WS_TABSTOP
  PUSHBUTTON "Suspend 2", IDD_SUSPEND2, 10, 75, 42, 12,
                WS_CHILD | WS_VISIBLE | WS_TABSTOP
  PUSHBUTTON "Resume 2", IDD_RESUME2, 10, 90, 42, 12,
                WS_CHILD | WS_VISIBLE | WS_TABSTOP
  LISTBOX IDD_LB1, 65, 11, 63, 42, LBS_NOTIFY |
          WS_VISIBLE | WS_BORDER | WS_VSCROLL | WS_TABSTOP
  LISTBOX IDD_LB2, 65, 61, 63, 42, LBS_NOTIFY |
          WS_VISIBLE | WS_BORDER | WS_VSCROLL | WS_TABSTOP
  CTEXT "Thread 1", IDD_TEXT1, 140, 22, 24, 18
  CTEXT "Thread 2", IDD_TEXT2, 140, 73, 24, 18
  CTEXT "Thread Priority", IDD_TEXT3, 65, 0, 64, 10
}


ThreadPanelMenu ACCELERATORS
{
  VK_F2, IDM_THREAD, VIRTKEY
  VK_F3, IDM_PANEL, VIRTKEY
  "^X", IDM_EXIT
  VK_F1, IDM_HELP, VIRTKEY
}
```

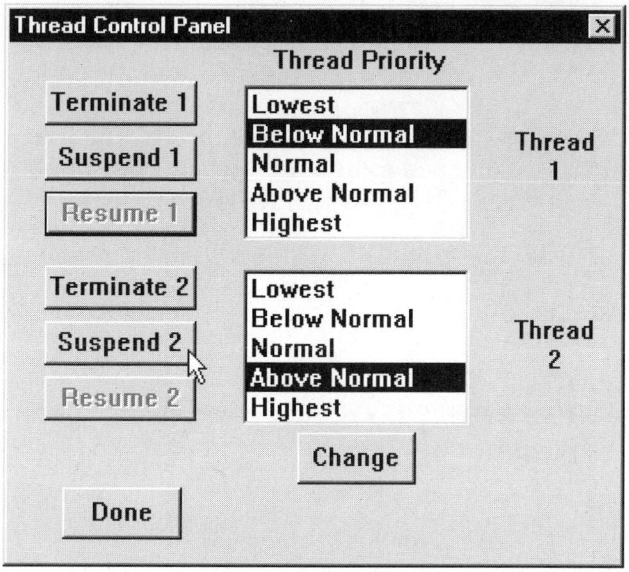

Sample output
from the
thread control
panel sample
program
Figure 16-2.

A Closer Look at the Thread Control Panel

Let's take a closer look at the thread control panel. To begin, notice that the
program defines several global variables that are used by the control panel.
They are

```
DWORD Tid1, Tid2; /* thread IDs */
HANDLE hThread1, hThread2; /* thread handles */

int ThPriority1, ThPriority2; /* thread priorities */
int suspend1 = 0, suspend2 = 0; /* thread states */

char priorities[NUMPRIORITIES][80] = {
  "Lowest",
  "Below Normal",
  "Normal",
  "Above Normal",
  "Highest"
};
```

Here, **Tid1** and **Tid2** will hold the IDs of the two threads. **hThread1** and **hThread2** are the handles to the two threads of execution. These handles store the values returned by **CreateThread( )** when the threads are created. **ThPriority1** and **ThPriority2** hold the current priority settings of the threads. The variables **suspend1** and **suspend2** are used by the control panel to store the state of each thread. The **priorities** array holds strings that will be used to initialize the list boxes used inside the control panel dialog box. These describe the priority settings of each string.

The program also defines the following macros:

```
#define NUMPRIORITIES 5
#define OFFSET 2
```

NUMPRIORITIES defines the number of priorities a thread may have. Using the control panel, you can set a thread to one of the following priorities.

THREAD_PRIORITY_HIGHEST

THREAD_PRIORITY_ABOVE_NORMAL

THREAD_PRIORITY_NORMAL

THREAD_PRIORITY_BELOW_NORMAL

THREAD_PRIORITY_LOWEST

The other two thread priority settings:

THREAD_PRIORITY_TIME_CRITICAL

THREAD_PRIORITY_IDLE

are not supported because, relative to the control panel, they are of little practical value. For example, if you want to create a time-critical application, you are better off making its priority class time-critical. However, you may want to try adding these settings on your own.

OFFSET defines an offset that will be used to translate between list box indexes and thread priorities. You should recall that normal priority has the value zero. In this example, the highest priority is **THREAD_PRIORITY_ HIGHEST**, which is 2. The lowest priority is **THREAD_PRIORITY_**

LOWEST, which is −2. Since list box indexes begin at zero, the offset is used to convert between indexes and priority settings.

The thread control panel is activated by the dialog function shown here.

```
/* Thread control panel dialog box. */
LRESULT CALLBACK ThreadPanel(HWND hdwnd, UINT message,
                             WPARAM wParam, LPARAM lParam)
{
  long i;
  HANDLE hpbRes, hpbSus;

  switch(message) {
    case WM_INITDIALOG:
      /* initialize list boxes */
      for(i=0; i<NUMPRIORITIES; i++) {
        SendDlgItemMessage(hdwnd, IDD_LB1,
            LB_ADDSTRING, 0, (LPARAM) priorities[i]);
        SendDlgItemMessage(hdwnd, IDD_LB2,
            LB_ADDSTRING, 0, (LPARAM) priorities[i]);
      }

      /* get current priority */
      ThPriority1 = GetThreadPriority(hThread1) + OFFSET;
      ThPriority2 = GetThreadPriority(hThread2) + OFFSET;

      /* update list box */
      SendDlgItemMessage(hdwnd, IDD_LB1, LB_SETCURSEL,
                         (WPARAM) ThPriority1, 0);
      SendDlgItemMessage(hdwnd, IDD_LB2, LB_SETCURSEL,
                         (WPARAM) ThPriority2, 0);

      /* set suspend and resume buttons for first thread */
      hpbSus = GetDlgItem(hdwnd, IDD_SUSPEND1);
      hpbRes = GetDlgItem(hdwnd, IDD_RESUME1);
      if(suspend1) {
        EnableWindow(hpbSus, 0); /* disable Suspend */
        EnableWindow(hpbRes, 1); /* enable Resume */
      }
      else {
        EnableWindow(hpbSus, 1); /* enable Suspend */
        EnableWindow(hpbRes, 0); /* disable Resume */
      }

      /* set suspend and resume buttons for second thread */
```

```
   hpbSus = GetDlgItem(hdwnd, IDD_SUSPEND2);
   hpbRes = GetDlgItem(hdwnd, IDD_RESUME2);
   if(suspend2) {
     EnableWindow(hpbSus, 0); /* disable Suspend */
     EnableWindow(hpbRes, 1); /* enable Resume */
   }
   else {
     EnableWindow(hpbSus, 1); /* enable Suspend */
     EnableWindow(hpbRes, 0); /* disable Resume */
   }

   return 1;
case WM_COMMAND:
  switch(wParam) {
    case IDD_TERMINATE1:
      TerminateThread(hThread1, 0);
      return 1;
    case IDD_TERMINATE2:
      TerminateThread(hThread2, 0);
      return 1;
    case IDD_SUSPEND1:
      SuspendThread(hThread1);
      hpbSus = GetDlgItem(hdwnd, IDD_SUSPEND1);
      hpbRes = GetDlgItem(hdwnd, IDD_RESUME1);
      EnableWindow(hpbSus, 0); /* disable Suspend */
      EnableWindow(hpbRes, 1); /* enable Resume */
      suspend1 = 1;
      return 1;
    case IDD_RESUME1:
      ResumeThread(hThread1);
      hpbSus = GetDlgItem(hdwnd, IDD_SUSPEND1);
      hpbRes = GetDlgItem(hdwnd, IDD_RESUME1);
      EnableWindow(hpbSus, 1); /* enable Suspend */
      EnableWindow(hpbRes, 0); /* disable Resume */
      suspend1 = 0;
      return 1;
    case IDD_SUSPEND2:
      SuspendThread(hThread2);
      hpbSus = GetDlgItem(hdwnd, IDD_SUSPEND2);
      hpbRes = GetDlgItem(hdwnd, IDD_RESUME2);
      EnableWindow(hpbSus, 0); /* disable Suspend */
      EnableWindow(hpbRes, 1); /* enable Resume */
      suspend2 = 1;
      return 1;
    case IDD_RESUME2:
```

```
         ResumeThread(hThread2);
         hpbSus = GetDlgItem(hdwnd, IDD_SUSPEND2);
         hpbRes = GetDlgItem(hdwnd, IDD_RESUME2);
         EnableWindow(hpbSus, 1); /* enable Suspend */
         EnableWindow(hpbRes, 0); /* disable Resume */
         suspend2 = 0;
         return 1;
       case IDOK: /* actually change priorities */
         ThPriority1 = SendDlgItemMessage(hdwnd, IDD_LB1,
                           LB_GETCURSEL, 0, 0);
         ThPriority2 = SendDlgItemMessage(hdwnd, IDD_LB2,
                           LB_GETCURSEL, 0, 0);
         SetThreadPriority(hThread1, ThPriority1-OFFSET);
         SetThreadPriority(hThread2, ThPriority2-OFFSET);
         return 1;
       case IDCANCEL:
         EndDialog(hdwnd, 0);
         return 1;
     }
   }
   return 0;
}
```

When the control panel begins, it performs the following sequence:

1. It initializes the two list boxes used by the panel.
2. It obtains the current priority setting for each thread.
3. It highlights each thread's priority within the list boxes.
4. If a thread is suspended, then the appropriate Suspend push button is disabled. Otherwise, the corresponding Resume button is disabled. The state of the push buttons is set using **EnableWindow( )**. (See the In Depth box.)

After the dialog box has been initialized, you may change a thread's priority by first selecting the new setting in its priorities list box and then pressing the Change button. Remember, the new priority setting that you select does not become active until you press Change.

You can suspend a thread by pressing its Suspend push button. The global variables **suspend1** and **suspend2** hold the current suspend status of each thread. Zero means the thread is running. Nonzero means that the thread is suspended. To resume a suspended thread, press its Resume button. The purpose of **suspend1** and **suspend2** is to disable the Suspend buttons when the dialog box is initialized. Remember, for any given thread, there must be one call to **ResumeThread( )** for each call to **SuspendThread( )** in order to restart it. By disabling a thread's Suspend button after it has been suspended, you can prevent multiple calls to **SuspendThread( )**. Since the control panel can be closed and then reopened during the execution of the threads, the state of the Suspend and Resume buttons must be set whenever the panel is initialized. These variables are reset each time a new set of threads is started.

You can terminate a thread by pressing its Terminate button. Once a thread has been terminated, it cannot be resumed. Notice that the control panel uses **TerminateThread( )** to halt execution of a thread. As mentioned earlier, this function must be used with care. If you use the control panel to experiment with threads of your own, you will want to make sure that no harmful side effects are possible.

Before moving on, you might want to experiment with the preceding program, noticing the effects of the different priority settings.

IN DEPTH

Disabling Controls

Sometimes you will have a control that is not applicable to all situations. The Suspend and Resume push buttons in the thread control panel are examples. When a control is not applicable, it can—and should—be disabled. A control that is disabled is displayed in gray and may not be selected. To disable a control, use the **EnableWindow( )** API function, shown here:

BOOL EnableWindow(HWND *hCntl*, BOOL *How*);

Here, *hCntl* specifies the handle of the window to be affected. (Remember, controls are simply specialized windows.) If *How* is nonzero, then the control is enabled—that is, activated. If *How* is zero, the control is disabled. The function returns nonzero if the control was already disabled and zero if the control was previously enabled.

On your own, you might want to try disabling and enabling various controls used by the other examples in this book.

Synchronization

Synchronization is the mechanism that allows you to control the execution of two or more threads.

When using multiple threads or processes, it is sometimes necessary to coordinate the activities of two or more. This process is called *synchronization*. The most common reason for this is when two or more threads need access to a shared resource that may only be used by one thread at a time. For example, when one thread is writing to a file, a second thread must be prevented from doing so at the same time. The mechanism that prevents this is called *serialization*. Another reason for synchronization is when one thread is waiting for an event that is caused by another thread. In this case, there must be some means by which the first thread is held in a suspended state until the event has occurred.

Before beginning, let's define some terms. There are two general states that a task may be in. First, it may be *executing* (or ready to execute as soon as it obtains its time slice). Second, a task may be *blocked*, awaiting some resource or event, in which case its execution is *suspended* until the needed resource is available or the event occurs.

If you are not familiar with the need for synchronization and the serialization problem or its most common solution, the semaphore, the next section discusses it. (If this is familiar territory for you, skip ahead.)

Understanding the Synchronization Problem

Windows 98 must provide special services that allow access to a shared resource to be serialized, because without help from the operating system, there is no way for one process or thread to know that it has sole access to a resource. To understand this, imagine that you are writing programs for a multitasking operating system that does not provide any synchronization support. Further imagine that you have two concurrently executing processes, A and B, both of which, from time to time, require access to some resource R (such as a disk file) that must only be accessed by one task at a time. As a means of preventing one program from accessing R while the other is using it, you try the following solution. First, you establish a variable called **flag** that can be accessed by both programs. Your programs initialize **flag** to 0. Next, before using each piece of code that accesses R, you wait for **flag** to be cleared, then set **flag**, access R, and finally clear **flag**. That is, before either program accesses R, it executes this piece of code:

```
while(flag) ; /* wait for flag to be cleared */
flag = 1; /* set flag */
```

```
/* ... access resource R ... */

flag = 0; /* clear the flag */
```

The idea behind this code is that neither process will access R if **flag** is set. Conceptually, this approach is in the spirit of the correct solution. However, in actual fact it leaves much to be desired for one simple reason: it won't always work! Let's see why.

Using the code just given, it is possible for both processes to access R at the same time. The **while** loop is, in essence, performing repeated load and compare instructions on **flag**—in other words, it is testing **flag**'s value. When **flag** is cleared, the next line of code sets **flag**'s value. The trouble is that it is possible for these two operations to be performed in two different time slices. Between the two time slices, the value of **flag** might have been accessed by a different process, thus allowing R to be used by both processes at the same time. To understand this, imagine that process A enters the **while** loop and finds that **flag** is 0, which is the green light to access R. However, before it can set **flag** to 1, its time slice expires and process B resumes execution. If B executes its **while**, it too will find that **flag** is not set and assume that it is safe to access R. However, when A resumes, it will also begin accessing R. The crucial aspect of the problem is that the testing and setting of **flag** do not comprise one uninterruptable operation. Rather, as just illustrated, they can be separated by a time slice. No matter how you try, there is no way, using only application-level code, that you can absolutely guarantee that one and only one process will access R at one time.

A semaphore synchronizes access to a resource.

The solution to the synchronization problem is as elegant as it is simple. The operating system (in this case Windows 98) provides a routine that in one uninterrupted operation tests and, if possible, sets a flag. In the language of operating systems engineers, this is called a *test and set* operation. For historical reasons, the flags used to control serialization and provide synchronization between threads (and processes) are called *semaphores*. The semaphore is at the core of Windows 98's synchronization system.

Windows 98 Synchronization Objects

Windows 98 supports five types of synchronization objects. The first type is the classic semaphore. A semaphore can be used to allow a limited number of processes or threads access to a resource. When using a semaphore, the resource can be either completely serialized, in which case one and only one thread or process can access it at any one time, or the semaphore can be used

16

to allow no more than a small number of processes or threads access at any one time. Semaphores are implemented using a counter that is decremented when a task is granted the semaphore and incremented when the task releases it.

The second synchronization object is the *mutex* semaphore. A mutex semaphore is used to serialize a resource so that one and only one thread or process can access it at any one time. In essence, a mutex semaphore is a special-case version of a standard semaphore.

The third synchronization object is the *event object*. It can be used to block access to a resource until some other thread or process signals that it may be used—that is, an event object signals that a specified event has occurred.

The fourth synchronization object is the *waitable timer*. A waitable timer blocks a thread's execution until a specific time. These objects offer some exciting possibilities, especially for background tasks.

You can prevent a section of code from being used by more than one thread at a time by making it into a *critical section* using a critical section object. Once a critical section is entered by one thread, no other thread may use it until the first thread has left the critical section. (Critical sections apply only to threads within a process.)

With the exception of critical sections, the other synchronization objects can be used to serialize threads within a process or processes themselves. In fact, semaphores are a common and simple means to interprocess communication.

This chapter describes how to create and use a semaphore, an event object, and a waitable timer. After you understand these synchronization objects, the mutex semaphore and the critical section will be easy for you to master on your own. Remember, at the core of all of synchronization, either implicitly or explicitly, is the concept of the semaphore, so we will begin there.

Using a Semaphore to Synchronize Threads

Before you can use a semaphore, you must create one using **CreateSemaphore( )**, whose prototype is shown here.

```
HANDLE CreateSemaphore(LPSECURITY_ATTRIBUTES lpSecAttr,
                       LONG InitialCount,
                       LONG MaxCount,
                       LPSTR lpszName);
```

Here, *lpSecAttr* is a pointer to the security attributes. Since Windows 98 ignores security, *lpSecAttr* should be **NULL**.

A semaphore can allow one or more tasks access to an object. The number allowed is determined by the value of *MaxCount*. If this value is 1, then the semaphore acts much like a mutex semaphore, allowing one and only one thread or process access to the resource at any one time.

Semaphores use a counter to keep track of how many tasks have currently been granted access. If the count is zero, no further access can be granted until one task releases the semaphore. If the count is greater than zero, the semaphore is said to be *signaled,* which means that another thread may be granted access. Each time a thread is granted access, the count is decremented. The initial count of the semaphore is specified in *InitialCount*. If this value is zero, then initially all objects waiting on the semaphore will be blocked until the semaphore is released elsewhere by your program. Typically, this value is set initially to 1 or more, indicating that the semaphore can be granted to at least one task. In any event, *InitialCount* must be non-negative and less than or equal to the value specified in *MaxCount*.

The *lpszName* parameter points to a string that becomes the name of the semaphore object. Semaphores are global objects that may be used by other processes. As such, when two processes each open a semaphore using the same name, both are referring to the same semaphore. In this way, two processes can be synchronized. The name may also be **NULL**, in which case, the semaphore is localized to one process. If *lpszName* specifies the name of an already existent semaphore, then *InitialCount* and *MaxCount* are not used.

The **CreateSemaphore( )** function returns a handle to the semaphore if successful or **NULL** on failure.

Once you have created a semaphore, you use it by calling two related functions: **WaitForSingleObject( )** and **ReleaseSemaphore( )**. The prototypes for these functions are shown here:

```
DWORD WaitForSingleObject(HANDLE hObject, DWORD dwHowLong);

BOOL ReleaseSemaphore(HANDLE hSema, LONG Count,
                      LPLONG lpPrevCount);
```

WaitForSingleObject( ) waits on a semaphore (or other type of synchronization object). It does not return until the object it is waiting on becomes available or a time-out occurs. For semaphores, *hObject* is the handle to a semaphore created earlier. The *dwHowLong* parameter specifies, in milliseconds, how long the calling routine will wait. Once that time has elapsed, a time-out error will be returned. To wait indefinitely, use the value **INFINITE**. The function returns **WAIT_OBJECT_0** when successful—that is, when access is granted. It returns **WAIT_TIMEOUT** when time-out is reached. If the previous owner of the semaphore terminates before releasing the semaphore, then **WAIT_ABANDONED** is returned. Each time **WaitForSingleObject( )** succeeds, the counter associated with the semaphore is decremented.

ReleaseSemaphore( ) releases the semaphore and allows another thread to use it. Here, *hSema* is the handle to the semaphore. The *Count* parameter determines what value will be added to the semaphore counter. Typically, this value is 1. The *lpPrevCount* parameter points to a variable that will receive the previous semaphore count. If you don't need this count, pass **NULL** for this parameter. The function returns nonzero if successful and zero on failure.

The following program demonstrates how to use a semaphore. It reworks the first multithreaded example program so that the two threads will not execute concurrently—that is, it forces the threads to be serialized. Notice that the semaphore handle is a global variable that is created when the window is first created. This allows it to be used by all threads (including the main thread) in the program. The program uses the same header and resource file as shown earlier.

```
/* A multithreaded program that uses a semaphore. */

#include <windows.h>
#include "thread.h"

#define MAX 5000

LRESULT CALLBACK WindowFunc(HWND, UINT, WPARAM, LPARAM);
DWORD WINAPI MyThread1(LPVOID param);
DWORD WINAPI MyThread2(LPVOID param);

char szWinName[] = "MyWin"; /* name of window class */

char str[255]; /* holds output strings */

DWORD Tid1, Tid2; /* thread IDs */

HANDLE hSema; /* handle to semaphore */
```

```
int WINAPI WinMain(HINSTANCE hThisInst, HINSTANCE hPrevInst,
                   LPSTR lpszArgs, int nWinMode)
{
  HWND hwnd;
  MSG msg;
  WNDCLASSEX wcl;
  HACCEL hAccel;

  /* Define a window class. */
  wcl.cbSize = sizeof(WNDCLASSEX);

  wcl.hInstance = hThisInst; /* handle to this instance */
  wcl.lpszClassName = szWinName; /* window class name */
  wcl.lpfnWndProc = WindowFunc; /* window function */
  wcl.style = 0; /* default style */

  wcl.hIcon = LoadIcon(NULL, IDI_APPLICATION); /* standard icon */
  wcl.hIconSm = LoadIcon(NULL, IDI_APPLICATION); /* small icon */
  wcl.hCursor = LoadCursor(NULL, IDC_ARROW); /* cursor style */

  wcl.lpszMenuName = "ThreadMenu"; /* main menu */
  wcl.cbClsExtra = 0; /* no extra */
  wcl.cbWndExtra = 0; /* information needed */

  /* Make the window white. */
  wcl.hbrBackground = (HBRUSH) GetStockObject(WHITE_BRUSH);

  /* Register the window class. */
  if(!RegisterClassEx(&wcl)) return 0;

  /* Now that a window class has been registered, a window
     can be created. */
  hwnd = CreateWindow(
    szWinName, /* name of window class */
    "Use a Semaphore", /* title */
    WS_OVERLAPPEDWINDOW, /* window style - normal */
    CW_USEDEFAULT, /* X coordinate - let Windows decide */
    CW_USEDEFAULT, /* Y coordinate - let Windows decide */
    CW_USEDEFAULT, /* width - let Windows decide */
    CW_USEDEFAULT, /* height - let Windows decide */
    HWND_DESKTOP, /* no parent window */
    NULL, /* no override of class menu */
    hThisInst, /* handle of this instance of the program */
    NULL /* no additional arguments */
  );
```

```
        /* Load accelerators. */
        hAccel = LoadAccelerators(hThisInst, "ThreadMenu");

        /* Display the window. */
        ShowWindow(hwnd, nWinMode);
        UpdateWindow(hwnd);

        /* Create the message loop. */
        while(GetMessage(&msg, NULL, 0, 0))
        {
          if(!TranslateAccelerator(hwnd, hAccel, &msg)) {
            TranslateMessage(&msg); /* translate keyboard messages */
            DispatchMessage(&msg); /* return control to Windows 98 */
          }
        }
        return msg.wParam;
}

/* This function is called by Windows 98 and is passed
   messages from the message queue.
*/
LRESULT CALLBACK WindowFunc(HWND hwnd, UINT message,
                            WPARAM wParam, LPARAM lParam)
{
  int response;

  switch(message) {
    case WM_CREATE:
      hSema = CreateSemaphore(NULL, 1, 1, NULL);
      break;
    case WM_COMMAND:
      switch(LOWORD(wParam)) {
        case IDM_THREAD:
          CreateThread(NULL, 0, (LPTHREAD_START_ROUTINE)MyThread1,
                       (LPVOID) hwnd, 0, &Tid1);
          CreateThread(NULL, 0, (LPTHREAD_START_ROUTINE)MyThread2,
                       (LPVOID) hwnd, 0, &Tid2);
          break;
        case IDM_EXIT:
          response = MessageBox(hwnd, "Quit the Program?",
                                "Exit", MB_YESNO);
          if(response == IDYES) PostQuitMessage(0);
          break;
        case IDM_HELP:
```

```
        MessageBox(hwnd,
                   "F1: Help\nF2: Demonstrate Threads",
                   "Help", MB_OK);
          break;
      }
      break;
    case WM_DESTROY: /* terminate the program */
      PostQuitMessage(0);
      break;
    default:
      /* Let Windows 98 process any messages not specified in
      the preceding switch statement. */
      return DefWindowProc(hwnd, message, wParam, lParam);
  }
  return 0;
}

/* A thread of execution within the process. */
DWORD WINAPI MyThread1(LPVOID param)
{
  int i;
  HDC hdc;

  /* wait for access to be granted */
  if(WaitForSingleObject(hSema, 10000)==WAIT_TIMEOUT) {
    MessageBox((HWND)param, "Time Out Thread 1",
               "Semaphore Error", MB_OK);
    return 0;
  }

  for(i=0; i<MAX; i++) {

    if(i==MAX/2) {
      /* Release at half way point.  This allows
         MyThread2 to run. */
      ReleaseSemaphore(hSema, 1, NULL);

      /* Next, once again wait for access to be granted. */
      if(WaitForSingleObject(hSema, 10000)==WAIT_TIMEOUT) {
        MessageBox((HWND)param, "Time Out Thread 1",
                   "Semaphore Error", MB_OK);
        return 0;
      }
    }
```

```
    wsprintf(str, "Thread 1: loop # %5d ", i);
    hdc = GetDC((HWND) param);
    TextOut(hdc, 1, 1, str, lstrlen(str));
    ReleaseDC((HWND) param, hdc);
  }

  ReleaseSemaphore(hSema, 1, NULL);

  return 0;
}

/* Another thread of execution within the process. */
DWORD WINAPI MyThread2(LPVOID param)
{
  int i;
  HDC hdc;

  /* wait for access to be granted */
  if(WaitForSingleObject(hSema, 10000)==WAIT_TIMEOUT) {
    MessageBox((HWND)param, "Time Out Thread 2",
               "Semaphore Error", MB_OK);
    return 0;
  }

  for(i=0; i<MAX; i++) {
    wsprintf(str, "Thread 2: loop # %5d ", i);
    hdc = GetDC((HWND) param);
    TextOut(hdc, 1, 20, str, lstrlen(str));
    ReleaseDC((HWND) param, hdc);
  }

  ReleaseSemaphore(hSema, 1, NULL);

  return 0;
}
```

A Closer Look at the Semaphore Program

In the program, **hSema** holds the handle to a semaphore that is used to serialize the two threads. When execution begins, **MyThread1( )** is activated before **MyThread2( )**. Therefore, when **MyThread1( )** is created, it immediately acquires the semaphore and begins execution. When **MyThread2( )** is created, it cannot acquire the semaphore, so it enters a wait state. Meanwhile, when the **for** loop inside **MyThread1( )** reaches

MAX/2, it releases the semaphore. This allows **MyThread2( )** to acquire it and begin execution. **MyThread1( )** then enters a wait state. Finally, **MyThread2( )** finishes and releases the semaphore. This allows **MyThread1( )** to resume.

Here are some experiments to try. First, since the program only allows one thread access to the semaphore at any one time, try substituting a mutex semaphore. Second, try allowing multiple instances of the threads to execute by increasing the count associated with **hSema** to 2 or 3. Observe the effect.

Using an Event Object

As explained earlier, an event object is used to notify one thread or process when an event has occurred. To create an event object, use the **CreateEvent( )** API function shown here:

HANDLE CreateEvent(LPSECURITY_ATTRIBUTES *lpSecAttr*,
                     BOOL *Manual*,
                     BOOL *Initial*,
                     LPSTR *lpszName*);

Here, *lpSecAttr* is a pointer to security attributes, which is ignored by Windows 98 and should be **NULL**. The value of *Manual* determines how the event object will be affected after the event has occurred. If *Manual* is nonzero, then the event object is reset only by a call to **ResetEvent( )**. Otherwise, the event object is reset automatically after a blocked thread is granted access. The value of *Initial* specifies the initial state of the object. If it is nonzero, the event object is set (the event is signaled). If it is zero, the event object is cleared (the event is not signaled).

The *lpszName* parameter points to a string that becomes the name of the event object. Event objects are global objects that may be used by other processes. As such, when two processes each open an event object using the same name, both are referring to the same object. In this way, two processes can be synchronized. The name may also be **NULL**, in which case the object is localized to one process.

CreateEvent( ) returns a handle to the event object if successful and **NULL** otherwise.

Once an event object has been created, the thread (or process) that is waiting for the event to occur simply calls **WaitForSingleObject( )** using the handle of the event object as the first parameter. This causes execution of that thread or process to suspend until the event occurs.

To signal that an event has occurred, use the **SetEvent( )** function, shown here.

BOOL SetEvent(HANDLE *hEventObject*);

Here, *hEventObject* is the handle of a previously created event object. When this function is called, the first thread or process waiting for the event will return from **WaitForSingleObject( )** and begin execution.

To see how an event object operates, modify the preceding program as follows. First, declare a global handle called **hEvent**. Next, add the following line inside the **WM_CREATE** case statement:

```
hEvent = CreateEvent(NULL, FALSE, FALSE, NULL);
```

Finally, change **MyThread1( )** and **MyThread2( )** to that shown here.

```
/* First thread of execution. */
DWORD WINAPI MyThread1(LPVOID param)
{
  int i;
  HDC hdc;

  /* wait for access to be granted */
  if(WaitForSingleObject(hEvent, 10000)==WAIT_TIMEOUT) {
    MessageBox((HWND)param, "Time Out Thread 1",
               "Event Error", MB_OK);
    return 0;
  }

  for(i=0; i<MAX; i++) {
    wsprintf(str, "Thread 1: loop # %5d ", i);
    hdc = GetDC((HWND) param);
    TextOut(hdc, 1, 1, str, lstrlen(str));
    ReleaseDC((HWND) param, hdc);
  }

  return 0;
}

/* Second thread of execution. */
DWORD WINAPI MyThread2(LPVOID param)
{
  int i;
  HDC hdc;
```

```
for(i=0; i<MAX; i++) {
  wsprintf(str, "Thread 2: loop # %5d ", i);
  hdc = GetDC((HWND) param);
  TextOut(hdc, 1, 20, str, lstrlen(str));
  ReleaseDC((HWND) param, hdc);
}

/* send event notification */
SetEvent(hEvent);

return 0;
}
```

Now, when the program executes, **MyThread1( )** is blocked until
MyThread2( ) completes and signals that it is done.

Using a Waitable Timer

Although timers are available for all versions of Windows, the *waitable timer*
is a recent addition. While it is possible to link a semaphore with a standard
timer, the waitable timer makes this process much more convenient.
Waitable timers are exciting because they will make it easier to automate all
types of background tasks.

PORTABILITY: Waitable timers were first added by Windows NT 4.
They are not supported by Windows 95 or Windows 3.1.

When you create a waitable timer, you are creating a timer that will run in
the background until a predetermined time is reached. A thread can wait on
that timer using the standard **WaitForSingleObject( )** function. The thread
will be blocked until the timer goes off.

Waitable timers are created using the **CreateWaitableTimer( )** function,
shown here.

HANDLE CreateWaitableTimer(LPSECURITY_ATTRIBUTES *lpSecAttr*,
                            BOOL *Manual*, LPCSTR *lpszName*);

Here, *lpSecAttr* points to the security descriptor, which is ignored by Windows 98 and should be **NULL**. If *Manual* is nonzero, the timer must be manually reset after each timing period. If it is zero, the timer is automatically reset. The *lpszName* parameter points to the name of the timer. To create an unnamed timer, pass **NULL** for this parameter. Named timers can be shared with other processes. Unnamed ones are local to the process in which they were created. The function returns a handle to the waitable timer if successful or **NULL** on failure.

Once a timer has been created, it is inactive. To set the timer, call **SetWaitableTimer( )**. Its prototype is shown here.

```
BOOL SetWaitableTimer(HANDLE hWaitTimer,
                      const LARGE_INTEGER *TargetTime,
                      LONG Period,
                      PTIMERAPCROUTINE lpTimerFunc,
                      LPVOID Param,
                      BOOL Unsuspend);
```

Here, *hWaitTimer* is the handle of the timer object. The *TargetTime* specifies the time at which the timer will go off. The value in *Period* specifies the length of time, in milliseconds, between timer activations. If *Period* is zero, the timer only goes off once. *lpTimerFunc* points to a function that will be called when the timer goes off. This function is optional. If no such function is needed, specify **NULL** for *lpTimerFunc*. The value specified by *Param* is passed to the timer function. If *Unsuspend* is nonzero, a computer that has been operating in low-power mode will be resumed. **SetWaitableTimer( )** returns nonzero if successful and zero on failure.

Timer functions must have this prototype:

```
VOID (APIENTRY *PTIMERAPCROUTINE) TimerFunc(
      LPVOID Param, DWORD LowTime, DWORD HighTime);
```

Here, *Param* is the value passed by **SetWaitableTimer( )**. The values in *LowTime* and *HighTime* contain the termination time in the format compatible with that contained in a **FILETIME** structure. (Time formats are described below.) Frankly, most applications of a waitable timer will not need to use a timer function.

When calling **SetWaitableTimer( )**, the target time is specified as a **LARGE_INTEGER**. This union represents time as a 64-bit integer that is compatible with the way time is represented in a **FILETIME** structure. Both structures are shown here.

```
typedef struct _FILETIME {
  DWORD dwLowDateTime; /* low-order 32-bits */
  DWORD dwHightDateTime; /* high-order 32-bits */
} FILETIME;

typedef union _LARGE_INTEGER {
  struct {
    DWORD LowPart;
    LONG HighPart;
  };
  LONGLONG QuadPart;
} LARGE_INTEGER;
```

A **FILETIME** structure contains the number of 100 nanosecond units that have passed since January 1, 1601.

Win32 provides functions to convert time as represented by a **FILETIME** structure from or to a more convenient form. Perhaps the easiest way to set the target time of a waitable timer is to first describe the time using a **SYSTEMTIME** structure and then convert that structure into a **FILETIME** structure (which can be assigned to a **LARGE_INTEGER**). Recall from Chapter 14 that the **SYSTEMTIME** structure is defined like this:

```
typedef struct _SYSTEMTIME {
  WORD wYear; /* year */
  WORD wMonth; /* month (1 through 12) */
  WORD wDayOfWeek; /* day of week (0 through 6) */
  WORD wDay; /* day of month (1 through 31) */
  WORD wHour; /* hour */
  WORD wMinute; /* minutes */
  WORD wSecond; /* seconds */
  WORD wMilliseconds; /* milliseconds */
} SYSTEMTIME;
```

Once you have initialized the fields of a **SYSTEMTIME** structure to the desired target time, you can then call **SystemTimeToFileTime( )** to convert the time into a **FILETIME** structure. The prototype for **SystemTimeToFileTime( )** is shown here:

BOOL SystemTimeToFileTime(CONST SYSTEMTIME *lpSysTime,
    FILETIME *lpFileTime);

The function returns nonzero if successful and zero on failure.

For most uses of a waitable timer, you will not actually have to manually set all of the fields in the **SYSTEMTIME** structure. Usually, you can obtain the current system time and then just advance the time by the desired amount. For example, if you wanted to create a timer that would go off in one hour, you would first obtain the current time and then increase the **wHour** field appropriately. To obtain the current system time, use **GetSystemTime( )**, shown here:

VOID GetSystemTime(SYSTEMTIME *lpSysTime);

The current time of the system is returned in the structure pointed to by *lpSysTime*. The time is specified in UTC (Coordinated Universal Time), which is essentially Greenwich Mean Time.

The following program demonstrates the use of a waitable timer. Each time you press F2, a thread of execution is created. Inside this thread, a waitable timer is created and given a target time that is 10 seconds in the future. Next, the window is minimized and the thread waits on that timer. When the time interval has elapsed, the window is restored, a beep is sounded, and the thread resumes execution. The beep is produced by calling the API **MessageBeep( )** function. Notice the definition of **_WIN32_WINDOWS** at the top of the program. Since waitable timers are quite new, this definition may be required to ensure that the appropriate header information is included.

```
/* Demonstrate a waitable timer */

/* The following is needed to ensure that waitable
   timer API functions are available for Windows 98. */
#define _WIN32_WINDOWS 0x0500

#include <windows.h>
#include "thread.h"

#define MAX 10000

LRESULT CALLBACK WindowFunc(HWND, UINT, WPARAM, LPARAM);
DWORD WINAPI MyThread1(LPVOID param);

char szWinName[] = "MyWin"; /* name of window class */

char str[255]; /* holds output strings */
```

```
DWORD Tid1; /* thread IDs */

HANDLE hWaitTimer; /* handle to semaphore */

int WINAPI WinMain(HINSTANCE hThisInst, HINSTANCE hPrevInst,
                   LPSTR lpszArgs, int nWinMode)
{
  HWND hwnd;
  MSG msg;
  WNDCLASSEX wcl;
  HACCEL hAccel;

  /* Define a window class. */
  wcl.cbSize = sizeof(WNDCLASSEX);

  wcl.hInstance = hThisInst; /* handle to this instance */
  wcl.lpszClassName = szWinName; /* window class name */
  wcl.lpfnWndProc = WindowFunc; /* window function */
  wcl.style = 0; /* default style */

  wcl.hIcon = LoadIcon(NULL, IDI_APPLICATION); /* standard icon */
  wcl.hIconSm = LoadIcon(NULL, IDI_APPLICATION); /* small icon */
  wcl.hCursor = LoadCursor(NULL, IDC_ARROW); /* cursor style */

  wcl.lpszMenuName = "WaitTimerMenu"; /* main menu */
  wcl.cbClsExtra = 0; /* no extra */
  wcl.cbWndExtra = 0; /* information needed */

  /* Make the window white. */
  wcl.hbrBackground = (HBRUSH) GetStockObject(WHITE_BRUSH);

  /* Register the window class. */
  if(!RegisterClassEx(&wcl)) return 0;

  /* Now that a window class has been registered, a window
     can be created. */
  hwnd = CreateWindow(
    szWinName, /* name of window class */
    "Use a Waitable Timer", /* title */
    WS_OVERLAPPEDWINDOW, /* window style - normal */
    CW_USEDEFAULT, /* X coordinate - let Windows decide */
    CW_USEDEFAULT, /* Y coordinate - let Windows decide */
    CW_USEDEFAULT, /* width - let Windows decide */
    CW_USEDEFAULT, /* height - let Windows decide */
```

```
        HWND_DESKTOP, /* no parent window */
        NULL, /* no override of class menu */
        hThisInst, /* handle of this instance of the program */
        NULL /* no additional arguments */
    );

    /* Load accelerators. */
    hAccel = LoadAccelerators(hThisInst, "WaitTimerMenu");

    /* Display the window. */
    ShowWindow(hwnd, nWinMode);
    UpdateWindow(hwnd);

    /* Create the message loop. */
    while(GetMessage(&msg, NULL, 0, 0))
    {
        if(!TranslateAccelerator(hwnd, hAccel, &msg)) {
            TranslateMessage(&msg); /* translate keyboard messages */
            DispatchMessage(&msg); /* return control to Windows 98 */
        }
    }
    return msg.wParam;
}

/* This function is called by Windows 98 and is passed
   messages from the message queue.
*/
LRESULT CALLBACK WindowFunc(HWND hwnd, UINT message,
                            WPARAM wParam, LPARAM lParam)
{
    int response;

    switch(message) {
        case WM_CREATE:
            /* create the timer */
            hWaitTimer = CreateWaitableTimer(NULL, 1, NULL);
            break;
        case WM_COMMAND:
            switch(LOWORD(wParam)) {
                case IDM_THREAD:
                    CreateThread(NULL, 0, (LPTHREAD_START_ROUTINE)MyThread1,
                                 (LPVOID) hwnd, 0, &Tid1);
                    break;
                case IDM_EXIT:
```

```
            response = MessageBox(hwnd, "Quit the Program?",
                                  "Exit", MB_YESNO);
            if(response == IDYES) PostQuitMessage(0);
            break;
          case IDM_HELP:
            MessageBox(hwnd,
                       "F1: Help\nF2: Demonstrate Timer",
                       "Help", MB_OK);
            break;
      }
      break;
    case WM_DESTROY: /* terminate the program */
      PostQuitMessage(0);
      break;
    default:
      /* Let Windows 98 process any messages not specified in
      the preceding switch statement. */
      return DefWindowProc(hwnd, message, wParam, lParam);
  }
  return 0;
}

/* Demonstrate waitable timer. */
DWORD WINAPI MyThread1(LPVOID param)
{
  int i;
  HDC hdc;
  SYSTEMTIME systime;
  FILETIME filetime;
  LARGE_INTEGER li;

  /* add 10 seconds onto current system time */
  GetSystemTime(&systime);
  SystemTimeToFileTime(&systime, &filetime);
  li.LowPart = filetime.dwLowDateTime;
  li.HighPart = filetime.dwHighDateTime;
  li.QuadPart += 100000000L;

  /* set the timer */
  SetWaitableTimer(hWaitTimer, &li,
                   0, NULL, NULL, 0);

  /* minimize the window until the timer expires */
  ShowWindow((HWND) param, SW_MINIMIZE);
```

```
/* wait for timer */
if(WaitForSingleObject(hWaitTimer, 100000)==WAIT_TIMEOUT) {
    MessageBox((HWND)param, "Time Out Thread 1",
              "Timer Error", MB_OK);
    return 0;
}

/* beep and restore window */
MessageBeep(MB_OK);
ShowWindow((HWND) param, SW_RESTORE);

hdc = GetDC((HWND) param);
for(i=0; i<MAX; i++) {
    wsprintf(str, "Thread 1: loop # %5d ", i);
    TextOut(hdc, 1, 1, str, lstrlen(str));
}
ReleaseDC((HWND) param, hdc);

return 0;
}
```

This program uses the same THREAD.H header file described earlier. It uses
this resource file.

```
#include <windows.h>
#include "thread.h"

WaitTimerMenu MENU
{
  POPUP "&Options" {
    MENUITEM "&Waitable Timer\tF2", IDM_THREAD
    MENUITEM "E&xit\tCtrl+X", IDM_EXIT
  }
  MENUITEM "&Help", IDM_HELP
}

WaitTimerMenu ACCELERATORS
{
  VK_F2, IDM_THREAD, VIRTKEY
  "^X", IDM_EXIT
  VK_F1, IDM_HELP, VIRTKEY
}
```

Uses for Waitable Timers

Waitable timers offer some interesting possibilities. For example, you could use one to create a computerized alarm clock. To do so, create a dialog box that allows the user to set the desired alarm time. Then use that time to initialize a waitable timer. You could also use a waitable timer to help create automated backup or file transfer utilities. Although these types of tasks have always been possible by using normal timers in conjunction with other synchronization objects, the waitable timer simplifies them.

IN DEPTH

The MessageBeep( ) Function

In the waitable timer example, the computer's bell was sounded by calling the **MessageBeep( )** API funciton. This is a simple but useful function you will probably find handy in many situations. Its prototype is shown here.

    BOOL MessageBeep(UINT *Sound*);

Here, *Sound* specifies the type of sound that you want to make. It can be −1, which produces a standard beep, or one of these built-in values.

MB_ICONASTERISK	MB_ICONEXCLAMATION	MB_ICONHAND
MB_ICONQUESTION	MB_OK	

MB_OK also produces a standard beep. **MessageBeep( )** returns nonzero if successful or zero on failure.

Creating a Separate Task

Although Windows 98's thread-based multitasking will have the most direct impact on how you program, it is, of course, still possible to utilize process-based multitasking where appropriate. When using process-based multitasking, instead of starting another thread within the same program, one program starts the execution of another program. In Windows 98, this is

16

accomplished using the **CreateProcess( )** API function, whose prototype is shown here.

```
BOOL CreateProcess(LPCSTR lpszName, LPSTR lpszComLine,
                LPSECURITY_ATTRIBUTES lpProcAttr,
                LPSECURITY_ATTRIBUTES lpThreadAttr,
                BOOL InheritAttr, DWORD How,
                LPVOID lpEnv, LPSTR lpszDir,
                LPSTARTUPINFO lpStartInfo,
                LPPROCESS_INFORMATION lpPInfo);
```

To start the execution of another program, call **Create-Process( )**.

The name of the program to execute, which may include a full path, is specified in the string pointed to by *lpszName*. Any command-line parameters required by the program are specified in the string pointed to by *lpszComLine*. However, if you specify *lpszName* as **NULL**, then the first token in the string pointed to by *lpszComLine* will be used as the program name. Thus, typically, *lpszName* is specified as **NULL** and the program name, and any required parameters are specified in the string pointed to by *lpszComLine*.

The *lpProcAttr* and *lpThreadAttr* parameters are used to specify any security attributes related to the process being created. For Windows 98, these parameters are ignored and should be specified as **NULL**. If *InheritAttr* is nonzero, handles in use by the creating process are inherited by the new process. If this parameter is zero, handles are not inherited.

By default, the new process is run "normally." However, the *How* parameter can be used to specify certain additional attributes that affect how the new process will be created. (For example, you could use *How* to specify a special priority for the process or to indicate that the process will be debugged.) If *How* is zero, the new process is created as a normal process.

The *lpEnv* parameter points to a buffer that contains the new process's environmental parameters. If this parameter is **NULL**, the new process inherits the creating process's environment.

The current drive and directory of the new process can be specified in the string pointed to by *lpszDir*. If this parameter is **NULL**, the current drive and directory of the creating process is used.

The parameter *lpStartInfo* is a pointer to a **STARTUPINFO** structure that contains information that determines how the main window of the new process will look. **STARTUPINFO** is defined as shown here:

```
typedef struct _STARTUPINFO {
  DWORD cb; /* size of STARTUPINFO */
  LPSTR lpReserved; /* must be NULL */
```

```
    LPSTR lpDesktop; /* name of desktop */
    LPSTR lpTitle; /* title of console (consoles only) */
    DWORD dwX; /* upper left corner of */
    DWORD dwY; /* new window */
    DWORD dwXSize; /* size of new window */
    DWORD dwYSize; /* size of new window */
    DWORD dwXCountChars; /* console buffer size */
    DWORD dwYCountChars; /* console buffer size */
    DWORD dwFillAttribute; /* initial text color and background */
    DWORD dwFlags; /* determines which fields are active */
    WORD wShowWindow; /* how window is shown, SW_SHOW, etc. */
    WORD cbReserved2; /* must be 0 */
    LPBYTE lpReserved2; /* must be NULL */
    HANDLE hStdInput; /* standard handles */
    HANDLE hStdOutput;
    HANDLE hStdError;
} STARTUPINFO;
```

The fields **dwX**, **dwY**, **dwXSize**, **dwYSize**, **dwXCountChars**,
dwYCountChars, **dwFillAttribute**, and **wShowWindow** are ignored
unless they are enabled by including the proper value as part of the **dwFlags**
field. The values for **dwFlags** are shown here:

Macro	Enables
STARTF_USESHOWWINDOW	**wShowWindow**
STARTF_USESIZE	**dwXSize** and **dwYSize**
STARTF_USEPOSITION	**dwX** and **dwY**
STARTF_USECOUNTCHARS	**dwXCountChars** and **dwYCountChars**
STARTF_USEFILLATTRIBUTE	**dwFillAttribute**
STARTF_USESTDHANDLES	**hStdInput**, **hStdOutput**, and **hStdError**

dwFlags may also include one or more of these values:

STARTF_FORCEONFEEDBACK	Feedback cursor is on.
STARTF_FORCEOFFFEEDBACK	Feedback cursor is off.

NOTE: The **lpTitle**, **dwXCountChars**, and **dwYCountChars** fields only apply to console applications, which were discussed in Chapter 15.

Generally, you will not need to use most of the fields in **STARTUPINFO** and you can allow most to be ignored. However, you must specify **cb**, which contains the size of the structure, and several other fields must be set to **NULL**.

The final parameter to **CreateProcess( )** is *lpPInfo*, which is a pointer to a structure of type **PROCESS_INFORMATION**, shown here:

```
typedef struct _PROCESS_INFORMATION {
  HANDLE hProcess; /* handle to new process */
  HANDLE hThread; /* handle to main thread */
  DWORD dwProcessId; /* ID of new process */
  DWORD dwThreadId; /* ID of new thread */
} PROCESS_INFORMATION;
```

Handles to the new process and the main thread of that process are passed back to the creating process in **hProcess** and **hThread**. The new process and thread IDs are returned in **dwProcessId** and **dwThreadId**. Your program can make use of this information or choose to ignore it.

CreateProcess( ) returns nonzero if successful and zero otherwise.

The following fragment illustrates the use of **CreateProcess( )**.

```
STARTUPINFO startinfo;
PROCESS_INFORMATION pinfo;
/* ... */
startinfo.cb = sizeof(STARTUPINFO);
startinfo.lpReserved = NULL;
startinfo.lpDesktop = NULL;
startinfo.lpTitle = NULL;
startinfo.dwFlags = STARTF_USESHOWWINDOW;
startinfo.cbReserved2 = 0;
startinfo.lpReserved2 = NULL;
startinfo.wShowWindow = SW_SHOW;
CreateProcess(NULL, "test.exe",
              NULL, NULL, 0, 0,
              NULL, NULL, &startinfo, &pinfo);
```

This starts the execution of a program called TEST.EXE, which must be in the current working directory of the parent process. The program is initially visible.

Once created, the new process is largely independent from the creating process. It is possible for the parent process to terminate the child, however. To do so, use the **TerminateProcess( )** API function.

PORTABILITY: Windows 3.1 does not support **CreateProcess( )**. To start another process in Window 3.1, the **WinExec( )** function is used. However, **WinExec( )** is obsolete and should not be used for Win32 programs. When porting older programs, be sure to replace any calls to **WinExec( )** with calls to **CreateProcess( )**.

In the next chapter we will examine one of Windows 98's most important subsystems: Help.

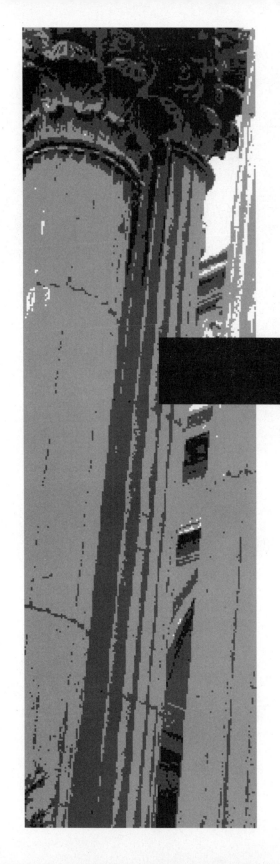

CHAPTER 17

Understanding the Help System

Windows 98 provides extensive support for online help. As you know from using Windows 98, nearly all applications provide the user with online instructions explaining how to use various features of the program. Most applications also provide online documentation that can be accessed via the help system. Frankly, it is not possible to write a top-notch professional Windows 98 program without providing extensive online help. The programming techniques necessary to accomplish this are described here.

Two Types of Help

Reference help supports online documentation. Context-sensitive help provides information related to a specific feature.

The Windows 98 help system supports two general categories of help. The first is essentially online documentation and is sometimes called *reference help*. It is accessed via the standard Help window, such as the one shown in Figure 17-1. Using the standard Help window, you can display various help topics, search for other topics, or view the contents of a help file. Reference help is used to display detailed descriptions of various features supported by the application or to act as the online version of the program's user manual. The second category of help is *context-sensitive*. Context-sensitive help is used to display a brief description of a specific program feature within a small window. An example is shown in Figure 17-2. Both types of help are required by a professional-quality Windows 98 application. As you will see, although different in style, both of these categories of help are handled in much the same way.

How the User Invokes Help

To properly implement the full Windows 98 help system, your program must support the four standard methods by which the user can invoke online help. Specifically, the user may obtain help by:

1. Clicking the right mouse button on an object.
2. Clicking on the **?** button and then clicking on an object.
3. Pressing F1.
4. Using a Help menu.

The first two methods are almost always used to invoke context-sensitive, pop-up help. In most situations, F1 is also used to invoke context-sensitive help. Occasionally, it invokes reference help. Selecting help through a menu usually invokes reference help.

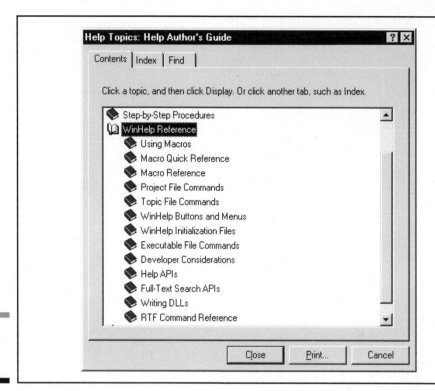

It is also permissible for the application itself to invoke help whenever it needs to do so. For example, a program might activate the help system when the user attempts an invalid operation.

Once the user has activated a help option, your application will respond to a help request by calling the **WinHelp( )** API function. This function manages all help requests. As you will see, it is a very versatile function. However, before examining **WinHelp( )**, you need to understand how to create a help file.

The Help File

At the core of the Windows 98 help system is the *help file*. Both context-sensitive and reference help utilize the help file. Help files are not text files. Rather, they are specially compiled files that have the .HLP file extension. To create a help file, you must first create an RTF (Rich Text Format) file that contains all of the help topics, plus formatting, indexing, and cross-

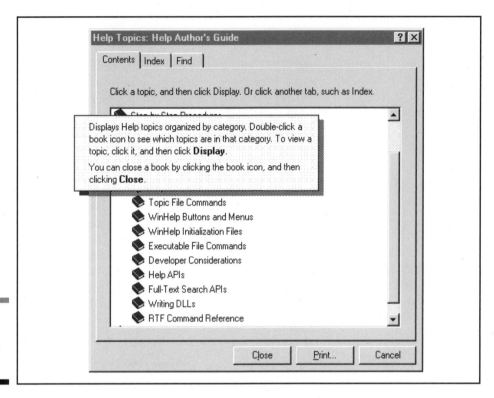

An example
of context-
sensitive help

Figure 17-2.

An RTF file
contains
formatting,
indexing, and
cross-referencing
information.

referencing information. This file will normally have the extension .RTF. This
file is then compiled using a help compiler. For example, the
help compiler for Windows 98 supplied with Microsoft's Visual C++ is
called HCW. The output of the help compiler is a .HLP file. Thus, relative
to the help compiler, the RTF file is the source file and the .HLP file is the
object file.

The Rich Text Format language contains a large number of commands. The
help compiler only accepts a subset of these commands. However, the help
system also recognizes several additional, help-related commands that are not
part of the general purpose RTF language. All RTF commands begin with a \.
For example, **b** is the RTF command for bold. It is far beyond the scope of
this chapter to discuss all of the commands. (Indeed, an entire book is
needed to fully describe the RTF language.) However, this chapter describes
the most important and commonly used commands relating to help files. If

you will be doing extensive work with help files, you will need to acquire a full description of the RTF language.

In addition to the RTF file, the help compiler also uses a project file. Typically, this is a file created by the help compiler. In it are various settings and values that relate to the help file. Help project files use the .HPJ extension.

17

Creating a Help File

As stated, the source code for a help file must be in rich text format. This means that creating the source code for a help file is a nontrivial task. Fortunately, there are three ways that you can create a help file. First, you can use a third-party automated Help authoring package. Second, you can use a text editor that generates RTF files. Third, you can use a standard text editor and manually embed RTF commands. If you will be preparing large and complex help files, the authoring package is probably the best alternative. However, for smaller applications, either of the other two choices is adequate. Since the one option that all readers will have is the third, that is the method that will be used here.

The General Form of a Help File

All help source files have certain basic elements in common. First, the entire file must be enclosed between curly braces. That is, it must begin with a { and end with a }. Immediately following the opening curly brace must be the **\rtf** command. This command identifies the file as a rich text format file and specifies which version of the Rich Text Format specification is being used. (Help files use version 1.) You must then define the character set used by the file. This will generally be the ANSI character set, which is specified using the **\ansi** command. You must also define the character fonts used by the file. This is done with the **\fonttbl** command. Thus, the general form of a help RTF file will look like this.

```
{\rtf1\ansi \fonttbl...
    Help File Contents
}
```

Within an RTF file, additional curly braces can be used to localize the effect of various RTF commands. In this capacity, the curly braces act much like they do in a C/C++ source file: they define a block.

Some RTF Commands

Before you can create even a simple help file, you need to know a few of the most important and common RTF commands. The ones used in this chapter are shown in Table 17-1. Each command is described here.

\ansi

The **\ansi** command specifies the ANSI character set. RTF files support other character sets, such as **\mac** (Macintosh character set) or **\pc** (OEM character set). However, the ANSI character set is the one that is generally used for help files.

RTF Command	Meaning
\ansi	Specifies the ANSI character set.
\b	Turns on boldface.
\b0	Turns off boldface.
\f*n*	Selects the font specified by *n*.
\fs*n*	Sets font size to *n*.
\fonttbl	Defines a font table.
\footnote	Specifies keywords and index topics.
\i	Turns on italics.
\i0	Turns off italics.
\page	Indicates the end of a topic.
\par	Indicates the end of a paragraph.
\rtf*n*	Specifies which RTF specification is being used.
\tab	Moves to next tab position.
\uldb	Marks a "hot spot" link to another topic.
\v	Creates a topic link (used in conjunction with **\uldb**).

Selected Help-Related RTF Commands
Table 17-1.

\b

The **\b** command turns on boldface. **\b0** turns it off. However, if the **\b** command is used within a block, only the text within that block is boldfaced and there is no need to use the **\b0** command. For example:

```
{\b this is bold} this is not
```

Here, only the text within the curly braces will be in boldface.

\fn

The **\fn** command selects a font. The font is specified by its number. The font must have been previously defined using a **\fonttbl** statement.

\fsn

The **\fsn** command sets the font size to that specified by *n*, which is expressed in half-point units. For example, **\fs24** sets the font size to 12 points.

\fonttbl

Before a font can be used, it must be included in a **\fonttbl** statement. It has the following general form:

```
{\fonttbl
 {\f1\family-name font-name;}
 {\f2\family-name font-name;}
 {\f3\family-name font-name;}
   .
   .
   .
 {\fn\family-name font-name;}
}
```

Here, *family-name* is the name of the font family (such as **froman** or **fswiss**) and *font-name* is the name of a specific font (such as Times New Roman, Arial, or Old English) within that family. The number of the font as specified in the **\f** statement will be used to select the font. A partial list of font families and names is shown here.

Family	Fonts
\froman	Times New Roman, Palatino
\fswiss	Arial
\fmodern	Courier New, Pica
\fscript	Cursive
\fdecor	Old English

For example, the following declares font 0 to be **\fswiss** Arial.

```
{\fonttbl {\f0\fswiss Arial;}}
```

\footnote

The **\footnote** statement is one of the most important RTF commands when creating a help file because it is used to specify topic names, context IDs, and browse sequences. The following forms of the **\footnote** command are used in this chapter.

${\footnote *string*}
K{\footnote *string*}
#{\footnote *string*}
+{\footnote *sequence-name:sequence-order*}
@(\footnote *string*)

The **$** form defines a title for a topic that is also displayed in the history window of the help system. The title can include spaces. A topic title identifies the topic.

The **K** form specifies that *string* is a keyword or phrase and can include spaces. Keywords are displayed as index entries. If the first character of the string is a K, then it must be preceded by an extra space. The **K** form can be used only if a topic title has been specified.

A browse sequence specifies a sequence of help topics.

The **#** defines a *context ID* that is used to create links and cross-references between topics. It is also used by your application program to access portions of the help file. In this form, *string* may not include spaces. As you will see, the context ID string is usually a macro that represents the ID value.

The **+** form defines a *browse sequence*. A browse sequence determines the linkage between topics when the browse arrows are pressed. (The browse arrows are the << and >> arrow buttons on the Help window's button bar.) In

The **Browsebuttons( )** macro must be included in your help project file to enable browse buttons.

this form, the content of *sequence-name* specifies the sequence, and *sequence-order* determines the position of the topic in that sequence. Browse sequences are performed in alphabetical order or numerical order based upon the values of *sequence-order*. A help file may have one or more browse sequences. To define several sequences, both the *sequence-name* and *sequence-order* specifiers in the **\footnote** command are required. If your help file has only one browse sequence, the *sequence-name* is not required. Examples of browse sequences are contained in the example help file shown later.

To cause browse buttons to be included in the standard Help window, you must include the **Browsebuttons( )** macro in the configuration section of the project file associated with a help file that defines a browse sequence.

The @ form of the **\footnote** command is used to embed a comment.

i

The **\i** command turns on italics. **\i0** turns it off. However, if the **\i** command is used within a block, only the text within that block is italicized and there is no need to use the **\i0** command.

page

The **\page** command signals the end of a topic.

par

The **\par** command marks the end of a paragraph. It also causes a line to be skipped. Thus, two **\par** commands in a row will skip two lines.

rtfn

The **\rtfn** command determines which RTF specification is being used. In this chapter, version 1 is used.

tab

The **\tab** command advances one tab stop.

uldb

To mark a *hot spot* link, specify it using the **\uldb** command. It has the following general form:

    \uldb *text*

The *text* will be shown in the standard hot spot color and font. This command is always used in conjunction with a \v command.

\v

The \v command specifies a link to another topic. It has the following general form:

   \v *context-ID*

Here, *context-ID* must be the same as specified in a #\footnote statement. This link is executed when the hot spot associated with the \v command is clicked by the user.

A Sample Help File

The following help file will be used by the example program shown later in this chapter. This file contains all the common components of a help file. Call this file HELPTEST.RTF.

```
{\rtf1\ansi
{\fonttbl{\f0\fswiss Arial;} {\f1\froman Times New Roman;}}
\fs40
\f1
@{\footnote This is a comment.  So is the following.}
@{\footnote Countdown Timer Help File.}
${\footnote Contents}
Timer Help Contents
\f0
\fs20
\par
\par
\tab{\uldb Main Menu \v MenuMain}
\par
\tab{\uldb Main Window \v MainWindow}
\par
\tab{\uldb Start Pushbutton \v PushButton1}
\par
\tab{\uldb Cancel PushButton \v PushButton2}
\par
\tab{\uldb Minimize Radio Button \v RadioButton1}
\par
\tab{\uldb Maximize Radio Button \v RadioButton2}
\par
```

```
\tab{\uldb As-is Radio Button \v RadioButton3}
\par
\tab{\uldb Set Delay Up-Down Control \v UpDown}
\par
\tab{\uldb Show Countdown Check Box \v CheckBox1}
\par
\tab{\uldb Beep at End Check Box \v CheckBox2}
\par
\par
\f1
\fs30
Select a Topic.
\fs20
\f0
\page
#{\footnote MenuMain}
${\footnote Main Menu}
K{\footnote Main Menu}
{\fs24\b Main Menu}
\par
\par
The main menu allows you to activate the timer,
activate the help system, display
information about this program, or terminate
the program.
\page
#{\footnote MenuMainPU}
This is the main menu for the program.
\page
#{\footnote RadioButton1}
${\footnote Minimize Radio Button}
K{\footnote Minimize Radio Button}
+{\footnote Radio:A}
{\fs24\b Minimize Radio Button}
\par
\par
The {\b Minimize} button minimizes the window
while the countdown is running.
\par
\par
See also {\uldb Maximize Radio Button \v RadioButton2}
\page
#{\footnote RadioButton1PU}
Select this to minimize the window while
the count down is running.
```

```
\page
#{\footnote RadioButton2}
${\footnote Maximize Radio Button}
K{\footnote Maximize Radio Button}
+{\footnote Radio:B}
{\fs24\b Maximize Radio Button}
\par
\par
The {\b Maximize} button maximizes the window
while the count down is running.
\par
\par
See also {\uldb As-is Radio Button \v RadioButton3}
\page
#{\footnote RadioButton2PU}
Select this to maximize the window while
the count down is running.
\page
#{\footnote RadioButton3}
${\footnote As-is Radio Button}
K{\footnote As-is Radio Button}
+{\footnote Radio:C}
{\fs24\b As-is Radio Button}
\par
\par
The {\b As-is} button leaves the window as-is
while the count down is running.
\par
\par
See also {\uldb Minimize Radio Button \v RadioButton1}
\page
#{\footnote RadioButton3PU}
Select this to leave the window as-is while
the count down is running.
\page
#{\footnote PushButton1}
${\footnote Start Push Button}
K{\footnote Start Push Button}
+{\footnote Push:A}
{\fs24\b Start Push Button}
\par
\par
The {\b Start} push button starts the timer.
\par
\par
```

```
See also {\uldb Cancel Push Button \v PushButton2}
\page
#{\footnote PushButton1PU}
Press this to start the timer.
\page
#{\footnote PushButton2}
${\footnote Cancel Push Button}
K{\footnote Cancel Push Button}
+{\footnote Push:B}
{\fs24\b Cancel Push Button}
\par
\par
The {\b Cancel} push button closes the timer dialog box.
\par
\par
See Also {\uldb Start Push Button \v PushButton1}
\page
#{\footnote PushButton2PU}
Press this to close the timer dialog box.
\page
#{\footnote MainWindow}
${\footnote Main Window}
K{\footnote Main Window}
{\fs24\b Main Window}
\par
\par
This is the main program window for the Countdown Timer.
\page
#{\footnote MainWindowPU}
Main window for the Countdown Timer program.
\page
#{\footnote DlgPU}
${\footnote DlgPU}
This is the Countdown Timer dialog box.
\page
#{\footnote UpDown}
${\footnote Delay UpDown Control}
K{\footnote Delay Updown Control}
{\fs24\b Delay UpDown Control}
\par
\par
The {\b Delay in Seconds} up-down control sets the
 number of seconds that the timer will count down.
\page
#{\footnote UpDownPU}
```

```
Use this to set the number of seconds to delay.
\page
#{\footnote CheckBox1}
${\footnote Show Countdown Check Box}
K{\footnote Show Countdown Check Box}
+{\footnote BOX:A}
{\fs24\b Show Countdown Check Box}
\par
\par
Checking the {\b Show Countdown} check box
causes the countdown to be displayed in the
up-down control as the timer runs.
\page
#{\footnote CheckBox1PU}
Check this to display countdown.
\page
#{\footnote CheckBox2}
${\footnote Beep at End Check Box}
K{\footnote Beep at End Check Box}
+{\footnote BOX:B}
{\fs24\b Beep at End Check Box}
\par
\par
Checking the {\b Beep at End} check box causes
a beep to sound when the count down is over.
\page
#{\footnote CheckBox2PU}
Check this to beep on completion.
\page
#{\footnote MenuDlgPU}
Activates the Countdown Timer dialog box.
\page
#{\footnote MenuExitPU}
Termintes the program.
\page
#{\footnote MenuHelpPU}
Activates the Help System.
\page
#{\footnote MenuAboutPU}
Displays information about the Countdown Timer.
\page
}
```

In this file, the **#\footnote** commands whose IDs end in **PU** are the entry points for context-sensitive, pop-up help. The other **#\footnote** commands are used to support reference help in the standard Help window.

After you have entered this file, you must compile it using the help compiler. Call the output file HELPTEST.HLP. This file will be used by the example program. However, before you compile the file, you must define the following MAP statements within the configuration section of the project file associated with HELPTEST.RTF. As you will soon see, these values will be used to support context-sensitive, pop-up help windows.

17

RadioButton1PU	400
RadioButton2PU	401
RadioButton3PU	402
CheckBox1PU	403
CheckBox2PU	404
UpDownPU	405
PushButton1PU	406
PushButton2PU	407
MainWindowPU	408
DlgPU	409
MenuDlgPU	410
MenuExitPU	411
MenuHelpPU	412
MenuAboutPU	413
MenuMainPU	414

The easiest way to define the MAP values is to include a map file in your help project. Map files use the following format to map values to identifiers.

identifier1	value1
identifier2	value2

identifier3   value3

.

.

.

identifierN   valueN

For example, here is the map file that you can use for the sample help file:

```
RadioButton1PU        400
RadioButton2PU        401
RadioButton3PU        402
CheckBox1PU           403
CheckBox2PU           404
UpDownPU              405
PushButton1PU         406
PushButton2PU         407
MainWindowPU          408
DlgPU                 409
MenuDlgPU             410
MenuExitPU            411
MenuHelpPU            412
MenuAboutPU           413
MenuMainPU            414
```

You must also activate the browse buttons in the standard Help window by including the **BrowseButtons( )** macro in the configuration section of your project file. Finally, if you want to give your help windows a title, you can specify one in the Options dialog box of the help compiler. If you don't specify a title, the default title "Windows Help" will be used. The title used in the examples is "Countdown Timer Help File."

When you compile this help file, call the output file HELPTEST.HLP. This file will need to be in the same directory as the executable version of the example program shown later in this chapter.

IN DEPTH

Help File Macros

The **BrowseButtons( )** macro is just one of many macros supported by the Windows 98 help system. Here are a few more.

Macro	Meaning
Annotate( )	Shows the Annotation box.
Back( )	Moves to the previous topic.
DisableButton(*ButtonID*)	Disables the standard help button specified by *ButtonID*.
EnableButton(*ButtonID*)	Enables the standard help button specified by *ButtonID*.
Exit( )	Terminates the help system.
GotoMark(*mark*)	Jumps to the marker previously set by **SaveMark( )**.
History( )	Shows the history list.
Next( )	Advances to the next topic in a browse sequence. Must be executed from within a valid browse sequence.
Prev( )	Returns to the previous topic in a browse sequence. Must be executed from within a valid browse sequence.
Print( )	Prints the current topic.
SaveMark(*mark*)	Saves the current help file position in the marker specified by *mark*.
TCard(*comID*)	Used with training card help. Sends the specified command ID to the invoking program in the *wParam* component of a **WM_TCARD** message.

Help macros can be executed in a variety of ways. Some, such as **BrowseButtons( )**, are specified within the help project file. Others can be executed from within the help file itself. To execute a macro from within a help file, use this form of the **\footnote** RTF command.

!{\footnote *macro*( )}

Here, *macro* is the name of the macro that you wish to execute. For example, this command activates the previous topic in a browse sequence.

```
!{\footnote prev()}
```

As you write more sophisticated help files, you will make use of several help macros because they expand your control over how the help information is presented to the user. You should spend some time exploring the help macros on your own.

Executing Help Using WinHelp( )

After you have created a help file and compiled it into its .HLP form, your application can access the information contained in it by invoking the **WinHelp( )** API function. Its prototype is shown here.

BOOL WinHelp(HWND hwnd, LPCSTR filename, UINT command,
DWORD extra);

Here, *hwnd* is the handle of the invoking window. The name of the help file being activated is specified in *filename*, which may include a drive and path specifier. Precisely what action the **WinHelp( )** function takes is determined by *command*.

The valid values for *command* are shown in the following table.

17

Command	Purpose
HELP_COMMAND	Executes a help macro.
HELP_CONTENTS	Obsolete; use **HELP_FINDER** instead.
HELP_CONTEXT	Displays a specified topic.
HELP_CONTEXTMENU	Displays context-sensitive help. This includes a "What's This?" menu.
HELP_CONTEXTPOPUP	Displays context-sensitive help.
HELP_FINDER	Displays the standard Help Topics window.
HELP_FORCEFILE	Forces correct file to be displayed.
HELP_HELPONHELP	Displays help information on Help. Requires that the WINHLP32.HLP file is available.
HELP_INDEX	Obsolete; use **HELP_FINDER** instead.
HELP_KEY	Displays a specific topic given its keyword.
HELP_MULTIKEY	Displays a specific topic given its alternative keyword.
HELP_PARTIALKEY	Displays a specific topic given a partial keyword.
HELP_QUIT	Closes the Help window.
HELP_SETCONTENTS	Sets the contents topic.
HELP_SETPOPUP_POS	Specifies the position of the next pop-up window displayed by the help system.
HELP_SETWINPOS	Determines the size and position of the Help window and displays it, if necessary.
HELP_TCARD	This command is ORed with other commands for training card help.
HELP_WM_HELP	Displays context-sensitive help.

Some commands require additional information. When this is the case, the additional information is passed in *extra*. The value of *extra* for each command is shown here.

Command	Meaning of *extra*
HELP_COMMAND	Pointer to string that contains macro.
HELP_CONTENTS	Not used; set to zero.
HELP_CONTEXT	Context ID of topic.
HELP_CONTEXTMENU	See text.
HELP_CONTEXTPOPUP	Context ID of topic.
HELP_FINDER	Not used; set to zero.
HELP_FORCEFILE	Not used; set to zero.
HELP_HELPONHELP	Not used; set to zero.
HELP_INDEX	Not used; set to zero.
HELP_KEY	Pointer to string that contains the keyword.
HELP_MULTIKEY	Pointer to **MULTIKEYHELP** structure.
HELP_PARTIALKEY	Pointer to string containing partial keyword.
HELP_QUIT	Not used; set to zero.
HELP_SETCONTENTS	Context ID of topic.
HELP_SETPOPUP_POS	Pointer to a **POINTS** structure.
HELP_SETWINPOS	Pointer to a **HELPWININFO** structure.
HELP_WM_HELP	See text.

For the **HELP_WM_HELP** and **HELP_CONTEXTMENU** commands, the meaning of *extra* is a little more detailed than it is for the other commands. For these two commands, *extra* is a pointer to an array of **DWORD** values. These values are organized into pairs. The first value specifies the ID of a control (such as a push button, edit box, etc.) or menu item. The second value specifies the context ID of the help information linked to that control. This array must end with two zero values. These two commands are used to support context-sensitive help and to help process **WM_HELP** and **WM_CONTEXTMENU** messages, which are described next.

17

Responding to WM_HELP and WM_CONTEXTMENU Messages

As mentioned near the beginning of this chapter, there are two broad categories of help: reference and context-sensitive. In a correctly written Windows 98 program, the user can activate reference help (that is, activate the standard Help window) by selecting Help from a menu or, in many situations, by pressing F1. Context-sensitive help is activated either by right-clicking on a control or window, by using the **?** button, or, in some situations, by pressing F1. (The distinction between the two uses of F1 is discussed in the following section.)

Since your program must respond differently to different types of help requests, there must be some way to tell them apart. And there is. When F1 is pressed or when the **?** button is used, a **WM_HELP** message is automatically sent to the active window. When the user right-clicks on a window or control, a **WM_CONTEXTMENU** message is sent to the window that contains the control. The proper processing of these two messages is crucial to the correct implementation of online help. Both messages will be examined here.

> Pressing F1 or using the ? button generates a **WM_HELP** message. Right-clicking generates a **WM_CONTEXT-MENU** message.

PORTABILITY: The **WM_HELP** and **WM_CONTEXTMENU** messages are supported by Windows 95 and Windows NT, but not by Windows 3.1. Therefore, when converting older programs to Windows 98, you will want to add support for these messages.

WM_HELP

Each time your program receives a **WM_HELP** command, **lParam** will contain a pointer to a **HELPINFO** structure that describes the help request. The **HELPINFO** structure is defined like this:

```
typedef struct tagHELPINFO
{
  UINT cbSize;
  int iContextType;
  int iCtrlId;
  HANDLE hItemHandle;
  DWORD dwContextId;
  POINT MousePos;
} HELPINFO;
```

Here, **cbSize** contains the size of the **HELPINFO** structure.

iContextType specifies the type of object for which help is being requested. If it is for a menu item, it will contain **HELPINFO_MENUITEM**. If it is for a window or control, it will contain **HELPINFO_WINDOW**. **iCtrlId** contains the ID of the control, window, or menu item.

hItemHandle specifies the handle of the control, window, or menu. **dwContextId** contains the context ID for the window or control. **MousePos** contains the current mouse position.

Most of the time, your program will respond to a **WM_HELP** message by displaying a pop-up window containing context-sensitive help. For example, to display context help about a control, your program must invoke **WinHelp( )** using the contents of **hItemHandle** as the window handle, i.e., the first parameter to **WinHelp( )**. (This will be the handle of the control.) You must specify **HELP_WM_HELP** as the command parameter and the address of the array of IDs as the extra parameter. (You will see an example of this in the example program.) Invoking **WinHelp( )** in this fashion causes it to search the array for the control ID that matches the control specified in **hItemHandle**. It then uses the corresponding context ID to obtain context-sensitive help. It displays this help in a pop-up window. It does not activate the standard Help window.

Although most often your program will respond to a **WM_HELP** message by displaying context-sensitive help, this will not always be the case. As mentioned earlier, pressing F1 may be used to invoke either reference help or context-sensitive help. Here is the distinction between the two uses. When the main window has input focus (and no child window, control, or menu is selected), then pressing F1 activates the standard Help window and displays reference help. However, pressing F1 when a control, menu, or child window is active causes context-sensitive help to be displayed. The theory behind these two uses is that when the user presses F1 from the topmost level, the user is desiring help about the entire program, not a part of it. When responding to this situation, you will invoke the full help system. However, when a control (or other child window) is active when F1 is pressed, the user is desiring help about that specific item and context-sensitive help is warranted.

Since F1 may be used to activate either reference help or context-sensitive help, you might be wondering how your program will tell the two types of requests apart. That is, pressing F1 causes a **WM_HELP** message to be sent no matter what type of help is being requested. The answer is quite simple: If the handle contained in **hItemHandle** is that of the main window, reference help will be displayed. Otherwise, invoke context sensitive help as described above.

WM_CONTEXTMENU

17

When the user right-clicks the mouse, your program receives a **WM_CONTEXTMENU** command. **wParam** will contain the handle of the control or window being queried. If the user clicked on a control, then respond by invoking **WinHelp( )** using **wParam** as the window handle (i.e., the first parameter to **WinHelp( )**). Specify **HELP_CONTEXTMENU** as the command parameter and the address of the array of IDs as the extra parameter. You will see an example of this command in the example program.

Including the ? Button

As mentioned, one way to activate context-sensitive help is through the **?** button. To include the **?** button in a window, you must include the extended style **WS_EX_CONTEXTHELP**. Since this is an extended style feature, you must create the window using **CreateWindowEx( )** rather than **CreateWindow( )**. To display the **?** button in a dialog box, include the **DS_CONTEXTHELP** style.

NOTE: Current Windows style guides recommend the **?** button primarily for use in dialog boxes. However, it can be used in a main window if the situation warrants.

A Help Demonstration Program

Now that you have learned about the various pieces and techniques involved in creating online help, it is time to put them to use. The following program implements a simple countdown timer. The timer lets you enter a delay interval in seconds and then counts down from the number of seconds you specified. The timer includes a number of options, such as displaying the countdown as it proceeds, sounding a beep on completion, and determining how the program's window is shown during the countdown. To keep count, the timer uses a standard Windows timer (as described in Chapter 3) that is set to go off every second. When the timer has counted the specified interval, the timer is stopped and the user is notified.

The program provides complete help for the countdown timer, demonstrating both reference help and context-sensitive help. It uses the help file shown earlier and illustrates various ways the file can be accessed using **WinHelp( )**. Sample output is shown in Figure 17-3.

```c
/* Demonstrating Help using a countdown timer. */

#include <windows.h>
#include <commctrl.h>
#include <string.h>
#include <stdio.h>
#include "timer.h"

#define MAXTIME 99

LRESULT CALLBACK WindowFunc(HWND, UINT, WPARAM, LPARAM);
BOOL CALLBACK DialogFunc(HWND, UINT, WPARAM, LPARAM);

char szWinName[] = "MyWin"; /* name of window class */

HINSTANCE hInst;

HWND hwnd;

/* map control IDs to context IDs */
DWORD HelpArray[] = {
  IDD_START, IDH_PB1,
  IDCANCEL, IDH_PB2,
  IDD_RB1, IDH_RB1,
  IDD_RB2, IDH_RB2,
  IDD_RB3, IDH_RB3,
  IDD_EB1, IDH_UPDOWN,
  IDD_UPDOWN, IDH_UPDOWN,
  IDD_CB1, IDH_CB1,
  IDD_CB2, IDH_CB2,
  0, 0
};

int WINAPI WinMain(HINSTANCE hThisInst, HINSTANCE hPrevInst,
                   LPSTR lpszArgs, int nWinMode)
{
```

```
MSG msg;
WNDCLASSEX wcl;
HACCEL hAccel;
INITCOMMONCONTROLSEX cc;

/* Define a window class. */
wcl.cbSize = sizeof(WNDCLASSEX);

wcl.hInstance = hThisInst; /* handle to this instance */
wcl.lpszClassName = szWinName; /* window class name */
wcl.lpfnWndProc = WindowFunc; /* window function */
wcl.style = 0; /* default style */

wcl.hIcon = LoadIcon(NULL, IDI_APPLICATION); /* standard icon */
wcl.hIconSm = LoadIcon(NULL, IDI_WINLOGO); /* small icon */
wcl.hCursor = LoadCursor(NULL, IDC_ARROW); /* cursor style */


wcl.lpszMenuName = "TimerMenu"; /* main menu */
wcl.cbClsExtra = 0; /* no extra */
wcl.cbWndExtra = 0; /* information needed */

/* Make the window white. */
wcl.hbrBackground = (HBRUSH) GetStockObject(WHITE_BRUSH);

/* Register the window class. */
if(!RegisterClassEx(&wcl)) return 0;

/* Now that a window class has been registered, a window
   can be created. */
hwnd = CreateWindow(
  szWinName, /* name of window class */
  "Demonstrate the Help System", /* title */
  WS_OVERLAPPEDWINDOW, /* window style - normal */
  CW_USEDEFAULT, /* X coordinate - let Windows decide */
  CW_USEDEFAULT, /* Y coordinate - let Windows decide */
  CW_USEDEFAULT, /* width - let Windows decide */
  CW_USEDEFAULT, /* height - let Windows decide */
  HWND_DESKTOP, /* no parent window */
  NULL, /* no override of class menu */
  hThisInst, /* handle of this instance of the program */
  NULL /* no additional arguments */
);

hInst = hThisInst; /* save the current instance handle */
```

```
  /* Load accelerators. */
  hAccel = LoadAccelerators(hThisInst, "TimerMenu");

  /* Initialize the common controls. */
  cc.dwSize = sizeof(INITCOMMONCONTROLSEX);
  cc.dwICC = ICC_UPDOWN_CLASS;
  InitCommonControlsEx(&cc);

  /* Display the window. */
  ShowWindow(hwnd, nWinMode);
  UpdateWindow(hwnd);

  /* Create the message loop. */
  while(GetMessage(&msg, NULL, 0, 0))
  {
    if(!TranslateAccelerator(hwnd, hAccel, &msg)) {
      TranslateMessage(&msg); /* translate keyboard messages */
      DispatchMessage(&msg); /* return control to Windows 98 */
    }
  }
  return msg.wParam;
}

/* This function is called by Windows 98 and is passed
   messages from the message queue.
*/
LRESULT CALLBACK WindowFunc(HWND hwnd, UINT message,
                            WPARAM wParam, LPARAM lParam)
{
  int response;

  switch(message) {
    case WM_HELP: /* user pressed F1 or used ? button */
      if(((LPHELPINFO) lParam)->iContextType ==
                            HELPINFO_MENUITEM) {
        /* request for help about menu */
        switch(((LPHELPINFO) lParam)->iCtrlId) {
          case IDM_DIALOG:
            WinHelp(hwnd, "helptest.hlp", HELP_CONTEXTPOPUP,
                    (DWORD) IDH_MENUDLG);
            break;
          case IDM_HELP:
            WinHelp(hwnd, "helptest.hlp", HELP_CONTEXTPOPUP,
                    (DWORD) IDH_MENUHELP);
            break;
```

```
        case IDM_HELPTHIS:
          WinHelp(hwnd, "helptest.hlp", HELP_CONTEXTPOPUP,
                  (DWORD) IDH_MENUABOUT);
          break;
        case IDM_EXIT:
          WinHelp(hwnd, "helptest.hlp", HELP_CONTEXTPOPUP,
                  (DWORD) IDH_MENUEXIT);
          break;
        default:
          /* menu bar selected, but no option highlighted */
          WinHelp(hwnd, "helptest.hlp", HELP_CONTEXTPOPUP,
                  (DWORD) IDH_MENUMAIN);
      }
    }
    else
      /* standard help for main window */
      WinHelp(hwnd, "helptest.hlp", HELP_KEY,
              (DWORD) "Main Window");
    break;
  case WM_CONTEXTMENU: /* user right-clicked mouse */
      /* context help about main window */
      WinHelp(hwnd, "helptest.hlp",
              HELP_CONTEXTPOPUP, IDH_MAIN);
    break;
  case WM_COMMAND:
    switch(LOWORD(wParam)) {
      case IDM_DIALOG:
        DialogBox(hInst, "TimerDB", hwnd, (DLGPROC) DialogFunc);
        break;
      case IDM_EXIT:
        response = MessageBox(hwnd, "Quit the Program?",
                              "Exit", MB_YESNO);
        if(response == IDYES) PostQuitMessage(0);
        break;
      case IDM_HELP:
        WinHelp(hwnd, "helptest.hlp", HELP_FINDER, 0);
        break;
      case IDM_HELPTHIS:
        MessageBox(hwnd, "Countdown Timer V1.0",
                   "About", MB_OK);
        break;
    }
    break;
  case WM_DESTROY: /* terminate the program */
    WinHelp(hwnd, "helptest.hlp", HELP_QUIT, 0);
```

```
        PostQuitMessage(0);
        break;
      default:
        /* Let Windows 98 process any messages not specified in
           the preceding switch statement. */
        return DefWindowProc(hwnd, message, wParam, lParam);
    }
    return 0;
}

/* Dialog function */
BOOL CALLBACK DialogFunc(HWND hdwnd, UINT message,
                         WPARAM wParam, LPARAM lParam)
{
  static long udpos = 1;
  static HWND hEboxWnd;
  static HWND udWnd;
  static int t;

  switch(message) {
    case WM_HELP: /* user pressed F1 or used ? button */
      /* context help about a control */
      WinHelp((HWND)((LPHELPINFO) lParam)->hItemHandle,
              "helptest.hlp", HELP_WM_HELP,
              (DWORD) HelpArray);
      return 1;
    case WM_CONTEXTMENU: /* user right-clicked mouse */
      if((HWND) wParam != hdwnd)
        /* context help about a control */
        WinHelp((HWND) wParam, "helptest.hlp",
                HELP_CONTEXTMENU, (DWORD) HelpArray);
      else
        /* context help about dialog window */
        WinHelp(hdwnd, "helptest.hlp",
                HELP_CONTEXTPOPUP, IDH_DLG);
      return 1;
    case WM_COMMAND:
      switch(LOWORD(wParam)) {
        case IDCANCEL:
          KillTimer(hdwnd, IDD_TIMER);
          WinHelp(hdwnd, "helptest.hlp", HELP_QUIT, 0);
          EndDialog(hdwnd, 0);
          return 1;
        case IDD_START: /* start the timer */
          SetTimer(hdwnd, IDD_TIMER, 1000, NULL);
```

17

```
        t = udpos = SendMessage(udWnd, UDM_GETPOS, 0, 0);

        if(SendDlgItemMessage(hdwnd,
              IDD_RB1, BM_GETCHECK, 0, 0) == BST_CHECKED)
          ShowWindow(hwnd, SW_MINIMIZE);
        else
        if(SendDlgItemMessage(hdwnd,
              IDD_RB2, BM_GETCHECK, 0, 0) == BST_CHECKED)
          ShowWindow(hwnd, SW_MAXIMIZE);
        return 1;
      }
      break;
    case WM_TIMER: /* timer went off */
      if(t==0) {
        KillTimer(hdwnd, IDD_TIMER);
        if(SendDlgItemMessage(hdwnd,
           IDD_CB2, BM_GETCHECK, 0, 0) == BST_CHECKED)
            MessageBeep(MB_OK);
        else
          MessageBox(hdwnd, "Timer Went Off", "Timer", MB_OK);
        SetDlgItemInt(hdwnd, IDD_EB1, udpos, 1);
        ShowWindow(hwnd, SW_RESTORE);
        return 1;
      }
      t--;

      /* see if countdown is to be displayed */
      if(SendDlgItemMessage(hdwnd,
            IDD_CB1, BM_GETCHECK, 0, 0) == BST_CHECKED) {
        SetDlgItemInt(hdwnd, IDD_EB1, t, 1);
      }
      return 1;
    case WM_INITDIALOG:
      hEboxWnd = GetDlgItem(hdwnd, IDD_EB1);
      udWnd = CreateUpDownControl(
                  WS_CHILD | WS_BORDER | WS_VISIBLE |
                  UDS_SETBUDDYINT | UDS_ALIGNRIGHT,
                  10, 10, 50, 50,
                  hdwnd, IDD_UPDOWN,
                  hInst, hEboxWnd,
                  MAXTIME, 1, udpos);

      /* check the As-Is radio button */
      SendDlgItemMessage(hdwnd, IDD_RB3, BM_SETCHECK, BST_CHECKED, 0);
      return 1;
```

```
  }
  return 0;
}
```

The program requires the following resource file.

```
#include "timer.h"
#include <windows.h>

TimerMenu MENU
{
  POPUP "&Dialog"
  {
    MENUITEM "&Timer\tF2", IDM_DIALOG
    MENUITEM "E&xit\tCtrl+X", IDM_EXIT
  }
  POPUP "&Help" {
    MENUITEM "&Help Topics", IDM_HELP
    MENUITEM "&About", IDM_HELPTHIS
  }
}


TimerMenu ACCELERATORS
{
  VK_F2, IDM_DIALOG, VIRTKEY
  "^X", IDM_EXIT
}


TimerDB DIALOG 18, 18, 130, 92
CAPTION "A Countdown Timer"
STYLE DS_MODALFRAME | WS_POPUP | WS_CAPTION |
      WS_SYSMENU | DS_CONTEXTHELP
{
  PUSHBUTTON "Start", IDD_START, 20, 60, 30, 14,
             WS_CHILD | WS_VISIBLE | WS_TABSTOP
  PUSHBUTTON "Cancel", IDCANCEL, 70, 60, 30, 14,
             WS_CHILD | WS_VISIBLE | WS_TABSTOP
  AUTOCHECKBOX "Show Countdown", IDD_CB1, 1, 20, 70, 10
  AUTOCHECKBOX "Beep At End", IDD_CB2, 1, 30, 50, 10
  AUTORADIOBUTTON "Minimize", IDD_RB1, 80, 20, 50, 10
  AUTORADIOBUTTON "Maximize", IDD_RB2, 80, 30, 50, 10
  AUTORADIOBUTTON "As-Is", IDD_RB3, 80, 40, 50, 10
  EDITTEXT IDD_EB1, 1, 1, 20, 12, ES_LEFT | WS_CHILD |
             WS_VISIBLE | WS_BORDER
```

```
    LTEXT "Delay in Seconds", IDD_TEXT1, 24, 2, 60, 14
}
```

The header file HELPTEST.H is shown here.

```
#define IDM_DIALOG      100
#define IDM_EXIT        101
#define IDM_HELP        102
#define IDM_HELPTHIS    103

#define IDD_START       200
#define IDD_TIMER       201

#define IDD_CB1         300
#define IDD_CB2         301
#define IDD_RB1         302
#define IDD_RB2         303
#define IDD_RB3         304
#define IDD_EB1         305
#define IDD_UPDOWN      306
#define IDD_TEXT1       307

#define IDH_RB1         400
#define IDH_RB2         401
#define IDH_RB3         402
#define IDH_CB1         403
#define IDH_CB2         404
#define IDH_UPDOWN      405
#define IDH_PB1         406
#define IDH_PB2         407
#define IDH_MAIN        408
#define IDH_DLG         409
#define IDH_MENUDLG     410
#define IDH_MENUEXIT    411
#define IDH_MENUHELP    412
#define IDH_MENUABOUT   413
#define IDH_MENUMAIN    414
```

A Closer Look at the Countdown Timer Program

The countdown timer works like this. The up-down control is used to set the delay. To start the timer, the user presses the Start button. This sets a timer that goes off once every second (1,000 milliseconds). The value of the counter variable **t** is set to the value determined by the position of the

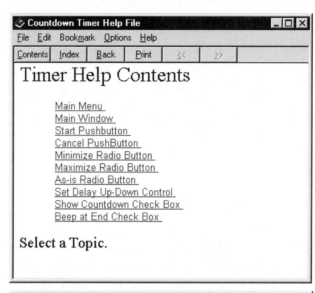

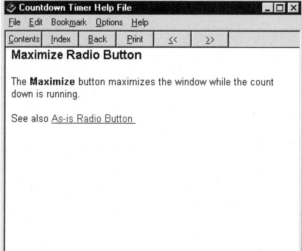

Sample output
from the Help
demonstration
program

Figure 17-3.

17

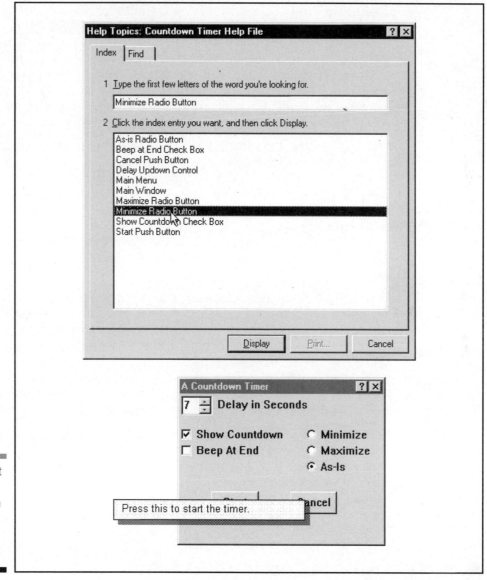

Sample output
from the Help
demonstration
program
(*continued*)
Figure 17-3.

up-down control. If the Minimize radio button is checked, the program windows are minimized. If the Maximize button is checked, the program windows are maximized. Otherwise, the program windows are left unchanged. Notice that the main window handle, **hwnd**, is used in the call to **ShowWindow( )** and not the dialog box handle, **hdwnd**. To minimize or maximize the program, the main window handle must be used—not the handle of the dialog box. Also, notice that **hwnd** is a global variable in this program. This allows it to be used inside **DialogFunc( )**.

Each time a **WM_TIMER** message is received, the value of **t** is checked. If the countdown has reached zero, the timer is killed, the up-down control is reset, and the window is restored to its former size, if necessary. If the Beep at End button is checked, the computer's speaker is beeped using a call to the API function **MessageBeep( )**. Otherwise, a message box informing the user that the specified time has elapsed is displayed. If there is still time remaining, the counter variable **t** is decremented. If the Show Countdown button is checked, the time remaining in the countdown is displayed inside the up-down control.

Most of the help-related features of the program should be clear. However, a few points warrant specific attention. First, consider the declaration of **HelpArray**. This is the array that maps control IDs to context IDs. In the HELPTEST.H header file, the **IDH_** macros are given the same values that you defined in the HELPTEST.PRJ file when you created the help file. Notice that both the up-down control and its buddy window map onto the same context ID. This is perfectly valid. If the same pop-up help message will be displayed for two or more controls, there is no reason to create duplicate messages.

Notice that the program includes the **?** button in the timer dialog box but not in the program's main window. This is in keeping with standard style guidelines. (The **?** is mostly for use in dialog boxes.) When using the **?**, it will only send messages to its own window. For example, try this experiment. Activate the dialog box and click on its **?** button. Next, move the pointer out of the dialog box. As you will see, the **?** disappears. The **?** applies only to the window in which it is defined.

Using Secondary Windows

It is possible to use a secondary Help window. A secondary window contains a button bar but not a menu bar. Thus it is smaller than the standard Help Topics window, but larger than a pop-up menu. A secondary Help window stays active until you close it, but it allows you to continue using your application. You have almost certainly seen secondary Help windows in action.

Using a secondary Help window is actually quite easy. First, you need to add one to your help project. To do so, simply specify its name and its type using the Windows option of the help compiler. You will have three choices of secondary window styles:

Procedure
Reference
Error Message

A procedure window is a small window that contains the buttons Help Topics, Back, and Options. It is positioned in the upper-right corner of the screen. A reference window also contains the Help Topics, Back, and Options buttons, but is a larger window. It is displayed with its upper-left corner near the top left portion of the screen. Error Message windows are small and contain no buttons.

To use a secondary window, you must include its name when specifying the name of the help file in the call to **WinHelp( )**, using this general form:

filename>windowname

For example, if a secondary window is called "HlpWin2", the following call will use that window to display context help about the Dialog entry in the main menu in the preceding program.

```
WinHelp(hwnd, "helptest.hlp>HlpWin2", HELP_CONTEXT,
               (DWORD) IDH_MENUDLG);
```

Assuming that "HlpWin2" is a procedure window, this will produce the window shown in Figure 17-4.

Secondary windows are easy to add, and enhance the look and feel of your application. You will want to experiment with them to find which style works best for the various needs of your program.

There is no question that online, context-sensitive help is an important part of any Windows 98 application. It is better to build support for help into your program from the start, rather than adding it later.

In the next chapter you will see how to print documents and utilize the common dialogs.

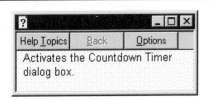

A secondary
Help window
Figure 17-4.

IN DEPTH

Training Card Help

There is a subcategory of reference help that you may find useful: *training card help*. You have almost certainly seen examples of training card help since it is used by Windows 98 itself. Training cards are sequenced, secondary Help windows that are used to guide a user through a complex process, one step at a time. (In a sense, training cards are to the Help system what Wizards are to dialog boxes.) The thing that makes training card help unique is that the training cards (i.e., secondary Help windows) may send messages to your program.

To activate training card help, you must call **WinHelp( )** using a secondary Help window and including the **HELP_TCARD** command. (The **HELP_TCARD** command is ORed with another **WinHelp( )** command.) Once training card help has been initialized, your program will receive **WM_TCARD** messages whenever the user causes the **TCard( )** help macro to execute. The **TCard( )** macro can be used to send either a standard ID, such as **IDOK** or **IDCANCEL**, or a help context ID.

When a **WM_TCARD** message is received, *wParam* will contain either one of the standard IDs or one of the following.

HELP_TCARD_DATA	A help context ID is being sent.
HELP_TCARD_NEXT	The user pressed the Next button.
HELP_TCARD_OTHER_CALLER	Another process is starting training card help. (Your program should send a **HELP_QUIT** | **HELP_TCARD** command in response.)

If *wParam* contains **HELP_TCARD_DATA**, *lParam* will contain the help context ID.

Training card help is an effective way of presenting a long series of instructions to the user. However, it takes significant effort—in terms of both programming and content—for it to be successful. But, for many applications, the effort is worth the reward.

17

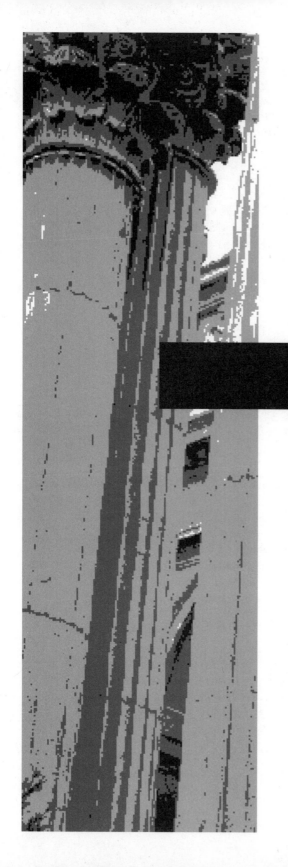

CHAPTER 18

Using the Printer

617

Prior to Windows, sending output to a printer was a fairly mundane and simple-to-perform task. Most output was character-oriented, and the printer could be easily driven using only a few lines of code. However, because of Windows' device-independent philosophy, its multitasking, and the need to translate graphical screen images into their printed forms, printing under Windows presents the programmer with a bit more of a challenge. This is especially true of Windows 98. Although printing is more complicated under Windows 98 than say, DOS, Windows 98 does provide significant built-in support for it. Also, once you have mastered the essentials, you will have no trouble adding print capabilities to any of your programs.

This chapter explains how to do the following:

♦ Print text
♦ Print graphical images
♦ Scale graphical images
♦ Create and install a printing abort function

These operations are the foundation of all printing jobs under Windows 98. The chapter concludes by developing a practical utility program that prints text files.

Before beginning, it is important to understand that when you print something, you will usually be sending output to the print spooler and not directly to the printer itself. Although it is possible for a user to tell Windows 98 to print directly to the printer, most users do not select this option because print spooling is a significant performance enhancer. Fortunately, whether output is managed by the spooler or sent directly to the printer has little or no effect on how you write a program. But the distinction is good to keep in mind.

Obtaining a Printer Device Context

A printer device context is required to output to a printer.

In the same way that a display device context describes and manages output to the screen, a printer device context describes and manages output to the printer. For this reason, you must obtain a printer device context before you can send output to the printer. There are two ways to obtain this device context: using **CreateDC( )** or using **PrintDlg( )**. Each is examined here.

CreateDC( )

The first way to obtain a printer device context is to use **CreateDC( )**. Its prototype is shown here:

HDC CreateDC(LPCSTR *NotUsed1*, LPCSTR *DevName*,
                        LPCSTR *NotUsed2*, CONST DEVMODE **DevMode*);

Here, *NotUsed1* is not used by Windows 98 and should be **NULL**. *DevName* specifies the name of the printer as shown in the list of printers displayed by the Add Printer wizard or shown in the Printers window when you select Printers from the Control Panel. *NotUsed2* must be **NULL**. *DevMode* points to a **DEVMODE** structure that contains initialization information. To use the default initialization, *DevMode* must be **NULL**. **CreateDC( )** returns a handle to the device context if successful or **NULL** on failure. After your application is through printing, delete the device context by calling **DeleteDC( ).**

PORTABILITY: In older versions of Windows, you need to specify a pointer to the name of the file that contains the printer device driver in *NotUsed1* and a pointer to the name of the printer port in *NotUsed2*. This is not the case with Windows 98.

In some cases, your application will need to obtain the name of the currently selected printer. To do this, use **EnumPrinters( )** to obtain the names of available printers.

CreateDC( ) is most often used when printing does not involve interaction with the user. Although such situations are not common, they are not rare, either. For example, a system log might be printed after midnight, when no user is present. However, for most purposes (and for the examples in this chapter), you will acquire a printer DC using another of Windows 98's API functions: **PrintDlg( )**.

PrintDlg( )

A common dialog box is a standard dialog box that is provided by Windows 98.

Most often, the easiest and best way to obtain a printer device context is to call **PrintDlg( )**. **PrintDlg( )** is one of Windows 98's *common dialog boxes*. Common dialog boxes are system-defined dialog boxes that your application may use to perform various common input tasks, such as obtaining a

18

filename, choosing a font, or setting a color. A common dialog box is activated by calling its API function.

PrintDlg( ) displays the standard Print common dialog box. You have certainly seen it in action because it is used by nearly all Windows applications. Its precise appearance varies, depending upon what options you select, but it will look something like that shown in Figure 18-1. The advantage of using **PrintDlg( )** to obtain a device context is that it gives the user control over the printing operation. To use **PrintDlg( )**, include COMMDLG.H in your program. **PrintDlg( )** is both powerful and flexible. The following discussion describes its basic operation. However, you will want to explore this function fully if you will be working extensively with printers and printing.

PORTABILITY: **PrintDlg( )** can also activate the Print Setup common dialog box. However, Print Setup is now obsolete. It has been superseded by the new Page Setup common dialog box. See the Page Setup In Depth box later in this chapter.

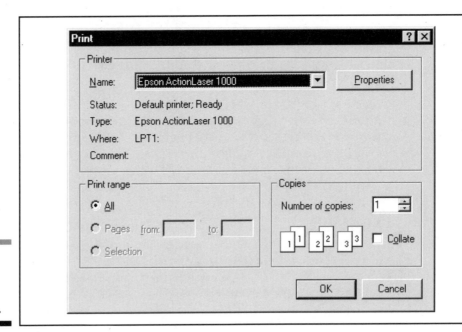

The Print common dialog box

Figure 18-1.

PrintDlg( ) has the following prototype:

BOOL PrintDlg(LPPRINTDLG *PrintDlg*);

It returns nonzero if the user terminates the dialog box by pressing OK. It returns zero if the user clicks Cancel (or presses ESC) or closes the box using the system menu. You must include COMMDLG.H in your program in order to use this function.

The contents of the **PRINTDLG** structure pointed to by *PrintDlg* determine how **PrintDlg( )** operates. This structure is defined like this:

18

```
typedef struct tagPD {
  DWORD lStructSize;
  HWND hwndOwner;
  HGLOBAL hDevMode;
  HGLOBAL hDevNames;
  HDC hDC;
  DWORD Flags;
  WORD nFromPage;
  WORD nToPage;
  WORD nMinPage;
  WORD nMaxPage;
  WORD nCopies;
  HINSTANCE hInstance;
  LPARAM lCustData;
  LPPRINTHOOKPROC lpfnPrintHook;
  LPSETUPHOOKPROC lpfnSetupHook;
  LPCSTR lpPrintTemplateName;
  LPCSTR lpSetupTemplateName;
  HGLOBAL hPrintTemplate;
  HGLOBAL hSetupTemplate;
} PRINTDLG;
```

lStructSize contains the size of the **PRINTDLG** structure. **hwndOwner** specifies the handle of the window that owns **PrintDlg( )**.

hDevMode specifies the handle of a global **DEVMODE** structure that is used to initialize the dialog box controls prior to the call and contains the state of the controls after the call. This field may also be specified as **NULL**. In this case, **PrintDlg( )** allocates and initializes a **DEVMODE** structure and returns a handle to it in the **hDevMode** member. The **DEVMODE** structure is not used by the examples in this chapter.

hDevNames contains the handle of a global **DEVNAMES** structure. This structure specifies the name of the printer driver, the name of the printer, and the name of the port. These names are used to initialize the **PrintDlg( )** dialog box. After the call, they will contain the corresponding names entered by the user. This field may also be specified as **NULL**. In this case, **PrintDlg( )** allocates and initializes a **DEVNAMES** structure and returns a handle to it. The **DEVNAMES** structure is not used by the examples in this chapter. When both **hDevNames** and **hDevMode** are **NULL**, the default printer is used.

After the call, **hDC** will contain either the printer device context or information context depending upon which value is specified in the **Flags** member. For the purposes of this chapter, **hDC** will contain a device context. (An information context simply contains information about a device context without actually creating one.)

nFromPage initializes the From edit box. On return, it will contain the starting page specified by the user. **nToPage** initializes the To edit box. On return, it will contain the ending page specified by the user.

nMinPage contains the minimum page number that can be selected in the From box. **nMaxPage** contains the maximum page number that can be selected in the To box.

nCopies initializes the Copies edit box. After the call, it will contain the number of copies to print as specified by the user. Your application must ensure that the number of copies requested by the user are actually printed.

hInstance contains the instance handle of an alternative dialog box specification if one is specified by the **lpPrintTemplateName** or **lpSetupTemplateName** members.

lCustData contains data that is passed to the optional functions pointed to by **lpfnPrintHook** or **lpfnSetupHook**.

lpfnPrintHook is a pointer to a function that preempts and processes messages intended for the Print dialog box. This element is used only if **Flags** contains the value **PD_ENABLEPRINTHOOK**. **lpfnSetupHook** is a pointer to a function that preempts and processes messages intended for the Print Setup dialog box. This element is used only if **Flags** contains the value **PD_ENABLESETUPHOOK**.

You can use a different layout (template) for the Print common dialog box. To do so, assign **lpPrintTemplateName** the address of the name of the dialog box resource that contains the new layout. **lpPrintTemplateName** is ignored unless **Flags** contains the value **PD_ENABLEPRINTTEMPLATE**.

You can use a different layout (template) for the Print Setup common dialog box. To do so, assign **lpSetupTemplateName** the address of the name of the dialog box resource that contains the new layout. **lpSetupTemplate-Name** is ignored unless **Flags** contains the value **PD_ENABLESETUP-TEMPLATE**.

You can also use a different template for the Print common dialog box by specifying its handle in **hPrintTemplate** and specifying the **PD_ENABLEPRINTTEMPLATEHANDLE** flag. Similarly, you can use a different template for the Print Setup common dialog box by specifying its handle in **hSetupTemplate** and specifying the **PD_ENABLESET-UPTEMPLATEHANDLE** flag. Otherwise, set these members to **NULL**.

 REMEMBER:　The Print Setup common dialog box is obsolete. Use Page Setup instead.

The **Flags** member contains values that determine precisely how the Print dialog box will behave and which fields will be active. On return, they will indicate the user's choices. It must be any valid combination of the values shown in Table 18-1.

As mentioned, on return the **hDC** member will contain the printer's device context. Using this context, you can output to the printer using functions such as **TextOut( )** or **BitBlt( )** that operate on device contexts. After your application is through printing, delete the printer device context by calling **DeleteDC( )**.

The Printer Functions

There are several functions that your program must use when printing. These functions are shown here.

```
int EndDoc(HDC hPrDC);
int EndPage(HDC hPrDC);
int StartDoc(HDC hPrDC, CONST DOCINFO *Info);
int StartPage(HDC hPrDC);
```

Flag	Effect
PD_ALLPAGES	Checks the All radio button. (This is the default.) On return, this flag will be set if the All radio button is selected.
PD_COLLATE	Checks the Collate Copies check box. On return, this flag will be set if Collate Copies is checked and the selected printer driver does not provide collation. In this situation, your program must perform collation manually.
PD_DISABLEPRINTTOFILE	Deactivates the Print to File check box.
PD_ENABLEPRINTHOOK	Enables the **lpfnPrintHook** member.
PD_ENABLEPRINTTEMPLATE	Uses alternative dialog box template specified by **lpPrintTemplateName**.
PD_ENABLEPRINTTEMPLATE-HANDLE	Uses alternative Print dialog box template specified by **hPrintTemplate**.
PD_ENABLESETUPHOOK	Enables the **lpfnSetupHook** member.
PD_ENABLESETUPTEMPLATE	Uses alternative dialog box template specified by **lpSetupTemplateName**.
PD_ENABLESETUPTEMPLATE-HANDLE	Uses alternative Setup dialog box template specified by **hSetupTemplate**.
PD_HIDEPRINTTOFILE	Suppresses the Print to File check box.
PD_NONETWORKBUTTON	Suppresses Network button.
PD_NOPAGENUMS	Deactivates the Pages radio button.
PD_NOSELECTION	Deactivates the Selection radio button.
PD_NOWARNING	No warning message is displayed when there is no default printer.
PD_PAGENUMS	Selects the Pages radio button. On return, this flag is set if the Pages radio button is selected.
PD_PRINTSETUP	Print Setup rather than Print dialog box is displayed. This option is obsolete. Use the Page Setup common dialog box instead.

The values
for the **Flags**
member of
PRINTDLG
Table 18-1.

Flag	Effect
PD_PRINTTOFILE	Checks the Print to File check box. On return, indicates that user desires output to be directed to a file.
PD_RETURNDC	Causes a device context to be returned in **hDC**.
PD_RETURNDEFAULT	On return, **hDevMode** and **hDevNames** will contain values for the default printer. No dialog box is displayed. **hDevMode** and **hDevNames** must be **NULL** when **PrintDlg( )** is called.
PD_RETURNIC	Causes an information context to be returned in **hDC**.
PD_SELECTION	Selects the Selection radio button. On return, this flag will be set if the Selection radio button is selected.
PD_SHOWHELP	Help button is displayed.
PD_USEDEVMODECOPIES-ANDCOLLATE PD_USEDEVMODECOPIES	Deactivates Number of Copies spin control and/or Collate check box if the printer driver does not support multiple copies or collation, respectively. If not set, the number of copies is contained in the **nCopies** member and the **PD_COLLATE** flag will be set if collation is required.

18

The values for the **Flags** member of **PRINTDLG** (*continued*)

Table 18-1.

In all cases, *hPrDC* is the handle of the printer device context. Also, in all cases, the functions return a nonzero, positive value if successful. On failure they return zero or less. A description of each function follows.

To start printing, you must first call **StartDoc( )**. **StartDoc( )** performs two functions. First, it starts a print job. Second, its return value is the job ID. Although the examples in this chapter do not require print job IDs, some applications will because the job ID is needed by some print-related functions. The *Info* parameter is a structure of type **DOCINFO**, which is defined like this:

```
typedef struct _DOCINFO {
  int cbSize;
  LPCSTR lpszDocName;
  LPCSTR lpszOutput;
  LPCSTR lpszDatatype;
  DWORD fwType;
} DOCINFO;
```

Here, **cbSize** must contain the size of the **DOCINFO** structure.
lpszDocName is a pointer to the name of the print job. **lpszOutput** is a
pointer to the name of the file that will receive printed output. However, to
send output to the printer device context specified by *hPrDC*, **lpszOutput**
must be **NULL**. **lpszDatatype** is a pointer to a string that identifies the type
of data used to record the print job. This member can be **NULL**. **fwType**
contains any additional data required by the print job.

To start printing, you must call **StartPage( )**. After each page is printed, you
must call **EndPage( )**. **EndPage( )** advances the printer to a new page. Once
your program is through printing, it must call **EndDoc( )**. Therefore, the
following outline shows the sequence required to print a page.

```
StartDoc(dc, &info);
StartPage(dc);
   /* print a page of data here */
EndPage(dc);
EndDoc(dc);
```

PORTABILITY: For Windows 3.1, the functions performed by
StartDoc( ), **StartPage( )**, **EndPage( )**, and **EndDoc( )** are accomplished
using escape codes. These codes are sent via the **Escape( )** function. The
Escape( ) function is obsolete, and you will seldom find it used in a
Windows 98 application. When converting older programs, you will want to
replace calls to **Escape( )** with the appropriate printer function.

A Simple Printing Example

Although there are many more details that are necessary to properly add
printing to a Windows 98 application, the functions described in the
preceding sections are sufficient to send text output to the printer. So, before
we move on, let's take a look at an example. The following program prints

18

lines of text on the printer. Note that this (and subsequent examples) make use of the virtual window technology developed in Chapter 8.

```c
/* A simple printing demonstration. */

#include <windows.h>
#include <string.h>
#include <commdlg.h>
#include "print.h"

#define NUMLINES 20

LRESULT CALLBACK WindowFunc(HWND, UINT, WPARAM, LPARAM);
void PrintInit(PRINTDLG *printdlg, HWND hwnd);

char szWinName[] = "MyWin"; /* name of window class */

int X = 0, Y = 0; /* current output location */
int maxX, maxY; /* screen dimensions */

HDC memDC; /* virtual device handle */
HBITMAP hBit; /* bitmap handle */
HBRUSH hBrush; /* brush handle */

PRINTDLG printdlg;
DOCINFO docinfo;

int WINAPI WinMain(HINSTANCE hThisInst, HINSTANCE hPrevInst,
                   LPSTR lpszArgs, int nWinMode)
{
  HACCEL hAccel;
  HWND hwnd;
  MSG msg;
  WNDCLASSEX wcl;

  /* Define a window class. */
  wcl.cbSize = sizeof(WNDCLASSEX);

  wcl.hInstance = hThisInst; /* handle to this instance */
  wcl.lpszClassName = szWinName; /* window class name */
  wcl.lpfnWndProc = WindowFunc; /* window function */
  wcl.style = 0; /* default style */

  wcl.hIcon = LoadIcon(NULL, IDI_APPLICATION); /* standard icon */
  wcl.hIconSm = LoadIcon(NULL, IDI_APPLICATION); /* small icon */
```

```
wcl.hCursor = LoadCursor(NULL, IDC_ARROW); /* cursor style */

wcl.lpszMenuName = "PrintDemoMenu";
wcl.cbClsExtra = 0; /* no extra */
wcl.cbWndExtra = 0; /* information needed */

/* Make the window white. */
wcl.hbrBackground = (HBRUSH) GetStockObject(WHITE_BRUSH);

/* Register the window class. */
if(!RegisterClassEx(&wcl)) return 0;

/* Now that a window class has been registered, a window
   can be created. */
hwnd = CreateWindow(
  szWinName, /* name of window class */
  "Using the Printer", /* title */
  WS_OVERLAPPEDWINDOW, /* standard window */
  CW_USEDEFAULT, /* X coordinate - let Windows decide */
  CW_USEDEFAULT, /* Y coordinate - let Windows decide */
  CW_USEDEFAULT, /* width - let Windows decide */
  CW_USEDEFAULT, /* height - let Windows decide */
  HWND_DESKTOP, /* no parent window */
  NULL, /* no override of class menu */
  hThisInst, /* handle of this instance of the program */
  NULL /* no additional arguments */
);

/* Load accelerators. */
hAccel = LoadAccelerators(hThisInst, "PrintDemoMenu");

/* Display the window. */
ShowWindow(hwnd, nWinMode);
UpdateWindow(hwnd);

/* Create the message loop. */
while(GetMessage(&msg, NULL, 0, 0))
{
  if(!TranslateAccelerator(hwnd, hAccel, &msg)) {
    TranslateMessage(&msg);
    DispatchMessage(&msg);
  }
}
return msg.wParam;
}
```

```
/* This function is called by Windows 98 and is passed
   messages from the message queue.
*/
LRESULT CALLBACK WindowFunc(HWND hwnd, UINT message,
                           WPARAM wParam, LPARAM lParam)
{
  HDC hdc;
  PAINTSTRUCT ps;
  int response;
  TEXTMETRIC tm;
  char str[80];
  int i;
  int copies;

  switch(message) {
    case WM_CREATE:
      /* get screen coordinates */
      maxX = GetSystemMetrics(SM_CXSCREEN);
      maxY = GetSystemMetrics(SM_CYSCREEN);

      /* create a virtual window */
      hdc = GetDC(hwnd);
      memDC = CreateCompatibleDC(hdc);
      hBit = CreateCompatibleBitmap(hdc, maxX, maxY);
      SelectObject(memDC, hBit);
      hBrush = (HBRUSH) GetStockObject(WHITE_BRUSH);
      SelectObject(memDC, hBrush);
      PatBlt(memDC, 0, 0, maxX, maxY, PATCOPY);

      /* get text metrics */
      GetTextMetrics(hdc, &tm);

      strcpy(str, "This is displayed in the main window.");
      for(i=0; i<NUMLINES; i++) {
        TextOut(memDC, X, Y, str, strlen(str)); /* output to memory */
        TextOut(hdc, X, Y, str, strlen(str)); /* output to window */
        /* advance to next line */
        Y = Y + tm.tmHeight + tm.tmExternalLeading;
      }

      ReleaseDC(hwnd, hdc);
      break;
    case WM_COMMAND:
      switch(LOWORD(wParam)) {
        case IDM_TEXT:
```

```
      X = Y = 0;

      /* initialize PRINTDLG struct */
      PrintInit(&printdlg, hwnd);

      if(!PrintDlg(&printdlg)) break;

      docinfo.cbSize = sizeof(DOCINFO);
      docinfo.lpszDocName = "Printing text";
      docinfo.lpszOutput = NULL;
      docinfo.lpszDatatype = NULL;
      docinfo.fwType = 0;

      /* get text metrics for printer */
      GetTextMetrics(printdlg.hDC, &tm);

      strcpy(str, "This is printed on the printer.");

      StartDoc(printdlg.hDC, &docinfo);

      for(copies=0; copies < printdlg.nCopies; copies++) {
        StartPage(printdlg.hDC);

        for(i=0; i<NUMLINES; i++) {
          TextOut(printdlg.hDC, X, Y, str, strlen(str));
          /* advance to next line */
          Y = Y + tm.tmHeight + tm.tmExternalLeading;
        }

        EndPage(printdlg.hDC);
      }

      EndDoc(printdlg.hDC);
      DeleteDC(printdlg.hDC);
      break;
    case IDM_EXIT:
      response = MessageBox(hwnd, "Quit the Program?",
                            "Exit", MB_YESNO);
      if(response == IDYES) PostQuitMessage(0);
      break;
    case IDM_HELP:
      MessageBox(hwnd, "Printing Demo", "Help", MB_OK);
      break;
  }
  break;
```

```
      case WM_PAINT: /* process a repaint request */
        hdc = BeginPaint(hwnd, &ps); /* get DC */

        BitBlt(hdc, ps.rcPaint.left, ps.rcPaint.top,
               ps.rcPaint.right-ps.rcPaint.left, /* width */
               ps.rcPaint.bottom-ps.rcPaint.top, /* height */
               memDC,
               ps.rcPaint.left, ps.rcPaint.top,
               SRCCOPY);

        EndPaint(hwnd, &ps); /* release DC */
        break;
      case WM_DESTROY: /* terminate the program */
        DeleteDC(memDC);
        PostQuitMessage(0);
        break;
      default:
        /* Let Windows 98 process any messages not specified in
           the preceding switch statement. */
        return DefWindowProc(hwnd, message, wParam, lParam);
  }
  return 0;
}

/* Initialize PRINTDLG structure. */
void PrintInit(PRINTDLG *printdlg, HWND hwnd)
{
  printdlg->lStructSize = sizeof(PRINTDLG);
  printdlg->hwndOwner = hwnd;
  printdlg->hDevMode = NULL;
  printdlg->hDevNames = NULL;
  printdlg->hDC = NULL;
  printdlg->Flags = PD_RETURNDC | PD_NOSELECTION |
                    PD_NOPAGENUMS | PD_HIDEPRINTTOFILE;
  printdlg->nFromPage = 0;
  printdlg->nToPage = 0;
  printdlg->nMinPage = 0;
  printdlg->nMaxPage = 0;
  printdlg->nCopies = 1;
  printdlg->hInstance = NULL;
  printdlg->lCustData = 0;
  printdlg->lpfnPrintHook = NULL;
  printdlg->lpfnSetupHook = NULL;
  printdlg->lpPrintTemplateName = NULL;
  printdlg->lpSetupTemplateName = NULL;
```

```
  printdlg->hPrintTemplate = NULL;
  printdlg->hSetupTemplate = NULL;
}
```

The program requires the following resource file.

```
#include <windows.h>
#include "print.h"

PrintDemoMenu MENU
{
  POPUP "&Printer Demo"
  {
    MENUITEM "Print &Text\tF2", IDM_TEXT
    MENUITEM "E&xit\tCtrl+X", IDM_EXIT
  }
  MENUITEM "&Help", IDM_HELP
}

PrintDemoMenu ACCELERATORS
{
  VK_F2, IDM_TEXT, VIRTKEY
  "^X", IDM_EXIT
}
```

The header file PRINT.H is shown here. In addition to the values used by the preceding program, it includes several values that will be used by subsequent programs in this chapter.

```
#define IDM_TEXT      100
#define IDM_BITMAP    101
#define IDM_EXIT      102
#define IDM_HELP      103
#define IDM_WINDOW    104
#define IDM_ENLARGE   105
#define IDM_PRINTFILE 106

#define IDD_EB1       200
#define IDD_EB2       201
#define IDD_UD1       202
#define IDD_UD2       202

#define IDD_TEXT1     210
#define IDD_TEXT2     211
```

A Closer Look at the First Printing Program

Relative to printing, the important part of the program occurs within the **IDM_TEXT** case. It is shown here for your convenience. This code is executed whenever the user selects Print Text from the Printer Demo menu.

```
case IDM_TEXT:
  X = Y = 0;

  /* initialize PRINTDLG struct */
  PrintInit(&printdlg, hwnd);

  if(!PrintDlg(&printdlg)) break;

  docinfo.cbSize = sizeof(DOCINFO);
  docinfo.lpszDocName = "Printing text";
  docinfo.lpszOutput = NULL;
  docinfo.lpszDatatype = NULL;
  docinfo.fwType = 0;

  /* get text metrics for printer */
  GetTextMetrics(printdlg.hDC, &tm);

  strcpy(str, "This is printed on the printer.");

  StartDoc(printdlg.hDC, &docinfo);

  for(copies=0; copies < printdlg.nCopies; copies++) {
    StartPage(printdlg.hDC);

    for(i=0; i<NUMLINES; i++) {
      TextOut(printdlg.hDC, X, Y, str, strlen(str));
      /* advance to next line */
      Y = Y + tm.tmHeight + tm.tmExternalLeading;
    }

    EndPage(printdlg.hDC);
  }

  EndDoc(printdlg.hDC);
  DeleteDC(printdlg.hDC);
  break;
```

Let's go through this code sequence step by step. First, **X** and **Y**, which are used to position text on both the printer and in a window, are reset to zero.

18

Next, a **PRINTDLG** structure is initialized by calling **PrintInit( )**. Notice that the Selection radio button and the Pages edit boxes are disabled. The Print to File check box is also hidden. These controls are not needed by the program. Next, **PrintDlg( )** is executed. Upon return, **printdlg.hDC** contains the device context of the printer selected by the user. Then a **DOCINFO** structure is initialized. Next, a call is made to **GetTextMetrics( )** using the printer device context. Since text is going to be printed, it is necessary to obtain the text metrics as they relate to the printer in order to correctly perform carriage return/linefeed sequences. These values will not be the same as those obtained when text is displayed on the screen inside the **WM_CREATE** case. This is an important point. The printer device context is separate and unique. It does not necessarily share any attributes in common with the window DCs used by the other parts of your program.

To start the printing process, **StartDoc( )** is called. Next, a loop is started that prints the number of copies requested by the user. This value is obtained from the **nCopies** member of **printdlg**. Since each copy will be on its own page, **StartPage( )** is called at the start of each iteration. Next, a few lines of text are sent to the printer. Notice that the device context obtained by calling **PrintDlg( )**, which is **printdlg.hDC**, is used as the target context for the **TextOut( )** function. Once you have a printer device context, it can be used like any other device context. At the end of each page, **EndPage( )** is called. When all printing is done, **EndDoc( )** is executed and the printer DC is deleted.

While this example is quite simple, it does illustrate all of the essential elements required to print a document on the printer. The remainder of this chapter shows you how to print bitmaps, add an abort box, and handle scaling. However, the fundamental approach to sending output to the printer will be the same.

IN DEPTH

The Common Dialog Boxes

The function **PrintDlg( )** is a specific example of a general class of built-in common dialog boxes. Windows 98 provides several common dialog boxes that your application may use to perform various common input tasks. A common dialog box is activated by calling an API function. (This differs from the common controls, which are windows that must be created.) To use a common dialog box, you must include COMMDLG.H in your program.

The common dialog boxes supported by Windows 98 are shown here.

Function	Dialog Box Activated
ChooseColor( )	Activates the Color dialog. This allows the user to choose a color or create a custom color.
ChooseFont( )	Activates the Font dialog. This allows the user to select a font.
FindText( )	Activates the Find dialog, which supports text searches.
GetFileTitle( )	Extracts a filename (i.e., file title) from a full path and drive specification.
GetOpenFileName( )	Activates the Open dialog. This allows the user to select a file to open.
GetSaveFileName( )	Activates the Save As dialog. This allows the user to select a file into which information will be saved.
PageSetupDlg( )	Activates the Page Setup dialog, which is used to specify the format of a printed page.
PrintDlg( )	Activates the Print dialog, which is used to print a file.
ReplaceText( )	Activates the Replace dialog, which supports text replacements.

While there is no technical reason that you cannot create your own dialog boxes to handle the types of input managed by the common dialogs, generally you should not. Instead, the common dialogs should be used by your program whenever one of the operations that they can perform is required. The reason for this is easy to understand: it is what the users of your programs have come to expect. Also, the common dialogs provide easy-to-use solutions to several fairly complex input situations. It is fortunate that they are built into Windows 98.

18

Printing Bitmaps

Since Windows 98 is a graphical operating system, it makes sense that you can print graphical output. And, indeed, this is the case. In fact, sending text output to the printer using **TextOut( )** as shown in the preceding example is the exception, not the rule. Most of the time, your program will need to render a printed version of a graphical bitmap. Keep in mind that this bitmap might contain text, but it will not be restricted to text. Fortunately, printing a bitmap is not in itself a difficult task. However, certain side issues need to be dealt with. First, before printing a bitmap, your program must determine whether the selected printer is capable of displaying graphical output. (Not all printers are.) Second, in order for the printed bitmap to have the same perspective that it does on the screen, some scaling of output might need to be performed. Finally, it is not possible to select a bitmap into a printer device context. (Bitmaps can only be selected into memory DCs.) Therefore, to print a bitmap implies that you will first need to select it into a compatible DC and then copy the contents of that DC to the printer DC using a function such as **StretchBlt( )**. Let's examine each of these issues.

Determining Printer Raster Capabilities

Not all printers can print bitmaps. For example, some printers can only print text. In the language of Windows 98, a printer that can print a bitmap is capable of raster operations. The term *raster* originally referred to video display devices. However, it has been generalized. In its current usage, if a device has raster capabilities, it can perform certain types of operations normally associated with a video display. In simple terms, if a printer has raster capabilities, it can display graphical output. Today, most commonly used printers have raster capabilities. However, since there are still many printers that do not, your program must check before attempting to print a bitmap. To do this, you will use the **GetDeviceCaps( )** function. Its prototype is shown here.

To print a bitmap, a printer must be capable of raster operations.

    int GetDeviceCaps(HDC *hdc*, int *attribute*);

Here, *hdc* is the handle of the device context for which information is being obtained. The value of *attribute* determines precisely what attribute about the device is retrieved. The function returns the requested information.

There are a large number of attributes that can be returned, and most are not relevant to this chapter. (However, you will want to explore **GetDeviceCaps( )**

on your own. It can obtain an amazing amount of information about a device.) The attribute that we will use to see if a printer is able to display a bitmap is **RASTERCAPS**. The return value will indicate what, if any, raster capabilities the printer has. It will be one or more of these values.

Value	Meaning
RC_BANDING	Printer DC requires banding support for graphics.
RC_BITBLT	Printer DC can be target of **BitBlt( )**.
RC_BITMAP64	Printer DC can handle bitmaps larger than 64K.
RC_DI_BITMAP	Printer DC supports device-independent bitmaps via the **SetDIBits( )** and **GetDIBits( )** functions.
RC_DIBTODEV	Printer DC supports **SetDIBitsToDevice( )**.
RC_FLOODFIL	Printer DC supports flood fills.
RC_PALETTE	Printer DC supports a palette.
RC_SCALING	Printer DC provides its own scaling capabilities.
RC_STRETCHBLT	Printer DC can be target of **StretchBlt( )**.
RC_STRETCHDIB	Printer DC can be target of **StretchDIBits( )**.

18

For the purposes of this chapter, we are interested in only two of these values: **RC_BITBLT** and **RC_STRETCHBLT**.

Maintaining Perspective

If you want the bitmap to look the same when printed as it does when displayed on the screen, you will need to scale the image appropriately when printing it. To accomplish this, you will need to know the resolution of both the screen and the printer. For this purpose, you will once again use the **GetDeviceCaps( )** function. To obtain the number of horizontal pixels-per-inch, specify **LOGPIXELSX** as the attribute. To retrieve the number of vertical pixels-per-inch, use **LOGPIXELSY**. For example, after these calls,

```
hres = GetDeviceCaps(hdc, LOGPIXELSX);
vres = GetDeviceCaps(hdc, LOGPIXELSY);
```

In order for a bitmap to look the same printed as it does on the screen, it must be scaled.

hres will contain the number of pixels-per-inch along the X axis, and **vres** will contain the number of pixels-per-inch along the Y axis for the device context specified by **hdc**.

Once you have found the resolution of both the video DC and the printer DC, you can compute a scaling factor. You will use this scaling factor in a call to **StretchBlt( )** to render the bitmap, in its correct perspective, on the printer.

StretchBlt( )

StretchBlt( ) copies a bitmap and is related to the **BitBlt( )** function described earlier in this book. However, in the process, **StretchBlt( )** expands or compresses the source bitmap so that it will fit and completely fill the target rectangle. Its prototype is

```
BOOL StretchBlt(HDC hDest, int DestX, int DestY,
                int DestWidth, int DestHeight,
                HDC hSource, int SourceX, int SourceY,
                int SourceWidth, int SourceHeight,
                DWORD dwHow);
```

Here, *hDest* is the handle of the target device context, and *DestX* and *DestY* are the upper-left coordinates at which point the bitmap will be drawn. The width and height of the bitmap are specified in *DestWidth* and *DestHeight*. The *hSource* parameter contains the handle of the source device context. *SourceX* and *SourceY* specify the upper-left coordinates in the bitmap at which point the copy operation will begin. The width and height of the source bitmap are passed in *SourceWidth* and *SourceHeight*. **StretchBlt( )** automatically expands (i.e., stretches) or contracts the source bitmap so that it will fit into the destination bitmap. This differs from the **BitBlt( )**, which performs no stretching or compressing.

StretchBit( ) is similar to BitBlt( ) except that it can expand or compress an image.

The value of *dwHow* determines how the bit-by-bit contents of the bitmap will actually be copied. It uses the same values as does the comparable parameter to **BitBlt( )**. Some of its most common values are shown here:

dwHow Macro	Effect
DSTINVERT	Inverts the bits in the destination bitmap.
SRCAND	ANDs bitmap with current destination.
SRCCOPY	Copies bitmap as is, overwriting previous contents.
SRCERASE	ANDs bitmap with the inverted bits of destination bitmap.
SRCINVERT	XORs bitmap with current destination.
SRCPAINT	ORs bitmap with current destination.

18

StretchBlt( ) is important when printing bitmaps because it allows you to scale the printed version. **StretchBlt( )** shrinks or enlarges the source bitmap, as needed, so that it fits the target rectangle. By applying the scaling factors to the dimensions of the target rectangle, you can use **StretchBlt( )** to scale the printed version of the bitmap. Keep in mind, however, that if no scaling is desired, your program can use **BitBlt( )** to copy a bitmap to the printer. But the printed version will not have the same perspective as the screen image. You will see examples of both in the program that follows.

Obtaining Printer-Compatible DCs

One small but sometimes irritating problem associated with printing bitmaps is that a bitmap can only be selected into a memory device context. Thus, you cannot select a bitmap directly into the printer DC obtained from **PrintDlg( )** or **CreateDC( )**. Instead, you will need to create a compatible memory DC, select the bitmap into that device context, and then copy it to the printer context using either **BitBlt( )** or **StretchBlt( )**.

There is one other complication. The bitmap that you want to print may not be compatible with the printer device context. When this is the case, you must also create a printer-compatible bitmap. Next, select that bitmap into the printer-compatible memory DC, copy the bitmap that you want to print into the printer-compatible bitmap, and then copy that bitmap to the printer

DC. If this all seems overly complicated, it is! Nevertheless, this is the way that Windows 98 is designed. However, as you will see, it is actually an easy process to implement.

A Bitmap Printing Demonstration Program

The following program adds two new features to the first printing example. One option prints a bitmap on the printer two ways: first, without performing any scaling, and then with the scaling factors applied, to maintain perspective. This option allows you to easily see the difference between scaled and nonscaled output. The other option lets you print the contents of the program's main window. This is simple to do because the program uses the virtual window technology. This means that the contents of the main window are also stored in a bitmap. Thus, to print the contents of the window is simply a special case of the general procedure used to print any bitmap. Sample output is shown in Figure 18-2.

```
/* A Bitmap Printing Demo Program. */

#include <windows.h>
#include <string.h>
#include <commdlg.h>
#include "print.h"

#define NUMLINES 25

#define BMPWIDTH 256
#define BMPHEIGHT 128

LRESULT CALLBACK WindowFunc(HWND, UINT, WPARAM, LPARAM);
void PrintInit(PRINTDLG *printdlg, HWND hwnd);

char szWinName[] = "MyWin"; /* name of window class */

int X = 0, Y = 0; /* current output location */
int maxX, maxY; /* screen dimensions */

HDC memDC, memPrDC; /* virtual device handles */
HBITMAP hBit, hBit2, hImage; /* bitmap handles */
HBRUSH hBrush; /* brush handle */

PRINTDLG printdlg;
DOCINFO docinfo;
```

```
int WINAPI WinMain(HINSTANCE hThisInst, HINSTANCE hPrevInst,
                   LPSTR lpszArgs, int nWinMode)
{
  HACCEL hAccel;
  HWND hwnd;
  MSG msg;
  WNDCLASSEX wcl;

  /* Define a window class. */
  wcl.cbSize = sizeof(WNDCLASSEX);

  wcl.hInstance = hThisInst; /* handle to this instance */
  wcl.lpszClassName = szWinName; /* window class name */
  wcl.lpfnWndProc = WindowFunc; /* window function */
  wcl.style = 0; /* default style */

  wcl.hIcon = LoadIcon(NULL, IDI_APPLICATION); /* standard icon */
  wcl.hIconSm = LoadIcon(NULL, IDI_APPLICATION); /* small icon */
  wcl.hCursor = LoadCursor(NULL, IDC_ARROW); /* cursor style */

  wcl.lpszMenuName = "PrintDemoMenu2";
  wcl.cbClsExtra = 0; /* no extra */
  wcl.cbWndExtra = 0; /* information needed */

  /* Make the window white. */
  wcl.hbrBackground = (HBRUSH) GetStockObject(WHITE_BRUSH);

  /* Register the window class. */
  if(!RegisterClassEx(&wcl)) return 0;

  /* Now that a window class has been registered, a window
     can be created. */
  hwnd = CreateWindow(
    szWinName, /* name of window class */
    "Using the Printer", /* title */
    WS_OVERLAPPEDWINDOW, /* standard window */
    CW_USEDEFAULT, /* X coordinate - let Windows decide */
    CW_USEDEFAULT, /* Y coordinate - let Windows decide */
    CW_USEDEFAULT, /* width - let Windows decide */
    CW_USEDEFAULT, /* height - let Windows decide */
    HWND_DESKTOP, /* no parent window */
    NULL, /* no override of class menu */
    hThisInst, /* handle of this instance of the program */
    NULL /* no additional arguments */
  );
```

```
      /* Load accelerators. */
      hAccel = LoadAccelerators(hThisInst, "PrintDemoMenu2");

      /* Load the bitmap. */
      hImage = LoadBitmap(hThisInst, "MyBP1"); /* load bitmap */

      /* Display the window. */
      ShowWindow(hwnd, nWinMode);
      UpdateWindow(hwnd);

      /* Create the message loop. */
      while(GetMessage(&msg, NULL, 0, 0))
      {
        if(!TranslateAccelerator(hwnd, hAccel, &msg)) {
          TranslateMessage(&msg);
          DispatchMessage(&msg);
        }
      }
      return msg.wParam;
}

/* This function is called by Windows 98 and is passed
   messages from the message queue.
*/
LRESULT CALLBACK WindowFunc(HWND hwnd, UINT message,
                            WPARAM wParam, LPARAM lParam)
{
  HDC hdc;
  PAINTSTRUCT ps;
  int response;
  TEXTMETRIC tm;
  char str[250];
  int i;
  int copies;
  double VidXPPI, VidYPPI, PrXPPI, PrYPPI;
  double Xratio, Yratio;
  RECT r;

  switch(message) {
    case WM_CREATE:
      /* get screen coordinates */
      maxX = GetSystemMetrics(SM_CXSCREEN);
      maxY = GetSystemMetrics(SM_CYSCREEN);

      /* create a virtual window */
```

```
      hdc = GetDC(hwnd);
      memDC = CreateCompatibleDC(hdc);
      hBit = CreateCompatibleBitmap(hdc, maxX, maxY);
      SelectObject(memDC, hBit);
      hBrush = (HBRUSH) GetStockObject(WHITE_BRUSH);
      SelectObject(memDC, hBrush);
      PatBlt(memDC, 0, 0, maxX, maxY, PATCOPY);

      ReleaseDC(hwnd, hdc);
      break;
    case WM_COMMAND:
      switch(LOWORD(wParam)) {
        case IDM_TEXT: /* print text */
          X = Y = 0;

          /* initialize PRINTDLG struct */
          PrintInit(&printdlg, hwnd);

          if(!PrintDlg(&printdlg)) break;

          docinfo.cbSize = sizeof(DOCINFO);
          docinfo.lpszDocName = "Printing Text";
          docinfo.lpszOutput = NULL;
          docinfo.lpszDatatype = NULL;
          docinfo.fwType = 0;

          /* get text metrics for printer */
          GetTextMetrics(printdlg.hDC, &tm);

          strcpy(str, "This is printed on the printer.");

          StartDoc(printdlg.hDC, &docinfo);

          for(copies=0; copies < printdlg.nCopies; copies++) {
            StartPage(printdlg.hDC);

            for(i=0; i<NUMLINES; i++) {
              TextOut(printdlg.hDC, X, Y, str, strlen(str));
              /* advance to next line */
              Y = Y + tm.tmHeight + tm.tmExternalLeading;
            }

            EndPage(printdlg.hDC);
          }
```

18

```
      EndDoc(printdlg.hDC);
      DeleteDC(printdlg.hDC);
      break;
    case IDM_BITMAP: /* print a bitmap */
      /* initialize PRINTDLG struct */
      PrintInit(&printdlg, hwnd);

      if(!PrintDlg(&printdlg)) break;

      docinfo.cbSize = sizeof(DOCINFO);
      docinfo.lpszDocName = "Printing bitmaps";
      docinfo.lpszOutput = NULL;
      docinfo.lpszDatatype = NULL;
      docinfo.fwType = 0;

      if(!(GetDeviceCaps(printdlg.hDC, RASTERCAPS)
         & (RC_BITBLT | RC_STRETCHBLT))) {
         MessageBox(hwnd, "Cannot Print Raster Images",
                    "Error", MB_OK);
         break;
      }

      /* create a memory DC compatible with the printer */
      memPrDC = CreateCompatibleDC(printdlg.hDC);
      /* create a bitmap compatible with the printer DC */
      hBit2 = CreateCompatibleBitmap(printdlg.hDC, maxX, maxY);
      SelectObject(memPrDC, hBit2);

      /* put bitmap image into memory DC */
      SelectObject(memDC, hImage);

      /* copy bitmap to printer-compatible DC */
      BitBlt(memPrDC, 0, 0, BMPWIDTH, BMPHEIGHT,
             memDC, 0, 0, SRCCOPY);

      /* obtain pixels-per-inch */
      VidXPPI = GetDeviceCaps(memDC, LOGPIXELSX);
      VidYPPI = GetDeviceCaps(memDC, LOGPIXELSY);
      PrXPPI = GetDeviceCaps(printdlg.hDC, LOGPIXELSX);
      PrYPPI = GetDeviceCaps(printdlg.hDC, LOGPIXELSY);

      /* get scaling ratios */
      Xratio = PrXPPI / VidXPPI;
      Yratio = PrYPPI / VidYPPI;
```

```
SelectObject(memDC, hBit); /* restore virtual window */

StartDoc(printdlg.hDC, &docinfo);

for(copies=0; copies < printdlg.nCopies; copies++) {
  StartPage(printdlg.hDC);

  /* copy bitmap to printer DC, as-is */
  BitBlt(printdlg.hDC, 0, 0, BMPWIDTH, BMPHEIGHT,
         memPrDC, 0, 0, SRCCOPY);

  /* copy bitmap while maintaining perspective */
  StretchBlt(printdlg.hDC, 0, BMPHEIGHT + 100,
             (int) (BMPWIDTH*Xratio),
             (int) (BMPHEIGHT*Yratio),
             memPrDC, 0, 0,
             BMPWIDTH, BMPHEIGHT,
             SRCCOPY);

  EndPage(printdlg.hDC);
}

EndDoc(printdlg.hDC);
DeleteDC(memPrDC);
DeleteDC(printdlg.hDC);
break;
case IDM_WINDOW: /* print contents of window */
GetClientRect(hwnd, &r);
hdc = GetDC(hwnd);

/* display some text in the window */
GetTextMetrics(hdc, &tm);
X = Y = 0;
strcpy(str, "This is displayed in the main window.");
for(i=0; i<NUMLINES; i++) {
  TextOut(hdc, X, Y, str, strlen(str));
  TextOut(memDC, X, Y, str, strlen(str));
  /* advance to next line */
  Y = Y + tm.tmHeight + tm.tmExternalLeading;
}

/* display bitmap image in the window */
SelectObject(memDC, hImage);
BitBlt(hdc, 100, 100, BMPWIDTH, BMPHEIGHT,
       memDC, 0, 0, SRCCOPY);
```

18

```
/* save image in window for PAINT requests */
SelectObject(memDC, hBit);
BitBlt(memDC, 0, 0, r.right, r.bottom, hdc, 0, 0, SRCCOPY);

/* initialize PRINTDLG struct */
PrintInit(&printdlg, hwnd);

if(!PrintDlg(&printdlg)) break;

docinfo.cbSize = sizeof(DOCINFO);
docinfo.lpszDocName = "Printing Window";
docinfo.lpszOutput = NULL;
docinfo.lpszDatatype = NULL;
docinfo.fwType = 0;

/* obtain pixels-per-inch */
VidXPPI = GetDeviceCaps(memDC, LOGPIXELSX);
VidYPPI = GetDeviceCaps(memDC, LOGPIXELSY);
PrXPPI = GetDeviceCaps(printdlg.hDC, LOGPIXELSX);
PrYPPI = GetDeviceCaps(printdlg.hDC, LOGPIXELSY);

/* get scaling ratios */
Xratio = PrXPPI / VidXPPI;
Yratio = PrYPPI / VidYPPI;

if(!(GetDeviceCaps(printdlg.hDC, RASTERCAPS)
   & (RC_BITBLT | RC_STRETCHBLT))) {
   MessageBox(hwnd, "Cannot Print Raster Images",
              "Error", MB_OK);
   break;
}

StartDoc(printdlg.hDC, &docinfo);

for(copies=0; copies < printdlg.nCopies; copies++) {
  StartPage(printdlg.hDC);

  StretchBlt(printdlg.hDC, 0, 0,
             (int) (r.right*Xratio),
             (int) (r.bottom*Yratio),
             hdc, 0, 0, (int) r.right, (int) r.bottom,
             SRCCOPY);

  EndPage(printdlg.hDC);
}
```

```
                    EndDoc(printdlg.hDC);
                    DeleteDC(printdlg.hDC);
                    DeleteDC(memPrDC);
                    ReleaseDC(hwnd, hdc);
                    break;
                case IDM_EXIT:
                    response = MessageBox(hwnd, "Quit the Program?",
                                        "Exit", MB_YESNO);
                    if(response == IDYES) PostQuitMessage(0);
                    break;
                case IDM_HELP:
                    MessageBox(hwnd, "Printing Demo", "Help", MB_OK);
                    break;
            }
            break;
        case WM_PAINT: /* process a repaint request */
            hdc = BeginPaint(hwnd, &ps); /* get DC */

            BitBlt(hdc, ps.rcPaint.left, ps.rcPaint.top,
                    ps.rcPaint.right-ps.rcPaint.left, /* width */
                    ps.rcPaint.bottom-ps.rcPaint.top, /* height */
                    memDC,
                    ps.rcPaint.left, ps.rcPaint.top,
                    SRCCOPY);

            EndPaint(hwnd, &ps); /* release DC */
            break;
        case WM_DESTROY: /* terminate the program */
            DeleteDC(memDC);
            PostQuitMessage(0);
            break;
        default:
            /* Let Windows 98 process any messages not specified in
               the preceding switch statement. */
            return DefWindowProc(hwnd, message, wParam, lParam);
    }
    return 0;
}

/* Initialize PRINTDLG structure. */
void PrintInit(PRINTDLG *printdlg, HWND hwnd)
{
    printdlg->lStructSize = sizeof(PRINTDLG);
    printdlg->hwndOwner = hwnd;
    printdlg->hDevMode = NULL;
```

18

```
  printdlg->hDevNames = NULL;
  printdlg->hDC = NULL;
  printdlg->Flags = PD_RETURNDC | PD_NOSELECTION |
                    PD_NOPAGENUMS | PD_HIDEPRINTTOFILE;
  printdlg->nFromPage = 0;
  printdlg->nToPage = 0;
  printdlg->nMinPage = 0;
  printdlg->nMaxPage = 0;
  printdlg->nCopies = 1;
  printdlg->hInstance = NULL;
  printdlg->lCustData = 0;
  printdlg->lpfnPrintHook = NULL;
  printdlg->lpfnSetupHook = NULL;
  printdlg->lpPrintTemplateName = NULL;
  printdlg->lpSetupTemplateName = NULL;
  printdlg->hPrintTemplate = NULL;
  printdlg->hSetupTemplate = NULL;
}
```

This program requires the following resource file.

```
#include <windows.h>
#include "print.h"

MyBP1 BITMAP BP.BMP

PrintDemoMenu2 MENU
{
  POPUP "&Printer Demo"
  {
    MENUITEM "Print &Text\tF2", IDM_TEXT
    MENUITEM "Print &Bitmap\tF3", IDM_BITMAP
    MENUITEM "Print &Window\tF4", IDM_WINDOW
    MENUITEM "E&xit\tCtrl+X", IDM_EXIT
  }
  MENUITEM "&Help", IDM_HELP
}


PrintDemoMenu2 ACCELERATORS
{
  VK_F2, IDM_TEXT, VIRTKEY
  VK_F3, IDM_BITMAP, VIRTKEY
  VK_F4, IDM_WINDOW, VIRTKEY
  "^X", IDM_EXIT
}
```

18

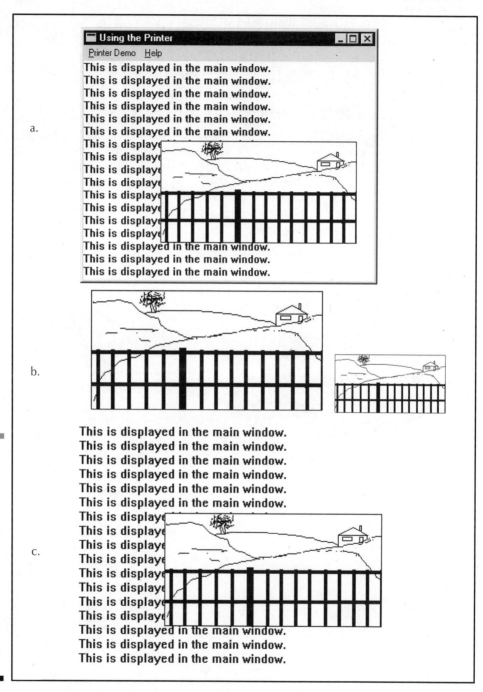

Sample
output from
the bitmap
printing
program.
(a) Window as
it appears on
the screen;
(b) Printed
bitmaps;
(c) Contents
of window
printed

Figure 18-2.

This program requires a bitmap for operation. As the program is written, the bitmap must be 256 pixels wide and 128 pixels high. However, if you change the definitions of **BMPWIDTH** and **BMPHEIGHT**, you can use any size bitmap you like. The bitmap must be stored in a file called BP.BMP.

A Closer Look at the Bitmap Printing Program

Let's begin by examining the **IDM_BITMAP** case. This code is executed when the user selects the Print Bitmap option. It prints the bitmap stored in BP.BMP. This code is shown here for your convenience.

```
case IDM_BITMAP: /* print a bitmap */
  /* initialize PRINTDLG struct */
  PrintInit(&printdlg, hwnd);

  if(!PrintDlg(&printdlg)) break;

  docinfo.cbSize = sizeof(DOCINFO);
  docinfo.lpszDocName = "Printing bitmaps";
  docinfo.lpszOutput = NULL;
  docinfo.lpszDatatype = NULL;
  docinfo.fwType = 0;

  if(!(GetDeviceCaps(printdlg.hDC, RASTERCAPS)
     & (RC_BITBLT | RC_STRETCHBLT))) {
     MessageBox(hwnd, "Cannot Print Raster Images",
               "Error", MB_OK);
     break;
  }

  /* create a memory DC compatible with the printer */
  memPrDC = CreateCompatibleDC(printdlg.hDC);
  /* create a bitmap compatible with the printer DC */
  hBit2 = CreateCompatibleBitmap(printdlg.hDC, maxX, maxY);
  SelectObject(memPrDC, hBit2);

  /* put bitmap image into memory DC */
  SelectObject(memDC, hImage);

  /* copy bitmap to printer-compatible DC */
  BitBlt(memPrDC, 0, 0, BMPWIDTH, BMPHEIGHT,
        memDC, 0, 0, SRCCOPY);

  /* obtain pixels-per-inch */
```

```
VidXPPI = GetDeviceCaps(memDC, LOGPIXELSX);
VidYPPI = GetDeviceCaps(memDC, LOGPIXELSY);
PrXPPI = GetDeviceCaps(printdlg.hDC, LOGPIXELSX);
PrYPPI = GetDeviceCaps(printdlg.hDC, LOGPIXELSY);

/* get scaling ratios */
Xratio = PrXPPI / VidXPPI;
Yratio = PrYPPI / VidYPPI;

SelectObject(memDC, hBit); /* restore virtual window */

StartDoc(printdlg.hDC, &docinfo);

for(copies=0; copies < printdlg.nCopies; copies++) {
  StartPage(printdlg.hDC);

  /* copy bitmap to printer DC, as-is */
  BitBlt(printdlg.hDC, 0, 0, BMPWIDTH, BMPHEIGHT,
         memPrDC, 0, 0, SRCCOPY);

  /* copy bitmap while maintaining perspective */
  StretchBlt(printdlg.hDC, 0, BMPHEIGHT + 100,
             (int) (BMPWIDTH*Xratio),
             (int) (BMPHEIGHT*Yratio),
             memPrDC, 0, 0,
             BMPWIDTH, BMPHEIGHT,
             SRCCOPY);

  EndPage(printdlg.hDC);
}

EndDoc(printdlg.hDC);
DeleteDC(memPrDC);
DeleteDC(printdlg.hDC);
break;
```

After the printer DC has been acquired and **docinfo** has been initialized, a
call is made to **GetDeviceCaps( )** to determine if the printer supports the
necessary raster operations. Remember, if the printer cannot print graphics,
it cannot print a bitmap. Assuming that the printer can print the bitmap,
a printer-compatible memory DC (**memPrDC**) and bitmap (**hBit2**)
are created. The use of **maxX** and **maxY** for the dimensions of the printer-
compatible bitmap is suitable for all bitmaps that are not larger than the
size of the screen. (Of course, if you want to print a larger bitmap, these

dimensions would need to be larger.) Next, **hbit2** is selected into the printer-compatible memory DC.

The bitmap to be displayed (whose handle is **hImage**) is selected into the memory device context described by **memDC**. This is the same memory DC used to support the virtual window system that handles **WM_PAINT** messages. It is simply doing double-duty at this point. (A separate memory DC could have been created for this purpose, but to do so seemed unnecessarily inefficient.) Next, the bitmap is copied from **memDC** into **memPrDC**. The reason for this intermediate step is that the bitmap stored in BP.BMP is compatible with a video device context, not a printer device context. Thus, it cannot be directly selected into **memPrDC**.

The next step computes the scaling ratios. To do this, the number of pixels-per-inch for the screen and the printer are obtained, and a scaling factor is computed.

Finally, the bitmap can be sent to the printer. First, it is copied as is, using **BitBlt( )**. This causes the bitmap to be printed without adjusting for the perspective differences between the two devices. Next, the bitmap is printed using **StretchBlt( )** and applying the scaling factors. As you can see, the scaled bitmap closely resembles the way the bitmap looks when displayed on the screen.

The code inside the **IDM_WINDOW** is similar to that inside the **IDM_BITMAP** case just described. You should have no trouble understanding it.

IN DEPTH

Using the Page Setup Common Dialog Box

Windows 98 provides another common dialog box that helps support printing: Page Setup. It allows the user to specify the following print-related items.

◆   The size of the paper being used.

◆   The paper source (such as the paper tray).

◆ The orientation of the printed image (landscape or portrait).

◆ The left, right, top, and bottom margins.

To activate the Page Setup common dialog box, call **pageSetupDlg( )**, shown here:

BOOL PageSetupDlg(LPPAGESETUPDLG *lpPSD*);

The function returns nonzero if the user presses the OK button to close the dialog box or zero if the user pressed Cancel (or on error).

lpPSD points to a **PAGESETUPDLG** structure, which is defined like this:

```
typedef struct tagPSD {
  DWORD lStructSize; /* size of PAGESETUPDLG */
  HWND hwndOwner; /* handle of owner */
  HGLOBAL hDevMode; /* handle of DEVMODE structure */
  HGLOBAL hDevNames; /* handle of DEVNAMES structure */
  DWORD Flags; /* various initialization flags */
  POINT ptPaperSize; /* size of paper */
  RECT rtMinMargin; /* minimum acceptable margins */
  RECT rtMargin; /* margins */
  HINSTANCE hInstance; /* handle for lpPageSetupTemplateName */
  LPARAM lCustData; /* data for lpfnPageSetupHook */
  LPPAGESETUPHOOK lpfnPageSetupHook; /* alternative hook function */
  LPPAGEPAINTHOOK lpfnPagePaintHook; /* alternative paint function */
  LPCSTR lpPageSetupTemplateName; /* alternative template name */
  HGLOBAL hPageSetupTemplate; /* alternative template handle
} PAGESETUPDLG;
```

Many of the fields in **PRINTSETUPDLG** are the same as those used by **PRINTDLG**. However, notice these: **ptPaperSize**, **rtMinMargin**, and **rtMargin**. On return, **ptPaperSize** will contain the size of the paper selected by the user in either thousandths of an inch or hundredths of millimeters. **rtMinMarg** specifies the minimum margin sizes that the user may select. **rtMargin** specifies the initial margins and on return will contain the margins selected by the user.

The following fragment displays the default Page Setup dialog box.

18

```
PAGESETUPDLG psd;
/* ... */
psd.lStructSize = sizeof(PAGESETUPDLG);
psd.hwndOwner = hwnd;
psd.hDevMode = psd.hDevNames = NULL;
psd.Flags = 0;
PageSetupDlg(&psd);
```

This displays the dialog box shown here:

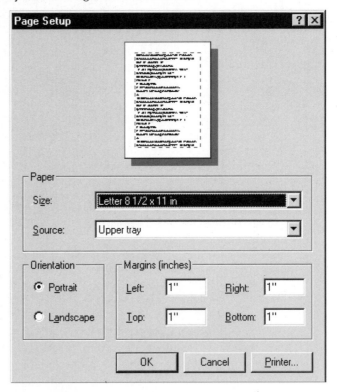

You might want to experiment with the Page Setup dialog box. It supports a number of useful options.

Adding an Abort Function

The preceding examples sent output to the printer and forgot about it. That is, as far as the program was concerned, once the output was sent to the printer, its job was done. However, for real applications, things cannot be this simple. Sometimes an error occurs while printing and a print job must be stopped. Sometimes the user will change his or her mind and want to cancel a print job. To handle such situations, your program must supply a printer abort function and a modeless dialog box that allow the user to cancel a print job before it is complete. According to standard Windows style, all programs must supply such a feature. In this section, you will see how to accomplish this.

A printing abort function allows printing to be canceled by the user.

18

SetAbortProc( )

To install an abort function, your program must call **SetAbortProc( )**. Its prototype is shown here:

    int SetAbortProc(HDC *hPrDC*, ABORTPROC *AbortFunc*);

Here, *hPrDC* is the handle of the printer device context. *AbortFunc* is the name of the abort function that is being installed. The function returns a value that is greater than zero if successful or **SP_ERROR** on failure.

All abort functions have the following prototype:

    BOOL CALLBACK AbortFunc(HDC *hPrDC*, int *Code*);

When called, *hPrDC* will contain the handle for the printer device context. *Code* will be zero unless an error has occurred. Your application can watch this value and take appropriate action when an error is detected. The function must return nonzero to continue printing or zero to stop.

Inside the abort function, you must implement a message loop. However, instead of using **GetMessage( )** to retrieve messages, you must use **PeekMessage( )** with the **PM_REMOVE** option instead. The reason for this is that **GetMessage( )** waits for a message if one is not already in the message queue, while **PeekMessage( )** does not. Thus, a skeletal abort function looks like this:

```
/* Printer abort function. */
BOOL CALLBACK AbortFunc(HDC hdc, int err)
{
  MSG message;

  /* if err is other than zero, handle the error */

  while(PeekMessage(&message, NULL, 0, 0, PM_REMOVE)) {
    if(!IsDialogMessage(hDlg, &message)) {
      TranslateMessage(&message);
      DispatchMessage(&message);
    }
  }

  return printOK; /* printOK is a global variable */
}
```

PeekMessage( )
is similar to
GetMessage( )
except that it
does not wait
for a message
to be queued.

The handle of the modeless dialog box that is used to cancel the print job must be stored in **hDlg**. The global variable **printOK** must be initially set to nonzero. However, if the user cancels the print job, this variable will be set to zero. This action is accomplished by a modeless dialog box, which is described next.

The Cancel Printing Dialog Box

After the abort function has been installed, your program must activate a modeless dialog box that allows the user to cancel the print job. Although this dialog box can contain additional features and controls, it must contain at least one button, called Cancel, that cancels the print job. When the user presses Cancel, the dialog box sets a global variable to zero. This global variable must be the same one returned by the abort function described in the preceding section.

A Complete Printing Example

The following program adds an abort function to the preceding program. It also adds one other element: an enlarging option. Using this option, you can set scale factors for the X and Y dimensions. By default, these factors are 1 and thus no enlargement takes place. However, they can be set anywhere between 1 and 10. Using these factors, you can print a bitmap up to ten times as large as its original size. You can also enlarge only one dimension. Sample output from the program is shown in Figure 18-3.

```
/* Using an Abort Function and Enlargement. */

#include <windows.h>
#include <string.h>
#include <commdlg.h>
#include <commctrl.h>
#include "print.h"

#define NUMLINES 25
#define SCALEMAX 10

#define BMPWIDTH 256
#define BMPHEIGHT 128

LRESULT CALLBACK WindowFunc(HWND, UINT, WPARAM, LPARAM);
BOOL CALLBACK EnlargeDialog(HWND, UINT, WPARAM, LPARAM);
void PrintInit(PRINTDLG *printdlg, HWND hwnd);

BOOL CALLBACK AbortFunc(HDC hdc, int err);
LRESULT CALLBACK KillPrint(HWND, UINT, WPARAM, LPARAM);

char szWinName[] = "MyWin"; /* name of window class */

int X = 0, Y = 0; /* current output location */
int maxX, maxY; /* screen dimensions */

HDC memDC, memPrDC; /* store the virtual device handle */
HBITMAP hBit, hBit2, hImage; /* bitmap handles */
HBRUSH hBrush; /* store the brush handle */

PRINTDLG printdlg;
DOCINFO docinfo;

HINSTANCE hInst;

int Xenlarge = 1, Yenlarge = 1;

int printOK = 1;

HWND hDlg = NULL;

int WINAPI WinMain(HINSTANCE hThisInst, HINSTANCE hPrevInst,
                   LPSTR lpszArgs, int nWinMode)
{
  HACCEL hAccel;
```

```
HWND hwnd;
MSG msg;
WNDCLASSEX wcl;
INITCOMMONCONTROLSEX cc;

/* Define a window class. */
wcl.cbSize = sizeof(WNDCLASSEX);

wcl.hInstance = hThisInst; /* handle to this instance */
wcl.lpszClassName = szWinName; /* window class name */
wcl.lpfnWndProc = WindowFunc; /* window function */
wcl.style = 0; /* default style */

wcl.hIcon = LoadIcon(NULL, IDI_APPLICATION); /* standard icon */
wcl.hIconSm = LoadIcon(NULL, IDI_APPLICATION); /* small icon */
wcl.hCursor = LoadCursor(NULL, IDC_ARROW); /* cursor style */

wcl.lpszMenuName = "PrintDemoMenu3";
wcl.cbClsExtra = 0; /* no extra */
wcl.cbWndExtra = 0; /* information needed */

/* Make the window white. */
wcl.hbrBackground = (HBRUSH) GetStockObject(WHITE_BRUSH);

/* Register the window class. */
if(!RegisterClassEx(&wcl)) return 0;

/* Now that a window class has been registered, a window
   can be created. */
hwnd = CreateWindow(
  szWinName, /* name of window class */
  "Using the Printer", /* title */
  WS_OVERLAPPEDWINDOW, /* standard window style */
  CW_USEDEFAULT, /* X coordinate - let Windows decide */
  CW_USEDEFAULT, /* Y coordinate - let Windows decide */
  CW_USEDEFAULT, /* width - let Windows decide */
  CW_USEDEFAULT, /* height - let Windows decide */
  HWND_DESKTOP, /* no parent window */
  NULL, /* no override of class menu */
  hThisInst, /* handle of this instance of the program */
  NULL /* no additional arguments */
);

hInst = hThisInst;
```

```
/* Load accelerators. */
hAccel = LoadAccelerators(hThisInst, "PrintDemoMenu3");

/* Load the bitmap. */
hImage = LoadBitmap(hThisInst, "MyBP1"); /* load bitmap */

/* Initialize the common controls. */
cc.dwSize = sizeof(INITCOMMONCONTROLSEX);
cc.dwICC = ICC_UPDOWN_CLASS;
InitCommonControlsEx(&cc);

/* Display the window. */
ShowWindow(hwnd, nWinMode);
UpdateWindow(hwnd);

/* Create the message loop. */
while(GetMessage(&msg, NULL, 0, 0))
{
  if(!TranslateAccelerator(hwnd, hAccel, &msg)) {
    TranslateMessage(&msg);
    DispatchMessage(&msg);
  }
}
  return msg.wParam;
}

/* This function is called by Windows 98 and is passed
   messages from the message queue.
*/
LRESULT CALLBACK WindowFunc(HWND hwnd, UINT message,
                            WPARAM wParam, LPARAM lParam)
{
  HDC hdc;
  PAINTSTRUCT ps;
  int response;
  TEXTMETRIC tm;
  char str[250];
  int i;
  int copies;
  double VidXPPI, VidYPPI, PrXPPI, PrYPPI;
  double Xratio, Yratio;
  RECT r;

  switch(message) {
    case WM_CREATE:
```

```
        /* get screen coordinates */
        maxX = GetSystemMetrics(SM_CXSCREEN);
        maxY = GetSystemMetrics(SM_CYSCREEN);

        /* create a virtual window */
        hdc = GetDC(hwnd);
        memDC = CreateCompatibleDC(hdc);
        hBit = CreateCompatibleBitmap(hdc, maxX, maxY);
        SelectObject(memDC, hBit);
        hBrush = (HBRUSH) GetStockObject(WHITE_BRUSH);
        SelectObject(memDC, hBrush);
        PatBlt(memDC, 0, 0, maxX, maxY, PATCOPY);

        ReleaseDC(hwnd, hdc);
        break;
    case WM_COMMAND:
      switch(LOWORD(wParam)) {
        case IDM_ENLARGE:
          DialogBox(hInst, "EnlargeDB", hwnd, (DLGPROC) EnlargeDialog);
          break;
        case IDM_TEXT: /* print text */
          X = Y = 0;

          /* initialize PRINTDLG struct */
          PrintInit(&printdlg, hwnd);

          if(!PrintDlg(&printdlg)) break;

          docinfo.cbSize = sizeof(DOCINFO);
          docinfo.lpszDocName = "Printing Text";
          docinfo.lpszOutput = NULL;
          docinfo.lpszDatatype = NULL;
          docinfo.fwType = 0;

          StartDoc(printdlg.hDC, &docinfo);

          strcpy(str, "This is printed on the printer.");

          /* get text metrics for printer */
          GetTextMetrics(printdlg.hDC, &tm);

          printOK = 1;
          SetAbortProc(printdlg.hDC, (ABORTPROC) AbortFunc);
          hDlg = CreateDialog(hInst, "PrCancel", hwnd, (DLGPROC) KillPrint);
```

```
for(copies=0; copies < printdlg.nCopies; copies++) {
  StartPage(printdlg.hDC);

  for(i=0; i<NUMLINES; i++) {
    TextOut(printdlg.hDC, X, Y, str, strlen(str));
    /* advance to next line */
    Y = Y + tm.tmHeight + tm.tmExternalLeading;
  }

  EndPage(printdlg.hDC);
}

if(printOK) {
  DestroyWindow(hDlg);
  EndDoc(printdlg.hDC);
}

DeleteDC(printdlg.hDC);
break;
case IDM_BITMAP: /* print a bitmap */
  /* initialize PRINTDLG struct */
  PrintInit(&printdlg, hwnd);

  if(!PrintDlg(&printdlg)) break;

  docinfo.cbSize = sizeof(DOCINFO);
  docinfo.lpszDocName = "Printing bitmaps";
  docinfo.lpszOutput = NULL;
  docinfo.lpszDatatype = NULL;
  docinfo.fwType = 0;

  if(!(GetDeviceCaps(printdlg.hDC, RASTERCAPS)
      & (RC_BITBLT | RC_STRETCHBLT))) {
    MessageBox(hwnd, "Cannot Print Raster Images",
               "Error", MB_OK);
    break;
  }

  /* create a memory DC compatible with the printer */
  memPrDC = CreateCompatibleDC(printdlg.hDC);
  /* create a bitmap compatible with the printer DC */
  hBit2 = CreateCompatibleBitmap(printdlg.hDC, maxX, maxY);
  SelectObject(memPrDC, hBit2);
```

```
/* put bitmap image into memory DC */
SelectObject(memDC, hImage);

/* copy bitmap to printer-compatible DC */
BitBlt(memPrDC, 0, 0, BMPWIDTH, BMPHEIGHT,
       memDC, 0, 0, SRCCOPY);

/* obtain pixels-per-inch */
VidXPPI = GetDeviceCaps(memDC, LOGPIXELSX);
VidYPPI = GetDeviceCaps(memDC, LOGPIXELSY);
PrXPPI = GetDeviceCaps(printdlg.hDC, LOGPIXELSX);
PrYPPI = GetDeviceCaps(printdlg.hDC, LOGPIXELSY);

/* get scaling ratios */
Xratio = PrXPPI / VidXPPI;
Yratio = PrYPPI / VidYPPI;

SelectObject(memDC, hBit); /* restore virtual window */

StartDoc(printdlg.hDC, &docinfo);

printOK = 1;
SetAbortProc(printdlg.hDC, (ABORTPROC) AbortFunc);
hDlg = CreateDialog(hInst, "PrCancel", hwnd, (DLGPROC) KillPrint);

for(copies=0; copies < printdlg.nCopies; copies++) {
  StartPage(printdlg.hDC);

  /* copy bitmap to printer DC using enlargement
     factors but no perspective scaling */
  StretchBlt(printdlg.hDC, 0, 0,
             BMPWIDTH * Xenlarge,
             BMPHEIGHT * Yenlarge,
             memPrDC, 0, 0, BMPWIDTH, BMPHEIGHT, SRCCOPY);

  /* enlarge bitmap while maintaining perspective */
  StretchBlt(printdlg.hDC, 0, BMPHEIGHT+100*Yenlarge,
             (int) (BMPWIDTH*Xratio*Xenlarge),
             (int) (BMPHEIGHT*Yratio*Yenlarge),
             memPrDC, 0, 0,
             BMPWIDTH, BMPHEIGHT,
             SRCCOPY);

  EndPage(printdlg.hDC);
}
```

```
          if(printOK) DestroyWindow(hDlg);

          EndDoc(printdlg.hDC);
          DeleteDC(printdlg.hDC);
          DeleteDC(memPrDC);
          break;
    case IDM_WINDOW: /* print contents of window */
        GetClientRect(hwnd, &r);
        hdc = GetDC(hwnd);

        /* display some text in the window */
        GetTextMetrics(hdc, &tm);
        X = Y = 0;
        strcpy(str, "This is displayed in the main window.");
        for(i=0; i<NUMLINES; i++) {
          TextOut(hdc, X, Y, str, strlen(str));
          TextOut(memDC, X, Y, str, strlen(str));
          /* advance to next line */
          Y = Y + tm.tmHeight + tm.tmExternalLeading;
        }

        /* display bitmap image in the window */
        SelectObject(memDC, hImage);
        BitBlt(hdc, 100, 100, 256, 128,
              memDC, 0, 0, SRCCOPY);

        /* save image in window for PAINT requests */
        SelectObject(memDC, hBit);
        BitBlt(memDC, 0, 0, r.right, r.bottom, hdc, 0, 0, SRCCOPY);

        /* initialize PRINTDLG struct */
        PrintInit(&printdlg, hwnd);

        if(!PrintDlg(&printdlg)) break;

        docinfo.cbSize = sizeof(DOCINFO);
        docinfo.lpszDocName = "Printing Window";
        docinfo.lpszOutput = NULL;
        docinfo.lpszDatatype = NULL;
        docinfo.fwType = 0;

        /* obtain pixels-per-inch */
        VidXPPI = GetDeviceCaps(memDC, LOGPIXELSX);
        VidYPPI = GetDeviceCaps(memDC, LOGPIXELSY);
        PrXPPI = GetDeviceCaps(printdlg.hDC, LOGPIXELSX);
```

```
      PrYPPI = GetDeviceCaps(printdlg.hDC, LOGPIXELSY);

      /* get scaling ratios */
      Xratio = PrXPPI / VidXPPI;
      Yratio = PrYPPI / VidYPPI;

      if(!(GetDeviceCaps(printdlg.hDC, RASTERCAPS)
         & (RC_BITBLT | RC_STRETCHBLT)))
      {
        MessageBox(hwnd, "Cannot Print Raster Images",
                   "Error", MB_OK);
        break;
      }

      StartDoc(printdlg.hDC, &docinfo);

      printOK = 1;
      SetAbortProc(printdlg.hDC, (ABORTPROC) AbortFunc);
      hDlg = CreateDialog(hInst, "PrCancel", hwnd, (DLGPROC) KillPrint);

      for(copies=0; copies < printdlg.nCopies; copies++) {
        StartPage(printdlg.hDC);

        StretchBlt(printdlg.hDC, 0, 0,
                   (int) (r.right*Xratio) * Xenlarge,
                   (int) (r.bottom*Yratio) * Yenlarge,
                   hdc, 0, 0,
                   (int) r.right, (int) r.bottom,
                   SRCCOPY);

        EndPage(printdlg.hDC);
      }

      if(printOK) DestroyWindow(hDlg);

      EndDoc(printdlg.hDC);
      DeleteDC(printdlg.hDC);
      DeleteDC(memPrDC);
      ReleaseDC(hwnd, hdc);
      break;
    case IDM_EXIT:
      response = MessageBox(hwnd, "Quit the Program?",
                            "Exit", MB_YESNO);
      if(response == IDYES) PostQuitMessage(0);
      break;
```

```
        case IDM_HELP:
          MessageBox(hwnd, "Printing Demo", "Help", MB_OK);
          break;
    }
    break;
  case WM_PAINT: /* process a repaint request */
    hdc = BeginPaint(hwnd, &ps); /* get DC */

    BitBlt(hdc, ps.rcPaint.left, ps.rcPaint.top,
           ps.rcPaint.right-ps.rcPaint.left, /* width */
           ps.rcPaint.bottom-ps.rcPaint.top, /* height */
           memDC,
           ps.rcPaint.left, ps.rcPaint.top,
           SRCCOPY);

    EndPaint(hwnd, &ps); /* release DC */
    break;
  case WM_DESTROY: /* terminate the program */
    DeleteDC(memDC);
    PostQuitMessage(0);
    break;
  default:
    /* Let Windows 98 process any messages not specified in
       the preceding switch statement. */
    return DefWindowProc(hwnd, message, wParam, lParam);
  }
  return 0;
}

/* Initialize PRINTDLG structure. */
void PrintInit(PRINTDLG *printdlg, HWND hwnd)
{
  printdlg->lStructSize = sizeof(PRINTDLG);
  printdlg->hwndOwner = hwnd;
  printdlg->hDevMode = NULL;
  printdlg->hDevNames = NULL;
  printdlg->hDC = NULL;
  printdlg->Flags = PD_RETURNDC | PD_NOSELECTION |
                    PD_NOPAGENUMS | PD_HIDEPRINTTOFILE;
  printdlg->nFromPage = 0;
  printdlg->nToPage = 0;
  printdlg->nMinPage = 0;
  printdlg->nMaxPage = 0;
  printdlg->nCopies = 1;
  printdlg->hInstance = NULL;
```

```
  printdlg->lCustData = 0;
  printdlg->lpfnPrintHook = NULL;
  printdlg->lpfnSetupHook = NULL;
  printdlg->lpPrintTemplateName = NULL;
  printdlg->lpSetupTemplateName = NULL;
  printdlg->hPrintTemplate = NULL;
  printdlg->hSetupTemplate = NULL;
}

/* Enlargement factor dialog function */
BOOL CALLBACK EnlargeDialog(HWND hdwnd, UINT message,
                            WPARAM wParam, LPARAM lParam)
{
  static int tempX=1, tempY=1;

  static long temp;
  static HWND hEboxWnd1, hEboxWnd2;
  static HWND udWnd1, udWnd2;
  int low=1, high=SCALEMAX;


  switch(message) {
    case WM_INITDIALOG:
      hEboxWnd1 = GetDlgItem(hdwnd, IDD_EB1);
      hEboxWnd2 = GetDlgItem(hdwnd, IDD_EB2);
      udWnd1 = CreateUpDownControl(
                    WS_CHILD | WS_BORDER | WS_VISIBLE |
                    UDS_SETBUDDYINT | UDS_ALIGNRIGHT,
                    10, 10, 50, 50,
                    hdwnd,
                    IDD_UD1,
                    hInst,
                    hEboxWnd1,
                    SCALEMAX, 1, Xenlarge);

      udWnd2 = CreateUpDownControl(
                    WS_CHILD | WS_BORDER | WS_VISIBLE |
                    UDS_SETBUDDYINT | UDS_ALIGNRIGHT,
                    10, 10, 50, 50,
                    hdwnd,
                    IDD_UD2,
                    hInst,
                    hEboxWnd2,
                    SCALEMAX, 1, Yenlarge);
```

18

```
            tempX = Xenlarge;
            tempY = Yenlarge;
            return 1;
        case WM_VSCROLL: /* process up-down control */
            if(udWnd1==(HWND)lParam)
              tempX = GetDlgItemInt(hdwnd, IDD_EB1, NULL, 1);
            else if(udWnd2==(HWND)lParam)
              tempY = GetDlgItemInt(hdwnd, IDD_EB2, NULL, 1);
            return 1;
        case WM_COMMAND:
          switch(LOWORD(wParam)) {
            case IDOK:
              Xenlarge = tempX;
              Yenlarge = tempY;
            case IDCANCEL:
              EndDialog(hdwnd, 0);
              return 1;
          }
          break;
    }
    return 0;
}

/* Printer abort function. */
BOOL CALLBACK AbortFunc(HDC hdc, int err)
{
  MSG message;

  while(PeekMessage(&message, NULL, 0, 0, PM_REMOVE)) {
    if(!IsDialogMessage(hDlg, &message)) {
      TranslateMessage(&message);
      DispatchMessage(&message);
    }
  }

  return printOK;
}

/* Let user kill print process. */
LRESULT CALLBACK KillPrint(HWND hdwnd, UINT message,
                           WPARAM wParam, LPARAM lParam)
{
  switch(message) {
    case WM_COMMAND:
      switch(LOWORD(wParam)) {
```

```
        case IDCANCEL:
          printOK = 0;
          DestroyWindow(hDlg);
          hDlg = NULL;
          return 1;
      }
      break;
  }
  return 0;
}
```

The resource file for the program is shown here.

```
#include <windows.h>
#include "print.h"

MyBP1 BITMAP BP.BMP

PrintDemoMenu3 MENU
{
  POPUP "&Printer Demo"
  {
    MENUITEM "&Enlarge\tF2", IDM_ENLARGE
    MENUITEM "Print &Text\tF3", IDM_TEXT
    MENUITEM "Print &Bitmap\tF4", IDM_BITMAP
    MENUITEM "Print &Window\tF5", IDM_WINDOW
    MENUITEM "E&xit\tCtrl+X", IDM_EXIT
  }
  MENUITEM "&Help", IDM_HELP
}

PrintDemoMenu3 ACCELERATORS
{
  VK_F2, IDM_ENLARGE, VIRTKEY
  VK_F3, IDM_TEXT, VIRTKEY
  VK_F4, IDM_BITMAP, VIRTKEY
  VK_F5, IDM_WINDOW, VIRTKEY
  "^X", IDM_EXIT
}

EnlargeDB DIALOG 10, 10, 97, 77
CAPTION "Enlarge Printer Output"
STYLE WS_POPUP | WS_SYSMENU | WS_VISIBLE
{
  PUSHBUTTON "OK", IDOK, 10, 50, 30, 14,
```

```
                    WS_CHILD | WS_VISIBLE | WS_TABSTOP
     PUSHBUTTON "Cancel", IDCANCEL, 55, 50, 30, 14,
                    WS_CHILD | WS_VISIBLE | WS_TABSTOP
     LTEXT "X Scale Factor", IDD_TEXT1,  15, 1, 25, 20
     LTEXT "Y Scale Factor", IDD_TEXT2,  60, 1, 25, 20
     EDITTEXT IDD_EB1, 15, 20, 20, 12, ES_LEFT | WS_CHILD |
             WS_VISIBLE | WS_BORDER
     EDITTEXT IDD_EB2, 60, 20, 20, 12, ES_LEFT | WS_CHILD |
             WS_VISIBLE | WS_BORDER
}

PrCancel DIALOG 10, 10, 100, 40
CAPTION "Printing"
STYLE WS_CAPTION | WS_POPUP | WS_SYSMENU | WS_VISIBLE
{
   PUSHBUTTON "Cancel", IDCANCEL, 35, 12, 30, 14,
             WS_CHILD | WS_VISIBLE | WS_TABSTOP

}
```

18

A Practical Example: Printing a Text File

To conclude this chapter we will look at a practical example: the printing of a text file. The program that follows allows the user to select a text file to be printed and then prints the file. Multiple copies may be printed. This example is a useful utility in its own right. It can also provide the foundation for your own file-printing tasks. Before a file can be printed, two additional pieces of information need to be known: the size of a page of paper and the name of the file.

Obtaining the Size of a Page

In the previous examples, the size of a page of paper in the printer was simply ignored because all output fit on a standard-sized page. However, in order to print a multipage document, it is necessary to know how long a page is. Although not required by the following example, you may also need to know how wide a page is. To obtain these dimensions, you will once again use the **GetDeviceCaps( )** function. To find the length of a printed page, use the **VERTRES** attribute. This causes the length of the page in pixels to be returned. To find the width of a page, use **HORZRES**. Using these dimensions, you can determine when one page ends and another begins. You can also determine when output exceeds the width of a page.

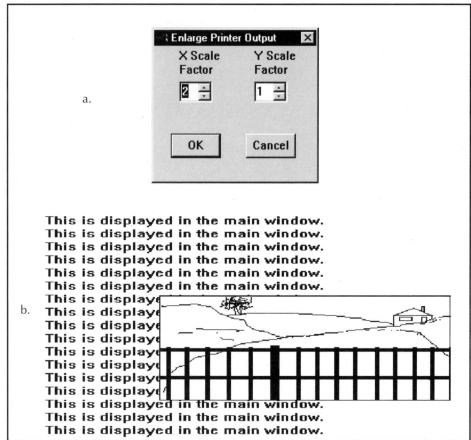

Sample output
from the final
printing
demonstration
program.
(a) The
Enlargement
dialog box;
(b) Contents of
screen printed
with a 2X
enlargement
factor along
the X-axis

Figure 18-3.

Obtaining a File Name

GetOpenFile-
Name( )
activates
the standard
Open common
dialog box.

The file printing program allows the user to select the file to be printed. It
does this using another of Windows 98's common dialog boxes: Open. The
Open dialog box is used to input the name of a file to be opened. It allows a
user to select a filename either by typing it or selecting it from a list. The user
may also change directories or drives. The Open dialog box used by the
following program is shown in Figure 18-4. The Open dialog box is activated
by calling the **GetOpenFileName( )** API function. Its prototype is shown
here:

BOOL GetOpenFileName(LPOPENFILENAME *lpBuf*);

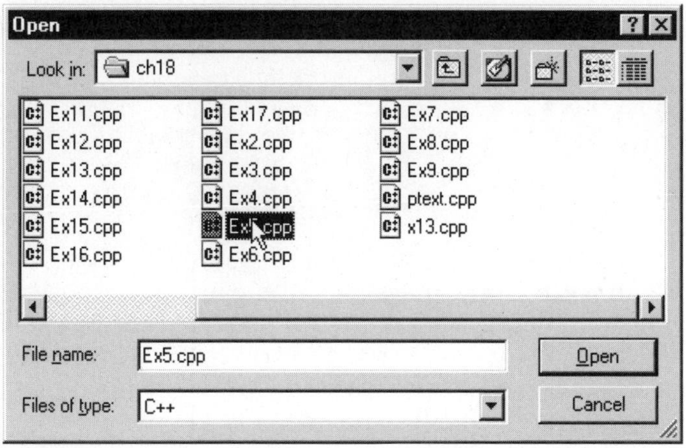

The Open
common
dialog box
Figure 18-4.

Here, *lpBuf* is a pointer to a structure of type **OPENFILENAME**. The function
returns nonzero if a valid filename is specified by the user and zero otherwise.

The **OPENFILENAME** structure pointed to by *lpBuf* must be initialized prior
to calling **GetOpenFileName( )**. Upon return, the filename specified by the
user, and several other pieces of information, will be contained in that
structure. The **OPENFILENAME** structure is defined like this:

```
typedef struct tagOFN
{
  DWORD lStructSize;
  HWND hwndOwner;
  HINSTANCE hInstance;
  LPCSTR lpstrFilter;
  LPSTR lpstrCustomFilter;
  DWORD nMaxCustFilter;
  DWORD nFilterIndex;
  LPSTR lpstrFile;
  DWORD nMaxFile;
  LPSTR lpstrFileTitle;
  DWORD nMaxFileTitle;
  LPCSTR lpstrInitialDir;
  LPCSTR lpstrTitle;
  DWORD Flags;
  WORD nFileOffset;
```

```
    WORD nFileExtension;
    LPCSTR lpstrDefExt;
    LPARAM lCustData;
    LPOFNHOOKPROC lpfnHook;
    LPCSTR   lpTemplateName;
} OPENFILENAME;
```

Each element of **OPENFILENAME** is described here.

lStructSize must contain the size of the **OPENFILENAME** structure.
hwndOwner must contain the handle of the window that owns the dialog
box. If **Flags** contains either **OFN_ENABLETEMPLATE** or
OFN_ENABLETEMPLATEHANDLE, then **hInstance** specifies a handle
that defines an alternative dialog box template. Otherwise, **hInstance** is not
used.

lpstrFilter must point to an array that contains pairs of strings that define a
filename filter. The pairs of strings must be organized like this:
"description""mask", where the description identifies the type of files matched
by the mask. For example, "C Files""*.C" specifies the description *C Files* and
the mask **.C*. The last two strings in the array must be null in order to
terminate the list. The names of the filters are displayed in a drop-down list
from which the user may choose. If this element is **NULL**, no filename filter
is used.

lpstrCustomFilter points to a static array that will be used to store a file
filter entered by the user. This array must initially contain a description and
file filter using the format just described. However, after the user selects a
filename, the new filter is copied into the array. If **lpstrCustomFilter**
is **NULL**, this element is ignored. The array must be 40 characters (or
more) long.

nMaxCustFilter specifies the size of the array pointed to by
lpstrCustomFilter. This value is needed only if **lpstrCustomFilter**
is not **NULL**.

nFilterIndex specifies which pair of strings pointed to by **lpstrFilter** will
provide the initial file filter and description when the dialog box is first
displayed. The value 1 corresponds to the first pair, the value 2 to the
second pair, and so on. This value is ignored if **lpstrFilter** is **NULL**. If
nFilterIndex is zero, the strings pointed to by **lpstrCustomFilter**
are used.

lpstrFile points to an array that will receive the complete file, path, and
drive of the filename selected by the user. The array may contain an initial

filename that will be used to initialize the filename edit box or it may point to a null string.

nMaxFile specifies the size of the array pointed to by **lpstrFile**. The array should be at least 256 bytes long so as to accommodate the longest possible filename.

lpstrFileTitle points to an array that receives the filename (without path or drive information) of the file selected by the user. If the filename by itself is not needed, this field may be **NULL**.

nMaxFileTitle specifies the size of the array pointed to by **lpstrFileTitle**.

lpstrInitialDir points to an array that contains the directory that will first be used when the dialog box is activated. If **lpstrInitialDir** is **NULL**, the current directory is used. However, if no files in the current directory match the specified file filter, the user's personal files directory is used.

PORTABILITY: In Windows 95 and Windows NT 4 and earlier, if **lpstrInitialDir** is **NULL**, the current directory is used in all cases.

18

lpstrTitle points to a string that will be used as the title for the dialog box. The default title is used if **lpstrTitle** is **NULL**. For the **GetOpenFileName( )** function, the default title is "Open".

The **Flags** element is used to set various options inside the dialog box. **GetOpenFilename( )** supports numerous options. Several of the most commonly used are shown here. You can OR together two or more flags if necessary.

Flags	Effect
OFN_ENABLEHOOK	Allows the function pointed to by **lpfnHook** to be used.
OFN_ENABLETEMPLATE	Allows alternative dialog box template to be used. In this case, **hInstance** specifies the instance handle of the module that contains the dialog box specified by **lpTemplateName**.

Flags	Effect
OFN_ENABLETEMPLATEHANDLE	Allows alternative dialog box template to be used. In this case, **hInstance** is the handle to a region of memory that contains the dialog box template.
OFN_FILEMUSTEXIST	User may only specify existent files.
OFN_HIDEREADONLY	Causes the read-only check box to be suppressed.
OFN_NOCHANGEDIR	Current directory remains unchanged by user selection.
OFN_PATHMUSTEXIST	User may only specify existent paths.

The **nFileOffset** element receives the index of the start of the filename within the string returned in the array pointed to by **lpstrFile**. (Remember, this array will contain drive and path information in addition to the filename.)

nFileExtension receives the index of the file extension within the string returned in the array pointed to by **lpstrFile**.

lpstrDefExt points to an array that contains a default extension that is appended to the filename entered by the user when no extension is included. (The extension should be specified without a leading period.) This field can be **NULL**.

lCustData contains data that is passed to the optional function pointed to by **lpfnHook**.

lpfnHook is a pointer to a function that preempts and processes messages intended for the dialog box. This element is only used if **Flags** contains the value **OFN_ENABLEHOOK**.

lpTemplateName points to the name of an alternative dialog box template. **hInstance** must be the handle to the module that contains the dialog box resource. **lpTemplateName** is ignored unless **Flags** contains the value **OFN_ENABLETEMPLATE**.

Although **OPENFILENAME** contains many members, several of them can be set to either zero or **NULL**. Others are ignored unless their associated flag is included. Thus, it is not as difficult to use **GetOpenFileName( )** as it may at first seem.

NOTE: The complement to **GetOpenFileName( )** is **GetSaveFileName( )**. It works in much the same way except that the standard Save As dialog box is displayed.

The Print Text File Program

Here is the complete text file printing program. To print a file, select Print Text File from the Print menu. You will then see the Open dialog box and can select the file to print. Once you have selected a file, the Print dialog box is displayed and your file will be printed. Remember, this program can only print plain text files. For example, it will print the source code files for the programs in this book. But it will not be able to print most word processor files that include special format codes.

```c
/* Print a Text File */

#include <windows.h>
#include <string.h>
#include <commdlg.h>
#include <stdio.h>
#include "print.h"

LRESULT CALLBACK WindowFunc(HWND, UINT, WPARAM, LPARAM);
void PrintInit(PRINTDLG *printdlg, HWND hwnd);
BOOL CALLBACK AbortFunc(HDC hdc, int err);
LRESULT CALLBACK KillPrint(HWND, UINT, WPARAM, LPARAM);

char szWinName[] = "MyWin"; /* name of window class */

PRINTDLG printdlg;
DOCINFO docinfo;

HINSTANCE hInst;

int printOK = 1;

HWND hDlg = NULL;

int WINAPI WinMain(HINSTANCE hThisInst, HINSTANCE hPrevInst,
```

```
                    LPSTR lpszArgs, int nWinMode)
{
  HACCEL hAccel;
  HWND hwnd;
  MSG msg;
  WNDCLASSEX wcl;

  /* Define a window class. */
  wcl.cbSize = sizeof(WNDCLASSEX);

  wcl.hInstance = hThisInst; /* handle to this instance */
  wcl.lpszClassName = szWinName; /* window class name */
  wcl.lpfnWndProc = WindowFunc; /* window function */
  wcl.style = 0; /* default style */

  wcl.hIcon = LoadIcon(NULL, IDI_APPLICATION); /* standard icon */
  wcl.hIconSm = LoadIcon(NULL, IDI_APPLICATION); /* small icon */
  wcl.hCursor = LoadCursor(NULL, IDC_ARROW); /* cursor style */

  wcl.lpszMenuName = "PrintFile";
  wcl.cbClsExtra = 0; /* no extra */
  wcl.cbWndExtra = 0; /* information needed */

  /* Make the window white. */
  wcl.hbrBackground = (HBRUSH) GetStockObject(WHITE_BRUSH);

  /* Register the window class. */
  if(!RegisterClassEx(&wcl)) return 0;

  /* Now that a window class has been registered, a window
     can be created. */
  hwnd = CreateWindow(
    szWinName, /* name of window class */
    "Print a Text File", /* title */
    WS_OVERLAPPEDWINDOW, /* standard window style */
    CW_USEDEFAULT, /* X coordinate - let Windows decide */
    CW_USEDEFAULT, /* Y coordinate - let Windows decide */
    CW_USEDEFAULT, /* width - let Windows decide */
    CW_USEDEFAULT, /* height - let Windows decide */
    HWND_DESKTOP, /* no parent window */
    NULL, /* no override of class menu */
    hThisInst, /* handle of this instance of the program */
    NULL /* no additional arguments */
  );
```

```
      hInst = hThisInst;

      /* Load accelerators. */
      hAccel = LoadAccelerators(hThisInst, "PrintFile");

      /* Display the window. */
      ShowWindow(hwnd, nWinMode);
      UpdateWindow(hwnd);

      /* Create the message loop. */
      while(GetMessage(&msg, NULL, 0, 0))
      {
        if(!TranslateAccelerator(hwnd, hAccel, &msg)) {
          TranslateMessage(&msg);
          DispatchMessage(&msg);
        }
      }
      return msg.wParam;
    }


    /* This function is called by Windows 98 and is passed
       messages from the message queue.
    */
    LRESULT CALLBACK WindowFunc(HWND hwnd, UINT message,
                                  WPARAM wParam, LPARAM lParam)
    {
      int response;
      TEXTMETRIC tm;
      char str[250];
      int i;
      int copies;
      static int Y = 0;

      OPENFILENAME fname;
      char filename[64]; /* file name */
      static char fn[256]; /* full path name */
      char filefilter[] = "Text\0*.TXT\0C\0*.C\0C++\0*.CPP\0\0\0";
      static FILE *fp;
      int numlines;

      switch(message) {
        case WM_COMMAND:
          switch(LOWORD(wParam)) {
            case IDM_PRINTFILE:
              /* first, get the name of the file to be printed. */
```

```
/* initialize the OPENFILENAME struct */
fname.lStructSize = sizeof(OPENFILENAME);
fname.hwndOwner = hwnd;
fname.lpstrFilter = filefilter;
fname.nFilterIndex = 1;
fname.lpstrFile = fn;
fname.nMaxFile = sizeof(fn);
fname.lpstrFileTitle = filename;
fname.nMaxFileTitle = sizeof(filename)-1;
fname.Flags = OFN_FILEMUSTEXIST | OFN_HIDEREADONLY;
fname.lpstrCustomFilter = NULL;
fname.lpstrInitialDir = NULL;
fname.lpstrTitle = NULL;
fname.lpstrDefExt = NULL;
fname.lCustData = 0;

if(!GetOpenFileName(&fname)) /* get the file name */
  break;

if((fp=fopen(fn, "r"))==NULL) {
  MessageBox(hwnd, fn, "Cannot Open File", MB_OK);
  break;
}

/* initialize PRINTDLG struct */
PrintInit(&printdlg, hwnd);

if(!PrintDlg(&printdlg)) break;

docinfo.cbSize = sizeof(DOCINFO);
docinfo.lpszDocName = "Printing File";
docinfo.lpszOutput = NULL;
docinfo.lpszDatatype = NULL;
docinfo.fwType = 0;

StartDoc(printdlg.hDC, &docinfo);

/* get text metrics for printer */
GetTextMetrics(printdlg.hDC, &tm);

/* determine number of lines per page */
numlines = GetDeviceCaps(printdlg.hDC, VERTRES);
numlines = numlines / (tm.tmHeight + tm.tmExternalLeading);
```

```
      printOK = 1;
      SetAbortProc(printdlg.hDC, (ABORTPROC) AbortFunc);
      hDlg = CreateDialog(hInst, "PrCancel", hwnd,
                          (DLGPROC) KillPrint);

      /* now, actually print the file */
      for(copies=0; copies < printdlg.nCopies; copies++) {
        StartPage(printdlg.hDC);
        Y = 0;
        i = 0;

        do {
          fgets(str, 80, fp); /* get a line of text */
          str[strlen(str)-1] = 0; /* remove cr-lf */

          /* send this line to the printer */
          TextOut(printdlg.hDC, 0, Y, str, strlen(str));

          /* advance to next line */
          Y = Y + tm.tmHeight + tm.tmExternalLeading;
          i++;

          /* see if at end of page */
          if(numlines == i) {
            EndPage(printdlg.hDC);
            i = 0; Y = 0;
            StartPage(printdlg.hDC);
          }
        } while(!feof(fp));
        EndPage(printdlg.hDC);
        rewind(fp);
      }

      if(printOK) {
        DestroyWindow(hDlg);
        EndDoc(printdlg.hDC);
      }

      DeleteDC(printdlg.hDC);
      fclose(fp);

      break;
    case IDM_EXIT:
      response = MessageBox(hwnd, "Quit the Program?",
```

```
                                        "Exit", MB_YESNO);
            if(response == IDYES) PostQuitMessage(0);
            break;
          case IDM_HELP:
            MessageBox(hwnd, "Printing a Text File",
                       "Help", MB_OK);
            break;
      }
      break;
    case WM_DESTROY: /* terminate the program */
      PostQuitMessage(0);
      break;
    default:
      /* Let Windows 98 process any messages not specified in
         the preceding switch statement. */
      return DefWindowProc(hwnd, message, wParam, lParam);
  }
  return 0;
}

/* Initialize PRINTDLG structure. */
void PrintInit(PRINTDLG *printdlg, HWND hwnd)
{
  printdlg->lStructSize = sizeof(PRINTDLG);
  printdlg->hwndOwner = hwnd;
  printdlg->hDevMode = NULL;
  printdlg->hDevNames = NULL;
  printdlg->hDC = NULL;
  printdlg->Flags = PD_RETURNDC | PD_NOSELECTION |
                    PD_NOPAGENUMS | PD_HIDEPRINTTOFILE;
  printdlg->nFromPage = 0;
  printdlg->nToPage = 0;
  printdlg->nMinPage = 0;
  printdlg->nMaxPage = 0;
  printdlg->nCopies = 1;
  printdlg->hInstance = NULL;
  printdlg->lCustData = 0;
  printdlg->lpfnPrintHook = NULL;
  printdlg->lpfnSetupHook = NULL;
  printdlg->lpPrintTemplateName = NULL;
  printdlg->lpSetupTemplateName = NULL;
  printdlg->hPrintTemplate = NULL;
  printdlg->hSetupTemplate = NULL;
}
```

```
/* Printer abort function. */
BOOL CALLBACK AbortFunc(HDC hdc, int err)
{
  MSG message;

  while(PeekMessage(&message, NULL, 0, 0, PM_REMOVE)) {
    if(!IsDialogMessage(hDlg, &message)) {
      TranslateMessage(&message);
      DispatchMessage(&message);
    }
  }

  return printOK;
}

/* Let user kill print process. */
LRESULT CALLBACK KillPrint(HWND hdwnd, UINT message,
                           WPARAM wParam, LPARAM lParam)
{
  switch(message) {
    case WM_COMMAND:
      switch(LOWORD(wParam)) {
        case IDCANCEL:
          printOK = 0;
          DestroyWindow(hDlg);
          hDlg = NULL;
          return 1;
      }
      break;
  }
  return 0;
}
```

The program uses the same PRINT.H header file shown earlier. It uses the following resource file.

```
#include <windows.h>
#include "print.h"

MyBP1 BITMAP BP.BMP

PrintFile MENU
{
  POPUP "&Print"
  {
```

```
      MENUITEM "&Print Text File\tF2", IDM_PRINTFILE
      MENUITEM "E&xit\tCtrl+X", IDM_EXIT
   }
   MENUITEM "&Help", IDM_HELP
}


PrintFile ACCELERATORS
{
   VK_F2, IDM_PRINTFILE, VIRTKEY
   "^X", IDM_EXIT
}


PrCancel DIALOG 10, 10, 100, 40
CAPTION "Printing"
STYLE WS_CAPTION | WS_POPUP | WS_SYSMENU | WS_VISIBLE
{
   PUSHBUTTON "Cancel", IDCANCEL, 35, 12, 30, 14,
              WS_CHILD | WS_VISIBLE | WS_TABSTOP
}
```

A Closer Look at the File Printing Program

The operation of most of the program should be clear, but let's look at a couple of areas. To begin, notice how the array **filefilter** is initialized. Remember, the array pointed to by **lpstrFilter** must contain pairs of strings. In the program, it is initialized to hold three file extensions: .TXT, .C, and .CPP.

Once a filename has been obtained, it is used to open the file for printing. Observe that in this case, the entire drive, path, and filename contained in **fn** and pointed to by **lpstrFile** are used. If you wanted to restrict files to the current directory, then the contents of **filename** (pointed to by **lpstrFileTitle**) could have been used.

Before the printing begins, the length of a page in lines is computed. This is accomplished by obtaining the length of a page in pixels and then dividing that value by the height of a line of text.

Inside the print loop, lines of text are read from the file and sent to the printer. Each time a line is read, the line counter **i** is incremented. When a page full of text has been printed (i.e., when **i** equals **numlines**), a new page is started and the various counters are reset.

In this example, the length of a line is restricted to 80 characters and standard width paper is assumed. Thus, there is no need to obtain the width of a page. However, as an experiment you might want to try changing the program so that it automatically truncates long lines that exceed the page width.

Some Things to Try

When it comes to printing, there is virtually no end to things with which you can experiment. Here are some ideas. Try adding page numbers and margins. Try printing color images. If your printer only supports black and white, experiment with different color translations and shades of gray. Another interesting challenge is to print sideways on the page. This is useful for wide printouts. It is possible to allow the user to select a range of pages to print. You should try to implement this on your own.

In the next chapter you will see how to handle the system registry and learn to create screen savers.

18

CHAPTER 19

Using the System Registry and Creating Screen Savers

This chapter discusses two topics that at first may seem unrelated: *screen savers* and the *system registry*. But the ability to understand and use the registry is necessary for the creation of all but the most simple screen savers. The reason for this is that a typical screen saver needs to store configuration information. The screen saver uses this information to configure itself each time it pops up. Under Windows 98, the proper place to store such information is in the system registry. In fact, screen savers are one of the few smaller applications that make use of the registry, and they serve as excellent practical examples of registry utilization.

Although screen savers are some of the simpler Windows 98 applications that you will write, they are also some of the most interesting from the programmer's point of view. They are also the one type of application that virtually all programmers want to write. Indeed, it is rare to find a programmer who has not thought about creating his or her own screen saver. While screen savers were initially invented to prevent phosphor burn on idle screens, they have taken on a life of their own. Today, most screen savers provide either an entertaining message, an interesting graphics display, a company logo, or a humorous animated sequence. As you will see, creating your own screen saver is one of the easier Windows 98 programming tasks.

The system registry is a much more mundane topic. It is also one of the more important Windows 98 programming issues. As you probably know, the registry was designed to take the place of .INI initialization files. It stores information about the state and configuration of your computer and of its software. Most programmers are initially intimidated by the registry, but it is really quite easy to use.

This chapter develops two simple screen savers. The first is nonconfigurable and does not use the registry. Its purpose is to introduce the basic elements common to all screen savers. The second screen saver can be configured and stores its configuration information in the registry. Keep in mind that neither screen saver generates interesting, engaging, or exciting output. They simply illustrate the mechanics involved in creating a screen saver. However, you can use these examples as starting points from which you can develop your own.

PORTABILITY: If you have written a screen saver for Windows 3.1 or used the registry under Windows 3.1, beware: both are somewhat different under Windows 98. Screen savers are a little easier to implement, and the registry supports some new API functions.

Screen Saver Fundamentals

One reason that a screen saver is one of the easiest Windows 98 applications to program is that it does not create a main window. Instead, it uses the desktop (that is, the entire screen) as its window. It also does not contain a **WinMain( )** function or need to create a message loop. In fact, a screen saver requires only three functions, two of which may be empty placeholders.

When creating screen savers, you must include SCRNSAVE.H and link in SCRNSAVE.LIB.

When you create a screen saver, your program must include the header file SCRNSAVE.H and you must include SCRNSAVE.LIB when linking. The screen saver library provides the necessary support for screen savers. This is why your screen saver code need only contain three functions. The rest of the details are handled by the screen saver library.

The Screen Saver Functions

The three functions that every screen saver must provide are shown here.

Function	Purpose
ScreenSaverProc( )	This is the screen saver's window procedure. It is passed messages and must respond appropriately.
ScreenSaverConfigureDialog( )	This is the dialog function for the screen saver's configuration dialog box. It can be empty if no configuration is supported.
RegisterDialogClasses( )	This function is used to register custom class types. It will be empty if no custom classes are used.

Although the names of these functions are defined by Windows 98, you must supply the functions themselves in the source code to your screen saver. (That is, they are not provided by Win32.) Let's take a closer look at these three functions now.

ScreenSaverProc( ) is a window procedure. Its prototype is shown here:

LRESULT WINAPI ScreenSaverProc(HWND *hwnd*, UINT *message*,
                     WPARAM *wParam*, LPARAM *lParam*);

It is passed messages in the same way as other window procedures. There is one important difference, however. If the function does not process a

message, it must call **DefScreenSaverProc( )** rather than
DefWindowProc( ). Also, the window handle passed to
ScreenSaverProc( ) in *hwnd* is the handle for the entire screen. That is,
it is the handle of the desktop. Your screen saver will make use of this fact.

ScreenSaverConfigureDialog( ) is the dialog box function that handles
the screen saver's configuration dialog box. It has the following prototype:

> BOOL WINAPI ScreenSaverConfigureDialog(HWND *hdwnd*,
> UINT *message*, WPARAM *wParam*,
> LPARAM *lParam*);

If your screen saver does not require configuration, the only thing this
function must do is return zero. If the screen saver supports a configuration
dialog box, it must be defined in the screen saver's resource file and given the
ID value of **DLG_SCRNSAVECONFIGURE**. This value is defined in
SCRNSAVE.H as 2003.

RegisterDialogClasses( ) is used to register custom window classes, such as
custom controls. It has this prototype:

> BOOL WINAPI RegisterDialogClasses(HANDLE *hInst*);

If your screen saver does not use custom window classes, simply return
nonzero.

As mentioned, **ScreenSaverProc( )** will call **DefScreenSaverProc( )** if it
does not process a message. The prototype for **DefScreenSaverProc( )** is
shown here:

> LRESULT WINAPI DefScreenSaverProc(HWND *hwnd*, UINT *message*,
> WPARAM *wParam*, LPARAM *lParam*);

Two Screen Saver Resources

All screen savers must define two special resources: an icon and a string.
The icon, whose ID must be **ID_APP**, is used to identify the screen saver.
The string resource, whose identifier must be **IDS_DESCRIPTION**,
contains a description of the screen saver. This string must be no more
than 24 characters long. **ID_APP** and **IDS_DESCRIPTION** are defined
in SCRNSAVE.H.

String resources are defined in a resource file using the **STRINGTABLE**
statement. It has this general form.

```
STRINGTABLE
{
  ID1  "string"
  ID2  "string"
  .
  .
  .
  IDn  "string"
}
```

Here, *ID* is the identifier associated with the string. Your program can refer to a string resource by its ID value. A program can load a string resource by calling **LoadString( )**. However, for the purposes of a screen saver, the **IDS_DESCRIPTION** string is not used by the screen saver itself. Rather, it simply provides a description of the screen saver.

Other Programming Considerations

SCRNSAVE.H defines several global variables. The one of interest to us in this chapter is **hMainInstance**. This will contain the instance handle of the screen saver. This handle will be needed if your screen saver creates a window, for example. Other global variables are defined within SCRNSAVE.H, which may be useful to your screen saver. You will want to examine the contents of this header file.

A screen saver is driven by a timer.

All screen savers are driven by a timer. Each time the timer goes off, the screen saver receives a **WM_TIMER** message and updates the screen display. Your screen saver must start the timer when it is first activated and destroy the timer when it is destroyed. (Timers were described in Chapter 3.)

After you have compiled the screen saver, you must rename it so that it has the .SCR rather than .EXE extension. Next, copy the renamed screen saver into the proper directory. For most users, the directory that holds screen savers will be WINDOWS\SYSTEM. (The easiest way to determine which directory to use is to see which one holds the screen savers currently installed on your system.) Once you have renamed and copied the screen saver to the proper directory, you can select your new screen saver using the control panel.

Creating a Minimal Screen Saver

We will begin by creating a bare bones screen saver. It simply displays a text-based message that moves about the screen. It cannot be configured and does not use the **ScreenSaverConfigureDialog( )** function. It does, however, illustrate the basic elements of a screen saver. Here is the complete listing for the minimal screen saver.

```c
/* A miminal screen saver. */
#include <windows.h>
#include <scrnsave.h>

/* This is the message displayed on the screen. */
char str[80] = "Windows 98 Screen Saver #1";

/* This is timer delay. */
int delay = 200;

/* Screen Saver Function */
LRESULT WINAPI ScreenSaverProc(HWND hwnd, UINT message,
                               WPARAM wParam, LPARAM lParam)
{
  static HDC hdc;
  static unsigned int timer;
  static RECT scrdim;
  static SIZE size;
  static int X = 0, Y = 0;
  static HBRUSH hBlkBrush;
  static TEXTMETRIC tm;

  switch(message) {
    case WM_CREATE:
      timer = SetTimer(hwnd, 1, delay, NULL);
      hBlkBrush = (HBRUSH) GetStockObject(BLACK_BRUSH);
      break;
    case WM_ERASEBKGND:
      hdc = GetDC(hwnd);

      /* get coordinates of screen */
      GetClientRect(hwnd, &scrdim);

      /* erase the screen */
      SelectObject(hdc, hBlkBrush);
      PatBlt(hdc, 0, 0, scrdim.right, scrdim.bottom, PATCOPY);

      /* get and save height and length of string */
      GetTextMetrics(hdc, &tm);
      GetTextExtentPoint32(hdc, str, strlen(str), &size);
```

```
        ReleaseDC(hwnd, hdc);
        break;
    case WM_TIMER:
        hdc = GetDC(hwnd);

        /* erase previous output */
        SelectObject(hdc, hBlkBrush);
        PatBlt(hdc, X, Y, X + size.cx, Y + size.cy, PATCOPY);

        /* move string to new location */
        X += 10; Y += 10;
        if(X > scrdim.right) X = 0;
        if(Y > scrdim.bottom) Y = 0;

        /* output string */
        SetBkColor(hdc, RGB(0, 0, 0));
        SetTextColor(hdc, RGB(0, 255, 255));
        TextOut(hdc, X, Y, str, strlen(str));

        ReleaseDC(hwnd, hdc);
        break;
    case WM_DESTROY:
        KillTimer(hwnd, timer);
        break;
    default:
        return DefScreenSaverProc(hwnd, message, wParam, lParam);
    }

    return 0;
}

/* Placeholder Dialog Box Function */
BOOL WINAPI ScreenSaverConfigureDialog(HWND hdwnd, UINT message,
                                  WPARAM wParam, LPARAM lParam)
{
    return 0;
}

/* No classes to register. */
BOOL WINAPI RegisterDialogClasses(HANDLE hInst)
{
    return 1;
}
```

The screen saver requires the following resource file.

```
#include <windows.h>
#include <scrnsave.h>

ID_APP ICON SCRICON.ICO

STRINGTABLE
{
  IDS_DESCRIPTION "My Screen Saver #1"
}
```

As this resource file implies, you will need to create an icon for your screen saver. Save it in a file called SCRICON.ICO.

A Closer Look at the First Screen Saver

Each time the screen saver is activated, it receives two messages. The first is **WM_CREATE**. Your screen saver must use this message to perform any initializations it requires, as well as to start the timer. In this example, the timer has a period of 200 milliseconds. Thus, it will interrupt the screen saver five times a second. The black brush is also obtained when the screen saver is created.

The next message received by your screen saver is **WM_ERASEBKGND**. When this message is received, your screen saver must clear the entire screen. There are, of course, several ways to do this. The method employed by the example is to obtain the coordinates of the screen, select the black brush, and then use **PatBlt( )** to fill the specified region with black (i.e., nothing). Remember, *hwnd* contains the handle of the desktop, so the call to **GetClientRect( )** returns the dimensions of the entire screen.

Since the message displayed by the screen saver does not change, its dimensions are also obtained and stored when **WM_ERASEBKGND** is received.

Each time the timer goes off, **WM_TIMER** is sent to the screen saver. In response, the screen saver first erases the message from its current location, advances the location counters, and then redisplays the message.

When the user presses a key or moves the mouse, the screen saver receives a **WM_DESTROY** message. When this occurs, the screen saver must cancel the timer and perform any other shutdown tasks.

Since this screen saver has no user-configurable data or custom control classes, the functions **ScreenSaverConfigureDialog( )** and **RegisterDialogClasses( )** are simply placeholders.

Problems with the First Screen Saver

While the preceding screen saver shows the basics, it is inadequate for actual use. First, the message displayed on the screen cannot be changed. Second, the delay period is fixed. Both of these items are subject to personal taste and should be configurable by the user. Fortunately, it is easy to add this capability to the screen saver. However, doing so raises one interesting problem: Where is the configuration data going to be stored? To allow the screen saver to be configured requires that the delay time and the message be stored on disk somewhere. When the screen saver executes, it must be able to retrieve these settings. While it is certainly possible, in this simple case, to store the information in a normal data file, a better solution exists. Therefore, before developing a configurable screen saver, a short discussion of one of Windows 98's most important facilities is required.

19

Understanding the System Registry

As pointed out by the preceding section, when a program contains configurable options, there must be some way to store them. In the early days of computing, each program would create its own, special data file that contained its configuration settings. Such files often used file extensions such as .CFG or .DAT. (In fact, you can still find examples of these types of files, although they are getting increasingly rare.) While such an individualized approach was adequate for operating systems such as DOS, it was not appropriate for multitasking systems, such as Windows. For example, it was possible for two or more programs to use the same name for their configuration files, causing confusion. To solve this problem, early versions of Windows created the .INI file extension, which was reserved for program initialization files. Windows also defined its own initialization file, called WIN.INI. Applications were free to use this file to hold their own configuration information or to create their own, private .INI files.

The system registry stores configuration information.

While .INI files helped bring order to configuration files, they were not a perfect solution. One reason is that it was still possible for two different applications to use the same name for their .INI files. Also, when a computer had several applications loaded onto it, there were often a very large number of .INI files. Further, in some cases it was beneficial for one program to know if another program was also installed on the system. Using .INI files, this was not always an easy thing to determine. To finally solve the configuration file problem, Microsoft abandoned .INI files entirely and invented an entirely new approach called the *system registry*, or just *registry* for short. While the registry was partially supported by Windows 3.1, it was enhanced for Windows 95 and Windows NT. Windows 98 uses essentially the same registry structure as Windows 95. It is important to understand that Windows 98 still supports the older .INI files. However, for new applications, you must use the registry to hold configuration information.

For various reasons, the registry has gotten the reputation of being difficult to use and understand. However, this reputation is not deserved. Indeed, the truth is quite the contrary. As you will see, using the registry is straight-forward. Once you have mastered only a few new API functions, you will have no trouble using it.

PORTABILITY: The registry was largely ignored under Windows 3.1 and most Windows 3.1 programs do no use it. However, under Windows 98, all new applications are expected to use the registry. You should make this change when porting older programs.

The Registry Structure

The registry is a special, hierarchical database maintained by Windows 98 that stores information related to three entities: the user, the machine, and the installed software. For the most part, it stores configuration settings relating to these items. The information stored in the registry is in its binary form. For this reason there are only two ways by which you may alter or examine the contents of the registry: by using REGEDIT, the standard registry editor, or by using the registry management API functions. You cannot, for example, edit the registry using a text editor.

The registry is a set of keys structured as a tree. A *key* is, for practical purposes, a node in the tree. The name of a key is essentially the name of a node. A key may be empty, have subkeys, or contain values. Typically, these values consist of configuration information for a program. Thus, to use the registry, your program will create a key and store its configuration information under that key. When it needs this information, it will look up the key and then read the information. If the user changes the configuration settings, your program will simply write those new values to the registry. Using the registry really is just this easy.

A registry key is
~~is a node in the~~ a node in the
registry tree.

The Built-in Keys

The registry contains six built-in keys. Each key forms the root node for its own subtree of keys. The names of the built-in keys are shown here.

Key	Purpose
HKEY_CLASSES_ROOT	Holds information used by OLE. Also defines associations between file extensions and applications.
HKEY_CURRENT_CONFIG	Current hardware configuration.
HKEY_CURRENT_USER	Holds information related to the current user. This is where user-related, application program configuration information is usually stored.
HKEY_LOCAL_MACHINE	Holds information about the system, including the installed software, network preferences, and other system-wide, hardware-related information.
HKEY_USERS	Holds the preferences for each user of the machine.
HKEY_DYN_DATA	Holds dynamic data.

19

These six keys are always open and may be used by your application. However, generally, an application will only use two of these keys: **HKEY_LOCAL_MACHINE**, which is used to store any system-wide configuration options relating to the machine, and **HKEY_CURRENT_ USER**, which is used to store configuration options relating to the user.

Typically, an installation program will create a key under **HKEY_LOCAL_ MACHINE**, which contains the name and version number of an application package, plus the name of the company that created the application. Other application-related data may also be stored under **HKEY_LOCAL_ MACHINE**. Under **HKEY_CURRENT_USER**, a program will store configuration options selected by the user. Default user configuration information may also be written under this key when the program is installed. Typically, the application will use this information when it begins execution. The configuration data for the screen saver will be stored under this key.

Since the screen saver in this chapter is a simple example program, it doesn't require any special installation. Thus, we won't be using **HKEY_LOCAL_MACHINE**. However, the techniques used to read and write data to and from the registry using this key are the same as for **HKEY_CURRENT_USER**.

There are several standard subkeys that will normally be found in the registry. For example, under **HKEY_CURRENT_USER**, some of the standard subkeys are **Software**, **Control Panel**, and **Network**. When you add the configuration settings for a new program to the registry, you will typically do so under the **Software** subkey of **HKEY_CURRENT_USER**. Although the standard subkeys will exist on all computers running Windows 98, they are not automatically open.

Since the registry is a set of hierarchical trees, you will need to specify a full path to the key that you want. Key paths are similar in concept to directory paths. Each key is separated from the one preceding it using a backslash (\) character. For example, if you access a key called **Screensaver** under the **Software** subkey of **HKEY_CURRENT_USER**, the key path will look like this:

    HKEY_CURRENT_USER\Software\Screensaver

A key may also include a period.

Recall that in C/C++, the backslash character signals the start of an escape sequence when used in a string. Therefore, when specifying a string in a C/C++ program that contains a backslash, you must use two backslashes for each backslash character you need. For example, to specify the preceding path as a C/C++ string, use the following:

    "HKEY_CURRENT_USER\\Software\\Screensaver"

If you forget to use the two backslashes, your registry functions will not work properly.

In Windows terminology, a *hive* is a key hierarchy that typically descends directly from either **HKEY_LOCAL_MACHINE** or **HKEY_USERS**. Some registry operations operate on hives. For example, you can save or load a hive.

Registry Values

The registry allows several different types of data to be stored as values under a key. When you store or retrieve data, you must specify its name and its type. Table 19-1 shows the types of data supported by the registry. You will always add a value to the registry under a key that you have defined. There is no concept of simply adding a value to the registry by itself.

Creating and Opening a Key

All registry operations take place relative to an open key. The six predefined keys described earlier are always open. Therefore, you will use one of the predefined keys as the starting point when opening any other key. To open an existing key, use **RegOpenKeyEx( )**. Its prototype is shown here:

```
LONG RegOpenKeyEx(HKEY hKey, LPCSTR lpszSubKey,
                  DWORD NotUsed, REGSAM Access,
                  PHKEY Result);
```

Here, *hKey* is the handle of an already open key, which may be one of the predefined keys. The key being opened must be a subkey of *hKey*. The name

Data Type	Meaning
REG_BINARY	Generic type used to specify any binary data.
REG_DWORD	Long, unsigned integer.
REG_DWORD_LITTLE_ENDIAN	Long, unsigned integer stored with least-significant byte first. This is called *little-endian* format.
REG_DWORD_BIG_ENDIAN	Long, unsigned integer stored with most-significant byte first. This is called *big-endian* format.
REG_EXPAND_SZ	A string that contains unexpanded environmental variables.
REG_LINK	A Unicode symbolic link.
REG_MULTI_SZ	An array of strings. The last two strings must be null.
REG_NONE	Undefined type.
REG_RESOURCE_LIST	A resource list for a device driver.
REG_SZ	Normal, null-terminated string.

The Data Types Supported by the Registry

Table 19-1.

of the subkey is pointed to by *lpszSubKey*. *NotUsed* is reserved and must be zero. *Access* determines the access privileges for the subkey handle. This value can be any combination of the values shown in Table 19-2. *Result* is a pointer to a variable that, on return, contains the handle of the subkey.

The function returns **ERROR_SUCCESS** if successful. On failure, an error code is returned. The function fails if the specified key does not exist.

Although you can use **RegOpenKeyEx( )** to open a registry key, you will probably find that more often you will use another registry function called **RegCreateKeyEx( )**. This function serves a dual purpose: It will open an already existing key or, if the specified key does not it exist, it will create it. Its prototype is shown here:

```
LONG RegCreateKeyEx(HKEY hKey, LPCSTR lpszSubKey,
                    DWORD NotUsed, LPSTR lpszClass,
                    DWORD How, REGSAM Access,
                    LPSECURITY_ATTRIBUTES SecAttr,
                    PHKEY Result, LPDWORD WhatHappened);
```

Access Value	Purpose
KEY_ALL_ACCESS	Allows all accesses.
KEY_CREATE_LINK	Allows the creation of a symbolic link.
KEY_CREATE_SUB_KEY	Allows the creation of subkeys.
KEY_ENUMERATE_SUB_KEYS	Allows the enumeration of subkeys.
KEY_EXECUTE	Allows read access.
KEY_NOTIFY	Allows change notification.
KEY_QUERY_VALUE	Allows read-access to subkey data.
KEY_READ	Allows all read accesses. Same as **KEY_ENUMERATE_SUB_KEYS	KEY_NOTIFY	KEY_QUERY_VALUE.**
KEY_SET_VALUE	Allows write-access to subkey data.
KEY_WRITE	Allows all write accesses. Same as **KEY_CREATE_SUB_KEY	KEY_SET_VALUE.**

Key Access
Privilege
Values
Table 19-2.

Here, *hKey* is the handle of an open key. *lpszSubKey* is a pointer to the name of the key to open or create. *NotUsed* is reserved and must be zero. *lpszClass* is a pointer to the class or object type for the key. This value is only used for keys being created and can be a string of your own choosing.

For Windows 98, the value of *How* should be

> **REG_OPTION_NON_VOLATILE**

This creates a nonvolatile key that is stored on disk. This is the default.

Access determines the access privileges of the key. It may be any valid combination of the values shown in Table 19-2.

SecAttr is a pointer to a **SECURITY_ATTRIBUTES** structure that defines the security descriptor for the key. For Windows 98, this value should be **NULL**.

On return, the variable pointed to by *Result* will contain the handle of the key that has just been created or opened. *WhatHappened* is a pointer to a variable that, on return, describes which action took place. It will be either **REG_CREATED_NEW_KEY**, if a new key was created, or **REG_OPENED_EXISTING_KEY**, if an already existing key was opened.

RegCreateKeyEx( ) can create several keys at the same time. For example, if *SubKey* contains the string "\\CoName\\AppName", then the keys **CoName** and **AppName** are created if they do not already exist.

The function returns **ERROR_SUCCESS** if successful. On failure, an error code is returned.

PORTABILITY: Windows 3.1 does not support any of the registry functions that end in **Ex**. For example, it does not support **RegCreateKeyEx( )**. Instead, older applications use **RegCreateKey( )**. When converting older applications, you will want to watch for opportunities to convert older functions into their Windows 98, **Ex** form.

Storing Values

Once you have obtained an open key, you can store values under it. To do this, use **RegSetValueEx( )**. Its prototype is shown here:

```
LONG RegSetValueEx(HKEY hKey, LPCSTR lpszName,
                DWORD NotUsed, DWORD DataType,
                CONST LPBYTE lpValue, DWORD SizeOfValue);
```

19

hKey is the handle of an open key that has been opened with
KEY_SET_VALUE access rights. *lpszName* is a pointer to the name of the
value. If this name does not already exist, it is added to the key. *NotUsed* is
currently reserved and must be set to zero.

DataType specifies the type of data that is being stored. It must be one of the
values specified in Table 19-1. *lpValue* is a pointer to the data being stored.
SizeOfValue specifies the size of this data (in bytes). For string data, the
null-terminator must also be counted.

For example, the following call to **RegSetValueEx( )** stores the string "This
is a test" in the value **StringTest**.

```
strcpy(str, "This is a test");
RegSetValueEx(hRegKey, "StringTest", 0, REG_SZ,
              (LPBYTE) str, strlen(str)+1);
```

As mentioned, notice that the null terminator must be counted as part of the
size of a string. This is why 1 is added to the value of **strlen( )**.

RegSetValueEx( ) returns **ERROR_SUCCESS** if successful. On failure, it
returns an error code.

Retrieving Values

Once you have stored a value in the registry, it can be retrieved at any time
by your program (or by any other program). To do so, use the
RegQueryValueEx( ) function, shown here:

LONG RegQueryValueEx(HKEY *hKey*, LPSTR *lpszName*,
                    LPDWORD *NotUsed*, LPDWORD *DataType*,
                    LPBYTE *Value*, LPDWORD *SizeOfData*);

hKey is the handle of an open key, which must have been opened with
KEY_QUERY_VALUE access privileges. *lpszName* is a pointer to the name of
the value desired. This value must already exist under the specified key.
NotUsed is currently reserved and must be set to **NULL**.

DataType is a pointer that, on return, contains the type of the value being
retrieved. This will be one of the values shown in Table 19-1. *Value* is a
pointer to a buffer that, on return, contains the data associated with the
specified value. *SizeOfData* is a pointer to a variable that contains the size of
the buffer in bytes. On return, *SizeOfData* will point to the number of bytes
stored in the buffer.

For example, the following call to **RegQueryValueEx( )** retrieves the string associated with the value **StringTest**.

```
char str[80];
long size = 80;
RegQueryValueEx(hRegKey, "StringTest", NULL, REG_SZ,
                (LPBYTE) str, &size);
```

RegQueryValueEx( ) returns **ERROR_SUCCESS** if successful. On failure, it returns an error code.

Closing a Key

To close a key, use **RegCloseKey( )**, shown here:

LONG RegCloseKey(HKEY *hKey*);

Here, *hKey* is the handle of the key being closed. The function returns **ERROR_SUCCESS** if successful, or an error code on failure.

IN DEPTH

Some Additional Registry Functions

Although the registry functions described in this chapter are the only ones needed by the configurable screen saver, there are several other registry-related functions that you will want to explore on your own. Here are some of the other, commonly used ones.

Function	Purpose
RegDeleteKey( )	Deletes a key.
RegDeleteValue( )	Deletes a value.
RegEnumKeyEx( )	Enumerates the subkeys of a given key.
RegEnumValue( )	Enumerates the values associated with a given key.
RegLoadKey( )	Loads a key subtree (i.e., a hive) from a file.

Function	Purpose
RegQueryInfoKey( )	Obtains detailed information about a key.
RegSaveKey( )	Saves an entire subtree (i.e., a hive), beginning at the specified key, to a file. Values are also saved.

One good way to learn more about the registry is to write a program that enumerates and displays all of the keys and values it contains. When experimenting with the registry, remember one caution: do not change its values. Doing so may stop your computer from working.

Using REGEDIT

Your program interacts with the registry using the registry API functions. However, if you want to examine (or even alter) the contents of the registry, you may do so using REGEDIT. REGEDIT displays the registry, including all keys and values. You can add, delete, and modify both keys and values. Normally, you will not want to manually change the registry. If you do so incorrectly, your computer might stop working! However, using REGEDIT to view the structure and contents of the registry is completely safe and it will give you a concrete understanding of the registry's organization.

Creating a Configurable Screen Saver

To transform the simple screen saver shown at the start of this chapter into a configurable one, three additions must be made. First, a configuration dialog box must be defined in the screen saver's resource file. Second, the **ScreenSaverConfigureDialog( )** function must be filled in. Third, the configuration settings must be stored in the registry and retrieved each time the screen saver executes. Here is the complete program that contains these enhancements.

NOTE: The following program uses a spin control, which is a common control. For this reason, you will need to include COMCTL32.LIB when linking.

```c
/* A Configurable Screen Saver */
#include <windows.h>
#include <scrnsave.h>
#include <commctrl.h>
#include <string.h>
#include "scr.h"

#define DELAYMAX 999
#define MSGSIZE 80

/* This is the screen saver's message. */
char str[MSGSIZE+1] = "Windows 98 Screen Saver #2";

/* This is timer delay. */
long delay;

unsigned long datatype, datasize;
unsigned long result;

/* This is a registry key. */
HKEY hRegKey;

/* Screen Saver Function */
LRESULT WINAPI ScreenSaverProc(HWND hwnd, UINT message,
                               WPARAM wParam, LPARAM lParam)
{
  static HDC hdc;
  static unsigned int timer;
  static RECT scrdim;
  static SIZE size;
  static int X = 0, Y = 0;
  static HBRUSH hBlkBrush;
  static TEXTMETRIC tm;

  switch(message) {
    case WM_CREATE:
      /* open screen saver key or create, if necessary */
      RegCreateKeyEx(HKEY_CURRENT_USER,
          "Software\\HSPrograms\\Screensaver",
          0, "Screen Saver", 0, KEY_ALL_ACCESS,
          NULL, &hRegKey, &result);

      /* if key was created */
      if(result==REG_CREATED_NEW_KEY) {
        /* set its initial value */
```

```
    delay = 100;
    RegSetValueEx(hRegKey, "delay", 0,
        REG_DWORD, (LPBYTE) &delay, sizeof(DWORD));
    RegSetValueEx(hRegKey, "message", 0,
        REG_SZ, (LPBYTE) str, strlen(str)+1);
  }
  else { /* key was already in registry */
    /* get delay value */
    datasize = sizeof(DWORD);
    RegQueryValueEx(hRegKey, "delay", NULL,
        &datatype, (LPBYTE) &delay, &datasize);

    /* get message */
    datasize = MSGSIZE;
    RegQueryValueEx(hRegKey, "message", NULL,
        &datatype, (LPBYTE) str, &datasize);
  }

  RegCloseKey(hRegKey);

  timer = SetTimer(hwnd, 1, delay, NULL);
  hBlkBrush = (HBRUSH) GetStockObject(BLACK_BRUSH);
  break;
case WM_ERASEBKGND:
  hdc = GetDC(hwnd);

  /* Get coordinates of screen */
  GetClientRect(hwnd, &scrdim);

  /* erase the screen */
  SelectObject(hdc, hBlkBrush);
  PatBlt(hdc, 0, 0, scrdim.right, scrdim.bottom, PATCOPY);

  /* get and save height and length of string */
  GetTextMetrics(hdc, &tm);
  GetTextExtentPoint32(hdc, str, strlen(str), &size);

  ReleaseDC(hwnd, hdc);
  break;
case WM_TIMER:
  hdc = GetDC(hwnd);

  /* erase previous output */
  SelectObject(hdc, hBlkBrush);
  PatBlt(hdc, X, Y, X + size.cx, Y + size.cy, PATCOPY);
```

```
      /* move string to new location */
      X += 10; Y += 10;
      if(X > scrdim.right) X = 0;
      if(Y > scrdim.bottom) Y = 0;

      /* output string */
      SetBkColor(hdc, RGB(0, 0, 0));
      SetTextColor(hdc, RGB(0, 255, 255));
      TextOut(hdc, X, Y, str, strlen(str));

      ReleaseDC(hwnd, hdc);
      break;
    case WM_DESTROY:
      KillTimer(hwnd, timer);
      break;
    default:
      return DefScreenSaverProc(hwnd, message, wParam, lParam);
  }

  return 0;
}

/* Configuration Dialog Box Function */
BOOL WINAPI ScreenSaverConfigureDialog(HWND hdwnd, UINT message,
                  WPARAM wParam, LPARAM lParam)
{
  static HWND hEboxWnd;
  static HWND udWnd;
  INITCOMMONCONTROLSEX cc;

  switch(message) {
    case WM_INITDIALOG:
      /* initialize common controls */
      cc.dwSize = sizeof(INITCOMMONCONTROLSEX);
      cc.dwICC = ICC_UPDOWN_CLASS;
      InitCommonControlsEx(&cc);

      /* open screen saver key or create, if necessary */
      RegCreateKeyEx(HKEY_CURRENT_USER,
         "Software\\HSPrograms\\Screensaver",
         0, "Screen Saver", 0, KEY_ALL_ACCESS,
         NULL, &hRegKey, &result);

      /* if key was created */
      if(result==REG_CREATED_NEW_KEY) {
```

```
      /* set its initial value */
      delay = 100;
      RegSetValueEx(hRegKey, "delay", 0,
         REG_DWORD, (LPBYTE) &delay, sizeof(DWORD));
      RegSetValueEx(hRegKey, "message", 0,
         REG_SZ, (LPBYTE) str, strlen(str)+1);
    }
    else { /* key was already in registry */
      /* get delay value */
      datasize = sizeof(DWORD);
      RegQueryValueEx(hRegKey, "delay", NULL,
         &datatype, (LPBYTE) &delay, &datasize);

      /* get message */
      datasize = MSGSIZE;
      RegQueryValueEx(hRegKey, "message", NULL,
         &datatype, (LPBYTE) str, &datasize);
    }

    /* create delay spin control */
    hEboxWnd = GetDlgItem(hdwnd, IDD_EB1);
    udWnd = CreateUpDownControl(
                WS_CHILD | WS_BORDER | WS_VISIBLE |
                UDS_SETBUDDYINT | UDS_ALIGNRIGHT,
                20, 10, 50, 50,
                hdwnd,
                IDD_UPDOWN,
                hMainInstance,
                hEboxWnd,
                DELAYMAX, 1, delay);

    /* initialize edit box with current message */
    SetDlgItemText(hdwnd, IDD_EB2, str);

    return 1;
  case WM_COMMAND:
    switch(LOWORD(wParam)) {
      case IDOK:
        /* set delay value */
        delay = GetDlgItemInt(hdwnd, IDD_EB1, NULL, 1);

        /* get message string */
        GetDlgItemText(hdwnd, IDD_EB2, str, MSGSIZE);
```

```
                 /* update registry */
                 RegSetValueEx(hRegKey, "delay", 0,
                    REG_DWORD, (LPBYTE) &delay, sizeof(DWORD));
                 RegSetValueEx(hRegKey, "message", 0,
                    REG_SZ, (LPBYTE) str, strlen(str)+1);

                 /* fall through to next case ... */
              case IDCANCEL:
                RegCloseKey(hRegKey);
                EndDialog(hdwnd, 0);
                return 1;
            }
          break;
      }
    return 0;
}

/* No classes to register. */
BOOL WINAPI RegisterDialogClasses(HANDLE hInst)
{
  return 1;
}
```

The resource file required by the program is shown here.

```
// Dialog box for screen saver.
#include <windows.h>
#include <scrnsave.h>
#include "scr.h"

ID_APP ICON SCRICON.ICO

STRINGTABLE
{
  IDS_DESCRIPTION "My Screen Saver #2"
}

DLG_SCRNSAVECONFIGURE DIALOGEX 18, 18, 110, 60
CAPTION "Set Screen Saver Options"
STYLE DS_MODALFRAME | WS_POPUP | WS_VISIBLE | WS_CAPTION |
      WS_SYSMENU
{
```

```
PUSHBUTTON "OK", IDOK, 20, 40, 30, 14,
          WS_CHILD | WS_VISIBLE | WS_TABSTOP
PUSHBUTTON "Cancel", IDCANCEL, 60, 40, 30, 14,
          WS_CHILD | WS_VISIBLE | WS_TABSTOP
EDITTEXT IDD_EB1, 5, 5, 24, 12, ES_LEFT | WS_CHILD |
        WS_VISIBLE | WS_BORDER
EDITTEXT IDD_EB2, 5, 20, 65, 12, ES_LEFT | WS_CHILD |
         WS_VISIBLE | WS_BORDER | ES_AUTOHSCROLL |
         WS_TABSTOP
LTEXT "Delay in milliseconds", IDD_TEXT1, 35, 7, 100, 12
LTEXT "Message", IDD_TEXT2, 76, 22, 30, 12
}
```

The header file SCR.H is shown here.

```
#define IDD_EB1      200
#define IDD_EB2      201

#define IDD_UPDOWN   202

#define IDD_TEXT1    203
#define IDD_TEXT2    204
```

A Closer Look at the Configurable Screen Saver

Let's begin by examining the **ScreenSaverConfigureDialog( )** function.
This dialog function allows two items to be configured: the delay period
and the message that is displayed. It is shown here for your convenience.
When this dialog function is executed, it produces the dialog box shown in
Figure 19-1.

```
/* Configuration Dialog Box Function */
BOOL WINAPI ScreenSaverConfigureDialog(HWND hdwnd, UINT message,
                  WPARAM wParam, LPARAM lParam)
{
  static HWND hEboxWnd;
  static HWND udWnd;
  INITCOMMONCONTROLSEX cc;

  switch(message) {
    case WM_INITDIALOG:
      /* initialize common controls */
      cc.dwSize = sizeof(INITCOMMONCONTROLSEX);
      cc.dwICC = ICC_UPDOWN_CLASS;
```

```
InitCommonControlsEx(&cc);

/* open screen saver key or create, if necessary */
RegCreateKeyEx(HKEY_CURRENT_USER,
   "Software\\HSPrograms\\Screensaver",
   0, "Screen Saver", 0, KEY_ALL_ACCESS,
   NULL, &hRegKey, &result);

/* if key was created */
if(result==REG_CREATED_NEW_KEY) {
  /* set its initial value */
  delay = 100;
  RegSetValueEx(hRegKey, "delay", 0,
     REG_DWORD, (LPBYTE) &delay, sizeof(DWORD));
  RegSetValueEx(hRegKey, "message", 0,
     REG_SZ, (LPBYTE) str, strlen(str)+1);
}
else { /* key was already in registry */
  /* get delay value */
  datasize = sizeof(DWORD);
  RegQueryValueEx(hRegKey, "delay", NULL,
     &datatype, (LPBYTE) &delay, &datasize);

  /* get message */
  datasize = MSGSIZE;
  RegQueryValueEx(hRegKey, "message", NULL,
     &datatype, (LPBYTE) str, &datasize);
}

/* create delay spin control */
hEboxWnd = GetDlgItem(hdwnd, IDD_EB1);
udWnd = CreateUpDownControl(
              WS_CHILD | WS_BORDER | WS_VISIBLE |
              UDS_SETBUDDYINT | UDS_ALIGNRIGHT,
              20, 10, 50, 50,
              hdwnd,
              IDD_UPDOWN,
              hMainInstance,
              hEboxWnd,
              DELAYMAX, 1, delay);

/* initialize edit box with current message */
SetDlgItemText(hdwnd, IDD_EB2, str);

return 1;
```

```
      case WM_COMMAND:
        switch(LOWORD(wParam)) {
          case IDOK:
            /* set delay value */
            delay = GetDlgItemInt(hdwnd, IDD_EB1, NULL, 1);

            /* get message string */
            GetDlgItemText(hdwnd, IDD_EB2, str, MSGSIZE);

            /* update registry */
            RegSetValueEx(hRegKey, "delay", 0,
              REG_DWORD, (LPBYTE) &delay, sizeof(DWORD));
            RegSetValueEx(hRegKey, "message", 0,
               REG_SZ, (LPBYTE) str, strlen(str)+1);

            /* fall through to next case ... */
          case IDCANCEL:
            RegCloseKey(hRegKey);
            EndDialog(hdwnd, 0);
            return 1;
        }
      break;
  }
  return 0;
}
```

When the dialog box is first executed, it receives the standard
WM_INITDIALOG message. First, the common controls are initialized. The
dialog box then opens or creates the registry key **Screensaver**, which is a
subkey of **HSPrograms**, which, in turn, is a subkey of **Software** under the
built-in key **HKEY_CURRENT_USER**. That is, the key path being opened
(or created) is

HKEY_CURRENT_USER\Software\HSPrograms\Screensaver

If the specified key does not already exist in the registry (as it won't when you
first run the screen saver), then **RegCreateKeyEx( )** creates it for you. If it
does already exist, then the key path is opened. The registry path created by
the program (as displayed by REGEDIT) is shown in Figure 19-2.

After **RegCreateKeyEx( )** returns, the contents of **result** are examined to
determine whether the key was created or opened. If the key was created, the
registry is given initial, default values for the delay period and the message.
Otherwise, those values are read from the registry.

19

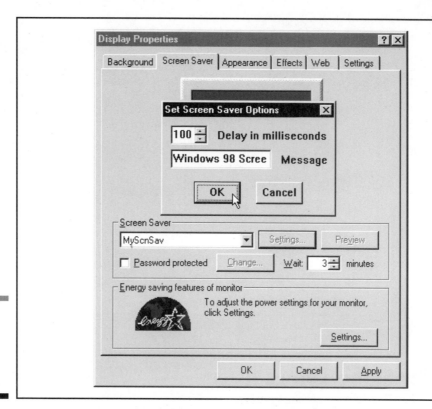

The screen
saver
configuration
dialog box
Figure 19-1.

Once the initialization information has been obtained, the dialog box
creates a spin control, which is used to set the delay period, and an edit box,
which is used to set the message. The box also contains two buttons. If the
user selects Cancel, any changes made by the user are ignored. If the user
presses OK, the contents of the spin control and edit box are used to update
the registry.

Now, look at the code inside the **WM_CREATE** statement of
ScreenSaverProc( ). This code performs exactly the same registry sequence
as the dialog box. Of course, instead of being used to allow the user to view
and/or modify the configuration, **ScreenSaverProc( )** uses the registry
information to control the execution of the screen saver. One other point:
Since it is possible that the user will execute the screen saver without
ever having activated the configuration dialog box, the code inside
WM_CREATE must also be able to create the screen saver keys and set
the values. That is, you cannot simply assume that the key **Software\
HSPrograms\Screensaver** and the values **delay** and **message** are already
in the registry.

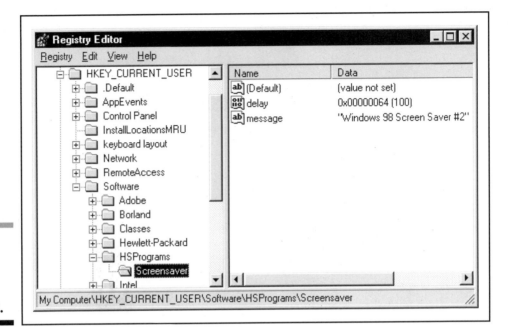

The registry
path created
by the
screen saver

Figure 19-2.

Some Things to Try

The first thing that you will probably want to try is having the screen saver
generate a more interesting graphics display. The purpose of this chapter was
to explain the system registry and the mechanics of screen savers. It was not
to create an exciting screen saver—this is left to you! One easy starting point
is to create a full-screen bitmap and use it as a backdrop. Of course, you must
alter the backdrop, too. Otherwise the screen saver won't actually "save" the
screen. If you have a scanner, then a simple yet effective way to create a
custom screen saver is to display a digitized photo.

Because the configurable screen saver is an example program, no entries
under **HKEY_LOCAL_MACHINE** relating to the program were made in the
registry. Normally, entries are made under this key by installation programs
when you install large applications. For fun, you might want to write your
own installation program that installs the screen saver and its icon, adding
an entry under **HKEY_LOCAL_MACHINE** in the process. To add an
application under **HKEY_LOCAL_MACHINE**, use a key path similar
to the one shown here:

HKEY_LOCAL_MACHINE\Software\YourName\AppName\Version

CHAPTER 20

Supercharging Menus

W̶e will now return to one of the most fundamental elements of a Windows program: the menu. Even though the topic of menus may seem rather tame, this is only a surface impression. The menuing subsystem supports a substantial number of sophisticated and advanced features. In this chapter we will explore two general categories of enhanced menus: dynamic and free-floating, pop-up menus. You will also see how to modify the options on the menu bar at run time. All of these give you extended control over the contents of your application's menus and the way such menus can be used. The skillful application of these features allows you to supercharge the menus associated with any application.

Dynamic Menus

A dynamic menu responds to changing conditions at run time.

Although most simple Windows 98 applications statically define their menus in resource files, more sophisticated applications frequently need to add or delete menu items dynamically, during run time, in response to changing program conditions. For example, a word processor may define different options in its File menu, depending upon the type of file being edited. A compiler may include one set of debugging options for C code and another for C++ programs. Menus that change in response to conditions that occur at run time are called *dynamic menus*. The advantage of dynamic menus is that they present the user with a list of options that are appropriate to the current state of the program.

Windows 98 includes several menu management API functions that allow you manipulate the contents of menus during the execution of your program. The ones used by this chapter are **InsertMenuItem( )**, **EnableMenuItem( )**, **DeleteMenu( )**, **GetMenu( )**, **GetSubMenu( )**, **CheckMenuItem( )**, and **CheckMenuRadioItem( )**.

Adding an Item to a Menu

To add an item to a menu at run time, use **InsertMenuItem( )**, shown here:

```
BOOL InsertMenuItem(HMENU hMenu, UINT Where,
                    BOOL How, LPMENUITEMINFO MenuInfo);
```

InsertMenuItem( ) adds an item to the menu whose handle is specified by *hMenu*. The new menu item is inserted into the menu immediately before the item specified by *Where*. The precise meaning of *Where* is determined by the value of *How*. If *How* is nonzero, then *Where* must contain the index at which point the new item is inserted. (Indexing begins at zero.) If *How* is zero, then

Where must contain the menu ID of an existing item at which point the new item is inserted. The menu item being added is defined by the **MENUITEMINFO** structure pointed to by *MenuInfo*. **MENUITEMINFO** is defined like this:

```
typedef struct tagMENUITEMINFO
{
  UINT cbSize;
  UINT fMask;
  UINT fType;
  UINT fState;
  UINT wID;
  HMENU hSubMenu;
  HBITMAP hbmpChecked;
  HBITMAP hbmpUnchecked;
  DWORD dwItemData;
  LPSTR dwTypeData;
  UINT cch;
} MENUITEMINFO;
```

20

Here, **cbSize** must contain the size of the **MENUITEMINFO** structure.

The value of **fMask** determines which of the other members of **MENUITEMINFO** contain valid information when setting menu information. That is, it determines which of the other members are active. (It is also used to specify which members will be loaded when menu information is retrieved.) It must be a combination of one or more of these values.

fMask Value	Activates
MIIM_CHECKMARKS	**hbmpChecked** and **hbmpUnchecked**
MIIM_DATA	**dwItemData**
MIIM_ID	**wID**
MIIM_STATE	**fstate**
MIIM_SUBMENU	**hSubMenu**
MIIM_TYPE	**fType** and **dwTypeData**

The type of the menu item is determined by **fType**. It can be any valid combination of the following values.

fType Value	Meaning
MFT_BITMAP	The low-order word of **dwTypeData** specifies a bitmap handle. The menu item is displayed as a bitmap.
MFT_MENUBARBREAK	For menu bar, causes the item to be put on a new line. For pop-up menus, causes the item to be put in a different column. In this case, the item is separated using a bar.
MFT_MENUBREAK	Same as **MFT_MENUBARBREAK** except that no separator bar is used.
MFT_OWNDERDRAW	Owner-drawn item.
MFT_RADIOCHECK	Radio button check mark style is used when the item is selected rather than the normal menu check mark. **hbmpChecked** must be NULL.
MFT_RIGHTJUSTIFY	For menu bars only. Right-justifies the item. Subsequent items are also right-justified.
MFT_RIGHTORDER	Menus descend right-to-left. Supports right-to-left reading languages.
MFT_SEPARATOR	Places a horizontal dividing line between menu items. The values in **dwTypeData** and **cch** are ignored. This type cannot be used for menu bar items.
MFT_STRING	**dwTypeData** is a pointer to a string that describes the menu item.

The state of the menu item is determined by **fState**. It can be any valid combination of the following values.

fState Value	Meaning
MFS_CHECKED	Item is checked.
MFS_DEFAULT	Item is the default selection.
MFS_DISABLED	Item is disabled.

fState Value	Meaning
MFS_ENABLED	Item is enabled. Items are enabled by default.
MFS_GRAYED	Item is disabled and grayed.
MFS_HILITE	Item is highlighted.
MFS_UNCHECKED	Item is unchecked.
MFS_UNHILITE	Item is unhighlighted. Items are unhighlighted by default.

The ID value associated with the menu item is specified in **wID**.

If the item being inserted is a pop-up submenu, its handle must be in **hSubMenu**. Otherwise, this value must be **NULL**.

You can specify bitmaps that will be used to indicate a menu item's checked and unchecked state in **hbmpChecked** and **hbmpUnchecked**. To use the default check mark, specify **NULL** for both of these members.

The value of **dwItemData** is application-dependent. If unused, set this value to zero.

The menu item itself is specified in **dwTypeData**. It will be either a pointer to a string or the handle of a bitmap, depending upon the value of **fType**.

When a menu item is being retrieved, **cch** will contain the length of the string if **fType** is **MFT_STRING**. The value of **cch** is ignored when the menu item is being set.

InsertMenuItem( ) returns nonzero if successful and zero on failure.

PORTABILITY: **InsertMenuItem( )** is not supported by Windows 3.1. Instead, menu items were dynamically inserted into a menu using **AppendMenu( )** or **InsertMenu( )**. While these functions are still supported by Windows 98, the use of **InsertMenuItem( )** is recommended.

Deleting a Menu Item

To remove a menu item, use the **DeleteMenu( )** function, shown here:

```
BOOL DeleteMenu(HMENU hMenu, UINT ItemID, UINT How);
```

20

Here, *hMenu* specifies the handle of the menu to be affected. The item to be removed is specified in *ItemID*. The value of *How* determines how *ItemID* is interpreted. If *How* is **MF_BYPOSITION**, then the value in *ItemID* must be the index of the item to be deleted. This index is the position of the item within the menu, with the first menu item being zero. If *How* is **MF_BYCOMMAND**, then *ItemID* is the ID associated with the menu item. **DeleteMenu( )** returns nonzero if successful and zero on failure.

If the menu item deleted is itself a pop-up submenu, then that pop-up menu is also destroyed. There is no need to call **DestroyMenu( )**. (**DestroyMenu( )** is described in Chapter 4.)

Obtaining a Handle to a Menu

As you have just seen, to add or delete a menu item requires a handle to the menu. To obtain the handle of the main menu, use **GetMenu( )**, shown here:

HMENU GetMenu(HWND *hwnd*);

GetMenu( ) obtains the handle of a window's main menu.

GetMenu( ) returns the handle of the menu associated with the window specified by *hwnd*. It returns **NULL** on failure.

Given a handle to a window's main menu, you can easily obtain the handles of the pop-up submenus contained in the main menu by using **GetSubMenu( )**. Its prototype is shown here:

GetSubMenu( ) obtains the handle of a pop-up submenu.

HMENU GetSubMenu(HMENU *hMenu*, int *ItemPos*);

Here, *hMenu* is the handle of the parent menu, and *ItemPos* is the position of the desired pop-up menu within the parent window. (The first position is zero.) The function returns the handle of the specified pop-up menu or **NULL** on failure.

Obtaining the Size of a Menu

Frequently, when working with menus dynamically, you will need to know how many items are in a menu. To obtain the number of menu items, use **GetMenuItemCount( )**, shown here:

int GetMenuItemCount(HMENU *hMenu*);

Here, *hMenu* is the handle of the menu in question. The function returns –1 on failure.

Enabling and Disabling a Menu Item

Sometimes a menu item will only apply to certain situations and not to others. In such cases, you may wish to temporarily disable an item, enabling it later. To accomplish this, use the **EnableMenuItem( )** function, shown here:

BOOL EnableMenuItem(HMENU *hMenu*, UINT *ItemID*, UINT *How*);

The handle of the menu is passed in *hMenu*. The item to be enabled or disabled is specified in *ItemID*. The value of *How* determines two things. First, it specifies how *ItemID* is interpreted. If *How* contains **MF_BYPOSITION**, then the value in *ItemID* must be the index of the item to be deleted. This index is the position of the item within the menu, with the first menu item being zero. If *How* contains **MF_BYCOMMAND**, then *ItemID* is the ID associated with the menu item. The value in *How* also determines whether the item will be enabled or disabled, based upon which of the following values are present.

MF_DISABLED	Disables the new menu item.
MF_ENABLED	Enables the new menu item.
MF_GRAYED	Disables the menu item and turns it gray.

To construct the desired value of *How*, OR together the appropriate values.

EnableMenuItem( ) returns the previous state of the item or –1 on failure.

GetMenuItemInfo( ) and SetMenuItemInfo( )

Sometimes you will want to obtain detailed information about or make detailed adjustments to a menu. The easiest way to do this is to use the menu management functions, **GetMenuItemInfo( )** and **SetMenuItemInfo( )**, whose prototypes are shown here:

BOOL GetMenuItemInfo(HMENU *hMenu*, UINT ItemID,
                   BOOL *How*, LPMENUITEMINFO *MenuInfo*);

BOOL SetMenuItemInfo(HMENU *hMenu*, UINT *ItemID*,
                   BOOL *How*, LPMENUITEMINFO *MenuInfo*);

These functions get and set all of the information associated with a menu item. The menu containing the item is specified by *hMenu*. The menu item is specified by *ItemID*. The precise meaning of *ItemID* is determined by the value of *How*. If *How* is nonzero, *ItemID* must contain the index of the item. If *How* is zero, *ItemID* must contain the menu ID of the item. For **GetMenuItemInfo( )**, the **MENUITEMINFO** structure pointed to by *MenuInfo* will receive the current information about the item. For **SetMenuItemInfo( )**, the contents of the structure pointed to by *MenuInfo* will be used to set the menu item's information.

Both functions return nonzero if successful and zero on failure.

As you can guess, you could use **SetMenuItemInfo( )** to perform relatively simple menu management functions, such as enabling or disabling a menu item. However, using **SetMenuItemInfo( )** and **GetMenuItemInfo( )** for these types of operations is inefficient. They should be reserved for more complex or subtle menu manipulations.

Dynamically Adding Menu Items

Now that the basic menu management functions have been discussed, it's time to see them in action. Let's begin with dynamically inserting and deleting an item. To do this, we will use a simple program that draws various GDI objects in the main window. The program contains two menus. The first is called Options; the second is Draw. The Options menu lets the user select various options relating to the program. The Draw menu lets the user select which object will be drawn. The following program demonstrates dynamic menu management by adding an item to or deleting an item from its Options menu. Pay special attention to the **IDM_ADDITEM** and **IDM_DELITEM** cases inside **WindowFunc( )**. This is the code that adds or deletes a menu item. Sample output is shown in Figure 20-1.

```
/* Dynamically managing menus. */

#include <windows.h>
#include "menu.h"

LRESULT CALLBACK WindowFunc(HWND, UINT, WPARAM, LPARAM);

char szWinName[] = "MyWin"; /* name of window class */

int WINAPI WinMain(HINSTANCE hThisInst, HINSTANCE hPrevInst,
                   LPSTR lpszArgs, int nWinMode)
{
  HWND hwnd;
  MSG msg;
```

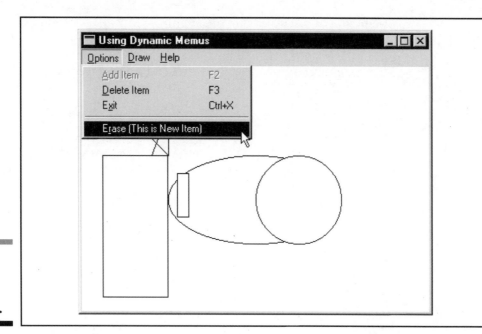

Adding
menu items
dynamically
Figure 20-1.

```
WNDCLASSEX wcl;
HACCEL hAccel;

/* Define a window class. */
wcl.cbSize = sizeof(WNDCLASSEX);

wcl.hInstance = hThisInst; /* handle to this instance */
wcl.lpszClassName = szWinName; /* window class name */
wcl.lpfnWndProc = WindowFunc; /* window function */
wcl.style = 0; /* default style */

wcl.hIcon = LoadIcon(NULL, IDI_APPLICATION); /* standard icon */
wcl.hIconSm = LoadIcon(NULL, IDI_APPLICATION); /* small icon */
wcl.hCursor = LoadCursor(NULL, IDC_ARROW);  /* cursor style */

wcl.lpszMenuName = "DynMenu"; /* main menu */
wcl.cbClsExtra = 0; /* no extra */
wcl.cbWndExtra = 0; /* information needed */

/* Make the window white. */
wcl.hbrBackground = (HBRUSH) GetStockObject(WHITE_BRUSH);
```

```
  /* Register the window class. */
  if(!RegisterClassEx(&wcl)) return 0;

  /* Now that a window class has been registered, a window
     can be created. */
  hwnd = CreateWindow(
    szWinName, /* name of window class */
    "Using Dynamic Memus", /* title */
    WS_OVERLAPPEDWINDOW, /* standard window */
    CW_USEDEFAULT, /* X coordinate - let Windows decide */
    CW_USEDEFAULT, /* Y coordinate - let Windows decide */
    CW_USEDEFAULT, /* width - let Windows decide */
    CW_USEDEFAULT, /* height - let Windows decide */
    HWND_DESKTOP, /* no parent window */
    NULL, /* no override of class menu */
    hThisInst, /* handle of this instance of the program */
    NULL /* no additional arguments */
  );

  /* Load the keyboard accelerators. */
  hAccel = LoadAccelerators(hThisInst, "DynMenu");

  /* Display the window. */
  ShowWindow(hwnd, nWinMode);
  UpdateWindow(hwnd);

  /* Create the message loop. */
  while(GetMessage(&msg, NULL, 0, 0))
  {
    if(!TranslateAccelerator(hwnd, hAccel, &msg)) {
      TranslateMessage(&msg); /* translate keyboard messages */
      DispatchMessage(&msg); /* return control to Windows 98 */
    }
  }
  return msg.wParam;
}

/* This function is called by Windows 98 and is passed
   messages from the message queue.
*/
LRESULT CALLBACK WindowFunc(HWND hwnd, UINT message,
                            WPARAM wParam, LPARAM lParam)
{
  HDC hdc;
```

20

```
RECT rect;
HMENU hmenu, hsubmenu;
int response;
int count;
MENUITEMINFO miInfo;

switch(message) {
  case WM_COMMAND:
    switch(LOWORD(wParam)) {
      case IDM_ADDITEM: /* dynamically add menu item */
        /* get handle of main menu */
        hmenu = GetMenu(hwnd);

        /* get handle of 1st popup menu */
        hsubmenu = GetSubMenu(hmenu, 0);

        /* get number of items in the popup */
        count = GetMenuItemCount(hsubmenu);

        /* append a separator */
        miInfo.cbSize = sizeof(MENUITEMINFO);
        miInfo.fMask = MIIM_TYPE;
        miInfo.fType = MFT_SEPARATOR;
        miInfo.fState = 0;
        miInfo.wID = 0;
        miInfo.hSubMenu = NULL;
        miInfo.hbmpChecked = NULL;
        miInfo.hbmpUnchecked = NULL;
        miInfo.dwItemData = 0;
        miInfo.dwTypeData = 0;
        InsertMenuItem(hsubmenu, count, 1, &miInfo);

        /* append new menu item */
        miInfo.fMask = MIIM_TYPE | MIIM_ID;
        miInfo.fType = MFT_STRING;
        miInfo.wID = IDM_NEW;
        miInfo.dwTypeData = "E&rase (This is New Item)";
        InsertMenuItem(hsubmenu, count+1, 1, &miInfo);

        /* deactivate the Add Item option */
        EnableMenuItem(hsubmenu, IDM_ADDITEM,
                    MF_BYCOMMAND | MF_GRAYED);

        /* activate the Delete Item option */
        EnableMenuItem(hsubmenu, IDM_DELITEM,
```

```
                        MF_BYCOMMAND | MF_ENABLED);
    break;
case IDM_DELITEM: /* dynamically delete menu item */
  /* get handle of main menu */
  hmenu = GetMenu(hwnd);

  /* get handle of 1st popup menu */
  hsubmenu = GetSubMenu(hmenu, 0);

  /* delete the new item and the separator */
  count = GetMenuItemCount(hsubmenu);
  DeleteMenu(hsubmenu, count-1, MF_BYPOSITION | MF_GRAYED);
  DeleteMenu(hsubmenu, count-2, MF_BYPOSITION | MF_GRAYED);

  /* reactivate the Add Item option */
  EnableMenuItem(hsubmenu, IDM_ADDITEM,
                 MF_BYCOMMAND | MF_ENABLED);

  /* deactivate the Delete Item option */
  EnableMenuItem(hsubmenu, IDM_DELITEM,
                 MF_BYCOMMAND | MF_GRAYED);
  break;
case IDM_EXIT:
  response = MessageBox(hwnd, "Quit the Program?",
                        "Exit", MB_YESNO);
  if(response == IDYES) PostQuitMessage(0);
  break;
case IDM_NEW: /* erase window */
  hdc = GetDC(hwnd);
  GetClientRect(hwnd, &rect);
  SelectObject(hdc, GetStockObject(WHITE_BRUSH));
  PatBlt(hdc, 0, 0, rect.right, rect.bottom, PATCOPY);
  ReleaseDC(hwnd, hdc);
  break;
case IDM_LINES:
  hdc = GetDC(hwnd);
  MoveToEx(hdc, 10, 10, NULL);
  LineTo(hdc, 100, 100);
  LineTo(hdc, 100, 50);
  LineTo(hdc, 50, 180);
  ReleaseDC(hwnd, hdc);
  break;
case IDM_ELLIPSES:
  hdc = GetDC(hwnd);
  Ellipse(hdc, 100, 100, 300, 200);
```

```
          Ellipse(hdc, 200, 100, 300, 200);
          ReleaseDC(hwnd, hdc);
          break;
        case IDM_RECTANGLES:
          hdc = GetDC(hwnd);
          Rectangle(hdc, 100, 100, 24, 260);
          Rectangle(hdc, 110, 120, 124, 170);
          ReleaseDC(hwnd, hdc);
          break;
        case IDM_HELP:
          MessageBox(hwnd, "Try Adding a Menu Item",
                     "Help", MB_OK);
          break;
      }
      break;
    case WM_DESTROY: /* terminate the program */
      PostQuitMessage(0);
      break;
    default:
      /* Let Windows 98 process any messages not specified in
         the preceding switch statement. */
      return DefWindowProc(hwnd, message, wParam, lParam);
  }
  return 0;
}
```

20

The resource file required by the program is shown here.

```
// Dynamic Menus
#include <windows.h>
#include "menu.h"

DynMenu MENU
{
  POPUP "&Options"
  {
    MENUITEM "&Add Item\tF2", IDM_ADDITEM
    MENUITEM "&Delete Item\tF3", IDM_DELITEM, GRAYED
    MENUITEM "E&xit\tCtrl+X", IDM_EXIT
  }
  POPUP "&Draw"
  {
    MENUITEM "&Lines\tF4", IDM_LINES
    MENUITEM "&Ellipses\tF5", IDM_ELLIPSES
```

```
      MENUITEM "&Rectangles\tF6", IDM_RECTANGLES
  }
  MENUITEM "&Help", IDM_HELP
}


// Define menu accelerators
DynMenu ACCELERATORS
{
  VK_F2, IDM_ADDITEM, VIRTKEY
  VK_F3, IDM_DELITEM, VIRTKEY
  "^X", IDM_EXIT
  VK_F4, IDM_LINES, VIRTKEY
  VK_F5, IDM_ELLIPSES, VIRTKEY
  VK_F6, IDM_RECTANGLES, VIRTKEY
  VK_F1, IDM_HELP, VIRTKEY
}
```

The MENU.H header file is shown here. It also includes a few values that are used by later programs in this chapter.

```
#define IDM_EXIT         100
#define IDM_LINES        101
#define IDM_ELLIPSES     102
#define IDM_RECTANGLES   103
#define IDM_HELP         104

#define IDM_ADDITEM      200
#define IDM_DELITEM      201

#define IDM_NEW          300
#define IDM_NEW2         301
#define IDM_NEW3         302
```

A Closer Look at the First Dynamic Menu Program

Most of this program is straightforward and easy to understand. When the program first begins, the Options menu initially contains only three selections: Add Item, Delete Item, and Exit. Initially, Delete Item is grayed and therefore may not be selected. To add the Erase option, select Add Item. After the Erase item has been dynamically added to the menu, the Delete Item option is activated and the Add Item option is grayed. When Delete Item is selected, Erase is removed from the menu, Add Item is reactivated, and Delete Item is once again grayed. This procedure prevents the new menu item from being added or deleted more than once.

Look closely at the code under **IDM_ADDITEM**. Notice how the handle to the Options pop-up menu is obtained. First, you must retrieve the handle of its outer menu, which in this case is the program's main menu, using **GetMenu( )**. Next, you must use **GetSubMenu( )** to obtain the handle of its first pop-up menu, which is Options. Next, the program must obtain a count of the number of items in the menu. This step is technically unnecessary since, in this simple example, we already know this value. This step is included for the sake of illustration because, in a real-world program, you may not always know how many items a menu contains. Next, the program adds a separator and then the Erase menu item itself.

Creating Dynamic Pop-up Menus

20

To create a pop-up menu, use CreatePopup-Menu( ).

In addition to creating new menu items, you can dynamically create an entire pop-up menu. (That is, you can create a pop-up menu at run time.) Once you have created the menu, it can then be added to an existing menu. To dynamically create a pop-up menu, you first use the API function **CreatePopupMenu( )**, shown here:

    HMENU CreatePopupMenu(void);

This function creates an empty menu and returns a handle to it. After you have created a menu, you add items to it using **InsertMenuItem( )**. Once the menu is fully constructed, you can add it to an existing menu, also using **InsertMenuItem( )**.

Menus created using **CreatePopupMenu( )** must be destroyed. If the menu is attached to a window, it will be destroyed automatically. A menu is also automatically destroyed when it is removed from a parent menu by a call to **DeleteMenu( )**. Dynamic menus can also be destroyed explicitly by calling **DestroyMenu( )**.

The following program is an enhanced version of the preceding program. It dynamically creates a pop-up menu that contains three items: Erase, Black Pen, and Red Pen. Selecting Erase erases the window. Choosing Black Pen selects the black pen (which is the default pen). Choosing Red Pen selects the red pen. After a pen has been selected, it is used to draw the shapes available in the Draw menu. Pay close attention to the way that the pop-up menu is constructed and attached to the Options menu.

```
/* Adding a popup menu. */

#include <windows.h>
#include "menu.h"

LRESULT CALLBACK WindowFunc(HWND, UINT, WPARAM, LPARAM);

char szWinName[] = "MyWin"; /* name of window class */

int WINAPI WinMain(HINSTANCE hThisInst, HINSTANCE hPrevInst,
                   LPSTR lpszArgs, int nWinMode)
{
  HWND hwnd;
  MSG msg;
  WNDCLASSEX wcl;
  HACCEL hAccel;

  /* Define a window class. */
  wcl.cbSize = sizeof(WNDCLASSEX);

  wcl.hInstance = hThisInst; /* handle to this instance */
  wcl.lpszClassName = szWinName; /* window class name */
  wcl.lpfnWndProc = WindowFunc; /* window function */
  wcl.style = 0; /* default style */

  wcl.hIcon = LoadIcon(NULL, IDI_APPLICATION); /* standard icon */
  wcl.hIconSm = LoadIcon(NULL, IDI_APPLICATION); /* small icon */
  wcl.hCursor = LoadCursor(NULL, IDC_ARROW); /* cursor style */

  wcl.lpszMenuName = "DynPopUpMenu"; /* main menu */
  wcl.cbClsExtra = 0; /* no extra */
  wcl.cbWndExtra = 0; /* information needed */

  /* Make the window white. */
  wcl.hbrBackground = (HBRUSH) GetStockObject(WHITE_BRUSH);

  /* Register the window class. */
  if(!RegisterClassEx(&wcl)) return 0;

  /* Now that a window class has been registered, a window
     can be created. */
  hwnd = CreateWindow(
    szWinName, /* name of window class */
    "Adding a Popup Menu", /* title */
    WS_OVERLAPPEDWINDOW, /* standard window */
```

```
        CW_USEDEFAULT, /* X coordinate - let Windows decide */
        CW_USEDEFAULT, /* Y coordinate - let Windows decide */
        CW_USEDEFAULT, /* width - let Windows decide */
        CW_USEDEFAULT, /* height - let Windows decide */
        HWND_DESKTOP, /* no parent window */
        NULL, /* no override of class menu */
        hThisInst, /* handle of this instance of the program */
        NULL /* no additional arguments */
      );

      /* Load the keyboard accelerators. */
      hAccel = LoadAccelerators(hThisInst, "DynPopUpMenu");

      /* Display the window. */
      ShowWindow(hwnd, nWinMode);
      UpdateWindow(hwnd);

      /* Create the message loop. */
      while(GetMessage(&msg, NULL, 0, 0))
      {
        if(!TranslateAccelerator(hwnd, hAccel, &msg)) {
          TranslateMessage(&msg); /* translate keyboard messages */
          DispatchMessage(&msg); /* return control to Windows 98 */
        }
      }
      return msg.wParam;
}

/* This function is called by Windows 98 and is passed
   messages from the message queue.
*/
LRESULT CALLBACK WindowFunc(HWND hwnd, UINT message,
                            WPARAM wParam, LPARAM lParam)
{
  HDC hdc;
  HMENU hmenu, hsubmenu;
  RECT rect;
  static HMENU hpopup;
  int response;
  int count;
  MENUITEMINFO miInfo;
  static HPEN hCurrentPen, hRedPen;

  switch(message) {
    case WM_CREATE:
```

```
      /* create red pen */
      hRedPen = CreatePen(PS_SOLID, 1, RGB(255, 0, 0));
      /* get black pen */
      hCurrentPen = (HPEN) GetStockObject(BLACK_PEN);
      break;
case WM_COMMAND:
    switch(LOWORD(wParam)) {
      case IDM_ADDITEM: /* dynamically add popup menu */
        /* get handle of main menu */
        hmenu = GetMenu(hwnd);

        /* get handle of 1st popup menu */
        hsubmenu = GetSubMenu(hmenu, 0);

        /* get number of items in the menu */
        count = GetMenuItemCount(hsubmenu);

        /* create new popup menu */
        hpopup = CreatePopupMenu();

        /* add items to dynamic popup menu */
        miInfo.cbSize = sizeof(MENUITEMINFO);
        miInfo.fMask = MIIM_TYPE | MIIM_ID;
        miInfo.fType = MFT_STRING;
        miInfo.wID = IDM_NEW;
        miInfo.hSubMenu = NULL;
        miInfo.hbmpChecked = NULL;
        miInfo.hbmpUnchecked = NULL;
        miInfo.dwItemData = 0;
        miInfo.dwTypeData = "&Erase";
        InsertMenuItem(hpopup, 0, 1, &miInfo);

        miInfo.dwTypeData = "&Black Pen";
        miInfo.wID = IDM_NEW2;
        InsertMenuItem(hpopup, 1, 1, &miInfo);

        miInfo.dwTypeData = "&Red Pen";
        miInfo.wID = IDM_NEW3;
        InsertMenuItem(hpopup, 2, 1, &miInfo);

        /* append a separator */
        miInfo.cbSize = sizeof(MENUITEMINFO);
        miInfo.fMask = MIIM_TYPE;
        miInfo.fType = MFT_SEPARATOR;
        miInfo.fState = 0;
```

20

```
miInfo.wID = 0;
miInfo.hSubMenu = NULL;
miInfo.hbmpChecked = NULL;
miInfo.hbmpUnchecked = NULL;
miInfo.dwItemData = 0;
InsertMenuItem(hsubmenu, count, 1, &miInfo);

/* append popup menu to main menu */
miInfo.fMask = MIIM_TYPE | MIIM_SUBMENU;
miInfo.fType = MFT_STRING;
miInfo.hSubMenu = hpopup;
miInfo.dwTypeData = "&This is New Popup";
InsertMenuItem(hsubmenu, count+1, 1, &miInfo);

/* deactivate the Add Popup option */
EnableMenuItem(hsubmenu, IDM_ADDITEM,
               MF_BYCOMMAND | MF_GRAYED);

/* activate the Delete Popup option */
EnableMenuItem(hsubmenu, IDM_DELITEM,
               MF_BYCOMMAND | MF_ENABLED);
break;
case IDM_DELITEM: /* dynamically delete popup menu */
  /* get handle of main menu */
  hmenu = GetMenu(hwnd);

  /* get handle of 1st popup menu */
  hsubmenu = GetSubMenu(hmenu, 0);

  /* delete the new popup menu and the separator */
  count = GetMenuItemCount(hsubmenu);
  DeleteMenu(hsubmenu, count-1, MF_BYPOSITION | MF_GRAYED);
  DeleteMenu(hsubmenu, count-2, MF_BYPOSITION | MF_GRAYED);

  /* reactivate the Add Popup option */
  EnableMenuItem(hsubmenu, IDM_ADDITEM,
                 MF_BYCOMMAND | MF_ENABLED);

  /* deactivate the Delete Popup option */
  EnableMenuItem(hsubmenu, IDM_DELITEM,
                 MF_BYCOMMAND | MF_GRAYED);
  break;
case IDM_EXIT:
  response = MessageBox(hwnd, "Quit the Program?",
                        "Exit", MB_YESNO);
```

```
        if(response == IDYES) PostQuitMessage(0);
        break;
      case IDM_NEW: /* erase */
        hdc = GetDC(hwnd);
        GetClientRect(hwnd, &rect);
        SelectObject(hdc, GetStockObject(WHITE_BRUSH));
        PatBlt(hdc, 0, 0, rect.right, rect.bottom, PATCOPY);
        ReleaseDC(hwnd, hdc);
        break;
      case IDM_NEW2: /* select black pen */
        hCurrentPen = (HPEN) GetStockObject(BLACK_PEN);
        break;
      case IDM_NEW3: /* select red pen */
        hCurrentPen = hRedPen;
        break;
      case IDM_LINES:
        hdc = GetDC(hwnd);
        SelectObject(hdc, hCurrentPen);
        MoveToEx(hdc, 10, 10, NULL);
        LineTo(hdc, 100, 100);
        LineTo(hdc, 100, 50);
        LineTo(hdc, 50, 180);
        ReleaseDC(hwnd, hdc);
        break;
      case IDM_ELLIPSES:
        hdc = GetDC(hwnd);
        SelectObject(hdc, hCurrentPen);
        Ellipse(hdc, 100, 100, 300, 200);
        Ellipse(hdc, 200, 100, 300, 200);
        ReleaseDC(hwnd, hdc);
        break;
      case IDM_RECTANGLES:
        hdc = GetDC(hwnd);
        SelectObject(hdc, hCurrentPen);
        Rectangle(hdc, 100, 100, 24, 260);
        Rectangle(hdc, 110, 120, 124, 170);
        ReleaseDC(hwnd, hdc);
        break;
      case IDM_HELP:
        MessageBox(hwnd, "Try Adding a Menu", "Help", MB_OK);
        break;
    }
    break;
  case WM_DESTROY: /* terminate the program */
    DeleteObject(hRedPen);
```

```
          PostQuitMessage(0);
          break;
       default:
          /* Let Windows 98 process any messages not specified in
             the preceding switch statement. */
          return DefWindowProc(hwnd, message, wParam, lParam);
     }
   return 0;
}
```

The header file MENU.H is the same as was used before. However, this program uses the following resource file.

```
// Dynamic Popup Menus
#include <windows.h>
#include "menu.h"

DynPopUpMenu MENU
{
  POPUP "&Options"
  {
    MENUITEM "&Add Popup\tF2", IDM_ADDITEM
    MENUITEM "&Delete Popup\tF3", IDM_DELITEM, GRAYED
    MENUITEM "E&xit\tCtrl+X", IDM_EXIT
  }
  POPUP "&Draw"
  {
    MENUITEM "&Lines\tF4", IDM_LINES
    MENUITEM "&Ellipses\tF5", IDM_ELLIPSES
    MENUITEM "&Rectangles\tF6", IDM_RECTANGLES
  }
  MENUITEM "&Help", IDM_HELP
}

// Define menu accelerators
DynPopUpMenu ACCELERATORS
{
  VK_F2, IDM_ADDITEM, VIRTKEY
  VK_F3, IDM_DELITEM, VIRTKEY
  "^X", IDM_EXIT
  VK_F4, IDM_LINES, VIRTKEY
  VK_F5, IDM_ELLIPSES, VIRTKEY
  VK_F6, IDM_RECTANGLES, VIRTKEY
  VK_F1, IDM_HELP, VIRTKEY
}
```

20

Sample output from this program is shown in Figure 20-2.

Most of the program is straightforward. However, notice one important point. The **MIIM_SUBMENU** flag must be set and the handle of the pop-up menu must be in **hSubMenu** when a pop-up menu is inserted into a menu.

Checking Menu Items

It is possible to display a check mark next to a menu item. This is useful when a menu item represents an option that can be set. As you saw in the description of **MENUITEMINFO**, it is possible to check a menu item when it is first created. It is also possible to check a menu item later. There are two ways to do this. First, you can use the **SetMenuItemInfo( )** function described earlier. However, an easier way is to use the **CheckMenuItem( )** function, shown here:

DWORD CheckMenuItem(HMENU *hMenu*, UINT *ItemID*, UINT *How*);

Here, *hMenu* is the handle to the menu. The item to be checked or cleared is specified in *ItemID*. The value of *How* determines two things. First, it specifies how *ItemID* is interpreted. If *How* contains **MF_BYPOSITION**, then the

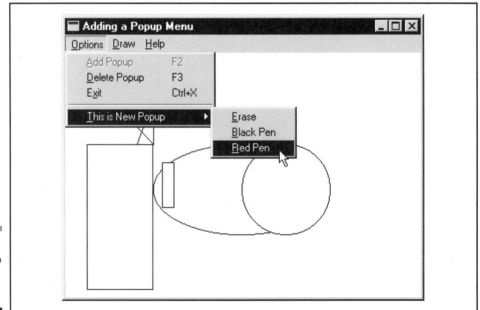

A dynamically created pop-up menu

Figure 20-2.

value in *ItemID* must be the index of the item. This index is the position of the item within the menu, with the first menu item being zero. If *How* contains **MF_BYCOMMAND**, then *ItemID* is the ID associated with the menu item. The value in *How* also determines whether the item will be checked or cleared, based upon which of the following values are present.

MF_CHECKED	Checks the menu item.
MF_UNCHECKED	Clears the menu item.

To construct the desired value of *How*, OR together the appropriate values. The previous check-state of the item is returned.

To see the effect of checking menu items, substitute the following **case** statements into the preceding program. Each time you select an item from the Draw menu, the item is checked. The item is cleared if you erase the window. The sample output in Figure 20-3 shows how the Draw menu looks after the Rectangles and Lines items have been selected.

20

```
case IDM_NEW: /* erase */
  /* get handle to 2nd popup menu */
  hmenu = GetMenu(hwnd);
  hsubmenu = GetSubMenu(hmenu, 1);
  /* uncheck drawing options */
  CheckMenuItem(hsubmenu, IDM_LINES,
              MF_BYCOMMAND | MF_UNCHECKED);
  CheckMenuItem(hsubmenu, IDM_ELLIPSES,
              MF_BYCOMMAND | MF_UNCHECKED);
  CheckMenuItem(hsubmenu, IDM_RECTANGLES,
              MF_BYCOMMAND | MF_UNCHECKED);

  hdc = GetDC(hwnd);
  GetClientRect(hwnd, &rect);
  SelectObject(hdc, GetStockObject(WHITE_BRUSH));
  PatBlt(hdc, 0, 0, rect.right, rect.bottom, PATCOPY);
  ReleaseDC(hwnd, hdc);
  break;
case IDM_LINES:
  /* get handle to 2nd popup menu */
  hmenu = GetMenu(hwnd);
  hsubmenu = GetSubMenu(hmenu, 1);
  CheckMenuItem(hsubmenu, IDM_LINES,
              MF_BYCOMMAND | MF_CHECKED);
```

```
    hdc = GetDC(hwnd);
    SelectObject(hdc, hCurrentPen);
    MoveToEx(hdc, 10, 10, NULL);
    LineTo(hdc, 100, 100);
    LineTo(hdc, 100, 50);
    LineTo(hdc, 50, 180);
    ReleaseDC(hwnd, hdc);
    break;
  case IDM_ELLIPSES:
    /* get handle to 2nd popup menu */
    hmenu = GetMenu(hwnd);
    hsubmenu = GetSubMenu(hmenu, 1);
    CheckMenuItem(hsubmenu, IDM_ELLIPSES,
                    MF_BYCOMMAND | MF_CHECKED);

    hdc = GetDC(hwnd);
    SelectObject(hdc, hCurrentPen);
    Ellipse(hdc, 100, 100, 300, 200);
    Ellipse(hdc, 200, 100, 300, 200);
    ReleaseDC(hwnd, hdc);
    break;
  case IDM_RECTANGLES:
    /* get handle to 2nd popup menu */
    hmenu = GetMenu(hwnd);
    hsubmenu = GetSubMenu(hmenu, 1);
    CheckMenuItem(hsubmenu, IDM_RECTANGLES,
                    MF_BYCOMMAND | MF_CHECKED);

    hdc = GetDC(hwnd);
    SelectObject(hdc, hCurrentPen);
    Rectangle(hdc, 100, 100, 24, 260);
    Rectangle(hdc, 110, 120, 124, 170);
    ReleaseDC(hwnd, hdc);
    break;
```

Using Radio Menu Items

Radio menu
items are
mutually
exclusive menu
options.

Although menu check marks like those shown in the preceding section are quite useful, they are not the best option when you are dealing with a set of mutually exclusive menu items. For example, in the sample program you can select either the red pen or the black pen—but not both. While it would be possible to indicate the current selection using normal menu check marks, doing so would require the program to manually check one option and uncheck the other. Fortunately, it is possible to let Windows 98 handle these

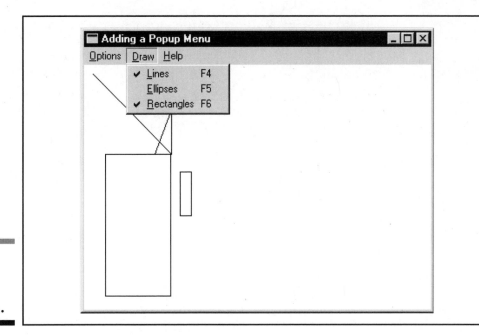

Using check
marks with
menu items
Figure 20-3.

details by using *radio menu items*. Radio menu items represent a set of
mutually exclusive menu options and are similar to radio buttons. When
your program checks one radio menu item, the previously checked item in its
group is automatically unchecked. Radio menu items are surprisingly easy to
use. The only restriction is that all radio items must be consecutive within
a menu.

You can treat any consecutive group of menu items as radio items by calling
CheckMenuRadioItem( ), shown here:

BOOL CheckMenuRadioItem(HMENU *hMenu*, UINT *StartID*,
                    UINT *EndID*, UINT *ItemID*, UINT *How*);

Here, *hMenu* is the handle to the menu. The first radio item in the group is
specified by *StartID*. The last of the group is passed in *EndID*. The item to be
checked is specified in *ItemID*. Any previously selected item is unchecked. If
How contains **MF_BYPOSITION**, the values in *StartID*, *EndID*, and *ItemID*
must be the indexes of the items. If *How* contains **MF_BYCOMMAND**, these
values represent the IDs associated with the menu items. In either case, the
items or command IDs must be consecutive. The function returns nonzero if
successful and zero on failure.

When you call **CheckMenuRadioItem( )**, it automatically sets the
MFT_RADIOCHECK flag associated with the item being set. It also clears
any check marks associated with any other items within the specified range.
Thus, within the range, only the specified item will be checked.

To see radio menu items in action, substitute the following cases into the
preceding program. They cause the Red Pen and Black Pen options to be
treated as radio menu items. The effect of this change is shown in
Figure 20-4.

```
case IDM_ADDITEM: /* dynamically add popup menu */
  /* get handle of main menu */
  hmenu = GetMenu(hwnd);

  /* get handle of 1st popup menu */
  hsubmenu = GetSubMenu(hmenu, 0);

  /* get number of items in the menu */
  count = GetMenuItemCount(hsubmenu);

  /* create new popup menu */
  hpopup = CreatePopupMenu();

  /* add items to dynamic popup menu */
  miInfo.cbSize = sizeof(MENUITEMINFO);
  miInfo.fMask = MIIM_TYPE | MIIM_ID;
  miInfo.fType = MFT_STRING;
  miInfo.wID = IDM_NEW;
  miInfo.hSubMenu = NULL;
  miInfo.hbmpChecked = NULL;
  miInfo.hbmpUnchecked = NULL;
  miInfo.dwItemData = 0;
  miInfo.dwTypeData = "&Erase";
  InsertMenuItem(hpopup, 0, 1, &miInfo);

  /* add a separator in popup menu */
  miInfo.cbSize = sizeof(MENUITEMINFO);
  miInfo.fMask = MIIM_TYPE;
  miInfo.fType = MFT_SEPARATOR;
  InsertMenuItem(hpopup, 1, 1, &miInfo);

  miInfo.dwTypeData = "&Black Pen";
  miInfo.fMask = MIIM_TYPE | MIIM_ID;
  miInfo.fType = MFT_STRING;
```

```
      miInfo.wID = IDM_NEW2;
      InsertMenuItem(hpopup, 2, 1, &miInfo);

      miInfo.dwTypeData = "&Red Pen";
      miInfo.wID = IDM_NEW3;
      InsertMenuItem(hpopup, 3, 1, &miInfo);

      /* append a separator */
      miInfo.cbSize = sizeof(MENUITEMINFO);
      miInfo.fMask = MIIM_TYPE;
      miInfo.fType = MFT_SEPARATOR;
      miInfo.fState = 0;
      miInfo.wID = 0;
      miInfo.hSubMenu = NULL;
      miInfo.hbmpChecked = NULL;
      miInfo.hbmpUnchecked = NULL;
      miInfo.dwItemData = 0;
      InsertMenuItem(hsubmenu, count, 1, &miInfo);

      /* append popup menu to main menu */
      miInfo.fMask = MIIM_TYPE | MIIM_SUBMENU;
      miInfo.fType = MFT_STRING;
      miInfo.hSubMenu = hpopup;
      miInfo.dwTypeData = "&This is New Popup";
      InsertMenuItem(hsubmenu, count+1, 1, &miInfo);

      /* deactivate the Add Popup option */
      EnableMenuItem(hsubmenu, IDM_ADDITEM,
                     MF_BYCOMMAND | MF_GRAYED);

      /* activate the Delete Popup option */
      EnableMenuItem(hsubmenu, IDM_DELITEM,
                     MF_BYCOMMAND | MF_ENABLED);

      /* radio check the current pen */
      if(hCurrentPen == hRedPen)
        CheckMenuRadioItem(hsubmenu, IDM_NEW2, IDM_NEW3,
                           IDM_NEW3, MF_BYCOMMAND);
      else
        CheckMenuRadioItem(hsubmenu, IDM_NEW2, IDM_NEW3,
                           IDM_NEW2, MF_BYCOMMAND);
      break;
    case IDM_NEW2: /* select black pen */
      /* get handle of popup menu */
      hmenu = GetMenu(hwnd);
```

```
      hsubmenu = GetSubMenu(hmenu, 0);

      /* radio check the black pen */
      CheckMenuRadioItem(hsubmenu, IDM_NEW2, IDM_NEW3,
                         IDM_NEW2, MF_BYCOMMAND);

      hCurrentPen = (HPEN) GetStockObject(BLACK_PEN);
      break;
  case IDM_NEW3: /* select red pen */
    /* get handle of popup menu */
    hmenu = GetMenu(hwnd);
    hsubmenu = GetSubMenu(hmenu, 0);

    /* radio check the red pen */
    CheckMenuRadioItem(hsubmenu, IDM_NEW2, IDM_NEW3,
                       IDM_NEW3, MF_BYCOMMAND);

    hCurrentPen = hRedPen;
    break;
```

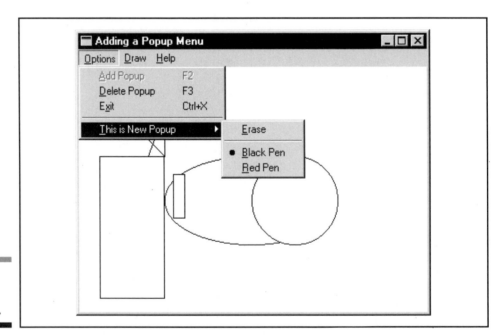

Using radio
menu items
Figure 20-4.

When you try these changes, notice that initially the Black Pen item is checked with the radio-style check mark. When you change to the red pen, the Red Pen item will be checked and the mark from Black Pen will be automatically removed. Observe that the radio menu items are set off in their own group by the addition of a separator. This is good practice when using radio menu items.

Using radio menu items is an excellent way to represent mutually exclusive options. Not only does it give immediate, visual feedback to the user that one and only one of these items may be selected, but it also simplifies your code because Windows 98 automatically handles the unchecking process for you.

Using Floating Menus

Floating menus are not attached to the menu bar.

Although stand-alone, or *floating,* pop-up menus have been available to Windows programmers for quite some time, they continue to increase in popularity and importance. One reason for this is that all current versions of Windows display a floating menu when you click the right mouse button on the desktop. Also, most professionally written applications now utilize floating menus. Frankly, it is hard to imagine creating a modern Windows 98 application that does not support floating menus.

Floating menus are also called *context menus* and *shortcut menus*. This book will use the term *floating menu* because it is the most descriptive.

20

Activating a Floating Menu

A floating menu is activated using **TrackPopupMenuEx( )**. Its prototype is shown here:

```
BOOL TrackPopupMenuEx(HMENU hMenu, UINT Flags, int X, int Y,
                      HWND hwnd, LPTPMPARMS OffLimits);
```

Here, *hMenu* is the handle of the menu that will be activated.

Various options are specified in *Flags*. This parameter may be any valid (i.e., non-mutually exclusive) combination of the values shown in Table 20-1. You may specify zero for *Flags*. Doing so causes the default configuration to be used.

Flags Value	Meaning
TPM_BOTTOMALIGN	Floating menu pops up with bottom edge at *Y*.
TPM_CENTERALIGN	Floating menu pops up centered left-to-right relative to *X*.
TPM_HORIZONAL	If the menu cannot be fully displayed at the location specified by *X* and *Y*, the horizontal alignment of the menu is given priority.
TPM_LEFTALIGN	Floating menu pops up with left side at *X*. (This is the default.)
TPM_LEFTBUTTON	Left mouse button operates the menu. (This is the default.)
TPM_NONOTIFY	Menu does not send notification messages.
TPM_RETURNCMD	The ID of the item selected is returned.
TPM_RIGHTALIGN	Floating menu pops up with right side at *X*.
TPM_RIGHTBUTTON	Right mouse button operates the menu.
TPM_TOPALGIN	Floating menu pops up with top edge at *Y*. (This is the default.)
TPM_VCENTERALIGN	Floating menu pops up centered top-to-bottom relative to *Y*.
TPM_VERTICAL	If the menu cannot be fully displayed at the location specified by *X* and *Y*, the vertical alignment of the menu is given priority.

The values
for the *Flags*
parameter of
**TrackPopup-
MenuEx( )**
Table 20-1.

The location *on the screen* at which to display the menu is specified in *X* and *Y*. Therefore, these coordinates are in terms of screen units, not window or dialog units. To convert between screen and window units, use either the **ClientToScreen( )** or the **ScreenToClient( )** function. (See the In Depth box.) In its default configuration, **TrackPopupMenuEx( )** displays the menu with its upper-left corner at the location specified by *X* and *Y*. However, you can use the *Flags* parameter to alter this placement.

The handle of the window that invokes **TrackPopupMenuEx( )** must be passed in *hwnd*.

You may specify a portion of the screen that is off-limits to the floating menu. To do so, specify the extent of that region in the **TPMPARAMS** structure pointed to by *OffLimits*. **TPMPARAMS** is defined like this:

```
typedef struct tagTPMPARAMS
{
  UINT cbSize;
  RECT rcExclude;
} TPMPARAMS;
```

Here, **cbSize** must contain the size of the **TPMPARAMS** structure. **rcExclude** must contain the coordinates of the excluded region. The coordinates specified in **rcExclude** must be in terms of screen units. *OffLimits* may be **NULL** if no part of the screen is being excluded.

TrackPopupMenuEx( ) returns nonzero if successful and zero on failure. However, if **TPM_RETURNCMD** is specified in *Flags*, then the ID of the menu item selected is returned. Zero is returned if no item is chosen.

 PORTABILITY: In Windows 3.1, floating menus were activated using **TrackPopupMenu( )**. This function is still supported by Windows 98. However, the new function **TrackPopupMenuEx( )** is recommended because it gives you more control.

Demonstrating Floating Menus

The following program modifies the previous program by making the Draw menu into a floating, pop-up menu. Thus, it is no longer part of the menu bar. Instead, it is activated by pressing the right mouse button. When this occurs, the floating menu is displayed at the location of the mouse pointer when the button was pressed. Sample output is shown in Figure 20-5.

```
/* Floating Menus */

#include <windows.h>
```

20

```
#include <string.h>
#include <stdio.h>
#include "menu.h"

LRESULT CALLBACK WindowFunc(HWND, UINT, WPARAM, LPARAM);

char szWinName[] = "MyWin"; /* name of window class */

HINSTANCE hInst;

int WINAPI WinMain(HINSTANCE hThisInst, HINSTANCE hPrevInst,
                   LPSTR lpszArgs, int nWinMode)
{
  HWND hwnd;
  MSG msg;
  WNDCLASSEX wcl;
  HACCEL hAccel;

  /* Define a window class. */
  wcl.cbSize = sizeof(WNDCLASSEX);

  wcl.hInstance = hThisInst; /* handle to this instance */
  wcl.lpszClassName = szWinName; /* window class name */
  wcl.lpfnWndProc = WindowFunc; /* window function */
  wcl.style = 0; /* default style */

  wcl.hIcon = LoadIcon(NULL, IDI_APPLICATION); /* standard icon */
  wcl.hIconSm = LoadIcon(NULL, IDI_APPLICATION); /* small icon */
  wcl.hCursor = LoadCursor(NULL, IDC_ARROW);  /* cursor style*/

  wcl.lpszMenuName = "FloatMenu"; /* main menu */
  wcl.cbClsExtra = 0; /* no extra */
  wcl.cbWndExtra = 0; /* information needed */

  /* Make the window white. */
  wcl.hbrBackground = (HBRUSH) GetStockObject(WHITE_BRUSH);

  /* Register the window class. */
  if(!RegisterClassEx(&wcl)) return 0;

  /* Now that a window class has been registered, a window
     can be created. */
  hwnd = CreateWindow(
    szWinName, /* name of window class */
    "Using a Floating Popup Menu", /* title */
```

```
        WS_OVERLAPPEDWINDOW, /* standard window */
        CW_USEDEFAULT, /* X coordinate - let Windows decide */
        CW_USEDEFAULT, /* Y coordinate - let Windows decide */
        CW_USEDEFAULT, /* width - let Windows decide */
        CW_USEDEFAULT, /* height - let Windows decide */
        HWND_DESKTOP, /* no parent window */
        NULL, /* no override of class menu */
        hThisInst, /* handle of this instance of the program */
        NULL /* no additional arguments */
    );

    /* Load the keyboard accelerators. */
    hAccel = LoadAccelerators(hThisInst, "FloatMenu");

    hInst = hThisInst; /* save instance handle */

    /* Display the window. */
    ShowWindow(hwnd, nWinMode);
    UpdateWindow(hwnd);

    /* Create the message loop. */
    while(GetMessage(&msg, NULL, 0, 0))
    {
      if(!TranslateAccelerator(hwnd, hAccel, &msg)) {
        TranslateMessage(&msg); /* translate keyboard messages */
        DispatchMessage(&msg); /* return control to Windows 98 */
      }
    }
    return msg.wParam;
}

/* This function is called by Windows 98 and is passed
   messages from the message queue.
*/
LRESULT CALLBACK WindowFunc(HWND hwnd, UINT message,
                            WPARAM wParam, LPARAM lParam)
{
  HDC hdc;
  HMENU hmenu, hsubmenu;
  RECT rect;
  static HMENU hpopup;
  int response;
  int count;
  MENUITEMINFO miInfo;
  POINT pt;
```

```
static HPEN hCurrentPen, hRedPen;

switch(message) {
  case WM_CREATE:
    /* create red pen */
    hRedPen = CreatePen(PS_SOLID, 1, RGB(255, 0, 0));
    /* get black pen */
    hCurrentPen = (HPEN) GetStockObject(BLACK_PEN);
    break;
  case WM_COMMAND:
    switch(LOWORD(wParam)) {
      case IDM_ADDITEM: /* dynamically add popup menu */
        /* get handle of main menu */
        hmenu = GetMenu(hwnd);

        /* get handle of 1st popup menu */
        hsubmenu = GetSubMenu(hmenu, 0);

        /* get number of items in the menu */
        count = GetMenuItemCount(hsubmenu);

        /* create new popup menu */
        hpopup = CreatePopupMenu();

        /* add items to dynamic popup menu */
        miInfo.cbSize = sizeof(MENUITEMINFO);
        miInfo.fMask = MIIM_TYPE | MIIM_ID;
        miInfo.fType = MFT_STRING;
        miInfo.wID = IDM_NEW;
        miInfo.hSubMenu = NULL;
        miInfo.hbmpChecked = NULL;
        miInfo.hbmpUnchecked = NULL;
        miInfo.dwItemData = 0;
        miInfo.dwTypeData = "&Erase";
        InsertMenuItem(hpopup, 0, 1, &miInfo);

        miInfo.dwTypeData = "&Black Pen";
        miInfo.wID = IDM_NEW2;
        InsertMenuItem(hpopup, 1, 1, &miInfo);

        miInfo.dwTypeData = "&Red Pen";
        miInfo.wID = IDM_NEW3;
        InsertMenuItem(hpopup, 2, 1, &miInfo);

        /* append a separator */
```

```
                miInfo.cbSize = sizeof(MENUITEMINFO);
                miInfo.fMask = MIIM_TYPE;
                miInfo.fType = MFT_SEPARATOR;
                miInfo.fState = 0;
                miInfo.wID = 0;
                miInfo.hSubMenu = NULL;
                miInfo.hbmpChecked = NULL;
                miInfo.hbmpUnchecked = NULL;
                miInfo.dwItemData = 0;
                InsertMenuItem(hsubmenu, count, 1, &miInfo);

                /* append popup menu to main menu */
                miInfo.fMask = MIIM_TYPE | MIIM_SUBMENU;
                miInfo.fType = MFT_STRING;
                miInfo.hSubMenu = hpopup;
                miInfo.dwTypeData = "&This is New Popup";
                InsertMenuItem(hsubmenu, count+1, 1, &miInfo);

                /* deactivate the Add Popup option */
                EnableMenuItem(hsubmenu, IDM_ADDITEM,
                             MF_BYCOMMAND | MF_GRAYED);

                /* activate the Delete Popup option */
                EnableMenuItem(hsubmenu, IDM_DELITEM,
                             MF_BYCOMMAND | MF_ENABLED);
                break;
          case IDM_DELITEM: /* dynamically delete popup menu */
                /* get handle of main menu */
                hmenu = GetMenu(hwnd);

                /* get handle of 1st popup menu */
                hsubmenu = GetSubMenu(hmenu, 0);

                /* delete the new popup menu and the separator */
                count = GetMenuItemCount(hsubmenu);
                DeleteMenu(hsubmenu, count-1, MF_BYPOSITION | MF_GRAYED);
                DeleteMenu(hsubmenu, count-2, MF_BYPOSITION | MF_GRAYED);

                /* reactivate the Add Popup option */
                EnableMenuItem(hsubmenu, IDM_ADDITEM,
                             MF_BYCOMMAND | MF_ENABLED);

                /* deactivate the Delete Popup option */
                EnableMenuItem(hsubmenu, IDM_DELITEM,
                             MF_BYCOMMAND | MF_GRAYED);
```

```
  break;
case IDM_EXIT:
  response = MessageBox(hwnd, "Quit the Program?",
                        "Exit", MB_YESNO);
  if(response == IDYES) PostQuitMessage(0);
  break;
case IDM_NEW: /* erase */
  hdc = GetDC(hwnd);
  GetClientRect(hwnd, &rect);
  SelectObject(hdc, GetStockObject(WHITE_BRUSH));
  PatBlt(hdc, 0, 0, rect.right, rect.bottom, PATCOPY);
  ReleaseDC(hwnd, hdc);
  break;
case IDM_NEW2: /* select black pen */
  hCurrentPen = (HPEN) GetStockObject(BLACK_PEN);
  break;
case IDM_NEW3: /* select red pen */
  hCurrentPen = hRedPen;
  break;
case IDM_LINES:
  hdc = GetDC(hwnd);
  SelectObject(hdc, hCurrentPen);
  MoveToEx(hdc, 10, 10, NULL);
  LineTo(hdc, 100, 100);
  LineTo(hdc, 100, 50);
  LineTo(hdc, 50, 180);
  ReleaseDC(hwnd, hdc);
  break;
case IDM_ELLIPSES:
  hdc = GetDC(hwnd);
  SelectObject(hdc, hCurrentPen);
  Ellipse(hdc, 100, 100, 300, 200);
  Ellipse(hdc, 200, 100, 300, 200);
  ReleaseDC(hwnd, hdc);
  break;
case IDM_RECTANGLES:
  hdc = GetDC(hwnd);
  SelectObject(hdc, hCurrentPen);
  Rectangle(hdc, 100, 100, 24, 260);
  Rectangle(hdc, 110, 120, 124, 170);
  ReleaseDC(hwnd, hdc);
  break;
case IDM_HELP:
  MessageBox(hwnd, "Try Pressing Right Mouse Button",
             "Help", MB_OK);
```

```
              break;
          }
          break;
        case WM_RBUTTONDOWN: /* popup floating menu */

          /* convert window coordinates to screen coordinates */
          pt.x = LOWORD(lParam);
          pt.y = HIWORD(lParam);
          ClientToScreen(hwnd, &pt);

          /* get handle of draw menu */
          hmenu = LoadMenu(hInst, "Draw");

          /* get 1st popup menu */
          hsubmenu = GetSubMenu(hmenu, 0);

          /* activate floating popup menu */
          TrackPopupMenuEx(hsubmenu, 0, pt.x, pt.y,
                           hwnd, NULL);
          DestroyMenu(hmenu);
          break;
        case WM_DESTROY: /* terminate the program */
          DeleteObject(hRedPen);
          PostQuitMessage(0);
          break;
        default:
          /* Let Windows 98 process any messages not specified in
             the preceding switch statement. */
          return DefWindowProc(hwnd, message, wParam, lParam);
    }
    return 0;
}
```

20

The program uses the same MENU.H file shown in previous programs. It requires this resource file.

```
// Floating Menus
#include <windows.h>
#include "menu.h"

FloatMenu MENU
{
  POPUP "&Options"
  {
    MENUITEM "&Add Popup\tF2", IDM_ADDITEM
```

```
        MENUITEM "&Delete Popup\tF3", IDM_DELITEM, GRAYED
        MENUITEM "E&xit\tCtrl+X", IDM_EXIT
    }
  MENUITEM "&Help", IDM_HELP
}

// This menu will popup
Draw MENU
{
  POPUP "&Draw" {
    MENUITEM "&Lines\tF4", IDM_LINES
    MENUITEM "&Ellipses\tF5", IDM_ELLIPSES
    MENUITEM "&Rectangles\tF6", IDM_RECTANGLES
  }
}

// Define menu accelerators
FloatMenu ACCELERATORS
{
  VK_F2, IDM_ADDITEM, VIRTKEY
  VK_F3, IDM_DELITEM, VIRTKEY
  "^X", IDM_EXIT
  VK_F4, IDM_LINES, VIRTKEY
  VK_F5, IDM_ELLIPSES, VIRTKEY
  VK_F6, IDM_RECTANGLES, VIRTKEY
  VK_F1, IDM_HELP, VIRTKEY
}
```

Notice that in this version, the Draw menu is not part of the main, menu bar menu. Instead, it is a stand-alone menu. Thus, it will not be displayed until it is invoked.

A Closer Look at the Floating Menu Program

Most of the program is unchanged from its previous version. (To keep the code easy to follow, neither check marks nor radio menu items are used. You might want to try adding these on your own.) However, notice the code under **WM_RBUTTONDOWN**. It is used to activate the Draw menu. It is shown here for your convenience.

```
case WM_RBUTTONDOWN: /* popup floating menu */

  /* convert window coordinates to screen coordinates */
  pt.x = LOWORD(lParam);
  pt.y = HIWORD(lParam);
```

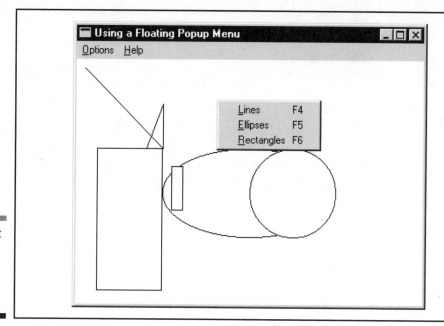

Sample output
from the
floating menu
program
Figure 20-5.

```
ClientToScreen(hwnd, &pt);

/* get handle of draw menu */
hmenu = LoadMenu(hInst, "Draw");

/* get 1st popup menu */
hsubmenu = GetSubMenu(hmenu, 0);

/* activate floating popup menu */
TrackPopupMenuEx(hsubmenu, 0, pt.x, pt.y,
                 hwnd, NULL);
DestroyMenu(hmenu);
break;
```

This code causes the Draw menu to pop up with its upper-left corner
positioned at the location of the mouse when the right button is pressed.
However, since the coordinates specified in **TrackPopupMenuEx( )** are in
terms of screen units, the program must convert the mouse's location (which
is in window units) into screen units using **ClientToScreen( )**. Next, the
menu must be loaded, using **LoadMenu( )**, and its first (and only) pop-up
menu obtained. After these steps have been taken, the menu can be
displayed.

IN DEPTH

Translating Between Screen and Window Coordinates

As you know, the location of a point within a window is given in window coordinates. Thus, no matter where a window is on the screen, the location of a point within that window will always have the same coordinates. As convenient as this is, sometimes you will need to know the absolute screen coordinate of a location that is specified in terms of window coordinates, or vice versa. As the floating menu program illustrates, one of the most common reasons to obtain the screen coordinates of a point is to position a window at a specific screen location. Whatever the case, Windows provides functions that translate between screen and window (also called *client*) coordinates. They are shown here:

BOOL ClientToScreen(HWND *hwnd*, POINT **lpLoc*);

BOOL ScreenToClient(HWND *hwnd*, POINT **lpLoc*);

ClientToScreen( ) is called with a window coordinate in the structure pointed to by *lpLoc* and returns the corresponding screen coordinate in that structure. The handle of the window in which the point lies is passed in *hwnd*. The function returns nonzero if successful and zero on failure.

ScreenToClient( ) is called with a screen coordinate in the structure pointed to by *lpLoc* and returns the corresponding window coordinate in that structure. The handle of the window in which the point lies is passed in *hwnd*. The function returns nonzero if successful and zero on failure.

Changing the Menu Bar

Before concluding this chapter we will examine one more menu-related technique: changing the contents of the menu bar itself. Menu items are added to the menu bar in exactly the same way that they are added to any other menu. There is only one additional action your program must take: It must redraw the menu bar in order for the changes to be displayed. To accomplish this, call **DrawMenuBar( )**, shown here:

BOOL DrawMenuBar(HWND *hwnd*);

Here, *hwnd* specifies the handle of the window whose menu bar will be redrawn. The function returns nonzero if successful and zero on failure.

To try modifying the contents of the menu bar, change the **IDM_ADDITEM** handler in the preceding program so that it looks like this.

```
/* dynamically add a popup menu to menu bar*/
case IDM_ADDITEM:
  /* get handle of menu bar */
  hmenu = GetMenu(hwnd);

  /* get number of items in the menu bar */
  count = GetMenuItemCount(hmenu);

  /* create new popup menu */
  hpopup = CreatePopupMenu();
  /* add items to dynamic popup menu */
  miInfo.cbSize = sizeof(MENUITEMINFO);
  miInfo.fMask = MIIM_TYPE | MIIM_ID;
  miInfo.fType = MFT_STRING;
  miInfo.wID = IDM_NEW;
  miInfo.hSubMenu = NULL;
  miInfo.hbmpChecked = NULL;
  miInfo.hbmpUnchecked = NULL;
  miInfo.dwItemData = 0;
  miInfo.dwTypeData = "&Erase";
  InsertMenuItem(hpopup, 0, 1, &miInfo);

  miInfo.dwTypeData = "&Black Pen";
  miInfo.wID = IDM_NEW2;
  InsertMenuItem(hpopup, 1, 1, &miInfo);

  miInfo.dwTypeData = "&Red Pen";
  miInfo.wID = IDM_NEW3;
  InsertMenuItem(hpopup, 2, 1, &miInfo);

  /* append popup menu to menu bar */
  miInfo.fMask = MIIM_TYPE | MIIM_SUBMENU;
  miInfo.fType = MFT_STRING;
  miInfo.hSubMenu = hpopup;
  miInfo.dwTypeData = "&New Popup";
  InsertMenuItem(hmenu, count+1, 1, &miInfo);

  /* get handle of 1st popup menu */
  hsubmenu = GetSubMenu(hmenu, 0);
  /* deactivate the Add Popup option */
```

20

```
EnableMenuItem(hsubmenu, IDM_ADDITEM, MF_BYCOMMAND | MF_GRAYED);
/* activate the Delete Popup option */
EnableMenuItem(hsubmenu, IDM_DELITEM, MF_BYCOMMAND | MF_ENABLED);

/* redraw the menu bar */
DrawMenuBar(hwnd);
break;
```

After making these changes, the pop-up menu will be added to the menu bar instead of the first drop-down menu. You should also make similar changes to the **IDM_DELITEM** handler so that it deletes the selection from the menu bar. Figure 20-6 shows what the menu bar looks like after adding the new item.

If you want to make extensive changes to the contents of the menu bar, you might want to use **SetMenu( )** instead of making the changes individually. **SetMenu( )** replaces the main menu of a window with another. It has this prototype:

BOOL SetMenu(HWND *hwnd*, HMENU *hMenu*);

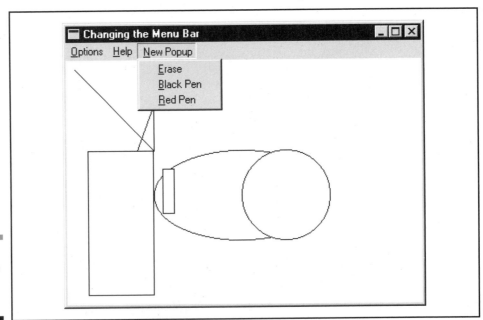

Changing the
contents of the
menu bar
Figure 20-6.

Here, *hwnd* is the handle of the window being affected and *hMenu* is the handle of the new menu. The old menu should be destroyed by calling **DestroyMenu( )**. If you know that your application will need to use two or more different main menus, you could construct them in advance and then use **SetMenu( )** to swap them in, when needed. This approach will usually be more efficient than making many changes to the menu bar by hand.

Finally, if you want to dynamically create a main menu (i.e., a menu bar), use the **CreateMenu( )** function. Its prototype is shown here:

```
HMENU CreateMenu(void);
```

It returns a handle to an empty menu that you must then fill in using the same approach that you used for dynamic pop-up menus.

Some Things to Try

Here is an easy experiment to try. In the first example program in this chapter, the Erase option was added to or removed from the Options menu manually, by the user. This approach was used only for the sake of illustration. It is possible to add or remove the Erase option automatically, under program control. For example, when the window is empty (as it is when the program begins), do not display the Erase option. As soon as the user draws something in the window, activate Erase. Once the user has erased the window, deactivate the Erase option. Automating the inclusion of the Erase option in this way reflects the way that dynamic menus are used in real applications.

Try adding check marks and radio menu items to the floating pop-up menu example.

You will also want to try the various options available to the **TrackPopupMenuEx( )** function. Specifically, try defining an excluded region. Also, try having the menu aligned differently.

Finally, try integrating free-floating context menus with the Help system. For ideas about how this might be done, observe how commercial programs handle this situation.

CHAPTER 21

Multiple Monitors, DLLs, and ActiveX

We have come a long way from Chapter 1. If you have worked through the preceding 20 chapters, you are well on your way to becoming an accomplished Windows 98 programmer. But there are three more topics with which you need to be familiar. The first is how to take advantage of the multiple-monitor capability offered by Windows 98. The second is learning to create and use your own dynamic link libraries (DLLs). The third is ActiveX. The last two of these are large topics. In fact, a complete discussion of ActiveX requires more than one volume! For obvious reasons it is not possible to deal with these topics in great detail here. However, a general understanding is important, and an overview of each is presented.

Using Multiple Monitors

Although many of the enhancements that Windows 98 provides over Windows 95 occur "under the hood," there is one that stands out: support for multiple monitors. With Windows 98 it is possible to connect up to nine monitors to a single system. The additional monitors add to the display area, acting as one big screen. For example, when you put a second video card in your system and attach a monitor to it, you can use both monitors as a single large display surface. You can drag applications between the monitors and even split a window between the two. The more monitors you add, the more screen area you have. This offers some very pleasing options for developers. For example, you could move the debug window of your compiler to a second monitor. This would free up all of the primary monitor's workspace for your source code editor. Or, if you like to work online, you could have your browser on one monitor and your application development environment on another. Frankly, the potential for this capability is unlimited.

In this section we will explore the multiple-monitor APIs provided by Windows 98. As you will see, most applications will not need to be recoded to run under multi-monitor systems. In fact, for the most part, the addition of another monitor is handled automatically by Windows 98. However, if you wish to make explicit use of a monitor other than the main one, you will need to add a little extra code to your applications.

PORTABILITY: Multiple monitors and the functions and features used to support them are not supported by Windows 95, Windows 3.1, or versions of Windows NT prior to 5.

Virtual Display Space

When your system contains more than one monitor, a virtual display space is created that spans the monitors. This is also called the *virtual desktop* or the *virtual screen*. The size and shape of the virtual desktop is determined by how the monitors are arranged. For example, if you have two monitors and each has a resolution of 640 × 480, and two monitors are side-by-side, the size of the virtual desktop is 1280 × 480. If one monitor is directly over the other, the size of the virtual desktop is 640 × 960. It is important to understand that the virtual display space is a continuum that spans the monitors. Thus, it is possible to have windows that are larger than any single monitor.

The monitor arrangement is under user control and is accomplished using the Settings tab in the Display Properties property sheet. Figure 21-1 shows how this window appears when two monitors are used.

In all cases, the first (or primary) monitor is always located with its origin at 0, 0. (If it weren't, existing programs could not run right.) This implies that monitors positioned to the left or above the primary one will use negative coordinates. For example, if you have two monitors and the second monitor

21

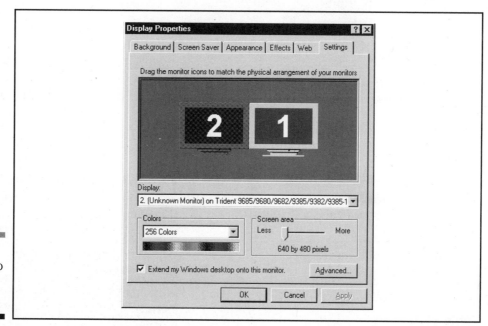

Figure 21-1.

is directly to the left of the primary monitor, and if both have resolutions of 640 × 480, then the origin of the virtual desktop is at –640, 0. The fact that virtual screen coordinates can potentially be negative must be taken into account by any code that uses screen coordinates for positioning windows.

To obtain the origin, width, and height of the virtual screen, use the **GetSystemMetrics( )** function with the following values.

SM_XVIRTUALSCREEN	Left coordinate of origin.
SM_YVIRTUALSCREEN	Top coordinate of origin.
SM_CXVIRTUALSCREEN	Width of virtual screen.
SM_CYVRITUALSCREEN	Height of virtual screen.

To obtain the number of monitors attached to the system, pass the value **SM_CMONITORS**

One last point: The monitors do not need to be directly side-by-side or directly over one another. They may be staggered. Thus, you cannot make simplistic assumptions about what will be visible just because you know the resolution of the monitors installed in a system.

The Multiple-Monitor API Functions

The multiple-monitor subsystem is supported by the five API functions shown in Table 21-1. Of these, we will be using **EnumDisplayMonitors( )**, **GetMonitorInfo( )**, and **MonitorFromWindow( )**. Each is examined next.

Function	Purpose
EnumDisplayMonitors( )	Enumerates information about the monitors installed in the computer.
GetMonitorInfo( )	Obtains information about a monitor given its handle.
MonitorFromPoint( )	Given a screen location, this function returns a handle to the monitor that contains the point.

The Multiple-Monitor API Functions

Table 21-1.

MonitorFromRect( )	Given a rectangular region, this function returns a handle to the monitor that contains the largest portion of that region.
MonitorFromWindow( )	Given a window handle, this function returns a handle to the monitor that contains the largest portion of that window.

The Multiple-
Monitor API
Functions
(*continued*)
Table 21-1.

EnumDisplayMonitors( )

EnumDisplayMonitors( ) obtains information about the monitors in the
system. Its prototype is shown here:

> BOOL EnumDisplayMonitors(HDC *hdc*, RECT **rect*,
> MONITORENUMPROC *enumFunc*,
> LPARAM *extra*);

21

Here, *hdc* contains either the DC of a specific region or **NULL**. If a device
context is passed, only those monitors that contain a portion of the DC
are enumerated. If *hdc* is **NULL**, the entire virtual screen is used. The *rect*
parameter specifies a clipping region within *hdc*. It can also be **NULL**. To
enumerate all monitors, both *hdc* and *rect* should be **NULL**. *enumFunc* is a
pointer to a callback function that will be called once for each monitor. The
value of *extra* is passed to *enumFunc*. The function returns nonzero if
successful and zero
on failure.

After **EnumDisplayMonitors( )** has been called, Windows 98
automatically calls the function pointed to by *enumFunc* one time for each
monitor it enumerates. This callback function has the following prototype.
(Of course, the name of the function may differ.)

> BOOL CALLBACK *enumFunc*(HMONITOR *hmon*, HDC *hdc*,
> RECT **rect*, LPARAM *extra*);

Here, *hmon* is the handle to the monitor being enumerated and *hdc* contains the
DC. The *hdc* parameter will be **NULL** if the *hdc* parameter to
EnumDisplayMonitors( ) was **NULL**. The coordinates in *rect* represent the
dimensions of the enumerated monitor if *hdc* is **NULL**. Otherwise, it contains
the portion of the region specified by the *rect* parameter to

EnumDisplayMonitors( ) that lies within the monitor. The value in *extra* contains the value that was specified in the call to **EnumDisplayMonitors( )**. Your function must return nonzero to continue the enumeration or zero to stop it.

GetMonitorInfo( )

GetMonitorInfo( ) obtains information about a specific monitor. Its prototype is shown here:

BOOL GetMonitorInfo(HMONITOR *hmon*, MONITORINFOEX **mi*);

Here, *hmon* is the handle to the monitor about which you wish to obtain information. The information about the monitor is returned in the **MONITORINFOEX** structure pointed to by *mi*. The function returns nonzero if successful and zero on failure.

The **MONITORINFOEX** structure is defined like this.

```
typedef struct tagMONITORINFOEX {
  DWORD cbSize;
  RECT rcMonitor;
  RECT rcWork;
  DWORD dwFlags;
  CHAR szDevice[CCJDEVICENAME];
} MONITORINFOEX;
```

Here, **cbSize** contains the size of the structure. This field must be set prior to calling **GetMonitorInfo( )**.

rcMonitor describes the bounding rectangle for the specified monitor in terms of virtual screen coordinates. Thus, if the monitor in question is directly left of the primary monitor and it has a resolution of 640×480, then the left, top coordinates in **rcMonitor** will be -640, 0, and its right, bottom coordinates will be 0, 480.

rcWork describes the work area of the monitor in terms of virtual screen coordinates.

If **dwFlags** contains **MONITORINFOF_PRIMARY**, then the monitor is the primary monitor.

The name of the monitor is found in **szDevice**.

NOTE: You can use a **MONITORINFO** structure in place of a **MONITORINFOEX** structure if you like. The only difference between the two is that **MONITORINFO** does not contain the **szDevice** field.

MonitorFromWindow( )

You can obtain the handle of the monitor that is displaying a window by calling **MonitorFromWindow( )**. Its prototype is shown here:

HMONITOR MonitorFromWindow(HWND *hwnd*, DWORD *retval*);

Here, *hwnd* is the handle of the window. The value passed in *retval* determines what the function returns if the specified window is not currently in any monitor. It can be one of these values.

MONITOR_DEFAULTTONEAREST

MONITOR_DEFAULTTONULL

MONITOR_DEFAULTTOPRIMARY

21

Using Multiple Monitors

The following program demonstrates various aspects of multiple monitors. For the sake of simplicity, the example assumes a system with two monitors, but you can easily change this. The program allows you to enumerate information about the monitors, position the program's window on either monitor, and obtain information about the current monitor. Sample output is shown in Figure 21-2.

```
/* Using Two Monitors */
#define WINVER 0x0500

#include <windows.h>
#include <string.h>
#include <stdio.h>
#include "mon2.h"

LRESULT CALLBACK WindowFunc(HWND, UINT, WPARAM, LPARAM);

char szWinName[] = "MyWin"; /* name of window class */
```

```
BOOL CALLBACK MonInfo(HMONITOR hMon, HDC hdc,
                      LPRECT rect, LPARAM extra);
BOOL CALLBACK DisplayMonInfo(HMONITOR hMon, HDC hdc,
                      LPRECT rect, LPARAM extra);

int monOrg[9][2]; /* max of 9 monitors */
int numMon = 0;

int WINAPI WinMain(HINSTANCE hThisInst, HINSTANCE hPrevInst,
                   LPSTR lpszArgs, int nWinMode)
{
  HWND hwnd;
  MSG msg;
  WNDCLASSEX wcl;
  HACCEL hAccel;

  /* Define a window class. */
  wcl.cbSize = sizeof(WNDCLASSEX);

  wcl.hInstance = hThisInst; /* handle to this instance */
  wcl.lpszClassName = szWinName; /* window class name */
  wcl.lpfnWndProc = WindowFunc; /* window function */
  wcl.style = 0; /* default style */

  wcl.hIcon = LoadIcon(NULL, IDI_APPLICATION); /* standard icon */
  wcl.hIconSm = LoadIcon(NULL, IDI_APPLICATION); /* small icon */
  wcl.hCursor = LoadCursor(NULL, IDC_ARROW); /* cursor style */

  wcl.lpszMenuName = "MonMenu"; /* main menu */
  wcl.cbClsExtra = 0; /* no extra */
  wcl.cbWndExtra = 0; /* information needed */

  /* Make the window white. */
  wcl.hbrBackground = (HBRUSH) GetStockObject(WHITE_BRUSH);

  /* Register the window class. */
  if(!RegisterClassEx(&wcl)) return 0;

  /* Now that a window class has been registered, a window
     can be created. */
  hwnd = CreateWindow(
    szWinName, /* name of window class */
    "Multiple Monitors", /* title */
    WS_OVERLAPPEDWINDOW, /* standard window */
```

```
            CW_USEDEFAULT, /* X coordinate - let Windows decide */
            CW_USEDEFAULT, /* Y coordinate - let Windows decide */
            CW_USEDEFAULT, /* width - let Windows decide */
            CW_USEDEFAULT, /* height - let Windows decide */
            HWND_DESKTOP, /* no parent window */
            NULL, /* no override of class menu */
            hThisInst, /* handle of this instance of the program */
            NULL /* no additional arguments */
        );

        /* Load the keyboard accelerators. */
        hAccel = LoadAccelerators(hThisInst, "DynPopUpMenu");

        /* Display the window. */
        ShowWindow(hwnd, nWinMode);
        UpdateWindow(hwnd);

        /* Create the message loop. */
        while(GetMessage(&msg, NULL, 0, 0))
        {
          if(!TranslateAccelerator(hwnd, hAccel, &msg)) {
            TranslateMessage(&msg); /* translate keyboard messages */
            DispatchMessage(&msg); /* return control to Windows 98 */
          }
        }
      return msg.wParam;
}

/* This function is called by Windows 98 and is passed
   messages from the message queue.
*/
LRESULT CALLBACK WindowFunc(HWND hwnd, UINT message,
                            WPARAM wParam, LPARAM lParam)
{
  HDC hdc;
  static char str1[255];
  char str2[255];
  PAINTSTRUCT paintstruct;
  int response;
  MONITORINFOEX mi;
  HMONITOR hMon;
  static int vTop, vLeft, vRight, vBottom;

  switch(message) {
    case WM_CREATE:
```

21

```
vTop = GetSystemMetrics(SM_YVIRTUALSCREEN);
vLeft = GetSystemMetrics(SM_XVIRTUALSCREEN);
vRight = GetSystemMetrics(SM_CXVIRTUALSCREEN);
vBottom = GetSystemMetrics(SM_CYVIRTUALSCREEN);

EnumDisplayMonitors(NULL, NULL, MonInfo, 0);

sprintf(str1,
        "%s%d,%d  %s%d  %s%d",
        "Virtual origin: ", vLeft, vTop,
        "Virtual width: ", vRight,
        "Virtual height: ", vBottom);

  break;
case WM_COMMAND:
  switch(LOWORD(wParam)) {
    case IDM_ENUM:
      EnumDisplayMonitors(NULL, NULL, DisplayMonInfo,
                          (LPARAM) hwnd);

      sprintf(str2, "%d", numMon);
      MessageBox(hwnd, str2, "Monitors in System",
              MB_OK);
      break;
    case IDM_MON1: /* move to primary monitor */
      /* monitor 1 is always located at 0, 0 */
      MoveWindow(hwnd, 100, 100, 450, 200, 1);
      break;
    case IDM_MON2: /* move to monitor 2 */
      MoveWindow(hwnd, monOrg[1][0]+100,
              monOrg[1][1]+100, 450, 200, 1);
      break;
    case IDM_CURMON:
      hMon = MonitorFromWindow(hwnd,
                              MONITOR_DEFAULTTOPRIMARY);
      mi.cbSize = sizeof(MONITORINFOEX);
      GetMonitorInfo(hMon, &mi);
      sprintf(str2,
              "%s\nOrigin: %d, %d\nWidth: %d\nHeight: %d",
              mi.szDevice,
              mi.rcMonitor.left, mi.rcMonitor.top,
              mi.rcMonitor.right, mi.rcMonitor.bottom);
      MessageBox(hwnd, str2, "Current Monitor", MB_OK);
      break;
    case IDM_EXIT:
```

```
            response = MessageBox(hwnd, "Quit the Program?",
                                  "Exit", MB_YESNO);
            if(response == IDYES) PostQuitMessage(0);
            break;
          case IDM_HELP:
            MessageBox(hwnd, "Try Moving the Window",
                    "Help", MB_OK);
            break;
      }
      break;
    case WM_PAINT:
      hdc = BeginPaint(hwnd, &paintstruct);
      TextOut(hdc, 0, 0, str1, strlen(str1));
      EndPaint(hwnd, &paintstruct);
      break;
    case WM_DESTROY: /* terminate the program */
      PostQuitMessage(0);
      break;
    default:
      /* Let Windows 98 process any messages not specified in
         the preceding switch statement. */
      return DefWindowProc(hwnd, message, wParam, lParam);
  }
  return 0;
}


/* Enumerate monitors and store origins. */
BOOL CALLBACK MonInfo(HMONITOR hMon, HDC hdc,
                      LPRECT rect, LPARAM extra)
{
  MONITORINFOEX mi;

  mi.cbSize = sizeof(MONITORINFOEX);
  GetMonitorInfo(hMon, &mi);
  monOrg[numMon][0] = mi.rcMonitor.left;
  monOrg[numMon][1] = mi.rcMonitor.top;
  numMon++;

  return TRUE;
}


/* Show info on all monitors in system. */
BOOL CALLBACK DisplayMonInfo(HMONITOR hMon, HDC hdc,
                             LPRECT rect, LPARAM hwnd)
{
```

21

```
MONITORINFOEX mi;
char str[255];

mi.cbSize = sizeof(MONITORINFOEX);
GetMonitorInfo(hMon, &mi);

mi.cbSize = sizeof(MONITORINFOEX);
GetMonitorInfo(hMon, &mi);
sprintf(str,
        "Origin: %d, %d\nWidth: %d\nHeight: %d",
        mi.rcMonitor.left, mi.rcMonitor.top,
        mi.rcMonitor.right, mi.rcMonitor.bottom);
MessageBox((HWND)hwnd, str, mi.szDevice, MB_OK);

return TRUE;
}
```

The resource file for the program is shown here.

```
// Use Multiple Monitors
#include <windows.h>
#include "mon2.h"

MonMenu MENU
{
  POPUP "&Options"
  {
    MENUITEM "&Enumerate\tF2", IDM_ENUM
    MENUITEM "&Primary Monitor\tF3", IDM_MON1
    MENUITEM "&Secondary Monitor\tF4", IDM_MON2
    MENUITEM "&Show Info\tF5", IDM_CURMON
    MENUITEM "E&xit\tCtrl+X", IDM_EXIT
  }
  MENUITEM "&Help", IDM_HELP
}

// Define menu accelerators
DynPopUpMenu ACCELERATORS
{
  VK_F1, IDM_HELP, VIRTKEY
  VK_F2, IDM_ENUM, VIRTKEY
  VK_F3, IDM_MON1, VIRTKEY
  VK_F4, IDM_MON2, VIRTKEY
  VK_F5, IDM_CURMON, VIRTKEY
```

```
    "^X", IDM_EXIT
}
```

The header file MON.H is shown here.

```
#define IDM_MON1     101
#define IDM_MON2     102
#define IDM_CURMON   103
#define IDM_EXIT     104
#define IDM_ENUM     105
#define IDM_HELP     106
```

A Closer Look at the Multiple-Monitor Program

Notice that the program defines **WINVER** with the value 0x0500. Since multiple monitors are quite new, your compiler may require this definition in order to compile the multiple-monitor API functions.

When **WindowFunc( )** receives a **WM_CREATE** message, it obtains the coordinates of the virtual desktop. It also enumerates the monitors, using the callback function **MonInfo( )**. **MonInfo( )** counts the monitors and stores the origin (in virtual screen coordinates) of each. Although the program only works with two monitors, this function will store the origins of all monitors in the system.

When you select Enumerate, the monitors are also enumerated. This time the callback function **DisplayMonInfo( )** is used and the information about each monitor is displayed.

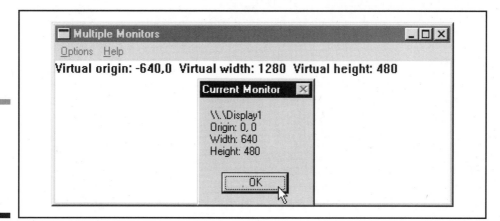

Sample output from the multiple-monitor program

Figure 21-2.

When you choose Secondary Monitor, the main window is moved to the second monitor. To move back, select Primary Monitor. The window is moved using the **MoveWindow( )** function, described earlier in this book. Notice that the primary monitor is always located at 0, 0. Thus, the coordinates to **MoveWindow( )** are "normal." However, the second monitor (and all others) must have its coordinates adjusted relative to the origin of the monitor. This is why the origin of the enumerated monitors is stored when the program starts running.

To obtain information about the monitor that the window is currently on, choose Show Info. The information is obtained by calling **GetMonitorInfo( )**.

Multiple monitors open the door to many exciting possibilities. Even though few users currently have more than one monitor, this situation will not take long to change. You should start thinking in terms of multiple-monitor systems now. Programs that take advantage of the multiple monitors will definitely have a competitive edge.

Creating DLLs

As you know, the Win32 API library is stored as a dynamic link library. This means that when your application program uses an API function, the code for that function is not actually added to your program's object file. Instead, loading instructions are supplied. Only when your program is loaded for execution are the dynamically linked API functions added. It is possible for you to create your own dynamic link libraries that work in the same way. As you will see, the process is easier than you might expect.

Dynamic Linking vs. Static Linking

Static linking takes place at compile time. Dynamic linking occurs at run time.

Before beginning, let's review the difference between static linking and dynamic linking. As just explained, dynamic linking occurs at run time. The code for dynamically linked functions does not appear in your program's .EXE file. By contrast, static linking occurs at compile time. The code for statically linked functions is physically added to your program's .EXE file. Functions that will be statically linked are usually stored in either .OBJ or .LIB files. For example, when you write a large program consisting of several separate compilation units (files), the linker will combine the .OBJ files for each module when it creates the .EXE file. In this case, the .EXE file will contain all of the code found in the .OBJ files.

When you use dynamic linking, the code for the functions that will be dynamically linked will be stored in a .DLL file that is separate from the rest of your program. As you will see, your program will link in a small amount of code that contains the loading instructions for the DLL functions, but the functions themselves will not be included.

Why Create a DLL?

You might be wondering why you would want to create your own dynamic link library. Frankly, for small programs there are no advantages. It is just easier to link all of the functions used by your program at compile time. However, for large software systems involving several components that share a custom function library, the advantages can be enormous. For example:

1. Placing functions in a DLL reduces the size of each component because the functions are not duplicated in each program when stored on disk. Although disk space is currently plentiful and cheap, it is still wrong to waste it.

2. Using DLLs makes upgrades easier. When a function stored in a normal library is changed, each program that uses that function must be relinked. When using dynamic linking, only the DLL file must be recompiled. All applications that use that DLL will automatically use the new version of the function the next time they are executed.

3. Using DLLs can make it easier to fix code "in the field." For example, if you have a misbehaving, mission-critical program, it is far easier to download a repaired dynamic link library than it is to download the entire application. This is quite important for programs used in remote environments, such as spacecraft, unmanned monitoring posts, and the like.

21

Of course, nothing is without its costs. The downside to using your own DLLs is that your program is now in two (or more) pieces. This makes the management of that program harder and does open up some failure paths. For example, if the dynamic link library is out of synch with the application, trouble is sure to follow. That said, when building large software systems, the benefits of dynamic linking exceed its negatives.

DLL Basics

Functions defined in a DLL must be exported.

Before looking at an example DLL, there are a few rules that apply to building and using DLLS with which you need to be familiar. First, any function contained in a DLL that will be called by code outside the DLL must be

Functions in DLLs must be imported by applications that use them.

exported. Second, to use a function contained in a DLL, you must *import* it. When using C/C++, export is accomplished using the **dllexport** keyword, and import is done with **dllimport**. **dllexport** and **dllimport** are extended keywords supported by both Microsoft Visual C++ and Borland C++.

PORTABILITY: In Windows 3.1, functions exported from DLLs had to be specified in the EXPORTS section of the .DEF file associated with the DLL. Although this is still allowed, **dllexport** provides a more convenient alternative.

The **dllexport** and **dllimport** keywords cannot be used by themselves. Instead, they need to be preceded by another extended keyword: _ _**declspec**. Its general form is shown here:

_ _declspec(*specifier*)

Here, *specifier* is a storage class specifer. For DLLs, *specifier* will be either **dllexport** or **dllimport**. For example, to export a function called **MyFunc( )**, you would use a line like this:

```
__declspec(dllexport) void MyFunc(int a)
```

To simplify the syntax of declaring imported and exported functions, most programmers create a macro name that can be substituted for the rather long _ _**declspec** specification. For example,

```
#define DllExport __declspec (dllexport)
```

Now, **MyFunc( )** can be exported using this simpler statement.

```
DllExport void MyFunc(int a)
```

If your DLL is compiled as a C++ program and you want it to also be usable by C programs, you will need to add the "C" linkage specification, as shown here:

```
#define DllExport extern "C" __declspec (dllexport)
```

If your DLL will be used by both C and C++ programs, specify C linkage for its functions.

This prevents the standard C++ *name mangling* (also called *name decoration*) from taking place. Name mangling is the process by which the name of a function is modified to include type-related information. This process is used to distinguish between different forms of overloaded functions, between member functions of different classes, functions in different name spaces, etc. We will include the C linkage specification for the examples in this book to avoid any possible troubles in this regard. (If you are compiling C programs, do not add **extern "C"** since it isn't needed and it will not be accepted by the compiler.)

At the time of this writing, the use of **dllimport** is technically not necessary for functions. It is strongly recommended because it allows more efficient code to be generated. **dllimport** is necessary when importing data, however.

When compiling a DLL, you must tell the compiler that a DLL is being created. The easiest way to do this is to simply specify that you are creating a DLL when creating a new project. If you are unsure about what compiler options to set, refer to your compiler's documentation.

After you have compiled a DLL, two files will be present. One will contain the DLL functions and will use the .DLL extension. The other will contain loading information for the functions and it will use the .LIB extension. You must link the .LIB file into any program that will be using your DLL.

The .DLL file must be in a directory where it will be found when your application is loaded. Windows 98 searches for DLLs in the following sequence. It first searches the directory that held the application. Next, it looks in the current working directory. Then it examines the standard DLL directory. Next, it searches the Windows directory. Finally, it searches any directories specified in the PATH variable. It is strongly suggested that when you are experimenting with DLLs, you keep them in the same directory as the application and not in any of the standard directories. This way, you avoid any chance of accidentally overwriting a DLL that is used by your system's software.

If a program requires a DLL that cannot be found, the program will not be executed and a message box will be displayed on the screen.

A Simple DLL

Let's begin by creating a very simple dynamic link library. Here is the source code for a DLL that contains only one function: **ShowMouseLoc( )**. This function displays the location of the mouse when a button-press message is

21

received. Recall that mouse button-press messages contain, in **lParam**, the coordinates of the mouse at the time at which the message was generated. To show the location of the mouse, pass this value to **ShowMouseLoc( )** along with the desired device context. The function displays the coordinates. As you can see, **ShowMouseLoc( )** is declared as an exported function.

```
/* A simple DLL. */
#include <windows.h>
#include <string.h>

#define DllExport extern "C" __declspec (dllexport)

/* This function displays the coordinates of the mouse
   at the point at which a mouse button was pressed.

   hdc:    Specifies the device context in which to
           output the coordinates.
   lParam: Specifies the value of lParam when the
           button was pressed.
*/
DllExport void ShowMouseLoc(HDC hdc, LPARAM lParam)
{
  char str[80];

  wsprintf(str, "Button is down at %d, %d",
           LOWORD(lParam), HIWORD(lParam));
  TextOut(hdc, LOWORD(lParam), HIWORD(lParam),
          str, strlen(str));
}
```

To follow along, enter this file now, calling it MYDLL.CPP. Next, create a DLL project. To do this using Visual C++, select Win32 Dynamic Link Library in the Projects tab of the New dialog box. Next, compile the library. This will result in these two files being created: MYDLL.DLL and MYDLL.LIB. As explained, the .DLL file will contain the dynamic link library itself. The .LIB file contains loading information that must be linked with any application that uses the library.

Creating a Header File

As it must for any other library function that it uses, your program must include the prototypes to functions contained in a DLL. This is why you must include WINDOWS.H in all Windows 98 programs, for example. The easiest way to include prototypes for the functions in your DLL is to create a companion header file. For example, the header file for MYDLL is shown here. To follow along with the example, call this file MYDLL.H.

```
#define DllImport extern "C" __declspec (dllimport)

DllImport void ShowMouseLoc(HDC hdc, LPARAM lParm);
```

Using the DLL

Once your dynamic link library has been compiled and put in the proper directory, and a header file has been created for it, it is ready for use. Here is a simple program that uses MYDLL.DLL. It merely displays the location of the mouse whenever the left or right mouse button is pressed. Sample output is shown in Figure 21-3. When you compile this program, you must be sure to include MYDLL.LIB in your link list. When you run the program, **ShowMouseLoc( )** will be automatically loaded from MYDLL.DLL when your program is executed.

```
/* Use ShowMouseLoc() from DLL */

#include <windows.h>
#include <string.h>
#include "mydll.h"

LRESULT CALLBACK WindowFunc(HWND, UINT, WPARAM, LPARAM);

char szWinName[] = "MyWin"; /* name of window class */

int WINAPI WinMain(HINSTANCE hThisInst, HINSTANCE hPrevInst,
                    LPSTR lpszArgs, int nWinMode)
{
  HWND hwnd;
  MSG msg;
  WNDCLASSEX wcl;

  /* Define a window class. */
  wcl.cbSize = sizeof(WNDCLASSEX);

  wcl.hInstance = hThisInst; /* handle to this instance */
  wcl.lpszClassName = szWinName; /* window class name */
  wcl.lpfnWndProc = WindowFunc; /* window function */
  wcl.style = 0; /* default style */

  wcl.hIcon = LoadIcon(NULL, IDI_APPLICATION); /* standard icon */
  wcl.hIconSm = LoadIcon(NULL, IDI_APPLICATION); /* small icon */
```

```
  wcl.hCursor = LoadCursor(NULL, IDC_ARROW); /* cursor style */

  wcl.lpszMenuName = NULL; /* no main menu */
  wcl.cbClsExtra = 0; /* no extra */
  wcl.cbWndExtra = 0; /* information needed */

  /* Make the window white. */
  wcl.hbrBackground = (HBRUSH) GetStockObject(WHITE_BRUSH);

  /* Register the window class. */
  if(!RegisterClassEx(&wcl)) return 0;

  /* Now that a window class has been registered, a window
     can be created. */
  hwnd = CreateWindow(
    szWinName, /* name of window class */
    "Demonstrate a DLL", /* title */
    WS_OVERLAPPEDWINDOW, /* window style - normal */
    CW_USEDEFAULT, /* X coordinate - let Windows decide */
    CW_USEDEFAULT, /* Y coordinate - let Windows decide */
    CW_USEDEFAULT, /* width - let Windows decide */
    CW_USEDEFAULT, /* height - let Windows decide */
    HWND_DESKTOP, /* no parent window */
    NULL, /* no override of class menu */
    hThisInst, /* handle of this instance of the program */
    NULL /* no additional arguments */
  );

  /* Display the window. */
  ShowWindow(hwnd, nWinMode);
  UpdateWindow(hwnd);

  /* Create the message loop. */
  while(GetMessage(&msg, NULL, 0, 0))
  {
    TranslateMessage(&msg); /* translate keyboard messages */
    DispatchMessage(&msg); /* return control to Windows 98 */
  }
  return msg.wParam;
}

/* This function is called by Windows 98 and is passed
   messages from the message queue.
*/
LRESULT CALLBACK WindowFunc(HWND hwnd, UINT message,
                            WPARAM wParam, LPARAM lParam)
```

```
{
  HDC hdc;

  switch(message) {
    case WM_RBUTTONDOWN: /* process right button */
      hdc = GetDC(hwnd); /* get DC */
      ShowMouseLoc(hdc, lParam); /* call DLL function */
      ReleaseDC(hwnd, hdc); /* Release DC */
      break;
    case WM_LBUTTONDOWN: /* process left button */
      hdc = GetDC(hwnd); /* get DC */
      ShowMouseLoc(hdc, lParam); /* call DLL function */
      ReleaseDC(hwnd, hdc); /* Release DC */
      break;
    case WM_DESTROY: /* terminate the program */
      PostQuitMessage(0);
      break;
    default:
       /* Let Windows 98 process any messages not specified in
          the preceding switch statement. */
      return DefWindowProc(hwnd, message, wParam, lParam);
  }
  return 0;
}
```

21

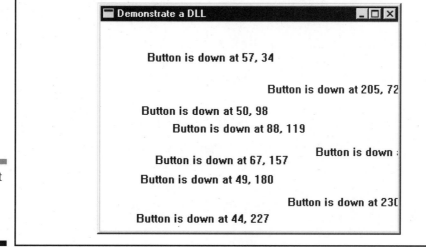

Sample output
from the first
DLL program

Figure 21-3.

Using DllMain( )

DllMain( )
provides
initialization
and termination
for a DLL.

Some DLLs will require special startup or shutdown code. To allow for this, all DLLs have a function, **DllMain( )**, that is called when the DLL is being initialized or terminated. This function is defined by you in your dynamic link library source file. However, if you don't define it, a default version is automatically provided by the compiler. This is why we did not need one for the preceding DLL. Of course, all but the simplest DLLs will provide their own.

DllMain( ) has the following prototype:

BOOL WINAPI DllMain(HANDLE *hInstance*, ULONG *What*,
                    LPVOID *NotUsed*);

When this function is called by Windows 98, *hInstance* is the instance handle of the DLL, *What* specifies what action is occurring, and *NotUsed* is reserved. The function must return nonzero if successful and zero on failure.

The value in *What* will be one of the following.

Value	Meaning
DLL_PROCESS_ATTACH	Process is beginning use of DLL.
DLL_PROCESS_DETACH	Process is releasing DLL.
DLL_THREAD_ATTACH	Process has created a new thread.
DLL_THREAD_DETACH	Process has destroyed a thread.

When *What* contains **DLL_PROCESS_ATTACH**, it means that a process has loaded the DLL. (In technical terms, it means that the library has been mapped into the process's address space.) If **DllMain( )** returns zero in response to this action, the process attempting to attach to the DLL is terminated. For each process that uses the DLL, **DllMain( )** will only be called once with **DLL_PROCESS_ATTACH**.

When *What* contains **DLL_PROCESS_DETACH**, the process no longer needs the DLL. This typically occurs when the process itself terminates. It also occurs when a DLL is being explicitly released.

When a process that has already attached a DLL creates a new thread, **DllMain( )** will be called with **DLL_THREAD_ATTACH**. When a thread is destroyed, **DllMain( )** is called with **DLL_THREAD_DETACH**. Multiple-thread attach and detach messages can be generated by a single process.

In general, your implementation of **DllMain( )** must take appropriate action based upon the contents of *What*, whenever it is called. Of course, such appropriate action may be to do nothing other than return nonzero.

Adding a DllMain( ) to MYDLL

To see exactly how and when **DllMain( )** is called, add **DllMain( )** to MYDLL.CPP, as shown here.

```
#include <windows.h>
#include <string.h>

#define DllExport extern "C" __declspec (dllexport)

/* This function is called during initialization and
   termination. */
BOOL WINAPI DllMain(HANDLE hInstance, ULONG what,
                    LPVOID Notused)
{
  switch(what) {
    case DLL_PROCESS_ATTACH:
      MessageBox(HWND_DESKTOP, "Process attaching DLL.",
                 "DLL Action", MB_OK);
      break;
    case DLL_PROCESS_DETACH:
      MessageBox(HWND_DESKTOP, "Process detaching DLL.",
                 "DLL Action", MB_OK);
      break;
    case DLL_THREAD_ATTACH:
      MessageBox(HWND_DESKTOP, "Thread attaching DLL.",
                 "DLL Action", MB_OK);
      break;
    case DLL_THREAD_DETACH:
      MessageBox(HWND_DESKTOP, "Thread detaching DLL.",
                 "DLL Action", MB_OK);
```

```
      break;
  }
  return 1;
}


/* This function displays the coordinates of the mouse
   at the point at which a mouse button was pressed.

   hdc:    Specifies the device context in which to
           output the coordinates.
   lParam: Specifies the value of lParam when the
           button was pressed.
*/
DllExport void ShowMouseLoc(HDC hdc, LPARAM lParam)
{
  char str[80];

  wsprintf(str, "Button is down at %d, %d",
           LOWORD(lParam), HIWORD(lParam));
  TextOut(hdc, LOWORD(lParam), HIWORD(lParam),
          str, strlen(str));
}
```

As you can see, each time **DllMain( )** is called, a message box is displayed
that explains why. Notice that **MessageBox( )** uses **HWND_DESKTOP** for
its first parameter. This allows the message box to be displayed independently
of any application, because **HWND_DESKTOP** refers to the screen.

One other point: **DllMain( )** is not exported from MYDLL because it is not
called by application programs. It is called by Windows 98 only.

Demonstrating DllMain( )

The following program demonstrates **DllMain( )**. As before, it uses the
ShowMouseLoc( ) function to display the location of the mouse when its
left or right button is pressed. However, it also creates another thread of
execution each time you press a key on the keyboard. When you run this
program, pay close attention to when and why **DllMain( )** is called. Sample
output is shown in Figure 21-4. Also, remember to link this program with
MYDLL.LIB.

```
/* Demonstrate DLL initialization. */

#include <windows.h>
#include <string.h>
#include <stdio.h>
#include "mydll.h"

#define MAX 10000

LRESULT CALLBACK WindowFunc(HWND, UINT, WPARAM, LPARAM);

DWORD WINAPI MyThread(LPVOID param);

char szWinName[] = "MyWin"; /* name of window class */

char str[255] = ""; /* holds output string */

DWORD Tid1; /* thread ID */

int WINAPI WinMain(HINSTANCE hThisInst, HINSTANCE hPrevInst,
                   LPSTR lpszArgs, int nWinMode)
{
  HWND hwnd;
  MSG msg;
  WNDCLASSEX wcl;

  /* Define a window class. */
  wcl.cbSize = sizeof(WNDCLASSEX);

  wcl.hInstance = hThisInst; /* handle to this instance */
  wcl.lpszClassName = szWinName; /* window class name */
  wcl.lpfnWndProc = WindowFunc; /* window function */
  wcl.style = 0; /* default style */

  wcl.hIcon = LoadIcon(NULL, IDI_APPLICATION); /* standard icon */
  wcl.hIconSm = LoadIcon(NULL, IDI_APPLICATION); /* small icon */
  wcl.hCursor = LoadCursor(NULL, IDC_ARROW); /* cursor style */

  wcl.lpszMenuName = NULL; /* no main menu */
  wcl.cbClsExtra = 0; /* no extra */
  wcl.cbWndExtra = 0; /* information needed */
```

```
/* Make the window white. */
wcl.hbrBackground = (HBRUSH) GetStockObject(WHITE_BRUSH);

/* Register the window class. */
if(!RegisterClassEx(&wcl)) return 0;

/* Now that a window class has been registered, a window
   can be created. */
hwnd = CreateWindow(
  szWinName, /* name of window class */
  "Using DllMain", /* title */
  WS_OVERLAPPEDWINDOW, /* window style - normal */
  CW_USEDEFAULT, /* X coordinate - let Windows decide */
  CW_USEDEFAULT, /* Y coordinate - let Windows decide */
  CW_USEDEFAULT, /* width - let Windows decide */
  CW_USEDEFAULT, /* height - let Windows decide */
  HWND_DESKTOP, /* no parent window */
  NULL, /* no override of class menu */
  hThisInst, /* handle of this instance of the program */
  NULL /* no additional arguments */
);

/* Display the window. */
ShowWindow(hwnd, nWinMode);
UpdateWindow(hwnd);

/* Create the message loop. */
while(GetMessage(&msg, NULL, 0, 0))
{
  TranslateMessage(&msg); /* translate keyboard messages */
  DispatchMessage(&msg); /* return control to Windows 98 */
}
return msg.wParam;
}

/* This function is called by Windows 98 and is passed
   messages from the message queue.
*/
LRESULT CALLBACK WindowFunc(HWND hwnd, UINT message,
                            WPARAM wParam, LPARAM lParam)
{
  HDC hdc;
```

```
        PAINTSTRUCT ps;

        switch(message) {
          case WM_RBUTTONDOWN: /* process right button */
            hdc = GetDC(hwnd); /* get DC */
            ShowMouseLoc(hdc, lParam); /* call DLL function */
            ReleaseDC(hwnd, hdc); /* Release DC */
            break;
          case WM_LBUTTONDOWN: /* process left button */
            hdc = GetDC(hwnd); /* get DC */
            ShowMouseLoc(hdc, lParam); /* call DLL function */
            ReleaseDC(hwnd, hdc); /* Release DC */
            break;
          case WM_CHAR: /* start a thread when a key is pressed */
            CreateThread(NULL, 0,
                         (LPTHREAD_START_ROUTINE)MyThread,
                         (LPVOID) hwnd, 0, &Tid1);
            break;
          case WM_PAINT:
            hdc = BeginPaint(hwnd, &ps);
            strcpy(str, "Press a key to start a thread.");
            TextOut(hdc, 1, 1, str, strlen(str));
            EndPaint(hwnd, &ps);
            break;
          case WM_DESTROY: /* terminate the program */
            PostQuitMessage(0);
            break;
          default:
             /* Let Windows 98 process any messages not specified in
                the preceding switch statement. */
             return DefWindowProc(hwnd, message, wParam, lParam);
        }
        return 0;
}

/* Another thread of execution. */
DWORD WINAPI MyThread(LPVOID param)
{
  int i;
  HDC hdc;

  for(i=0; i<MAX; i++) {
    sprintf(str, "In thread: loop # %5d ", i);
```

```
    hdc = GetDC((HWND) param);
    TextOut(hdc, 1, 20, str, strlen(str));
    ReleaseDC((HWND) param, hdc);
  }
  return 0;
}
```

When you run this program, you will see the "Process attaching DLL" message box when the program first begins. When you press a key, a new thread is started. This causes a "Thread attaching DLL" message box to be displayed. When the thread ends, the "Thread detaching DLL" message box is shown. When you terminate the program, the last thing you will see is the "Process detaching DLL" message box. You might want to experiment with this program a little, making sure you understand when and why **DllMain( )** is called.

Although you may not have an immediate need for one, custom DLLs offer valuable advantages in many situations. As you have seen, they are easy to create. You should have no reluctance to using one when the time comes.

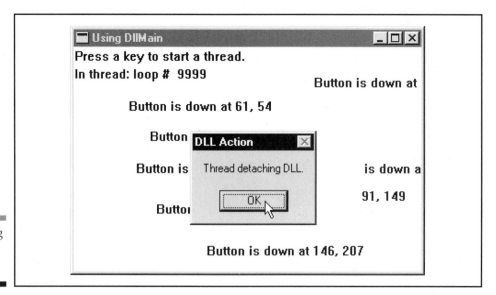

Demonstrating
DllMain( )
Figure 21-4.

IN DEPTH

Run-time Dynamic Linking

Most often, when you use functions defined in a DLL, your program calls those functions by name in its source code. This is the way all of the API functions have been called by the sample programs in this book and it is the way that **ShowMouseLoc( )** was called. When this is the case, the DLL that contains the functions is loaded when the application is loaded. This is called *load-time dynamic linking*. However, it is possible to load dynamic link libraries at run time.

If your application does not make explicit calls to one or more functions stored in a DLL, then that library will not, for obvious reasons, be loaded when your program begins execution. However, it is still possible to call functions contained in that DLL. To do so, your program must manually load the DLL and then obtain pointers to the functions that it wishes to use. This process is called *run-time dynamic linking*.

At the core of run-time dynamic linking are these three functions:

> HMODULE LoadLibrary(LPCSTR *DllName*);

> BOOL FreeLibrary(HMODLUE *hMod*);

> FARPROC GetProcAddress(HMODULE *hMod*, LPCSTR *FuncName*);

LoadLibrary( ) loads the DLL specified by *DllName* and returns a handle to it. **FreeLibrary( )** frees the DLL when it is no longer needed. **GetProcAddress( )** returns a pointer to the fuction named by *FuncName* that is contained in the DLL specified by *hMod*. Using this pointer, you can then call the desired function. Be careful, though. The name of the function must match exactly the name specified within the DLL. C++ name mangling may distort function names. You might want to avoid this by using the C linkage specification when you create your DLL functions.

To try run-time dynamic linking, make these changes to the second sample DLL program. First, define this global handle:

```
HMODULE hlib;
```

Next, add this sequence to **WinMain( )**, just before the message loop begins:

```
hlib = LoadLibrary("MYDLL.DLL");
if(!hlib) MessageBox(hwnd, "Cannot Load Library",
                     "Error", MB_OK);
```

Then, inside **WindowFunc( )**, define this function pointer:

```
 void (*f)(HDC, LPARAM);
```

Finally, change the mouse handlers as shown here.

```
   case WM_RBUTTONDOWN: /* process right button */
      hdc = GetDC(hwnd); /* get DC */

      /* get pointer to ShowMouseLoc */
      f = (void (*)(HDC, LPARAM)) GetProcAddress(hlib,
                  "ShowMouseLoc");

      /* call ShowMouseLoc */
      (*f)(hdc, lParam);

      ReleaseDC(hwnd, hdc); /* Release DC */
      break;
    case WM_LBUTTONDOWN: /* process left button */
      hdc = GetDC(hwnd); /* get DC */

      /* get pointer to ShowMouseLoc */
      f = (void (*)(HDC, LPARAM)) GetProcAddress(hlib,
                  "ShowMouseLoc");

      /* call ShowMouseLoc */
      (*f)(hdc, lParam);

      ReleaseDC(hwnd, hdc); /* Release DC */
      break;
```

You will also want to add a call to **FreeLibrary( )** when a **WM_DESTROY** message is received. After making these changes, the program will load the library dynamically and call **ShowMouseLoc( )** through a pointer rather than directly.

While you will normally use load-time dynamic linking, run-time linking does offer increased flexibility. For example, your application could take advantage of a DLL function if the DLL exists on the current machine. If it doesn't, the program could select an alternative.

A Jump Start to ActiveX

ActiveX is one of the most exciting disciplines in Windows programming, and it will play an increasingly important role in software development. Unfortunately, the ActiveX subsystem is both large and complex. To fully describe it would require a complete book. Frankly, if you want to create ActiveX applications, expect to spend at least a few weeks studying it. Although not difficult in concept, it is an extensive subject that requires some effort to master. With this in mind, the following discussion explains the essence of ActiveX and what benefits it offers programmers. This background will provide you with a "jump start" to the subject of ActiveX programming.

21

What Is ActiveX?

A software component is a small, reusable module of executable code that performs a well-defined function.

In the broadest sense, ActiveX is a set of methodologies and procedures that allow you to create *software components*. A software component is a reusable, self-contained module of code that may be used by another application. A software component can be "hooked onto" another application, providing additional control or functionality. Taken to its logical conclusion, an entire application could be constructed of nothing but software components "wired" together.

Software components have been one of the long sought-after goals of software engineering ever since there were computers. Although a conceptually powerful idea, component software remained a largely academic pursuit for several decades. In a world dominated by single-user, non-networked computers, component software was simply not a high priority. The reason for this is easy to understand: In a stand-alone system there is no easy way to acquire software components on demand. Thus, software for those machines was installed, intact and complete. If the user wanted to upgrade or enhance the software, he or she simply installed the latest version of the program. There was no concept of the user extending the functionality of an application by adding a component.

The key benefits of component software are best realized when a component can be acquired on demand, as needed—that is, when it can be dynamically downloaded. But this requires a means by which to acquire those components. For years, no such means existed. Of course, the advent of the Internet and the World Wide Web changed that. In the final analysis, it was the creation of the Internet that moved software components to the forefront of software engineering. Using the component software model, it is possible for a user to add functionality by adding components. At the time of this writing, we are just at the beginning of the component software revolution.

As it applies to ActiveX, a software component is called an *ActiveX control*. And, indeed, by far the most common use of ActiveX is to create an ActiveX control. Although ActiveX is not limited to controls, they are the reason ActiveX exists. They can be downloaded dynamically over the Internet and executed within all modern browsers. They can also be used by any OLE-compliant application.

OLE and ActiveX

OLE stands for object linking and embedding.

ActiveX is part of an evolutionary process that began with OLE, which stands for object linking and embedding. To understand ActiveX is to understand OLE, and vice versa. Since ActiveX begins with OLE, we will begin there, too.

In its original conception, OLE was designed to allow one application to link or embed information created by another application. When this is done, a *compound document* is created. A compound document is also referred to as an *OLE document*. While this original purpose of OLE is still supported, it is important to understand that OLE has gone through a rather extensive evolution. OLE version 1.0 was devised in 1991, but it was a seldom-used system. With the advent of OLE version 2, the capabilities and applicability of OLE took a quantum leap forward. Perhaps the single most important new feature of OLE 2 was the definition of the component object model (COM). It is this feature that ultimately led to the ActiveX technology.

In response to the Internet, Microsoft defined ActiveX in 1996. Based on OLE, it added support for Web-based applications. However, since it supports all of OLE, the term ActiveX has nearly supplanted the term OLE.

The Component Object Model

ActiveX is based upon the component object model (COM). This model
defines the way ActiveX-compliant applications interact with each other.
Specifically, it defines standard interfaces that one object can use to expose
its functionality to another. It is through these interfaces that one application
communicates with another.

In the component object model there are two types of applications:
containers and servers. In the simplest sense, a container is an application
that requires data, and a server is an application that supplies data. A
container can be a compound document. Another term for container is *client*.
The way that a container and server communicate is through the interfaces
defined by COM. These are the same interfaces used by an ActiveX control.
In fact, an ActiveX control is an in-process server (i.e., it runs within the
process that uses it).

COM Interfaces

21

The nature and contents of each interface are defined by the component
object model. An application that desires COM-compatibility simply
implements one or more of these interfaces. A COM interface is implemented
as a table of function pointers. These pointers point to the functions that
comprise the interface. To expose an interface, a server returns a pointer to
that interface's table. When a client seeks communication with a server, it
obtains a pointer to the server's interface table. The client may then call the
functions provided by the server through the pointers in the function table.
The client has no knowledge of or access to the details of the implementation
of the function it calls. It only knows that it is accessing a standard function
through a standard interface.

While there are several interfaces defined by COM, most ActiveX controls
will not implement them all. But the one interface they will all have is
called **IUnknown**. Using the **QueryInterface( )** function defined by
IUnknown, one application can find out what other interfaces are available
in another.

The fundamental value in interfaces is that one COM-compliant application
can take advantage of functionality provided by another COM-based
program. If you think about this for a moment, the implications are
enormous. It is easy to envision a computing universe populated with

components that a user can simply hook together as he or she sees fit. It is also easy to imagine smart components that will seek out and use other components when they require additional functionality. These possibilities are what make ActiveX controls so exciting.

Events, Properties, and Methods

In addition to using the standard COM interfaces, most ActiveX controls support three essential features: events, properties, and methods. An event is a message, a property is a data object, and a method is a function that may be executed. An ActiveX control sends a message to the container by generating an event. The container can alter the control by changing one of its properties or by calling one of its methods. These are the features that allow an ActiveX control to be active rather than passive.

Is ActiveX the Future of Windows?

Although OLE was initially designed only to support object linking and embedding, its role was dramatically expanded. The COM interface model defined for OLE went far beyond linking and embedding. ActiveX opened the door to the Internet and software components. Will this evolutionary process continue? The answer would seem to be Yes. Consider: The concepts contained in COM present an alternative, object-oriented way to view the entire Windows environment. It is possible that at some future time, the way that applications interface to Windows itself will be based upon something resembling COM. While it's too early to predict with certainty, it is safe to say at this point that ActiveX will be an important part of Windows programming well into the future.

What Next?

Windows 98 is a large and complex software system. There is much more to Windows 98 than can be described in any single book. Topics such as memory allocation, networking, telephony, and animation come to mind. Furthermore, large subsystems, such as COM/ActiveX, have exploded the amount of information that a Windows programmer needs to know. And the Web revolution continues to expand the Windows environment. But don't worry. Whatever your Windows 98 programming future holds, you now have the foundation upon which to pursue it.

Index

T